HOKUSAI
BEYOND THE GREAT WAVE

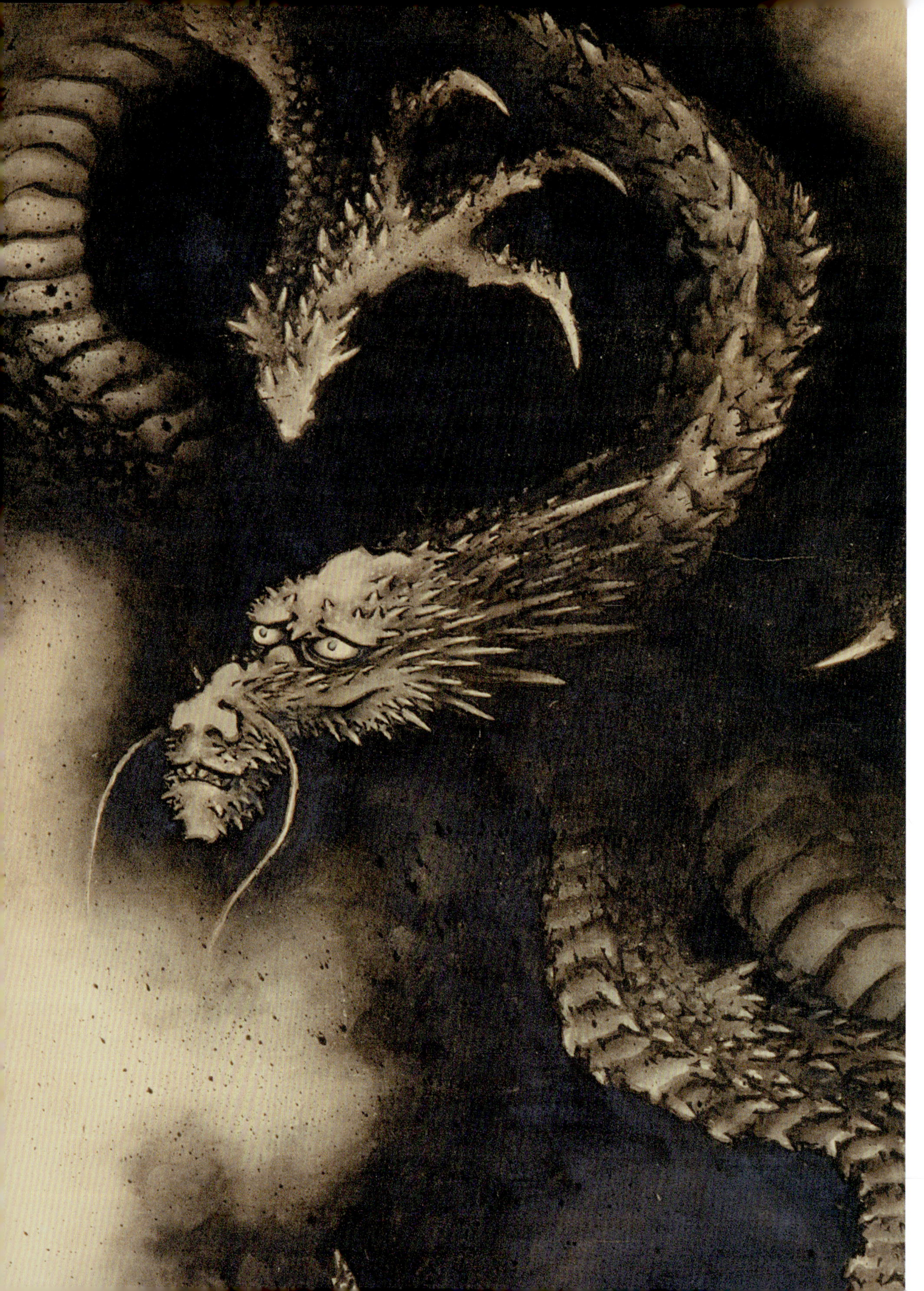

HOKUSAI

BEYOND THE GREAT WAVE

EDITED BY TIMOTHY CLARK

Thames &Hudson   The British Museum

This publication accompanies the exhibition 'Hokusai: beyond the Great Wave' at the British Museum from 25 May to 13 August 2017 and the exhibition 'Hokusai – Fuji o koete' at Abeno Harukas Art Museum, Osaka, from 6 October to 19 November 2017.

Supported by Mitsubishi Corporation
Research and publication supported by the Arts and Humanities Research Council

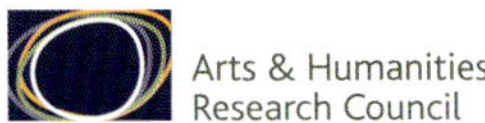

The exhibition at the British Museum has been made possible by the provision of insurance through the Government Indemnity Scheme. The British Museum would like to thank the Department for Culture, Media and Sport and Arts Council England for providing and arranging this indemnity.

First published in the United Kingdom in 2017 by Thames & Hudson Ltd, 6–24 Britannia Street, London WC1X 9JD in collaboration with the British Museum

First published in the United States of America in 2017 by Thames & Hudson Inc., 500 Fifth Avenue, New York, New York 10110

This compact hardback edition published in 2025

EU Authorized Representative: Interart S.A.R.L.
19 rue Charles Auray, 93500 Pantin, Paris, France
productsafety@thameshudson.co.uk
interart.fr

A CIP catalogue record for this book is available from the British Library

Library of Congress Control Number 2016952916

ISBN 978-0-500-48118-9

01

Printed and bound in China by C&C Offset Printing Co. Ltd

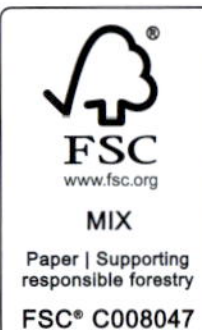

COVER

Katsushika Hokusai, *Under the wave off Kanagawa* ('The Great Wave'; detail), late 1831, colour woodblock, published by Nishimuraya Yohachi, 25.8 × 37.9 cm, British Museum, 2008,3008.1.JA, acquired with contributions from the Brooke Sewell Bequest and the Art Fund

FRONTISPIECE

Katsushika Hokusai, *Dragon in rain clouds* (detail), 1849, hanging scroll, ink and colour on paper, 120.5 × 42.5 cm, Musée national des arts asiatiques Guimet, Paris, MA.1217. Given by Norbert Lagane 2001.

NOTES TO THE READER

Names are given in the traditional Japanese order, family name followed by given name. Hokusai used many art names in addition.

All artworks are by Hokusai, unless another artist's name is given.

Katsushika (1), Katsushika (2), Katsushika (3) refer to the three generally accepted versions of this painting seal, thought to have been used by Hokusai in the periods, respectively: late 1810s–early 1830s; 1830s; and 1839–1847.

In pre-modern Japan, people were considered to be aged one when born and then their age increased by one year at each subsequent (lunar) New Year. Thus Hokusai, who died on the 18th day, fourth month, 1849, aged ninety by traditional Japanese reckoning, would have been eighty-eight by Western reckoning.

Dates in the traditional lunar calendar, such as 18th day, fourth month, 1849 are sometimes expressed in the catalogue in the form 1849/4/18. Fourth month, 1849 is sometimes expressed 1849/4.

The 'Provenance' and 'Literature' references in the catalogue section are not exhaustive. In each case only 3–4 of the most important references are given.

All works in the catalogue are on display at the British Museum, London, and Abeno Harukas Art Museum, Osaka, unless otherwise stated in the caption by 'London only' and 'Osaka only'. Works not on display are listed as 'Catalogue only'.

Contents

Sponsor's foreword

Mitsubishi Corporation is proud to support this new exhibition of the works of Katsushika Hokusai, one of the most famous of all Japanese artists, who has enjoyed a strong international reputation since the Japonisme era of the 1870s.

As an organization that has been involved in developing global trade for over sixty years, Mitsubishi Corporation's business is based upon strong foundations of international exchange and cultural understanding. Our sponsorship of the British Museum's Mitsubishi Corporation Japanese Galleries epitomizes our dedication to sharing Japan's culture with a global audience and enhancing appreciation for its rich heritage.

Now, we are delighted to be able to build upon our ongoing partnership with the British Museum by supporting this exhibition. It examines Hokusai's personal beliefs, and the nature of his highly individual artistic and spiritual quest, through major paintings, drawings, woodblock prints and illustrated books – many never seen before in the UK.

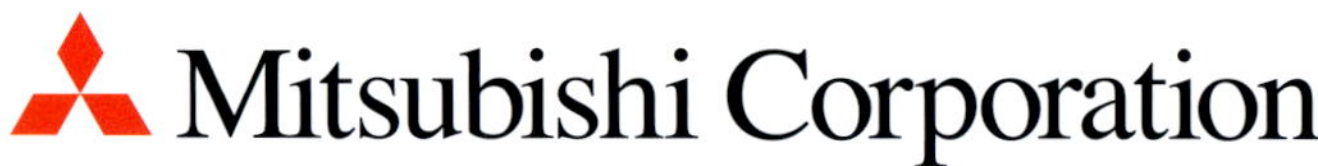

Director's foreword

'The Great Wave' has made Katsushika Hokusai (1760–1849) one of the best-loved artists in the world. Yet few in the UK have had the opportunity to admire the extraordinary paintings the artist created in his later years, when he was living with his daughter Eijo (Ōi, about 1800–after 1857), herself a talented painter, in humble rented dwellings in the great city of Edo, now Tokyo. This exhibition takes us beyond the iconic print, to explore Hokusai's artistic and spiritual journey during his last three, inspiring and innovative decades.

The British Museum purchased its first Hokusai print in 1860, just after Japan made the momentous decision to re-engage with the wider world after a long period of relative isolation. Major painted and printed Hokusai works came to the Museum from the collections of surgeon William Anderson in 1881 and novelist Arthur Morrison in 1906 and 1913. Further enriched by a substantial bequest of prints and drawings from the painters Charles Ricketts and Charles Shannon in 1937, the Museum staged a major exhibition of its Hokusai holdings in 1948, to mark the centenary of the artist's death. Many of Hokusai's important illustrated books were acquired from scholar Jack Hillier in 1979, and recent significant acquisitions have rounded out the collection – notably a fine, early impression of the Great Wave print, a purchase supported in 2008 by the Art Fund.

Our warm thanks go to Mitsubishi Corporation, who have sponsored this special exhibition and thereby made possible ambitious international loans. Their long-term support also underpins our permanent displays in the Mitsubishi Corporation Japanese Galleries.

The exhibition results from close collaboration with leading Hokusai scholar Dr Asano Shūgō, Director of the Abeno Harukas Art Museum, Osaka, where a related exhibition will be shown later this year. The exhibition is also informed by a ground-breaking research project, conducted jointly with SOAS University of London and funded by the Arts and Humanities Research Council. Inspirational Hokusai scholar, Dr Roger Keyes, has shared a lifetime of research with the project and assisted closely in shaping the exhibition.

Hokusai: beyond the Great Wave presents the fascinating story of an artist constantly innovating, overcoming the challenges of old age and often precarious life circumstances to produce sublime art. We thank the many lenders and scholars in Japan, Europe and the USA who have helped us to make the exhibition possible. We hope that you will be moved by what you see and learn.

Hartwig Fischer
Director, British Museum

Hokusai: the final years

Roger S. Keyes

Is any image in world art as immediately recognizable and as universally appealing as Hokusai's colour woodblock print of boats at sea, known throughout the English-speaking world as 'The Great Wave'? This famous print, prominently featured in this exhibition and publication, was designed by Katsushika Hokusai in his 'final years' (1820–1849). 'The Great Wave', though, compelling as it is, is only one of 3,000 colour prints that Hokusai designed during a seventy-year career. (He was born on 31 October 1760 and died on 10 May 1849, according to the European calendar of the day, and so lived to be ninety, according to the Japanese calendar.) In addition he drew illustrations for over 200 books, frequently in sets of many volumes. Hundreds of drawings and nearly 1,000 paintings also survive. Paintings were a major focus of the artist's work in his final years, particularly in his last decade, the 1840s, and they are an important feature here.

A master of collaboration, Hokusai worked with highly trained craftspeople, writers and other visual artists to produce a massive oeuvre at a consistently high level of quality. He also illustrated works by poets, novelists, essayists and anthologists, who valued his peerless intelligence, imagination and ingenuity. Hokusai himself was a prolific writer. He wrote stylish fiction, light verse, riddles and educated prose, including brush drawing manuals, a treatise on colour (cat. 211), a brief autobiographical note (Clark essay, p. 21; cats 176–182) and miscellaneous texts in Japanese and Chinese in many of his books.

Hokusai was adopted in childhood by an elite professional mirror-maker connected with the court of the then ruling shogun, Tokugawa Ieharu (reigned 1760–1786). He married young: his first wife seems to have died in 1785 after bearing three children; his second wife bore two or three more children before she too died in 1828. His early years as an artist were hard. From 1796, though, after dire spells of poverty, he achieved success, painting for patrons and designing hundreds of privately commissioned prints (*surimono*) for poets and performing artists. Around 1807 the next shogun, Tokugawa Ienari (reigned 1787–1837), commanded the artist to paint in his presence. This was a momentous occasion, and Hokusai concluded his demonstration by drawing a broad band of blue colour on a long sheet. Producing a live chicken from a basket, he dipped the bird's feet in red ink and marked the blue strip with them, titling the work 'Autumn leaves on the Tatsuta river'. In 1808 the artist was wealthy enough to purchase a house, and displayed paintings for sale to visitors.

Around the age of fifty, having completed a twenty-one day vigil, according to the temple where he undertook it, Hokusai was struck by lightning, which knocked him into a field. In the aftermath of this event he changed his life dramatically, curtailing his work and turning away from the literary and social world in which he had been a central figure. In 1812 the artist left Edo (present-day Tokyo) altogether, living for several months with a wealthy pupil in Nagoya, then travelling onwards to Kyoto (perhaps), Osaka and further reaches. In 1813 he returned to Edo, gave the name 'Hokusai' to a pupil and changed his own working name to 'Taito' (literally, 'Receiving the Big

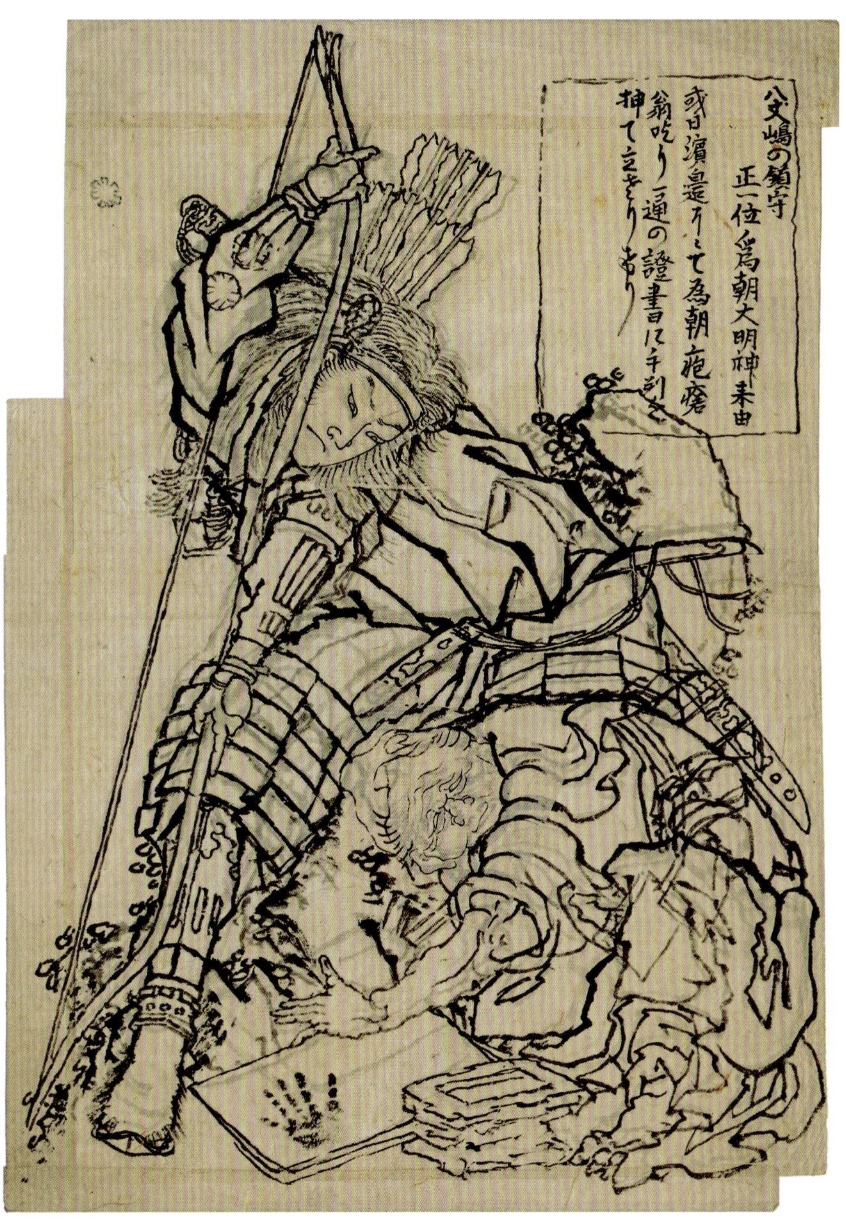

FIG 1

Attributed to Hokusai

Tametomo banishing the smallpox god

Late 1820s

Preparatory drawing, ink on paper, 38.3 × 26.0 cm

Private collection, UK

Dipper', more simply, 'Star-blessed'), intimating that after the lightning strike, the North Star, the principal object of his decades-long religious devotion, had saved his life.

From the New Year of 1820, the artist changed his name once again, this time to 'Iitsu' ('become one [with creation]', 'one again'). The name signalled that Hokusai in his sixty-first year was beginning his second cycle of sixty years. Of course he could not foresee how troubling and challenging the decade was to become. A beloved daughter died in 1821. His delinquent grandson saddled him with gambling debts. In 1828 his second wife died. In the late 1820s he suffered a stroke that permanently affected his drawing. Although he recovered and taught himself to draw again, he never regained his former fluency and he became more dependent on the assistance of his daughter Eijo (art name Ōi,

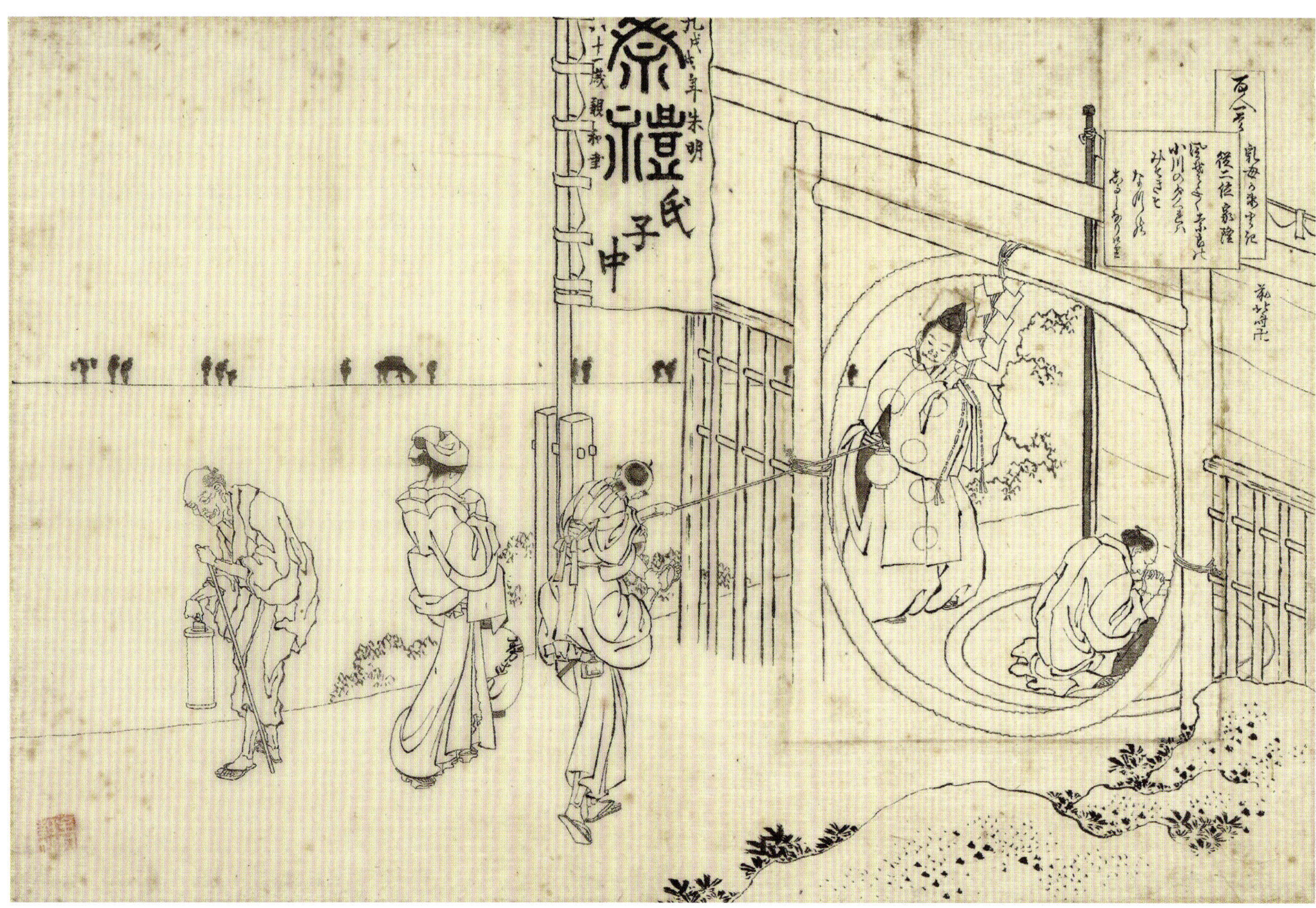

FIG 2

Poet 'Jūni'i Ietaka' from the series
One Hundred Poems by One Hundred
Poets, Explained by the Nurse
1838
Block-ready drawing, ink on paper,
25.6 × 37.5 cm
Freer-Sackler Gallery, Smithsonian
Institution, Washington, DC, Gift
of Charles Lang Freer, F1907.579

about 1800–after 1857), a gifted artist in her own right, to prepare final drawings for block cutters and to 'help' with paintings.

In the midst of this personal distress, however, drawing became a vehicle for discovery and personal guidance. As his new art name suggests, Hokusai believed that he 'became one' with his subjects by seeing them and drawing them. In the middle of the 1820s, he also realized that paintings like *Cormorant on a rock* (cat. 101) could 'make' his viewers 'one', both with the subject of the picture and also with his way of seeing – his 'vision'. In the late 1820s, his drawing of warrior hero Tametomo banishing the smallpox god (fig. 1) gave him the insight and guidance he needed to banish his grandson from Edo. This accomplished, he wrote to several publishers informing them that he was ready to work again. They replied immediately, and between 1830 and 1836 they and their colleagues published most of the colour prints in this exhibition.

In 1834 Hokusai changed his name for the last time. The reversed swastika symbol that he used was pronounced 'Manji' and meant 'everything', 'always' or 'all'. His last fifteen years saw repeated personal setbacks, but also an ever-deepening devotion to his art. *One Hundred Poems by One Hundred Poets, Explained by the Nurse* (cats 132–146) was the last set of colour prints Hokusai worked on, before an economic downturn interrupted its publication. Undaunted, the artist continued producing block-ready drawings for this set into the late 1830s, culminating in a remarkable allegory of his own life, dated 1838, portraying himself on one sheet as a child, an adult and an old man (fig. 2). In 1839, the year after Hokusai drew the allegory, a fire swept through his neighbourhood. He and his daughter Eijo saved their lives and fled, but sadly the wooden cart with all Hokusai's sketches, supplies and reference materials was lost in the blaze. In the ensuing decade, the artist devoted himself to painting, a story the exhibition aspires to tell. Many of the paintings in the exhibition are shown for limited periods, but all of them are illustrated in this book.

The exhibition and catalogue are arranged thematically into six sections. Here, there are short discussions of individual pictures and five essays about Hokusai's life and work in old age, his thought, his technique in woodblock prints and illustrated books, and his historical period and social networks. In conjunction with the exhibition we will be publishing online the full text of *Catalogue Raisonné of the Surviving Single Sheet Woodblock Prints of Katsushika Hokusai* by Roger Keyes and Peter Morse (unpublished manuscript, deposited at the Department of Asia, British Museum, 90 vols, 1972–2007). The continuing research project will result in a ground-breaking online Hokusai resource, including the first English translation of Iijima Kyoshin's indispensable biography, *Katsushika Hokusai den* (1893).

Late Hokusai, backwards

Timothy Clark

Hokusai believed that the older he got, the better his art became.[1] Prolonging
his life therefore became the artist's preoccupation, particularly after he turned
sixty-one in 1820. Since he was born in 1760, he had completed his first sixty-year
cycle as measured by the East Asian zodiac. He was thus 'one again' and also
'became one [with creation]' (Iitsu). Personal identification with a fixed point
of the cosmos – the North Star – had been one strategy since his younger days:
the name Hokusai, assumed in his late thirties in 1798, means 'North [Star] Studio'.[2]
Added alongside this in his older age was his identification with Mt Fuji, sacred
source of water and life. Lifelong faith in Nichiren Buddhism also served to keep
Hokusai spiritually focused and attuned, he believed, to all the manifestations
of creation. Many other powerful spiritual talismans were mobilized in his late
artistic repertoire, vehicles for expressing this unique mix of personal beliefs.
These included not only powerful mythical beings such as Shōki, the demon-queller,
and holy men such as monk Nichiren (1222–1282), but also proud solitary animals,
birds and mythical creatures – cormorants and eagles, tigers and dragons, Chinese
lions (fig. 3) and phoenixes. Staring out at us from all these beings is an intensely
inhabited gaze. They are all, in a sense, self-portraits of Hokusai wanting proudly
and forcefully to communicate with us. You and I commune, he insists, through
these extraordinary images.

For much of his career Hokusai was a busy commercial artist, designing
detailed block-ready drawings for colour woodblock prints and book illustrations,
at the employ of competing publishers. Painting was different.[3] Here he created
works directly, unmediated, and on subjects that mattered more personally to him.
The formats – fans, handscrolls, albums, hanging scrolls, folding screens and
even ceiling panels (cats 203, 204) – were generally larger too, giving greater scope
to Hokusai's constantly evolving explorations of form. Technically, some of
the late paintings are staggeringly complex, mobilizing a facility born of decades
of praxis. *Dragon in rain clouds* (cat. 223), for example, is painstakingly built up
from the ivory colour of the paper using progressively darker tones of ink.
Highlights on the head and scales of the dragon are reserved, unpainted paper.
The artist is therefore essentially working in reverse, conjuring intricate three-
dimensional forms out of his mind: these imaginary forms, moreover, do not
exist in our world.

Economic shocks occasioned by famines in the mid-1830s seem to have hastened
what was perhaps already Hokusai's personal inclination: to migrate away from
woodblock more definitively towards painting. Having said this, he still needed
to sell those paintings. This essay focuses on two key periods in Hokusai's later
career: his last three years, from 1847 to 1849, aged eighty-eight to ninety; and,
earlier, 1834 to 1836, when he was seventy-five to seventy-seven and first entering
what I will call deep old age.

The essay thus works backwards. This is done to highlight the extraordinary
single-mindedness, bravery and conviction that Hokusai poured into his late art.
For, truly, no one knows the hour of their death.

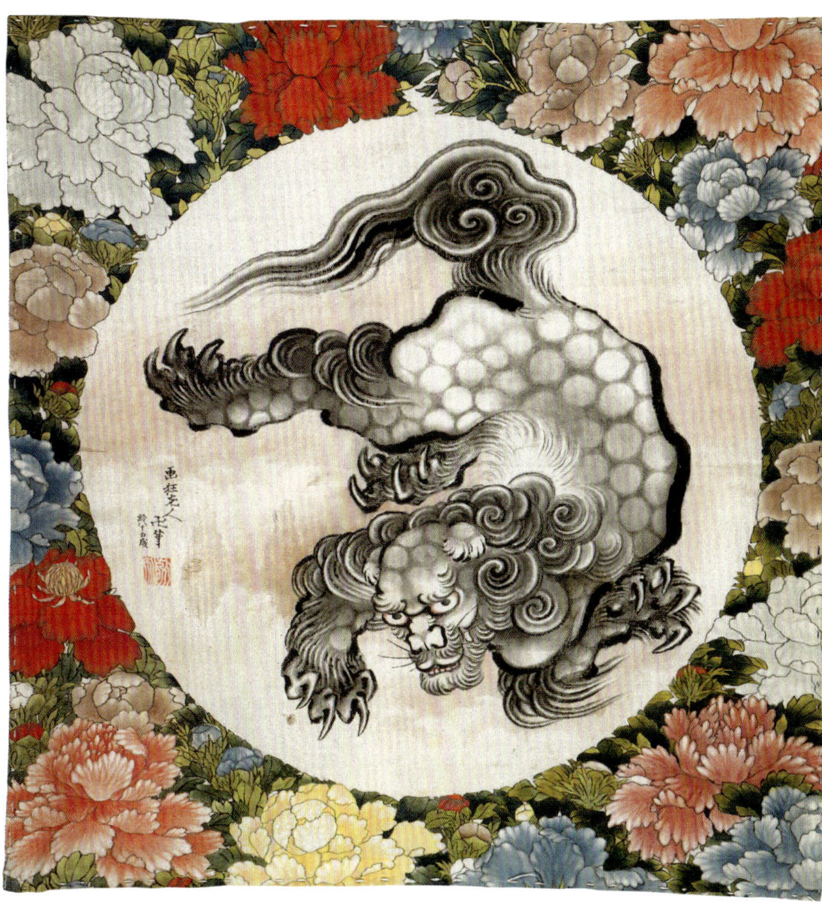

FIG 3

Chinese lion

1844

Painted wrapping cloth (*fukusa*),

ink and colour on crepe silk,

71.5 × 66.5 cm

Museum of Fine Arts, Boston,

William Sturgis Bigelow collection,

22.398

EIGHTY-EIGHT TO NINETY, 1847–1849

At the New Year of 1847, Hokusai turned eighty-eight. It was a goat year and the elderly artist 'tried out his brush' on New Year's day with an impromptu painting of a white goat (fig. 4). There would probably have been the customary 'rice longevity' (*beiju*) celebration for him; in written Chinese characters 'eighty-eight' 八十八 looks a bit like life-giving 'rice' 米.

Hokusai's signature on the goat painting is a little shaky. A letter that seems to have been written slightly earlier suggests the physical challenges he was facing. About a month before (6th day, twelfth month, 1846) he had written to his pupil Isai (Kamiyama Kumasaburō, 1821–1880) asking to borrow some money and noting, '… because my infirmity has recently returned, I could not brave the walk and was procrastinating'.[4] But he had not been too ill to work. At the beginning of the same letter he confirmed, 'the Hongō eagle painting [unidentified] is now complete'. Indeed, a few months previously, in a letter dated 13th day, eighth month, popular author Ryūtei Senka (1804–1868) had described Hokusai, then eighty-seven, at one of his good times: 'Even now he does trick paintings [*kyoku-gaki*] without glasses, and [detailed] block-ready drawings without stooping over. Last spring, in the rains, he walked from Nishi-Ryōgoku [his home?] as far as Nihonbashi. He was in fine fettle, and didn't feel tired.'[5] Back at the beginning of that year, though, things had not been so good. On the 9th day, first month, Hokusai had written to his pupil Honma Hokuyō (1822–1868), reporting that he

had been overwhelmed by a run of bad luck, including his daughter-in-law's
serious illness, and that he was thinking of moving in with his son Kase Sakijūrō
and his wife, who lived at a large samurai residence at Hongō Maruyama.[6]
The summer of 1846 was then unseasonably wet, with severe flooding in Edo.
From winter 1846 into the New Year of 1847, a smallpox epidemic raged.[7]
Hokusai produced at least two powerful paintings on silk in 1846 of Shōki
(the Chinese demon-queller Zhong Kui), painted in red so as to protect the
owner from misfortune and disease – especially smallpox (cats 160, 161).

Hokusai invariably included his age in painting signatures during his eighties
(and occasionally during his seventies). According to the most complete listing
– there is no catalogue raisonné of the paintings yet – thirty-two surviving brushed
works bear the 'eighty-eight' signature. The totals for each year in his eighties
are currently as follows, representing a range of painting formats from simple fans
to large hanging scrolls on silk. The twelve he painted in his final year were produced
in just over three months. Hokusai died on the 18th day of the fourth month, 1849.[8]

HOKUSAI'S AGE	NO. OF SURVIVING, DATED PAINTINGS
80	19
81	13
82	4
83	3
84	16
85	14
86	6
87	8
88	32
89	7
90	12

Given the generally high attrition rate of paintings from Hokusai's Edo – large
parts of the city have periodically been destroyed by fire, earthquake, floods and
(in 1945) bombing – the actual numbers of works originally painted by the artist
must have been very much larger.[9] In 1847, at any rate, on the surviving evidence,
he was almost twice as productive as in any other year during his eighties.

Hokusai's preoccupation with his legacy as a painter is also evident in a
publishing project from the same year. It was in 1847 that he must have finished
working on the painting manual *Picture Book: Essence of Colouring* (*Ehon saishiki tsū*,
cat. 211). Evidently planned since at least 1836,[10] the book was finally published in
two small, affordable volumes at the New Year, 1848.[11] After specific instructions
on the method of preparing certain pigments, illustrated examples are given of
how to colour about a hundred different motifs – mainly animals, birds and
plants. Many of these same motifs are found in the paintings of his last years:
the goat is in volume 2 (fig. 5). There are also descriptions of techniques imported
from Europe, such as 'oil painting' and copperplate printing. In a postscript to
volume 1, Hokusai expresses the desire to transmit to a wide audience his
practical experience accumulated over more than eighty years: '… from ninety
years I will keep on improving my style of painting. After I reach one hundred,
my only desire will be to revolutionize this vocation [painting]. You gentlemen
who live long [enough] will know that my words are not wrong.'[12] Hokusai

FIG 4 (OPPOSITE LEFT)

White goat
1847
Hanging scroll, ink and colour
on paper, 70.3 × 29.3 cm
Ichimura Tsugio collection, Japan

FIG 5 (OPPOSITE RIGHT)

Goat, from *Picture Book: Essence
of Colouring* (*Ehon saishiki tsū*)
1848
Illustrated book, vol. 2 (of 2),
woodblock, 18.0 × 13.0 cm (covers)
British Museum, 1979,0305,0.465

had published many brush drawing manuals in the course of his later career, from about 1812, but this was the first systematic attempt to teach his painting technique. At least two more volumes of the book were advertised, but sadly time ran out for him.

What were Hokusai's personal circumstances during these last years? The artist was famous for changing his rented lodgings even more frequently than he changed his art names. He was said to have moved thirty-four times by 1834, more than sixty times by 1843 and ninety-three times by 1848.[13] A fundamental document for visualizing Hokusai in his eighties is the annotated sketch (cat. 193) made from memory by his pupil Tsuyuki Kōshō (Iitsu III, died after 1893), which he gave to Iijima Kyoshin (1841–1901) when the latter was working on his *Biography of Katsushika Hokusai* (*Katsushika Hokusai den*, hereafter 'the biography'), published in 1893.[14] Hokusai, with the quilt of the heated brazier (*kotatsu*) covering his shoulders, crouches forwards to paint on what is likely paper, laid out on the tatami mats. Perhaps out of respect, his face is partly obscured by a wooden pillar. Hokusai is watched unsmilingly by his daughter Eijo (art name Ōi, about 1800– after 1857), who rests a hand on her long tobacco pipe. Her hair is cut *en brosse*, in an unconventional style. The text, reprinted in Iijima's biography, says that Hokusai stayed under the quilt from autumn through to spring, painting when he was awake and putting a pillow under his head when sleepy. Lice thrived in the quilt. In the corner of the room was a small area with floorboards rather than tatami, piled with rubbish – discarded wrappings of charcoal and food. Attached to the wall was an old wooden box for tangerines, with an image of monk Nichiren enshrined within (cat. 194), as well as a sign saying 'we strictly refuse [to paint] albums or fans'. The room is identified as a 'rented lodging at Hannoki Baba, Kamezawa-chō, in Honjo'. The biography adds that this was the period when each morning Hokusai would draw a Chinese lion or lion-dancer on a small piece of paper and throw it out of the window – to ward off evil.[15] Some of these Chinese lions survive, known as the 'Daily Exorcism' drawings,

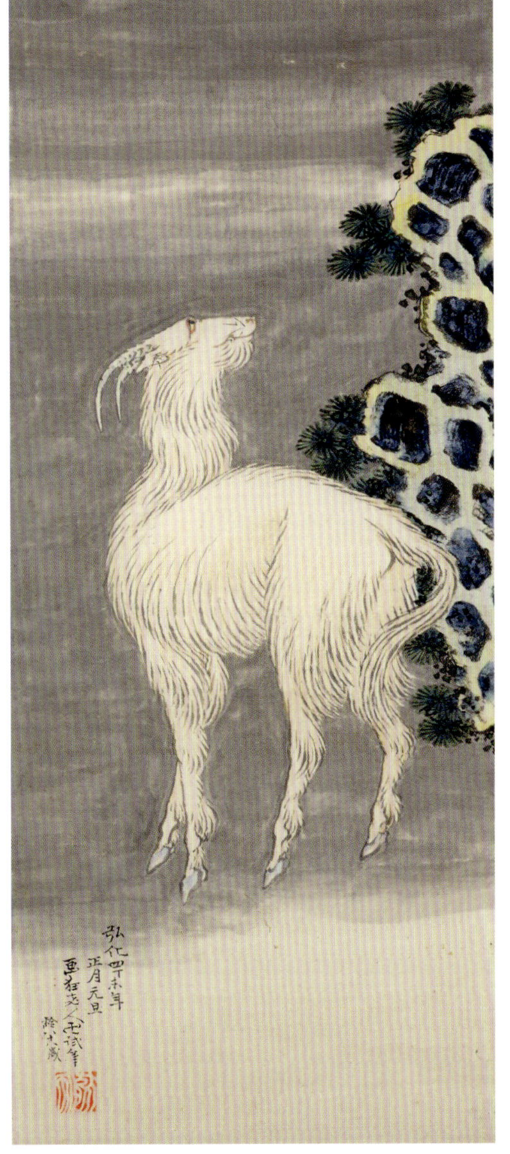

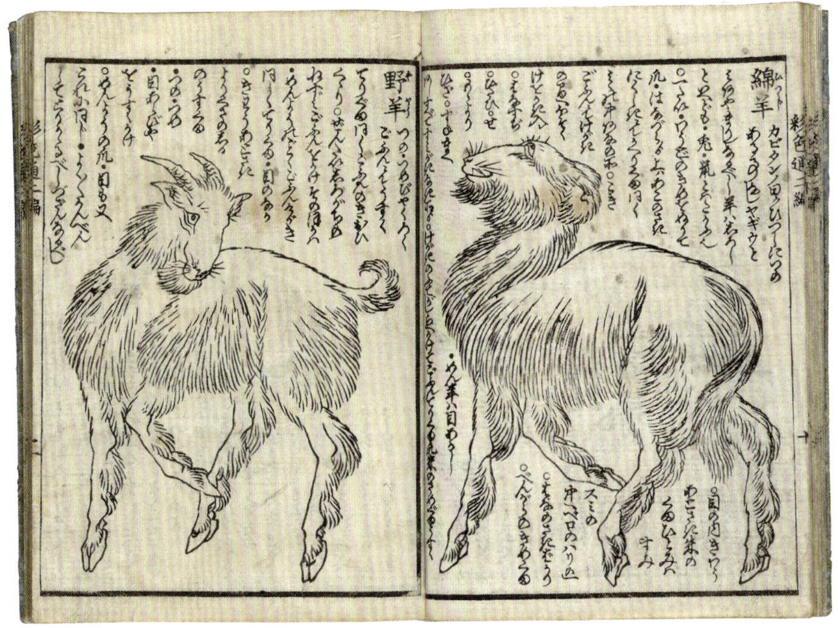

with dates ranging from late 1842 through to early 1844 (cats 191, 192). So Tsuyuki's sketch is thought to show Hokusai and Eijo around 1842–1843, when he was eighty-three or eighty-four and she is estimated to have been in her early forties.[16] Kamezawa-chō was just behind the timber yard of the shogunate, the samurai military government, in the heart of the Honjo-Fukagawa district on the east side of the Sumida river, the area where Hokusai was born, worked and resided in various places for much of his life. Kamezawa-chō is also the address given on a hilarious model 'memorandum' about collecting painting fees, which Hokusai playfully addressed to 'Mr so-and-so, of such-and-such a business'. Included in the note are thumbnail sketches by the artist of both himself and Eijo, with her distinctive pointed chin.[17]

Hokusai and Eijo apparently settled for a relatively long period at Kamezawa-chō. Other late addresses can be inferred from various pieces of evidence.[18] They are nearly all in the merchant-artisan districts of Honjo and Asakusa that straddled the Sumida river on its east and west sides, respectively:

1844/2	Mukōjima Koume-mura (Koume village) (east)
1844	Sensōji-mae (in front of Sensōji temple, Asakusa) (west)
1845	Honjo Banba-chō (east)
1845	Honjo Arai-machi (east)
1846/8/13	Nishi Ryōgoku (west)
1847/2/1	Tamachi 1-chōme, (probably in Asakusa) (west)
1848/6/5	Asakusa (west)
1848–1849	Asakusa Shōden-chō Henjō-in keidai (the precincts of Henjōin temple, Shōden-chō, Asakusa) (west, where Hokusai died)
1853/3/12	Asakusa Shōden-yokochō (west, Eijo's residence)

And, as mentioned above, in the first month of 1846, Hokusai may have been considering moving in with his son Sakijūrō and Sakijūrō's wife at Hongō Maruyama, on the west side of the river, closer to Edo castle.

Who was supporting the artist financially in his later years? One key relationship was with Takai Kōzan (1806–1883), the wealthy saké brewer and literatus from the town of Obuse in Shinano province (modern Nagano prefecture).[19] As described in greater detail elsewhere (pp. 50–53), Kōzan was instrumental in securing for Hokusai important commissions from the town to decorate two festival carts and the Ganshōin temple ceiling (cats 203, 204). The artist made several extended visits to Kōzan in Obuse, most likely in 1844 and again in 1845 – and perhaps on later occasions as well. Depending on the route, the journey from Edo took either four or five nights on foot. Another conduit for Hokusai's communication with Obuse was the firm of Jūhachiya. Originating in Obuse, the firm had a branch in Edo that traded in textiles and medicines, and also operated a courier service.[20] The Jūhachiya warehouse seems to have been in Hongin-chō, Nihonbashi, which, perhaps not coincidentally, was also the location of the Edo store of Nagoya publisher Eirakuya Tōshirō, a major publisher of Hokusai's books, including *Hokusai's Sketches* (*Hokusai manga*, cats 164, 165).

Sometime in 1847, Hokusai and Eijo (Ōi) gave to the samurai Miyamoto Shinsuke (1821–after 1871) of the Matsushiro domain (also in Shinano province, not far from Obuse) a group of more than 200 of his 'Daily Exorcism' drawings of Chinese lions and lion-dance performers (cats 191, 192).[21] These were offered in place of a painting commissioned at an earlier date that Hokusai had failed to complete. Accompanying the drawings was a short letter by the artist in which he thanks Miyamoto for accepting the works and says he 'is mopping the sweat from his brow', wondering how posterity will judge him.[22] Hokusai need not have worried, for the 'Daily Exorcism' drawings have always been considered among his most engaging works.

Fragments of evidence assembled by Hokusai scholar Kubota Kazuhiro point to the existence of a group or association (*shachū*) of individuals in Edo who were interested in acquiring paintings by Hokusai during his last years.[23] Key among these – either as a member of the group, or serving as an intermediary – was one 'Mr Nagakawa' (though the characters for his name can also be read Osagawa).[24] He is referred to in respectful terms, in association with a 'Mr Ogino', in the two letters that Hokusai wrote to his pupil Isai late in 1846 and early in 1847 – among the very last of the forty or so letters written by the artist that have survived. The letters imply that both Nagakawa and Ogino were regular visitors to Hokusai's residence. A few years later, after Hokusai's death, a certain Nagakawa Kamatarō of Honjo Hayashi-chō 2-chōme, close to Kamezawa-chō where Hokusai and Eijo had lived, appears several times in the collecting notes of Hokusai's former patron Takai Kōzan.[25] Between 1853 and 1855, Nagakawa supplied to Kōzan no fewer than twenty-three paintings by Hokusai and one by Ōi.[26] So perhaps this group or association, centred on the Honjo district where Hokusai had often resided, was a significant source of financial support to Hokusai and Ōi during the artist's last years.

The fluctuation in the known number of paintings by Hokusai from year to year in late old age surely reflects in part how busy the artist was with other work, and in part his state of health. There are relatively few paintings – seven – signed with the age 'eighty-nine'. Little is recorded about Hokusai's life in 1848. We know that he received his pupil Hokuyō twice at home, somewhere in Asakusa, in the sixth month, presenting him with the painting *Demon feasting* (cat. 208).[27] He may have enjoyed the opening-of-the-season kabuki performance at the Kawarazaki theatre in the eleventh month.[28] Old acquaintances Sekine Shisei (1825–1893) and Yomo no Umehiko (1822–1896) visited him at what was to prove his final residence, a house, probably rented, in the precincts of Henjōin temple, Shōden-chō, Asakusa.

There are rather more paintings than might be expected – twelve – bearing the signature 'ninety', given that Hokusai died in the fourth month of that year. We can surmise that a number of works may already have been at different stages of completion in the studio, and that paintings begun in 1848 were finished in the artist's final months in 1849. Ōi was at her father's side to give assistance. Did his situation in Henjōin temple perhaps permit him to make use of bigger spaces to work on larger paintings, such as the pair *Tiger in rain* and *Dragon in rain clouds* (cats 222, 223)? Final works from 1849 annotated with the months and days associated with zodiac animals (dragon, tiger) suggest that Hokusai was literally counting out the days and months that might be left to him (cats 221, 224). Following a short final illness, when the doctor advised that medicine could not help him, Hokusai's last words were recorded as follows: 'If heaven will extend my life by ten more years…', then, after a pause, 'If heaven will afford me five more years of life, then I'll manage to become a true artist.'

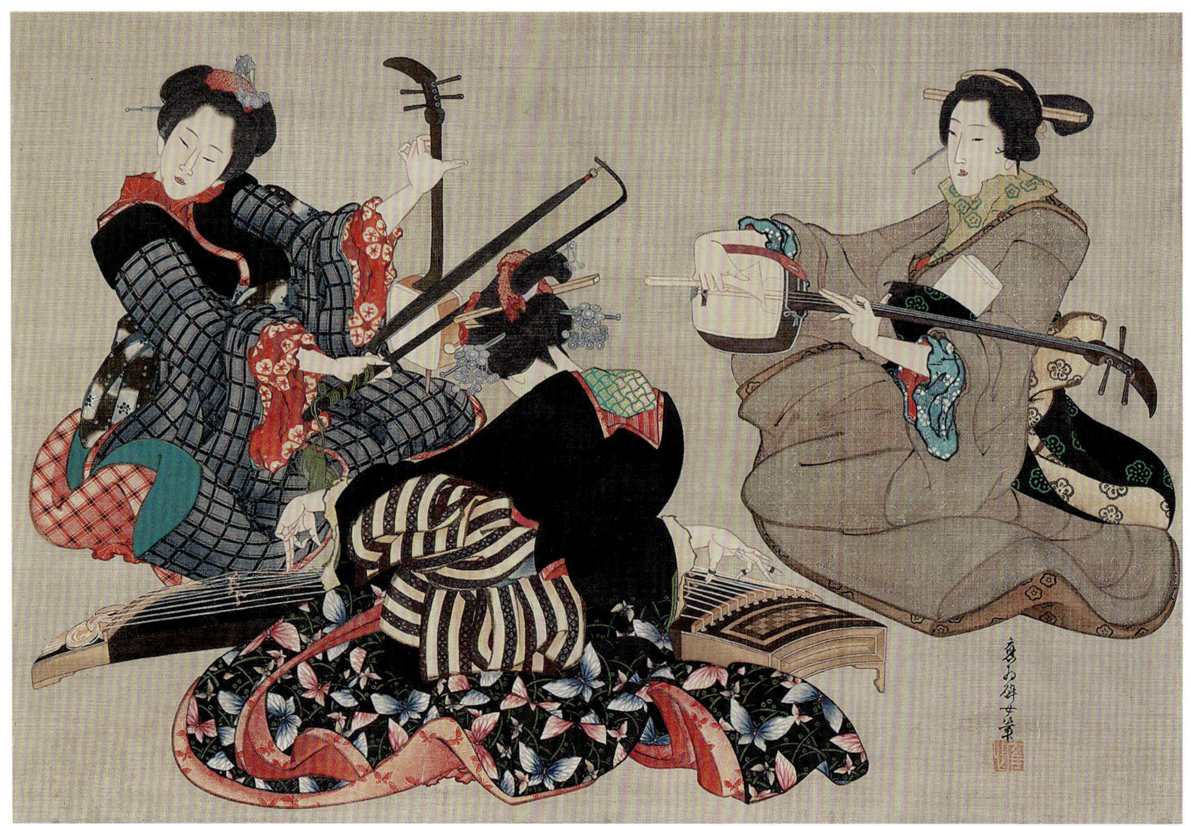

HOKUSAI AND EIJO (ŌI)

It was Eijo (alternatively O-Ei, Ōi), thought to be Hokusai's third daughter, from his second marriage, who sent a hurriedly written note to his pupil Hokushin when the artist died in the fourth month, 1849 (cat. 225). Although she was apparently living in close proximity with her father during his last decades, much about her life and work remains unclear. Even her birth and death dates are undetermined. In the handful of paintings and printed works signed with her own art name, Ōi (fig. 6, cats 195–198), she reveals herself to be an accomplished and distinctive artist. Recently, a comprehensive attempt has been made by Kubota Kazuhiro to assemble the known facts and to analyse Ōi's signed works.[29] Kubota proposes particular Ōi stylistic traits that he also detects in certain Hokusai-signed and unsigned works. He aims thereby to give more appropriate weight to the contribution that Ōi may have made, putatively, to the 'Hokusai' oeuvre in the later decades. The prime trait is an intricately detailed style that features modelling, highlights, shading and darkness in a manner that would have been considered 'European' in the contemporary Japanese context. Specific other mannerisms identified in Ōi works are long pointed fingers with only half-sketched nails, a stray lock of hair curling into the face, and the habit of including in the composition a prominent vertical architectural feature, such as a pillar. Such detective work, already begun by earlier scholars, discovers Ōi's hand in certain unsigned works dating from as early as the group of genre paintings produced for visiting Dutchmen in about 1824–1826 (cats 20–25). Kubota suggests that it was around 1824 that Eijo married the painter Tsutsumi (Minamisawa) Tōmei (worked about 1804–1830). The marriage soon ended in divorce, however, perhaps around 1827. Hokusai's second wife Koto (Eijo's mother) died in 1828, and this may have been when Eijo returned to live with her father. Her art name Ōi means 'following Iitsu', strongly suggesting that her artistic affiliation with her father was indeed formed during Hokusai's 'Iitsu' period (1820–1834). If Ōi was living with Hokusai from the late 1820s onwards, then she witnessed at close hand the creation of all the famous series of colour woodblock prints, notably *Thirty-Six Views of Mt Fuji* (1831–1833, cats 41–65).

Kubota's thesis is intricate and fascinating. But the question remains open as to whether we will ever be able to separate Ōi's hand from Hokusai's with any degree of certainty. Hokusai was Ōi's teacher and the dominant presence in their collaboration. Household income surely depended on that close collaboration and on Hokusai's name and fame. If the most accomplished of the unsigned genre paintings in 'European' style now in Leiden (cats 20–25) are in fact by Hokusai, then perhaps it was Ōi who learned that style from her father, rather than the other way round. In any event, the Hokusai–Ōi relationship is a vital factor to consider in assessing the artist's later years.

SEVENTY-FIVE TO SEVENTY-SEVEN (1834–1836)

At many junctures in his long career, Hokusai signalled an important new departure with a change of name. In 1834, at the age seventy-five, there was a complete overhaul.

On the colour prints that had been streaming from the printing blocks of publisher Nishimuraya Yohachi from about 1831 to 1834, the artist had settled into using 'Brush of Iitsu, the former Hokusai' (Saki no Hokusai Iitsu hitsu). Nearly all the print designs for which the artist is most celebrated appeared from this one firm in this short interval of years, their number and estimated year of publication as follows:[30]

> *Thirty-Six Views of Mt Fuji*, actually 46 designs, as the series was extended, about 1831–1833
> *Large flowers*, 10 designs, about 1831–1832
> *Tour of Waterfalls in Various Provinces*, 8 designs, about 1833
> *Wondrous Views of Famous Bridges in Various Provinces*, 11 designs, about 1834
> *Small flowers*, 10 designs, about 1834

Iitsu, as we have seen, was the new name Hokusai took in 1820 when he turned sixty-one, announcing that he was 'at one' with creation (in a Daoist sense) and also 'one again' – meaning that the sixty-year zodiac cycle of his birth had come round again (*kanreki*). The character 'rō', meaning old man, began to appear occasionally in Hokusai's signatures from 1821. Even though 'Hokusai' had ceased to be his main art name from about 1810 – and even though he had probably passed the name on to a pupil[31] – the artist and his publishers were loath to relinquish it altogether. The name Hokusai seems to have been the one that had most resonance with the public and it stuck. As the years passed, artist and publishers simply added new names to the ones he already had.

In 1834 he began to use the art name Manji, which would last until the end of his life.[32] The third month of that year saw the publication of the first volume of *One Hundred Views of Mt Fuji* (*Fugaku hyakkei*, cats 176–182), one of the greatest

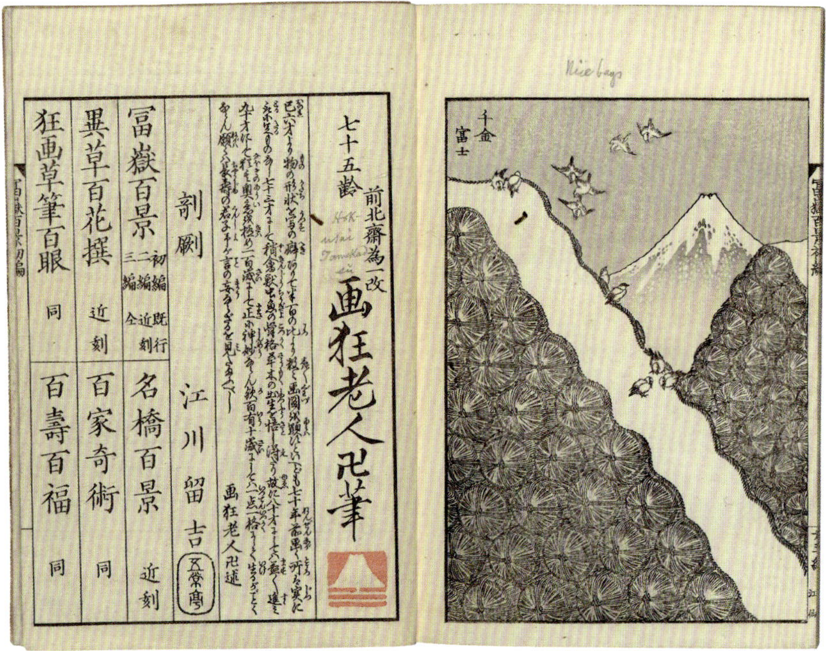

FIG 7

Colophon to volume 1 of *One Hundred Views of Mt Fuji* (*Fugaku hyakkei*)

Third month, 1834

Illustrated book, vol. 1 (of 3), woodblock, 22.7 × 15.7 cm (covers)

British Museum, 1979,0305,0.454.1

illustrated books ever.[33] The sacred mountain is shown in a dazzling range of guises and inventive compositions. Hokusai's block-ready drawings were interpreted in unparalleled fine cutting by a team led by the artist's block cutter of choice, Egawa Tomekichi. Volume 2 appeared exactly a year later and volume 3, after vicissitudes, around the time of Hokusai's death in 1849.[34] Unusually, some of the early stage preparatory drawings have survived for the designs in volume 2 (cats 177–182).[35] We savour the confidence of Hokusai's bold first thoughts, starting in red ink and then switching to black as his ideas gelled.

The signature at the back of published volume 1 was a long one: 'Brush of Manji, old man crazy to paint, changed from the former Hokusai Iitsu, aged seventy-five' (Nanajūgo rei / saki no Hokusai Iitsu aratame / Gakyō rōjin Manji hitsu) (fig. 7). Alongside new names are lined up the old, Hokusai and Iitsu. And the new signature was followed by a new painting seal of Mt Fuji above the ancient Chinese trigram for 'lake' from the *Book of Changes* (the *I Ching*). The combination of mountain plus lake forms a hexagram which has been interpreted, poignantly, to mean 'decrease' (Chinese: *sun*; Japanese: *son*).[36] Did Hokusai mean to suggest, therefore, that Mt Fuji transcends the limitations of personal decline?

Manji, the reverse swastika, is an ancient auspicious symbol in India and Buddhism. Its sound also means 'ten thousand things' – that is, 'everything'. Ten thousand is one hundred times one hundred, and since at least 1823, when Hokusai began to work regularly again with publisher Nishimuraya Yohachi, adverts continuously appeared for prints and books that would feature one hundred versions of all kinds of subject.[37] Mt Fuji was the only such project that came to full fruition – and that took fifteen years. Exploiting the virtuosity born of long experience, Hokusai in old age wanted to show off in his pictures how he could manipulate any form to reveal fundamental truths about the universe. There also seems to have been a kind of sympathetic magic at work. The longer (and deeper) he explored all the forms of creation, the longer he would live, and vice versa.

Gakyō rōjin literally means 'picture-mad-old-man', interpreted here to mean that Hokusai literally could not stop drawing and painting with his brush. The character 'kyō' may have had a more particular meaning for the artist, however. He had first adopted the name Gakyōjin ('picture-mad-man') in 1801 and flirted, briefly, with Gakyō rōjin ('picture-mad-old-man') in 1805, even though he was then only forty-four. Hokusai scholar Roger Keyes has suggested the following interpretation: 'Hokusai was surely reading the Confucian Analects in 1801–1802 when he adopted this name. He parodies passages from the Analects in his comic novel (*kibyōshi*) about food, *Buchōchō sokuseki ryori* (1803). Confucius uses 'kyō' to mean 'ardent', even 'passionate', and the word was used in this sense by Ming neo-Confucian writers like Wang Yangming (1472–1529, Japanese: Ōyōmei) who were widely read by Japanese intellectuals, including Hokusai, in the early 1800s.'[38]

In 1834, the new names featured prominently in the colophon to *One Hundred Views* (fig. 7). The boldest characters announce: 'Brush of Manji, old man crazy to paint', with the red Mt Fuji plus trigram seal beneath. The former names Hokusai and Iitsu are retained, but shunted to the right side, appearing in smaller script. It was important that the public was given time to get used to the artist's latest re-invention of his persona. Also in smaller script at the top is Hokusai's age, seventy-five years. Hokusai initiated this practice on a magnificent pair of painted screens, *Six Jewel Rivers* (Freer-Sackler Gallery, Smithsonian Institution, Washington, DC, F1904.204, 205), painted the previous year, 1833.[39] From eighty onwards, he would invariably write his age on paintings.

Immediately following the new signature in the colophon, to the left, is a text which has become rightly celebrated as Hokusai's personal artistic credo. From the vantage of seventy-five, the threshold of deep old age, he looks back dismissively over his long career, but anticipates future progress. The original text is here interleaved with several key career events:

> From the age of six I had a penchant for copying the form of things, and from about fifty [illustrated adventure stories, with author Bakin, cat. 14], my pictures were frequently published; but until the age of seventy [*Thirty-Six Views of Mt Fuji*, cats 41–65], nothing I drew was worthy of notice. At seventy-three years [*Large flowers* series, cats 82–88; beginning to draw *One Hundred Views of Mt Fuji*?, cats 176–182], I was somewhat able to fathom the growth of plants and trees, and the structure of birds, animals, insects and fish. Thus when I reach eighty years, I hope to have made increasing progress, and at ninety to see further into the underlying principles of things, so that at one hundred years I will have achieved a divine state in my art, and at one hundred and ten, every dot and every stroke will be as though alive. Those of you who live long enough, bear witness that these words of mine are not false (trans. Henry D. Smith II).[40]

The challenge to his readers to live long enough to witness the astounding progress to be made by the centenarian artist is similar to that in the text written aged eighty-eight for *Picture Book: Essence of Colouring* (see pp. 14–15 above). After seventy-five, Hokusai was in it for the long haul.

A glimpse into Hokusai's more worldly public activities can be gleaned from the chance survival of the advertising flier (*hikifuda*) for one of the popular so-called 'calligraphy and painting parties' (*shogakai*) at which he performed on the 16th day of the eighth month, 1834.[41] These were ticketed events at which the public could watch leading calligraphers and painters make impromptu art works, and request particular subjects to be done for them, for an additional fee, on the spot. The venue was generally a large restaurant with upstairs party rooms – in this case, the premises of Kawachiya Hanjirō at Yanagibashi. Sometimes the performers were raising funds for themselves. Such had been the case in 1808, when Hokusai had staged his own party at the very same restaurant to raise funds towards the new house he had just built in Kamezawa-chō – the neighbourhood he would later move back to with Eijo in 1843–1844 (see pp. 15–16 above). The 1834 event, however, billed 'to paint one thousand scrolls', was staged to raise funds for the popular author Hanagasa Bunkyō (1785–1860), who had lost his precious library to a fire and suffered serious ill health earlier in the year. Bunkyō would later write the text for the book *Biographies of Eccentric People of Japan*, probably published around the time of Hokusai's death in 1849, in which artist Utagawa Kuniyoshi (1797–1861) included a portrait of Hokusai painting (cat. 185).

In middle age, Hokusai had performed several tremendous feats of outdoor performance art, painting gigantic head-and-shoulders images of Daruma (Bodhidharma), founder of Zen Buddhism – first in the precincts of a temple in Edo in 1804 (cat. 163), and then again at a Nagoya temple in 1817.[42] But once he entered 'old age' in his sixties, it might have been assumed that Hokusai would leave energetic public performances behind. The advertising flier of 1834 suggests otherwise. It includes a comic, somewhat jaded, text by Hokusai himself:

> I have enjoyed painting since childhood. Yet, for more than seventy years now, I have not been able to fathom its depths. Over the years I have attended calligraphy and painting parties a hundred, maybe a thousand times. Personally, I have gotten bored with their games and these days I try to avoid them. Two or three of my associates plan an event to do one thousand paintings. I will demonstrate my paltry skill at trick paintings [fig. 8] and upside-down paintings, calling them, like a bad joke: 'One Hundred Unlettered Arts' [*Fugaku hyakugei*].[43] Will an old man's fighting strength be any use at the elbow of Mr Hanagasa?
>
> Old man of seventy-five / Iitsu, the former Hokusai[44]

Even allowing for the customary hyperbole ('hundred … thousand …') it is clear that Hokusai must have attended far more calligraphy and painting parties than we have record of. Interestingly, he here sticks to the former names that would have been much more familiar to the public. His pun on the title of *One Hundred Views of Mt Fuji* (*Fugaku hyakkei*) suggests that book was already becoming well known.

It is significant that we have concrete evidence that Hokusai was in Edo in the eighth month, 1834. According to the biography, around the winter of 1834 he 'went into hiding' (*senkyo*) in the coastal town of Uraga, Sagami province, on the Miura peninsula, about 50 kilometres (30 miles) southwest of Edo.[45] He even changed his name to the innocuous-sounding Miuraya Hachiemon, often used in letters from this time onwards. Various fragments of evidence, including a number of letters to the book publisher Kobayashi Shinbei (Sūzanbō) and other publishers, suggest that he stayed in Uraga on and off until the autumn of 1836.

Several possible explanations are given in the biography for this self-imposed exile: one of his children broke the law; a picture he drew contained something that infringed public morality; he was overwhelmed by debt; he was trying to avoid the problems arising from the dissolute lifestyle of his grandson (the son of Hokusai's pupil Yanagawa Shigenobu, who had already caused chronic problems for Hokusai in the late 1820s). But the specific reason is not known. One can surmise that it may have related in some way to the terrible crop failure and famine that afflicted the country in the middle years of the Tenpō era (1830–1844), especially from 1833 to 1836. This caused thousands of deaths and led to numerous rural revolts and urban riots, and the shogunate was regularly providing relief for up to 700,000 people.[46]

In his letters, Hokusai makes repeated pleas that the publishers will engage Egawa Tomekichi to carve the blocks for the illustrated books of Chinese warriors he is designing. He gives detailed instructions for the techniques of printing gradation to be used in these books, as well as specific corrections to the way he wants his faces carved in *Illustrated Anthology of Tang Poetry* (cat. 125); the publisher complied, and issued a corrected edition.[47] Other passing comments are significant. In a letter of the second month of 1835, to Kobayashi and two other book publishers, Hokusai says:

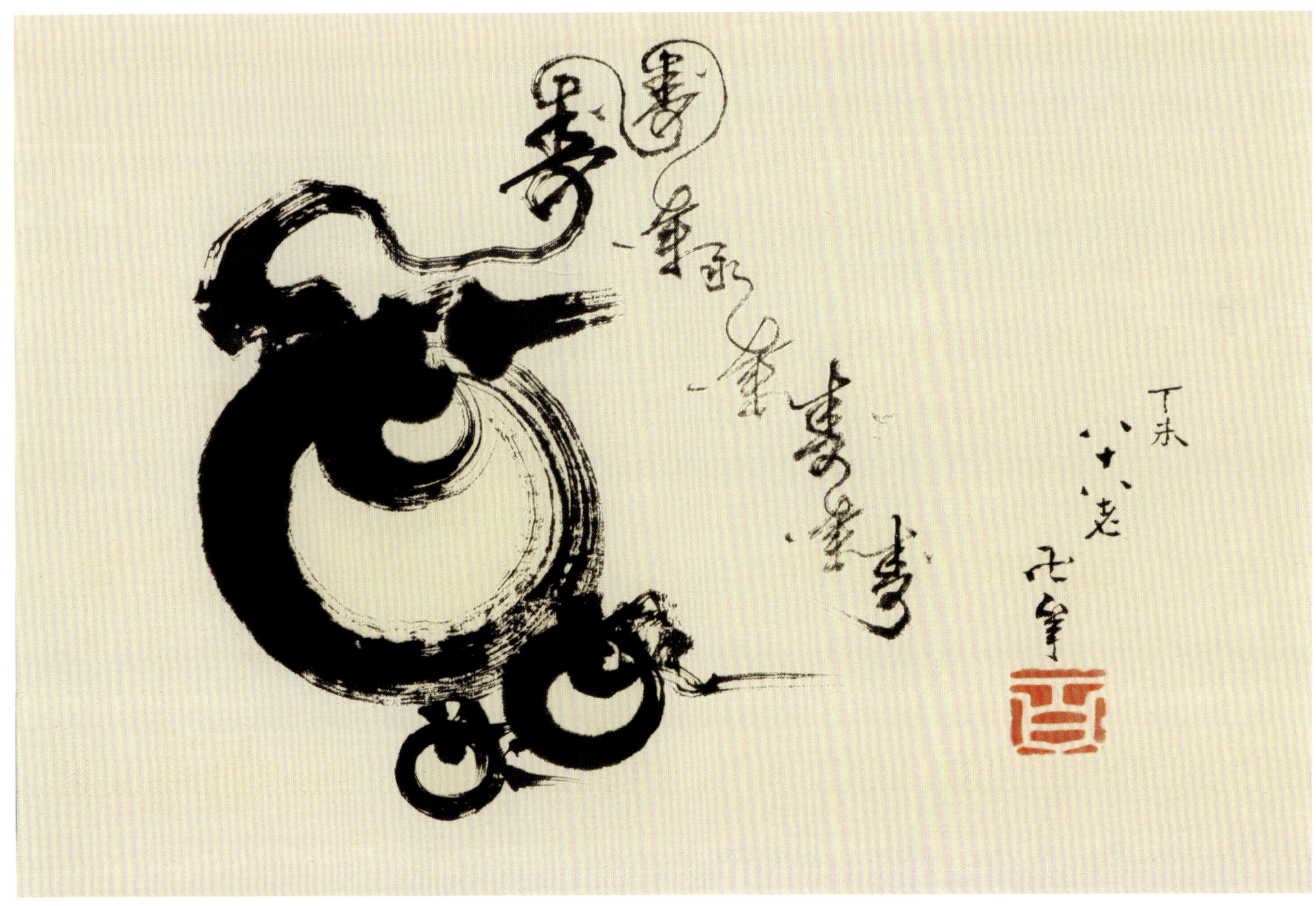

The new medium-size book *Shin hyakunin isshu* [*New One Hundred Poems by One Hundred Poets*] was commissioned from my daughter. However, after some discussion, I have decided to take it on myself. It will be started right after the warriors. The drawing fee will be according to the number of figures.[48]

The *One Hundred Poets* book project for Kobayashi does not seem to have materialized. But it may have triggered Hokusai's interest in working on a new series of large-sheet prints, *One Hundred Poems by One Hundred Poets, Explained by the Nurse* (cats 132–146), which would be the last major colour print series of his career.[49] The first five prints were issued by Nishimuraya Yohachi, then publication switched to Iseya Sanjirō for another twenty-two (plus one key-block proof), with both groups thought to have been issued in 1835–1836. Publication was then suspended, although Hokusai was continuing to prepare the remaining block-ready drawings as late as 1838 (sixty-three are known). It is fascinating to see Hokusai and Ōi discussing who will design what, and to know that Ōi was probably living with her father in Uraga.

In one letter to Kobayashi of the 17th day, first month, 1836, Hokusai promises that he will make a surreptitious visit to Edo the following month to stock up on art supplies:

> Around the beginning of the coming second month, my stock of brushes, paper, and pigments will be depleted. That will force this old man to return to Edo alone. I shall visit your store in secret then to give a more detailed account in person.[50]

Hokusai's personal fortunes in the 1830s must have been closely entwined with those of Nishimuraya Yohachi who, as we have seen, published nearly all his sheet prints in these years. Yohachi was also surely the leading presence in the project to publish volumes 1 and 2 of *One Hundred Views of Mt Fuji*. However, the prominence given in the colophons to an otherwise unknown publisher, Nishimura Yūzō – who must have been a relative – has led to the suggestion that Yohachi's business was in trouble and he needed additional capital.[51] This, rather than any economic dislocation caused by the Tenpō famine, may explain why, even though the outline blocks had probably been cut by 1835, publication of volume 3 had to be postponed by some fifteen years. When it finally appeared in about 1849, this final volume was fully resourced by the aggressively acquisitive publisher of Nagoya and Edo, Eirakuya Tōshirō. The last dated business advertisement for Nishimuraya Yohachi was in 1836. A letter of that year by author Takizawa Bakin (1767–1848) mentioned that already in 1835 the firm had been on the verge of 'putting up the shutters' (*to o tatesōrō yōsu*) and only able to continue in business by refinancing their debts.[52] Another Bakin letter of 1840 suggests that by then Yohachi was practically in hiding.[53] Thus, many of the frequent changes of direction in Hokusai's art while he was working within the world of print and book publication must have been dictated as much by commercial factors as by his personal artistic quest. The shift, broadly, from landscape and nature prints and books for Nishimuraya Yohachi in the early 1830s, to China-related books for Kobayashi Shinbei in the mid-1830s is just such a case in point.

Among the Nishimuraya advertisements appearing in the back of volume 2 of *One Hundred Views of Mt Fuji*, published in the third month, 1835, is one for a

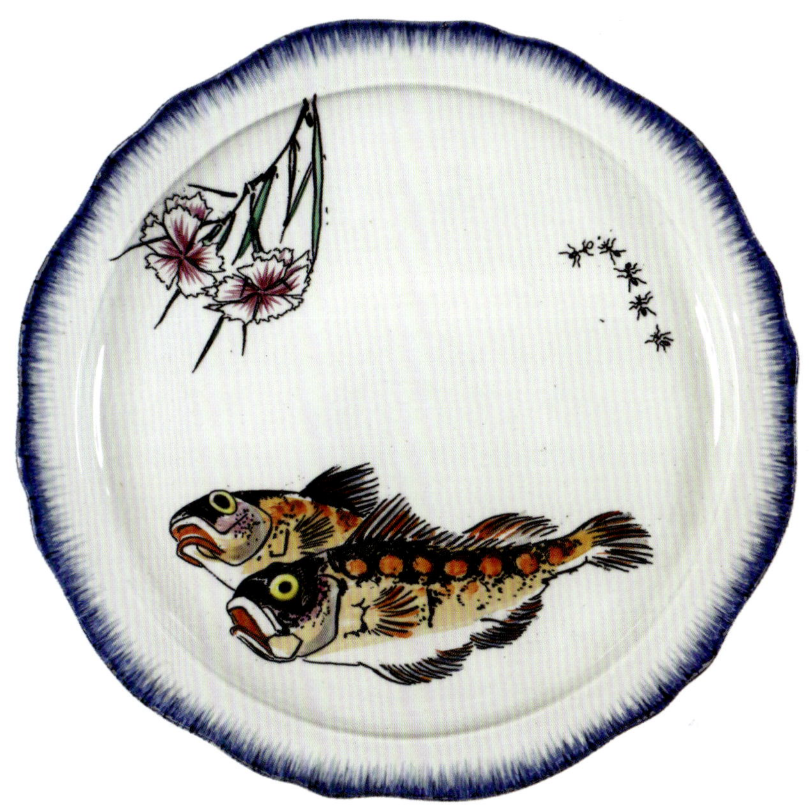

work entitled 'Picture Book Hand-Painted Folding Album' (*Ehon nikuhitsu gajō*).[54] This is thought to correspond to extant albums (three versions are known) in which ten nature and still-life subjects are repeated, with minor variations and in different orders, in painstakingly detailed ink and colour on thin paper (cat. 175). Each album is signed and sealed by Hokusai with the same form of names as the first two volumes of the *One Hundred Views* (1834–1835), so they are likely to be close in date, perhaps 1835–1836. According to the reminiscence of book publisher Shibaya Bunshichi, contained in the biography, it was by painting albums such as these that Hokusai was able to survive the worst privations of the famine in Edo:

> The year 1836 saw the famine spreading into many areas of the country, and the city of Edo could not escape. Many died of starvation and bodies were left in the street. Businesses were severely affected and many stores were as if closed. In such miserable conditions, people stopped buying luxury items such as colour prints or illustrated books.[55] No publisher dared to issue new prints. This made the lives of the artists particularly hard. In such dire conditions, Hokusai quickly came up with a life-saving idea. He gathered together all sorts of available paper – Chinese paper, official *hōsho* paper, *hanshi* paper for books – whatever was at hand, and piled it by his desk. Using all his skill and energy, he painted landscapes, figures, flowers and birds, plants and trees, following wherever the brush led. He then added covers to make folding albums and displayed them at various book and print stores. Since his name was already well known

by then, a few people began to purchase them, even in the midst of the famine. Thanks to this, Hokusai was able to escape starvation. Quite a few such books survive. The title on the cover is 'Hand-Painted Picture Book'.[56]

A worse personal disaster was to follow in a few years' time. At some point in 1839, the residence of Hokusai and Eijo at Honjo Daruma-yokochō burned to the ground.[57] Although in the past the artist had miraculously been able to escape the conflagrations that regularly destroyed large swathes of the city, on this occasion all his possessions were lost apart from the painting brushes that he grabbed as he jumped out of the building. The losses included a treasured collection of reference sketches that he had copied from old and new, Japanese and Chinese, even European pictures. In the past, they had almost filled a cart when he had transported them from lodging to lodging. Now Hokusai, aged eighty, and Eijo were reduced to near nakedness: they looked like beggars. This was the state in which Hokusai faced what would be his final decade.

EPILOGUE: WORLD ARTIST

From his twenties onwards, Hokusai adopted elements of European-style art that were crucial to the development of his own works – most importantly a sense of deep perspective, as epitomized by 'The Great Wave' (cat. 51). He knew that the genre paintings he created in European-influenced style for the visiting Dutch East India Company (VOC) officials in about 1824–1826 would find their way to Holland (cats 20–25).[58] But he can have had no inkling of how far and how quickly his reputation would spread in the half a century after his death in 1849. Within a few years, collectors in Japan were actively seeking out Hokusai paintings, and in 1900 the first major exhibition would be staged in Tokyo devoted to the artist's painted works.[59] This was in some part the result of his by then established international reputation. In 1843, volume 6 of *Hokusai's Sketches* (*Hokusai manga*) had been the first Hokusai work to find its way into the Print Room of the Bibliothèque nationale in Paris.[60] In 1859, the Japanese port of Yokohama was opened to international trade, following more than two centuries during which contacts with the outside world had been strictly regulated, with a newly established quarter for foreign residents there. Popular ukiyo-e ('floating world') prints and illustrated books began to flood out of the country. In 1860, the British Museum purchased its first Hokusai print.[61] Around 1866, the French artist Félix Bracquemond (1833–1914) was copying designs from *Hokusai's Sketches* (*Hokusai manga*) to decorate the so-called 'Rousseau' dinner service (fig. 9).[62] This would be displayed to acclaim at the Exposition Universelle d'Art et d'Industrie held in 1867, as were two illustrated books by Hokusai, *Hokusai's Sketches* (*Hokusai manga*, cats 164, 165) and *Ehon Musashi abumi*, which were among sixty titles sent by the shogunate for display in Paris.[63] The exhibition helped inaugurate Japonisme, the cultural movement inspired by enthusiasm for the art and design of Japan, which would soon flourish in many countries, with Hokusai as its standard-bearer.[64] But that is another story.

NOTES

1   For a general account of Hokusai's later career, see Lane 1989, especially chapters 21–23.

2   For more on the meaning of Hokusai's various art names, and his spiritual beliefs, see Suwa 2001.

3   The most comprehensive guide to Hokusai's paintings is Nagata 2000.

4   Inoue 1941. I am grateful to Robert Campbell and Yamamoto Yoshitaka for helping me to decipher Hokusai's two late letters to Isai.

5   Nagata 1997, pp. 138–139; Timothy Clark translation.

6   There is also a passing reference to Sakijūrō in the letter to Isai from the twelfth month. Originally named Takichirō, Hokusai's second son from his second marriage had been adopted into the samurai Kase family by 1819 and went on to have a successful career as a low-ranking direct vassal of the shogun, dying in 1861. Takemura 2010, p. 17.

7   *Edogaku jiten* 1984, chronology, pp. 837–838.

8   These statistics are from a personal communication from Asano Shūgō, 2014. Kubota 1989, vol. 95, pp. 26–27 lists 28 works with the 88 signatures; however, these have not all been examined.

9   See n. 26 below.

10   I am grateful to Ellis Tinios for pointing out the likely reference to this work in *Shoshoku ehon shin hinagata* 1836.

11   The work is fully illustrated and transcribed in Nagata *Edehon* 1985–1986, vol. 3, pp. 115–220, 230–270, 284–286. See also Retta 1994.

12   Nagata *Edehon* 1985–1986, vol. 3, p. 285; Timothy Clark translation.

13   Nagata 1997, pp. 114, 136, 141.

14   Iijima 1999, pp. 199–203; Kubota 2015, no. 16.

15   Iijima 1999, pp. 231–232.

16   Kubota 2015, p. 73.

17   Paris 2014, no. 537; Kubota 2015, no. 27.

18   I am grateful to Yasuhara Akio and Roger Keyes for sharing information about Hokusai's various addresses; personal communication, 2015.

19   Kubota 1989; Kobayashi 1996–1997; Hokusaikan 2015.

20   Kubota 1989, vol. 95, pp. 8–9.

21   Murayama 1906; Taki 1906; Christie's 1997; Hashimoto 2012.

22   Christie's 1997, pp. 24–25.

23   Kubota 1989, vol. 96, pp. 3–8.

24   See n. 4 above. The reading of the name remains tentative.

25   Kubota 1989, vol. 96, pp. 4–5, 17–22.

26   The worst destruction from the great Ansei earthquake and fire of 1855/10/2 was suffered on the eastern side of the Sumida river. So it was fortuitous that so many of Hokusai's paintings had been taken out of Edo before that date.

27   HK 15, Feb. 1980, pp. 4–11.

28   Nagata 1997, p. 141.

29   Kubota 1989, vol. 96, pp. 6–11; Kubota 2015.

30   See Asano commentaries in 'Worlds seen', pp. 140–205.

31   See Takemura Makoto, 'Nidai Hokusai ni tsuite', HK 54, Jan. 2015, pp. 4–46.

32   Hokusai had already used the name Manji in the composition of *senryū* comic poetry since about 1823, when he was sixty-four.

33   Suzuki 1986; Smith 1988; Nagata 2008.

34   Nagata 2008, pp. 42–49.

35   Guimet 2008, nos 95–100.

36   Smith 1988, p. 15; Roger Keyes, personal communication, 2016.

37   Smith 1988, pp. 14–16; Nagata 2008, pp. 17–20.

38   Roger Keyes, personal communication, 2016.

39   Nagata 2000, nos 78–89; Freer-Sackler 2006, no. 49.

40   Smith 1988, p. 7; Timothy Clark annotations.

41   Nagata Seiji, '(*Sekijō kihitsu*) *Gafuku senmai-kaki* hikifuda ni tsuite', in HK 46, Jan. 2011, pp. 4–15.

42   Nagoya 1991, pp. 181–183.

43   A pun on *Fugaku hyakkei* (*One Hundred Views of Mt Fuji*).

44   Timothy Clark translation.

45   Iijima 1999, pp. 141–160.

46   *Edogaku jiten* 1984, chronology, pp. 830–832.

47   Tinios 2015 (English); Tinios 2016 (Japanese).

48   Iijima 1999, p. 146; translation slightly adapted from Yasuhara 2015.

49   Morse 1989; Morse 1992; Nagata 2008, p. 11; Machotka 2009.

50   Iijima 1999, p. 148; translation slightly adapted from Yasuhara 2015.

51   Nagata 2008, pp. 11–12, 23–26.

52   Nagata 2008, p. 11.

53   Ibid., p. 25.

54   Itō 2000.

55   Analysis of the data provided by *Kotenseki sōgō mokuroku* suggests that the number of books published in Edo in each year during the 1830s seems to have been little affected by the Tenpō famine; Ellis Tinios, personal communication, 2016.

56   Iijima 1999, pp. 162–163; translation slightly adapted from Yasuhara 2015.

57   Iijima 1999, pp. 164–166.

58   Matthi Forrer, 'Katsushika Hokusai to Shiiboruto no deai', in Edo Tokyo 2007, pp. 11–39; also 'Katsushika Hokusai meeting with Siebold', in English Text Supplement, pp. 3–20.

59   Fenollosa 1901.

60   Paris 2014, p. 13.

61   1860,0414,0.321, purchased from the dealer Colnaghi in London.

62   Paris 2014, p. 15.

63   Nihon Shiseki Kyōkai, eds, *Tokugawa Akitake taiō kiroku* 2, 1932; repr. Tōkyō Daigaku Shuppankai, 1973, pp. 156–157. I am grateful to Ellis Tinios for bringing this to my attention, personal communication, 2016.

64   Guth 2015.

Hokusai's thought

Angus Lockyer

In what sense was Hokusai a thinker? He was well connected with writers and publishers, composing the occasional story for an illustrated book and participating enthusiastically in poetry circles during his middle decades. He may have studied with priests and scholars, to discover more about the religious and historical themes with which he populated his paintings and drawings. But he does not seem to have spent any time in the intellectual salons and academies of his day, or to have left behind essays or commentaries engaging with the religious, philosophical and political debates of the day.[1] His medium was brush and ink. With these he sought to translate the manifold phenomena of the world – large and small, visible and invisible – on to paper and silk, thereby revealing their power and wonder.

In doing so, however, Hokusai was also making claims about the world in which he lived. His extraordinary productivity, the diversity of his themes and styles, his determination to continue creating images for as long as he could – all of this suggests an unflagging will to understand the world through his brush. His vision was a compelling one at the time – even as it evolved from the popular, this-worldly concerns of his earlier years to an increasing focus on the spiritual significance of this and other worlds – and it remains a compelling one today. If we want to understand why Hokusai's pictures continue to move us, then we have to try to grasp how he understood the world and what he was trying to say – in other words, his thought.

We should resist the temptation, however, to confine Hokusai and his pictures within our own habitual ways of seeing. We might want to classify his multiple views of Mt Fuji in terms of landscape, for example, and thereby place them in a familiar story, which leads from the classical literary invocation of famous places, through an early modern travel boom, to modern preoccupations with topographical accuracy and romantic interiority. Or we might suggest that Hokusai depicted Fuji as a proto-national icon, building on the sacramental rites of the religious associations centred on the mountain, and thereby laying the ground for its investiture as a focus for ethnic identification. But doing so betrays the coherence and consistency of Hokusai's vision. It also makes it impossible to grasp why images produced in early nineteenth-century, pre-industrial Japan continue to find resonance in our post-industrial present.

SEARCHING FOR COMMUNION

We should start with faith. We know that, like many artists and performers in early modern Japan, Hokusai was a member of the Nichiren sect of Buddhism (cats 4, 157, 215). His biographer, Iijima Kyoshin (1841–1901), tells us that Hokusai made pilgrimages to famous Nichiren temples on the outskirts of Edo and that he could often be seen walking through the streets lost in the recitation of a mantra from the *Lotus Sutra*, the central text of that faith.[2] Tsuyuki Kōshō (Iitsu III, died after 1893), a pupil of Hokusai and the source of the anecdote about the mantra, also provided Iijima with a famous sketch, showing Hokusai and Ōi in their lodgings, with a statue of Nichiren enshrined in a box that had been used for tangerines (cat. 193). Hokusai's own late, great painting of Nichiren

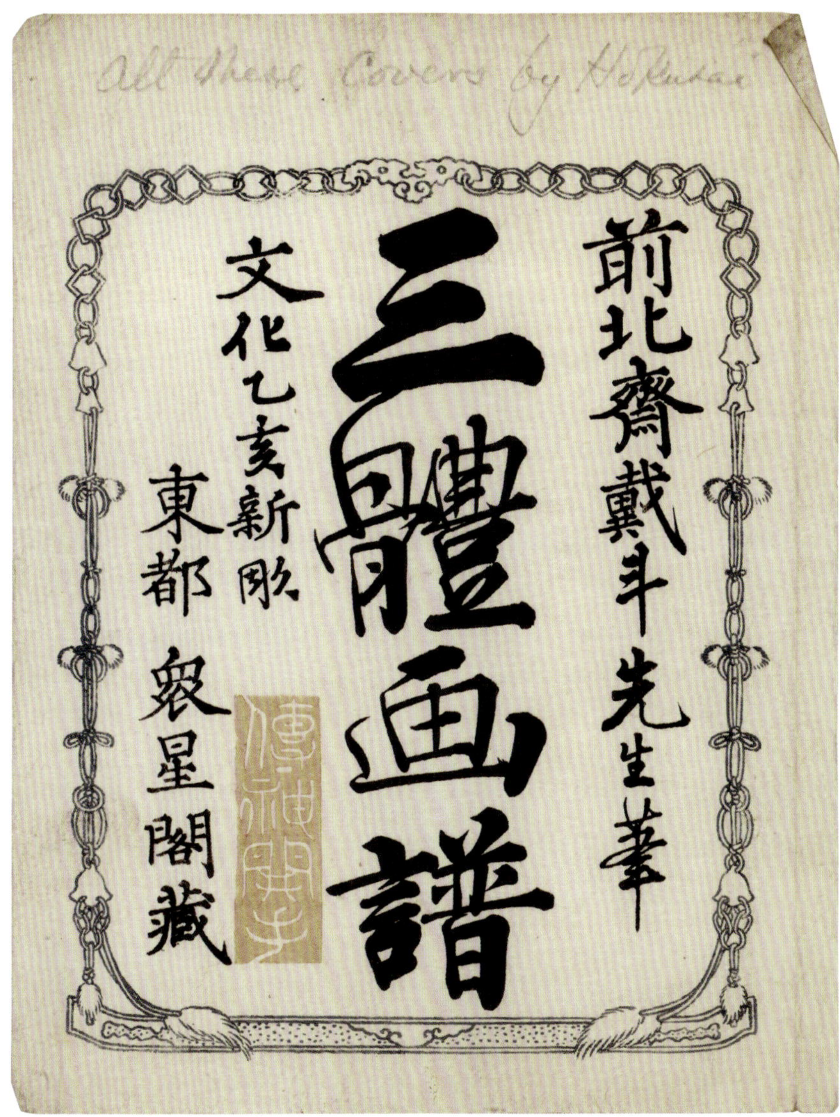

FIG 10

Wrapper for the book *(Denshin kaishu) Santai gafu*

1815

Colour woodblock, 22.5 × 16.8 cm

Museum of Fine Arts, Boston,

William Sturgis Bigelow collection,

11.45725

and a seven-headed dragon deity (cat. 215) is surely evidence of his belief in the enduring truth of the monk's gospel in a world of never-ending change.

We also know that Hokusai was a believer in the Bodhisattva Myōken, a deity associated with the North Star and Nichiren, and was a frequent visitor to the Myōken hall at Hosshōji, a Nichiren temple on the east side of Edo (cat. 2). Myōken seems to have been particularly important earlier in Hokusai's career, when he was struggling to make ends meet, and a number of his art names, including Hokusai, derived from his worship of the North Star.[3] Finally, Hokusai's work itself seems testament to some kind of belief in Mt Fuji as an enduring constant, through which it might be possible to transcend the present (cats 36 ff., 176–182, 221).

It is too easy, though, to fold these facts into an anodyne account of belief. The work of Hokusai's brush could simply be interpreted in line with the doctrinal and institutional preoccupations of traditional religious studies, thereby confining Hokusai within the limits of a particular faith or sect. In such a straightforward interpretation we might elaborate the nested hierarchy within which Myōken, as an associate of Nichiren, confirms Hokusai's identification as Buddhist. We might also want to determine whether or not he was indeed a member of a Fuji confraternity (*Fuji-kō*), in which case he must surely have engaged in their devotional practices and believed with them in the redemptive power of the mountain.

We need to remember, however, that religion in Japan had long been combinatory rather than exclusive.[4] The unseen world of deities and spirits was made up not of mutually jealous gods, but was rather a social network, making it possible to draw on multiple sources and forces in order to navigate the perils and possibilities of this life. Certainly, Hokusai seems to have had no problem in crossing doctrinal boundaries. His own family temple, Seikyōji, where he is buried, is affiliated with the Pure Land, rather than the Nichiren, sect. We know that he studied with Ogino Yaokichi (1781–1843), a Buddhist scholar affiliated with the Tendai school.[5] He also consulted with Kameda Bōsai (1752–1836), a Confucian scholar, in his search for new art names.[6] The profusion of gods in his work indicates his willingness to explore without prejudice the world of belief, however quickly we might want to assign the various deities to clear-cut categories.

More important and immediate, Hokusai's world was that of popular religion (*minshū shūkyō*). As this would suggest, his faith was in part a matter of praying for practical benefits – asking Myōken for success as an artist in his younger years, for example, or imploring the gods as he aged that he might live to be one hundred.[7] But this was not simply a matter of petitioning through occasional prayer to a separate, distant religious realm. The gods were ever-present in late Tokugawa Japan, such that each year and every day had its significance, aligned with the stars, to be decoded with almanacs.[8] Hokusai himself was well attuned to the importance of calendrical markers, not least the New Year, whether for urbane celebration (cats 7, 147), commercial opportunity (cat. 166) or spiritual renewal (cat. 224). And in this world, calibrated and tuned to the music of the spheres, practice was primary. Belief was not a matter of thinking the right thing, so that one's actions were insured, but of doing something repeatedly, thereby producing the desired result (cat. 191). The desire – as well as the result – for Hokusai, seems to have been communion with the world around him, and with other worlds which he could not visit in his lifetime, but which he could bring to life by putting brush to paper, repeatedly.

Equally important, Hokusai sought to pass on the possibility of communion to the world at large. A number of his drawing manuals, notably *Hokusai's Sketches* (*Hokusai manga*), came in wrappers bearing a red seal with the characters *denshin kaishu* (fig. 10). Earlier usage suggests it may be possible to translate this phrase prosaically as 'a picture primer'. It is hard, though, not to see other meanings suggested by the characters: 'transmitting' not the material form, but 'the spirit' of things, by 'opening one's hands' in petition to the gods and with generosity to the world.

AT HOME IN THE WORLD

For Hokusai, then, the boundary between the seen and the unseen was a permeable one. Perhaps more accurately, he lived at a time when the distinction between real and imagined worlds, which serves to structure our imagination, was less significant. Other distinctions, which we might assume to be foundational, were therefore hazy, too. Had he lived on into the late 1800s, Hokusai would have seen the emergence of a world in which the lines between present and past, us

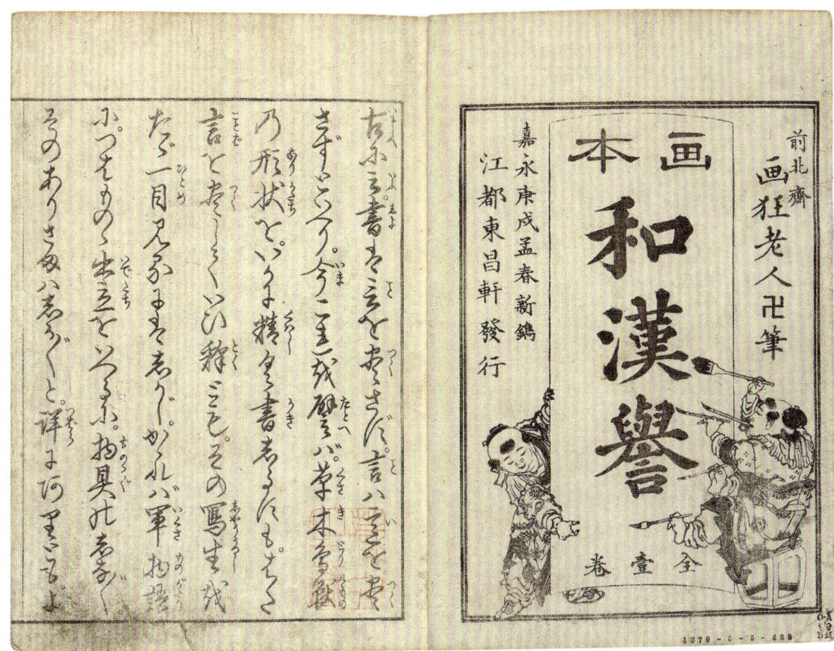

and them, would harden and be taken as absolute. His own world, by contrast, was one where horizons were local, but information abundant. The visible world may have been restricted to the one accessible on foot, but knowledge in late Edo society was encyclopaedic, providing access to an extraordinary catalogue of facts and figures about other times and places. And Hokusai's work is testament to the ease with which he was able to travel across boundaries, establishing connections where we might assume differences.

The most significant connections were with China. By the early 1800s, there were nativists in Japan who were trying to insist that the archipelago and the continent were two separate worlds. Educated people knew better. China was not, primarily, the country ruled at that point by the Manchu dynasty known as the Qing. Rather, that empire was a particular embodiment of a universal grammar that circumscribed the possibilities of this world.[9] Hokusai was therefore able to draw on a vast repository of cultural references, both to anchor his own practice (cat. 5) and to find an audience. Chinese poetry, for example, was a ready authority for one's choice of flowers to paint (cats 90–99). Japanese poetry had its own canon (cats 132–146), but Japanese poets took on added lustre when they could be seen in conversation with Chinese forebears (cats 123–129). Japanese warriors also had a long history of their own (cats 13, 131, 170, 171, 216), but were distinguished further when seen alongside their continental counterparts (cats 151, 169, fig. 11). And it was a tale of Chinese brigandage, *Outlaws of the Marsh*, that captivated the Japanese audience early in the nineteenth century, providing the raw material for one of Hokusai's longest-running publication projects (cat. 120).

Hokusai's thematic choices might easily be viewed in comfortably secular terms. His combining of Chinese and Japanese subjects followed conventional practice. He was a commercial artist, responding to the demands of the market. At a time of economic anxiety and political surveillance, it made sense to provide cultural consolation (through poetry) and reassurance (in the shape of heroes)

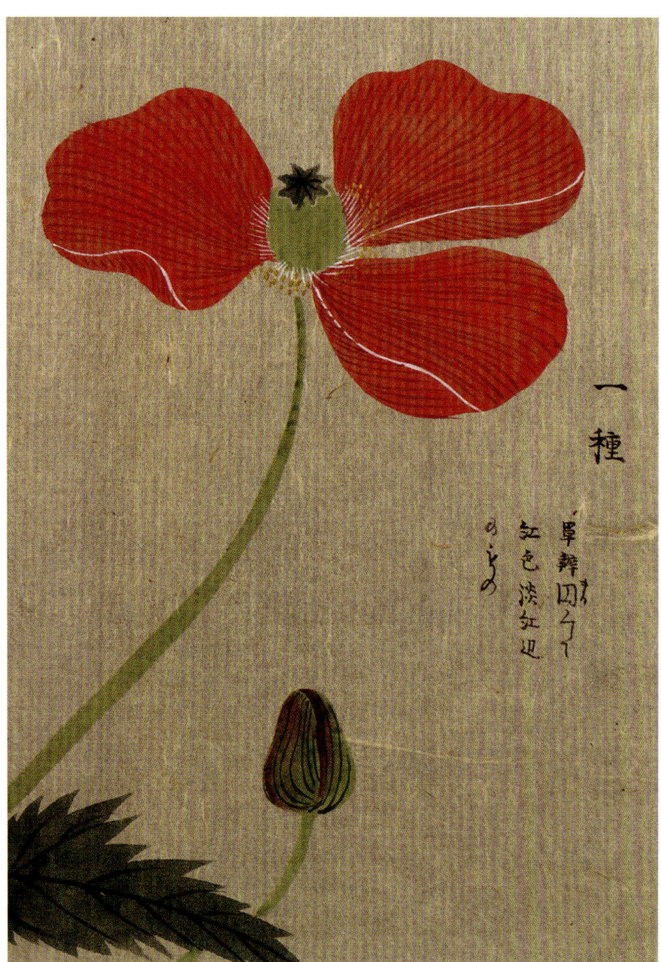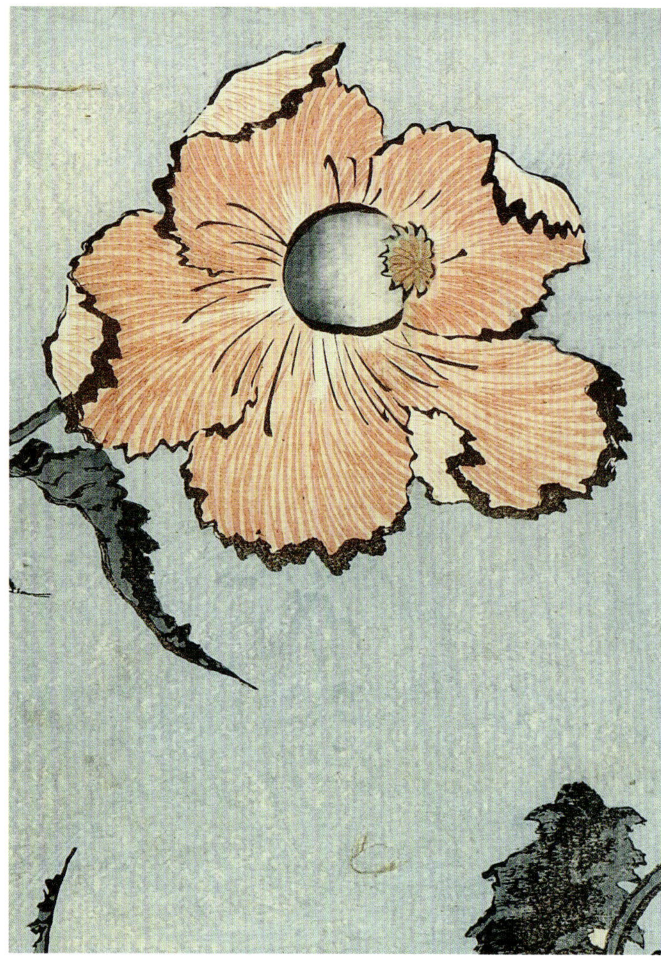

with examples that were drawn from times and places far away. Imposing our assumptions about history and geography like this, however, not only belies the ease with which Hokusai seems to have travelled across borders, it also discounts the immediacy and intimacy of the experience that he captures, for example, in the communion between a waterfall and the Chinese poet Li Bo (cats 123, 220).

THE FORMS OF THINGS

To understand this communion, we need to follow Hokusai carefully when he encourages us to look at things like waterfalls. From a distance or up close, he was determined to narrow the gap between us and what we might want to see simply as nature.

Hokusai was building on a long tradition of what we call landscape painting, but one that again came from China and often through literature, as with Li Bo. Famous places were made worthy of depiction by cultural precedent rather than empirical interest. Hokusai was departing from this – being both conversant with the past, but also engaged by the present – for example when he decided to make his own, new famous place (cat. 66). The story is further complicated because he was aware of and adept at European techniques, notably perspective drawing, with which to render a scene realistically (cats 20–25). Other artists

FIG 12 (ABOVE LEFT)
Iwasaki Kan'en (author and artist, 1786–1842)
'Poppy', in *Honzō zufu* (*Illustrated Manual of Plants*)
1828
Woodblock with hand colouring on paper, approx. 24.0 × 15.0 cm
Royal Botanic Gardens, Kew

FIG 13 (ABOVE RIGHT)
'Poppy' (detail; see cat. 83)
About 1831–1832
Colour woodblock, published by Nishimuraya Yohachi,
25.5 × 37.1 cm
British Museum 1960,0716,0.10, bequeathed by Morton Harcourt Sands

Notes

1 See Harry D. Harootunian, 'Late Tokugawa Thought and Culture,' in Marius B. Jansen, ed., *The Cambridge History of Japan*, vol. 5: *The Nineteenth Century*, Cambridge, Cambridge University Press, 1989, pp. 168–258.

2 Iijima 1999, pp. 203 and 207.

3 Iijima 1999, pp. 47 and 54.

4 Fabio Rambelli and Mark Teeuwen, eds, *Buddhas and Kami in Japan: Honji Suijaku as a Combinatory Paradigm*, New York and London, Routledge, 2002.

5 Iijima 1999, p. 203.

6 Iijima 1999, p. 54.

7 See also Ian Reader and George J. Tanabe, *Practically Religious: Worldly Benefits and the Common Religion of Japan*, Honolulu, University of Hawaii Press, 1998.

8 John Breen, 'Inside Tokugawa Religion: Stars, Planets and the Calendar-as-method', *Culture and Cosmos*, vol. 10, nos 1–2, 2006, pp. 63–78.

9 Harry D. Harootunian, 'The Functions of China in Tokugawa Thought,' in Akira Iriye, ed., *The Chinese and the Japanese: Essays in Cultural and Political Interactions*, Princeton, Princeton University Press, 1980, pp. 9–36; Marius B. Jansen, *China in the Tokugawa World*, Cambridge, MA, Harvard University Press, 1992; David Mervart, 'Meiji Japan's China Solution to Tokugawa Japan's China Problem', *Japan Forum*, vol. 27, no. 4, 2015, pp. 544–558.

10 Lane 1989, p. 241.

11 I am grateful to Roger Keyes for this insight, as well as the inspiration for the essay as a whole.

12 Maki Fukuoka, *The Premise of Fidelity: Science, Visuality, and Representing the Real in Nineteenth-Century Japan*, Stanford, Stanford University Press, 2012; Federico Marcon, *The Knowledge of Nature and the Nature of Knowledge in Early Modern Japan*, Chicago, University of Chicago Press, 2015.

were more content to adopt the custom of depicting what they saw in front of them, as Utagawa Hiroshige (1797–1858), for example, acknowledged.[10] Hokusai was after something different.

As with history, so with geography. Hokusai saw no need to restrict himself to what he could see, much less to depict what he saw as it appeared before his eyes. He was free to travel across the sea to provide a bird's-eye view of China (cat. 119). Here, he stuck close to his sources, given his audience's need for information about a place that remained for them out of reach. But the Tōkaidō highway, which linked Edo and Kyoto, was familiar (cat. 37). Hokusai was at liberty to distort the map to make his point. Mt Fuji not only occupied space in the physical landscape, it provided a spiritual anchor in relation to which the world was configured and a viewer could find their place. In *Thirty-Six Views of Mt Fuji*, Hokusai chronicled what Roger Keyes has characterized as 'the miraculous daily return of colour to the world' (cats 41–65). In *One Hundred Views of Mt Fuji*, he explored not only the material but also the spiritual dimensions of the mountain (cat. 176). Here and elsewhere, not least in his fascination with water (cat. 28 ff.), he returned repeatedly to the umbilical connection between stillness and movement – between the fixed and eternal truth of Fuji, for example, and the world of unceasing change.[11] By doing so, he sought to reveal how nature itself provides a connection to the divine (cats 206, 207).

This was no less the case when Hokusai turned to individual plants, birds and animals. As with nature writ large, he was drawing on East Asian traditions, for example that of bird-and-flower painting (cats 90–99), and on European techniques. This included the use of shading, with which to supplement the three traditional Japanese brush styles (formal, semi-cursive, and cursive: *shin*, *gyō*, *sō*) and so to animate his subjects (cats 82–88). The results, though, are far removed from the dead, decaying matter of European still lifes. They also seem to stand at some distance from the burgeoning Japanese practice of botanical illustration.[12]

To understand the difference, it is worth returning to Hokusai's own words, published as a postscript to *One Hundred Views of Mt Fuji* (Clark essay, p. 21, cat. 176). Sometimes characterized as autobiography, it is in fact a statement of intent. Hokusai turns his back on his past, dismissing the work of his first seven decades. It is only now, at the age of seventy-three, that he understands the true form of living things – how an animal's anatomy allows for movement, and the way plants come to be. But his focus is on the future. By ninety, he will see beyond surface and structure and into the 'essence' of things. By one hundred and ten, the marks he makes will themselves be alive. Hokusai is not talking about an invisible, prior world of inert, Platonic forms. His world comprises both visible beings and unseen forces. And he insists that drawing can bring both to life. His 'Poppy' (cat. 83) has been saved from the deadening, forensic brush of the botanical illustrator (figs 12 and 13). We can feel Hokusai in tune with the flower as it bends – and protests – turning its back on the wind. Equally, looking at the dragons that populate his final paintings (cats 215, 221, 223), we would be hard pressed to claim they have no place in the world in which we live.

The power of Hokusai's line

Matsuba Ryōko

Printing with woodblocks was the standard technology in Japan well into
the modern era. From gorgeous full-colour prints ('brocade prints') to simple,
inexpensive line-only programmes for the kabuki theatre, a wide range of
materials was produced using woodblocks. The industry reached its apogee
in terms of technical perfection and mass production in the early 1800s,
corresponding almost directly with Hokusai's mid- to late career.

The production process, managed by the publisher, who also bore the
financial risk, required the specialist trades of artist (and author in the case
of illustrated books), block cutter and printer (cat. 166). The artist would first
make preparatory drawings (*shita-e*) on a standard size of paper. After roughly
outlining the design with a charcoal stick (*yakifude*), the artist would then use
red for the underdrawing and for corrections, working towards a finished
outline drawing in black (cats 177–182). Finally, a thin sheet of paper was placed
over the preparatory drawing, and a neat, line-perfect drawing was produced
by tracing. This was the 'block-ready drawing' (*hanshita-e*). Thin Mino paper
was used, which was first polished using a boar's tusk until it took on a smooth,
shiny surface that could be drawn on with the brush without the ink catching
in the paper fibres.[1]

The finished drawing was then handed over to the block cutter, who pasted it
face-down on to a cherry woodblock and carefully cut away the background to
leave thin ridges of wood in relief that would print the lines of the finished work.
In the case of colour prints, this outline block was used to create a set of proof
prints (*kyōgō-zuri*), on which the artist indicated which colour should be printed
where. From these marked-up proofs a set of colour blocks was cut. The set
comprising outline block and colour blocks was then transferred to the printer,
and finished prints were printed on standard sizes of handmade paper.

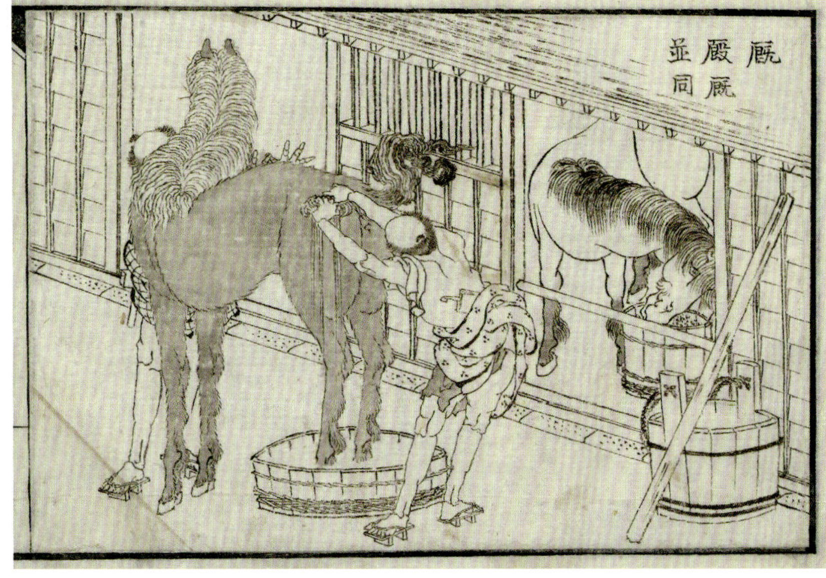

FIG 14

Drawings for a three-volume picture book
(detail)
1823–1835
Ink on paper, vol. 3 (of 3),
13.8 × 20.4 cm (covers)
Museum of Fine Arts, Boston,
1998.670.3, source unidentified

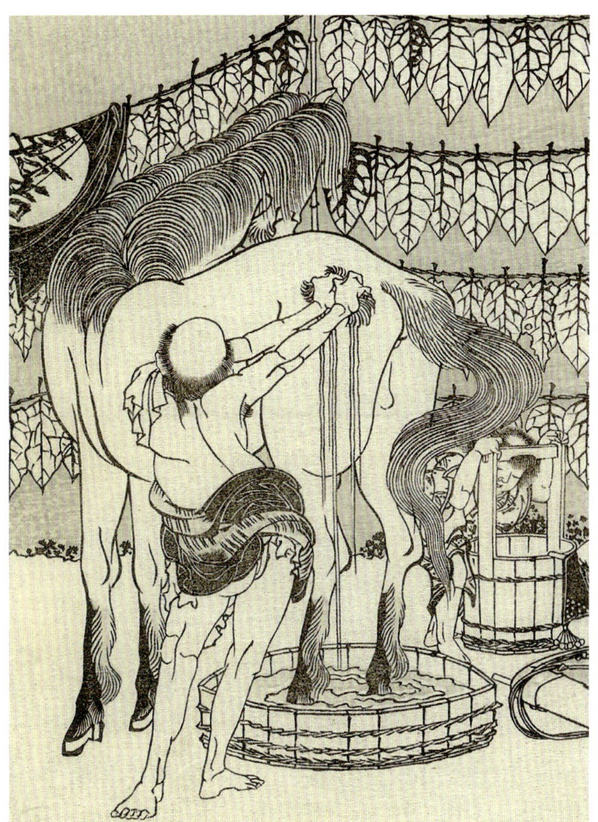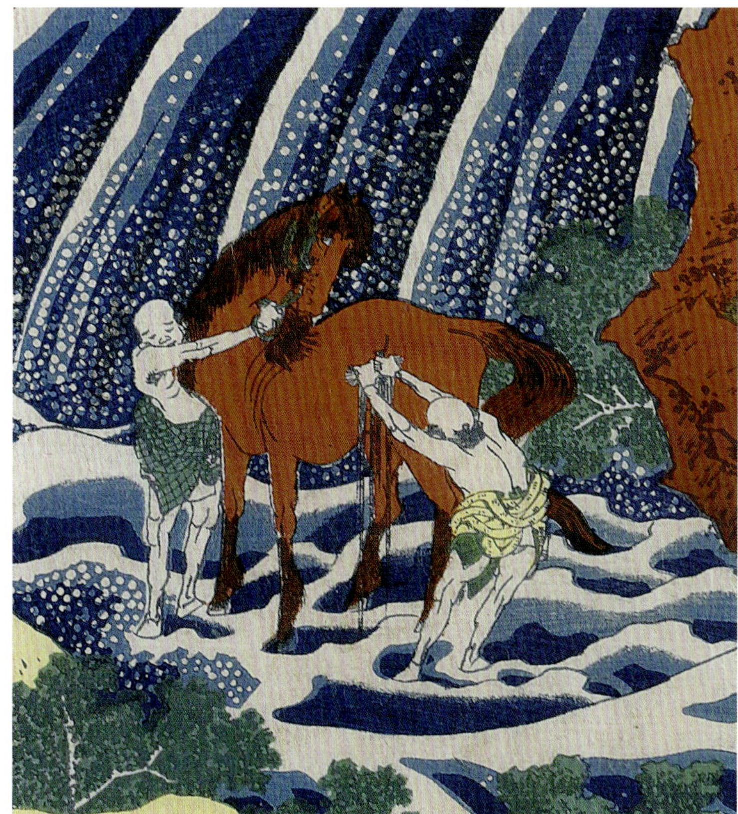

Ukiyo-e scholar Ishii Kendō noted that certain decisions were usually left up to the skill of the block cutter.[2] For instance, the artist did not draw every delicate hair line in a close-up portrait, but relied on the block cutter's skill to cut each strand. In his block-ready drawings (fig. 14), however, Hokusai drew incredibly fine lines for the hair on figures, fur on animals, patterns on objects, and the swell and foam of waves. It is as if he wanted to make sure that block cutters should not have to make any decisions of their own. According to the reminiscences of Sekine Shisei (1825–1893),[3] Hokusai always made a preparatory drawing, and if there was anything about this that did not please him, he would keep redrawing it until he was satisfied. And in truth, the perfection of Hokusai's surviving block-ready drawings is astounding. It must have been a source of regret to the artist that some of his block-ready drawings were never used. But fortunately for us, these surviving drawings allow us to examine the qualities of Hokusai's line and reveal the exacting technical standards he expected in the printed works of his later years.

A CHALLENGING LINE

In the 1830s, when he was in his seventies, Hokusai produced his most extraordinary print series and illustrated books. Beginning with the large-sheet colour woodblock series *Thirty-Six Views of Mt Fuji* (cats 41–65), he designed a succession of powerful single-sheet prints depicting famous places, warriors and birds-and-flowers. In the realm of illustrated books, the *Hokusai manga* series (cats 164, 165), which had reached preliminary completion in 1819 with volume 10, resumed publication. In 1834 Hokusai launched the first volume of his greatest

illustrated book, *One Hundred Views of Mt Fuji* (cat. 176). His designs in it called
for even more intricate details; Hokusai's demands on block cutters became
increasingly severe. In 1833 he was dissatisfied with the way the eyes and noses had
been cut for some of the pages in a volume of *Illustrated Anthology of Tang Poetry* (cat.
125). He demanded that the blocks be corrected; the publisher complied at once.[4]

We know from Hokusai's letters to publishers that he particularly trusted
the block-cutting skills of Egawa Tomekichi (worked 1820s–1830s).[5] Hokusai
and Egawa had already worked together on the production of the illustrated
book *Modern Designs for Combs and Tobacco Pipes* of 1823 (cats 29, 39), printed in
a small horizontal format that could handily be stored in a sleeve. The incredibly
fine patterns of the comb and pipe designs represented a new departure for
Hokusai. Cutting these intricate drawings into wooden printing blocks required
inordinate skill, and Egawa rose to Hokusai's challenge with extraordinarily fine
cutting of the lines. This must have been what convinced Hokusai that he should
work exclusively with Egawa on all important future works.

A significant difference in cutting skill is evident between Hokusai's single-sheet
landscape colour prints and his finest illustrated books. It is instructive to compare
Hokusai's block-ready drawing (fig. 14) of a scene of washing a horse for a book
that was never published (cat. 168) with a print version of a similar scene from an
illustrated book (fig. 15, from *One Hundred Views of Mt Fuji*, cat. 176) and a colour
woodblock print (fig. 16, from the series *Tour of Waterfalls in Various Provinces*, cat. 70)
– both printed versions were issued by the publisher Nishimuraya. According to
Higuchi Niyō (1863–1930), who was an ukiyo-e artist in his early career, it was the
custom to use less-skilled block cutters for landscape prints; in contrast, and
especially for Hokusai's illustrated books, book publishers employed high-calibre
block cutters who could work on both texts and images.[6] The fees of a master
block cutter such as Egawa Tomekichi were likely quite high. In Hokusai's letters,
he recommends that several publishers divide the cost of Egawa's fees between
them.[7] However, in the case of a series of single-sheet prints such as *Tour of*

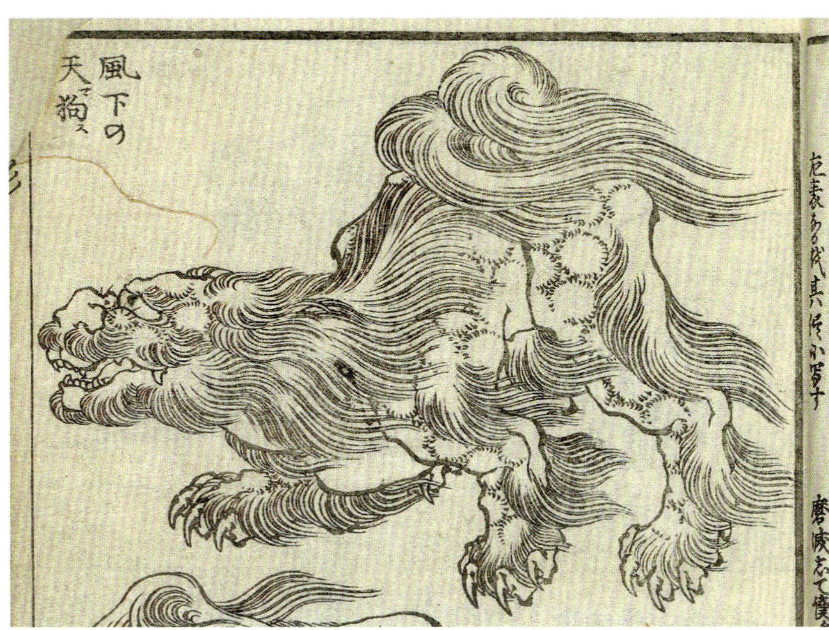

Waterfalls in Various Provinces (cats 66–71), which was issued by the Nishimuraya firm alone, it was probably not possible to engage the services of a block cutter of the calibre of Egawa. For Hokusai, who always wanted to have his drawn lines reproduced as faithfully as possible, it must have been more reassuring to work in the medium of the illustrated book than the large-sheet colour print.

At the same time as volumes 1 and 2 of *One Hundred Views of Mt Fuji* were being published in the mid-1830s, Hokusai was also engaged by the same publisher, Nishimuraya, to produce the series of large-sheet colour woodblock prints *One Hundred Poems by One Hundred Poets, Explained by the Nurse* (cats 132–146). The number of designs actually published was twenty-seven and, most unusually, some forty unpublished block-ready drawings have survived. One reason for the failure to publish the full series was surely the economic difficulties experienced by Nishimuraya in the mid-1830s.[8] But could another reason have been that it simply was not possible to inject sufficient capital into the project to be able to cut the extremely fine drawings well enough to satisfy Hokusai's demands?

In 1836, Egawa Tomekichi was engaged once again to cut the blocks for Hokusai's illustrated book *Picture Book for Various Crafts: New Models* (*Shoshoku ehon shin hinagata*). Included among Hokusai's illustrations is the ostentatious note 'abbreviated so as to avoid causing too much work during cutting', the implication being that he has refrained from drawing too much detail so as to lessen the burden on the block cutters. Furthermore, the following exchange appears in the final illustration,[9] beginning with a customer complaining, 'Hokusai, your pictures are too detailed. They are not pictures any more. Do something about it!' To which the response is, 'If your technique is clumsy to begin with, as you grow older it will very quickly get worse.… Day by day in my old age, I am developing my technique by building on my past failures. Even though I'm nearly eighty, my eyesight and the strength of my brush are no different from when I was young. Let me live to be a hundred and I will be without equal!' The declaration that he will live to be more than one hundred and become a true artist chimes with

FIG 17 (OPPOSITE)

Chinese lion, from *Picture Book for Various Crafts: New Models* (*Shoshoku ehon shin hinagata*) (detail)
1836
Illustrated book, woodblock, 22.0 × 16.0 cm (covers)
British Museum, 1979,0305,0.457

FIG 18 (RIGHT)

Chinese lion, from *Picture Book: Essence of Colouring* (*Ehon saishiki tsū*) (detail)
1848
Illustrated book, woodblock, vol. 2 (of 2), 18.0 × 13.0 cm (covers)
British Museum, 1979,0305,0.465.2

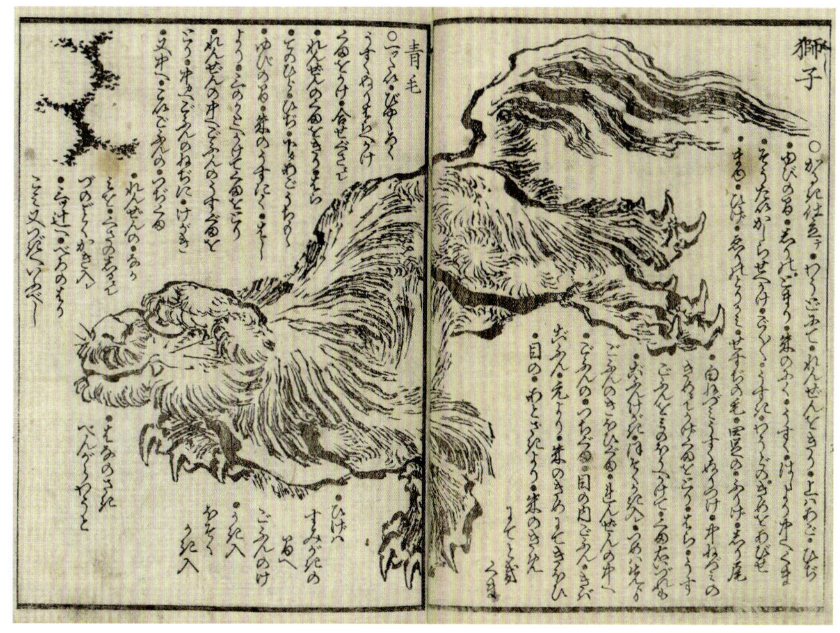

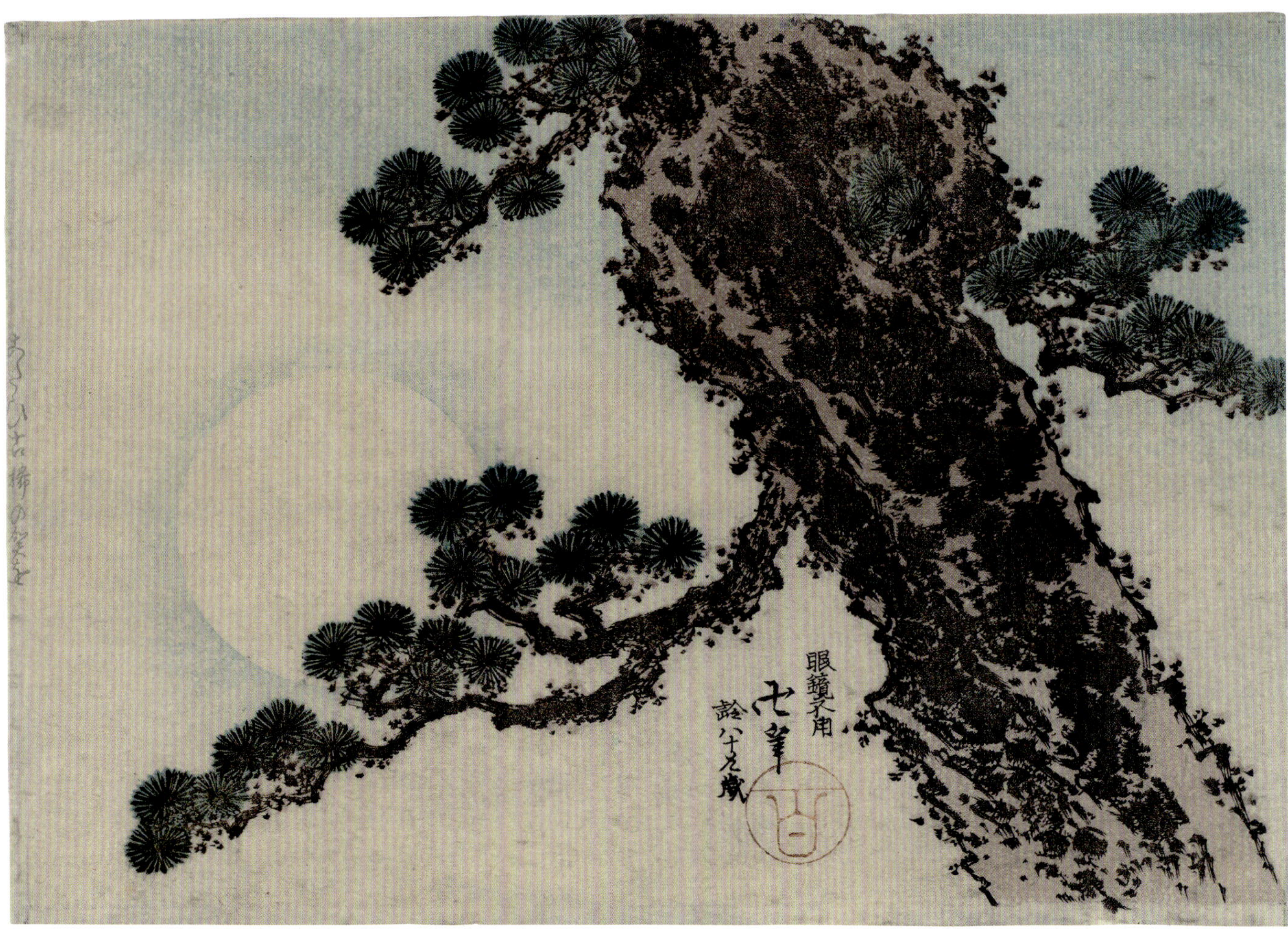

the famous colophon text of *One Hundred Views of Mt Fuji* (cat. 176 and p. 21). Hokusai fervently believed that accumulated life experience was constantly burnishing his technical skill. It was natural that his bodily strength would diminish as he grew older, but he resisted old age by maintaining the strength of his line.

A CRITICAL EYE

Hokusai was not only demanding of his publishers and block cutters, he also grew increasingly critical of his *own* compositions in later life. Several notations 'painted while drunk' are found in the illustrated books published in these years.[10] Iijima Kyoshin, author of the biography *Katsushika Hokusai den* (1893), weighs the evidence as to whether Hokusai, who had a reputation as a non-drinker, actually did or did not drink alcohol.[11] The inference is that the artist was using this claim as an excuse for what he regarded as a certain clumsiness in his drawing. Unlike her father, Hokusai's artist daughter Eijo (Ōi, about 1800–after 1857) is known to have enjoyed a drink, even sometimes signing her work with punning characters meaning 'drunken woman'. So it could also be conjectured that the 'painted while drunk' notations may indicate that Ōi was helping Hokusai with these particular illustrations and wanted this to be acknowledged in some way. The notations are clustered in the late 1830s and, whether Ōi was helping or not, the conclusion is

FIG 19

Pine tree and full moon
1848
Signature: Megane fuyō, Manji hitsu, yowai hachijūkyū sai ('Brush of Manji, aged eighty-nine, eye glasses not needed')
Seal: Hyaku ('Hundred')
Colour woodblock, 18.1 × 25.4 cm
Museum of Fine Arts, Boston, William S. and John T. Spaulding Collection, 21.10243

NOTES

1 Higuchi 1983, p. 88.

2 Ishii 1929, p. 20.

3 Iijima 1999, p. 215.

4 Tinios 2015, Tinios 2016.

5 Kobayashi 1996–1997, vol. 15, pp. 194–199. Egawa led a workshop of several craftspeople working under his name and direction and they divided the cutting work between them.

6 Higuchi 1983, pp. 118–119.

7 Iijima 1999, p. 143. This was possible in the case of illustrated books, which were often published by a consortium of different publishers.

8 The letter from Takizawa Bakin to Ozu Keiso, 21st day, sixth month, 1836. Shibata Mitsuhiko and Kanda Masayuki, eds, *Bakin shokan shūsei*, vol. 4, Tokyo, Yagi Shoten, 2003, p. 175.

9 The texts were translated into French in the book *Hokusai: Le vieux fou d'architecture* (*Shoshoku ehon* 28), Paris, Seuil, 2014.

10 Volume 49 of the illustrated adventure story *New Illustrated 'Outlaws of the Marsh'* (*Shinpen Suiko gaden*, 1835–1838, cat. 120); *Ehon Musashi abumi* (1836); *Ehon Wakan no homare* (1836; the publication date of *Ehon Wakan no homare* is 1850. However, the final illustration is signed 'Brush of Manji, Old Man Crazy to Paint, aged seventy-six years' and so the drawings must have been devised in 1835); and volume 6 of *Illustrated Life of Shakyamuni* (*Shaka go-ichidaiki zue*, 1845, cat. 158; preface dated 1838).

11 Iijima 1999, pp. 188–190.

12 Suzuki Jūzō suggested that the illustrations from part 7 of *New Illustrated 'Outlaws of the Marsh'* onwards were by Hokusai's pupil Taito II (Iijima 1999, p. 188). It has so far not been possible to find examples of illustrations actually signed by Taito II. However, there does indeed appear to be a change in style from part 7 onwards.

that on certain occasions during this period Hokusai was not able to draw lines in his block-ready drawings that completely satisfied him. In volumes 56–58 and 60 of part 6 of *New Illustrated 'Outlaws of the Marsh'*, published in 1838, the artist even added the note 'three pages in this volume were drawn from my sickbed'.[12]

There is a hiatus in Hokusai's production of woodblock prints and woodblock printed books after 1838, a subject that deserves a separate essay. Part of the explanation was certainly that the artist concentrated more and more on the production of paintings. But another reason may have been that Hokusai was no longer able freely to draw the fine lines demanded for a block-ready drawing. He had spent most of his working career designing illustrated books, so this development must surely have been disconcerting to him. As we know from letters Hokusai wrote in the 1830s, he viewed with an extremely critical eye the work of block cutters. Hokusai intuitively realized that he was racing against time, and he was determined that the printed works of his seventies would faithfully represent the height of his artistic achievement.

LIFE STRENGTH

The year 1848 saw the publication of the artist's last painting manual, *Picture Book: Essence of Colouring* (cat. 211). He was eighty-nine. If we examine the lines carefully we can see that the block cutter faithfully reproduced the way Hokusai had broken down any long lines in his block-ready drawings into smaller fragments. A comparison between a Chinese lion in *Picture Book for Various Crafts: New Models* (fig. 17), published in 1836, and the one in *Picture Book: Essence of Colouring* (fig. 18) of more than a decade later is instructive. Where the earlier image emphasizes the flowing movement of the carved steady lines, the later one conscientiously cuts each and every inflection of Hokusai's faltering lines. This shows the direct expression of Hokusai's actual brush power at this late date. Conflicting impulses are apparent in the work: on the one hand there is the stubborn desire as an artist to try out his strength one more time in his final years; on the other, he is facing up to the reality of growing old and seeking to disguise this.

A rare Hokusai *surimono* print, 'Pine tree and full moon' (fig. 19), was issued in 1848, the same year as *Picture Book: Essence of Colouring*. The signature includes 'eye glasses not needed' (*megane fuyō*), boasting the undimmed strength of the artist's eyesight. The textures of the tree bark and the individual pine needles are indeed painstakingly drawn. This insistence that his strength as an artist is undimmed recalls the comment of more than ten years earlier in *Picture Book for Various Crafts: New Models*: 'my eyesight and the strength of my brush are no different from when I was young'.

It is Hokusai's paintings that have received the most attention in assessments of the art of his later years. Yet when we review his career as a whole, he was most active – in terms of quantity – in the medium of illustrations for printed books. As he entered his final years, Hokusai's critical assessment of the qualities of his own line became ever sharper. However, as the artist himself became painfully aware, it became harder and harder for him to draw block-ready drawings as he wished them to be. Even as he felt a fading of his physical strength, Hokusai nevertheless used the 'hundred' seal following his signature, ever aspiring to reach the age of one hundred, perhaps even one hundred and ten. He was unshakeable in his belief that day by day his technical skill would get better and better. His undimmed eyes and continued mastery of his brush maintained the power of his line. It was this that gave Hokusai the strength to go on living.

Hokusai in old age – his ideas, his way
Asano Shūgō

From his youth Hokusai actively studied the painting styles of various schools, incorporating them to create his own unique artistic idiom, which is widely appreciated to the present day. His fierce dedication to painting is reflected by his use of *gakyō* ('crazy to paint') in two of his art names. But he was not just a painter. In the late 1790s and early 1800s, using the name Tokitarō Kakō, Hokusai both authored and created drawings for several books of comic fiction (*kibyōshi*). Later, in the 1820s and early 1830s, he composed comic haiku poetry (*zappai*). These literary activities throw a revealing light on Hokusai's stubborn determination in old age to have firm control over the artistic projects he undertook.

Tenri University Library, Nara, holds the rare preparatory drawings for a *kibyōshi* by Hokusai, *Muna zan'yō uso no tana-oroshi*, published in 1803. These show that Hokusai made numerous corrections and changes between the drawings and the published book. As long as he had agreement from the publisher, he was free to make any changes he wanted. This was not possible, however, when he had to collaborate with a separate author, for example Takizawa Bakin (1767–1848), with whom he often clashed.[1] This may have been the reason why Hokusai stopped drawing illustrations for *yomihon* adventure stories in his fifties, in order to concentrate on his own picture books and brush drawing manuals. Rather than endlessly making neat block-ready drawings from rough preparatory drawings by another author, he wanted to control the whole process himself. In old age, Hokusai was determined to carry through his own ideas, in his own way.

Hokusai illustrated three *yomihon* adventure stories after the age of sixty-one. The first was parts 2 to 6 of *New Illustrated 'Outlaws of the Marsh'* (*Shinpen suiko gaden*, 1829–1838, cat. 120).[2] Hokusai seems to have illustrated part 1 much earlier, from 1805, but as the story progressed in the 1830s, his idiosyncratic style became more and more pronounced. The second was *Picture Book: Military Chronicles of the Han and Chu* (*Ehon Kanso gundan*, 1843, 1845). The preface states that it was written by Tamenaga Shunsui (1790–1844) and others, but 'picture book' (*ehon*) in the title demonstrates the pre-eminence of Hokusai's illustrations, and it is his signature, 'Katsushika Iitsu Manji rōjin ga' (Drawn by old man Manji, Iitsu [of] Katsushika), that appears on the inside cover. The illustrations are also filled with his distinctive mannerisms of style, so we can presume he did not have to work from preparatory drawings supplied by the author(s) – everything was left up to Hokusai. Finally, *Illustrated Life of Shakyamuni* (*Shaka go-ichidaiki zue*, 1845, cat. 158) was authored by Yamada Isai (1788–1846). However, the gulf between its illustrations and traditional depictions of the life of Shakyamuni suggests that these, too, were left completely to Hokusai's invention. Apart from some *surimono* prints in the 1820s and his famous colour prints of the 1830s, Hokusai was concentrating all his artistic efforts on paintings, illustrated books and brush drawing manuals.

Block-ready drawings are normally destroyed during the process of cutting the printing blocks, but quite a number have survived for Hokusai's sheet prints and illustrated books. As suggested above, Hokusai was so particular about all the details of concept and execution that this must have led to disputes with publishers, particularly later in his career, when his demands resulted in higher fees for drawing and cutting and even in disagreements about content.[3] Only one set of early drawings survives,[4] but we know of seven substantial groups from the artist's later Iitsu and Manji periods, that is, from the 1820s through the 1840s.[5] It is revealing to examine one of these in greater detail: the block-ready drawings for a picture book, *Record of Shoguns of Great Japan, Collection One* (*Dai Nihon shōgun ki, shoshū*, 6 volumes, cat. 171), and the related preparatory drawings *Lives of Famous Generals of Japan* (*Nihon meishō den*, 3 volumes, cat. 170) – both in the collection of the Museum of Fine Arts, Boston.

'LIVES OF FAMOUS GENERALS OF JAPAN' AND 'RECORD OF SHOGUNS OF GREAT JAPAN, COLLECTION ONE'

Lives of Famous Generals of Japan is a set of three volumes, each with 'Drawings by Hokusai' (*Hokusai ga*) inscribed by hand on the cover and on a sheet with the title pasted inside. The volumes contain thirty-two double-page compositions of preparatory drawings. On the title page is the inscription, 'Preparatory drawings for block-ready drawings by Hokusai / These pictures were never made into blocks. They are a masterpiece for all ages.' *Record of Shoguns of Great Japan, Collection One* is a set of six loosely bound volumes, containing thirty-three double pages of block-ready drawings within printed page outlines, with the title on the edge of the page. The block-ready drawings are interleaved in the volumes with blank pages, presumably to make it easier to disassemble them when needed for cutting the blocks. There is one more drawing overall than in *Lives of Famous Generals*, but otherwise the two sets of volumes contain thirty-two corresponding pairs of preparatory drawings and block-ready drawings.

That *Record of Shoguns* was drawn by Hokusai himself can be demonstrated by comparison with his other warrior books of the 1830s.[6] First and foremost, in style and format – printed page outlines with edge-of-page title – they correspond exactly with the album of block-ready drawings *Picture Book: Japan and China in the Katsushika Style* (cat. 169), which in turn relates closely to the published warrior books *Picture Book of the Warrior Vanguard in Japan and China* (cat. 151) and *Ehon Musashi abumi*, both of 1836.[7] Further, *Record of Shoguns* is drawn in such a way that it was not intended as a simple black-and-white book, achieved in a single printing; rather, it would require an additional one or two printings in shades of grey. In this respect, it is like early printings of *Ehon Musashi abumi*, of 1836, and *Ehon Wakan no homare*, published posthumously in 1850. It is perhaps because Hokusai insisted on these expensive additional stages in the printing process that *Record of Shoguns* was never published.

There can be no doubt that Hokusai is also responsible for the preparatory drawings *Lives of Famous Generals*. They are full of the wonderful brush mannerisms only found in preparatory drawings by the master himself, and employ the same underdrawing in red ink and pale *sumi* (black) ink found in the surviving preparatory drawings for *One Hundred Views of Mt Fuji* (cats 177–182) and *One Hundred Poems by One Hundred Poets, Explained by the Nurse* (cats 132–146). Though clearly preparatory to *Record of Shoguns*, they include many details that were subsequently changed in the finished block-ready drawings. It is simply not possible that someone other than Hokusai could have drawn these, by working backwards from the finished block-ready drawings *Record of Shoguns*.

An important issue requiring further research is exactly when Hokusai did these preparatory and block-ready drawings. They do not seem to have the conspicuous sense of movement and the exaggerated contrasts between the figures seen in other warrior books of the Tenpō era (1830–1844). Therefore it is possible that they were done as early as the Bunsei era (1818–1830).

THE UNPUBLISHED WARRIOR BOOKS

Apart from one page, all the illustrations in both sets of drawings are annotated with a title, the majority of which relate to events of the Genpei civil wars of the late 1100s. The earliest, as titled in *Record of Shoguns*, are 'Yoritomo sends loyal troops to Izu to attack Yamaki Kanetaka' and 'Sadatsuna joins the allied armies and kills Nobutō' (17th day, eighth month, 1180). The latest is 'Yoritomo's battle group five attacks Yasuhira in Mutsu province' (eighth month, 1189). In broad terms then, the unpublished warrior books chronicle the founding of the Kamakura shogunate (1185–1333), from the time Minamoto no Yoritomo first raised his armies, through to his final victory in Mutsu province. The one illustration not connected to the Genpei wars is 'Legend of the deity Benzaiten of Enoshima summoning a five-headed poisonous dragon' (figs 20, 21). Enoshima is close to Kamakura, where the first shoguns were based, and this is perhaps why Hokusai chose this for the opening illustration of the book.

Apart from this picture of Benzaiten, we can trace the subjects of the other illustrations to medieval chronicles such as *Azuma kagami*, *Heike monogatari*, *Genpei seisuiki* and *Gikei ki*. The titles in the unpublished warrior books relate most closely, but not exclusively, to *Azuma kagami* (after 1266). For example, there is no specific entry in *Azuma kagami* for 'Heroic fighting by Sanada Yoichi Yoshitada', whereas there are references to this in *Heike monogatari* and *Genpei seisuiki*. The reasons for the discrepancies between the original sources and Hokusai's drawings are not entirely clear, but it is probable that he was also drawing on and incorporating material from popular contemporary sources. For example, 'Ushikawamaru enlists the help of Princess Minazuru to see the secret scroll' derives originally from the medieval *Gikei ki*, but it is more likely that Hokusai's direct source was the Edo period puppet and kabuki play *Kiichi Hōgen sanryaku no maki*. For some of the designs, it is clear that he referenced *Genpei seisuiki zue* (*Illustrated Rise and Fall of the Minamoto and Taira*), published in 1800.[8] Four of Hokusai's drawings are somewhat similar to the published illustrations in volumes 5 and 6 of this work. For example, the block-ready drawing 'Oblivious to the dangers of wind and waves, warrior hero Yoshitsune crosses to Shikoku' (fig. 22) relates to 'Enduring a storm, warrior general Yoshitsune crosses to Yashima' (fig. 23) in volume 5: the military crests on the sails of the three ships are identical in the two illustrations. Finally, 'Shimizu Yoshitaka enters Kamakura and has an audience with his stepmother Masako' does not appear in the medieval warrior tales, but is probably based on a popular tale such as *Shimizu kanja monogatari*.

INSCRIPTIONS IN THE UNPUBLISHED WARRIOR BOOKS

Of particular interest are the inscriptions written on small pieces of paper and pasted into *Lives of Famous Generals*, and the margin notes in *Record of Shoguns*. The inscriptions on the preparatory drawings show us Hokusai thinking through the design process. Figure 24 shows 'Defeated at the Battle of Ishibashiyama, Yoritomo hides in a fallen tree' from *Lives of Famous Generals*, in which Yoritomo and his followers hide in the hollow trunk of a large tree, with the forces of 'Ōba and Matano' shown in the background right.[9] The small vertical piece of paper

FIG 20 (RIGHT)

Attributed to Katsushika Hokusai
'Legend of the deity Benzaiten
of Enoshima summoning a
five-headed poisonous dragon'
(preparatory drawing), from
Lives of Famous Generals of Japan
About 1820–1835
Ink on paper, 23.5 × 16.4 cm
(covers)
Museum of Fine Arts, Boston,
2006.1863.1-3, source unidentified

FIG 21 (BELOW)

Attributed to Katsushika Hokusai
'Legend of the deity Benzaiten
of Enoshima summoning a five-
headed poisonous dragon' (block-
ready drawing), from *Record of
Shoguns of Great Japan, Collection One*
About 1820–1835
Ink on paper, 28.0 × 20.0 cm
(covers)
Museum of Fine Arts, Boston,
1998.669.1-6 , source unidentified

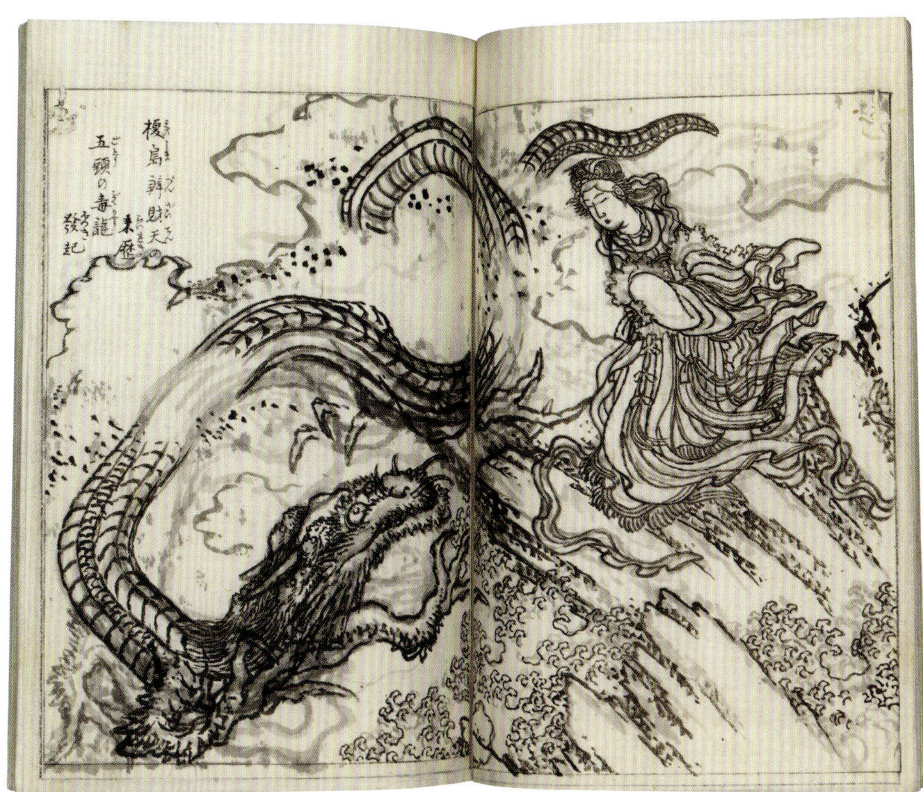

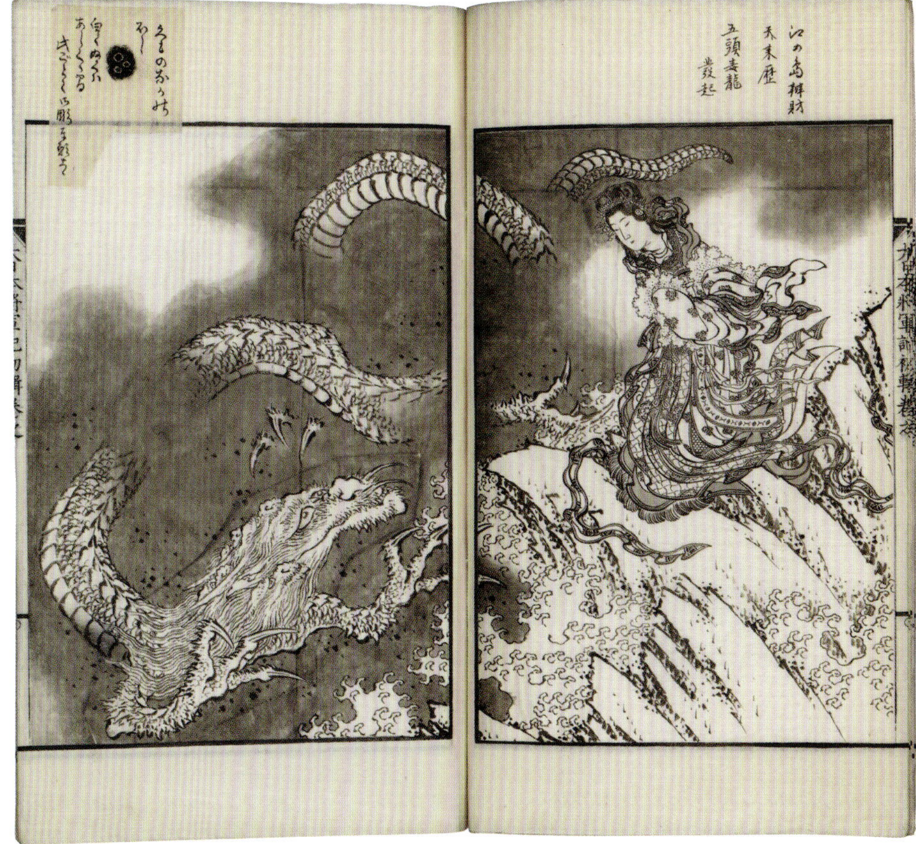

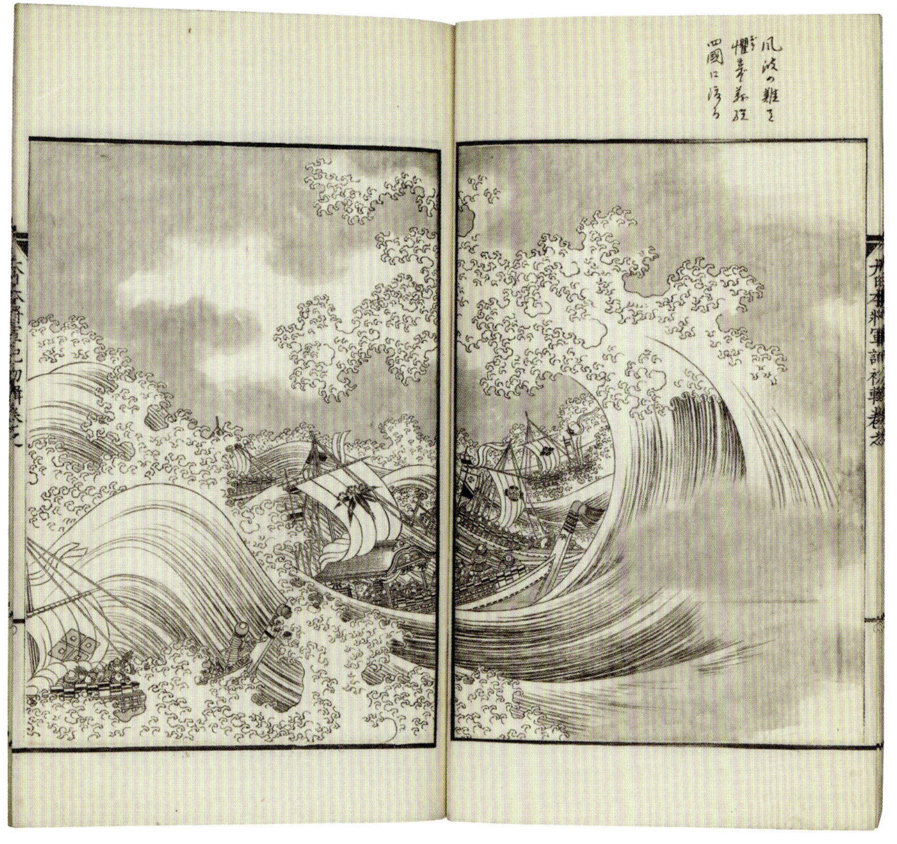

FIG 22 (LEFT)

Attributed to Katsushika Hokusai
'Oblivious to the dangers of wind and waves, warrior hero Yoshitsune crosses to Shikoku' (block-ready drawing), from *Record of Shoguns of Great Japan, Collection One*
About 1820–1835
Ink on paper, 28.0 × 20.0 cm (covers)
Museum of Fine Arts, Boston, 1998.669.1-6, source unidentified

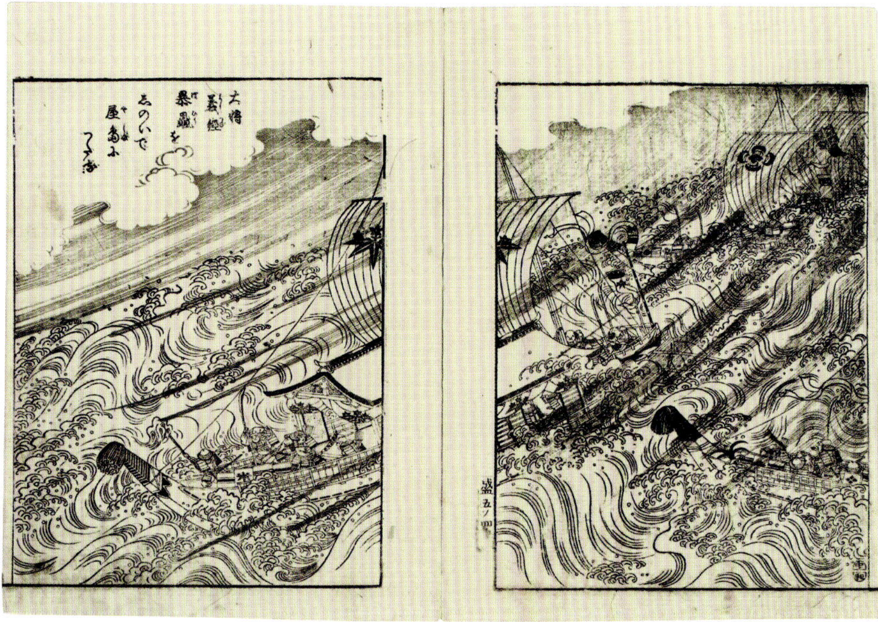

FIG 23 (BELOW)

Akisato Ritō (worked about 1780–1823, author), with Nishimura Chūwa (worked late 1700s–early 1800s) and Oku Bunmei (1773–1813, artists)
'Enduring a storm, warrior general Yoshitsune crosses to Yashima', from *Genpei seisuiki zue* (*Illustrated Rise and Fall of the Minamoto and Taira*), vol. 5
1800
Woodblock, illustrated book, 25.5 × 18.0 cm (covers)
National Institute of Japanese Literature, KG/159/Ak

pasted at top right is inscribed 'Yoritomo embarks ship at Manazuru-ga-saki?', then 'Hakone Eijitsu sends refreshments?', with an additional note, 'but this also appears in *Hyakushō den* [*Lives of One Hundred Generals*]'. The writing is the same as in the other inscriptions in *Lives of Famous Generals* and so must be Hokusai's. But what does this particular one mean? In the story, Hakone Eijitsu does indeed supply food to Yoritomo and his followers after they have escaped from Ōba Kagechika. And they do then cross by boat from Manazuru-ga-saki to Awa province (modern Chiba prefecture). If Hokusai wanted to depict the Battle of Ishibashiyama, the scene of Yoritomo and followers hiding in the fallen tree afterwards was the most obvious choice. So perhaps these inscriptions on slips of paper are suggestions to the publisher to consider alternative scenes? In the event, the scene of the fallen tree was chosen for the block-ready drawing in *Record of Shoguns*, albeit with the addition on the right of the composition of 'Kajiwara Kagetoki', who saves Yoritomo even though he is in the enemy camp. It is unclear which book '*Hyakushō den*' refers to, although *Nihon hyakushō den shō* (1667) does include some lines about the escape from Manazuru-ga-saki to Awa in the section 'Minamoto no Yoritomo'.[10]

In the notations on the block-ready drawings, by contrast, Hokusai specifies exactly how to translate the finished design on to the printed page. 'Legend of the deity Benzaiten of Enoshima summoning a five-headed poisonous dragon' (fig. 21), in *Record of Shoguns*, has an inscription slip on which Hokusai notes, 'The stars in the clouds should not be white dots. Please cut them like this', and then draws white circular shapes inside the dark *sumi* ink block for the clouds. Block cutting matching this can be found in the dark areas of 'The stone coffin shatters and hazy clouds appear', in the third supplementary volume of *Strange Tales of the Bow Moon* (cat. 14), as well as in the border of the mosquito net in the colour print

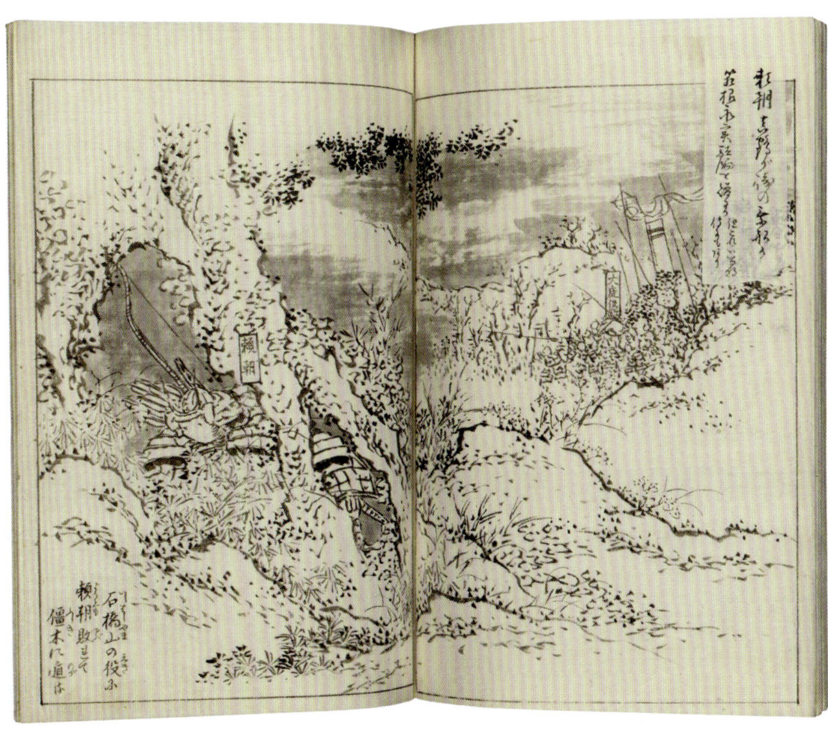

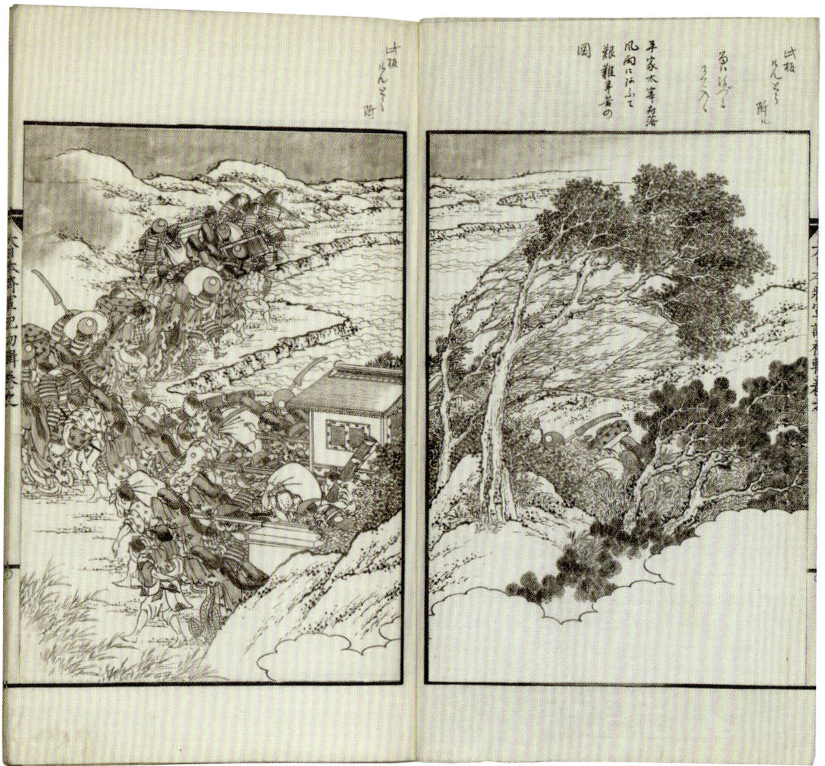

FIG 25

Attributed to Katsushika Hokusai
'Picture of the hardships and setbacks suffered by the Taira as they flee from Dazaifu and are assailed by wind and rain' (block-ready drawing), from *Record of Shoguns of Great Japan, Collection One*
About 1820–1835
Ink on paper, 28.0 × 20.0 cm (covers)
Museum of Fine Arts, Boston, 1998.669.1-6, source unidentified

'Kohada Koheiji', from the series *One Hundred Ghost Tales* (cat. 153). Hokusai also added notations above the block-ready drawing 'Picture of the hardships and setbacks suffered by the Taira as they flee from Dazaifu and are assailed by wind and rain' (fig. 25): 'Add registration marks [*kentō*] to this block' (twice, top right and top left), and 'Cut the rain into the grey block' (top right). The lines of the rain do not appear in the block-ready drawing, but they are present in the preparatory drawing. So it is clear that Hokusai is instructing the block cutter to prepare a block that will print the rain in grey. In fact, a total of four blocks would be needed to print this one illustration: the key (outline) block, the grey block, and one each to print, respectively, the gradation in the sky and the gradation in the clouds. This may be why the instruction 'Add registration marks to this block' is repeated twice.

The inscriptions in the unpublished warrior books emphasize to us just how particular Hokusai was about his illustrations: he constantly refers to various earlier sources in order to create his compositions, and then gives detailed instructions to the block cutter in order to realize them in print.

HOKUSAI'S PRIDE

From Hokusai's perspective it must have been a matter of regret that the preparatory and block-ready drawings were left unpublished. But for us, *Lives of Famous Generals of Japan* and *Record of Shoguns of Great Japan, Collection One* provide fascinating evidence of how particular he was about his ideas, how he researched existing sources, and how he specified the details of production. While he referred to other images, fundamentally Hokusai was only ever interested in creating new and original designs.

At about the same time that he was working on the unpublished warrior books, Hokusai was also preparing the block-ready drawings for the colour print series *One Hundred Poems by One Hundred Poets, Explained by the Nurse* (cats 132–146), most of which remained unpublished too. They have the same originality and painstaking attention to detail, and it is easy to imagine that this may have led to a dispute with the publisher. In a letter on the 17th day, fifth month, 1818 to the textile merchant Suzuki Bokushi (1770–1842), the author Bakin noted, 'There is no one in Edo apart from Hokusai I would have do these drawings. Last year he was being a bit awkward, so even though I have long admired him, I've kept my distance and have not made any requests of him since. And his fees are unusually high, which does not please the publishers.'[11] We get a vivid sense of Hokusai's pride, during his old age, and his determination to come up with his own ideas and to do things in his own way.

NOTES

1 Hokusai probably clashed with other authors, too. For example, the drawings for *Muna zan'yō* were originally done for the publisher Nishimuraya Yohachi, but the finished book was put out by Tsuruya Kiemon, suggesting that there was some kind of dispute.

2 The present author agrees with the theory that from part 7, this was not illustrated by Hokusai.

3 Hokusai successfully demanded of publisher Kobayashi Shinbei that some of the faces in the book *Illustrated Anthology of Tang Poetry (Tōshisen ehon)*, part 6, 1833, be recut and the book reprinted. See Tinios 2015, Tinios 2016, and pp. 23–24.

4 'Elegant Points around the Eastern Capital' (*Fūryū Tōto hōgaku*, cat. 2), from Hokusai's Shunrō period.

5 More than sixty block-ready drawings survive for the series *One Hundred Poems by One Hundred Poets, Explained by the Nurse* (Freer Gallery and other collections, cats 132–146); fourteen in the album *Collection of Block-Ready Drawings by Hokusai* (Private collection, Japan); two albums, for picture books and brush-drawing manuals, *Albums of Hokusai Sketches* (Metropolitan Museum, New York); *Album of Preparatory Drawings* (National Gallery, Prague); *Picture Book: Japan and China in the Katsushika Style* (Metropolitan Museum, cat. 169); *Drawings for a three-volume picture book* (Museum of Fine Arts, Boston, cats 30, 168); *Record of Shoguns* (Museum of Fine Arts, Boston, cat. 171).

6 There are a number of depictions by Hokusai of dancing *shirabyōshi* and female shrine attendants, notably 'Shirabyōshi' in *Ehon kōkyo*, volume 2 (1850), which are similar to the block-ready drawing 'Shizuka performs the dance *hōraku no mai* on the veranda of Tsurugaoka shrine'. The depiction of flames in 'Burning of the imperial residence at Yashima' is identical to that found in 'Xiao He, wise vassal of the Duke of Pei (Liu Bang), seizes documents from the Qin library rather than treasure', also in volume 2 of *Ehon kōkyo*.

7 *Record of Shoguns* (block-ready) has the titles – that is, descriptions of the picture content – written in the top margin of the page, exactly like the two published warrior books. One puzzle is prompted by the size of the printed outlines (about 28.3 × 14.3 cm / 11 × 5½ in.). If the titles were cut as written in the upper page margins then this would necessitate a book in the large *ōhon* format, rather than the more common *hanshibon* format. Since the titles are not drawn particularly neatly, perhaps the intention was, rather, to cut these titles into a separate block that would later be printed inside the pictures, after the illustrations had been printed and maybe after consultation with the publisher – although this would have added to the cost and technical difficulty of production. It is also worth noting that *Drawings for a three-volume picture book* (Museum of Fine Arts, Boston, cats 30, 168) are also drawn inside printed borders with a diagonal 'fish-tail' design at the top of the (blank) cartouche that would normally contain the edge-of-page book title. See Thompson 2016.

8 Akisato Ritō (worked about 1780–1828, author), with Nishimura Chūwa (worked late 1700s–early 1800s) and Oku Bunmei (1773–1813, artists), *Genpei seisuiki zue (Illustrated Rise and Fall of the Minamoto and Taira)*, 1800. Woodblock, *yomihon* illustrated book, 6 volumes, published by Nikyūdō, Kyoto.

9 Ōba Kagechika and Matano Kagehisa: it is unusual to find two linked family names in the cartouche within the picture, rather than the full name of a single warrior.

10 While there are several titles similar to *Hyakushō den*, none seem relevant in terms of episodes and illustrations. A title *Ehon hyakushō den* appears in the book catalogue *Shinsen shoseki mokuroku* of 1741, but no extant copies are known.

11 Shibata Mitsuhiko, Kanda Masayuki, *Bakin shokan shūsei*, vol. 1, Tokyo, Yagi Shoten, 2002, p. 39; transcription adapted by the present author.

Hokusai and late Tokugawa society
Alfred Haft

Besides his family and friends, perhaps nothing gave Hokusai more pleasure than dipping his brush in ink and painting. Particularly during his last years, he seems to have devoted nearly every waking moment to advancing his art. He was far from a recluse, however. In younger days he had participated in poetry clubs, staged his own public art performances and sought out the pleasure quarters. As time went on, although he was less socially active and visible, he continued to travel and to rely on an extensive social network. He thrived as an artist through engaging with the world. But what kind of world was this?

CHANGING SOCIETY

In 1615, the armies of shogun Tokugawa Ieyasu (1543–1616) vanquished the forces of the Toyotomi clan and brought peace to Japan under a system of military rule known as the Tokugawa shogunate. The system would last more than 200 years, throughout the Edo period (1615–1868), named after Ieyasu's capital city of Edo (now Tokyo). Ieyasu and his advisers seized the momentum of victory to organize Japanese society into four estates, in line with neo-Confucian thought: samurai, farmer, artisan and merchant. At the beginning of the Edo period, the estates were strictly divided. At the top of the social ladder, samurai enjoyed a regular stipend and the power of life-and-death over others, but they also had the responsibility of leading by moral example. Second in prestige, but tied to the land, farmers sometimes struggled to produce the rice yields their samurai masters relied on for income. Third, artisans of all kinds, including artists, provided the myriad services required by a newly leisured and wealthy society. Last in official ranking, merchants, brokers and salesmen tapped into the era's new networks of communications and transportation systems and expertly channelled goods to market. Despite occasional convulsions – notably the famines of 1732, 1782–1788 and the mid-1830s, and the government reforms of 1720, 1789 and 1842 – on the whole the system operated efficiently. Efficiently, perhaps, but not unchanged.

Rice yields grew rapidly early in the period but then levelled off, even as the expenses of the samurai lords (*daimyō*) and the overall population continued to rise. The increasing economic demands prompted social change. Responses from the poor included petitions and occasional riots; responses from the ruling samurai included heavy borrowing, which led to compounding debt and near financial ruin. By the early 1800s, with tacit official consent, *daimyō* in the various provinces had begun taking matters into their own hands, instituting reforms and promoting and managing local industries. Below them, not only were the samurai elite engaging in commerce, but also lower-ranking samurai were adopting the offspring of prosperous merchants and marrying their own children to them, while merchants now occasionally received the trappings of samurai. Even professional artisans felt the changes, as for example in 1837, when the Kyoto artist Gan Ku (died 1839) received the title Governor of Echizen province – governor being a position usually reserved for samurai. Hokusai himself saw his son adopted into a samurai family.[1] Over time the four estates thus shifted into a new alignment of parallel collaboration, each understood to serve an equally important social function (fig. 26).

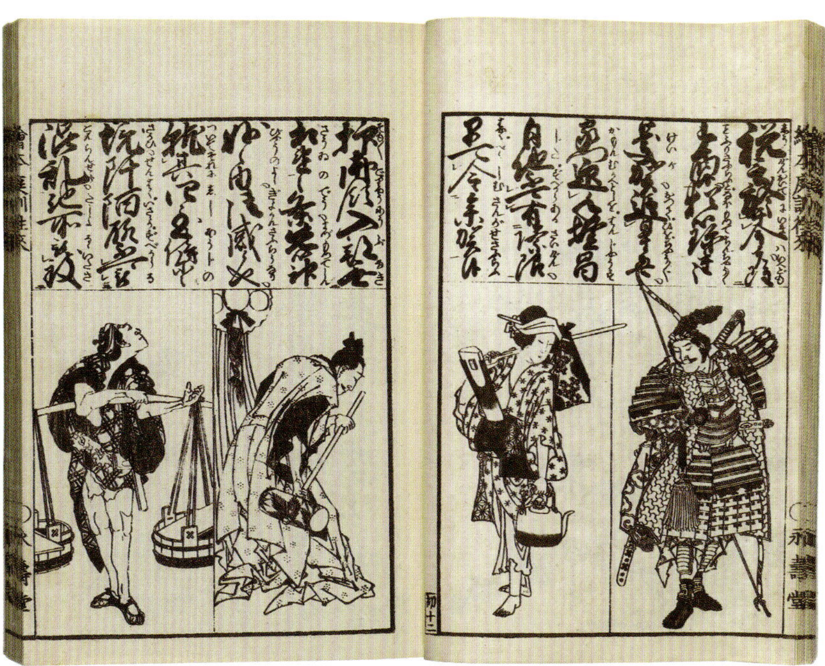

'The Four Estates', from *Ehon teikin ōrai* (from right: samurai, farmer, artisan, merchant)

1828

Woodblock, illustrated book,

22.0 x 15.0 cm (covers)

British Museum, 1979,0305,0.451

The rate of change accelerated in the unprecedented prosperity of the 1810s–1820s. Following the Tenmei famine (1782–1788), the Kansei reforms (1789–1792) and further retrenchment in the late 1790s–early 1800s, late Edo-period citizens embraced the finer things in life as never before, calling into question the moral foundations on which Tokugawa society was supposedly based. The long-serving, pleasure-loving eleventh shogun, Tokugawa Ienari (1773–1841; reigned 1787–1837), had a version of the Yoshiwara brothel district constructed within the grounds of Edo castle, maintained forty concubines and fathered fifty-five children by sixteen different wives.[2] Those with the means to do so followed suit. Over the first quarter of the nineteenth century, gourmet restaurants as well as Yoshiwara and various unofficial pleasure quarters enjoyed booming business. Metalworkers found a market not just for their sword fittings, but also for a variety of decorative objects including sword-guards (*tsuba*) encrusted with gold and precious alloys. Hokusai and his pupils, too, rode the wave of prosperity, as they numbered among Edo's most sought-after designers of privately commissioned woodblock prints (*surimono*), exquisitely crafted for members of comic poetry associations (*kyōka-ren*).[3]

Moreover, anyone desiring to learn a new skill or improve his or her education could choose from a variety of professional instructors. A who's-who for the city of Edo published around the 1830s–1840s names more than a thousand instructors in dozens of different fields.[4] Most numerous among them are teachers of *haikai* or linked sequences of short lyrical verses (*hokku*, today called haiku). Running a not-too-distant second are artists, subdivided into various specialties including 'Painting of the Eastern Capital' (*tōto-ga* or perhaps *Azuma-e*), the genre now called ukiyo-e ('pictures of the floating world'). Hokusai is listed here, along with such other contemporaries as the Utagawa-school artists Hiroshige (1797–1858), Kunisada (1786–1864) and Kuniyoshi (1797–1861). Official rhetoric organized education into two broad areas: military arts (*bu*) and cultural arts (*bun*). In this directory, however, one finds many more masters of culture – including Confucian scholars, Chinese-language poets, Japanese-language poets and calligraphers – than masters of military affairs; for example, Confucianists outnumber swordsmen sixteen to one, perhaps an indication of the priorities of the day. Also telling is the small category of individuals specializing in *fūryū*, meaning 'cultivation', 'refinement' or 'elegance'. The names in this category all end with a Chinese character that designates a high-ranking lord or government official (*kō*), perhaps suggesting that these were *daimyō* or retainers of the shogun, who after retiring found themselves at liberty to pursue cultivation and refinement as a profession.

AN INFLUENTIAL PATRON

In his decades of designing *surimono* and producing beautiful paintings, Hokusai encountered many adherents to the cause of cultivated refinement. They would have included perhaps a few samurai and certainly many wealthy merchants, but the most dedicated among them, and the most consequential for Hokusai's final years, was the saké manufacturer Takai Kōzan (1806–1883). Kōzan was born in Obuse, a village governed by Matsushiro domain (present-day Nagano prefecture), not far from the city of Nagano and the mountainous region of central Japan now called the Japan Alps. Nestled on the banks of the Chikuma river between two forested plateaus, and situated close to a fertile rice-growing area, Obuse had much nature but little culture to offer. It was also off the beaten track. A day's journey from it down a regional road ended in a junction with a regional highway still 300 kilometres (around 135 miles) from Edo, and 600 kilometres (around 270 miles) from Kyoto.[5] For four generations, the Takai family had been the leading saké producers in the area, and as heir, Kōzan was destined to take over the business. His grandfather recognized that he was unusually bright, and suggested that he first pursue an education in Kyoto. So in 1820 he headed for Japan's ancient capital, where over the next six years he engaged several of the city's leading cultural figures as his private tutors.[6] After a year spent back in Obuse in order to marry and to attend his grandfather's funeral, he returned to Kyoto with his wife Kazu (1810–1855) for additional study, before in 1833 he followed the Chinese-poetry specialist Yanagawa Seigan (1789–1858) to Edo. There, Kōzan explored neo-Confucianism and socialized with others from his home province, including the samurai Sakuma Shōzan (1811–1864) of Matsushiro domain, who had just arrived in the city to further his own education.[7]

It seems likely that Kōzan met Hokusai sometime during his first year in Edo. According to one report, they may have been introduced by a mutual friend, the trader Koyama Mon'uemon (dates unknown), whose business, the Jūhachjiya, specialized in silk textiles and pharmaceuticals and maintained shops in both Edo and Obuse.[8] The Jūhachjiya warehouse was located in Hongin-chō, a district in the centre of Edo just north of Nihonbashi, which also included the Edo branch of Eirakuya Tōshirō, the Nagoya publisher responsible for producing the wildly successful *Hokusai's Sketches* (*Hokusai manga*, cats 164, 165).[9] The details are unknown, but one can imagine Kōzan coming across Mon'uemon while exploring the city centre, and finding him a friendly source of news about his hometown. Hokusai may have liked to stop by when in the neighbourhood on other business, to study the medicines, or even just enjoy an occasional chat.

The presence of Hokusai's brush drawing manuals and *Thirty-Six Views of Mt Fuji* prints in bookshops across the city may also have already piqued Kōzan's curiosity about the artist. Whatever the case, it seems that at some point, Mon'uemon suggested that the two should meet.

Kōzan and Hokusai had evidently formed a friendship when towards the end of 1834 the artist, for unspecified but urgent reasons, left Edo to live in rural Uraga (see pp. 22–23). By the time he returned permanently, around the autumn of 1836, Kōzan had himself left Edo to return to Obuse, where at the height of the Tenpō famine he opened the doors of his family's rice storehouses to the starving. This probably drew the attention of the lord of Matsushiro domain, Sanada Yukitsura (1791–1852), who had already instituted a programme of comprehensive domain reform and economic development in the mid-1820s, and was now similarly engaged in aiding victims of the famine.[10] Yukitsura would become a senior councillor to the shogun in 1841, perhaps in recognition of his leadership. His appointment must have greatly boosted communications and eased conditions for travel between Edo and Matsushiro, presenting Kōzan with an unusual opportunity to bring the celebrated octogenarian Hokusai in person from Edo to his distant hometown. Hokusai and Kōzan had remained in contact over the previous years, with Kōzan facilitating local commissions and perhaps sending Hokusai gifts after a devastating fire in 1839 had destroyed nearly all the artist's possessions.[11]

Hokusai was an experienced traveller. In fact, he changed residences so often that one could say he lived his life on the road (see p. 16). He also made several extended journeys beyond Edo. For example, probably in 1812, from Nagoya he traced a broad circuit through the western provinces of Ise, Yoshino, Kii, Osaka and (perhaps) Kyoto before visiting Nagoya again on his way back to Edo.[12] In

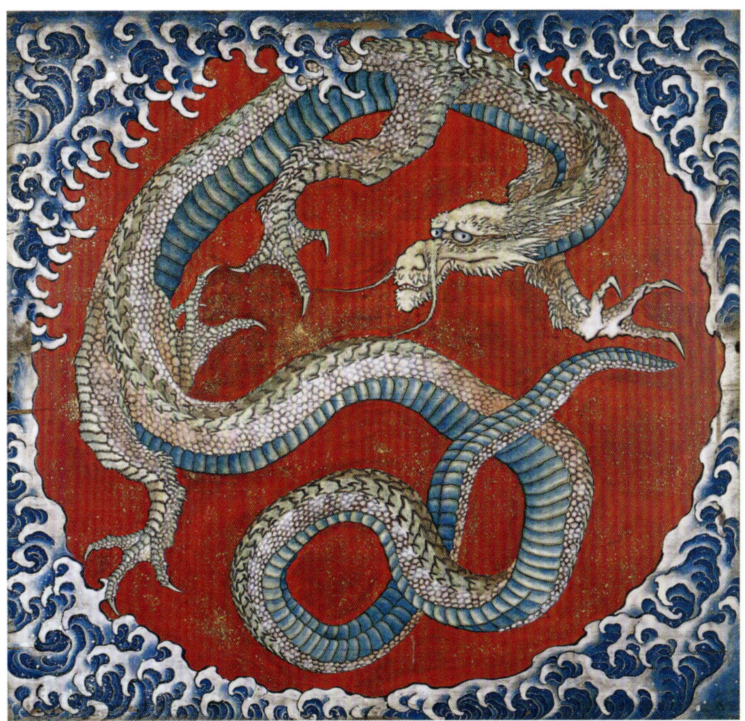

FIG 27

Coiled dragon

1844

Panel for Higashimachi festival cart, ink, colour and gold on paulownia wood, 123.0 × 126.5 cm

Higashimachi Neighbourhood Council, Obuse, Nagano Prefectural Treasure

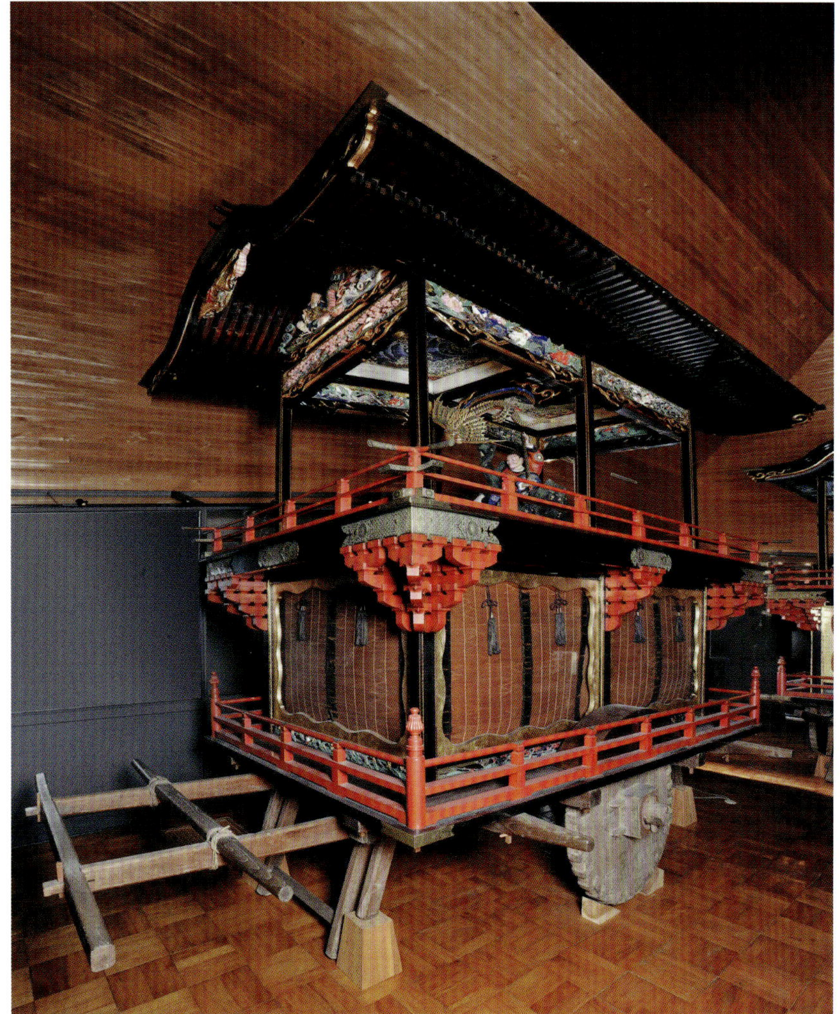

FIG 28

Kanmachi festival cart with wave ceiling panels by Hokusai
1845 (Hokusai panels)
Carved wood, pigment, lacquer, metal fittings, 4.84 × 3.85 × 2.40 m
Kanmachi Neighbourhood Council, Obuse, Nagano
Prefectural Treasure

1817, Hokusai made another extended visit to Nagoya, painting an enormous portrait of Daruma in front of a crowd in the precincts of Nishikakesho temple there.[13] His encounters with the people and the sometimes curious products of these regions proved memorable enough for him later to mention the trip in a design book, *Modern Designs for Combs and Tobacco Pipes* (1823; cats 29, 39). Hokusai's sojourn in Uraga, southwest of Edo, in the 1830s took him through several more provinces closer to home. By the early 1840s, however, the prospect of a trip to Obuse might have made even Hokusai think twice. Travel during the Edo period was, at best, less than easy or convenient, and it harboured genuine dangers, including bandits. As the author Takizawa Bakin (1767–1848) advised after returning from a trip to Kyoto and Osaka in the summer of 1802, 'Think of the road as enemy territory and always be on the look-out.'[14]

In the end, though, Kōzan's inducements proved irresistible. They included a studio prepared for the artist, Heki'i-ken (Blue Ripples Studio), as well as some major commissions. During the middle months of 1844, Hokusai produced two magnificent panel paintings – a dragon and a phoenix – for the ceiling of a festival cart sponsored by the Obuse neighbourhood of Higashimachi. The

NOTES

1 See the essay by Timothy Clark in this volume, pp. 12–27.

2 Hayashiya Tatsusaburō, 'Kasei bunka no rekishiteki ichi', in Hayashiya, ed., *Kasei bunka no kenkyū*, Tokyo, Iwanami Shoten, 1976, p. 31.

3 For English-language discussions of *surimono*, see especially the writings of Roger Keyes and John Carpenter.

4 *Edo genzon meika ichiran* (c. 1830s–1840s), in Mori Senzō, comp., *Kinsei jinmei roku shūsei*, vol. 2, Tokyo, Benseisha, 1976, pp. 300–318.

5 Distances derived from Kishii Yoshie, *Go kaidō saiken*, Tokyo, Seiabō, 1965, pp. 228–232.

6 For calligraphy Nukina Kaioku (1778–1863), for painting Gan Ku (who famously used only the most expensive available pigments), for classical Japanese studies Kido Chitate (1778–1845), and for classical Chinese studies Mashima Shōnan (1791–1839). Yamazaki Minoru, *Takai Kōzan monogatari*, Obuse, Takai Kōzan Kinenkan, 1995, p. 7.

7 Biographical information from ibid., pp. 7–8 ff.

8 Kubota 1989, pp. 8–9.

9 Ibid, p. 9. See also Clark essay, p. 16.

10 Nagano-ken, eds, *Nagano-ken shi: Tsūshi*, vol. 6, *Kinsei*, pt. 3, Nagano Kenshi Kankōkai, 1989, p. 420.

11 Kubota 1989, pp. 11–12.

12 Takeuchi Yoshinobu, 'Hokusai no Kansai ryokō o megutte', *Hokusai kenkyū* 30, Dec. 2001, p. 20.

13 Nagoya 1991, nos 221–223.

14 Takizawa Bakin, *Kiryō manroku*, in Herbert Plutschow, trans., *A Reader in Edo Period Travel*, Folkstone, Global Oriental, 2006, p. 244.

15 Hokusaikan 2015, p. 19.

16 Nagano-ken, p. 531.

17 This and the following information derived from Murayama Shungo, ed., *Katsushika Hokusai Nisshin joma chō*, Tokyo, Kokkasha, 1907, pp. 3–4 (accompanying English translation, *On Hokusai's "Daily Exorcisms"*, p. 3).

18 Kubota 2015, pp. 126–145.

two-storey cart had originally been built in 1805, but in 1844 the town decided it needed a complete renovation.[15] Hokusai not only conceived two remarkable designs for the paintings, but also employed an unusual technique: rather than applying pigments to a matte ground of shell-white, he combined them with a luminous binder of glue or oil and painted directly on the wood surface, making the paintings seem to pulse with light. The effect is particularly strong in the glowing red ground of the dragon painting (fig. 27).[16] The panels are framed by carved wood transoms depicting Chinese boys, and the ensemble would have formed an auspicious canopy for the festival dancers who performed directly beneath it, to music played by musicians seated behind bamboo curtains on the cart's lower level. The project was such a success that Kōzan brought Hokusai back the following year to design the ceiling panels for another festival cart, for the Kanmachi neighbourhood (fig. 28). This time the artist outdid himself with paintings that seem to condense the seas into two blue maelstroms (cats 206, 207).

A popular Edo artist causing a sensation in a small town could hardly have escaped the notice of local authorities for long. In Hokusai's case, sometime in 1844 or 1845, a samurai of Matsushiro domain named Miyamoto Shinsuke (1821–after 1871) made an appearance in Obuse and, intrigued by the master's style and popularity, requested a painting. Hokusai claimed to be overworked at the time, but promised to send something when he returned to Edo.[17] Later, in 1847, Hokusai and his daughter Eijo (Ōi, about 1800–after 1857) were living anonymously in Tamachi, a nondescript Edo neighbourhood north of Asakusa, when there came a knock at the door. Standing outside was Miyamoto, who had tracked them down to inquire about his painting. Hokusai once more claimed to be overworked. His daughter, though, may have thought it imprudent for an elderly artisan to try giving a determined samurai the brush-off twice, and (with Hokusai's consent) offered Miyamoto a stack of her father's brush drawings she had carefully preserved.

The drawings were the now-famous 'Daily Exorcisms' (*Nisshin joma*), pictures of animated Chinese lions and lion-dancers that Hokusai had produced on a daily basis from late 1842 through the following year (cats 191, 192). Miyamoto gladly accepted them, and later gave them to his son Chū, who had some of them bound into an album. For Eijo the drawings must have been a personal treasure, but she was willing to sacrifice them given the circumstances. Only a handful of her paintings (cats 195–197) and none of her personal possessions otherwise seem to have survived.[18] The 'Daily Exorcisms' – a rich record of artistic spirit and practice – may remain to us only as the result of a charged moment when artistic temperament, family ties and societal pressures came into conflict and found a resolution. In this perhaps unexpected way, the drawings bring together many threads from Hokusai's years of conversation with the brush, and from his decades of dialogue with the changing society in which he lived.

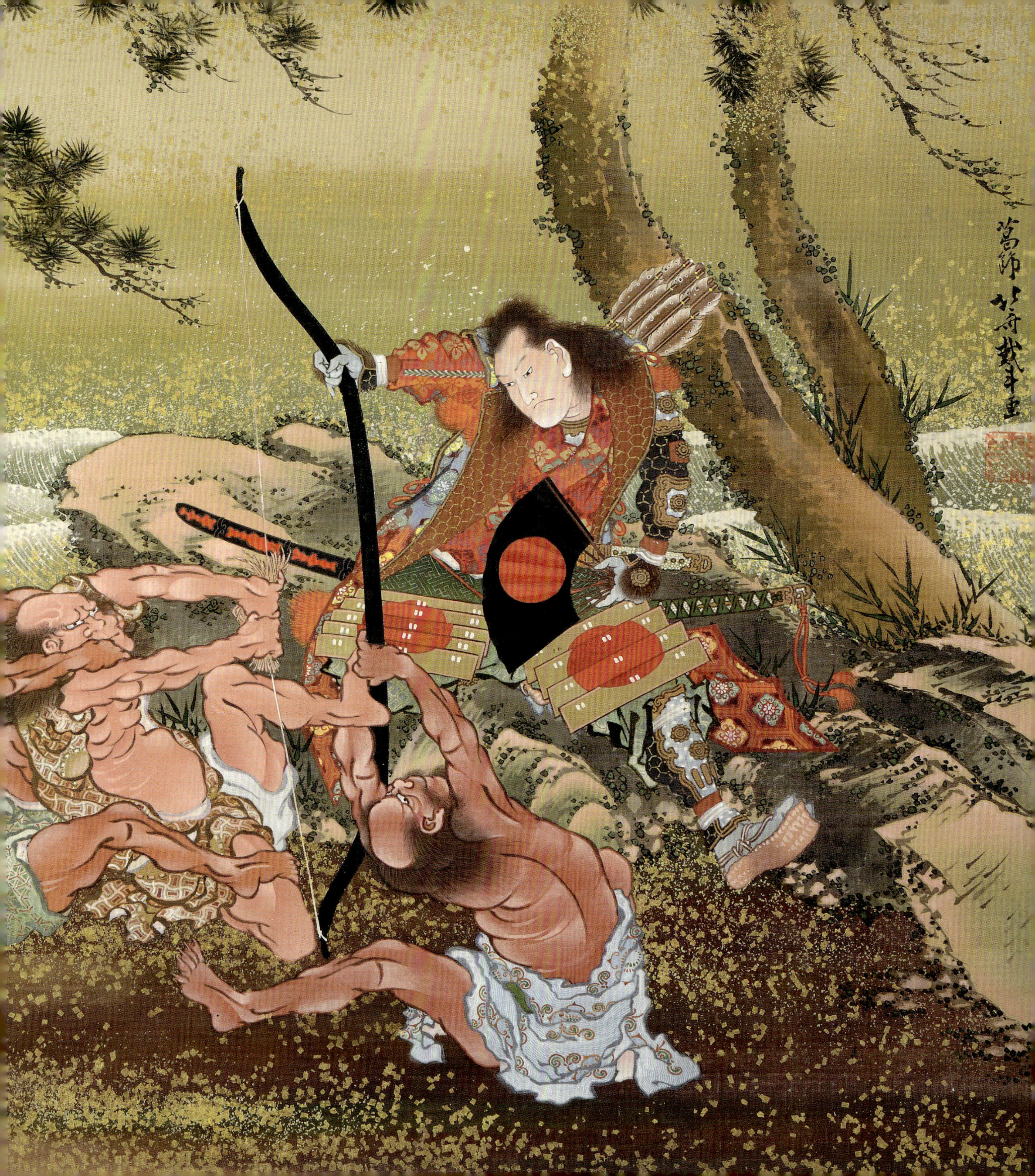

葛飾
北斎戴斗筆

Hokusai from twenty to sixty

By the time he reached sixty, Hokusai had been drawing for almost fifty-five years, having started at the age of six, as he himself declared (see Clark essay, p. 21), and a professional artist for over forty, adopting and leaving behind well over ten different art names along the way. Experimenting with style and self in this way prepared him in the final three decades of his life, after turning sixty-one, to create not only the printed masterpieces with which he is identified the world over, but also the extraordinary succession of paintings that are featured here.

Hokusai's early curiosity was stimulated by growing up in the Honjo district on the far bank of the Sumida river, which flowed through the flat lands to the east of Edo castle – a neighbourhood of artisans, craftspeople and other working classes. He worked as a delivery boy for a rental bookshop in his youth, and was thus able to study how word and image combined. In his mid-teens he was apprenticed to a woodblock cutter, making some of the blocks for a book on the pleasure quarters when he was only sixteen. Then, in about 1778, he became a pupil of Katsukawa Shunshō (died 1792), a leading ukiyo-e artist, known particularly for his prints of kabuki actors.

Under Shunshō, Hokusai took on the name Shunrō. Like his master, he focused on the theatre, producing actor prints in the characteristic manner of his school (cat. 1). This was hardly satisfying, and Hokusai was soon studying other traditions. The betrayal prompted his expulsion from the school, but this in turn inspired Hokusai to find his own path and forge his own style. His determination was underpinned by his devotion to Bodhisattva Myōken, a Buddhist deity associated with the North Star, whose temple at Yanagishima was much visited by artists and writers, and on whose power Hokusai continued to draw over the next few decades (cat. 2).

For some five years from 1794, Hokusai used the name Sōri, which announced his allegiance to the decorative, so-called 'Rinpa' style inaugurated in the early 1600s by Tawaraya Sōtatsu (about 1570–about 1640) and perfected by Ogata Kōrin (1658–1716) (cat. 7). His work ranged widely, however: he studied various Japanese and Chinese painting styles, as well as recently introduced European techniques, and began to experiment with landscape (cat. 17). Much of his livelihood, such as it was, came from his increasing involvement in literary circles, for whom he produced privately commissioned albums, prints (*surimono*) and other images, illustrating their 'crazy verse' (*kyōka*) (cat. 6). Hokusai's literary connections also led to a long series of collaborations with the leading authors and publishers of his day to create illustrated books (cat. 14).

By 1798, Hokusai's growing confidence was clear. His 'Shi zōka' seal announced his determination to serve 'creation' (cat. 5), and in the summer he declared his artistic independence, taking on two new names: Hokusai, the one by which he is best known today, and Tokimasa. Both underlined his dedication to the North Star (cat. 3). During the next decade he also frequently prefaced his signature with 'Gakyōjin' ('Man crazy to paint') (e.g. cat. 8). Hokusai's work between 1800 and 1810 was increasingly sought after, evident in the variety and quality of his commissions, from individual scroll paintings of beautiful women (*bijin-ga*) to intensive work for commercial publishers, illustrating the popular adventure stories of Takizawa Bakin (1767–1848). Artistically, he was rapidly evolving towards a distinctive style and a wide range of thematic preoccupations.

By the 1810s, Hokusai had synthesized his encyclopaedic command of artistic styles into his own, highly individual way of depicting the world and its people. The monumental figures of Tametomo and the islanders, set against an animated landscape (cat. 13), prefigure his way of brush drawing laid out in the serial picture book *Hokusai's Sketches* (*Hokusai manga*) from the middle of the decade (cats 164, 165), with examples ranging from divine beings and human types, to animal species, plant forms and natural features. Hokusai was interested in the common people and natural phenomena of this world, but he also saw how they connected easily to a world of mythic heroes and divine forces. He acknowledged the presence of the divine with a new name, Taito ('Receiving the Big Dipper'), which reaffirmed his devotion to the polar constellation and his faith in Myōken, as he entered his fifties. By the end of that decade of his life, he was ready to 'become one' ('Iitsu') with the world and to be reborn ('one again') as an artist from the age of sixty-one. **AL**

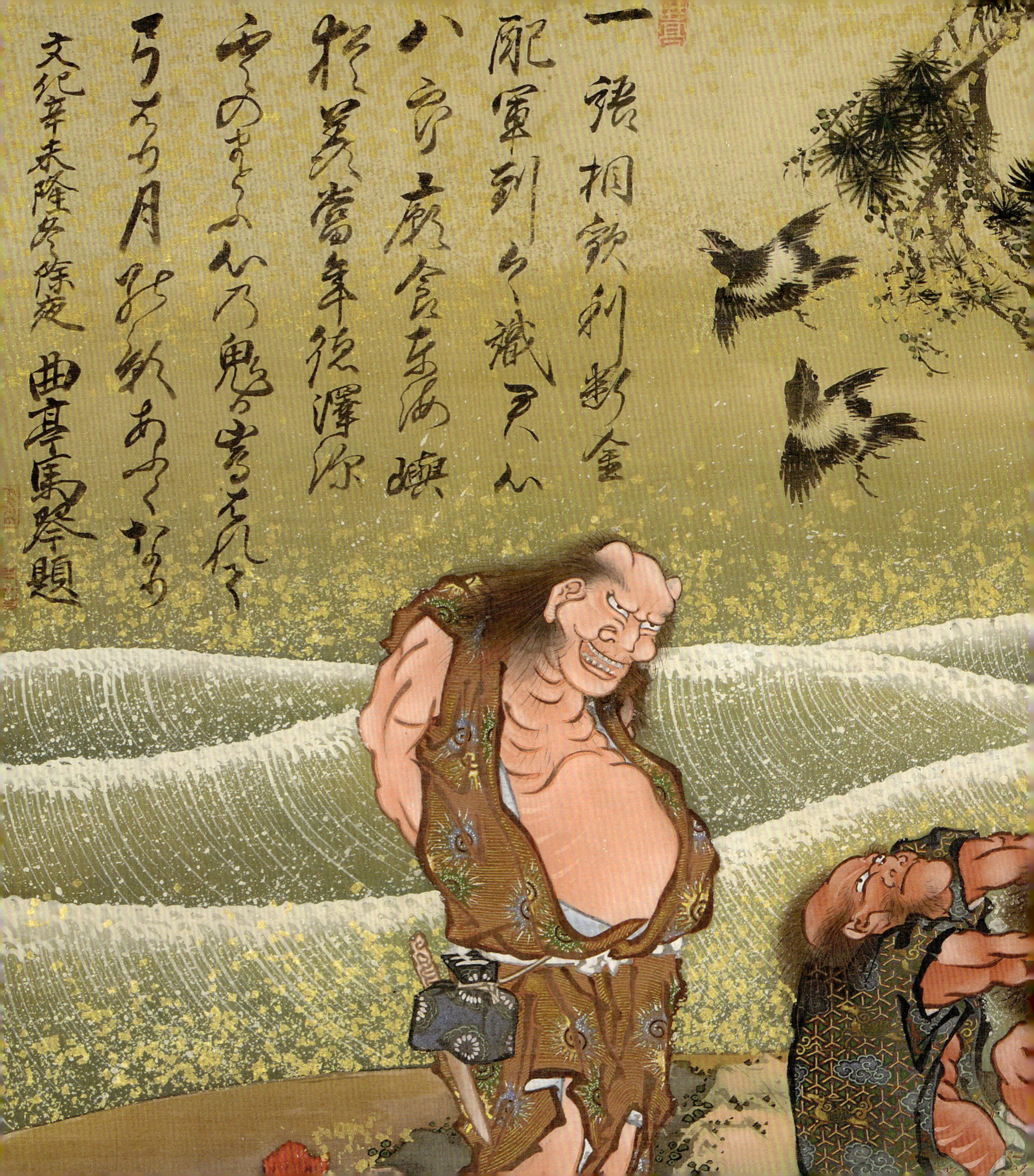

一張相欽利断金
配軍到々蔵戸ル
八斥上廏食在海嶼
扵炎當年後澤深
雫のまろひの鬼鳥居石戸
らうつ月光波あつなら
文化辛未隆冬除夜
曲亭馬琴題

Kabuki actor Segawa Kikunojō III as Oren

Eighth month, 1779
Signature: Katsukawa Shunrō ga
Colour woodblock, published by Iseya Kinbei
Literature: TNM 2005, no. 3; Keyes & Morse 2015,
no. 14202
Tokyo National Museum, A-10569-2864
Osaka only

This is one of four prints of kabuki actors that
mark the debut, in the eighth lunar month of 1779,
of the twenty-year-old artist who will in future become
famous as Hokusai. Following an apprenticeship as a
block cutter in his late teens, around 1778 Hokusai
is thought to have entered the studio of the leading
kabuki print artist Katsukawa Shunshō (died 1792).
Granted a character of his teacher's name, he was
known as Shunrō until about 1794. Segawa Kikunojō
III, a famous actor who specialized in female roles,
is here shown as Oren, daughter of samurai Masamune.
The print is produced to quite high standards, but is
printed with fewer colours and more text than similar
works designed by Shunshō and his pupils. On the
screen behind the actor is the first recorded image
of an angry wave by Hokusai. TC

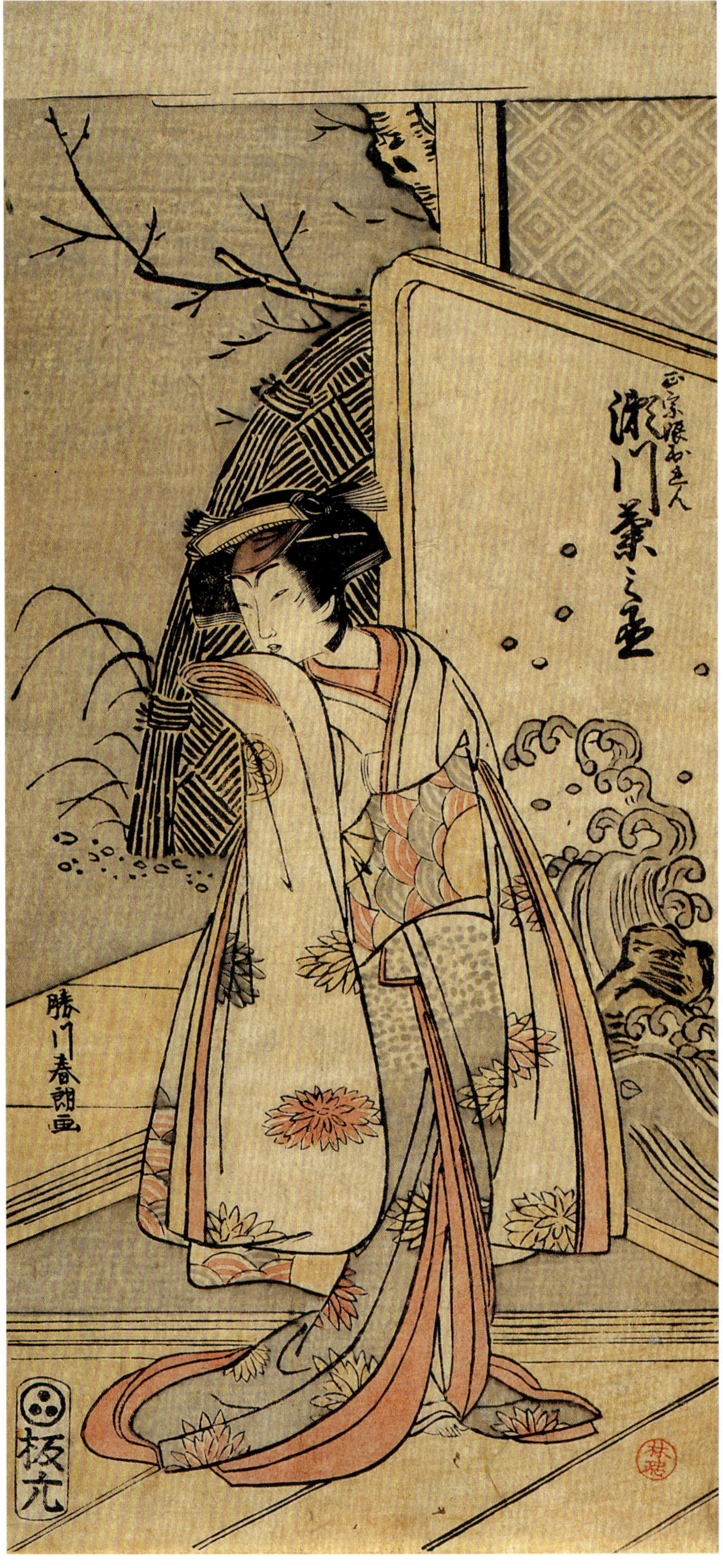

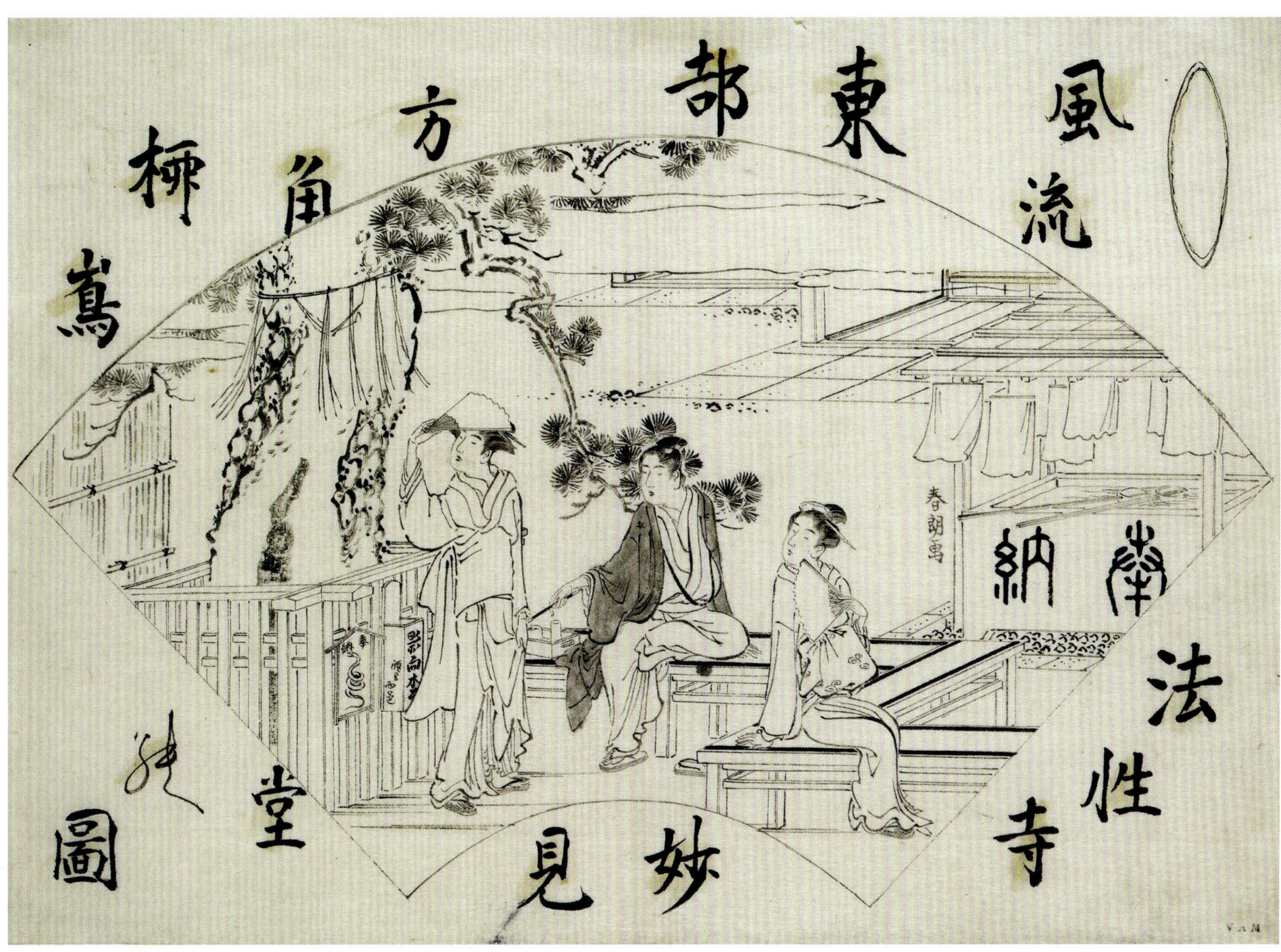

2

Myōkendō worship hall, Hosshōji temple, Yanagishima

1785–1787
Signature: Shunrō ga
Block-ready drawing, ink on paper, 18.9 × 25.7 cm
Literature: HUT 1987–1990, vol. 4, no. 7; Nagata 2000, p. 137; TNM 2005, no. 35
Victoria and Albert Museum, London, E.5087-1910

This is an important work from Hokusai's early period, when he used the art name Shunrō. Still worshipped today at the Myōkendō hall, Hosshōji temple, Yanagishima, Tokyo, is the Bodhisattva Myōken, deity of the North Star. Here Hokusai has depicted two young women and a young man admiring a sacred pine tree in the temple precincts. Attached to the railing is a votive painting of a white snake and a container for offerings, inscribed 'pine where the deity manifests' (*yōgō no matsu*), also 'Nishimura' – hinting that finished prints were intended to be published by the firm of Nishimuraya Yohachi. The art name Hokusai ('North Studio') derives from the Japanese name for the North Star (*hokushin*). Myōken worship similarly informs several of the artist's other names, such as Tokimasa and Taito. This block-ready drawing, from a group of ten, was for a series entitled 'Elegant Points around the Eastern Capital', but only three designs are known as finished prints. MR

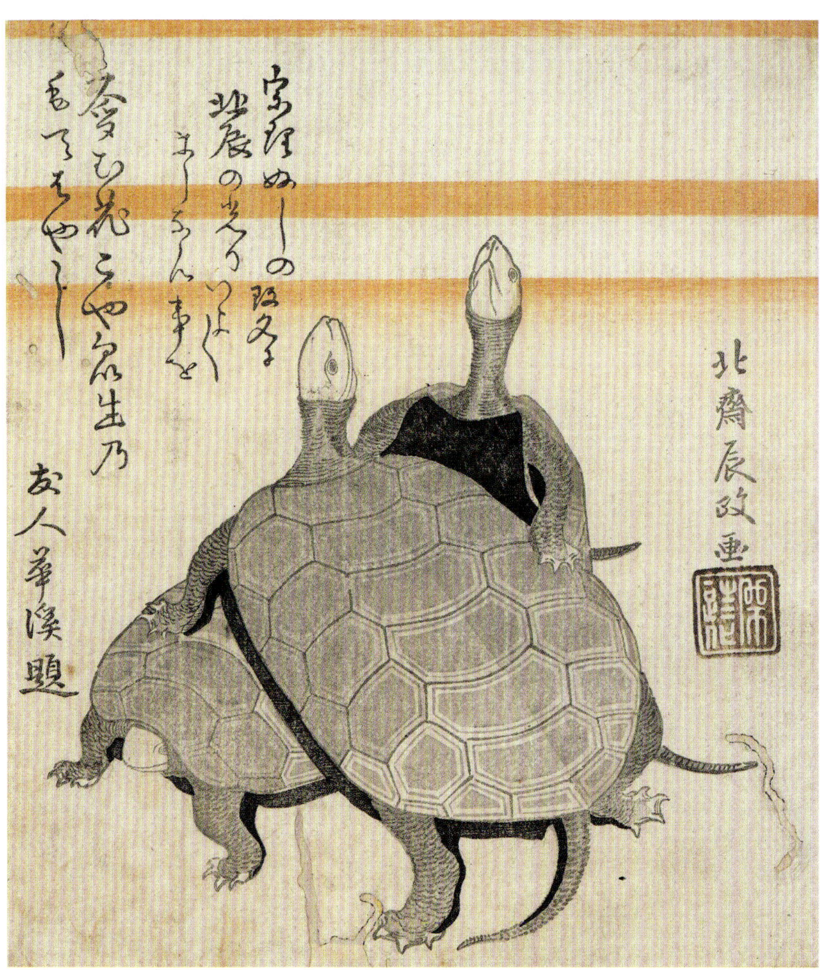

3

Three terrapins

1798

Signature: Hokusai Tokimasa ga

Seal: Shi zōka ('Creation is my master')

Inscription by Inaba Kakei

Surimono, colour woodblock, 17.8 × 15.4 cm

Literature: Tōbu 1993, no. 15; TNM 2005, no. 97; Paris 2014, no. 93; Keyes & Morse 2015, no. 2587

Private collection, Japan

Catalogue only

In the third month, 1798, Hokusai transferred the name Sōri to his pupil Sōji and took the new art names Hokusai and Tokimasa. The inscription, supplied by the calligrapher Inaba Kakei (died 1800), reads: 'Blossoming flowers and all denizens of the earth sing the praises of a future in which, with the change to a new holder of the name Sōri, the light of the North Star will shine with ever-increasing brilliance. Inscribed by Kakei, a friend.' *Hokushin* is the East Asian name for the North Star (Pole Star). This star is associated with Bodhisattva Myōken, a Buddhist deity who was an important focus of Hokusai's personal religious beliefs (cat. 2). In fact, Hokusai has here borrowed the star's name to form his own new art names: Hokusai ('North Studio') and Tokimasa (*toki* is an alternative reading of the character *shin*, star). The print therefore informs friends and acquaintances of the name-change, and so declares Hokusai to be an independent artist unaffiliated with any school. Two of the terrapins strain their necks energetically, even ambitiously, upwards. MR

4
Monk Nichiren

About 1811
Signature: Katsushika Hokusai Taito haiga
('Respectfully drawn by Katsushika Hokusai Taito')
Seal: [*kaō*]
Inscription by Anryūzan Nichiyō
Hanging scroll, ink, colour, gold and gold leaf
on paper, 40.6 × 20.3 cm
Provenance: Nasu Royal Museum (1996)
Literature: HK 21, Sept 1996, pp. 31–32; TNM 2005,
no. 243; Freer-Sackler 2006, no. 135
Hikaru Museum, Takayama

Monk Nichiren (1222–1282) founded a leading sect
of Japanese Buddhism. The ritual chant inscribed
on this painting was formulated by Nichiren himself:
'Praise the marvellous law of the *Lotus Sutra*' (*Namu
myōhō rengekyō*). Hokusai depicts Nichiren seated on a
rock reading a sutra, perhaps a reference to the occasion
when he preached at Matsuba-ga-yatsu, near Kamakura.
The name Anryūzan refers to the temple Jōonji in
Asakusa, Edo (modern Tokyo), where the inscriber
Nichiyō (died 1840) served as priest. Hokusai produced
several other paintings for Jōonji, suggesting personal
spiritual links to the Nichiren temples in Asakusa,
where he sometimes lived. Nichiren Buddhism was
closely allied to the worship of Bodhisattva Myōken,
a Buddhist deity of great importance to Hokusai, and
the Myōken worship hall at Yanagishima (cat. 2) stood
within the compound of a Nichiren temple. Early in
his career Hokusai created illustrations for a short
popular novel, *Life of Nichiren* (*Nichiren ichidai ki*, 1780). MR

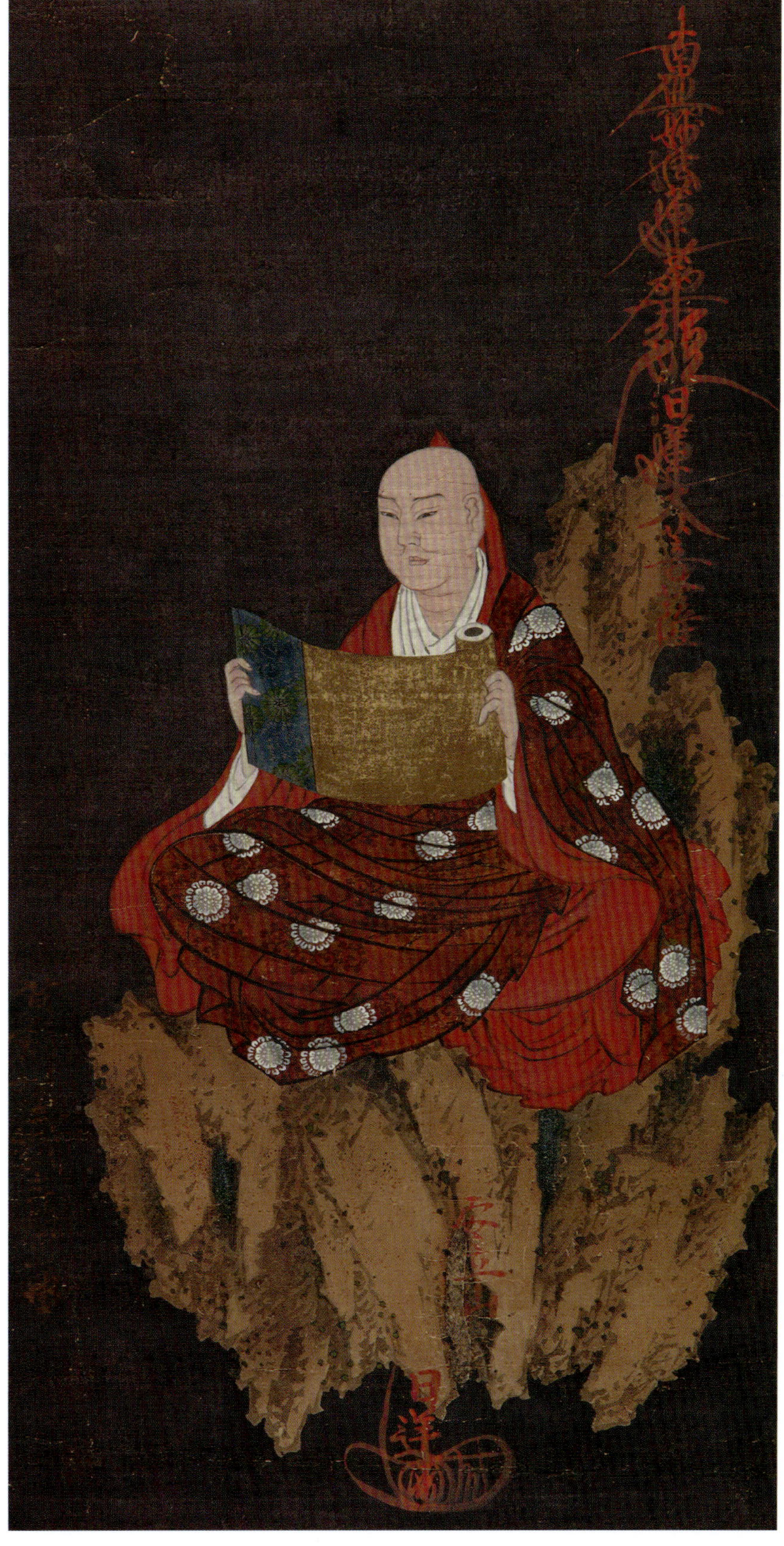

5

Chinese immortal Yuzhi and her dragon

About 1798

Signature: Hokusai Sōri ga

Seal: Shi zōka ('Creation is my master')

Pair of hanging scrolls, ink and colour on paper,

each about 125.4 × 56.5 cm

Provenance: Hayashi Tadamasa (1890);

Azabu Museum of Arts and Crafts

Literature: NUT 1994–1996, vol. 6, nos 54, 55;

Nagata 2000, no. 5. 14–15; Carpenter 2005, pp. 16–31,

cover

Private collection, USA

Classical China represented a great storehouse
of cultural legitimacy for Japanese artists, Hokusai
included. Yuzhi (Japanese: Gyokushi) is an immortal
in Chinese mythology, daughter of the Queen Mother
of the West. She rides a white dragon, and a hundred
birds gather when she plays her single-stringed *chin*,
a kind of harp. When he painted this, the artist had
just recently started using 'Hokusai' ('North Studio'),
the name referencing the North Star that will ultimately
make him famous around the world. His seal here
reads 'Creation is my master'. Approaching forty
and mobilizing all his painting skills learned to date,
Hokusai creates a powerfully mythic image – based
on an earlier book illustration by Tachibana Morikuni
(1679–1748) – that contrasts the poised and elegant
Chinese beauty with her obedient dragon. The paintings
were originally mounted on a two-panel folding screen. TC

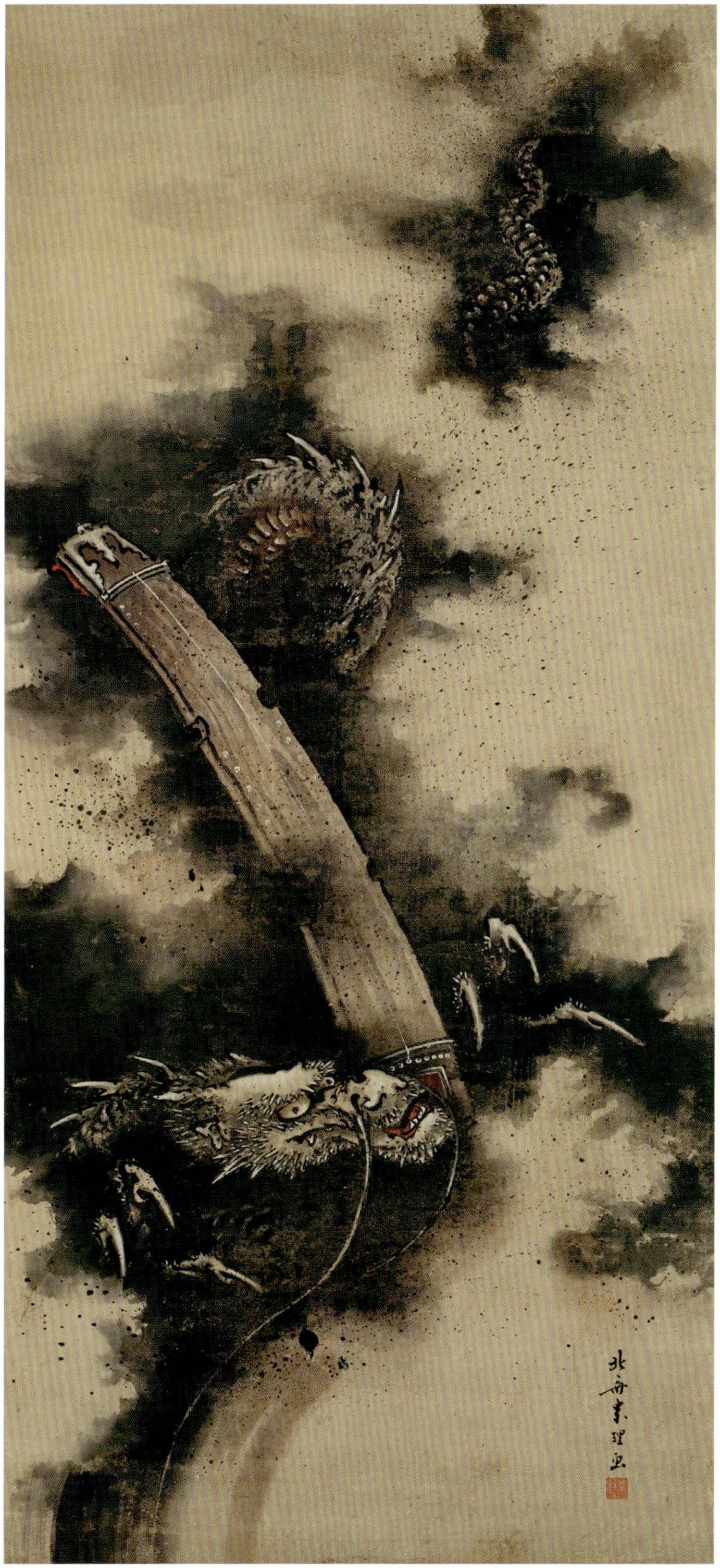

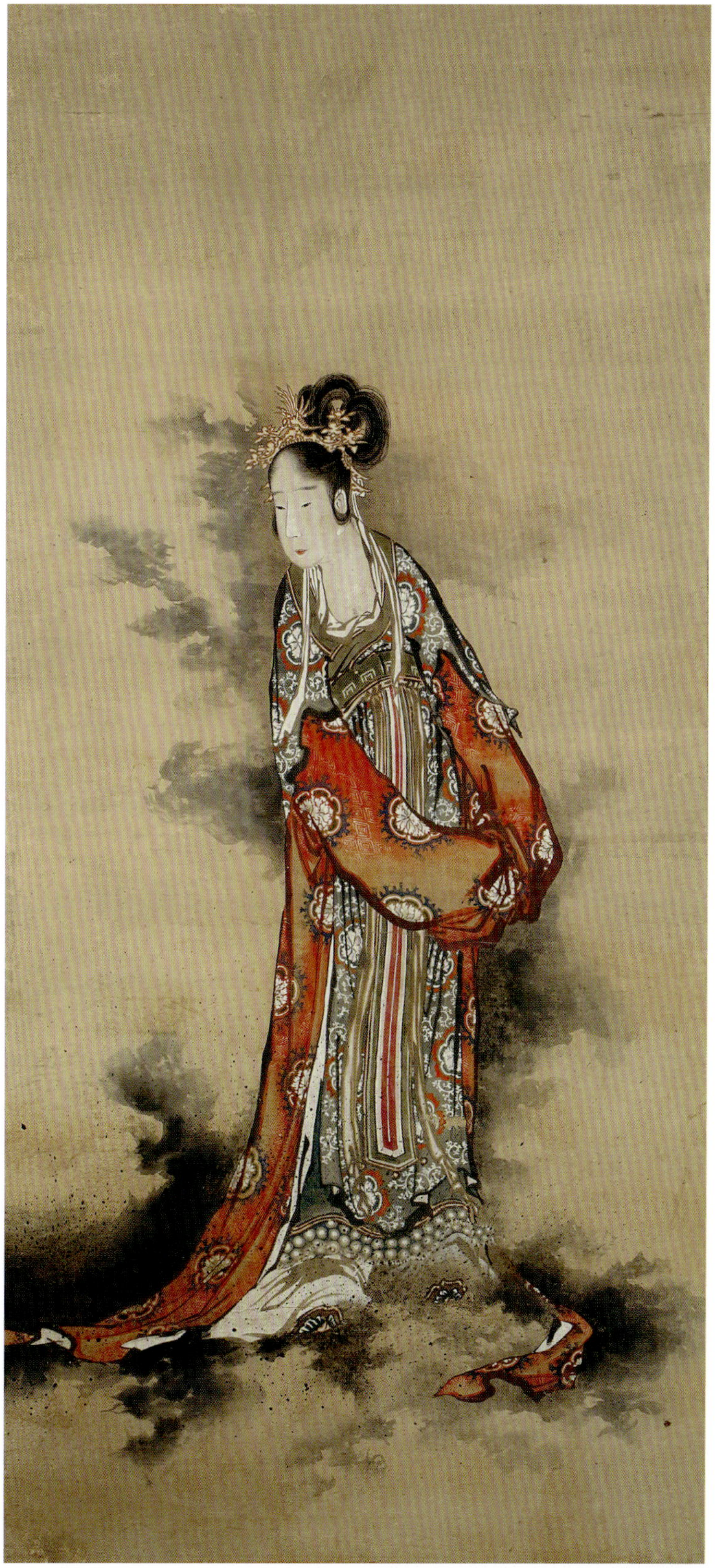

6
Flowering plum tree

About 1795–1798
Signature: Hokusai Sōri ga
Seal: Kanchi
Inscription by Yomo no Utagaki Magao
Hanging scroll, ink and shell-white on paper,
116.5 × 34.0 cm
Provenance: Louis Gonse; Janette Ostier; Ralph Harari
Literature: Goncourt 1896, p. 291; Clark 1992, no. 95;
Nagata 2000, no. 4
British Museum, 1982,0701,0.3, given by Dr and
Mrs Michael Harari
Osaka only

Attenuated branches of an old plum tree, painted in
ink with instinctual speed and skill, are topped by white
blossoms, each at a different stage of opening. Space
was left for the witty 'crazy verse' (*kyōka*) to be brushed
directly by poet Yomo no Utagaki Magao (1752–1829)
on the painting: 'First singing of the warbler / is more
impressive / than listening to parents' objections /
to getting up early / on a spring morning.' Particularly
during his thirties and forties, Hokusai intersected
with glittering circles of artists, poets and writers in Edo.
In paintings, specially commissioned prints (*surimono*)
and illustrations for printed poetry anthologies, he
created more than a thousand images that enhanced
the witty verses of these urbane poets. **TC**

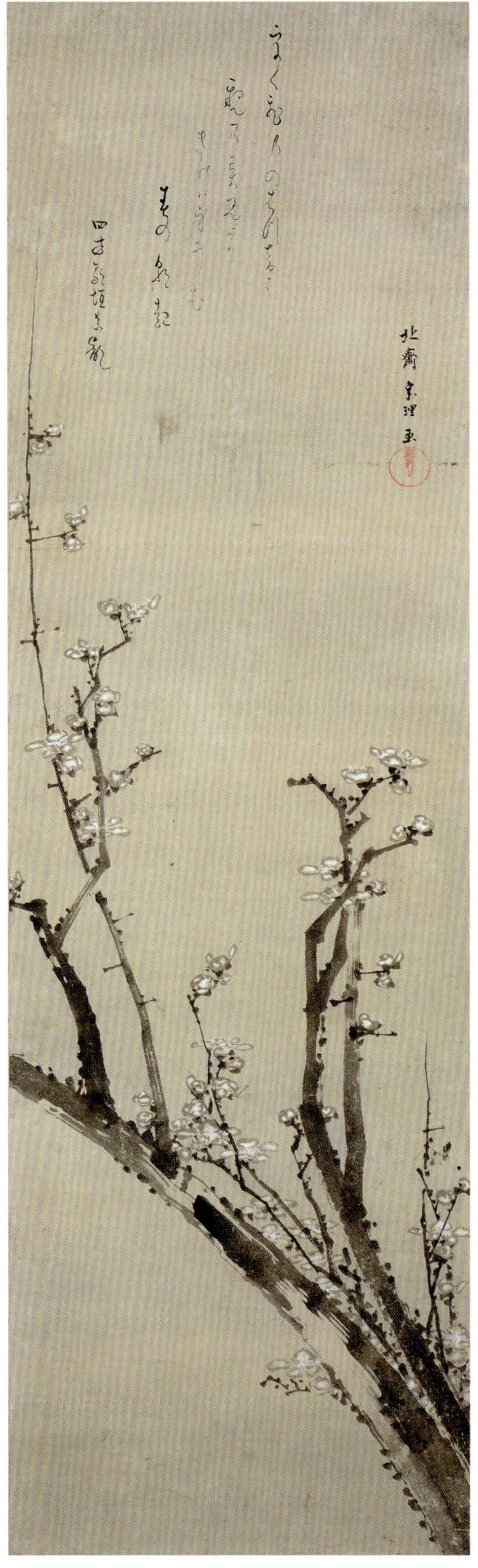

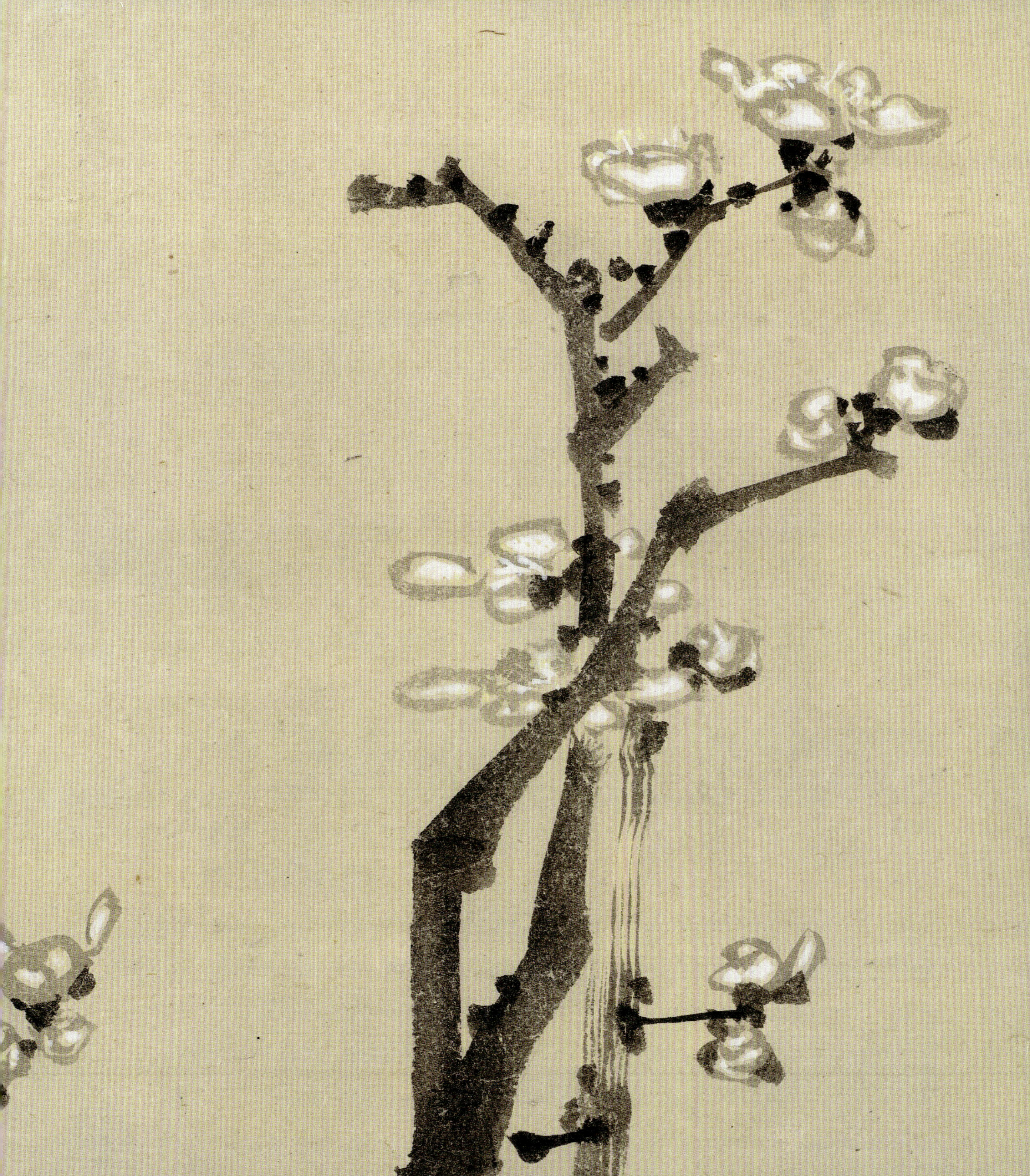

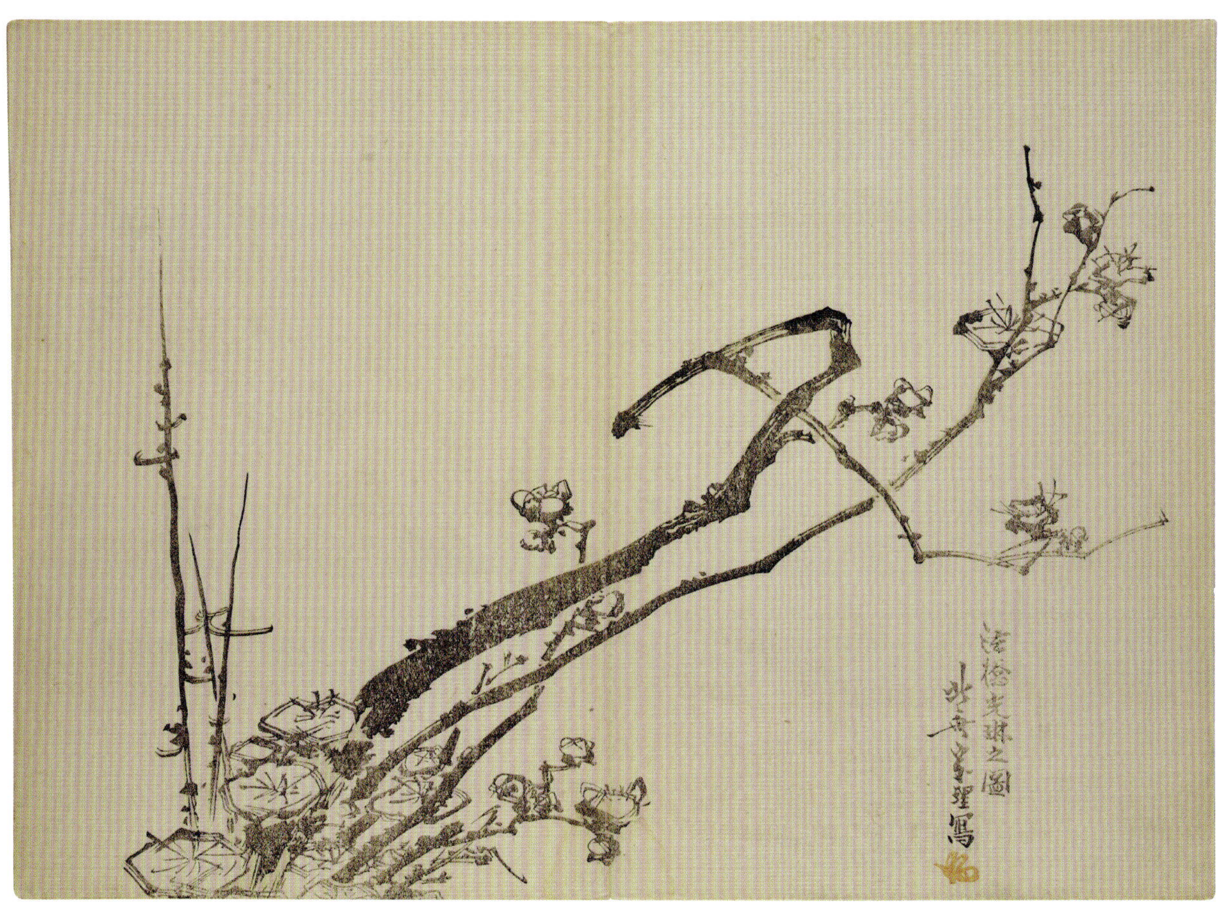

7

Flowering plum tree, from *Nightingale Deep in the Mountains (Miyama uguisu)*

New Year, 1798
Signature: Hokkyō Kōrin no zu / Hokusai Sōri sha
('Picture by Hokkyō Kōrin, copied by Hokusai Sōri')
Seal: [*kaō*]
Illustrated book, colour woodblock, 19.2 × 13.2 cm
(covers)
Provenance: Jack Hillier
Literature: Hillier 1980, no. 72; HUT 1987–1990, vol. 3,
no. 323; TNM 2005, no. 124
British Museum, 1979,0305,0.410
Osaka only

This may be the only surviving copy of this small,
privately printed anthology of 'crazy verses' (*kyōka*).
It was edited by a certain 'Ryūkasō Hirozumi' – his real
identity is unknown – and published at the New Year,
1798. Among thirteen page openings are two illustrations,
one each by Hokusai and his fellow floating world
(ukiyo-e) artist, Kitao Shigemasa (1739–1820). Hokusai
completed more than a thousand such commissions
for *surimono* and illustrations for poetry anthologies
during his thirties and forties. Here he claims stylistic
affiliation with the famous Rinpa school artist Ogata
Kōrin (1658–1716). Kōrin produced similar stylized
plum blossoms with broken outlines in his paintings. TC

Beauty with an umbrella under a willow

About 1801–1804
Signature: Gakyōjin Hokusai ga ('Drawn by Hokusai, man crazy to paint')
Seal: Tokimasa
Hanging scroll, ink and colour on silk, 84.3 × 25.4 cm
Literature: Sankei Shinbun 1977 [pages not numbered]; NU 1982, no. 2; Nagata 2000, BW no. 24; Paris 2014, no. 140; Hokusaikan 2015, pp. 36–37
Hokusai Museum, Obuse

A young woman looks back with a pensive expression as she walks in high clogs along a path, carrying a half-furled 'snake's-eye' umbrella. New green tresses on the aged willow and red azaleas coming into bloom on the grassy bank signal late spring. Her movement is momentarily arrested, encouraging us to identify with her enjoyment of the fresh breeze just after a shower. Paintings of beautiful women (*bijin-ga*) were a staple of most artists of the floating world (ukiyo-e) school. Hokusai painted the subject regularly into his sixties (cats 10, 11); however, the beauty paintings of his late thirties and forties are the most memorable. It was around the age of forty that the artist began to style himself 'man crazy to paint' (Gakyōjin). The name Tokimasa, like Hokusai, relates to his worship of the North Star and the cult of Bodhisattva Myōken (see cat. 2). TC

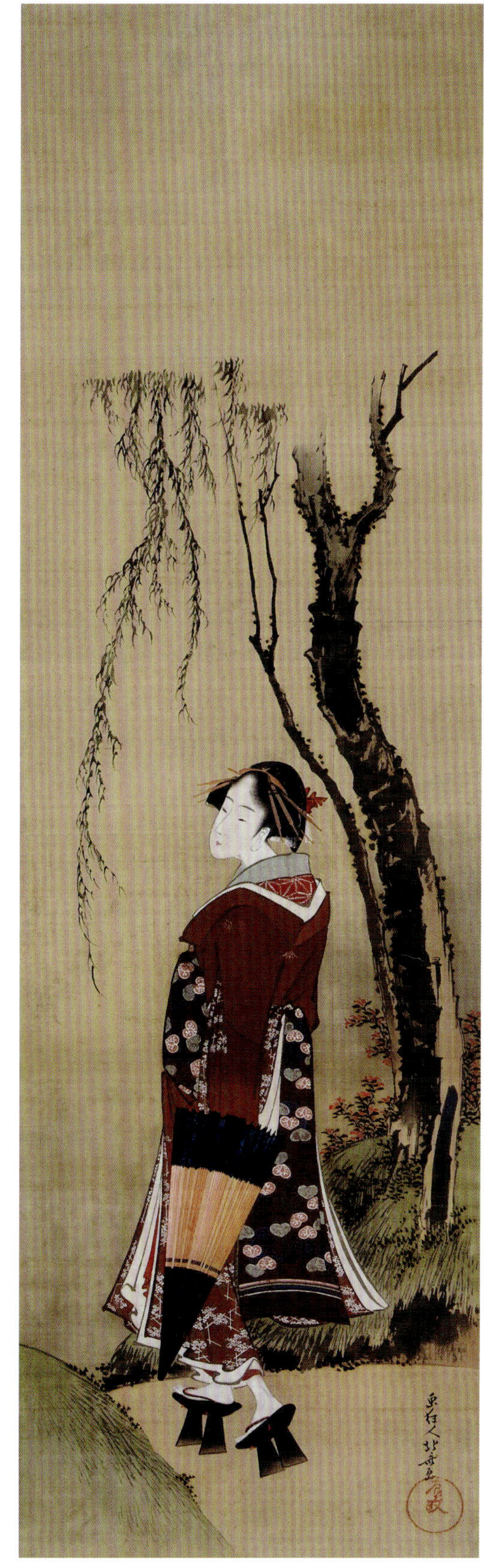

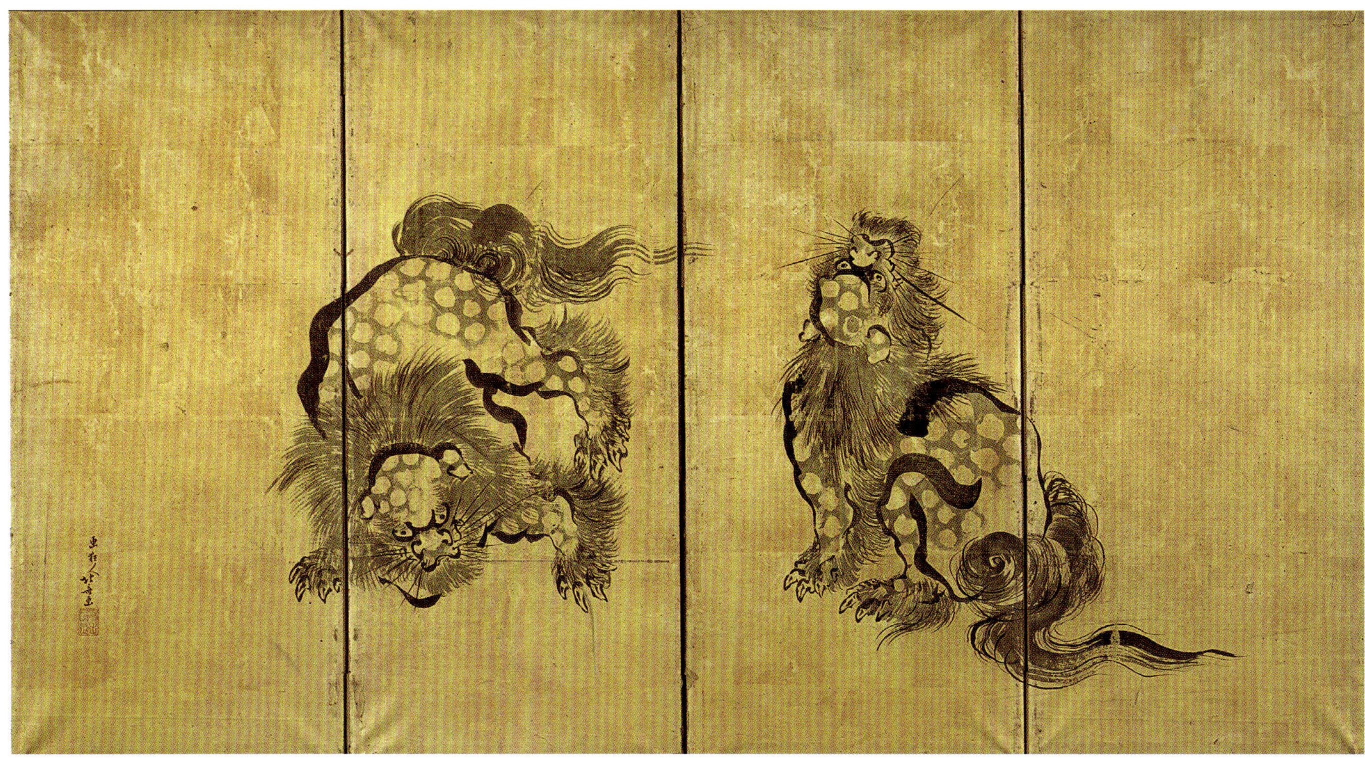

9
Mythical Chinese lions

About 1801–1804

Signature: Gakyōjin Hokusai ga ('Drawn by Hokusai, man crazy to paint')

Seal: Kimō dasoku ('Hair on the turtle, legs on the snake')

Four-panel folding screen, ink and gold leaf on paper, 54.2 × 97.2 cm

Literature: Tokyo National Museum, eds, *Nikuhitsu ukiyo-e*, Tokyo, 1993, no. 74; Nagata 2000, BW no. 47; TNM 2005, no. 188

Tokyo National Museum, A-896

Osaka only

The mythical Chinese lion, or *shishi*, is a protective being, typically represented in paired statues at the entrance to a temple or shrine. In the lion dance, performers wear fierce masks and mock-terrorize spectators. There is something inherently comic, even endearing about *shishi*. Here Hokusai has painted with freely flowing ink-strokes directly on to the gold-leaf-covered surface of a small, four-panel folding screen. One lion looks up quizzically, the other looks down. Perhaps the screen was originally used, it has been suggested, as the backdrop for a display of armour and other male symbols during the Boys' Festival, held each year in the fifth month (TNM 2005, no. 188). Regularly painting *shishi* would become an important talisman to ward off misfortune for Hokusai in old age (cat. 192). The painting seal used here – 'Hair on the turtle, legs on the snake' – alludes to the cult of Bodhisattva Myōken, which Hokusai followed, since a turtle and a snake are attributes of this Buddhist deity. TC

10

Two beauties

About 1801–1804
Signature: Gakyōjin Hokusai ga ('Drawn by Hokusai,
man crazy to paint')
Seal: Kimō dasoku ('Hair on the turtle, legs on
the snake')
Hanging scroll, ink and colour on silk, 110.6 × 36.7 cm
Literature: Ozaki 1967, no. 2; NU 1982, no. 2; TNM
2005, no. 159
MOA Museum of Art, Atami, Important Cultural
Property
Osaka only

The painting is a study in contrasts: a standing
courtesan in rich but casually worn night attire is
paired with a seated married woman in formal,
fashionable day wear. The courtesan rests her chin
on a raised hand wrapped inside her robes, apparently
lost in thought. The married woman holds one hand
up to her open mouth, in a gesture of surprise.
Although their forms overlap in complementary poses,
with the spreading skirts of both women anchoring
the composition, each figure seems psychologically
separate. We are invited into the intimate orbit
of both. Dark, saturated colours, and the sweeping
silhouette of the standing figure, in particular, recall
the influential late style of Kitagawa Utamaro (died
1806); yet Hokusai in his late thirties and forties created
a uniquely winsome and delicate ideal of female
beauty, as can be seen here. TC

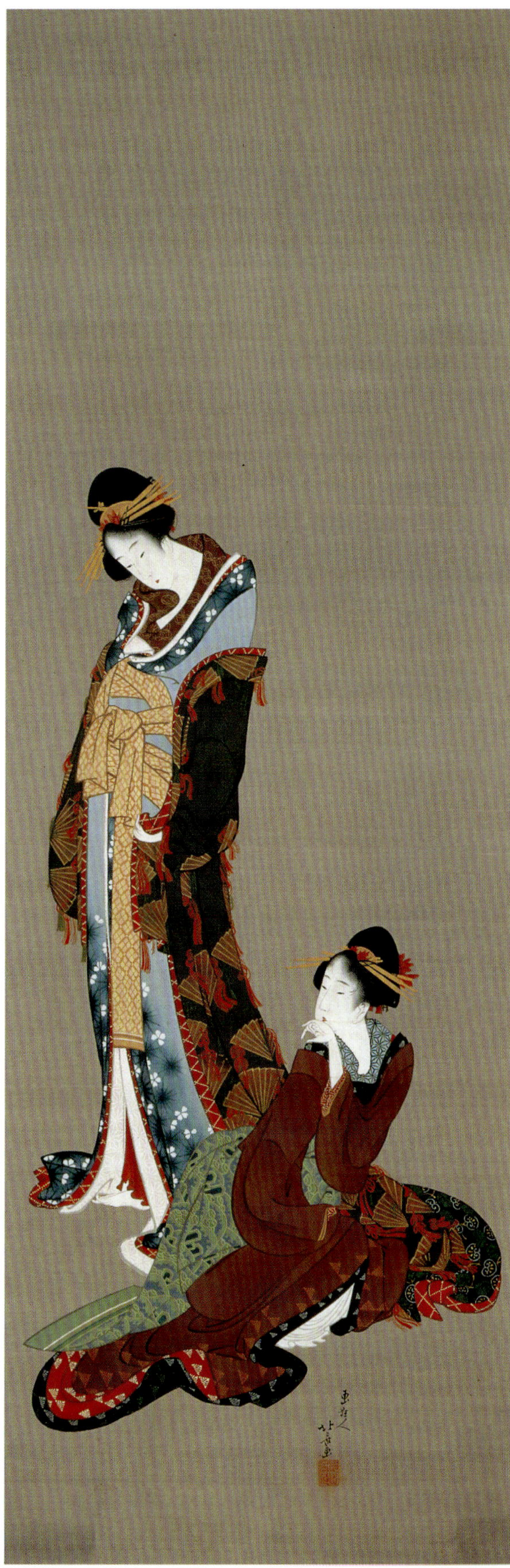

Beauty on a summer morning

About 1810
Signature: Katsushika Hokusai
Seal: Kimō dasoku ('Hair on the turtle, legs on
the snake')
Hanging scroll, ink and colour on silk, 86.1 × 32.4 cm
Provenance: Matsuki Zen'emon
Literature: *Kokka* 1121, Feb. 1989, pp. 23–24; Edo Tokyo
2007, no. 190
Okada Museum of Art, Hakone
London only

On a summer morning, a young woman stands looking
into a hand-mirror to arrange her hair. Her striped
outer robe is suspended from a decorative hanging
rack, and on the floor is the lacquered case for the
mirror, with a packet of tooth powder and a toothbrush
on top of it; fresh blossoms of morning glory grace
the blue-and-white porcelain bowl of water for rinsing
her mouth. Further emphasizing the summer season,
in a stoneware salver with cracked white glaze a pet
goldfish swims among waterweeds. The principal
satisfaction of the painting is the taut, arched pose
and flourishing sweep of the costume. Smoothly flowing
outlines of the thin checked robe are contrasted with
the eccentrically crinkled profile of the stiff brocade
sash. Hokusai's minute attention to detail in the
accessory objects parallels his work in still-life *surimono*
prints, of which he was designing hundreds in these
years (cats 115, 116). TC

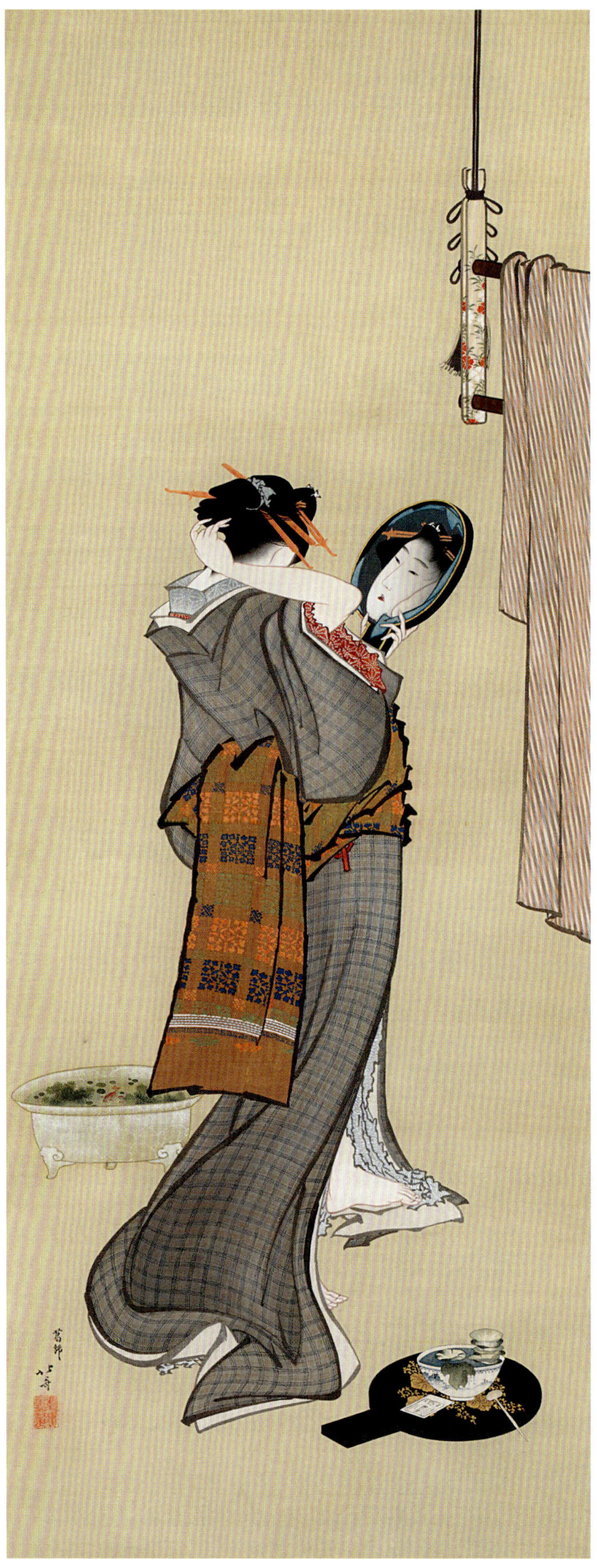

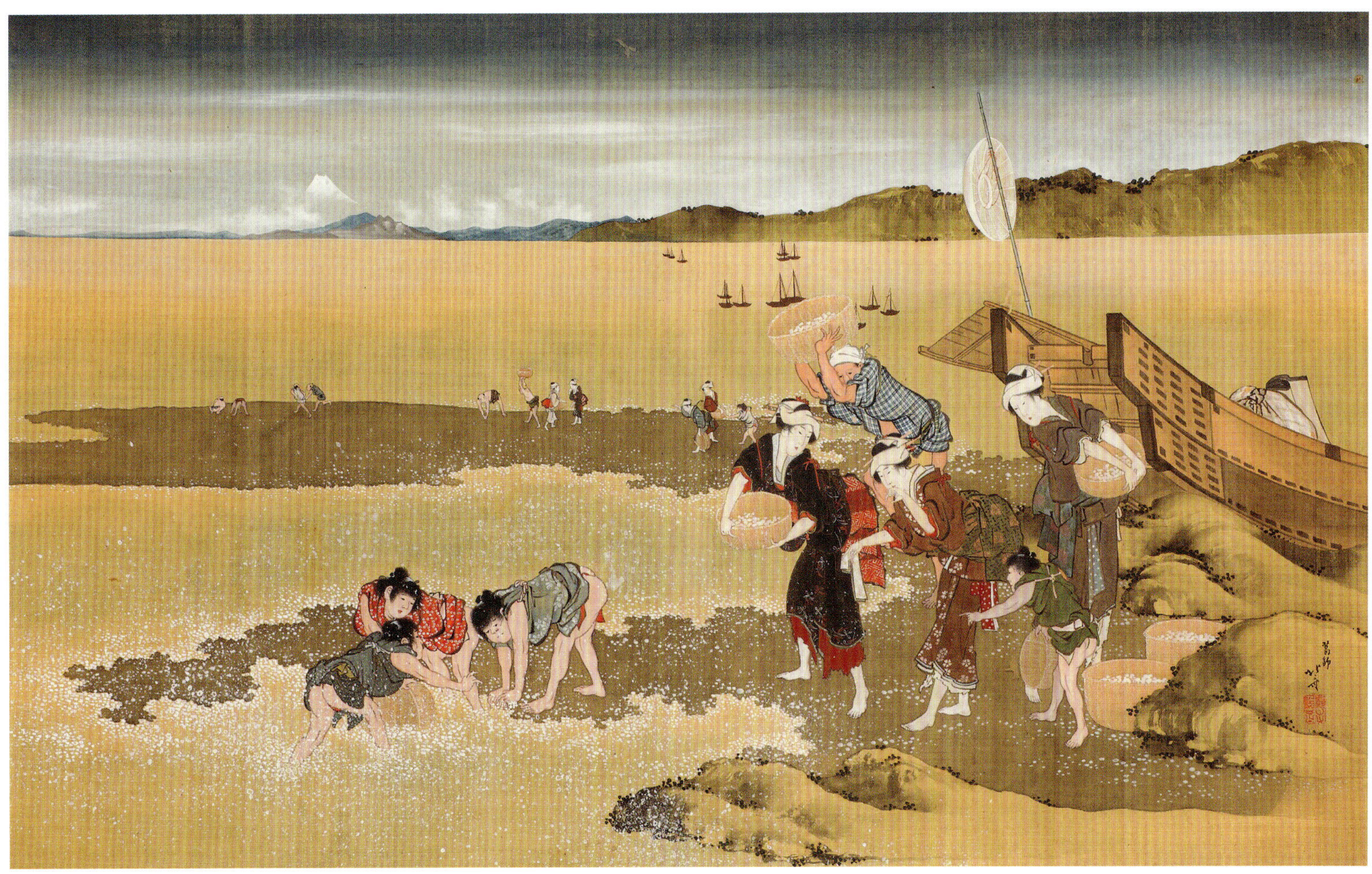

12

Shellfish gathering at low tide

About 1807–1810
Signature: Katsushika Hokusai
Seal: Kimō dasoku ('Hair on the turtle, legs on
the snake')
Hanging scroll, ink and colour on silk, 54.3 × 86.2 cm
Provenance: Kobayashi Bunshichi (?); Takeoka Toyota;
Nakajima Shōichirō
Literature: NU 1982, no. 20; Clark 1992, pp. 36–38,
fig. 24; Nagata 2000, BW no. 108; Osaka 2012, no. 51
Osaka City Museum of Fine Arts, Important Cultural
Property
Osaka only

People are out on mudflats at low tide, gathering
shellfish into baskets. A boat is pulled up on the rocks,
with a bundle and a mat inside and a hat hanging
from a bamboo pole. Three excited boys have caught
something in the shallows. An exact location cannot
be specified, although it is likely to be the coast of Edo
bay, with the peak of Mt Fuji visible above clouds on
the distant horizon. Judging by the degree of damage
to the 'Hair on the turtle, legs on the snake' painting
seal, this is a work of Hokusai's late forties. Transcending
earlier, more literal exercises in European-style
composition (cats 18, 19), here there is a satisfying
amalgam of the three broad traditions he has studied:
Western-influenced perspective, clouds and sky;
Chinese-style rock formations; and lively Japanese
ukiyo-e style figure painting. TC

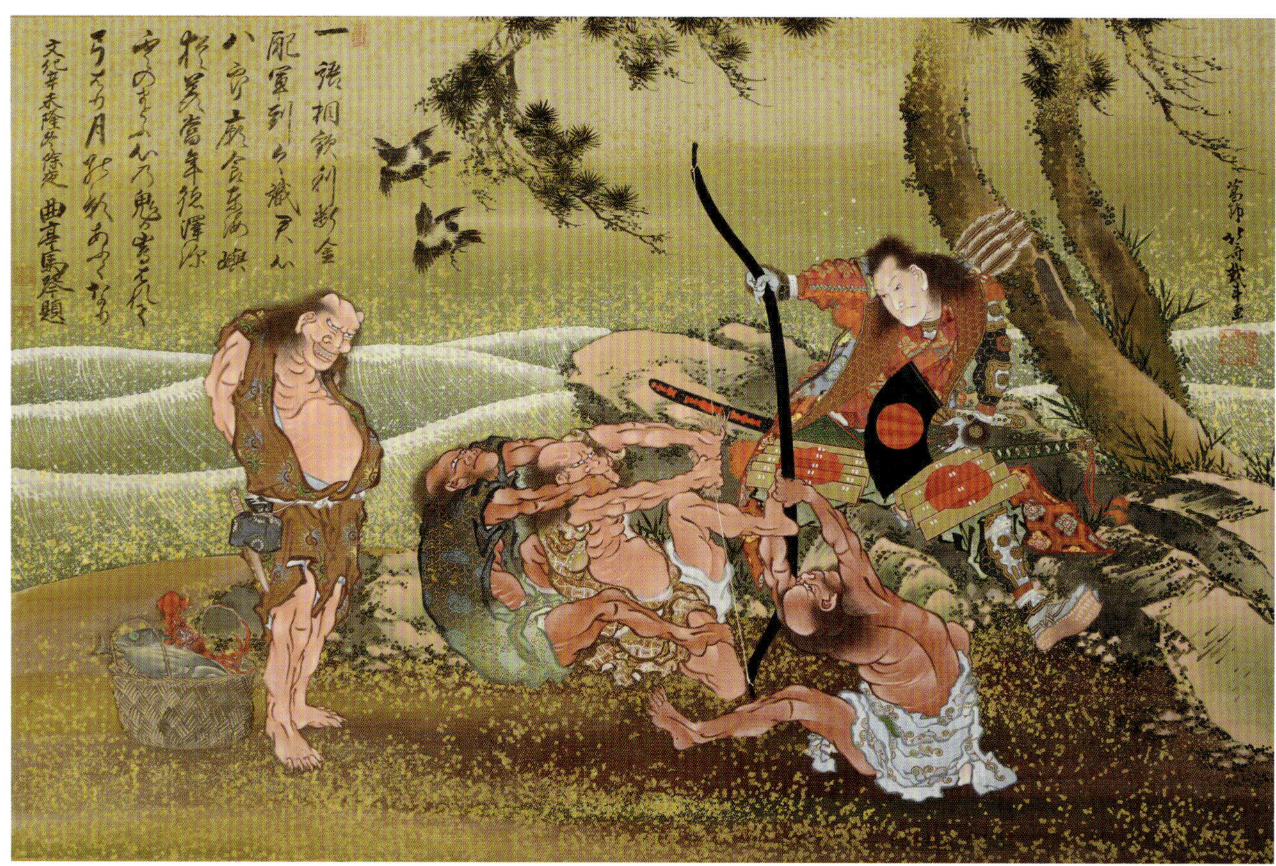

Warrior hero Tametomo and the inhabitants of Onoshima island

1811

Signature: Katsushika Hokusai Taito ga
('Drawn by Hokusai Taito of Katsushika')

Seal: Raishin ('Thunder tremor')

Inscription by Kyokutei (Takizawa) Bakin (1767–1848)

Hanging scroll, ink, colour, gold and gold leaf on silk,
54.9 × 82.1 cm

Provenance: Hirabayashi Shōgorō III (1854);
William Anderson

Literature: Narazaki Muneshige, ed., *Zaigai hihō* vol.
3: *Nikuhitsu ukiyo-e*, Tokyo, Gakken, 1969, p. 91, no. 88;
Mizuno Minoru, ed., *Zusetsu Nihon no koten*, vol. 19:
Kyokutei Bakin, Tokyo, Shūeisha, 1980, nos 22, 23; NU
1982, no. 26; Clark 1992, no. 96; Nagata 2000, no. 67
British Museum, 1881,1210,0.1747

Warrior hero Minamoto no Tametomo (1139–1170)
is so strong he can nonchalantly cool himself with his
war fan even as the inhabitants of Onoshima struggle
to pull the string on his mighty bow. The scene takes
place on a beach of this remote, mythical island, which
Tametomo will presently subdue. With its richly
layered colouring and extensive sprinklings of cut gold
leaf, this is technically one of the most complex
paintings by Hokusai. This reflects its commission by
the publisher Hirabayashi Shōgorō to mark completion
of the illustrated novel *Strange Tales of the Bow Moon* (cat.
14). The painting was then inscribed with a celebratory
Chinese-style poem by the book's author, Takizawa
Bakin (1767–1848). The name Taito ('Receiving the Big
Dipper') and the seal Raishin ('Thunder tremor') both
relate to the cult of Bodhisattva Myōken, the latter
particularly to an incident when the artist was struck by
lightning when returning after worship at the Myōken
hall in Yanagishima (Iijima 1999, p. 54). TC

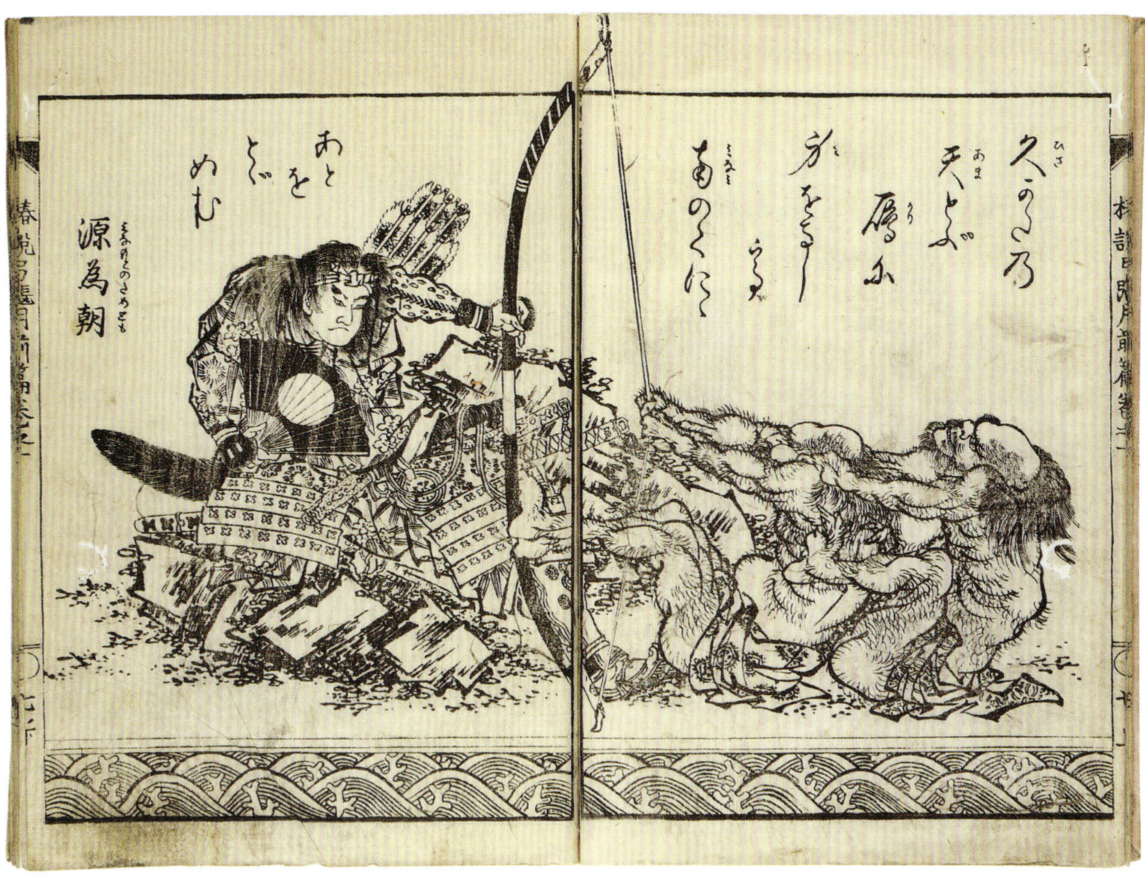

14

**Warrior hero Tametomo,
from *Strange Tales of the Bow Moon*
(*Chinsetsu yumiharizuki*), vol. 1**

1807
Signature: Katsushika Hokusai
Seal: Hokusai
Text by Takizawa Bakin (1767–1848)
Woodblock, illustrated book, vol. 1 (of 29), published
by Hirabayashi Shōgorō, 22.2 × 15.4 cm (covers)
Provenance: Jack Hillier
Literature: Mizuno Minoru, ed., *Zusetsu Nihon no koten*,
vol. 19: *Kyokutei Bakin*, Tokyo, Shūeisha, 1980, no. 301
British Museum, 1979,0305,0.488.1

In his forties, Hokusai, together with authors such
as Takizawa Bakin (1767–1848), played a leading role
in developing the genre of popular printed literature
called *yomihon*, literally, 'books to read'. These were
illustrated adventure stories, published serially, which
translated and adapted Chinese stories or spun
colourful yarns based on historical Japanese figures –
here the samurai warrior Minamoto no Tametomo
(1139–1170). In later periods Tametomo was venerated
as an extraordinarily strong super-hero, who subdued
a succession of remote islands on the periphery of
Japan (cat. 13). *Strange Tales of the Bow Moon* (*Chinsetsu
yumiharizuki*, 1807–1811), finally ran to twenty-nine
volumes and made the publisher Hirabayashi Shōgorō
a great deal of money. TC

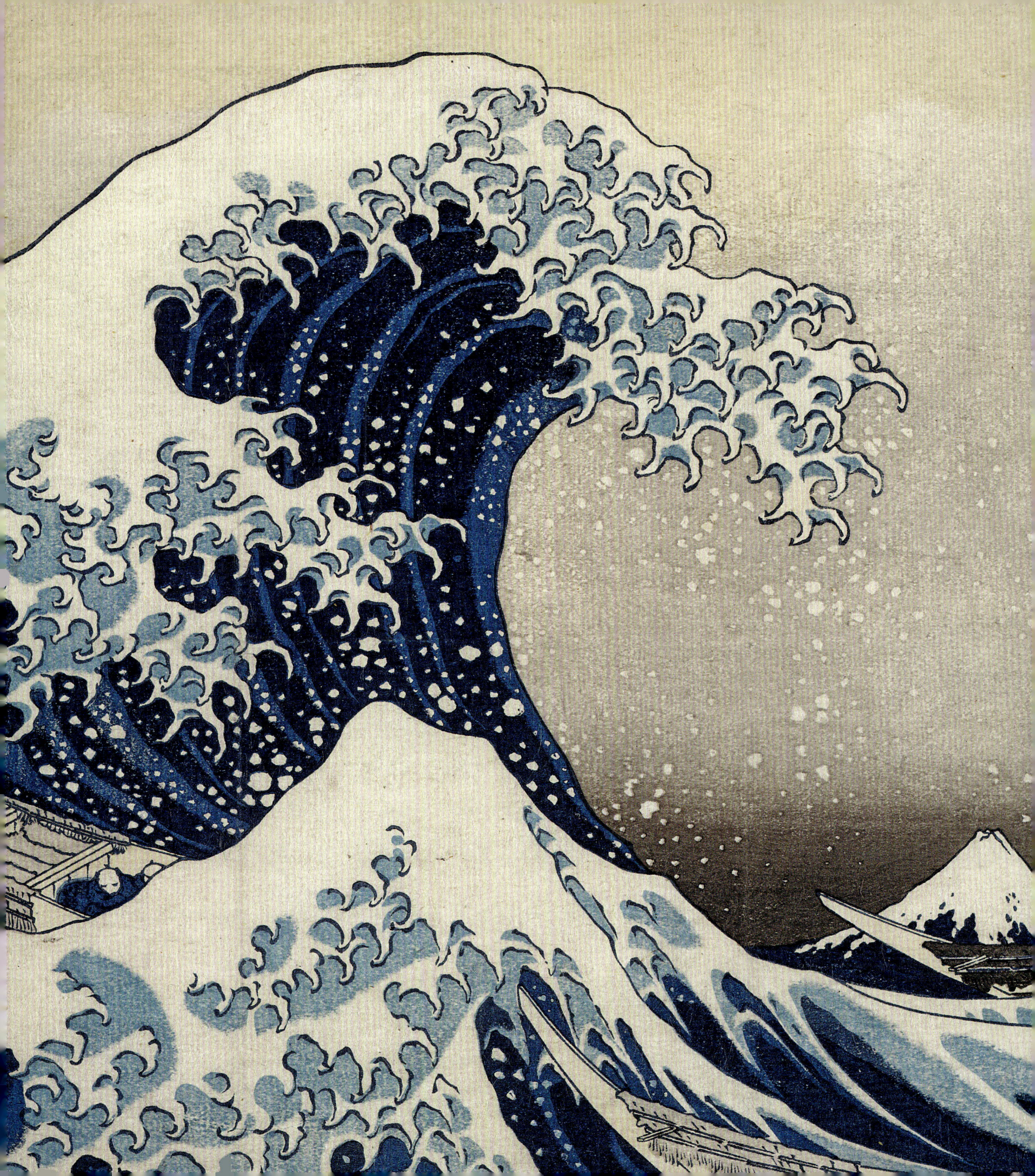

Mt Fuji and the Great Wave

By the Edo period (1615–1868), Mt Fuji was an object of popular religious devotion, laying the foundation for its role as a national icon in modern times. It had also long been depicted by artists. But Hokusai's interest was different from and his achievement transcended that of his predecessors. He depicted it a number of times before he turned fifty (cat. 36). But after he had reached sixty, Fuji began to take centre stage. The series that became *Thirty-Six Views of Mt Fuji* was a synthesis of all Hokusai had learned to that point, including from recent imports of European techniques and materials (cats 20–25 and 41–65, series introductions).

A few years later, around 1834, Hokusai declared a more personal identification with the mountain. Changing his name to Manji ('ten thousand things', 'everything'), he also began to use a stylized image of Fuji on a new seal. One of the first works bearing both was his greatest illustrated book, *One Hundred Views of Mt Fuji* (cats 35, 38, 176–182). *Thirty-Six Views* placed the mountain as the still centre of a teeming human landscape, but *One Hundred Views* suggested that its authority transcended the concerns of this world. Hokusai also returned to the mountain in his last few years, believing it to have life-prolonging powers (cats 209, 221).

Hokusai focused on Fuji in his seventies and early eighties, but he had been drawn to water, in all its forms, throughout his life. The East Asian landscape had long been defined in terms of mountains and rivers. Hokusai may have been the first, though, to explore fully the way a river animated a city (cat. 56), the liminal quality of the meeting between sea and land (cat. 32), and the inherent power and mystery of rivers (cat. 33), waterfalls (cats 66–72) and the ocean itself.

Hokusai's depiction of the ocean, particularly of waves, became ever more dynamic and animated over time (cats 1, 18, 19). 'The Great Wave' may be the most famous (cat. 51), but is only one example of his exploration of the relationship between sea, land and sky (e.g. cats 41–45). By the end of his life, Hokusai was focusing on the sea alone. In the 1840s, he combined waves and whirlpools, showing how the ocean in itself brought together the fury of waves and the stillness he had identified in Fuji, so providing a portal to another world (cats 206, 207). **AL**

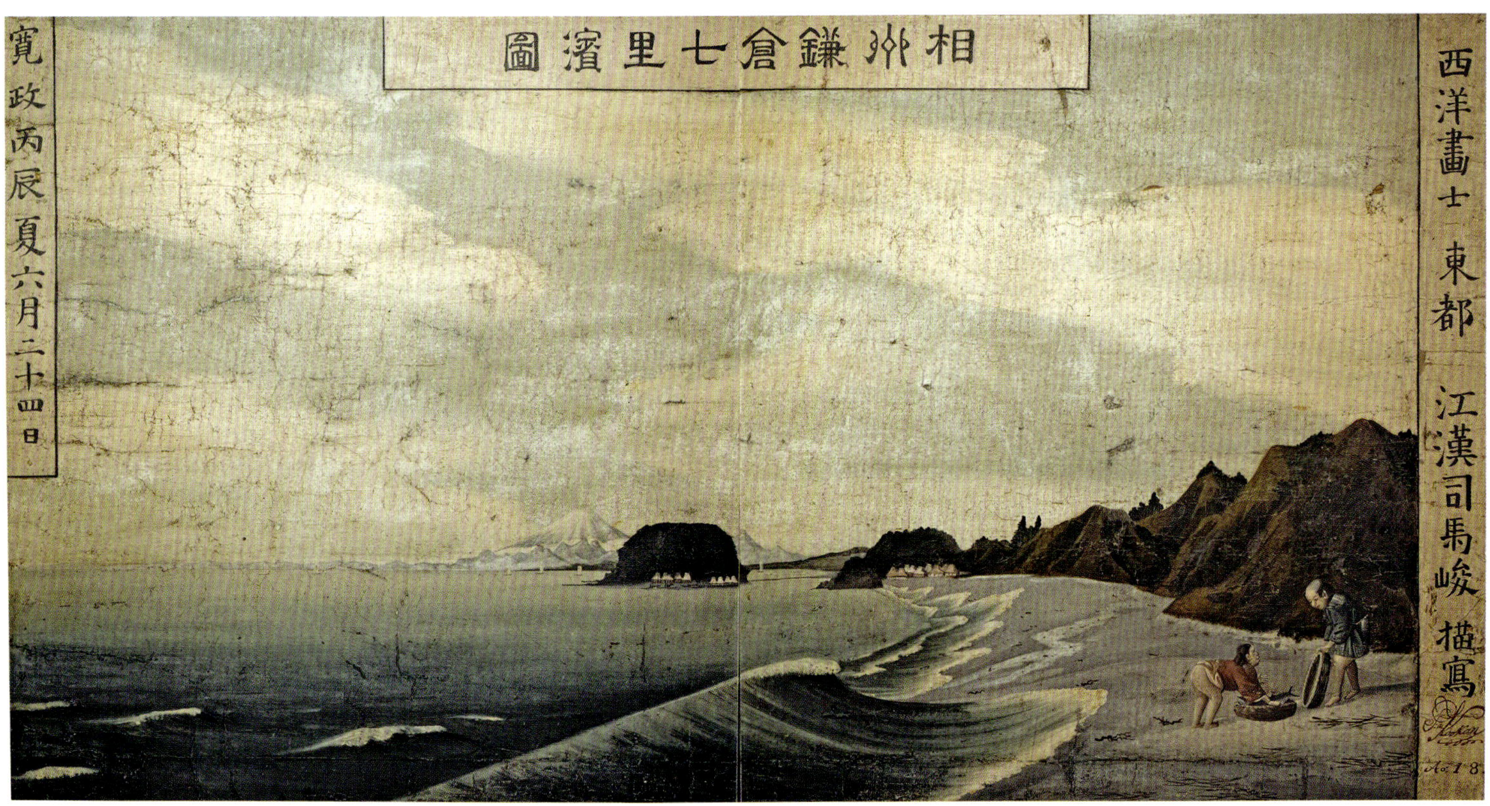

15

Shiba Kōkan (1747–1818)
**View of Shichirigahama beach,
Kamakura, Sagami province**

24th day, sixth month, 1796
Signature: Seiyō gashi Tōto Kōkan Shiba Shun byōsha
S:a.Kookan Ao:18 ('Depicted by Kōkan Shiba Shun
of the Eastern Capital [Edo], Western picture master')
Appended inscriptions by Ōta Nanpo (1749–1823)
and Nakai Tōdō (1758–1821)
Two-panel folding screen (originally a votive painting),
oil pigment on paper, 95.7 × 178.4 cm
Provenance: Atago shrine, Edo; publisher Seizandō
(by 1811); Ikenaga Hajime
Literature: Naruse Fujio, *Shiba Kōkan*, Tokyo, Yasaka
Shobō, 1995, no. 140
Kobe City Museum, Important Cultural Property
Osaka only

The view is from the beach at Kamakura, past
the island of Enoshima, towards a distant Mt Fuji.
Now mounted on a two-panel folding screen, Kōkan's
painting was originally hung framed under the eaves
of the votive picture hall at Atago shrine in Edo, where
Hokusai would surely have seen it. Presenting a deeply
receding perspective view with low horizon, using
pigments and techniques that imitated oil painting,
and even signing himself 'Western picture master',
Kōkan donated twelve similar views to shrines around
Japan, hoping to kick-start the revolution in European-
style picture-making that he longed for. Hokusai made
a close copy in woodblock in a printed album of the
following year (cat. 17), laying the foundations within
his own art for further development of European-
influenced style. He may have seen imported European
prints directly, but it was the example of successful
Japanese artists working in the foreign style that was
more significant. TC

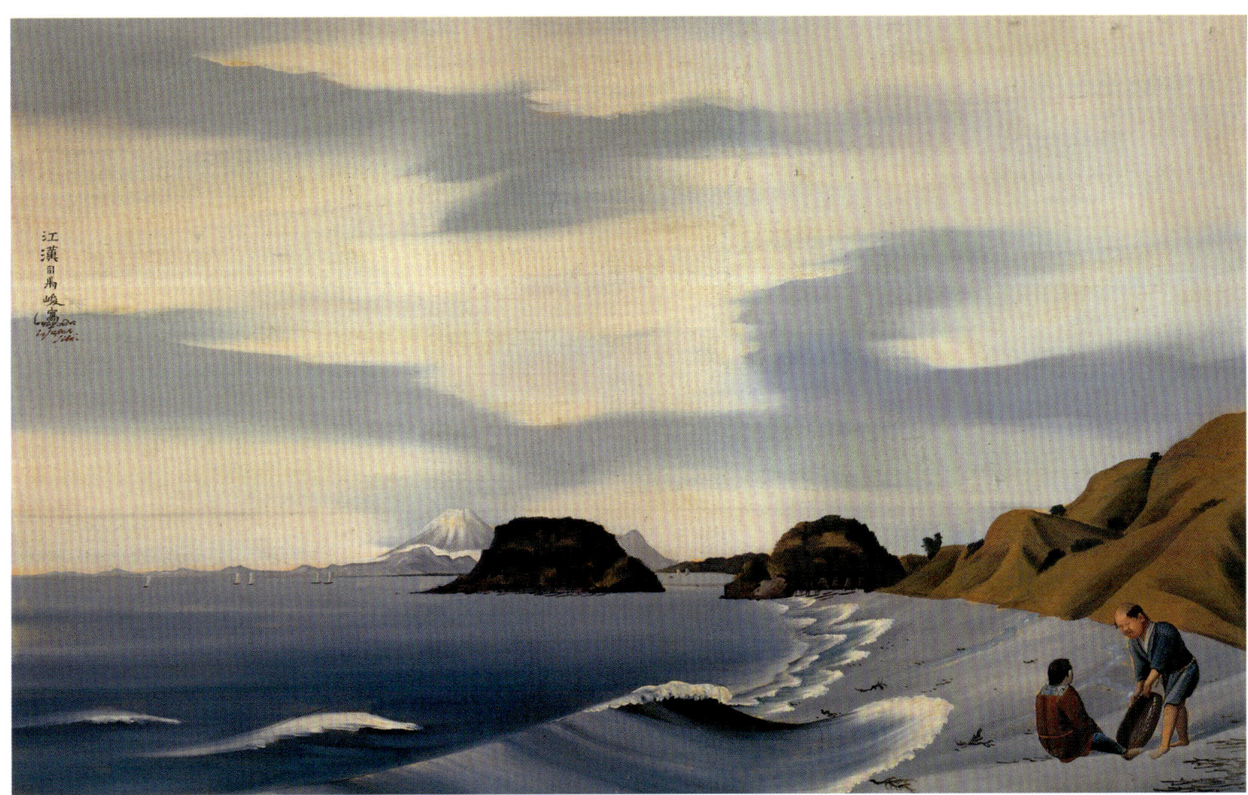

Shiba Kōkan (1747–1818)
Shichirigahama beach

Late Kansei era (1789–1801)
Signature: Kōkan Shiba Shun sha, Eerste Zonder
in Japan Siba. ('Painted by Kōkan Shiba Shun,
Siba the first unique person in Japan.')
Hanging scroll, oil pigment on silk, 47.0 × 73.7 cm
Literature: Naruse Fujio, ed., *Nihon bijutsu kaiga zenshū*,
vol. 25: *Shiba Kōkan*, Tokyo, Shūeisha, 1977, no. 10;
Narazaki Muneshige, ed., *Nikuhitsu ukiyo-e*, vol. 10,
Tokyo, Shūeisha, 1983, no. 51; Naruse Fujio, *Shiba
Kōkan*, Tokyo, Yasaka Shobō, 1995, no. 207
The Museum Yamato Bunkakan, Nara
London only

Kōkan's view is essentially the same as cat. 15, the most
famous version of the subject painted in 1796 for public
display at the Atago shrine, Edo. However, the state
of preservation of the colours here – Kōkan's version
of 'oil painting' – is very much better, featuring bright
blue in sea and sky. Votive paintings were generally
displayed at shrines in a roofed structure, the *emadō*,
which had no walls and was therefore open to the
elements. So the Atago shrine version is, inevitably,
in much poorer condition. Public familiarity with
the image apparently led to numerous commissions
and more than a dozen versions have been recorded
by Kōkan scholar Naruse Fujio. TC

Spring view, Enoshima,
from *Willow Tresses* (*Yanagi no ito*)

1797
Signature: Hokusai Sōri ga
Seals: Hokusai, Sōri
Album leaf, colour woodblock, published by Tsutaya
Jūzaburō, 24.9 × 38.0 cm
Provenance: Charles Ricketts & Charles Shannon
Literature: GUDHJ, vol. 7, p. 82; Nikkei 1998, no. 46
British Museum, 1937,0710,0.206, bequeathed by
Charles Shannon RA

Hokusai's printed spring view of a beach, with Mt Fuji
seen in the distance past the island of Enoshima, is
surely based on Kōkan's painting of the same subject
that was on public view at the Atago shrine, Edo,
from the previous year (cat. 15). In place of a humble
fisherman and his wife, however, we now find travellers
from the city, perhaps asking the way from local children.
The wave about to break on the shore also seems to
have caught Hokusai's attention, and is portrayed more
dynamically. It anticipates a sequence of wave imagery
that will culminate a quarter of a century later, around
1831, in the famous image 'The Great Wave' (cat. 51).
This is one of six plates by different artists illustrating
a de luxe album commissioned by the Asakusa group of
'crazy verse' (*kyōka*) poets, led by pawnbroker Asakusa
no Ichihito/Ichindo (1755–1820). TC

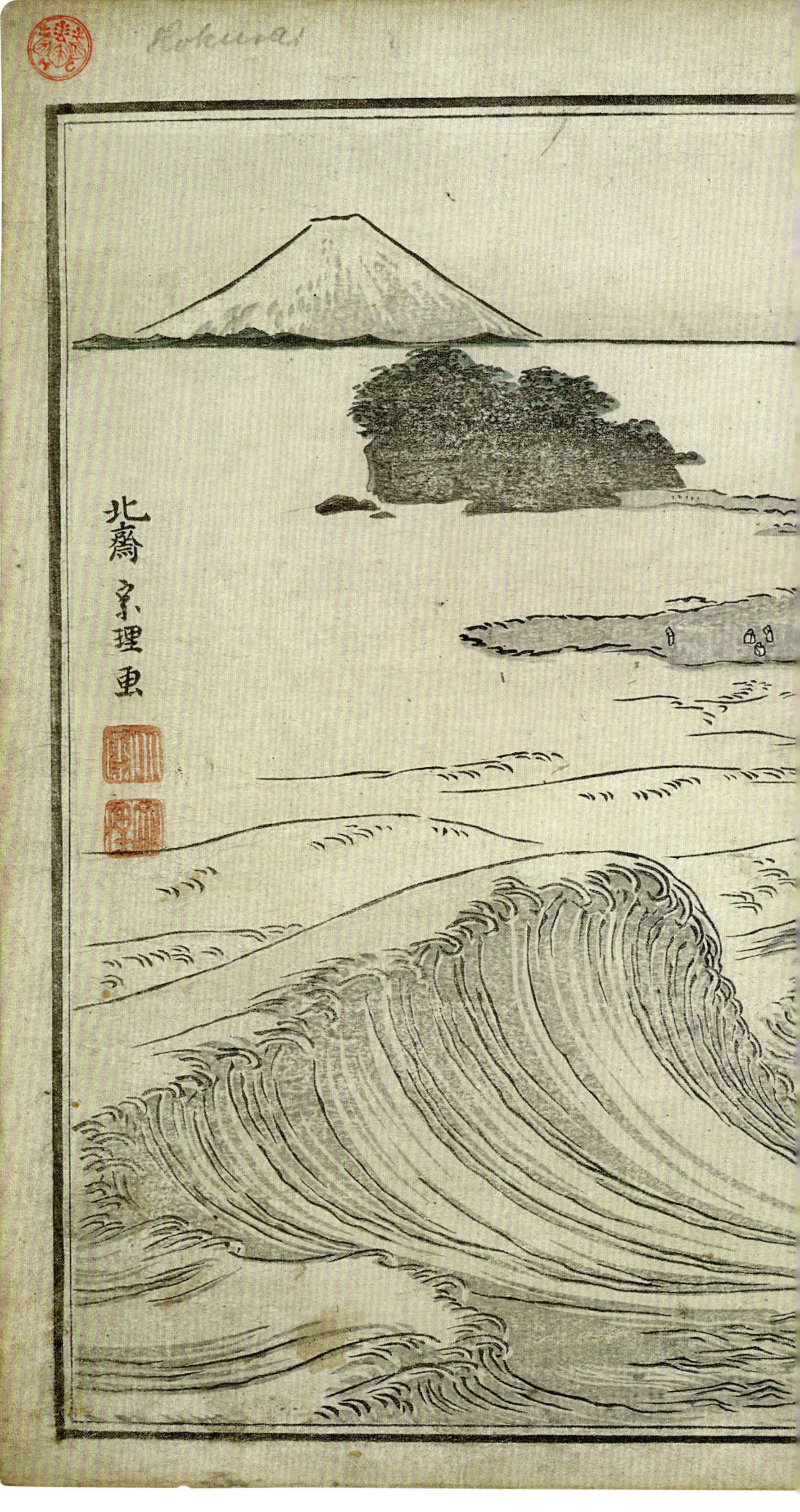

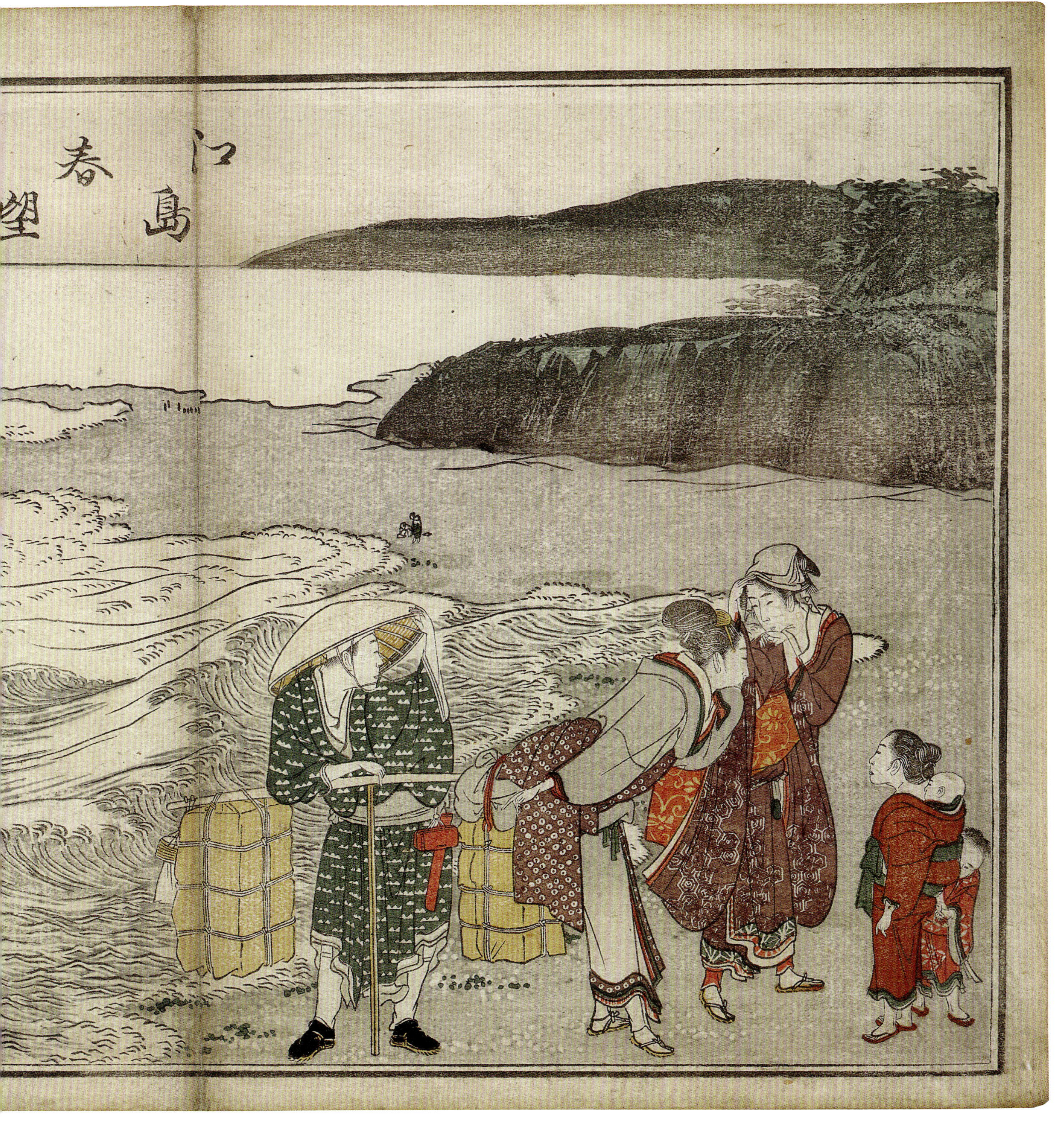

江島
春望

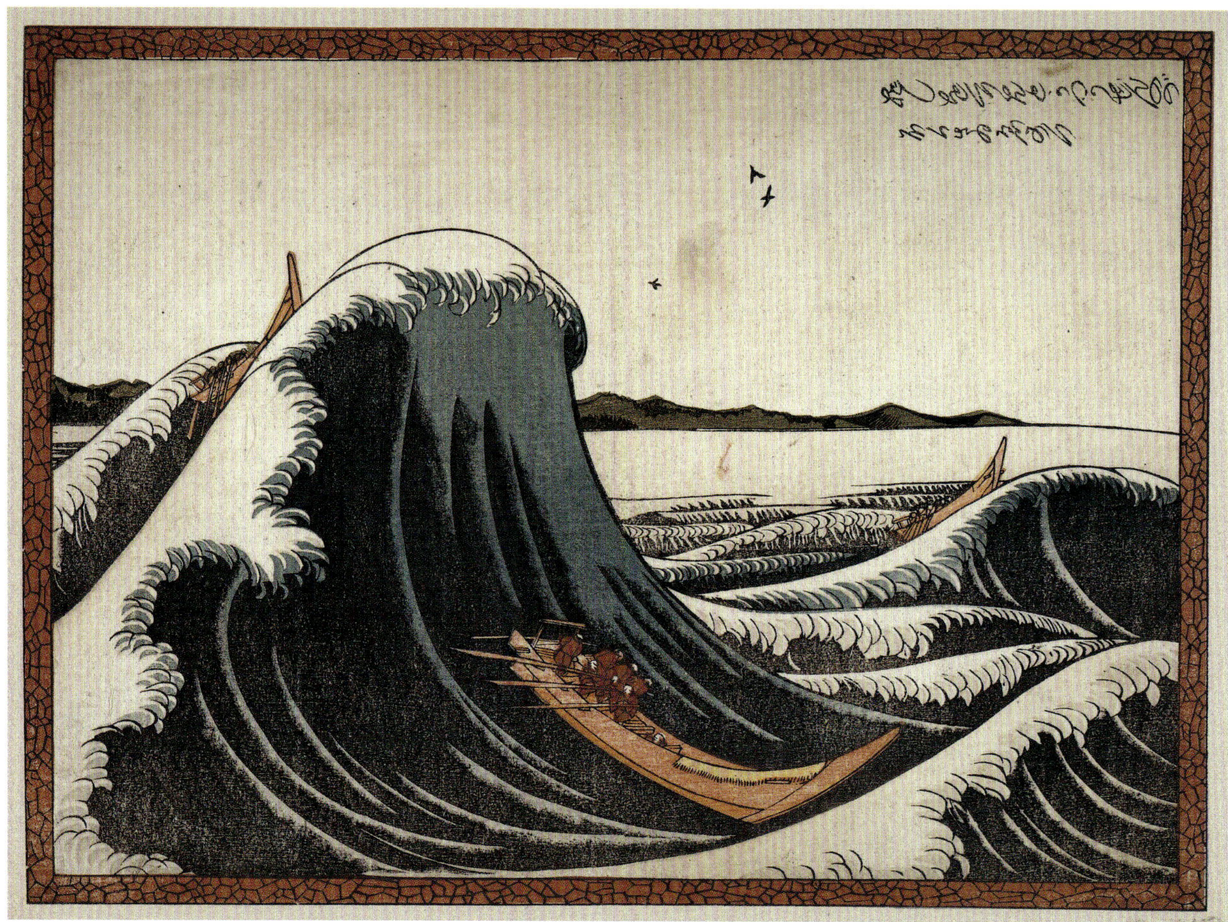

18

Fast skiffs navigating large waves (*Oshiokuri hatō tsūsen no zu*)

About 1804–1806

Signature: Hokusai egaku ('Drawn by Hokusai')

Colour woodblock, publisher unknown, 19.2 × 25.0 cm

Provenance: Maki Bokusen

Literature: Kamiya 1995; Edo Tokyo 2007, no. 78;

Keyes & Morse 2015, no. 534

Nagoya City Museum

London only

Three skiffs (*oshiokuri*) for high-speed delivery of fish to market in Edo are navigating a giant wave. This is the genesis of the famous 'The Great Wave' print (cat. 51) of some quarter of a century later, although here the wave seems frozen by comparison. Following the vogue for landscape/townscape images in 'European' style promoted by Shiba Kōkan (cats 15, 16), Hokusai produced several experimental sets in this idiom in his forties. Five recorded designs in the present set all show the environs of Edo. The title and signature are written in sideways *kana* syllables, imitating Dutch handwriting, and a 'picture frame' with crackled finish surrounds the perspective view, with its sombre *chiaroscuro* shading. This impression comes from an album of prints formerly owned by Hokusai's Nagoya pupil, Makino (or Maki) Bokusen (1775–1824). TC

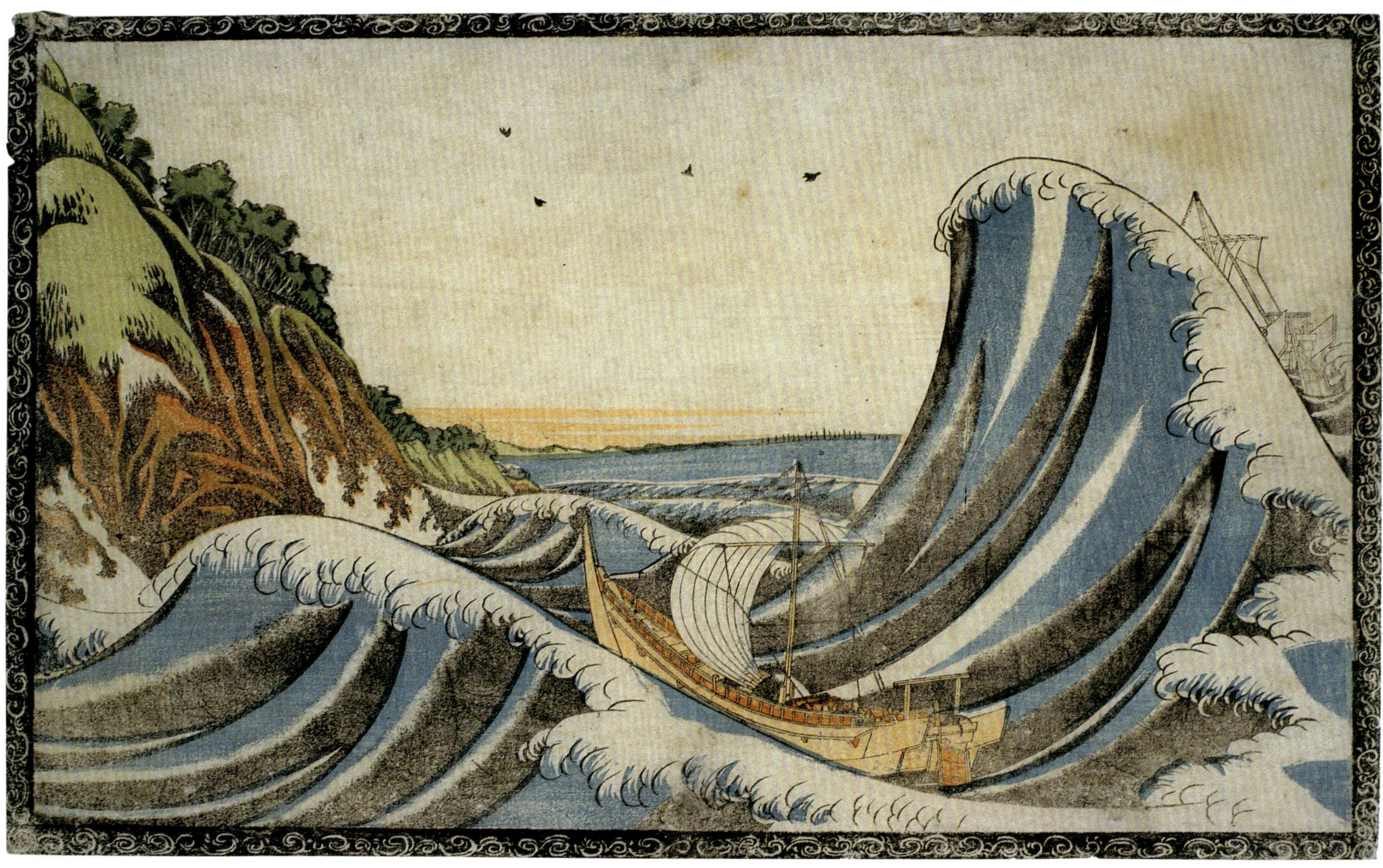

Honmoku, off Kanagawa
(*Kanagawa oki Honmoku no zu*)

About 1807–1809

Unsigned

Colour woodblock, publisher unknown, possibly
Sōshūya Yohei, 21.0 × 33.9 cm

Provenance: Irma and Edwin Grabhorn

Literature: Yamaguchi Keizaburō, ed., *Gurabuhōn
korekushon ukiyo-e meihin ten*, Tokyo, Asahi Shinbun, 1995,
no. 108; TNM 2005, no. 72; Keyes & Morse 2015,
no. 554

Kawasaki Isago-no-Sato Museum

London only

Two coastal cargo boats with sails navigate around a
giant wave, in a composition that is broadly the reverse
of cat. 18. There is a similar use of perspective,
low horizon and internal shading within the image
– Hokusai is experimenting with a European-influenced
style. An earlier printing of the design has a brown
(not black) 'picture frame' with white scrolling, and also
the printed title 'Honmoku, off Kanagawa' in the sky
(TNM 2005, no. 72). This suggests a more precise
location (Honmoku) for Hokusai's most famous print,
'Under the wave off Kanagawa' ('The Great Wave',
cat. 51) of some quarter of a century later. The gradation
(*ita-bokashi*) of the edge of the dark grey shading in
the cliffs and waves was achieved by the block cutter
sanding the edge of the cherry wood printing block,
according to tradition by using rough leaves of the
'Dutch rush' (*tokusa*). TC

Genre scenes in European-influenced style

These six paintings of genre scenes in European-influenced style (cats 20–25) are from a larger group of twenty-nine such works now in the National Museum of Ethnology, Leiden. A related group of twenty-five further works is in the Bibliothèque nationale, Paris. The Dutch East India Company (VOC) *kapitan* Jan Cock Blomhoff (1779–1863) is thought to have commissioned them from Hokusai during the company's Court Journey to Edo of 1822 – at which time Blomhoff would have supplied Hokusai with the Dutch paper the Leiden group are painted on. The finished paintings are presumed to have then been collected during the next Court Journey, in 1826, by *kapitan* Johan Willem de Sturler (1773–1855) and physician Philipp Franz von Siebold (1796–1866). They were taken out of Japan by De Sturler in 1826 and Von Siebold in 1829.

Although unsigned and unprecedented in the Hokusai oeuvre, nevertheless the style of many motifs and the skill – indeed the obsessive way in which many details are rendered – point strongly to the hand of Hokusai himself; at the very least to Hokusai as the master guiding completion of the commission. Hokusai specialist Matthi Forrer has argued for the participation in the project of Hokusai's pupils Totoya Hokkei (1780–1850), Taito II (worked about 1818–1854), and his daughter Ōi (about 1800–after 1857), and one of the paintings in Paris is signed by another pupil, Ōtsuka Dōan (Hachirō, 1795–1855) (Edo Tokyo 2007). More recently, Kubota Kazuhiro has proposed an even more significant role for Ōi in the execution of the paintings, including three of the works shown here (Kubota 2015).

Hokusai had already designed two small landscape series in the European-influenced style (cats 18, 19), learning also from the example of Shiba Kōkan (cats 15, 16). The presumed 1822 Dutch East India Company commission encouraged further, radical experiments in the European-influenced style – in terms of the adoption of vanishing-point perspective and the three-dimensional modelling and use of *chiaroscuro*. Painting on smoother, less absorbent Dutch paper may have encouraged the use of finer detail. The commission stimulated nothing short of a visual revolution in Hokusai's art, giving him the confidence to create some of his most famous colour prints in the 1830s. The frequent use of deep perspective in the *Thirty-Six Views of Mt Fuji* series of about 1831–1833 (cats 50, 60) is one striking result. Certain compositions in the *Thirty-Six Views* further develop specific subjects first realized in the paintings done for the Dutch. European-influenced volumetric style and the use of internal shadows would feature in later works by Ōi (for example *Display room in Yoshiwara at night*, cat. 195). TC

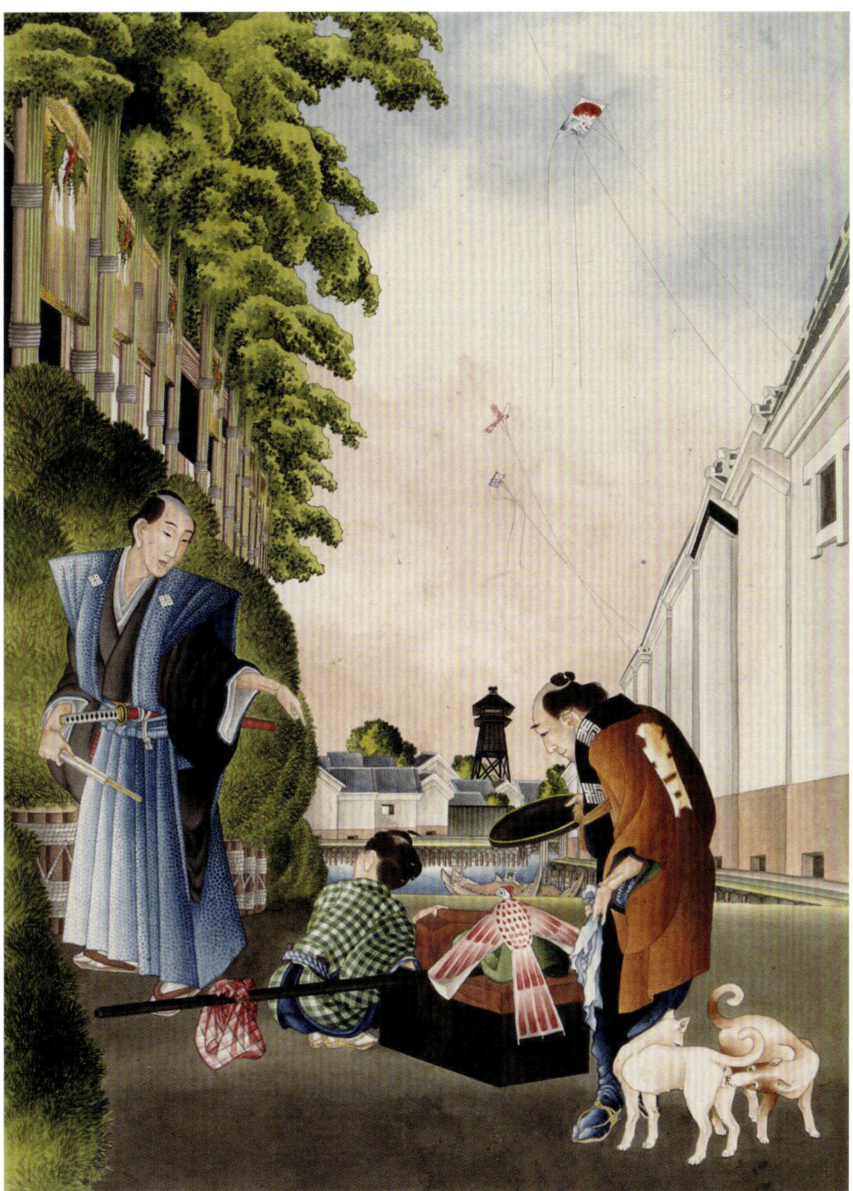

New Year scene

About 1824–1826
Unsigned (attributed to Hokusai)
Ink and colour on old Dutch paper ('J. C. Honig'),
39.8 × 28.4 cm
Provenance: Philipp Franz von Siebold
Literature: Edo Tokyo 2007, no. 1 (attr. Hokusai
and Ōi)
National Museum of Ethnology, Leiden,
RMVI-4482-L

A samurai dressed in formal attire for New Year
visits seems to be issuing orders to a tradesman holding
a tray and a boy who crouches next to a travelling
chest. New Year kites are flying in the pale blue and
roseate (dawn?) sky, and there is a bird kite resting
on a bundle on top of the chest. Dogs sniff each other.
Most striking of all is the deep perspective created
by the recession of the storehouses on the right and
the fence, high up on the left, with its progressively
diminishing decorations of bundles of new bamboo,
and lobsters and ferns. On the low horizon is a
fire-watch tower. The figures are more deeply coloured
on their right sides, suggesting internal lighting. TC

Sudden rain in the countryside

About 1824–1826
Unsigned (attributed to Hokusai)
Ink and colour on old Dutch paper ('J. C. Honig'),
27.2 × 39.8 cm
Provenance: Philipp Franz von Siebold
Literature: Edo Tokyo 2007, no. 13 (attr. Hokusai)
National Museum of Ethnology, Leiden,
RMV1-4482-A

Wind, rain, a thunder-dark sky with lightning above
the low horizon, figures scattering under umbrellas,
hats and a robe quickly pulled over the head – all is
drama and skilfully coordinated simultaneous action.
This is a revolutionary image in Japanese art, and a
later version of it in the print 'Ejiri, Suruga province'
(cat. 50), albeit more artfully composed, seems less
daring. Hokusai is tenacious in rendering each clump
of greenery, each leafy, wind-blown branch as if
individually alive. TC

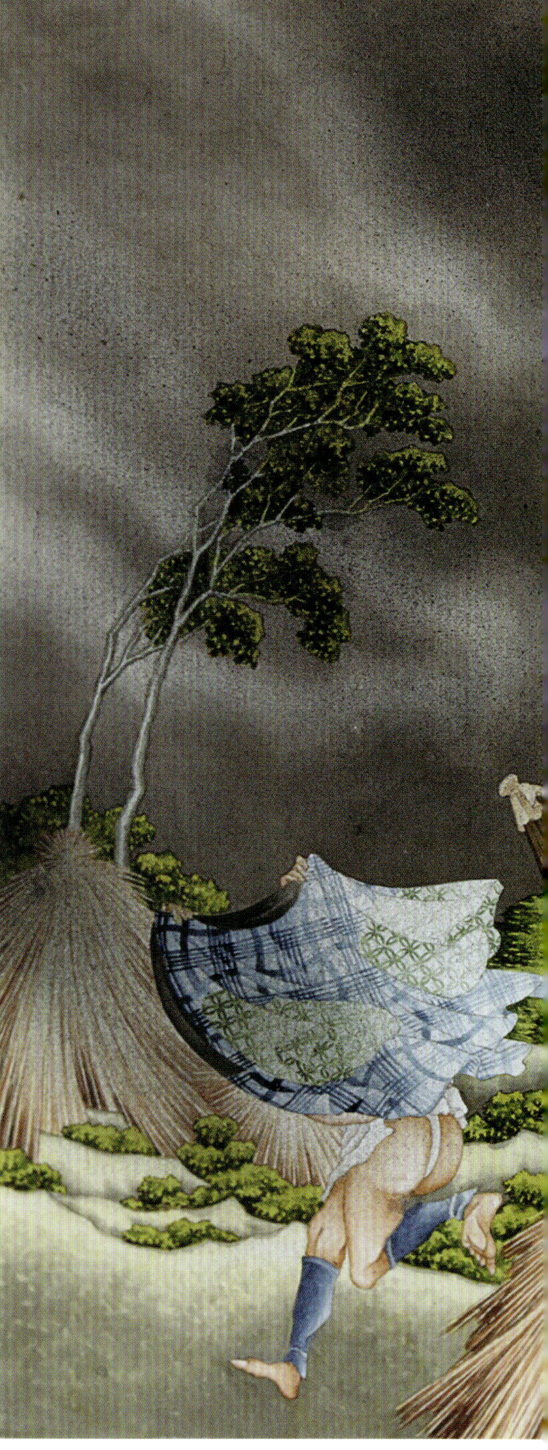

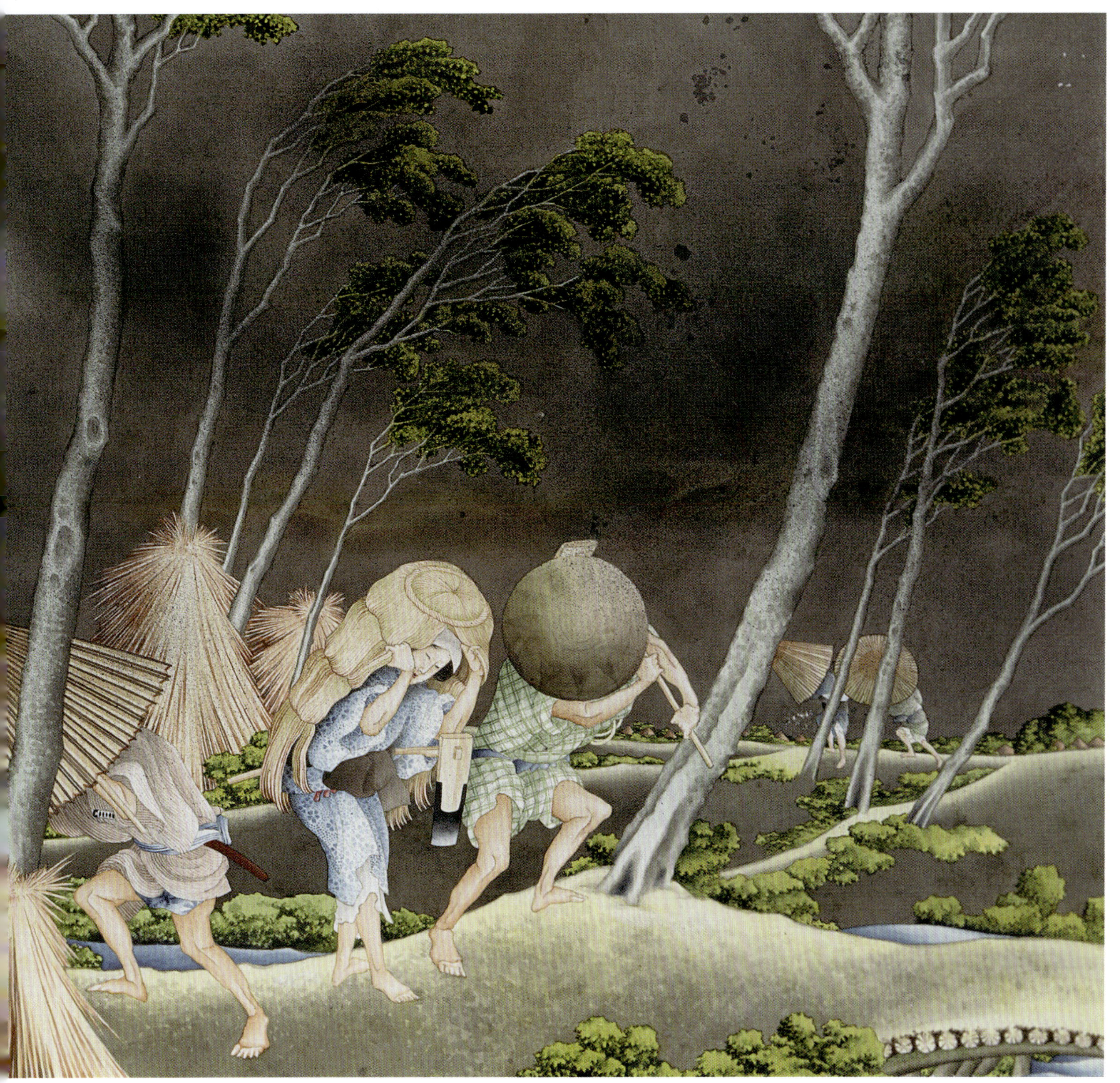

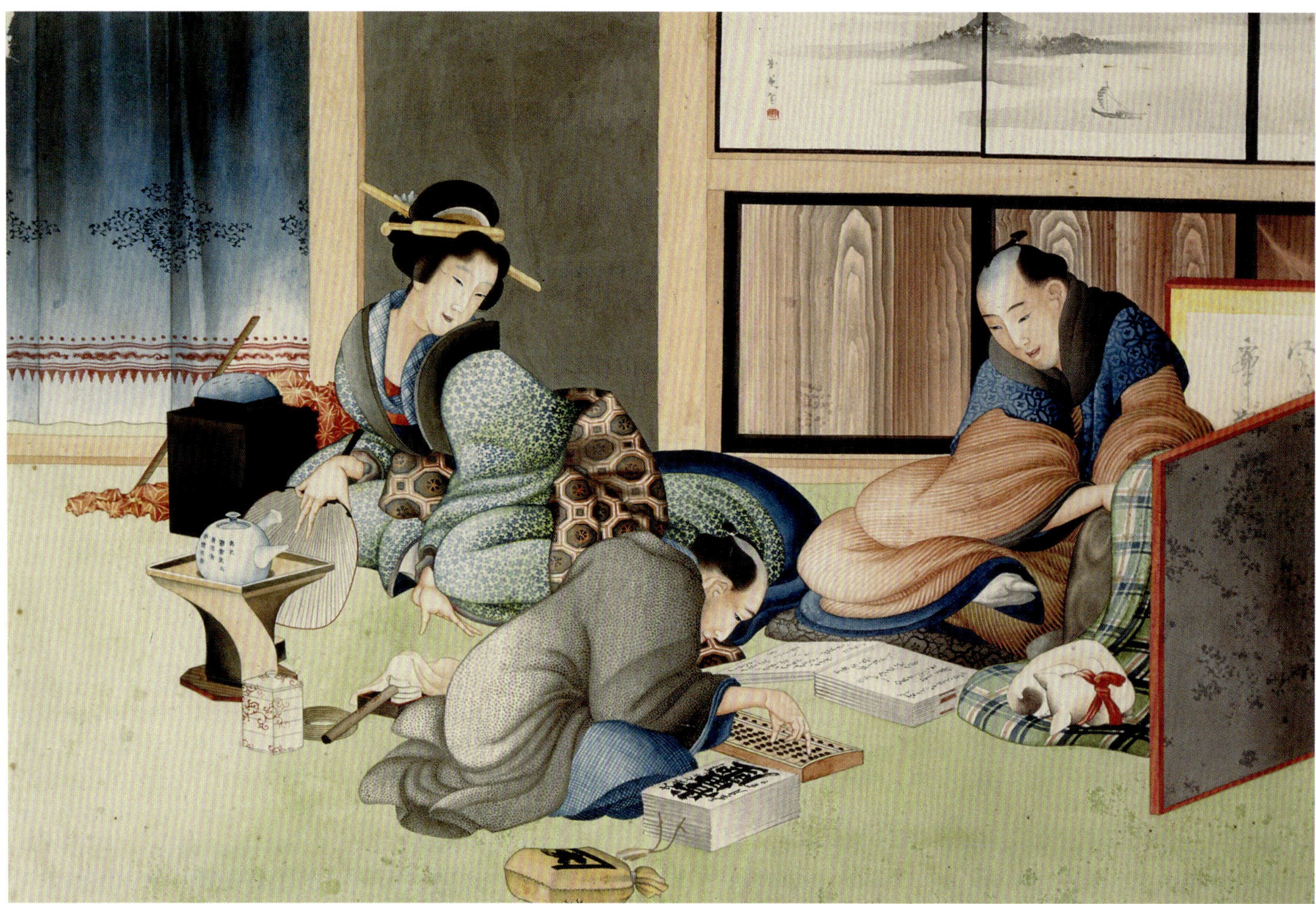

22

Year-end accounts

About 1824–1826
Unsigned (attributed to Hokusai)
Ink and colour on old Dutch paper ('J. C. Honig'),
27.8 × 40.1 cm
Provenance: Philipp Franz von Siebold
Literature: Edo Tokyo 2007, no. 4 (attr. Hokusai
and Ōi); Kubota 2015, no. 21 (attr. Ōi)
National Museum of Ethnology, Leiden,
RMV1-4482-C

A merchant with a cat next to a brazier, and the
merchant's wife with her sewing kit and service for
steeped tea, look on with satisfaction as their manager
pores over his abacus and account book – dated first
month, 1824 – reporting on the year-end accounts.
A two-panel folding screen surrounds the master, and
behind him are decoratively grained wooden cupboard
doors, and Chinese landscape ink paintings on the sliding
cupboard doors above. An indigo-dyed and patterned
split curtain leads into the next room, top left. This
complex grouping of figures and accessories, each with
its own patina and shading, is skilfully integrated. TC

23

Flower-viewing party

About 1824–1826
Unsigned (attributed to Hokusai)
Ink and colour on old Dutch paper ('J. C. Honig'),
40.0 × 27.2 cm
Provenance: Philipp Franz von Siebold
Literature: Edo Tokyo 2007, no. 2 (attr. Hokkei);
Kubota 2015, no. 22 (attr. Ōi)
National Museum of Ethnology, Leiden,
RMVı-4482-M

Two well-to-do merchant wives, accompanied by
a manservant and boy, are on a spring outing to enjoy
the blossoming cherry. The woman facing us has
shrugged off one sleeve of her outer robe in relaxation,
and both women hold pipes in their elongated fingers
(for Kubota, 2015, this is a stylistic trait of the work
of Hokusai's daughter Ōi). The servant carries a red
woollen rug and the boy an umbrella: there is surely
a picnic in their box and bundle. Multiple patterns
on the various robes are painted in painstaking detail
and with carefully gradated *chiaroscuro* effects. Each
beautiful blossom of the double-petalled cherry opens
at a different stage. Bright clumps of grass, each
varied, trail off into the distance. The spindly trunks
of the trees reappeared later in Hokusai's print 'Ejiri,
Suruga province' (cat. 50). TC

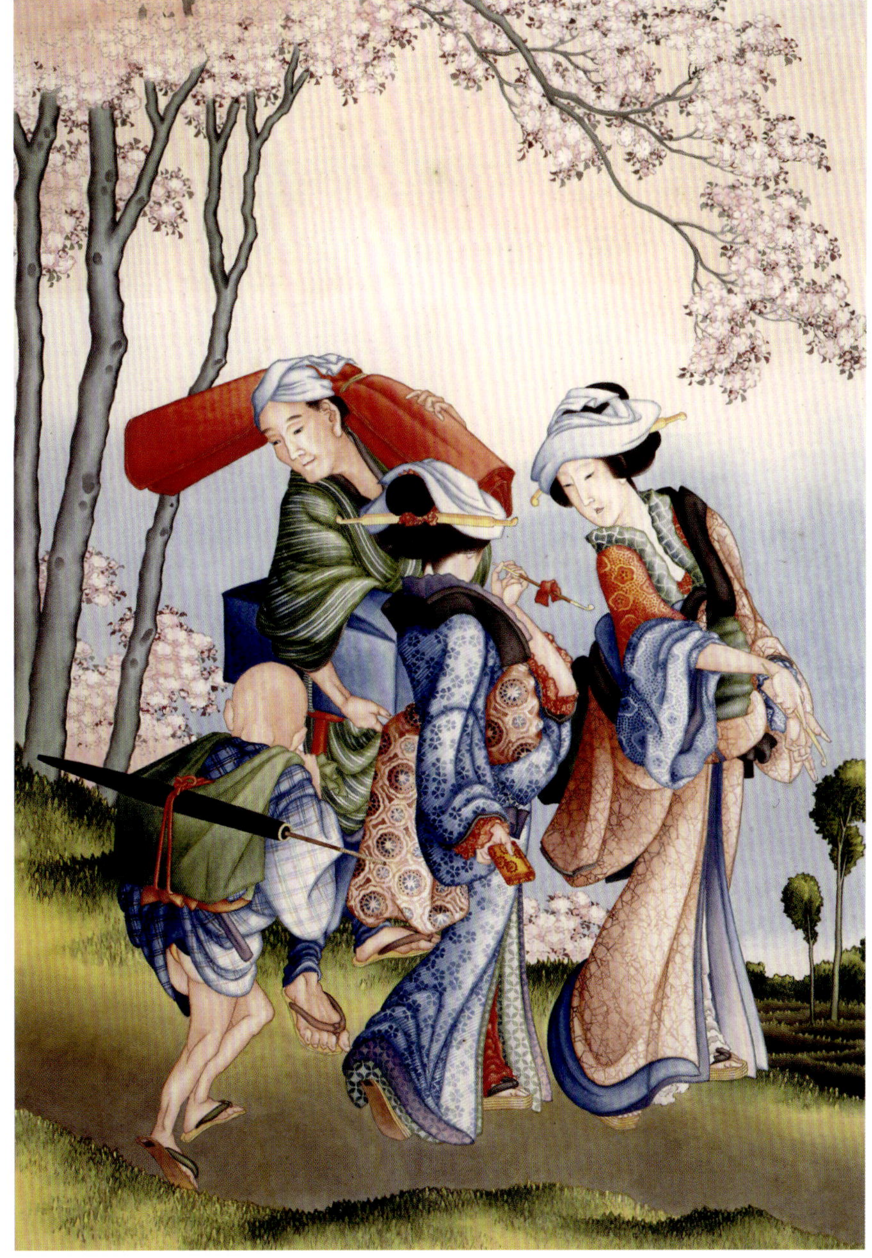

24

Boys' Festival

About 1824–1826
Unsigned (attributed to Hokusai)
Ink and colour on old Dutch paper ('J. C. Honig'),
40.2 × 27.6 cm
Provenance: Philipp Franz von Siebold
Literature: Edo Tokyo 2007, no. 3 (attr. Hokusai and
Ōi); Kubota 2015, no. 20 (attr. Ōi)
National Museum of Ethnology, Leiden,
RMVI-4482-H

Within the timber structure of a rooftop drying
platform, a young unmarried woman is removing
the tiny jacket of the baby boy she cradles in her
arms. The baby squirms, reaching down towards
his mother (?), who has bared her breast to feed him.
Banners with family crests and Shōki the demon-
queller (painted in red) and the flapping carp kite are
all decorations for the Boys' Festival in the fifth month.
Once again there is sensitive modelling of the facial
features and elaborate patterning and *chiaroscuro* on the
robes. The location and viewpoint is unconventional,
even eccentric. TC

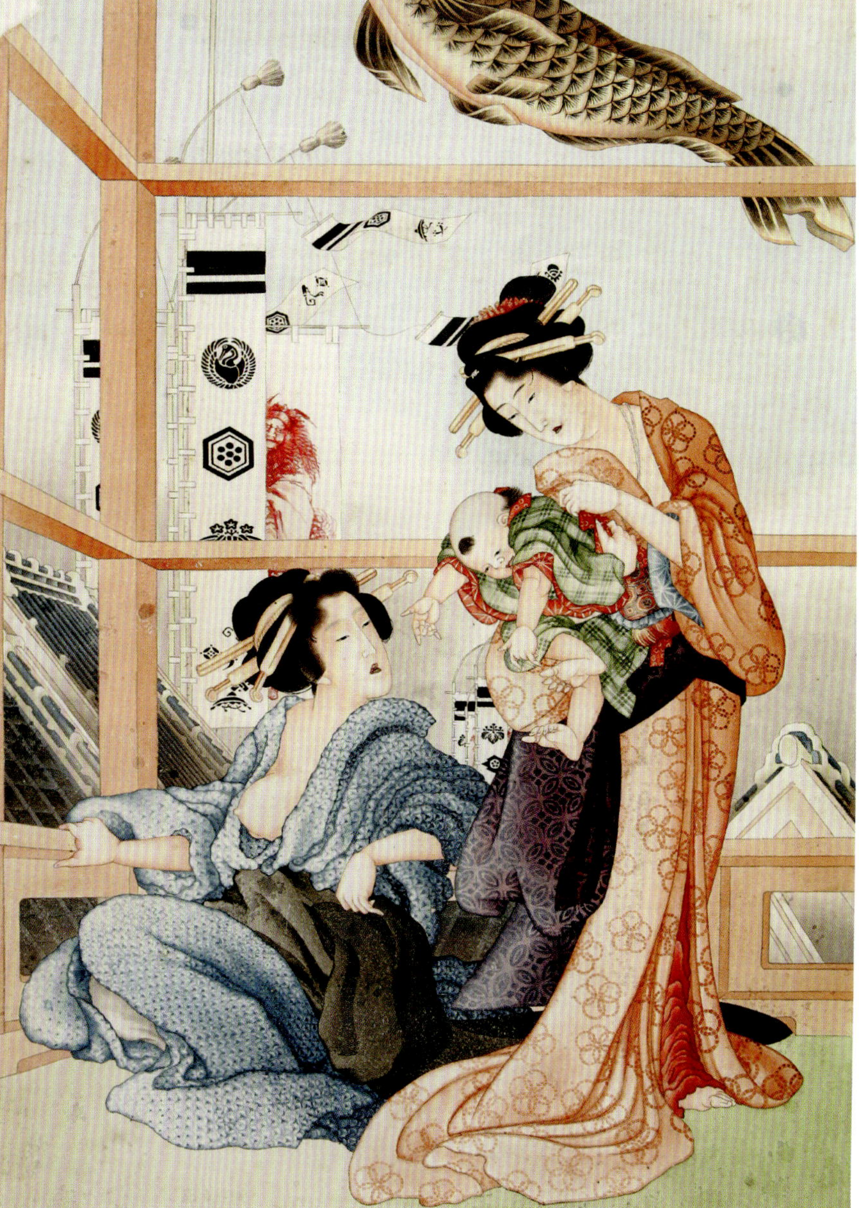

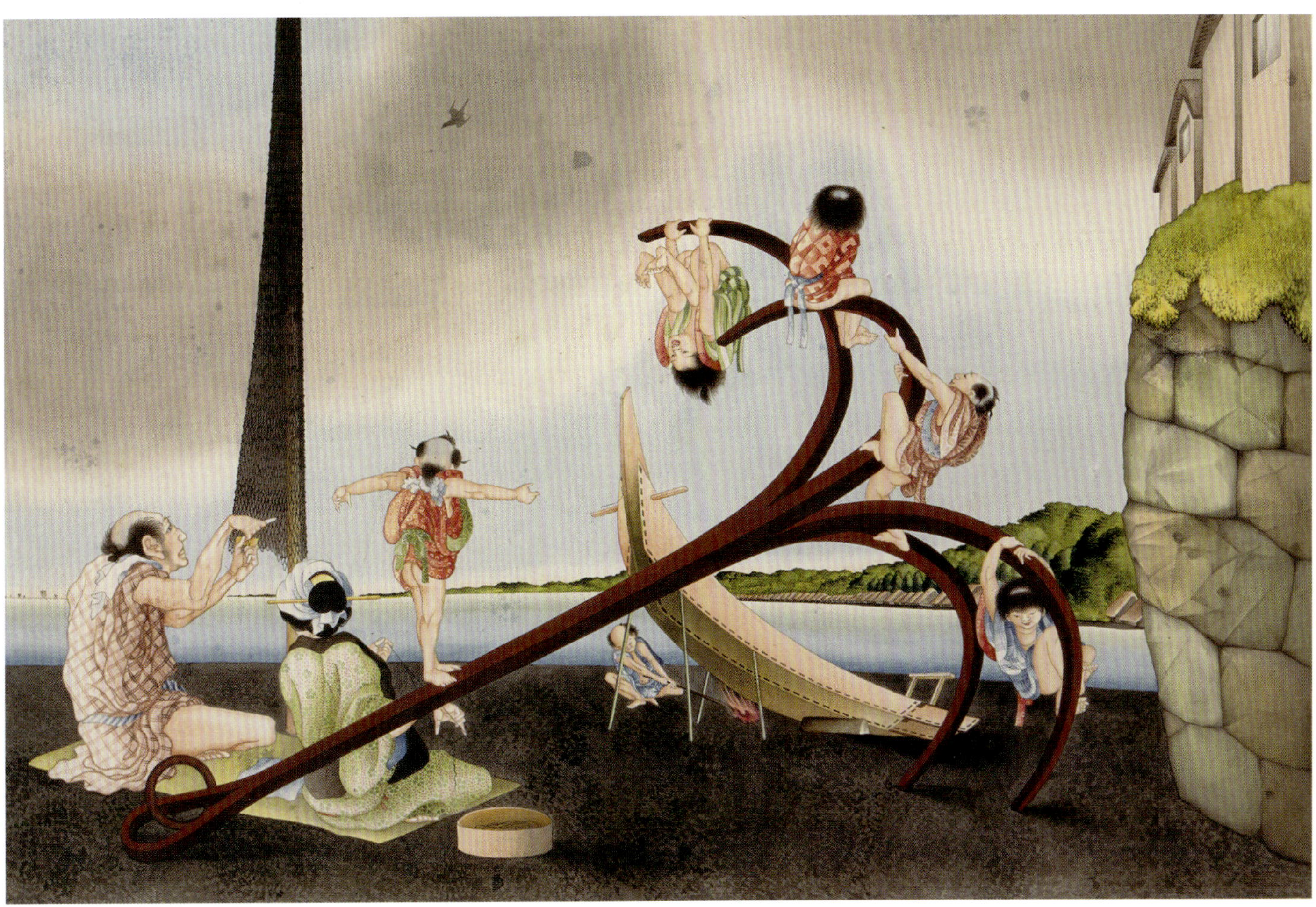

25
Fisherman's family

About 1824–1826
Unsigned (attributed to Hokusai)
Ink and colour on old Dutch paper ('J. C. Honig'),
27.6 × 40.2 cm
Provenance: Philipp Franz von Siebold
Literature: Edo Tokyo 2007, no. 10 (attr. Hokusai
and Ōi)
National Museum of Ethnology, Leiden,
RMV1-4482-K

A fisherman and his wife patiently knot a net, while
alongside five boys play on a large iron anchor pulled
up on to the beach. The swooping cuckoo in the sky
signifies the fourth month, early summer. In the middle
ground a man caulks the base of a boat. At right, a
row of small dwellings perches on top of a rampart
of eccentrically shaped rocks. In the distance are
more cottages lining the shore, and, far left, sails on
the horizon. Objects on the beach cast rudimentary
shadows. TC

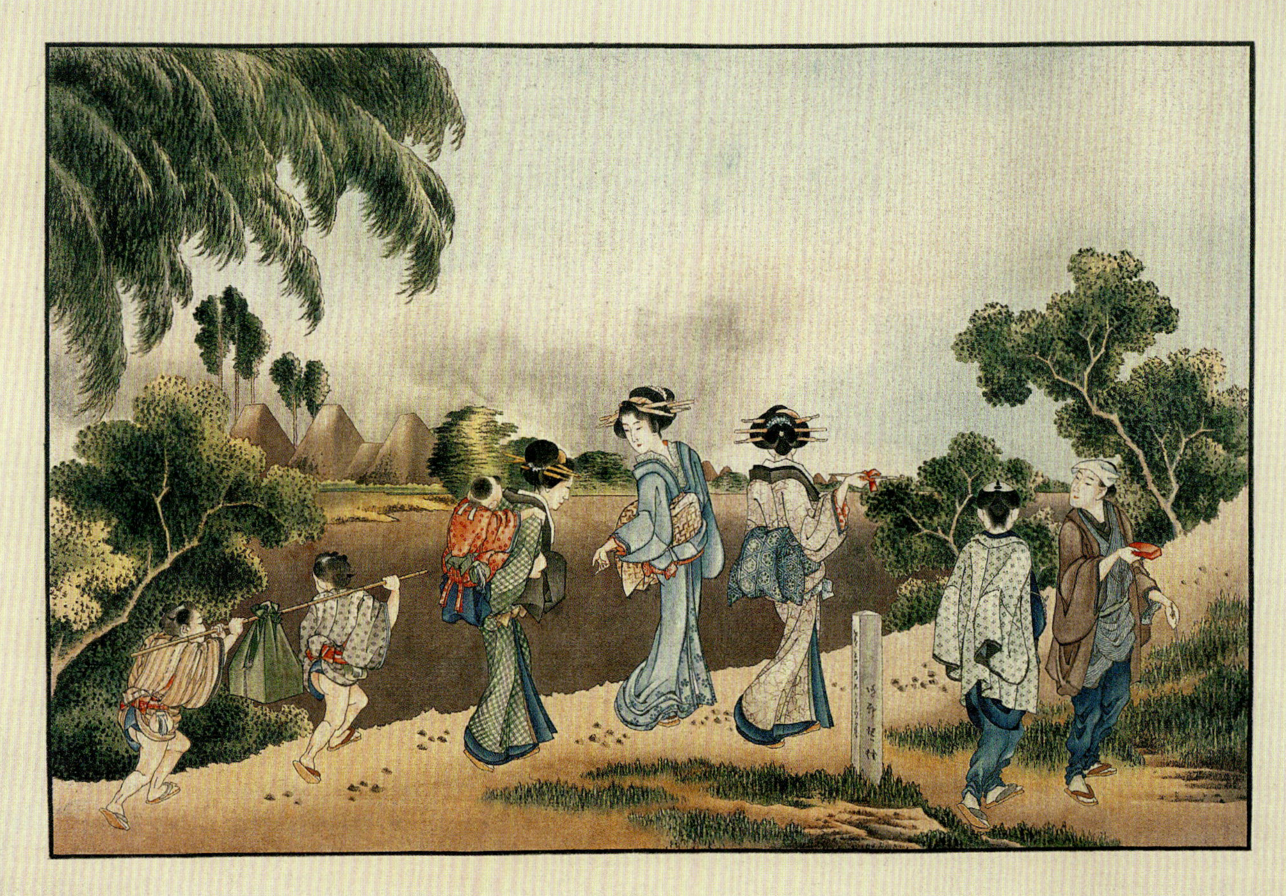

26

People enjoying an outing

1820s
Unsigned (attributed to Hokusai)
Ink and colour on paper, 31.8 × 45.7 cm
Literature: Kobayashi Tadashi, *Kokka* 1422, April 2014,
pp. 43–45, pl. 5
Private collection, Japan
Osaka only

Two well-dressed merchant women and two merchant men are enjoying a country outing, accompanied by a maidservant who carries a male infant on her back, and two boy servants who carry a bundle of picnic refreshments hanging from the bamboo pole resting on their shoulders. Across flooded (?) fields can be seen the roofs of a village in the distance. The motifs, technique, size and general atmosphere of this painting and the next link them closely to the group of twenty-nine genre scenes by Hokusai in European-influenced style now in Leiden (cats 20–25), and also to the group of twenty-five similar works in Paris (see the discussion on p. 82). The fact that cats 26 and 27 are painted on Japanese paper rather than old Dutch paper links them more specifically to the Paris group that were taken out of Japan by Johan Willem de Sturler in 1826 and donated by his son to the Bibliothèque nationale, Paris, in 1855. TC

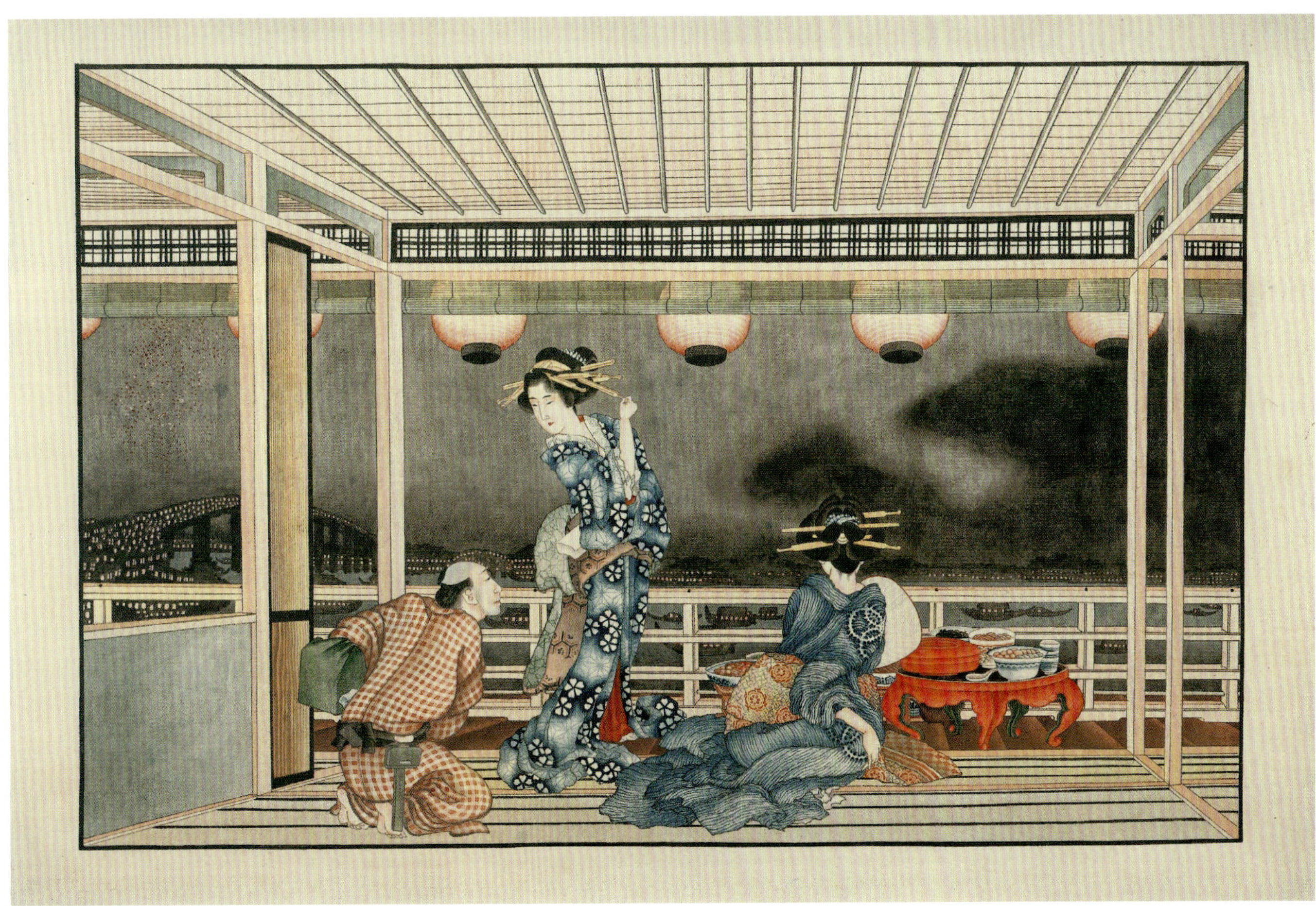

Restaurant overlooking the Sumida river

1820s

Unsigned (attributed to Hokusai)

Ink and colour on paper, 31.6 × 45.5 cm

Literature: Kobayashi Tadashi, *Kokka* 1422, April 2014, pp. 43–45, pl. 6

Private collection, Japan

Osaka only

An elegantly attired geisha (entertainer) has just arrived at a party room upstairs in a restaurant overlooking the Sumida river. She toys with her hairpin and seems to converse with the manservant who crouches carrying her *shamisen* (three-stringed banjo) in its case, wrapped in a cloth. The woman kneeling in a sinuous pose and staring out at the view is perhaps a waitress. Porcelain and lacquer bowls of food are placed ready on a red-lacquered low table – all depicted in minute detail, with the utmost precision. Effects such as the glimmering lanterns carried by the crowds on Ryōgoku bridge, above which fireworks are exploding in the sky, are unusual in Japanese art. Other European-influenced elements are the vanishing-point perspective implied by the architecture and the low horizon, the *chiaroscuro* modelling of the drapery and faces, and the sense of internal lighting cast by the hanging lanterns. TC

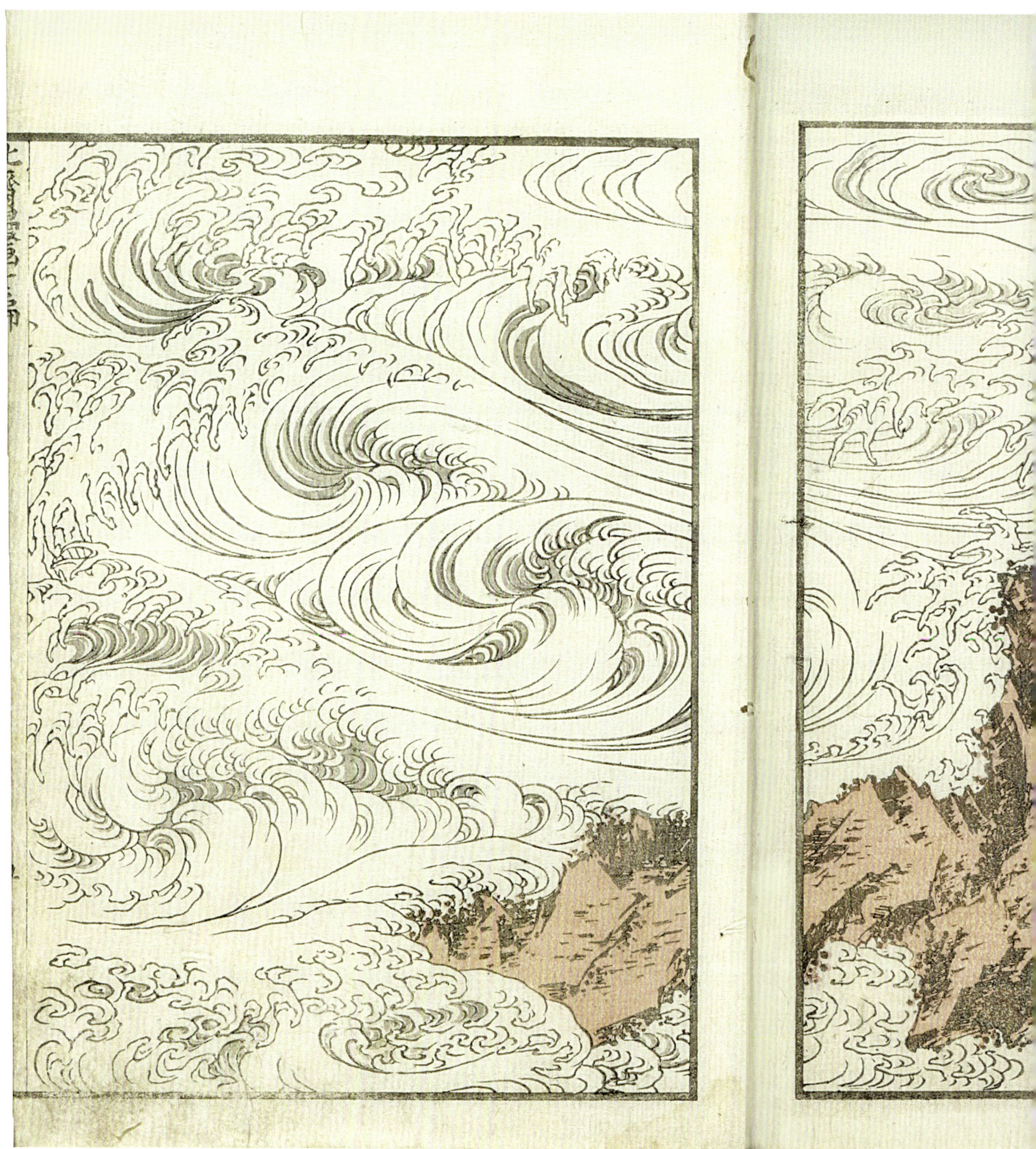

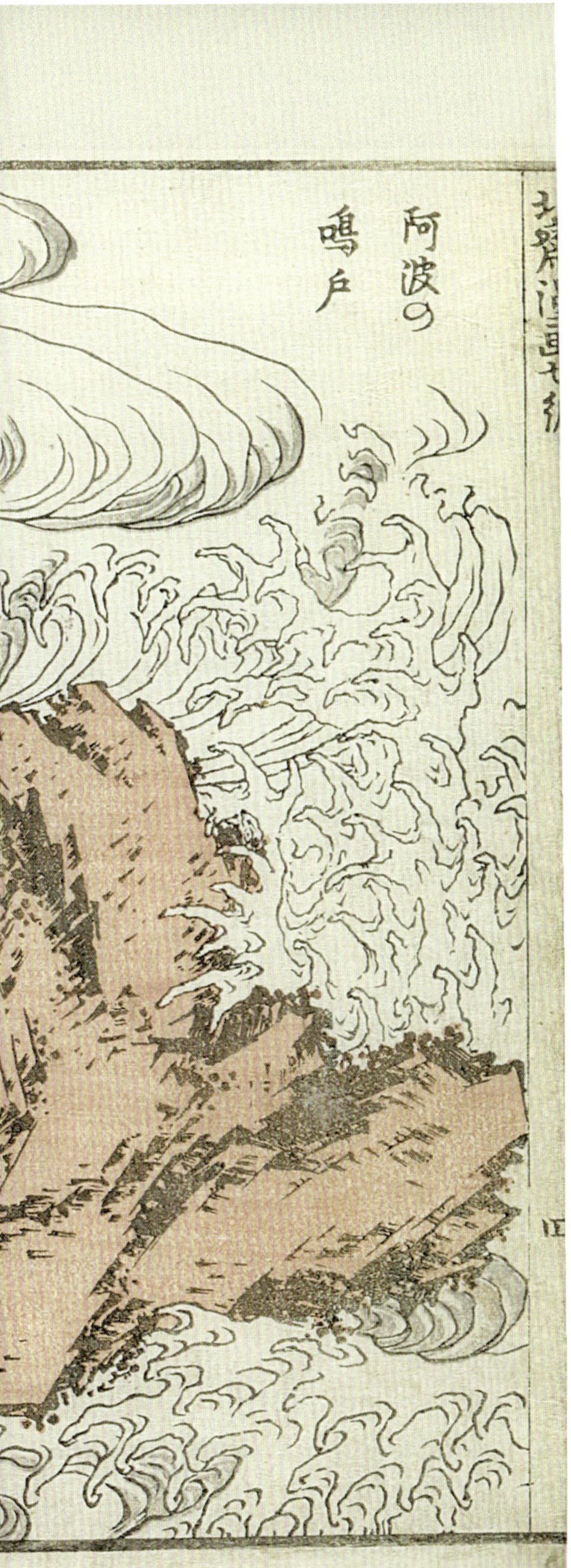

Whirlpools at Awa, from *Hokusai's Sketches* (*Hokusai manga*), vol. 7

New Year, 1817
Signature: Tōto gakō Hokusai aratame Katsushika
Taito ('Katsushika Taito, changed from Hokusai,
artist of the Eastern capital [Edo]')
Seal: Fujinoyama
Woodblock, illustrated book, vol. 7 (of 15), published
by Kadomaruya Jinsuke and others, 22.8 × 15.8 cm
(covers)
Literature: Michener 1958; Nagata *Manga*, 1986–1987,
vol. 2; Hashimoto 2005
Uragami Mitsuru collection, Japan

Roiling whirlpools splinter into fingers of foam against
a rock. The publisher's advert promised that this volume
of *Hokusai's Sketches* would 'depict views of wind, rain,
frost and snow at famous places in various provinces'
– here whirlpools in the 'thundering straits' of Awa,
between Awaji island and modern Tokushima prefecture
(Shikoku). After describing in his preface the delights
of scenery all over Japan, writer Shikitei Sanba
(1776–1822) concluded, 'rousing myself, I discovered
I had been [at my desk] by the window all along,
[asleep] with this little book as my pillow'. TC

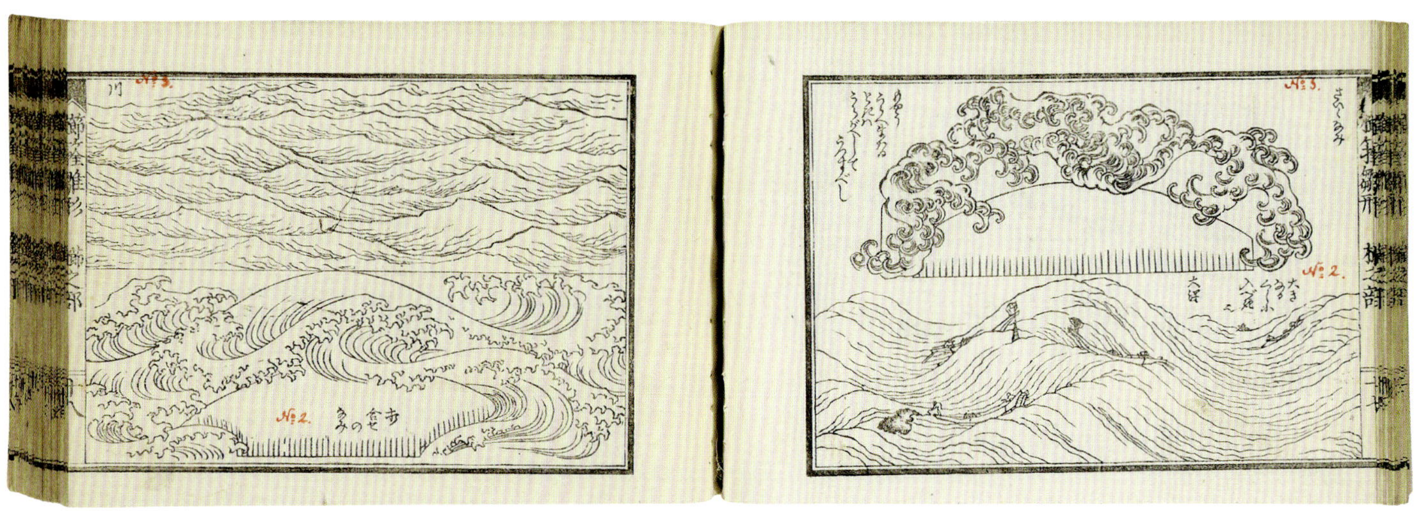

29

Carved waves, from *Modern Designs for Combs and Tobacco Pipes* (*Imayō sekkin hinagata*), vol. 1

Fifth month, 1823
Signature (preface): Saki no Hokusai aratame Katsushika Iitsu shi ('Written by the former Hokusai changed to Katsushika Iitsu')
Block cutter: Egawa Tomekichi
Woodblock, illustrated book, vol. 1 (of 3), published by Nishimuraya Yohachi and others, 12.8 × 18.6 cm (covers)
Provenance: Transferred from the Department of Oriental Manuscripts and Printed Books (now British Library), library stamp of 22 July 1868
Literature: Nagata Seiji, *Hokusai no edehon* 5, 1986
British Museum, 1915,0823,0.111

Volumes 1 and 2 of this book contain about 250 miniature designs for carved or lacquered wooden hair combs; volume 3 has some 160 designs for ornamented tobacco pipes. An instruction to the craftsperson, top right, says to flip the design for the reverse side of the comb; the bottom left design is 'Waves striking against each other'. There are prefaces by author Ryūtei Tanehiko (1783–1842) and Hokusai, and a postscript by 'crazy verse' (*kyōka*) poet Shakuyakutei Nagane (1767–1845). Adverts from publisher Nishimuraya Yohachi ambitiously promise works on themes including Mt Fuji (cats 41–65) and 'One hundred bridges at a glance' (cat. 74). This copy of the book was already in the British Museum by 1868. Certain pages were reproduced in Thomas Cutler, *A Grammar of Japanese Ornament and Design*, 1880. TC

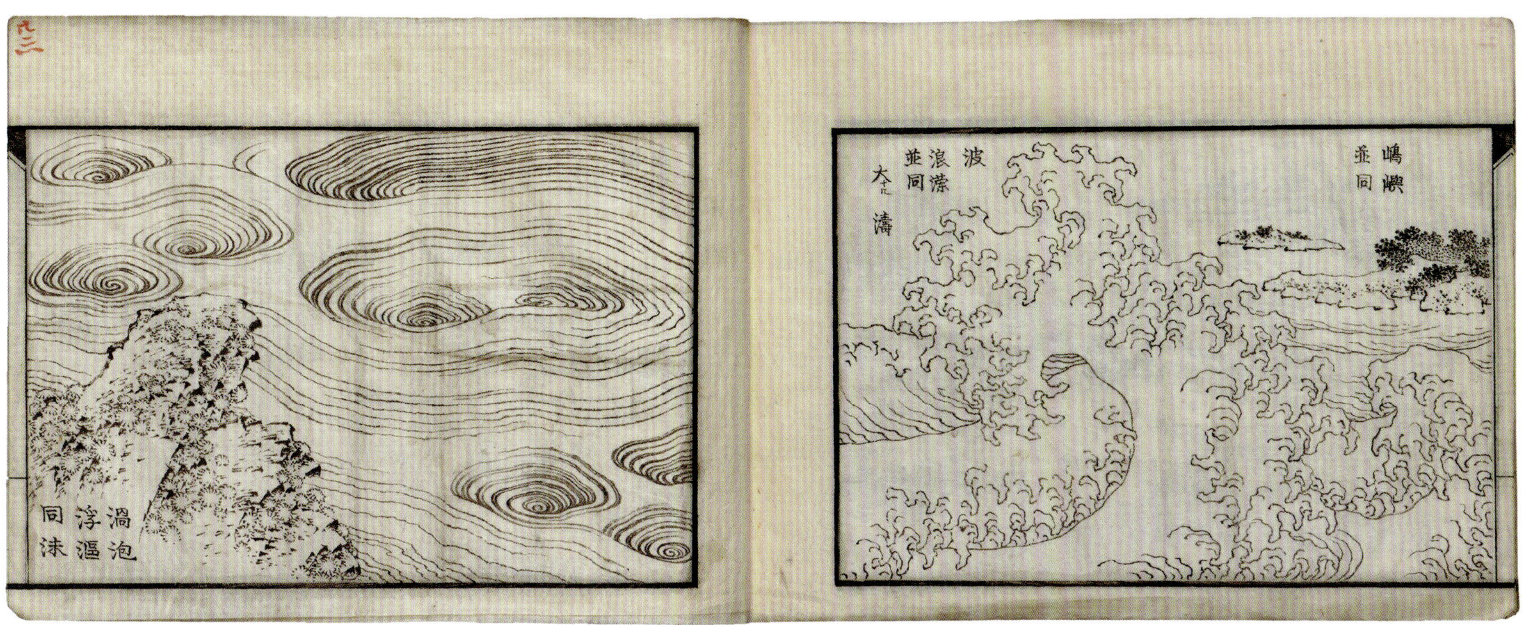

30

Waves and whirlpools, from *Drawings for a three-volume picture book*

1823–1835
Block-ready drawings, ink on paper, vol. 2 (of 3),
13.8 × 20.4 cm (covers)
Literature: Calza 2003, no. III.70.1–3; Boston 2013,
no. 141; Thompson 2015, no. 40; Thompson 2016
Museum of Fine Arts, Boston, 1998.670.2, source
unidentified
Osaka only

The double-page opening contrasts the splintering
spray from a wave hitting the coast on the right with
centripetal whirlpools on the left. The brush lines are
energetic yet extremely precise, as these are 'block-
ready' sketches, intended to be stuck face down on
to cherry wood printing blocks and destroyed when
the block cutter cuts through the back of the drawing.
This three-volume work (see also cat. 168) is a major
recent discovery in Hokusai's oeuvre. It contains an
encyclopaedic range of images of people working
at various trades, as well as flora, fauna, mythological
beasts, landscapes, deities and mythical beings.
Apparently it was intended as a further instalment
of Hokusai's printed brush drawing manuals, perhaps
building on the success of the first ten volumes of
Hokusai's Sketches (*Hokusai manga*, cats 164, 165). TC

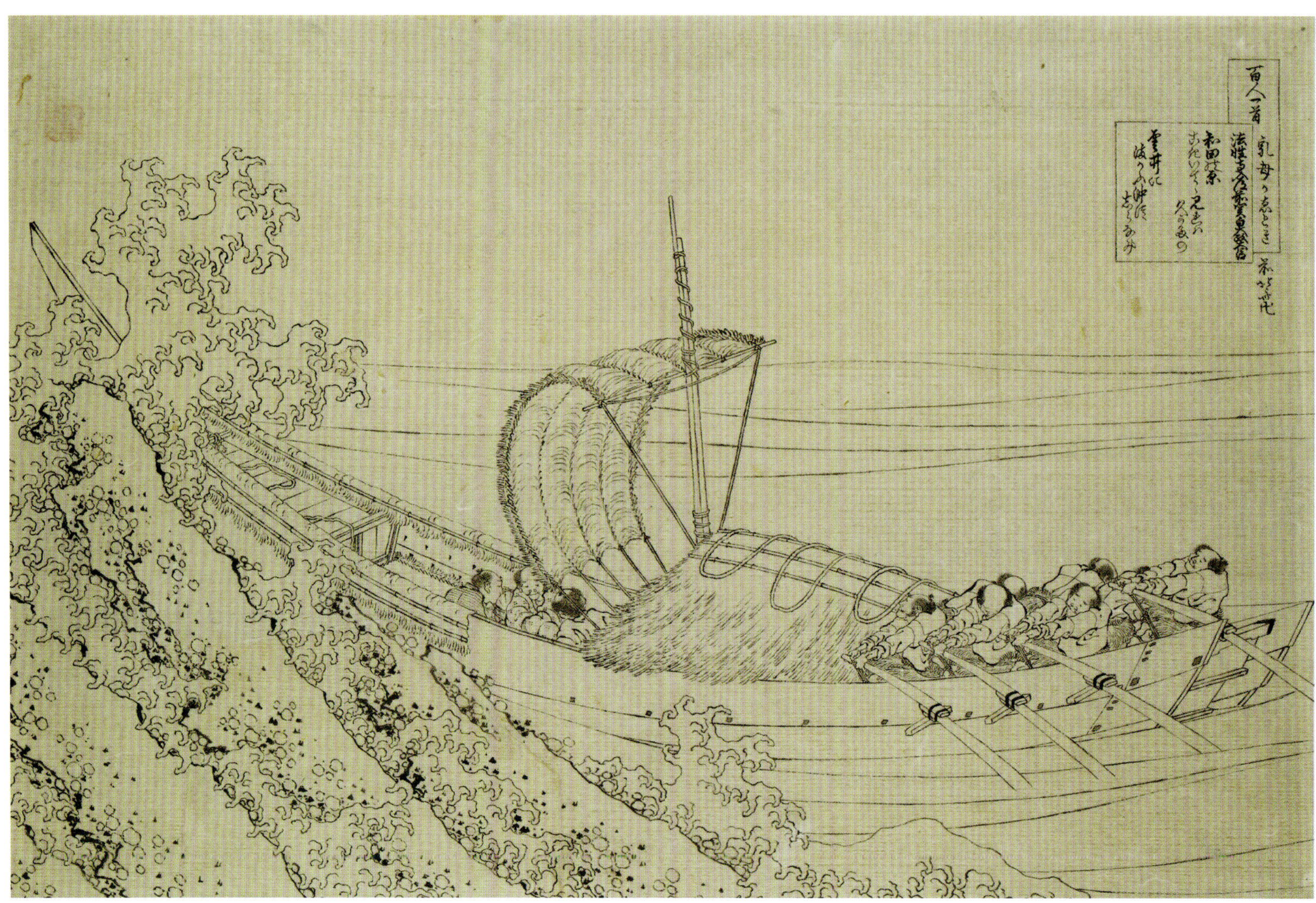

31

Block-ready drawing for 'Poet Fujiwara no Tadamichi', from the series *One Hundred Poems by One Hundred Poets, Explained by the Nurse*

About 1835–1838

Signature: Saki no Hokusai Manji ('Manji, the former Hokusai')

Block-ready drawing, ink on paper, 25.5 × 37.2 cm

Literature: HUT 1987–1990, vol. 4, no. 18; Morse 1989, no. 76; Mostow 1996, pp. 366–368; Keyes & Morse 2015, no. 76

Victoria and Albert Museum, London, E.3716-1910

A team of six oarsmen rows hard to steer a passenger boat away from treacherous rocks where waves are crashing and splintering. This is Hokusai's interpretation of a classical poem by Fujiwara no Tadamichi (1097–1164): 'As I row out into / the wide sea-plain and look / all around me – / the white waves of the offing / could be mistaken for clouds!', 'Former Prime Minister and Chancellor, the Hosshōji Buddhist Novice [Fujiwara no Tadamichi]' (trans. Joshua Mostow). Hokusai's vital contribution to the production of a colour woodblock print such as 'The Great Wave' (cat. 51) was a line-perfect block-ready drawing, or *hanshita-e*, like this one. Indeed, the hooked tentacles of wave foam drawn here are very close to 'The Great Wave' drawn just a few years earlier. Pasted face down on to the cherry wood printing block, the block cutter then cut through the back of the drawing, thereby destroying it. For more on the series *One Hundred Poems by One Hundred Poets, Explained by the Nurse* and why it was abandoned, see pp. 222–23 and cats 132–146. **TC**

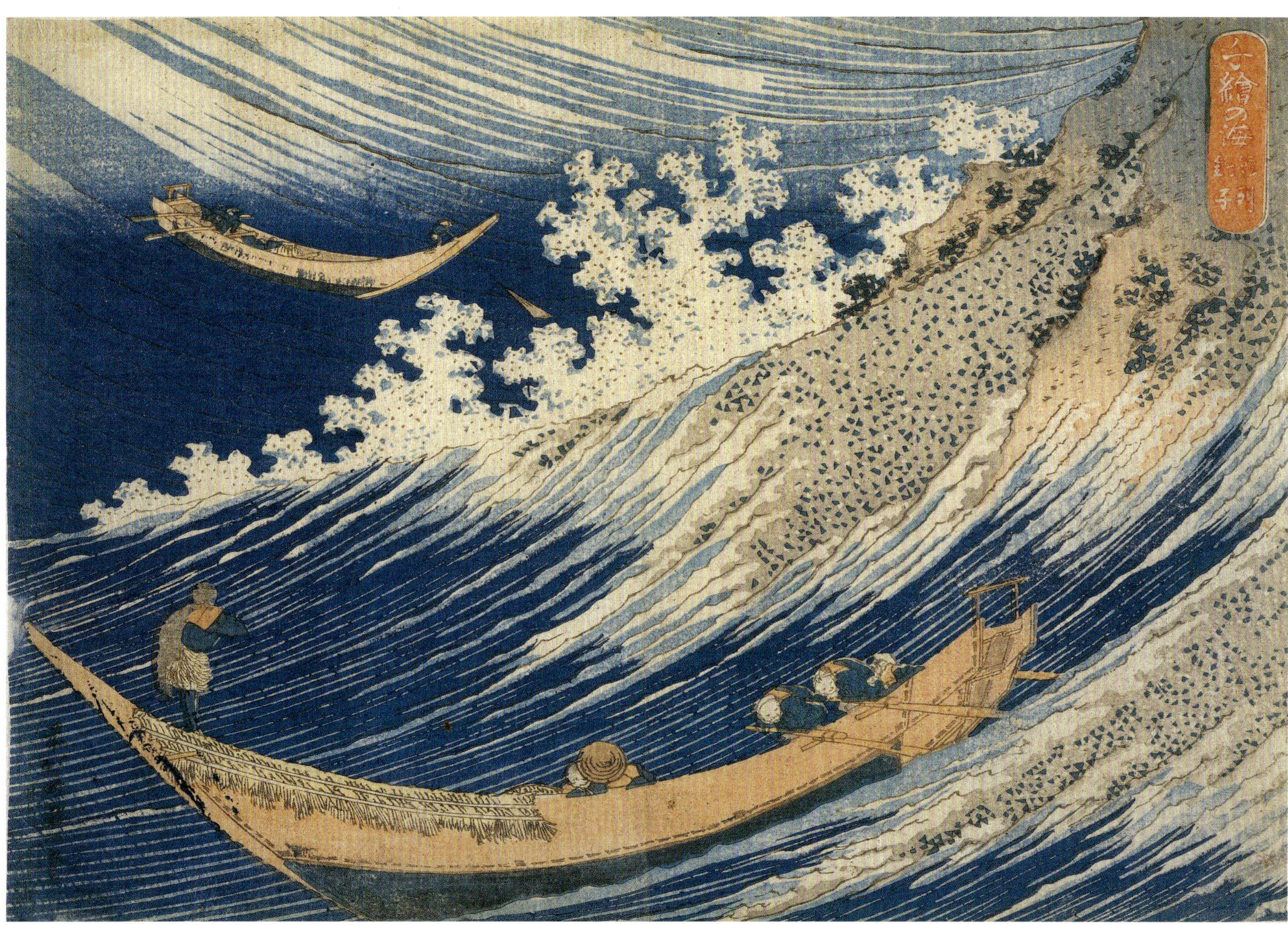

32

Chōshi in Sōshū province, from the series *A Thousand Pictures of the Sea* (*Chie no umi*)

About 1833
Signature: Saki no Hokusai Iitsu hitsu
('Brush of Iitsu, the former Hokusai')
Colour woodblock, published by Moriya Jihei,
17.8 × 25.0 cm
Literature: MSU 1991, no. 48; Keyes & Morse 2015,
no. 545
Chiba City Museum of Art

Two fishing skiffs battle in waves that crash and recede around a potentially treacherous rocky coast, the oarsmen bent forward and rowing at full strength. The design is arranged so as to suggest a powerful diagonal drag towards the bottom left corner. Chōshi was the most important fishing port in eastern Japan, at the mouth of the mighty Tone river where it flows into the Pacific. The series of ten medium-format (*chūban*) designs, plus proof prints for two more, features rivers and the sea, and those who labour on and around them. TC

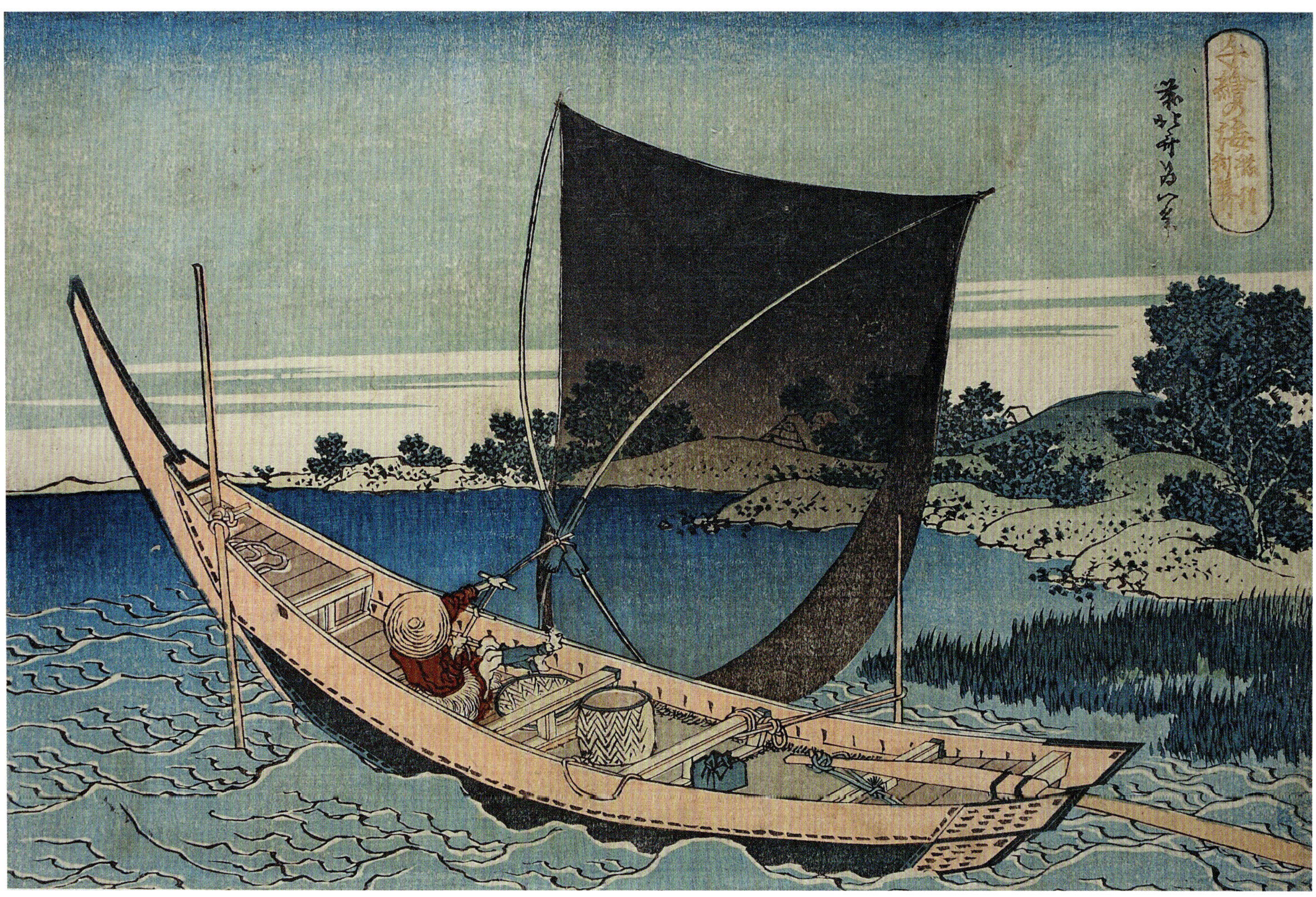

33

Tone river in Sōshū province, from the series *A Thousand Pictures of the Sea* (*Chie no umi*)

About 1833
Signature: Saki no Hokusai Iitsu hitsu ('Brush of Iitsu, the former Hokusai')
Colour woodblock, published by Moriya Jihei,
17.8 × 25.0 cm
Provenance: K. Murakami
Literature: MSU 1991, no. 54; Keyes & Morse 2015, no. 546
British Museum, 1930,1112,0.5

A fisherman braces his legs against the side of his boat as he pulls up a large scoop net. Through the delicately gradated net, a village can be glimpsed on the far riverbank. The location is the Tone river, perhaps its lower reaches. Hokusai designed a similar composition in volume 3 of *One Hundred Views of Mt Fuji* (cat. 176; published in about 1849, but probably already drawn by 1835). TC

34
Waves beating against cliffs

1846

Signature: Hachijūnana rō / Manji hitsu

('Brush of Manji, old man of eighty-seven')

Seal: Katsushika (3)

Hanging scroll, ink and colour on silk, 117.1 × 44.6 cm

Literature: Machida 2012, no. 322

Private collection, Japan

Osaka only

Waves crash against the rocky face of a cliff. The image
resembles 'Fuji from the sea' from the illustrated
book *One Hundred Views of Mt Fuji* (cat. 35) –
but more particularly 'Chōshi in Sōshū province',
from *A Thousand Pictures of the Sea* (cat. 32), both in the
way the waves dissolve into foam and in the overall
composition, evident when one focuses on the lighthouse,
top right; perhaps this painting depicts the same
geographical location. The following year, 1847,
Hokusai returned to the same subject in *Waves*
(Freer-Sackler Gallery, Smithsonian Institution,
Washington, DC, F1905.276). That painting shares
with this one the village huddled along the distant
shore, but there the wave breaks to the left, and
the foam tips of the wave echo the eagle-claw shape
of 'The Great Wave' (cat. 51). **AS**

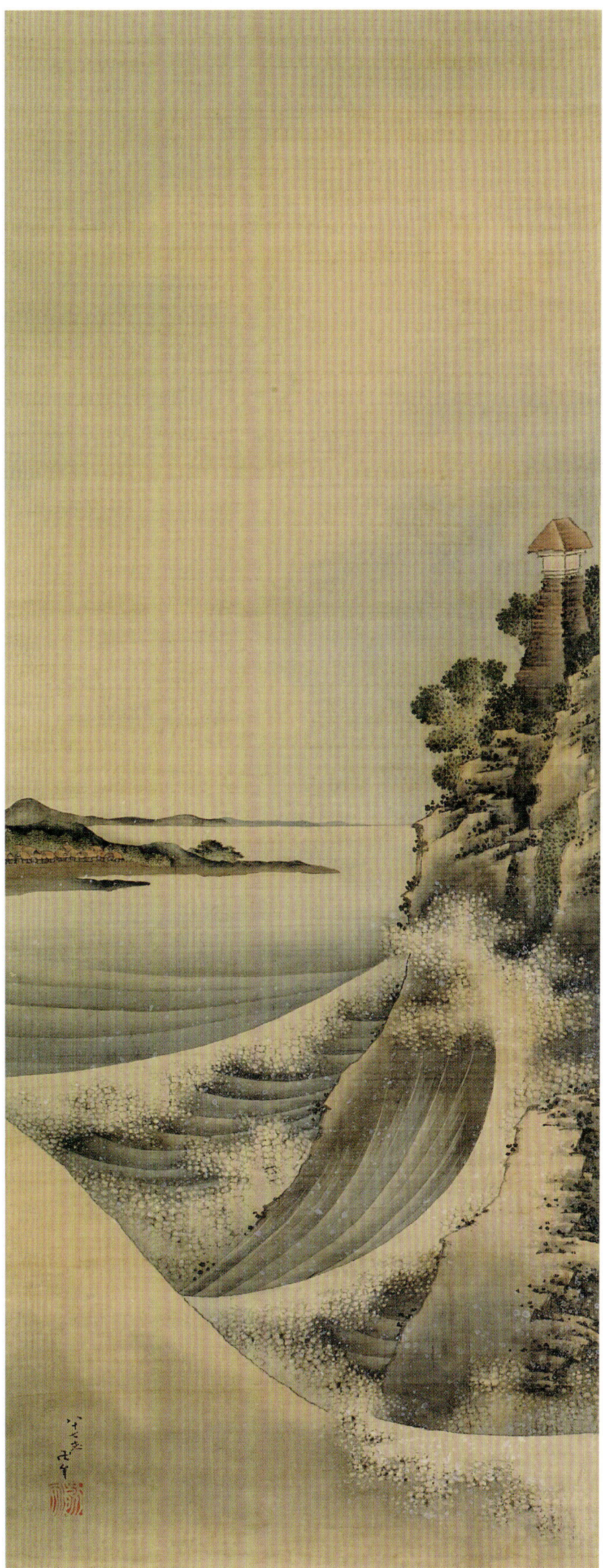

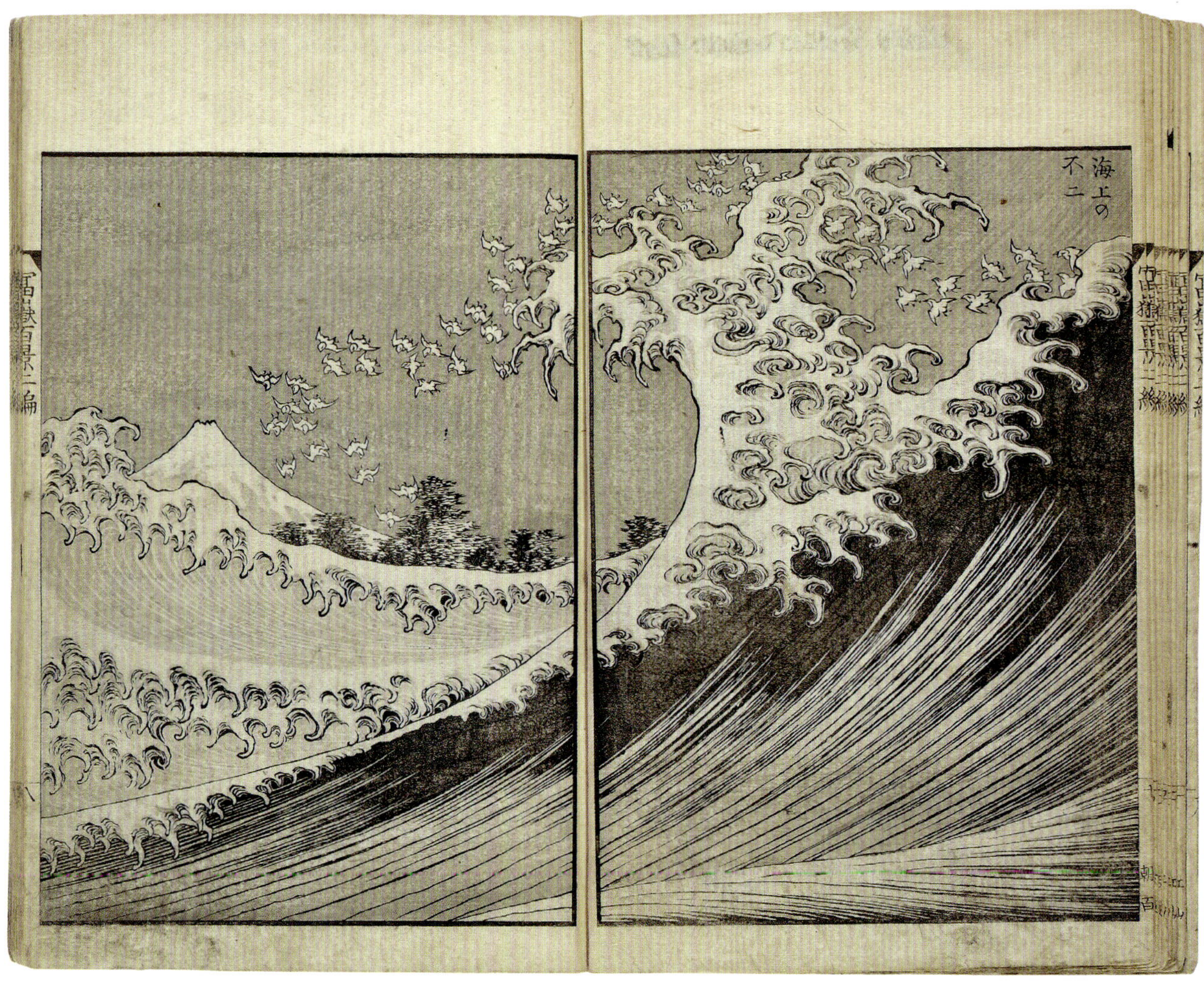

35
Fuji from the sea, from *One Hundred Views of Mt Fuji (Fugaku hyakkei)*

Third month, 1835
Signature: Nanajūroku rei / saki no Hokusai Iitsu aratame / Gakyō rōjin Manji hitsu ('Brush of Manji, old man crazy to paint, changed from the former Hokusai Iitsu, aged seventy-six')
Seal: Mt Fuji above trigram
Woodblock, illustrated book, vol. 2 (of 3), published by Nishimuraya Yūzō and others, 22.7 × 15.7 cm (covers)
Provenance: Jack Hillier
Literature: Smith 1988, pp. 118–119; HK 42, Oct. 2008, pp. 5–61
British Museum, 1979,0305,0.454.2

Just a few years after his famous print 'The Great Wave' (cat. 51), Hokusai produced a variation of the subject in this illustrated book, *One Hundred Views of Mt Fuji* (see also cats 176–182). Here, however, there is no human presence, rather a flock of plovers that suggest spray from the waves. Although the wave does not rear over us so threateningly, the tentacles of foam are coiled even more extravagantly than in 'The Great Wave' – a technical tour de force from block cutter Chōhyaku, whose name appears in the margin, bottom right. Chōhyaku is one of six named cutters who worked on this volume, under the direction of master cutter Egawa Tomekichi (worked 1820s–1830s). TC

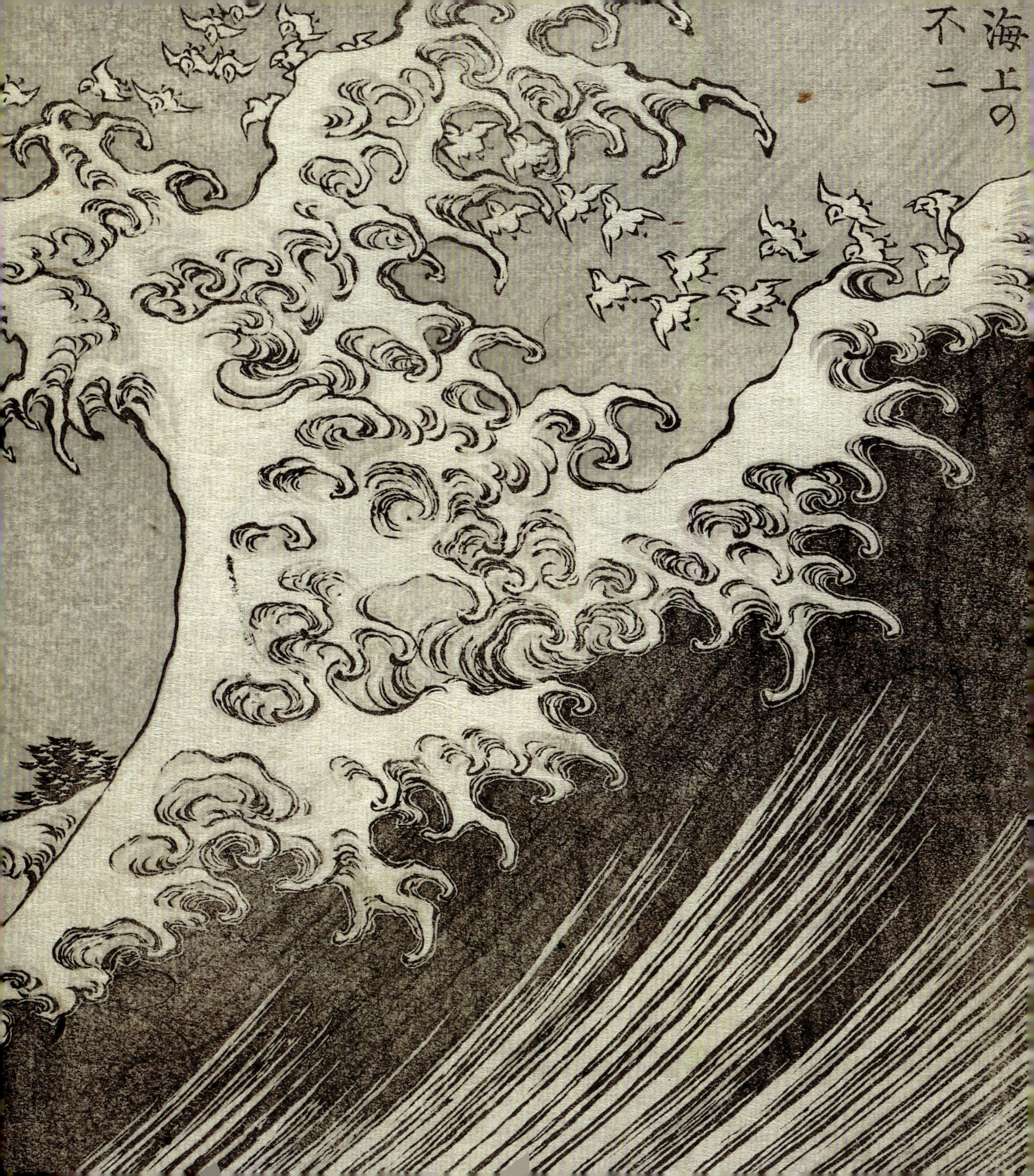

海上の不二

36
Boar hunt at the foot of Mt Fuji

Sixth month, 1806
Signature: Gakyōjin / Hokusai ryochū ga ('Painted
while travelling by Hokusai, man crazy to paint')
Seal: 'No in' ('Seal of') [hand-painted]
Framed votive panel, ink and colour on wood,
139.3 × 180.4 cm
Literature: Nishina 1971; HK 3, April 1973; NU 1982,
no. 13; Machida 2012, no. 82
Hie Jinja shrine, Kisarazu
Osaka only

Abraded by time, this magnificent votive panel (*ema*),
painted on wood, features the warrior Nitan no Shirō
drawing his sword to dispatch a charging wild boar,
which he daringly straddles. The mass of spears and
enclosures in the middle points to the large hunting
expedition led by shogun Minamoto no Yoritomo
(1147–1199) at the foot of Mt Fuji in 1193. Hokusai
is said to have painted the panel at the house of
the headman of Nagasuka village, Kazusa province
(modern Kisarazu city, Chiba prefecture), while he
was visiting in the summer of 1806. The composition is
particularly apposite – there is a spectacular view of
Mt Fuji from Kisarazu, across Tokyo bay. The dramatic,
forceful style is similar to that of the illustrations for
adventure stories (*yomihon*) that Hokusai was designing
at this time (cat. 14). TC

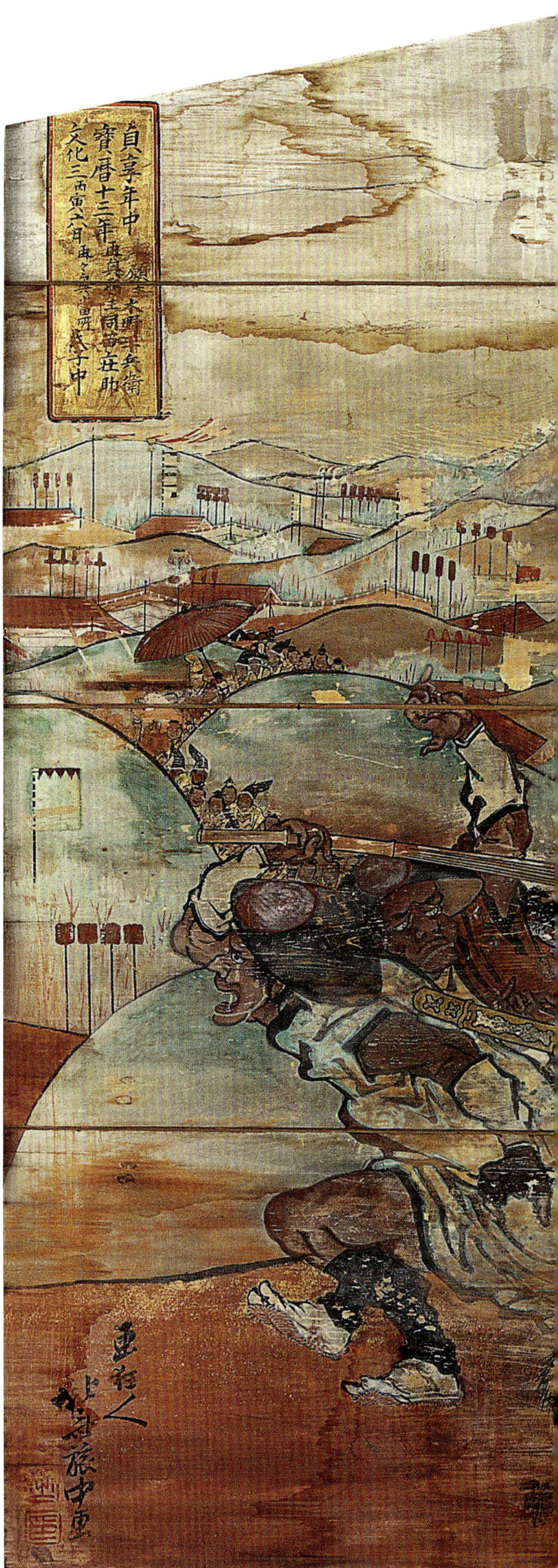

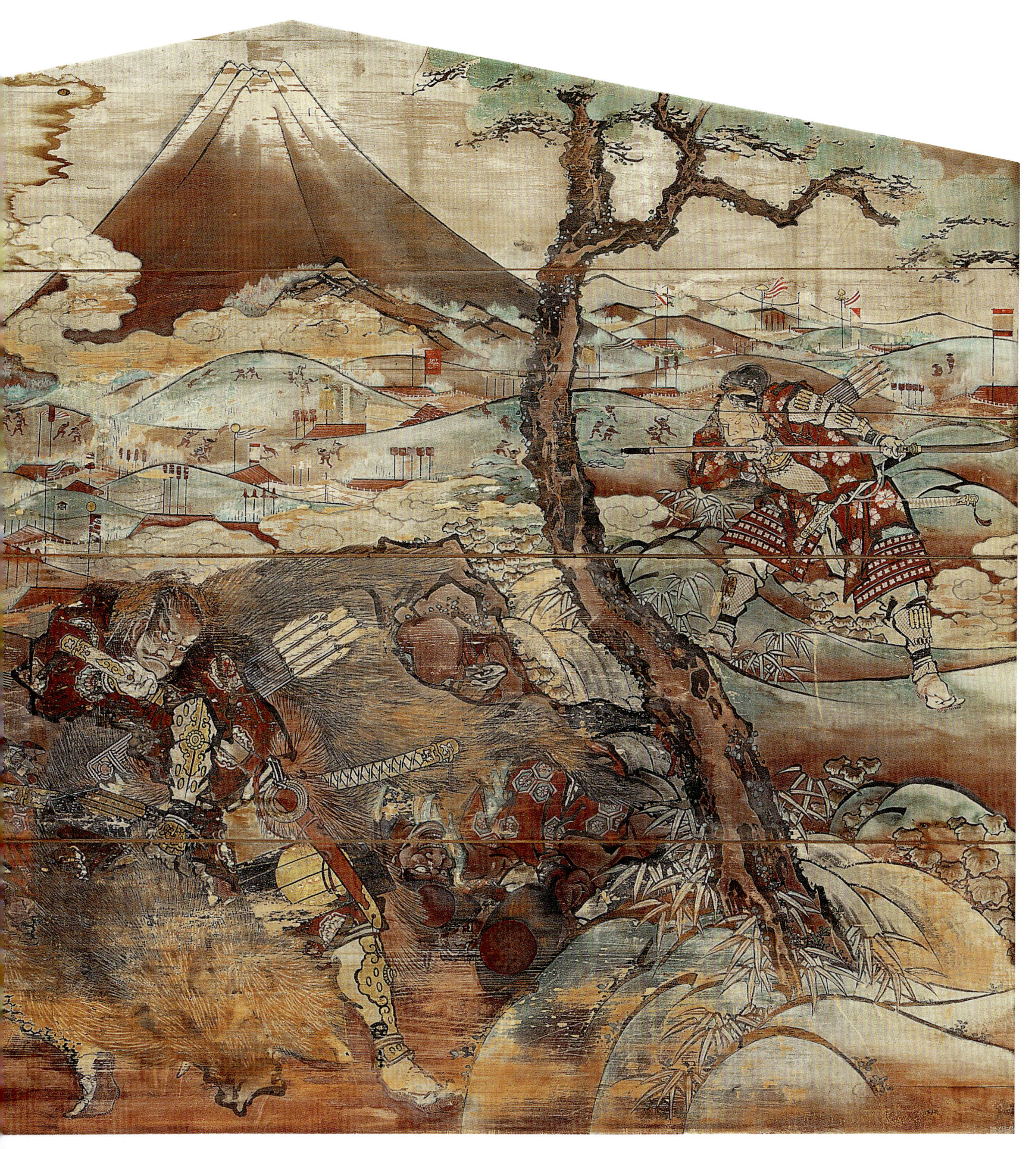

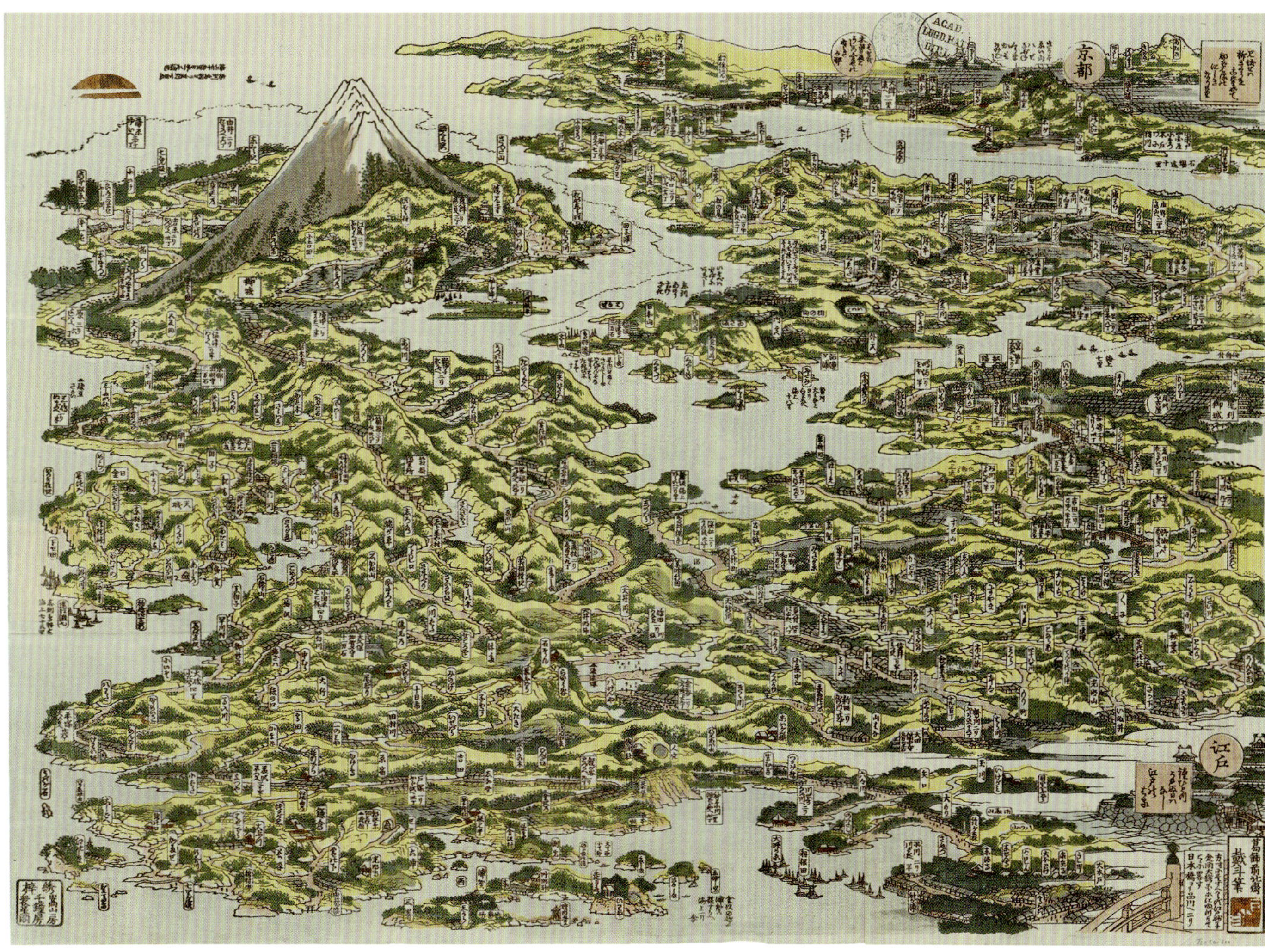

37

Famous places on the Tōkaidō highway at a glance

1818
Signature: Katsushika saki no Hokusai / Taito hitsu
('Brush of Taito, the former Hokusai, [of] Katsushika')
Seal: [unread]
Extra-large colour woodblock, published by
Shūseikaku (Kadomaruya Jinsuke) and others,
43.2 × 58.2 cm
Literature: Edo Tokyo 2007, no. 84; Paris 2014, no. 322;
Keyes & Morse 2015, no. 967
Leiden University Library, Ser. 373

Mt Fuji is by far the largest natural feature in the Japanese archipelago. Hokusai would have known the more literal bird's-eye views by his contemporary, Kuwagata Keisai (1764–1824). Here, however, the challenge for the artist – and the delight for the viewer – is a composition that manipulates the entire length of the Tōkaidō highway so as to fit it into the large, squarish format. The arterial 'East Sea Road' ran some 500 kilometres (310 miles) from Edo – in the bottom right – to Kyoto – top right. Hokusai has named each of the fifty-three officially designated post-stations and often captured in miniature some natural feature or manmade construction associated with the 'famous places' (*meisho*) along the route. Hokusai designed four such aerial views of different parts of Japan, and one imagining the whole of China (cat. 119). TC

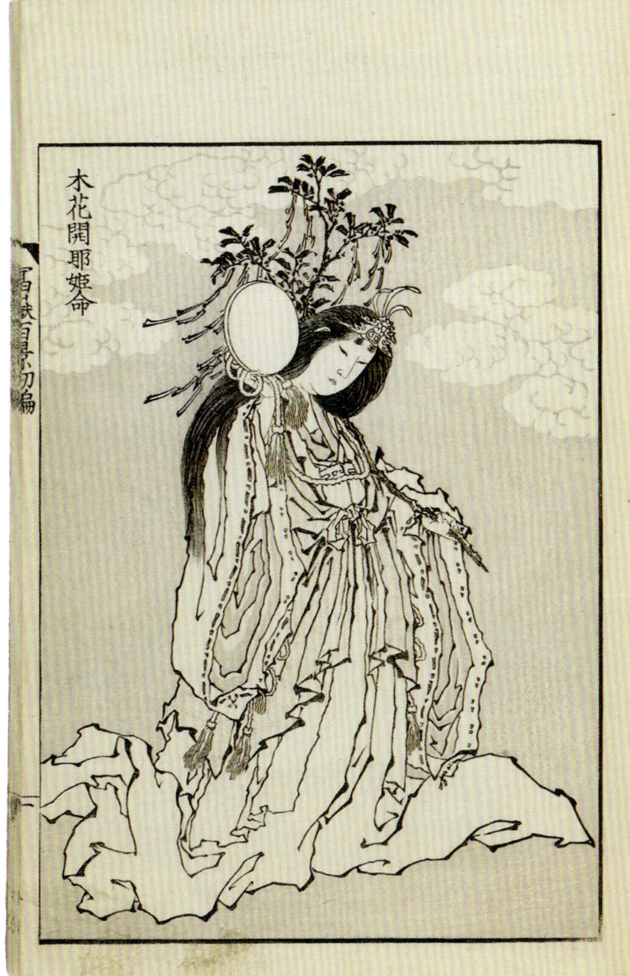
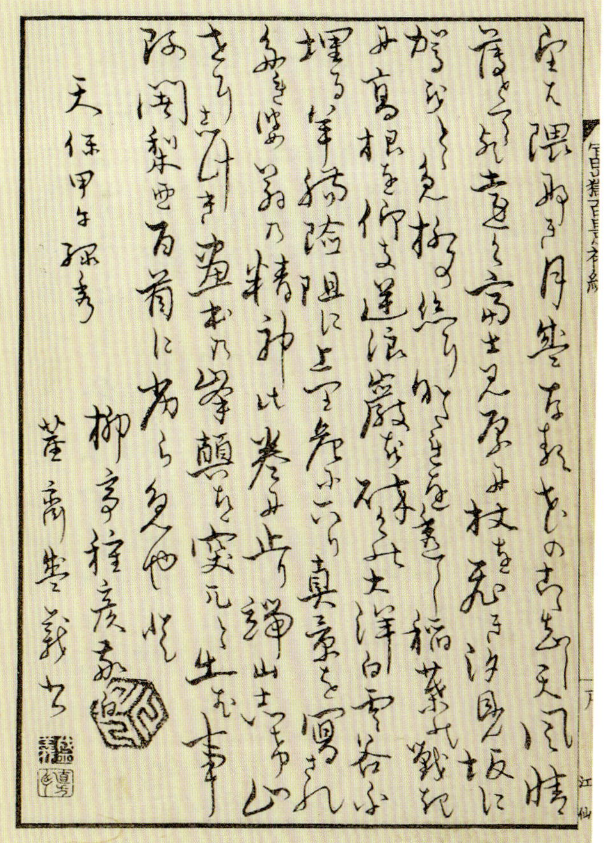

38

The deity Konohanasakuya-hime, from *One Hundred Views of Mt Fuji* (*Fugaku hyakkei*)

Third month, 1834
Signature: Nanajūgo rei / saki no Hokusai Iitsu aratame / Gakyō rōjin Manji hitsu ('Brush of Manji, old man crazy to paint, changed from the former Hokusai Iitsu, aged seventy-five')
Seal: Mt Fuji above trigram
Woodblock, illustrated book, vol. I (of 3), published by Nishimuraya Yūzō and others, 22.7 × 15.7 cm (covers)
Provenance: Jack Hillier
Literature: Smith 1988, pp. 194–195; HK 42, Oct. 2008, pp. 5–61
British Museum, 1979,0305,0.454.1

Mt Fuji was venerated as a deity in both the Buddhist and Shinto strands of Japanese belief – often closely intertwined. The female Shinto deity Konohanasakuya-hime ('Princess of the Flowering of Tree Blossoms'), native deity of the mountain, is shown in clouds, like the peak of Fuji, holding a sacred mirror and a branch of the *sakaki* tree. As the opening image of more than one hundred in the three-volume work, Mt Fuji is thereby immediately situated in the spiritual realm. For Hokusai personally, the mountain was a talisman of longevity, a possible fount of immortality. From this work onwards he regularly used the Buddhism-derived name Manji (literally, 'ten thousand things'), that is, 'everything'. TC

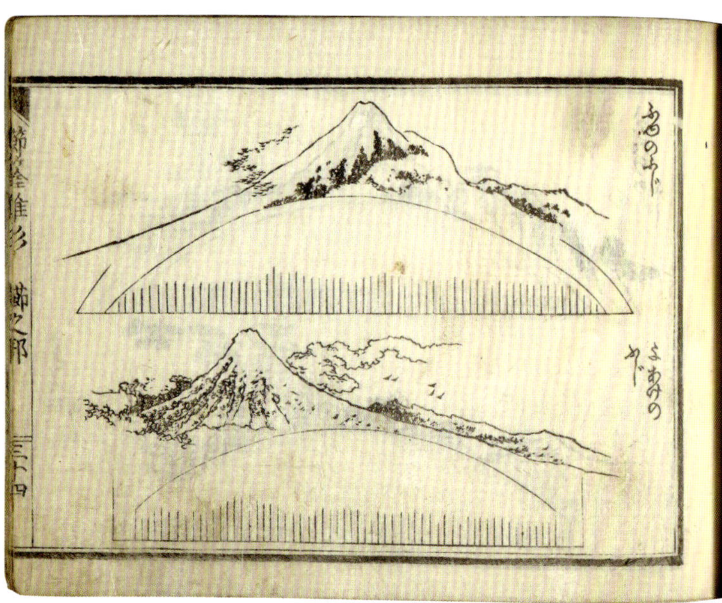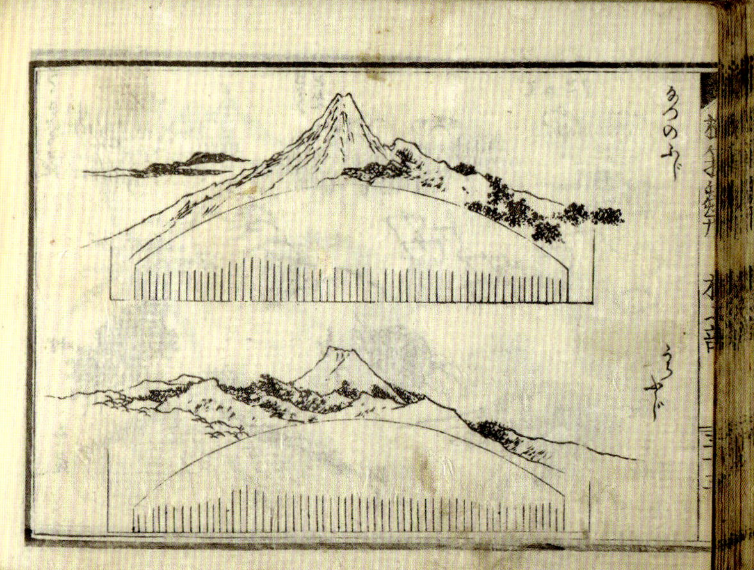

39

Mt Fuji combs, from *Modern Designs for Combs and Tobacco Pipes* (*Imayō sekkin hinagata*), vol. 1

Fifth month, 1823
Signature: Saki no Hokusai Iitsu sensei gazu
('Illustrations by Master Iitsu, the former Hokusai')
Woodblock, illustrated book, vol. 1 (of 3), published by
Nishimuraya Yohachi and others, 12.6 × 18.0 cm (covers)
Provenance: Jack Hillier
Literature: Nagata *Edehon* 1985–1986, vol. 5,
pp. 113–199, 259–263
British Museum, 1979,0305,0.432.1

Mt Fuji in various seasons and settings is used as designs for hair combs (clockwise, from top right): 'Fuji in summer', 'Fuji from the rear', 'Fuji in winter', Fuji at dawn', with four more Fuji designs on the next page opening. Advertisements at the back of the book promise ambitious future collaborations between publisher and artist, including an apparently unpublished set of prints, *Eight Forms of Fuji* (*Fugaku hattai*): 'Expressing with the tip of the brush how the landscape [*keshiki*] changes in the four seasons, fair weather, rain, wind, snow and mist, in accordance with heavenly creation [*ten no zōka*].' This may be the genesis of the later print series *Thirty-Six Views of Mt Fuji* (about 1831–1833, cats 41–65), but can stand equally well as a general statement of Hokusai's artistic credo in relation to the natural world around him. **TC**

40

Farmer washing taro

1831
Signature: Saki no Hokusai hitsu ('Brush of the
former Hokusai')
Seal: Nanajūni ō ('Old man of seventy-two')
Colour woodblock, published by Moriya Jihei,
23.5 × 16.7 cm
Literature: Yasuda 1971, fig. 13, pp. 139–141;
Keyes & Morse 2015, no. 1787
Museum of Fine Arts, Boston, 11.20399,
William Sturgis Bigelow collection
Osaka only

A man pauses from his work washing and pounding
taro (*imo*, a root vegetable) to gaze at a full moon over
the river. Flowering bush clover indicates autumn.
The print is from a series of ten medium-format (*chūban*)
prints with the unusual signature 'Saki no Hokusai
hitsu', all printed in shades of the chemical pigment
Prussian (Berlin) blue and published by Moriya Jihei.
The red seal here records Hokusai's age as seventy-two,
giving a secure publication date for the series. This also
corroborates the suggestion that the earliest designs
in the series *Thirty-Six Views of Mt Fuji* (cats 41–65),
also printed entirely in shades of blue – both Prussian
blue and indigo in that case – were probably issued
around the New Year of 1831. TC

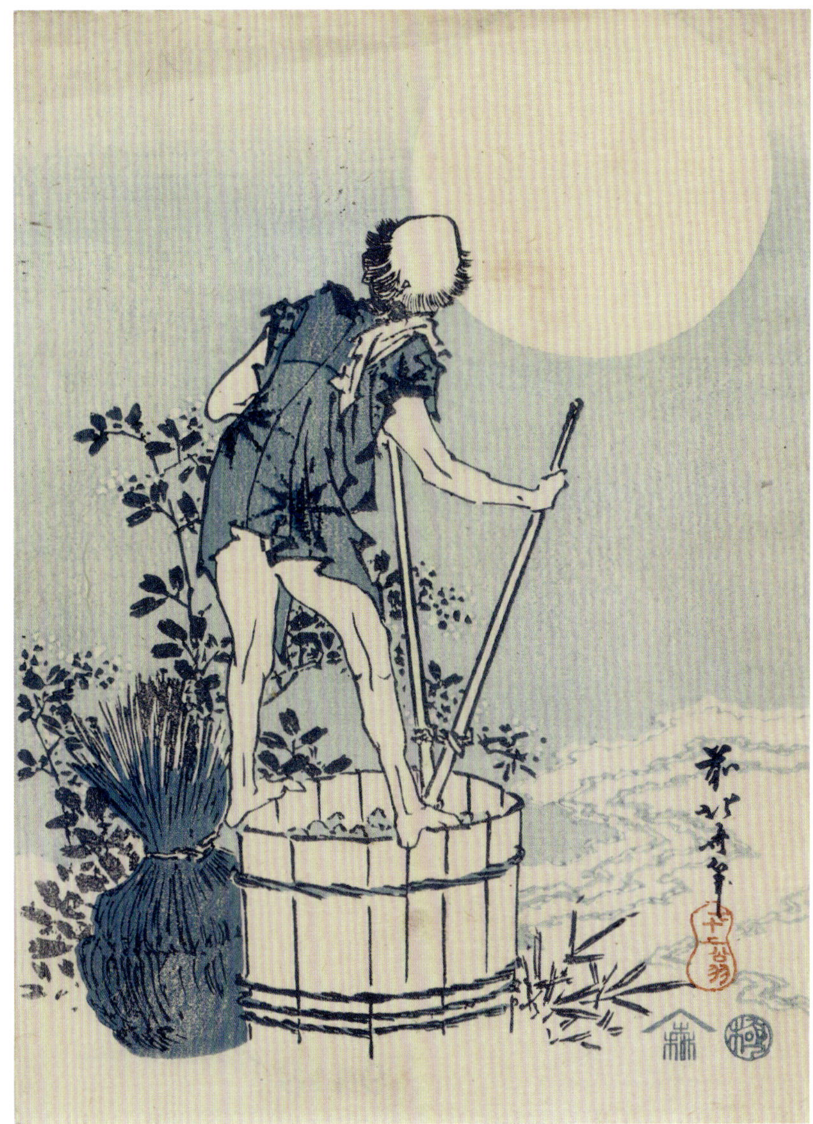

Thirty-Six Views of Mt Fuji (*Fugaku sanjūrokkei*)

At the New Year of 1831, Nishimuraya Yohachi published volume 12 of a
serial novel by Ryūtei Tanehiko (1783–1842) entitled *Shōhon-jitate*. On a sheet of
advertisements at the end of the book (fig. 29), Nishimuraya described for the
first time a new set of prints: '*Thirty-Six Views of Mt Fuji*, drawn by Old-man Iitsu,
the former Hokusai, printed in blue [*aizuri ichimai*], one view on each sheet,
published progressively. These pictures show how the form of Mt Fuji varies
from place to place, for example as seen from Shichirigahama beach [cat. 41]
or Tsukuda island [cat. 42], all different and particularly helpful to those studying
landscape. If carved progressively in this manner, they should even exceed one
hundred. They are not limited to thirty-six.' In fact, Hokusai designed and
Nishimuraya published, probably between 1831 and 1833, forty-six prints in this
famous set. Thirty-six, a canonical number in Japanese art and literature, drew
its authority from association with the Thirty-Six Immortals of classical Japanese
poetry (*sanjūrokkasen*). By 'blue prints', Nishimuraya meant pictures printed entirely
in shades of blue, a type of print popular in Edo in the late 1820s and early 1830s
(Smith 2005). Scientific analysis has shown that the *Thirty-Six Views* were printed
with both Prussian blue – a chemical pigment imported at this time from China
– and traditional indigo (Matsui 2005). Sometimes the two pigments were mixed.

Printing with different saturations of a single colour results in the effect of
seeing colour and form as one does in the hours just before dawn or after dusk,
when the eye perceives subtle differences in colour value, but without registering
differences in hue because of the dim light. Hokusai loved this grisaille-like
optical effect and the first five prints in the set were printed entirely in blue in
early impressions, as the publisher's advertisement indicated. Hokusai, a close
and meticulous observer, was aware that as the rising sun edged closer to the
horizon, colour gradually began to emerge from grey, turning foliage slightly
green, clouds a delicate pink and deep shadows black. Intrigued, he added one
of these colours to the full range of blues in each of the next five prints in the set.

At this point, the series dramatically departed from the publisher's announced
intention. In the third group of five, which includes 'Fuji from Tama river' and
'Clear day with a southern breeze' (cats 52, 53), the first rays of the rising sun
strike the earth, creating delicate, ephemeral, momentary effects. Then, in the
fourth group of five, the risen sun casts its full brilliance on the land, producing
deep shadows and dazzling, sometimes puzzling, highlights. Hokusai's first twenty
prints, in other words, chronicle the miraculous daily return of colour to the
world with the rebirth of the sun and the coming of light. In the last sixteen,
he explored the colour effects of full daylight on the urban and rural landscape.

Hokusai's association with Nishimura Yohachi I, the founder of this important
publishing firm, began as a young man in the middle of the 1780s, and continued
with his successor, Nishimuraya Yohachi II, into the first decade of the 1800s.
In the fifth month of 1823, after a hiatus, Nishimuraya Yohachi II published
Modern Designs for Combs and Tobacco Pipes (cats 29, 39), a three-volume book, which
included some ingenious views of Mt Fuji and an advertisement for a set of *Eight
Forms of Fuji (Fugaku hattai)*. Nishimuraya did not proceed with this Fuji publication
in the 1820s, but both artist and publisher had clearly planned a set of views of
Mt Fuji several years before they began collaborating on the *Thirty-Six Views* set.

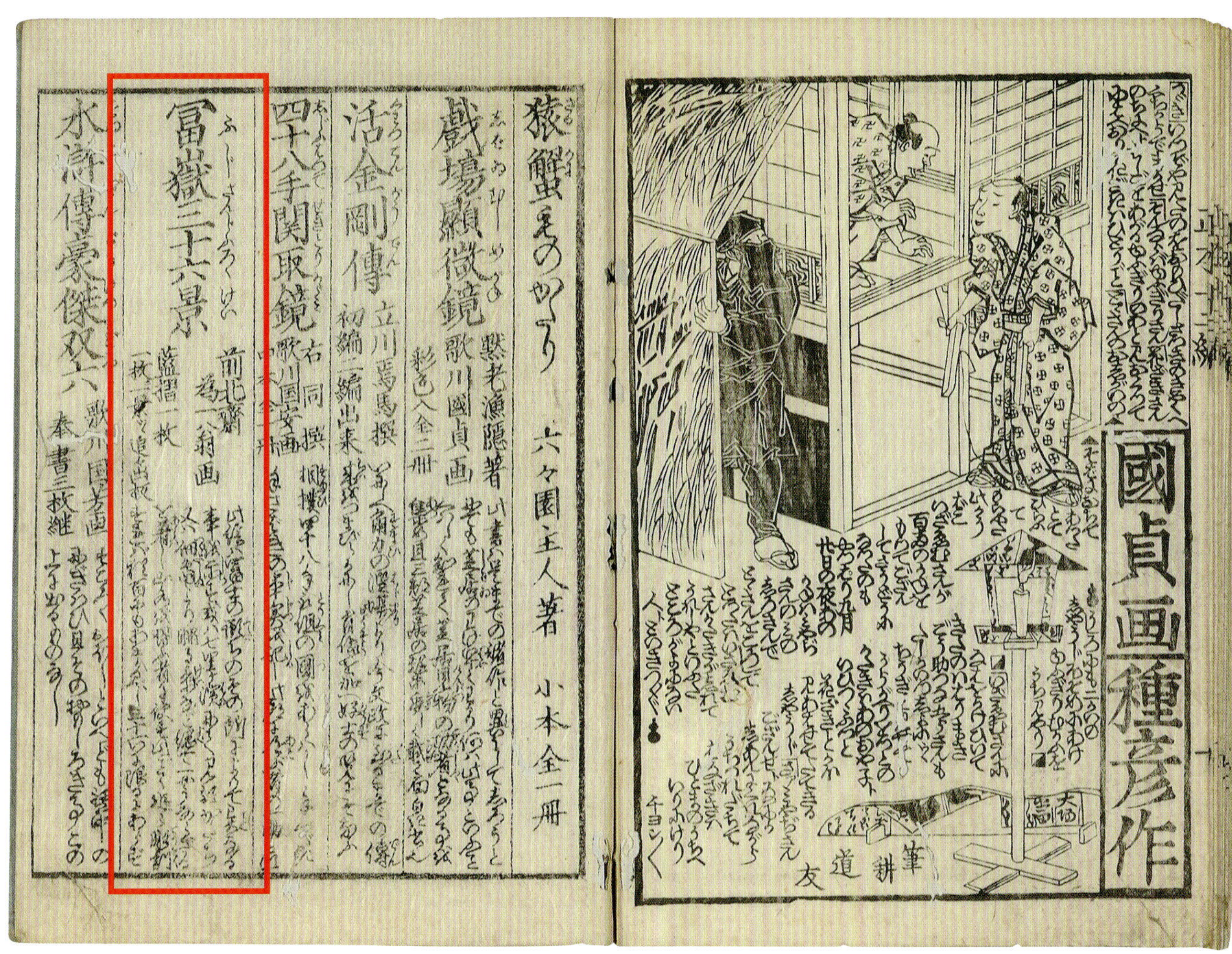

FIG 29

Ryūtei Tanehiko
(author, 1783–1842)
Shōhon-jitate, vol. 12
New Year, 1831
Illustrated novel, woodblock
Art Research Center,
Ritsumeikan University, Kyoto,
hayBK03-0544-06

It is possible that by early 1823 Hokusai had produced block-ready drawings of Mt Fuji for nine horizontal large-format (*ōban*) landscape prints, including 'Clear day with a southern breeze' (cats 52, 53) and 'Under the wave off Kanagawa' ('The Great Wave', cat. 51), which Nishimuraya eventually used in the *Thirty-Six Views* set. The artist signed these prints 'Hokusai aratame Iitsu hitsu', or 'Brush of Iitsu, changed from Hokusai'. This signature is commonly found on *surimono* published between 1823 and 1825. (It also appears on three Hokusai fan prints published in the summer of 1831, although he may have drawn these earlier.)

Nineteenth-century Edo publishers kept printing blocks as long as there was demand for a print. Hundreds of impressions of some of Hokusai's *Thirty-Six Views* have survived, suggesting that thousands of impressions were printed at the time – perhaps as many as 5,000–8,000 impressions of the most popular designs. Many surviving impressions are late, physically damaged or faded. The outlines of later impressions are often worn and they are printed with different colours that are not faithful to the artist's intention and lose the subtlety of the original printing effects. To understand what Hokusai was trying to achieve in his Fuji prints it is important to see the earliest possible impression of each, and ones that are unfaded, in order to appreciate Hokusai's colour sense. RK

41

Shichirigahama beach, Sagami province

Early 1831
Signature: Saki no Hokusai Iitsu hitsu ('Brush of Iitsu, the former Hokusai')
Colour woodblock, published by Nishimuraya Yohachi, 24.3 × 36.4 cm
Literature: MSU 1991, no. 24; Clark 2001, no. 45; Keyes & Morse 2015, no. 628
British Museum, 1907,0531,0.144, given by Sir Hickman Bacon

Shichirigahama ('Seven League beach') is a beach southwest of Kamakura that extends from Inamura point to Koshigoe, approximately 4.5 kilometres (3 miles) or seven old leagues (*ri*). The beach itself is invisible in Hokusai's view of Koshigoe village from a nearby hill. Other views from this beach past the island of Enoshima and towards Mt Fuji by Shiba Kōkan (1747–1818) and Hokusai are seen in cats 15–17. This is one of two blue (*aizuri*) prints mentioned by name in Nishimuraya's first advertisement of the set at the New Year, 1831. RK/TC

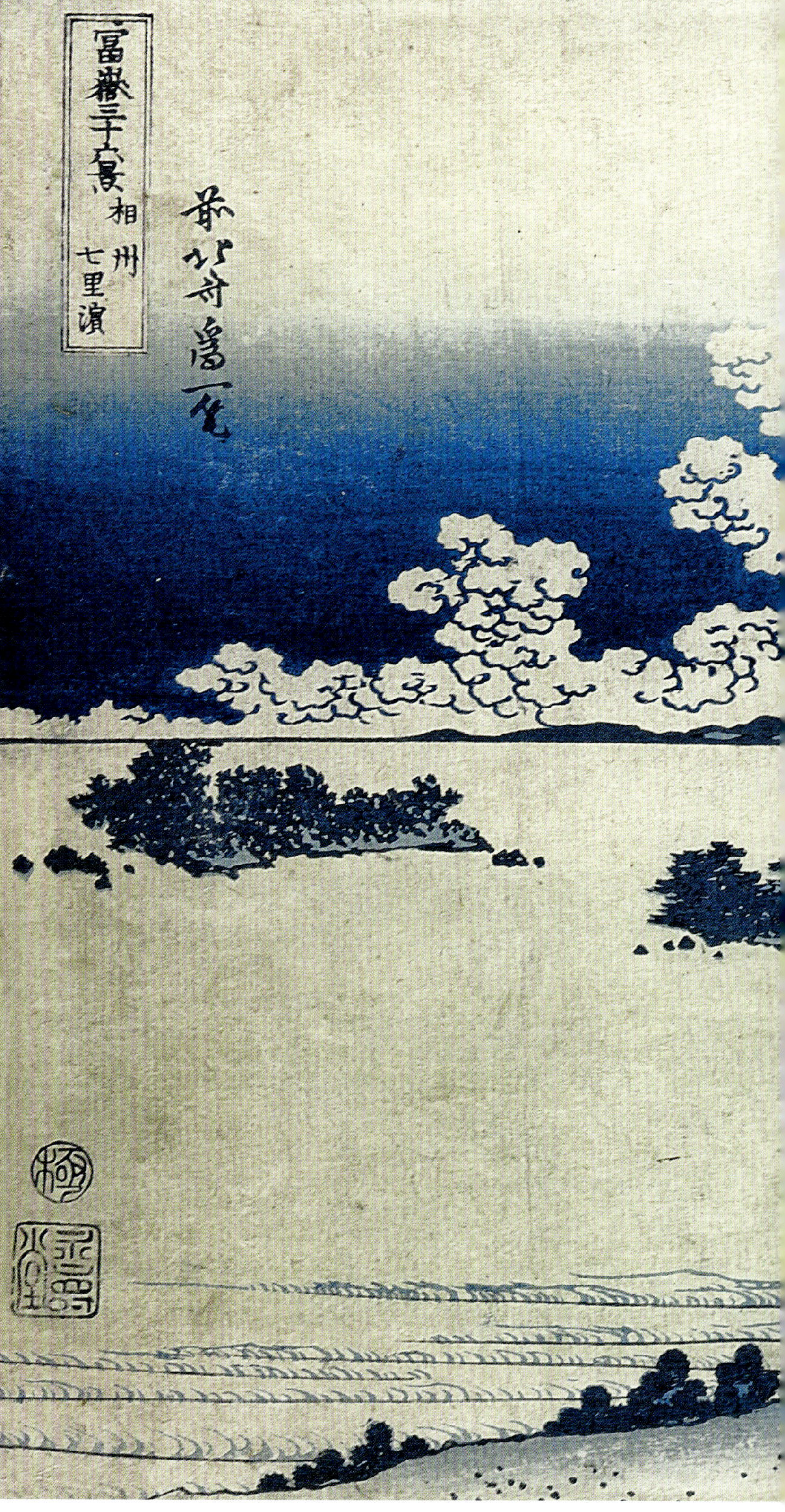

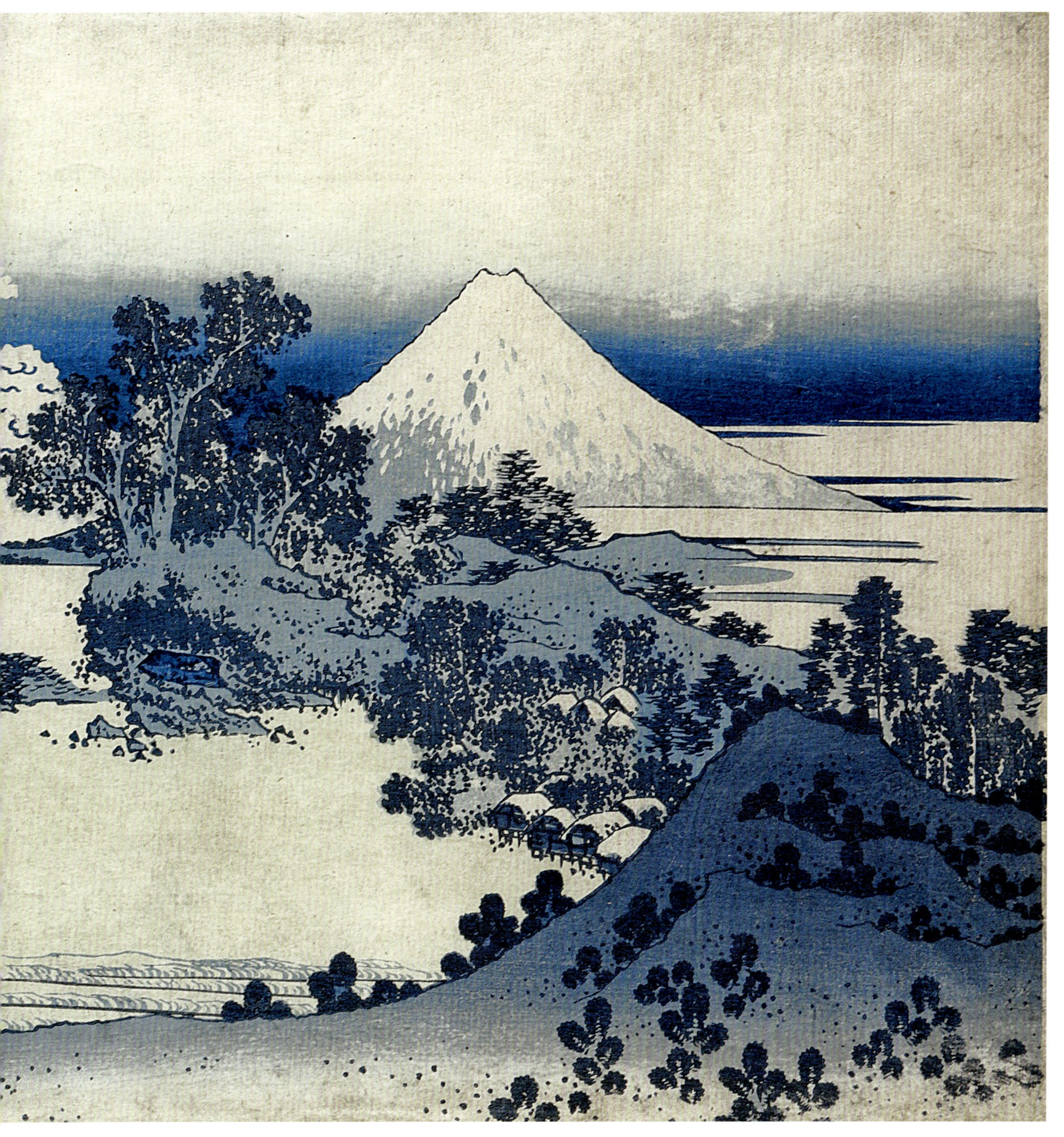

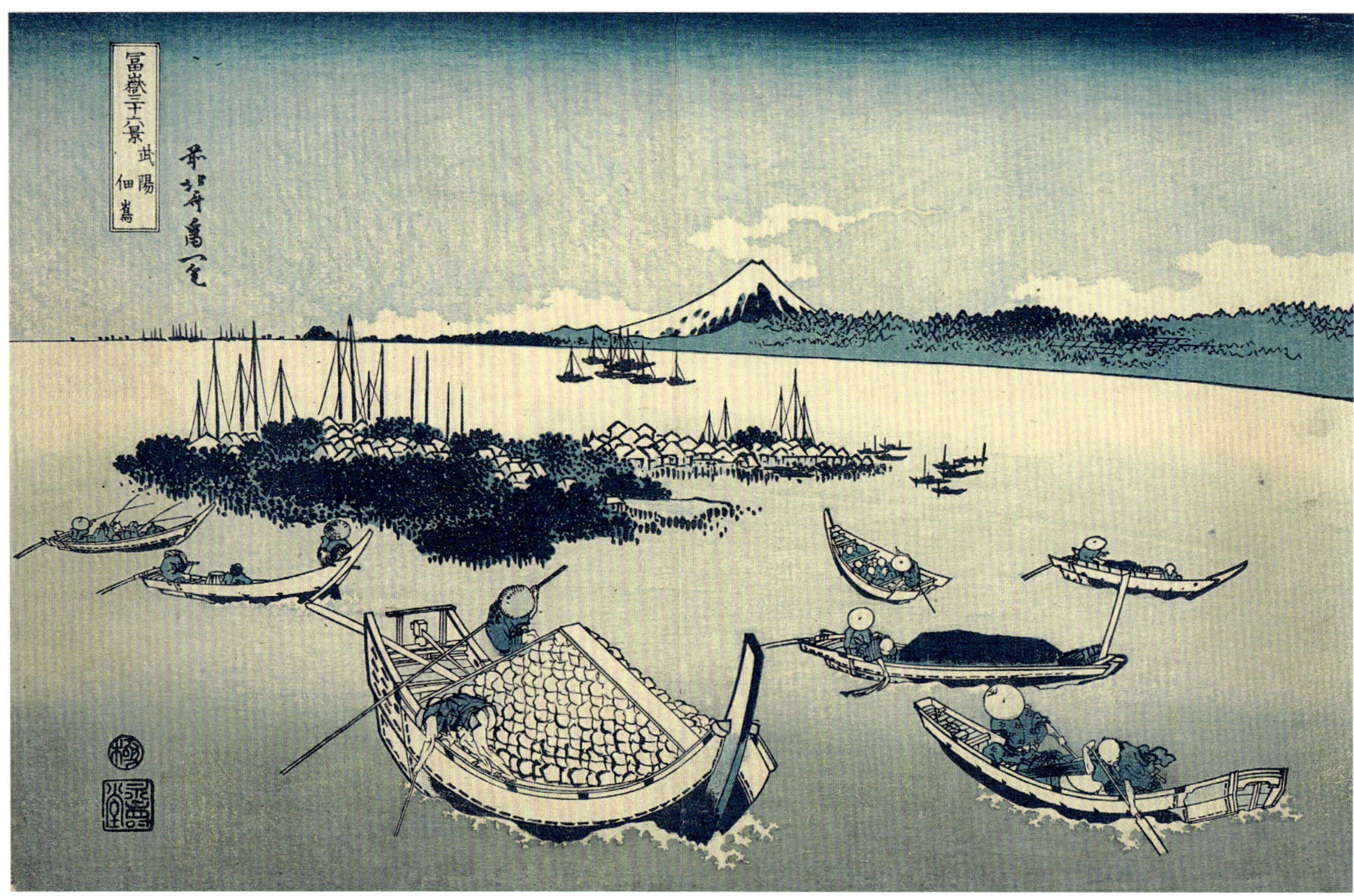

42

Tsukuda island, Musashi province

Early 1831
Signature: Saki no Hokusai Iitsu hitsu ('Brush of Iitsu, the former Hokusai')
Colour woodblock, published by Nishimuraya Yohachi, 25.4 × 38.7 cm
Literature: MSU 1991, no. 16; Clark 2001, no. 101; Keyes & Morse 2015, no. 620
Metropolitan Museum of Art, New York, JP2563, The Howard Mansfield Collection, Purchase, Rogers Fund, 1936

Tsukuda island was situated in Edo bay at the mouth of the Sumida river, home to a thriving fishing community. Here the bay is busy with a variety of passenger, pleasure and cargo boats. This is the second blue (*aizuri*) print mentioned by name in Nishimuraya's first advertisement of the set. Delicate gradated printing and small areas of overprinting expand even further the range of subtle shades of blue that are sensitively combined in the image. RK/TC

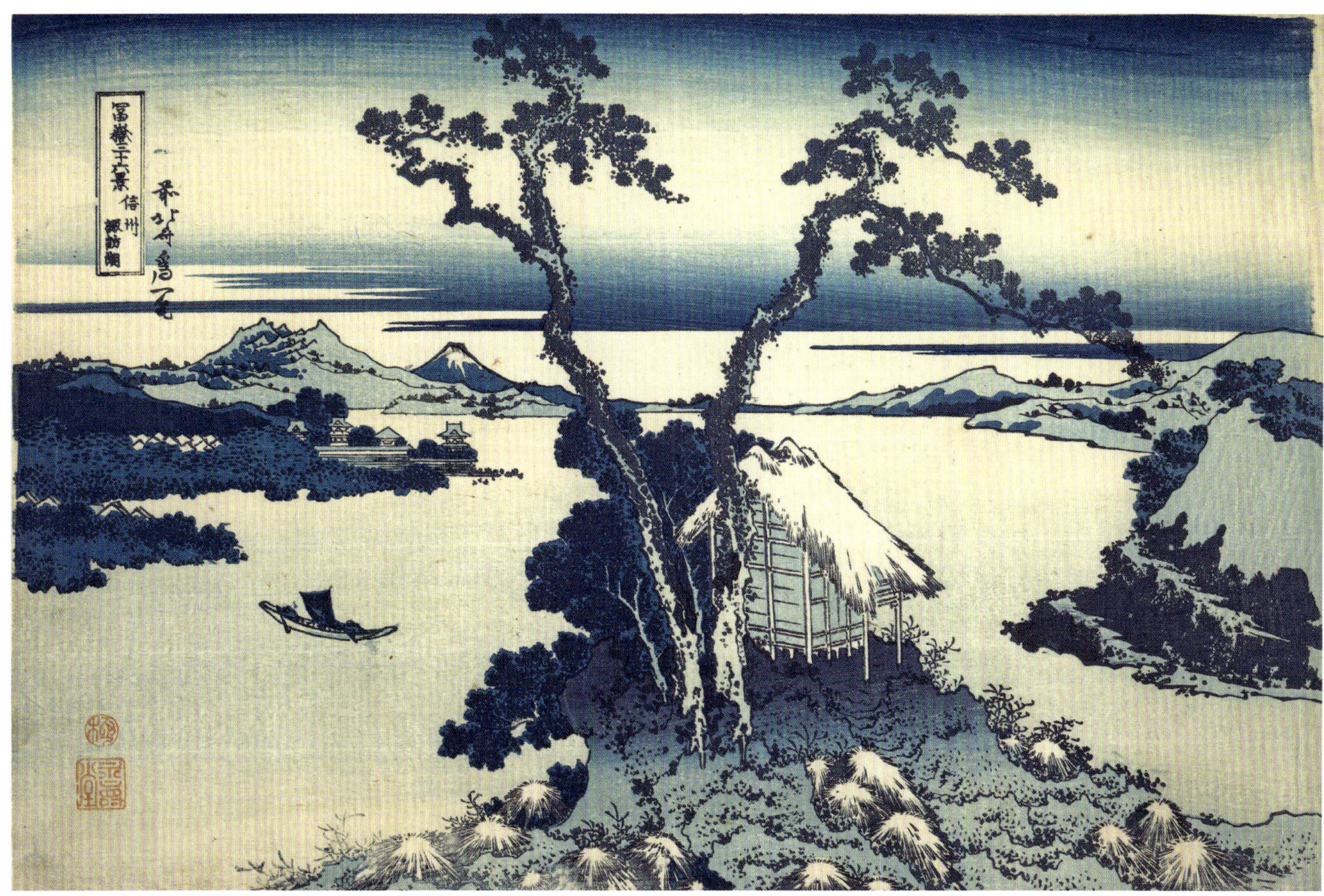

43

Lake Suwa, Shinano province

Early 1831
Signature: Saki no Hokusai Iitsu hitsu ('Brush of Iitsu,
the former Hokusai')
Colour woodblock, published by Nishimuraya Yohachi,
26.0 × 38.4 cm
Literature: MSU 1991, no. 44; Clark 2001, no. 47;
Keyes & Morse 2015, no. 648
Metropolitan Museum of Art, New York, JP2965,
Henry L. Phillips Collection, Bequest of Henry L.
Phillips, 1939

Lake Suwa, about 160 kilometres (100 miles) west of
Edo and 90 kilometres (56 miles) northwest of Mt Fuji,
is a large body of water surrounded by the mountains
of Shinano province (modern Nagano prefecture).
The view, printed entirely in shades of blue, is of
Takashima castle across the lake from a shrine on a
hilltop promontory with two large pines. This may
be an outlying part of the Great Shrine of Suwa on
the north shore of the lake, or the Kawaguchi Benten
shrine that Hokusai drew on his 1819 map of the
Kisokaidō highway (TNM 2005, nos 220–222).
As is often found in the *Thirty-Six Views*, the shape
of the thatched shrine building in the foreground
echoes the slopes of Mt Fuji. RK/TC

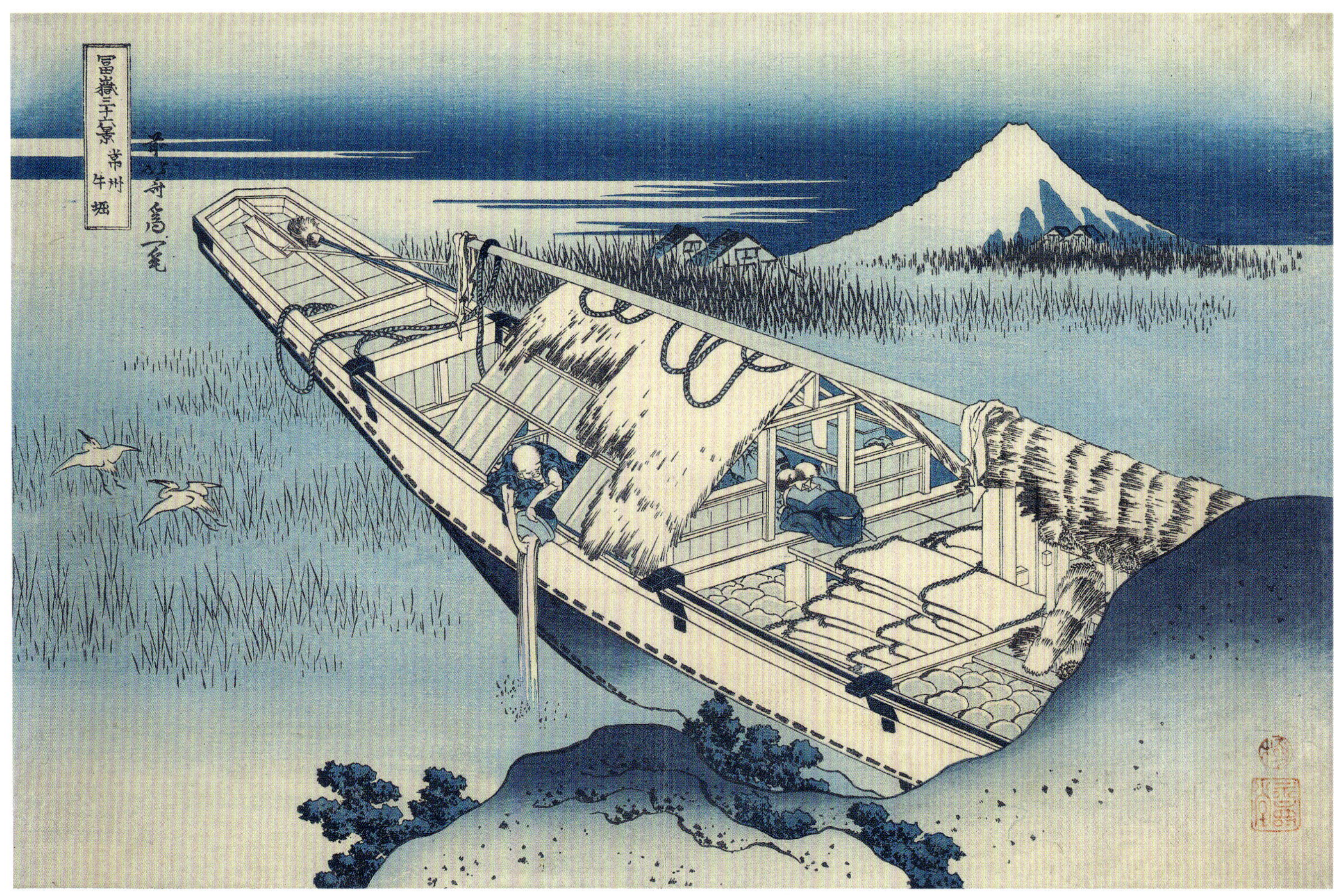# 44

Ushibori, Hitachi province

Early 1831
Signature: Saki no Hokusai Iitsu hitsu ('Brush of Iitsu, the former Hokusai')
Colour woodblock, published by Nishimuraya Yohachi, 25.4 × 28.1 cm
Literature: MSU 1991, no. 19; Clark 2001, no. 46; Keyes & Morse 2015, no. 623
Metropolitan Museum of Art, New York, JP2565, The Howard Mansfield Collection, Purchase, Rogers Fund, 1936

Ushibori is a harbour town about 75 kilometres (46 miles) northeast of Edo, on the south shore of Kasumigaura, a large marshy lake near the point where the Tone river meets the Pacific Ocean. This is the most remote location of the series. The man in the foreground is rinsing rice before dawn in preparation for the morning meal. It is unclear whether the rounded objects piled in the hold are cargo or ballast. RK/TC

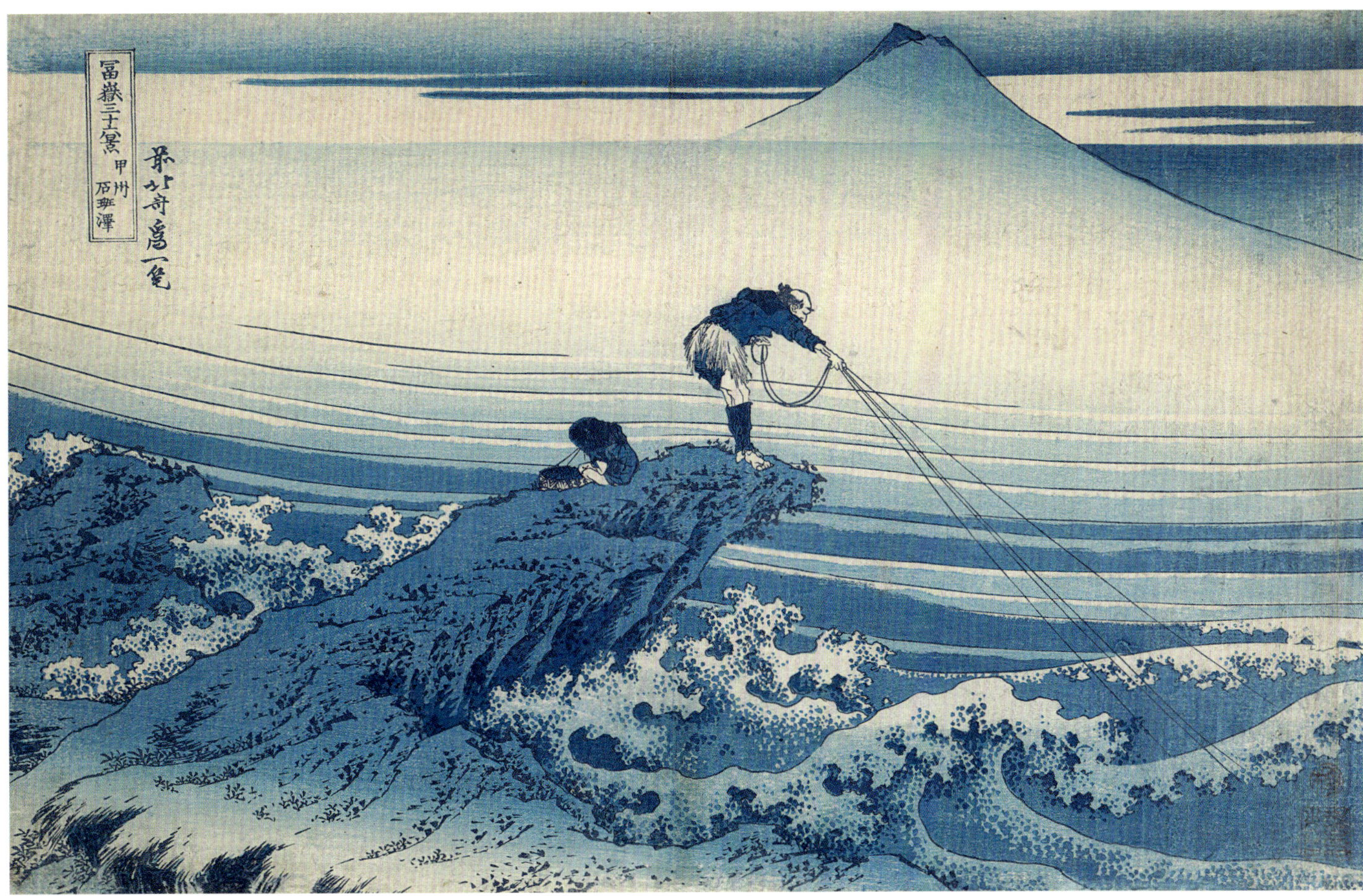

45

Kajikazawa, Kai province

Early 1831
Signature: Saki no Hokusai Iitsu hitsu ('Brush of Iitsu, the former Hokusai')
Colour woodblock, published by Nishimuraya Yohachi, 25.4 × 38.4 cm
Literature: MSU 1991, no. 45; Clark 2001, no. 48; Keyes & Morse 2015, no. 649
Metropolitan Museum of Art, New York, JP2581, The Howard Mansfield Collection, Purchase, Rogers Fund, 1936

Kajikazawa or 'Kajika marsh' is the area southwest of the city of Kōfu, where two swiftly flowing tributaries meet to become the Fuji river. A fisherman casts his nets from a rocky outcrop, accompanied by a boy with a basket. The view of Mt Fuji from the rear is less picturesque and the roiling spray is more evocative of ocean waves than river currents, creating a desolate atmosphere overall. Even among the early impressions rendered entirely in shades of blue, there is considerable variation in the tonalities and gradation of the printing. RK/TC

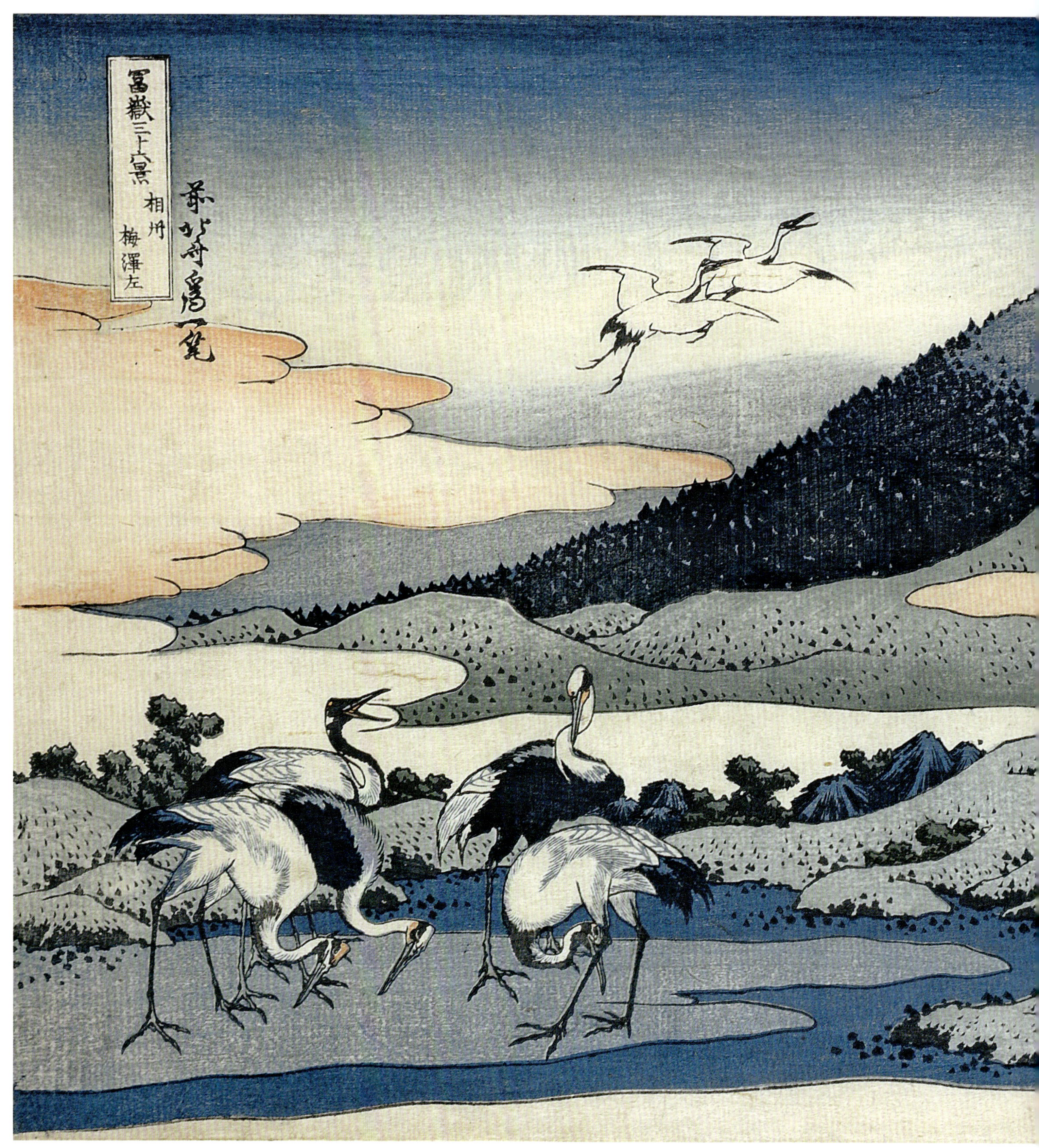

冨嶽三十六景
相州
梅澤左
葛飾北齋畫一覧

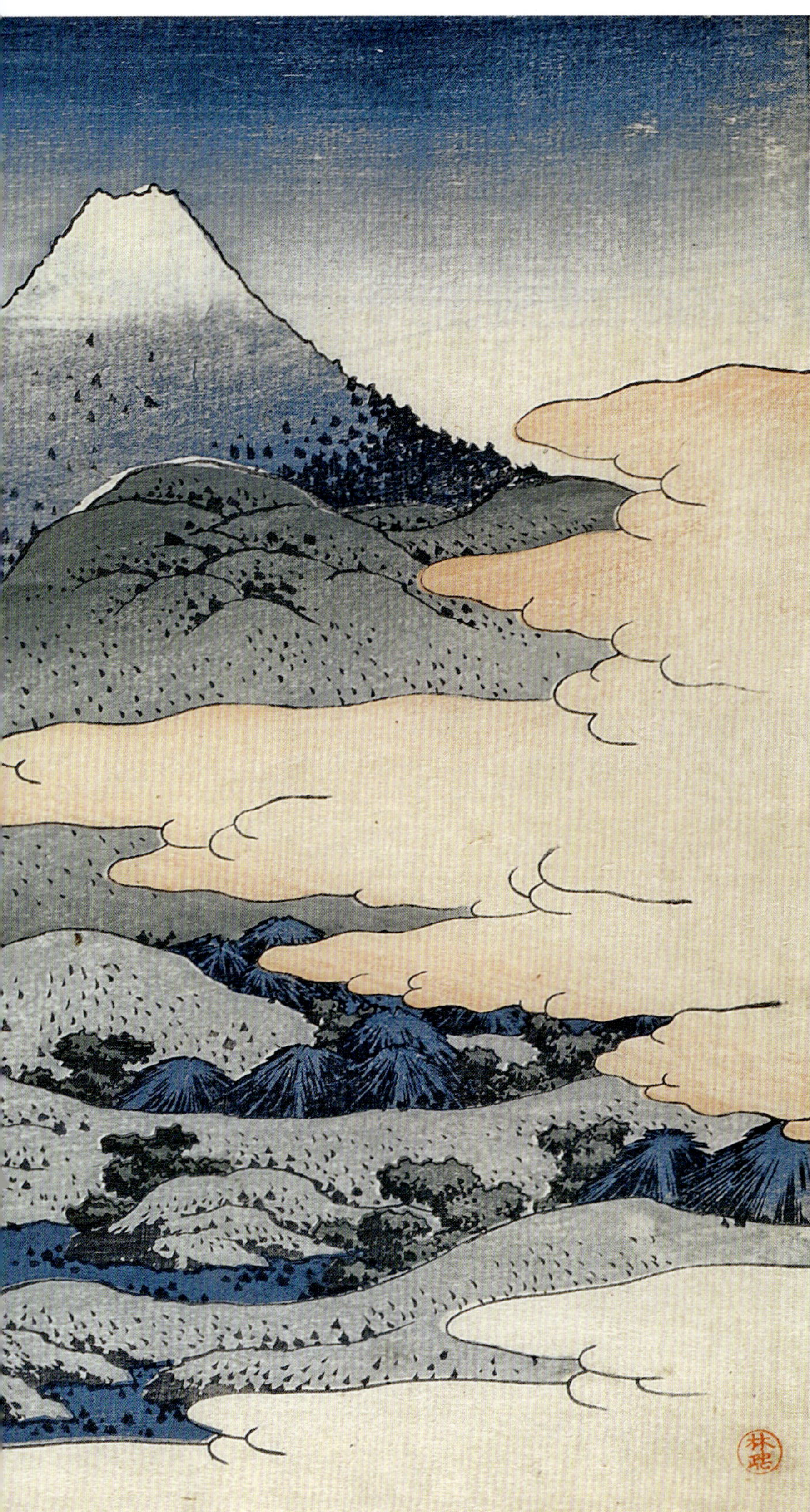

Umezawa manor, Sagami province

Early 1831
Signature: Saki no Hokusai Iitsu hitsu ('Brush of Iitsu, the former Hokusai')
Colour woodblock, published by Nishimuraya Yohachi, 25.6 × 38.1 cm
Provenance: Hayashi Tadamasa
Literature: MSU 1991, no. 27; Clark 2001, no. 49; Keyes & Morse 2015, no. 631
British Museum, 1928,0516,0.1

Clouds of pink-tinted morning mist part to reveal a blue Mt Fuji. Five auspicious cranes feed and preen in the foreground and another pair fly off towards the peak. Umezawa was a stopping place between Ōiso and Odawara on the Tōkaidō highway. It is now part of the modern city of Ninomiya, in Kanagawa prefecture. The last character in the printed title reads 'left' (*hidari*), but this is thought to be a block cutter's error for another character, perhaps *zai* or *shō*, meaning 'manor'. In the second group of five prints in the series, of which this is one, colour begins to creep into designs that are still predominantly blue. RK/TC

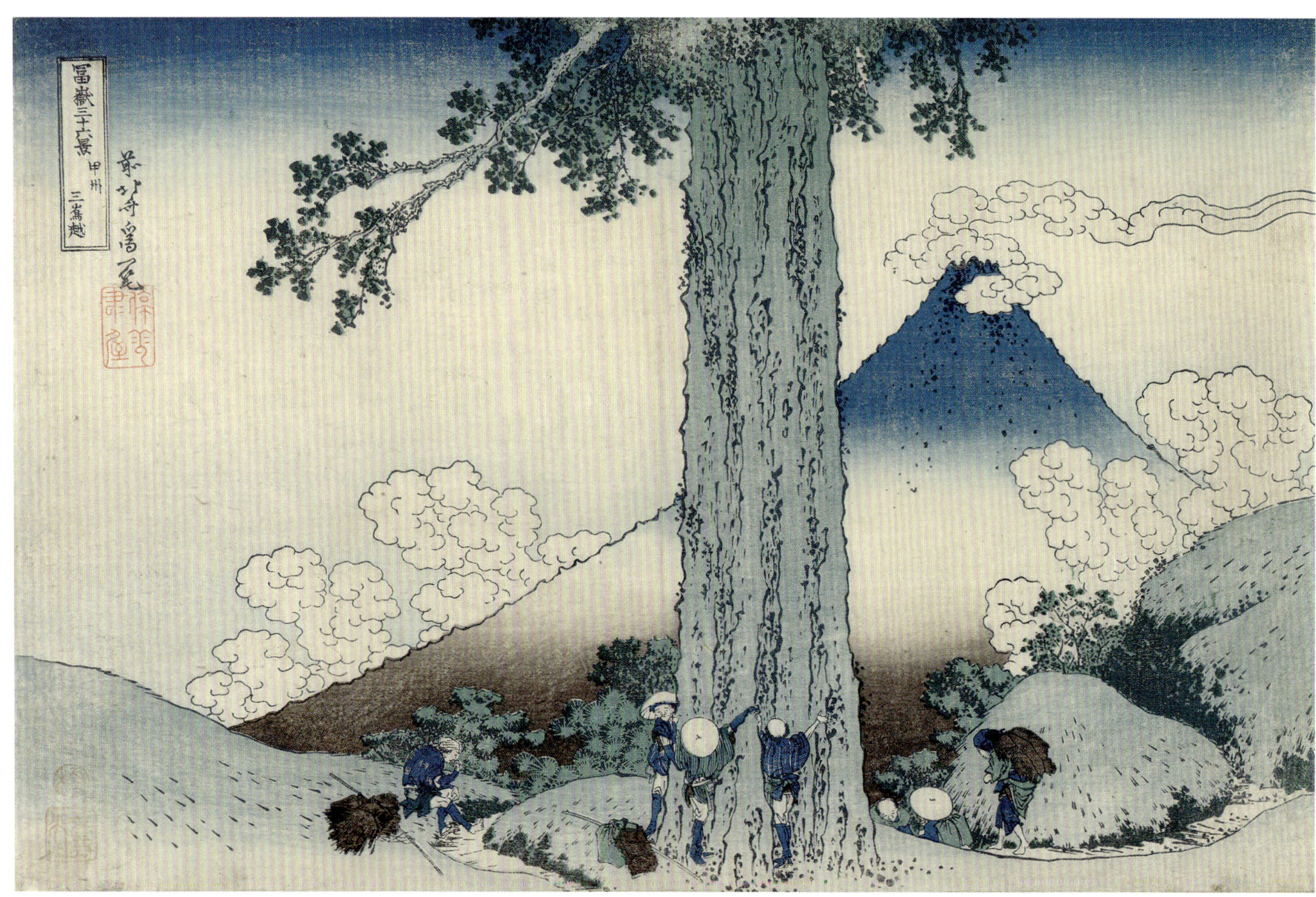

47
Mishima highroad, Kai province

Early 1831
Signature: Saki no Hokusai Iitsu hitsu ('Brush of Iitsu, the former Hokusai')
Colour woodblock, published by Nishimuraya Yohachi, 25.4 × 37.3 cm
Provenance: Charles Ricketts & Charles Shannon
Literature: MSU 1991, no. 29; Clark 2001, no. 51; Keyes & Morse 2015, no. 633
British Museum, 1937,0710,0.161, bequeathed by Charles Shannon RA

Mishima highroad ran from Kōfu through Misaka, Fuji Yoshida and Gotenba to the junction of the Tōkaidō highway at Mishima. Hokusai shows travellers measuring the girth of an old cryptomeria tree at Kagosaka pass, on the border of Kai and Suruga provinces, by encircling it with their outspread arms. The huge tree apparently dwarfs Mt Fuji and one dipping branch echoes the curving left slope of the mountain. Fuji's peak is capped with a 'hat' (*kasa*) cloud that trails almost as smoke would if the volcano were erupting. RK/TC

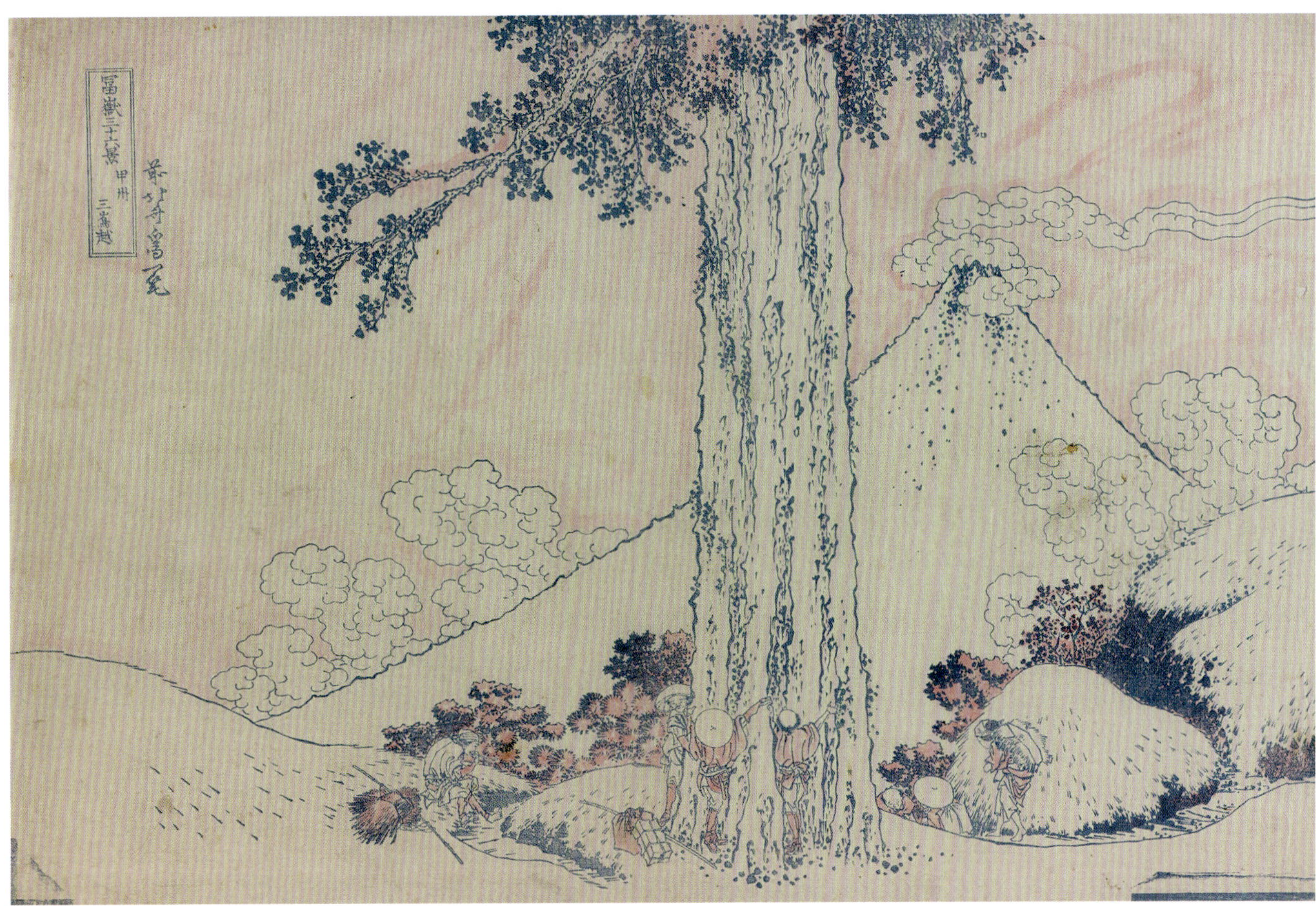

48

Mishima highroad, Kai province (proof print)

Early 1831

Signature: Saki no Hokusai Iitsu hitsu ('Brush of Iitsu, the former Hokusai')

Colour woodblock (proof), with slight hand-colouring, published by Nishimuraya Yohachi, 26.4 × 38.3 cm

Literature: MSU 1991, no. 29; Clark 2001, no. 51; Keyes & Morse 2015, no. 633

Ōta Memorial Museum of Art, Tokyo

London only

A feature of the series is that the outlines and text of the first thirty-six views were printed in blue, rather than the normal black. This rare surviving proof print (*kyōgō-zuri*) has certain areas marked by hand in pale red ink, which seem to indicate where dark green should be printed in the foreground and perhaps also where pale blue should be printed in the sky. The horizontal lines in the lower left and right corners are part of the *kentō* registration system. They first assist the block cutter in the making the colour blocks, and ultimately serve as a guide for correct placement of the paper during printing. (A similar mark is seen in the bottom right corner of cat. 49.) RK/TC

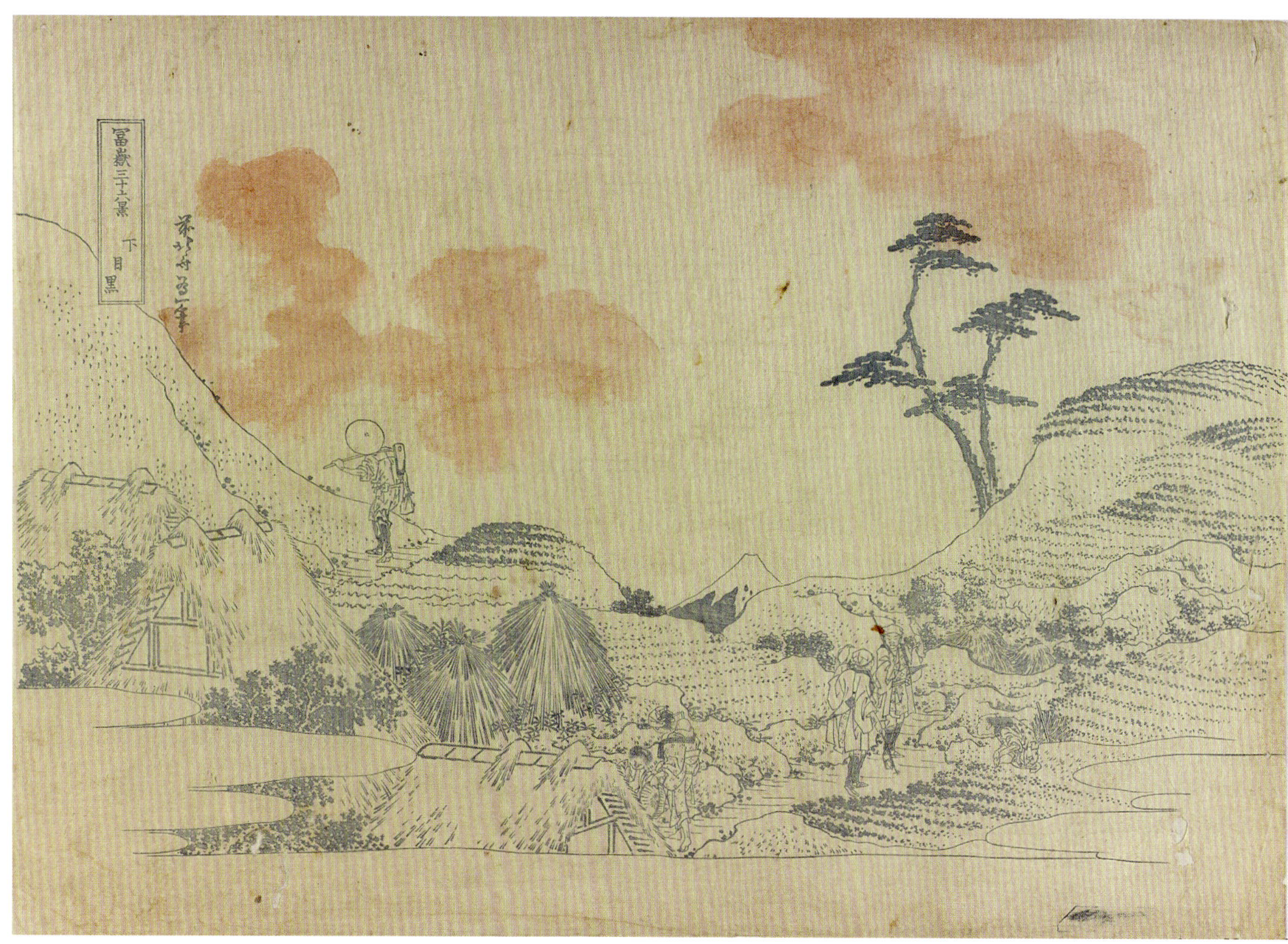

49
Shimo Meguro (proof print)

About 1832
Signature: Saki no Hokusai Iitsu hitsu ('Brush of Iitsu, the former Hokusai')
Colour woodblock (proof), with slight hand-colouring, published by Nishimuraya Yohachi, 27.5 × 37.6 cm
Literature: MSU 1991, no. 10; Clark 2001, no. 111; Keyes & Morse 2015, no. 614
Ōta Memorial Museum of Art, Tokyo
Osaka only

This, like the previous (cat. 48), is a proof of the key (outline) block printed in blue, with washes of pale red ink added by hand to indicate possible positions for clouds – never apparently realized in surviving impressions. Meguro, now part of Tokyo, was still a rural area in the 1830s. The road to the Fudō temple threads its way through hilly fields. RK/TC

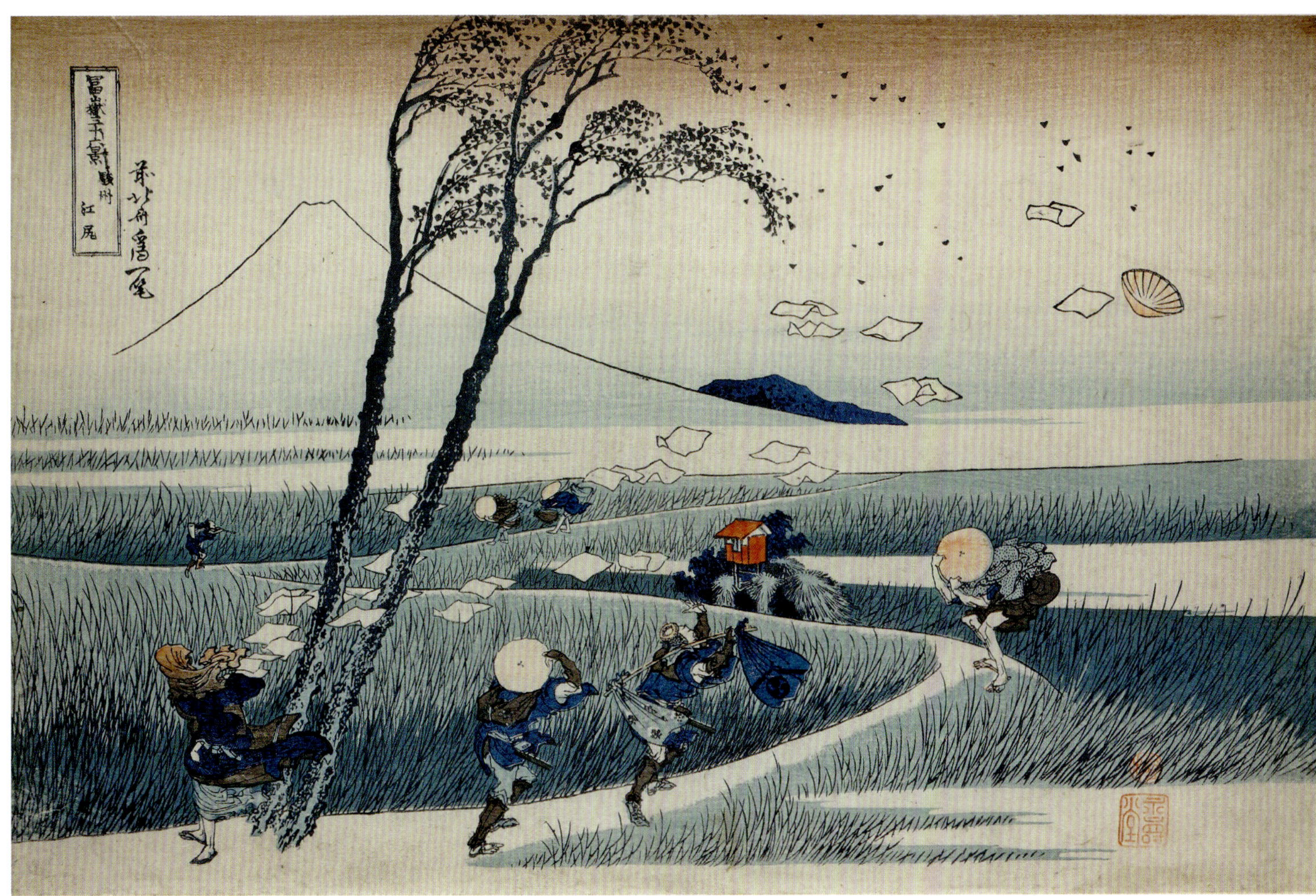

50

Ejiri, Suruga province

Early 1831
Signature: Saki no Hokusai Iitsu hitsu ('Brush of Iitsu, the former Hokusai')
Colour woodblock, published by Nishimuraya Yohachi, 25.7 × 38.1 cm
Literature: MSU 1991, no. 35; Clark 2001, no. 50; Keyes & Morse 2015, no. 639
British Museum, 1907,0531,0.545

Ejiri was a post-station on the Tōkaidō highway on the west side of Suruga bay, modern Shimizu ward in Shizuoka city. The desolate area shown here is thought to be around Uba-ga-ike ('Old Woman Pool'), with the road snaking through the marsh on raised dykes. Mt Fuji is drawn in silhouette, with a single line. Hokusai's brilliant conception shows the effects of a strong wind, stripping leaves from the bending trees and sending a stream of tissues and a lost travelling hat flying up into the sky. RK/TC

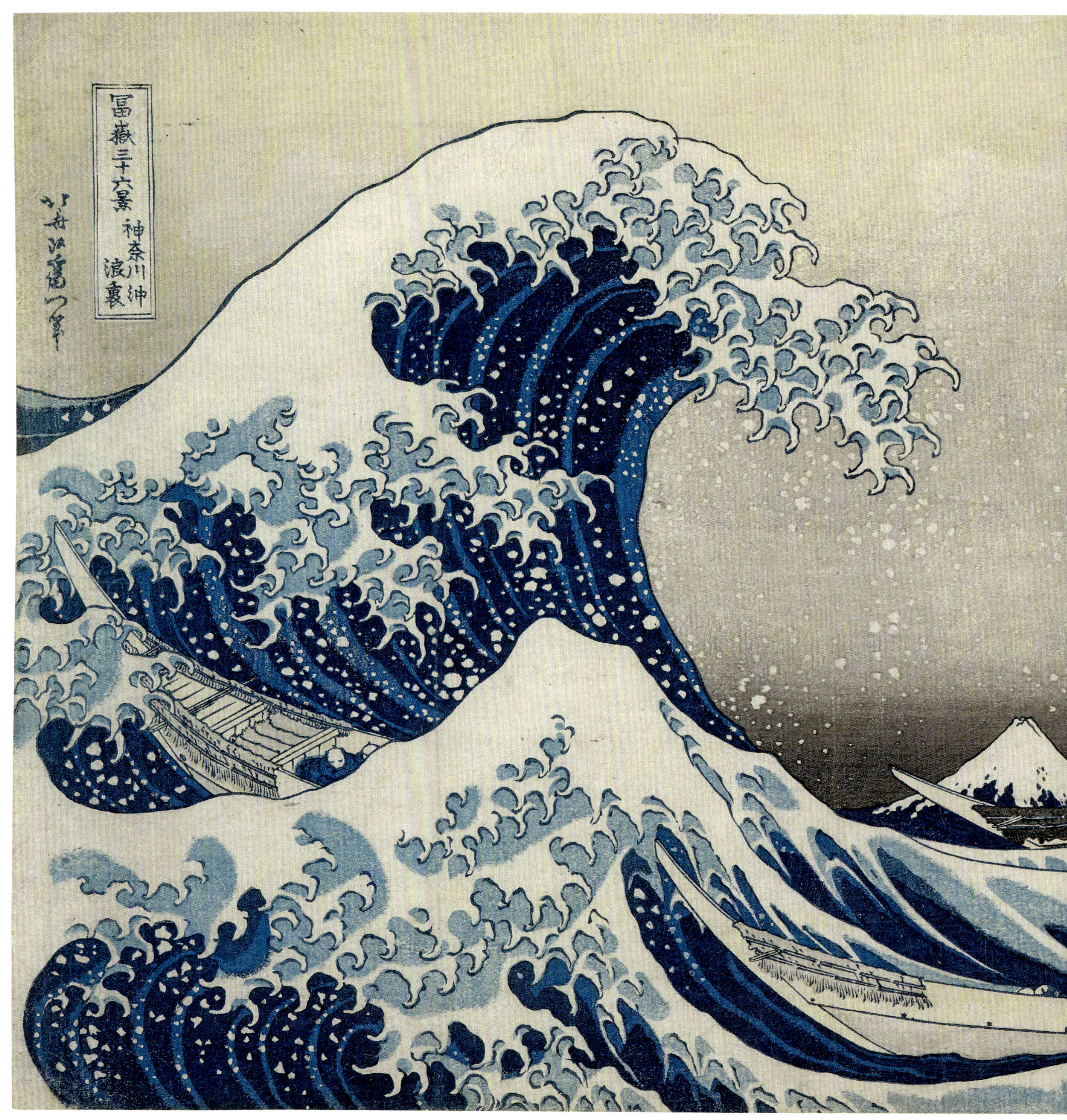

冨嶽三十六景 神奈川沖 浪裏
北斎改為一筆

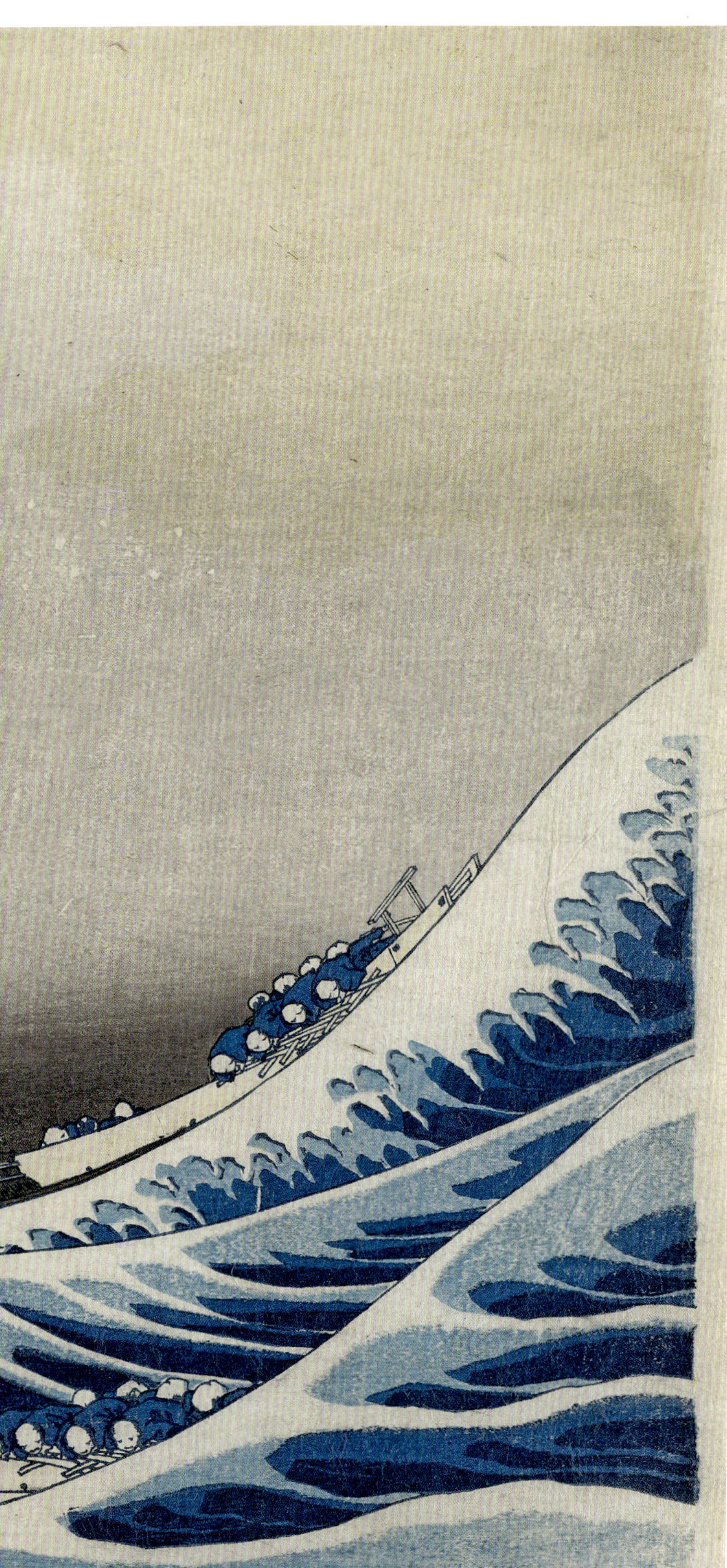

Under the wave off Kanagawa
('The Great Wave')

Late 1831
Signature: Hokusai aratame Iitsu hitsu ('Brush of Iitsu,
changed from Hokusai')
Colour woodblock, published by Nishimuraya Yohachi,
25.8 × 37.9 cm
Provenance: René Druart (1888–1961)
Literature: MSU 1991, no. 21; Clark 2001, no. 52;
Clark 2011; Guth 2015; Keyes & Morse 2015, no. 625
British Museum, 2008,3008.1.JA, acquired with
contributions from the Brooke Sewell Bequest and
the Art Fund

The 'Great Wave' dwarfs Mt Fuji. Spray falls from the
tentacles of the wave like snow on to the peak. The
whole picture is orchestrated to pay homage to the
steadfastness of the sacred mountain. Three swift boats
(*oshiokuri*), delivering fish to market in Edo, head
directly into a great storm wave out at sea off
Kanagawa. The oarsmen crouch forwards, ready to
battle heroically with the elemental power of the
ocean. Hokusai had rehearsed the wave several times
in his thirties and forties, when he was absorbing the
lessons of European-style perspective (cats 18, 19). To
this was added, in his old age, a veneration of Mt Fuji as
a talisman of longevity. The design may already have
been drawn in the early 1820s (see pp. 108–109). Then,
later in the decade, Prussian blue became available in
large quantities from China, providing a wonderfully
vibrant new pigment for sky and sea to add to the
traditional indigo. The series, of which this is the most
famous print, was one significant result. Over the years,
as many as 8,000 impressions of each design were
printed. For little more than the price of a double-
helping of noodles, anyone in Edo could purchase their
own impression of 'The Great Wave'. RK/TC

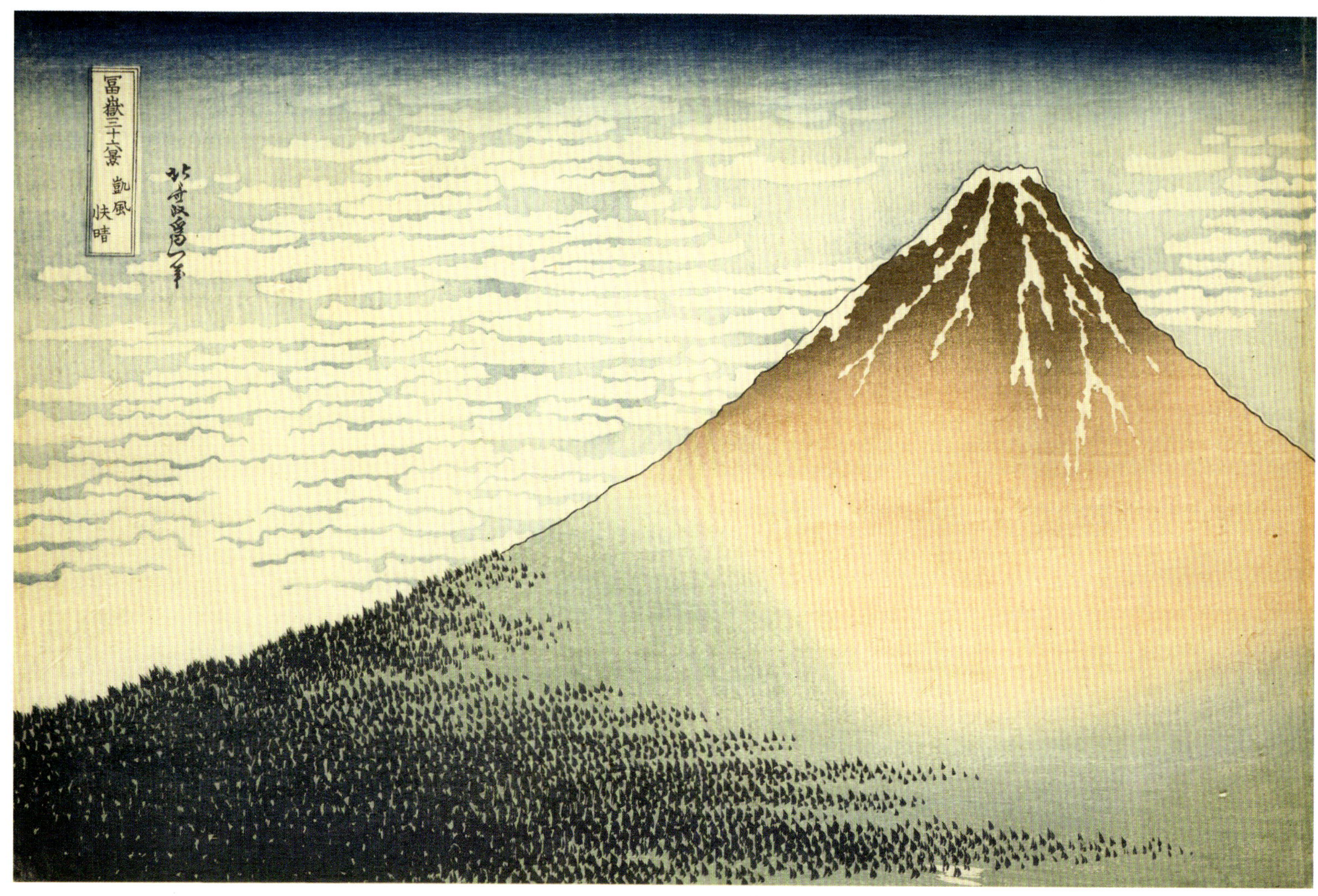

52

Clear day with a southern breeze ('Pink Fuji')

Late 1831

Signature: Hokusai aratame Iitsu hitsu ('Brush of Iitsu, changed from Hokusai')

Colour woodblock, published by Nishimuraya Yohachi, 25.5 × 37.9 cm

Literature: MSU 1991, no. 33; Kano 1994; Clark 2001, no. 53; Guimet 2008, no. 62b; Keyes 2008; Keyes & Morse 2015, no. 637

Musée national des arts asiatiques Guimet, Paris, AA.380, bequeathed by Mme Charles Jacquin 1938

London only

53

Clear day with a southern breeze ('Red Fuji')

Late 1831

Signature: Hokusai aratame Iitsu hitsu ('Brush of Iitsu, changed from Hokusai')

Colour woodblock, published by Nishimuraya Yohachi, 26.1 × 38.2 cm

Provenance: Arthur Morrison

Literature: MSU 1991, no. 33; Kano 1994; Clark 2001, no. 53; Keyes 2008; Keyes & Morse 2015, no. 637

British Museum, 1906,1220,0.525

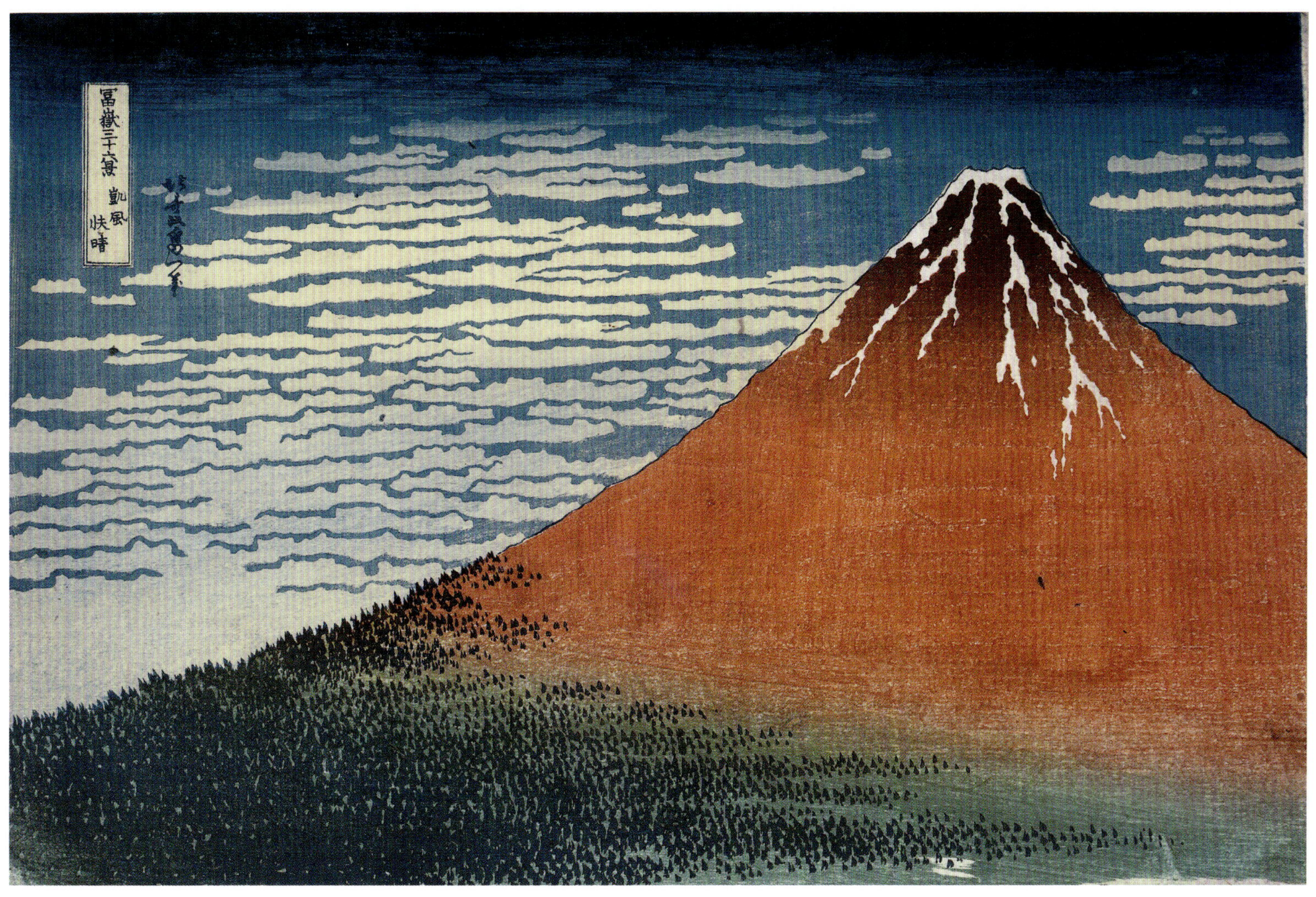

This may seem the most abstracted and monumental of Hokusai's many depictions of Mt Fuji, yet the effects the artist sought were quite specific (Keyes 2008). 'Southern breeze' is a phenomenon associated with late summer, when there is only a modicum of snow left around the summit of Fuji. In the earliest impressions the mountain is printed a delicate pinkish-brown, with a large expanse of green at the foot (cat. 52). We are looking at the eastern side of the mountain, just as the first rays of the sun, rising over the Pacific Ocean, strike the upper slopes and turn the black and grey ash a soft pink. The boundary of the light-struck area arcs because the mountain is a cone. This arc is lower at the right than the left, since the sun in summer rises north of east and therefore strikes the slopes at an oblique angle. The high altocumulus clouds of a 'mackerel sky' (sometimes called 'sardine

clouds', *iwashigumo*) dapple the morning sky and drift northwards, like a slow-moving shoal of fish. Surely instructed by the artist and the publisher, the printer purposely inked the pale blue sky block unevenly. This makes the morning sky look bright and the clouds seem to move. The printer also silhouetted just the mountain peak with a darker shade of blue, which brings the mountain forward. The print came to be known in modern times as 'Red Fuji' because a dark reddish-brown was commonly used for later impressions (cat. 53), combined with a darker blue sky. Many of the earlier special printing effects were simplified in later impressions; for example, the gradation between the reddish-brown and green on the mountain's slope became a straight diagonal – much quicker and easier for the printer. RK/TC

54
Sudden rain beneath the summit

Late 1831
Signature: Hokusai aratame Iitsu hitsu ('Brush of Iitsu, changed from Hokusai')
Colour woodblock, published by Nishimuraya Yohachi, 24.1 × 36.5 cm
Provenance: Arthur Morrison
Literature: MSU 1991, no. 32; Clark 2001, no. 54; Keyes & Morse 2015, no. 636
British Museum, 1906,1220,0.526

The artist imagines Fuji from the west, regarded as the 'back' view, on a late afternoon in summer, with the sun casting its shadow on clouds behind it. The 'white rain' (*haku'u*) of the Japanese title means a sudden downpour, and the dramatic flash of lightning on the lower slopes signals a summer storm down at the level of human habitation. The massive scale of the mountain dwarfs even the weather. It is equally monumental in composition as 'Clear day with a southern breeze' (cats 52, 53), and Hokusai's intention may have been to set up a series of contrasts between the two designs: front/back; morning/evening; fair weather/storm. RK/TC

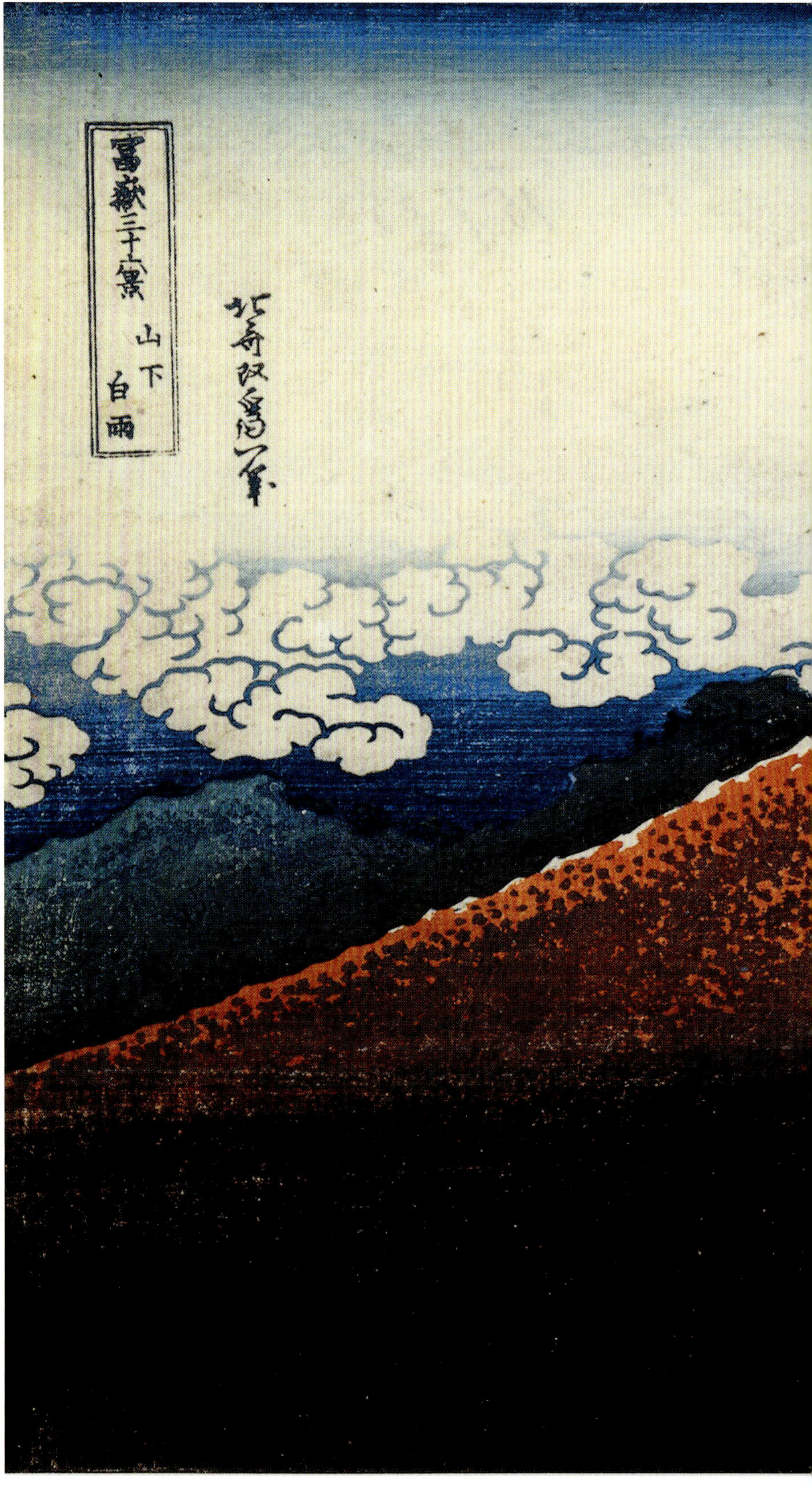

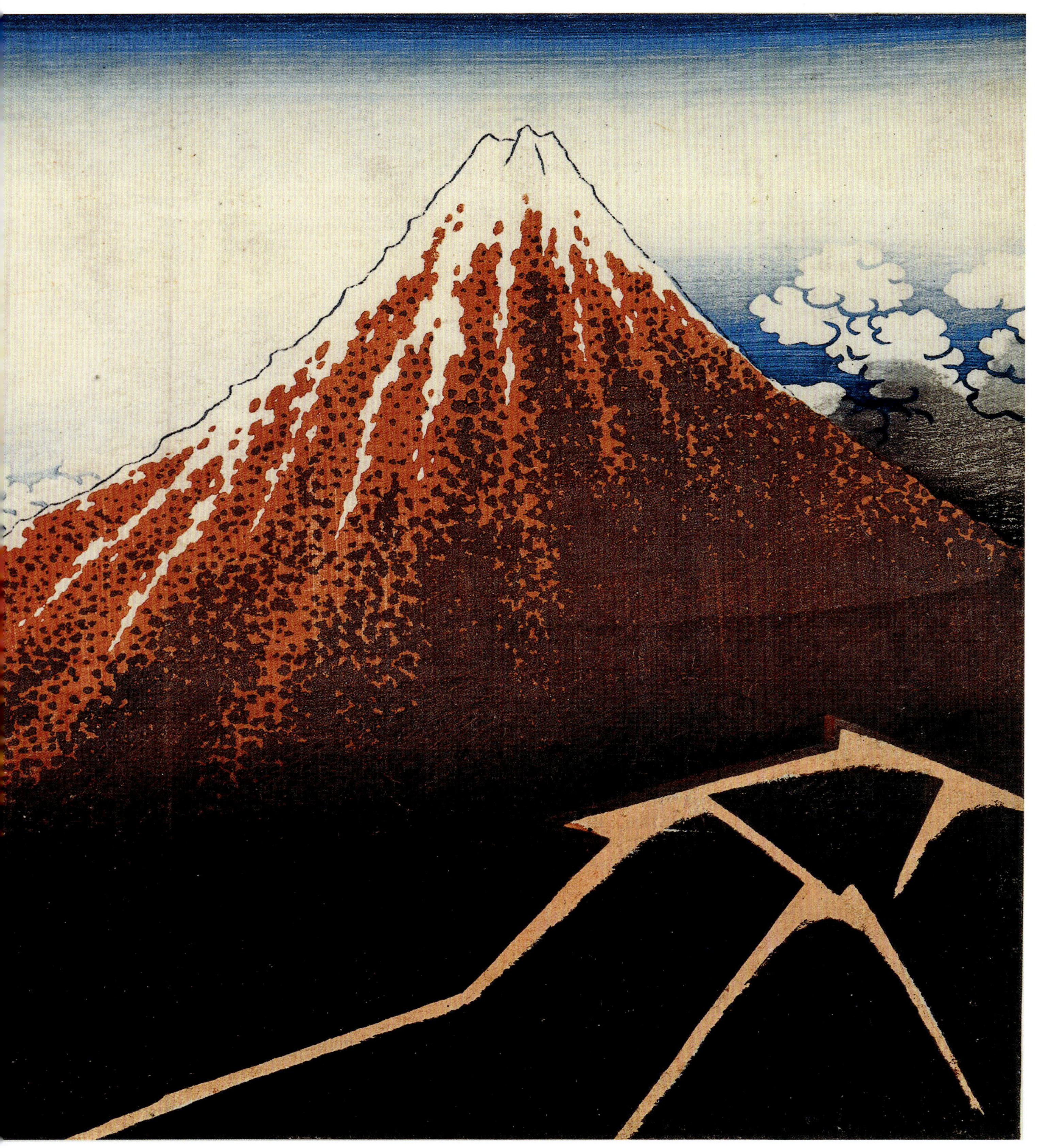

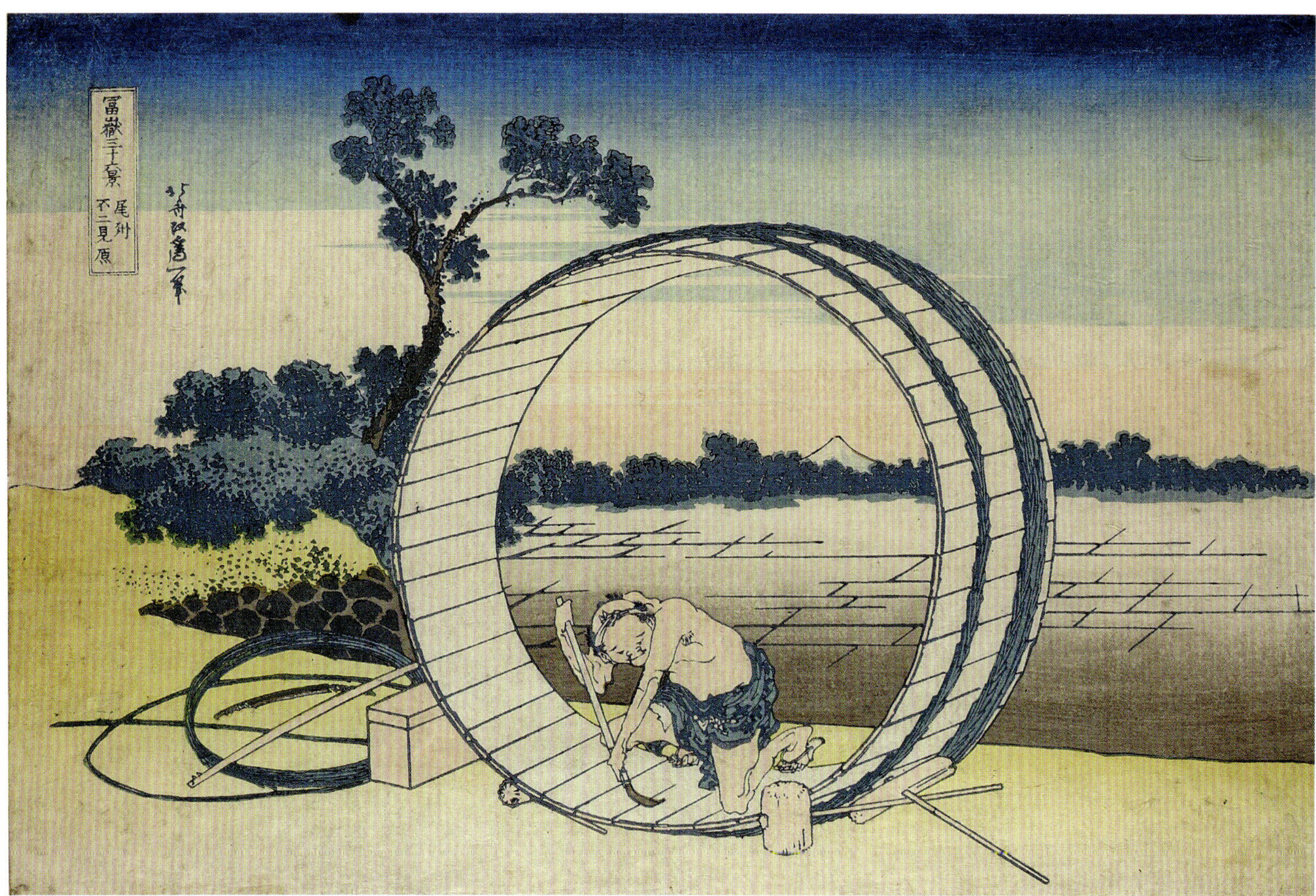

55

Fuji View moor, Owari province

Late 1831
Signature: Hokusai aratame Iitsu hitsu ('Brush of Iitsu,
changed from Hokusai')
Colour woodblock, published by Nishimuraya Yohachi,
25.8 × 37.7 cm
Provenance: Charles Ricketts & Charles Shannon
Literature: MSU 1991, no. 40; Clark 2001, no. 110;
Keyes & Morse 2015, no. 644
British Museum, 1937,0710,0.166, bequeathed by
Charles Shannon RA

Through the ellipse formed by a large wooden tub
under construction, we glimpse the tiny triangle of
Mt Fuji on the distant horizon. The barrel-maker planes
the wood intently, oblivious to the view – he can see it
any day. As so often in his pictures, Hokusai celebrates
the application and skill of people at work. Fujimigahara
('Fuji View moor') was on the road from Nagoya to
the Atsuta shrine. It is now part of Fujimi-chō in the
centre of Nagoya. RK/TC

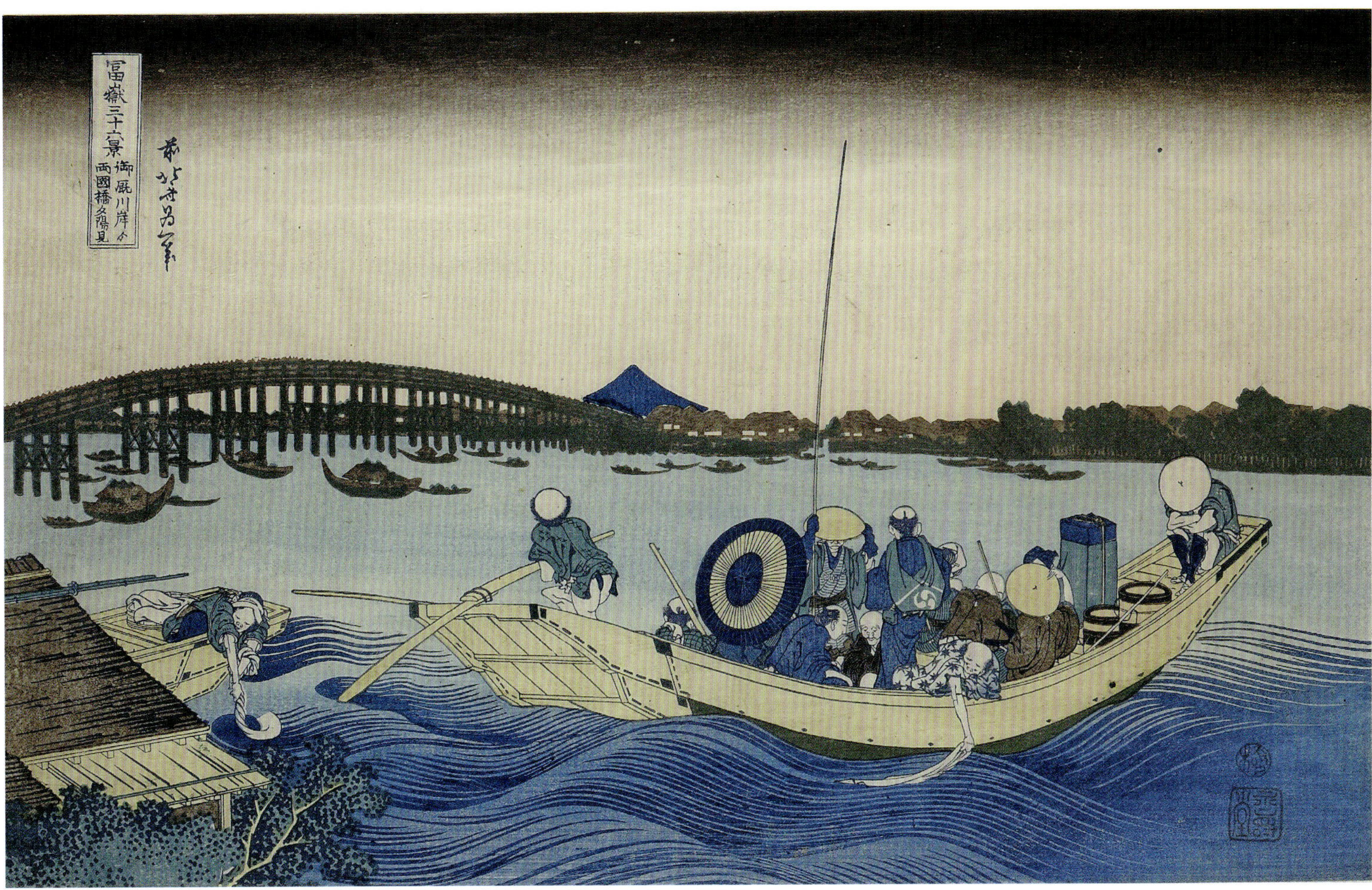

56
Viewing sunset over Ryōgoku bridge from the Onmaya ferry

About 1832
Signature: Saki no Hokusai Iitsu hitsu ('Brush of Iitsu, the former Hokusai')
Colour woodblock, published by Nishimuraya Yohachi, 24.6 × 37.8 cm
Provenance: Arthur Morrison
Literature: MSU 1991, no. 12; Clark 2001, no. 56; Keyes & Morse 2015, no. 616
British Museum, 1906,1220,0.550

The Onmaya ferry has just set out from Ishiwara-chō in Honjo on the far, east bank of the Sumida river. The government's stables had once been located in Miyoshi-chō on the opposite, west bank of the river, and the area came to be called Onmayagashi ('Stable embankment'). The disparate passengers with their varied loads are generally looking away from us, admiring Fuji silhouetted against the evening sky, just above Ryōgoku bridge. Hokusai skilfully captures the psychology of strangers brought together, who studiously ignore one another. The woman doing the washing in her boat is contrasted with the man in the ferry who idly trails his hand towel in the water. RK/TC

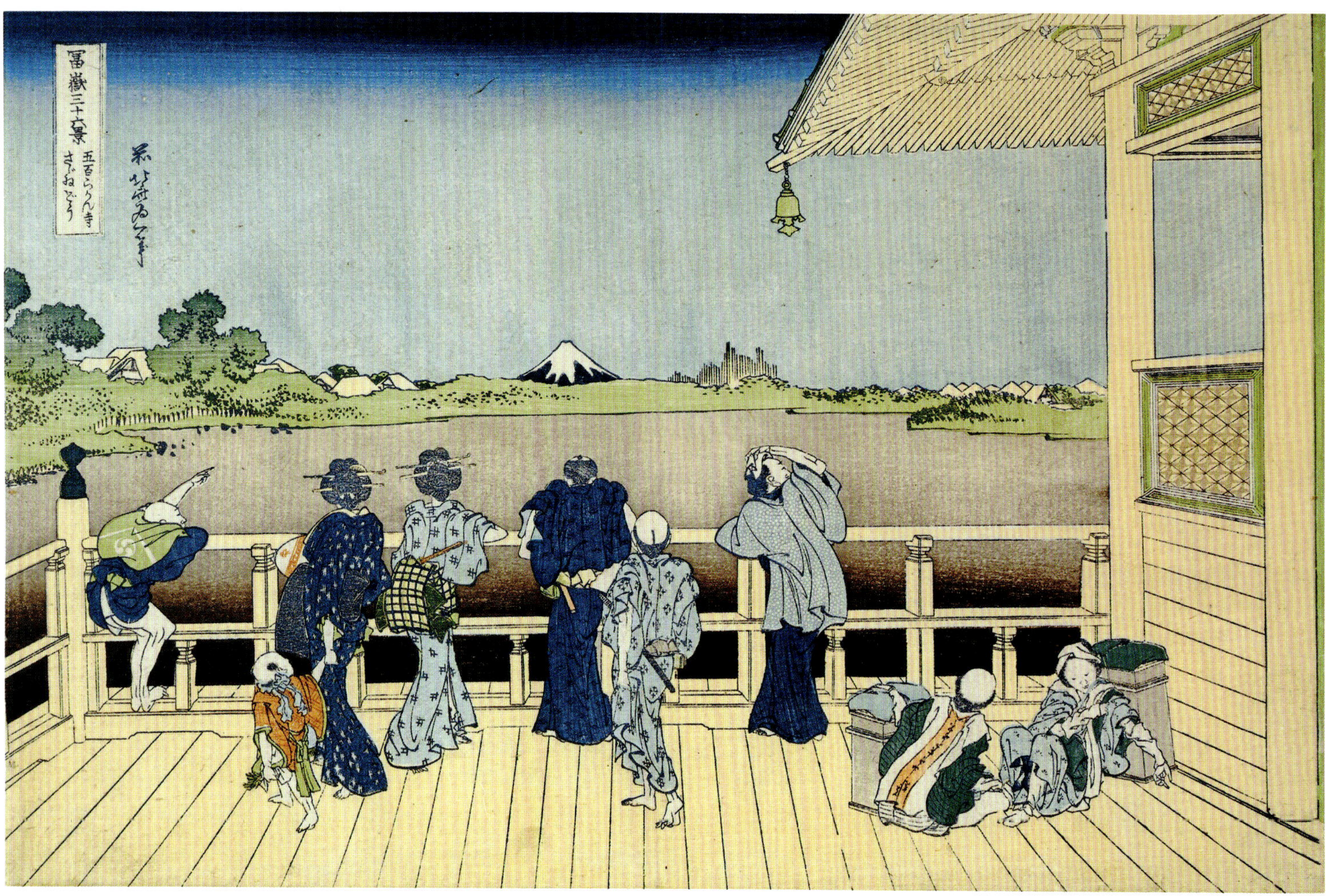

57

Sazai hall, Five Hundred Arhat temple

About 1832

Signature: Saki no Hokusai Iitsu hitsu ('Brush of Iitsu, the former Hokusai')

Colour woodblock, published by Nishimuraya Yohachi, 24.7 × 37.3 cm

Provenance: Arthur Morrison

Literature: MSU 1991, no. 7; Clark 2001, no. 57; Keyes & Morse 2015, no. 611

British Museum, 1906,1220,0.539

Two pilgrims, seated on the right, and a group of city dwellers and their children admire the view back over the city of Edo towards a distant Mt Fuji on the horizon. The converging lines of the architecture encourage us to do the same. The Ōbaku Zen sect temple Gohyaku-rakan-ji, 'temple of the five hundred arhats', was at that time located at Itsutsume village in Honjo, on the eastern outskirts of the city. In addition to five hundred expressively carved, life-size statues of the disciples of the Buddha ('arhats'), it boasted Sazai ('turban shell', or 'three turn') hall – where pilgrims ascended a spiral ramp through three floors and one hundred statues of Bodhisattva Kannon, to a viewing platform at the top. RK/TC

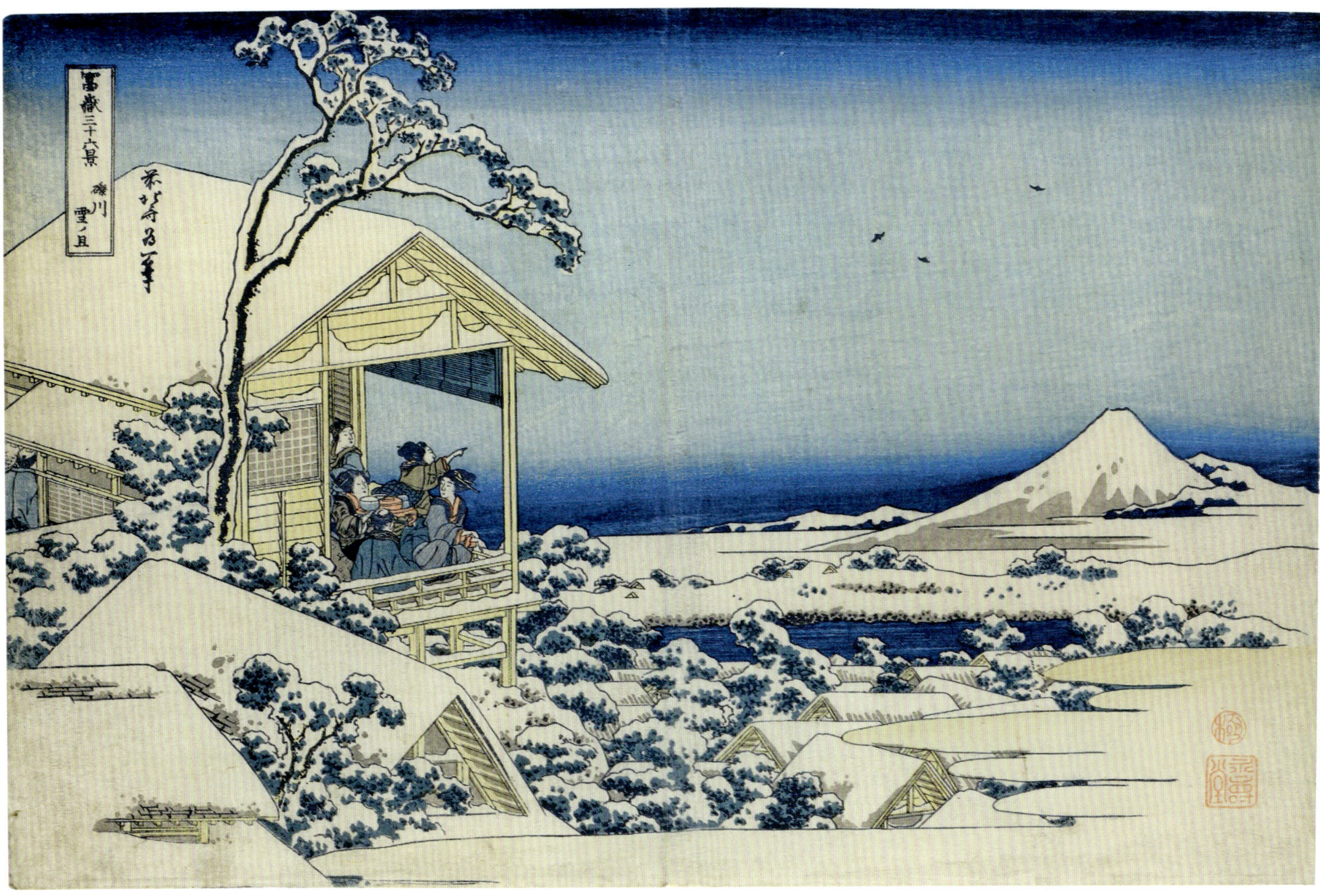

58

Snowy morning, Koishikawa

About 1832

Signature: Saki no Hokusai Iitsu hitsu ('Brush of Iitsu, the former Hokusai')

Colour woodblock, published by Nishimuraya Yohachi, 25.0 × 37.2 cm

Literature: MSU 1991, no. 11; Clark 2001, no. 58; Keyes & Morse 2015, no. 615

British Museum, 1927,0613,0.13, given by R. N. Shaw

After heavy overnight snow, an elegant party has assembled in a room with a fine vantage in the crisp early morning sunlight over snow-clad roofs and the Edo river towards Mt Fuji. One woman seems to point to three birds circling in the sky. Koishikawa, north of Suidōbashi, was an area of wealthy samurai residences and large religious holdings in the 1830s. Hokusai's view is thought to show the bustling neighbourhood in front of Denzūin temple. RK/TC

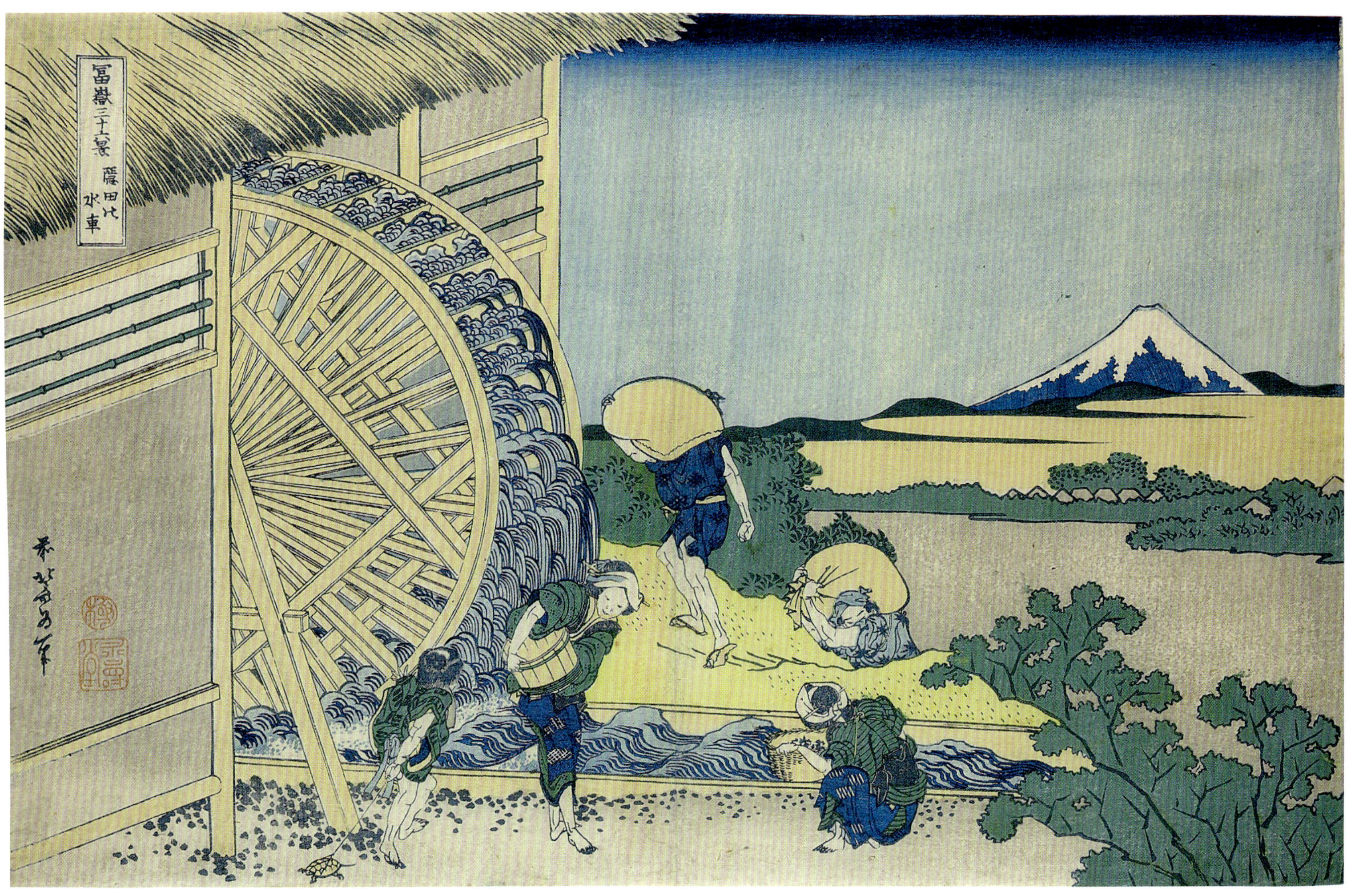

59

Onden waterwheel

About 1832
Signature: Saki no Hokusai Iitsu hitsu ('Brush of Iitsu,
the former Hokusai')
Colour woodblock, published by Nishimuraya Yohachi,
25.1 × 37.9 cm
Provenance: Charles Ricketts & Charles Shannon
Literature: MSU 1991, no. 9; Clark 2001, no. 59;
Keyes & Morse 2015, no. 613
British Museum, 1937,0710,0.164, bequeathed by
Charles Shannon RA

Two men carry sacks of grain up towards a mill, where
two women are busy next to the mill race. Work is
given priority, and only the small boy tugging his
obdurate terrapin on a string has the time to gaze at
Mt Fuji. Hokusai is careful to delineate how the gurgling
water starts to cascade as the waterwheel turns. Onden
was a farming village with many waterwheels on the
Shibuya river; it is now the bustling Harajuku and
Jingūmae districts of Tokyo. RK/TC

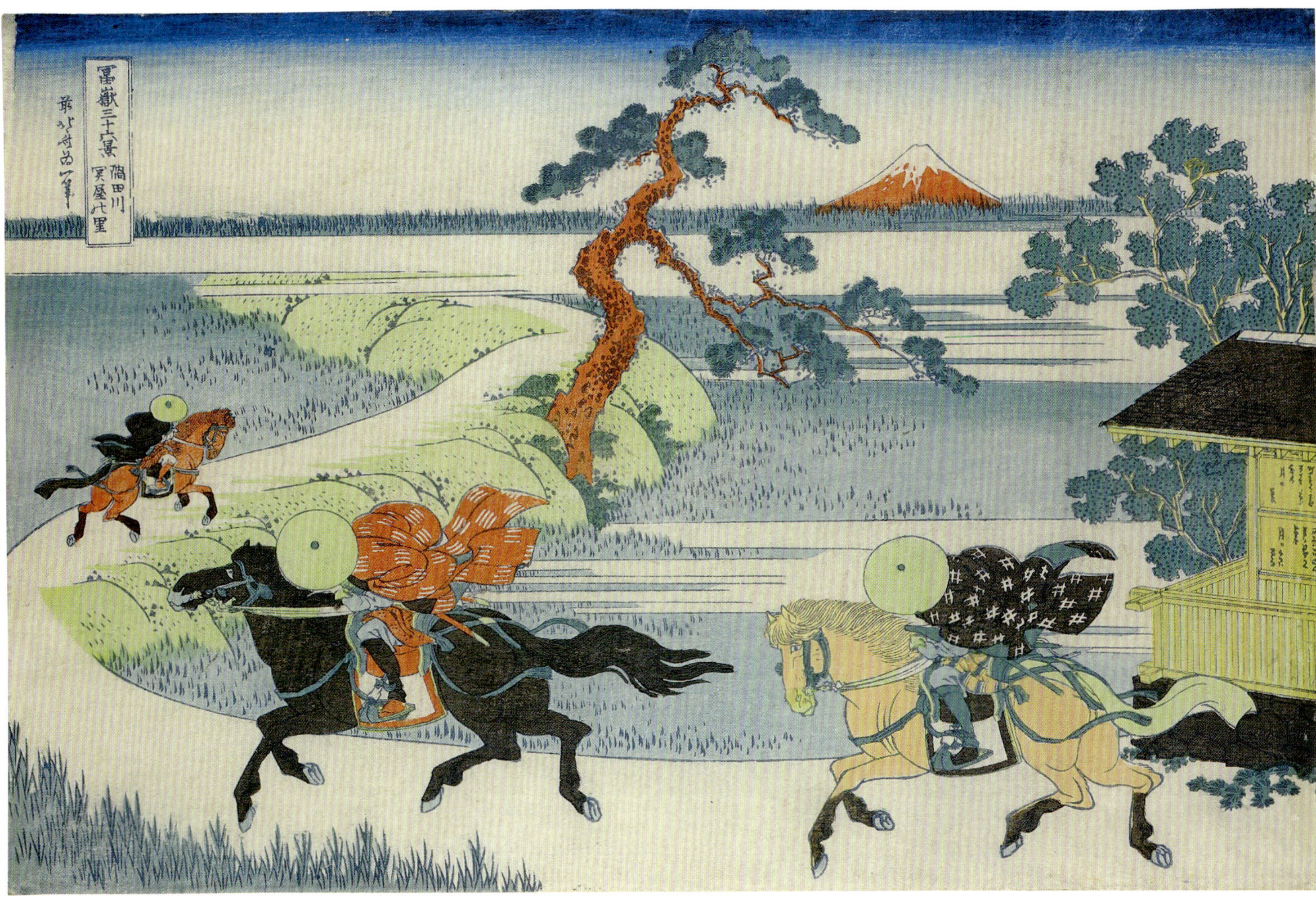

60

Sumida river, Sekiya villages

About 1832
Signature: Saki no Hokusai Iitsu hitsu ('Brush of Iitsu, the former Hokusai')
Colour woodblock, published by Nishimuraya Yohachi, 25.6 × 37.6 cm
Provenance: Charles Ricketts & Charles Shannon
Literature: MSU 1991, no. 13; Clark 2001, no. 61; Keyes & Morse 2015, no. 617
British Museum, 1937,0710,0.138, bequeathed by Charles Shannon RA

Three samurai horsemen, perhaps official messengers, race along the dykes through empty fields. The repeating forms of the horsemen, with their wind-blown robes, accentuate their speed. The notice boards on the right are for official proclamations, so this is a well-frequented highway. Early morning mists recede, but Mt Fuji is still catching the rays of the rising sun. Sekiya was a rural area on the north bank of the Sumida river between the Ayase river and Senju. RK/TC

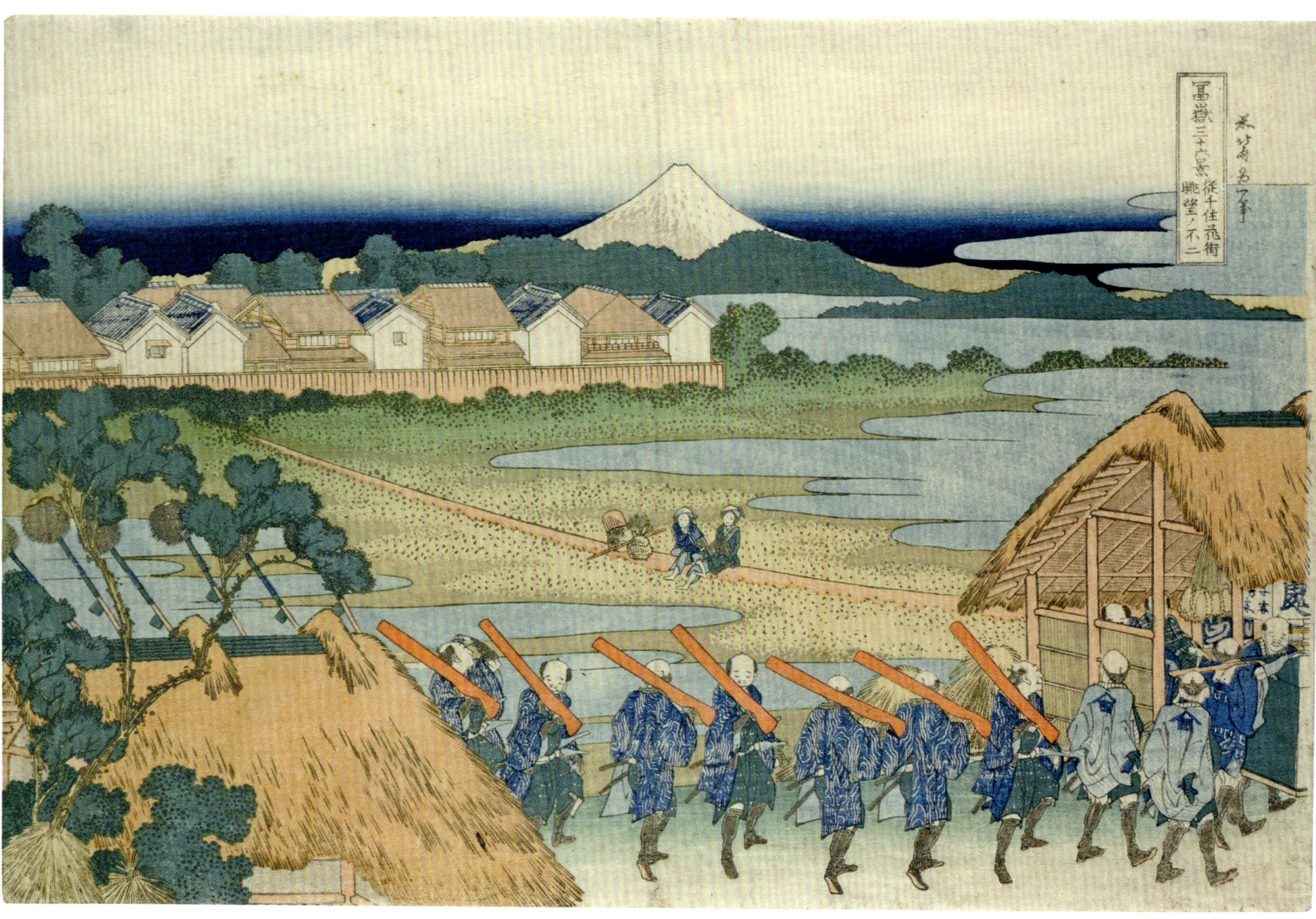

61

Fuji seen in the distance from Senju pleasure quarter

About 1833
Signature: Saki no Hokusai Iitsu hitsu ('Brush of Iitsu, the former Hokusai')
Colour woodblock, published by Nishimuraya Yohachi, 25.5 × 37.2 cm
Provenance: Charles Ricketts & Charles Shannon
Literature: MSU 1991, no. 15; Clark 2001, no. 64; Keyes & Morse 2015, no. 619
British Museum, 1937,0710,0.136, bequeathed by Charles Shannon RA

A feudal lord's procession marches towards Senju bridge and the highway to the north. Foot soldiers carry rifles in red cloth covers and are followed by spear-carriers. The regimentation of the samurai is contrasted with the relaxed poses of two farming women in the field and townsmen in a roadside shop, which sells straw sandals and other travel kit. The buildings in the background at left are Senju's brothel district, one of five in Edo licensed by the government. This is one of ten supplementary designs added to the series, probably in 1833, with black outlines replacing the earlier blue. RK/TC

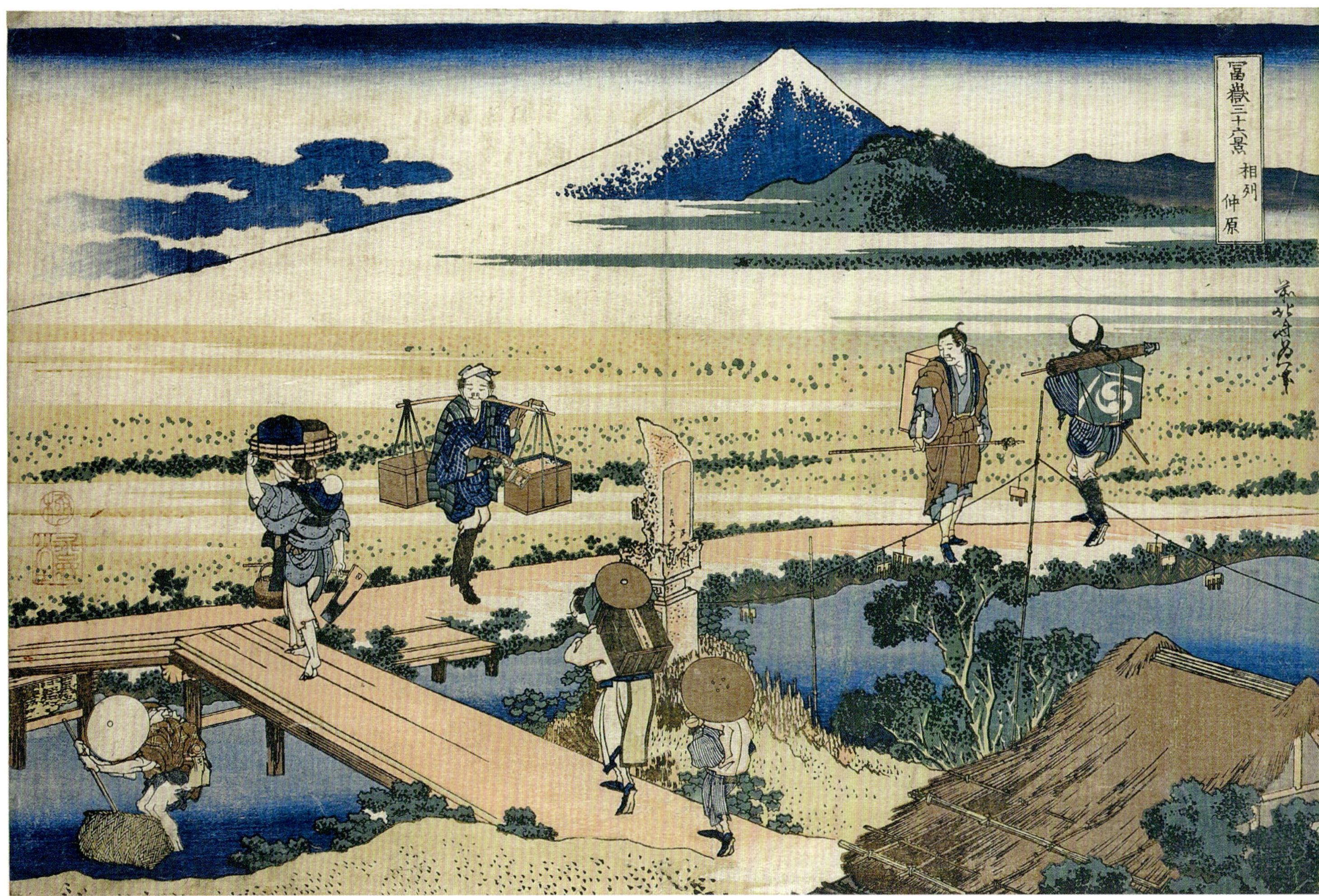

62

Nakahara, Sagami province

About 1833
Signature: Saki no Hokusai Iitsu hitsu ('Brush of Iitsu, the former Hokusai')
Colour woodblock, published by Nishimuraya Yohachi, 25.5 × 37.7 cm
Provenance: Charles Ricketts & Charles Shannon
Literature: MSU 1991, no. 26; Clark 2001, no. 66; Keyes & Morse 2015, no. 630
British Museum, 1937,0710,0.124, bequeathed by Charles Shannon RA
Osaka only

Nakahara was the first village on the road to Ōyama that branched off the Tōkaidō highway at Hiratsuka. The men carrying portable shrines on their backs are pilgrims to the Shingon sect temple on Mt Ōyama, which was only open to practitioners for a brief period in late summer. Beneath the bridge a man fishes for river shellfish. The roadside statue seems to be a replica of the stone Fudō that was worshipped at the mountain temple. The pack at the right is marked with the emblem of the publisher, Nishimuraya. RK/TC

63

Ōno Shinden, Suruga province

About 1833
Signature: Saki no Hokusai Iitsu hitsu ('Brush of Iitsu,
the former Hokusai')
Colour woodblock, published by Nishimuraya Yohachi,
25.0 × 36.7 cm
Literature: MSU 1991, no. 31; Clark 2001, no. 68;
Keyes & Morse 2015, no. 635
British Museum, 1907,0322,0.1, given by William
Cleverly Alexander

Farmers return home with their oxen heavily laden
with cut reeds. The setting sun catches the gathering
mists. Ōno Shinden is an area between Hara and
Yoshiwara on the Tōkaidō highway, almost due south
of Mt Fuji. It was famous for its clear, unobstructed
view of the mountain. Shinden means 'new rice fields',
but Hokusai has drawn empty marshland with egrets
in flight. RK/TC

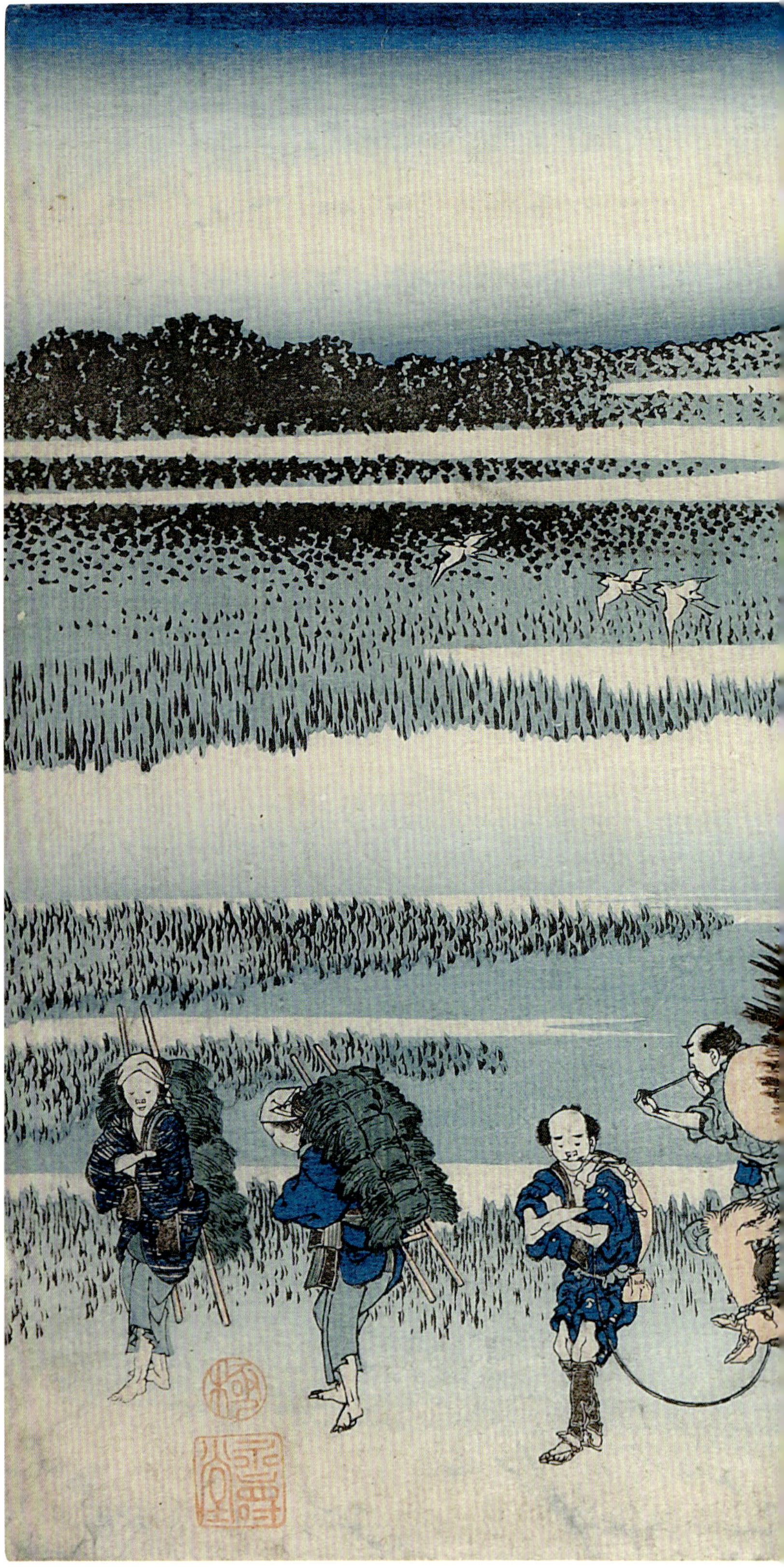

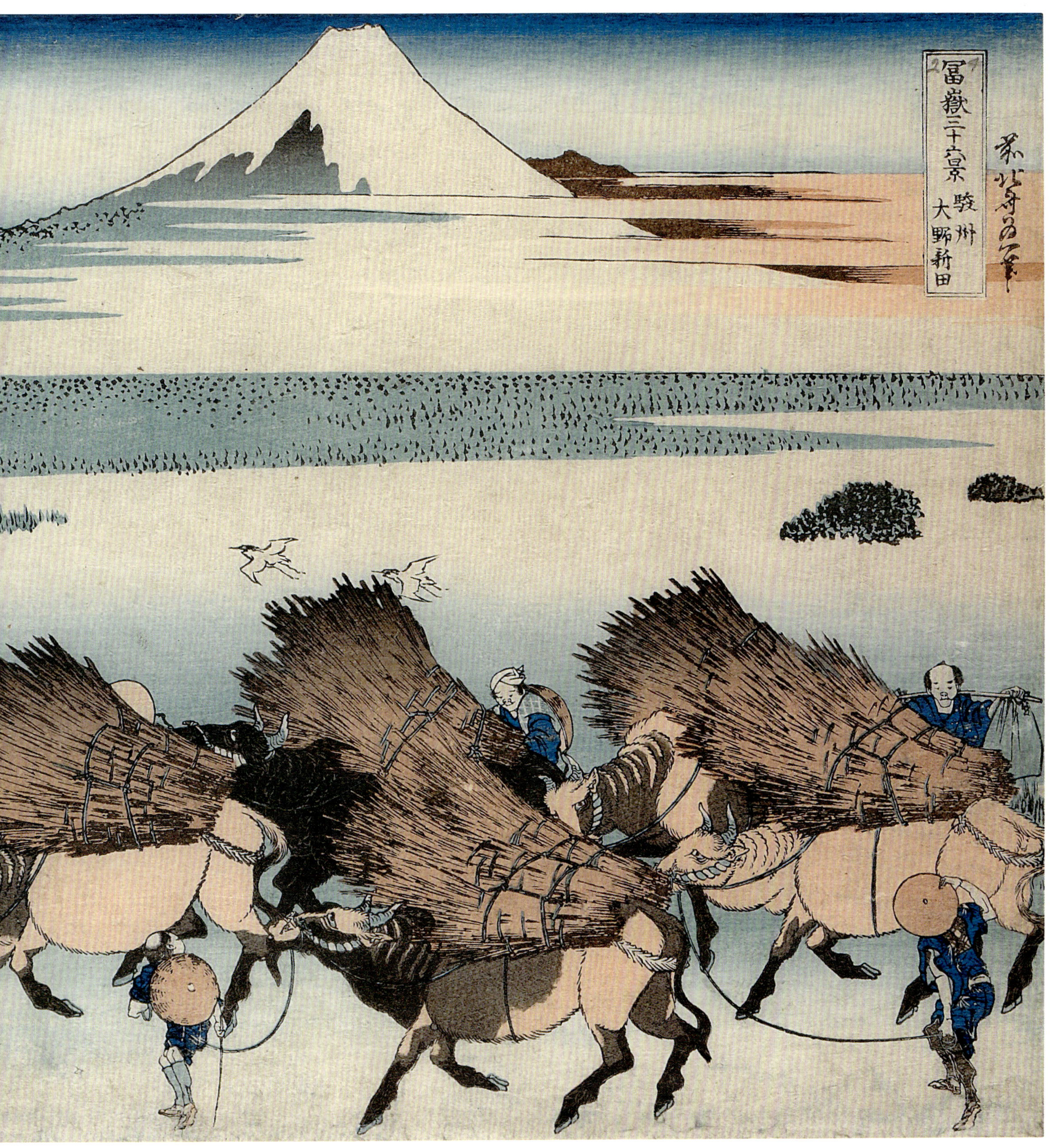

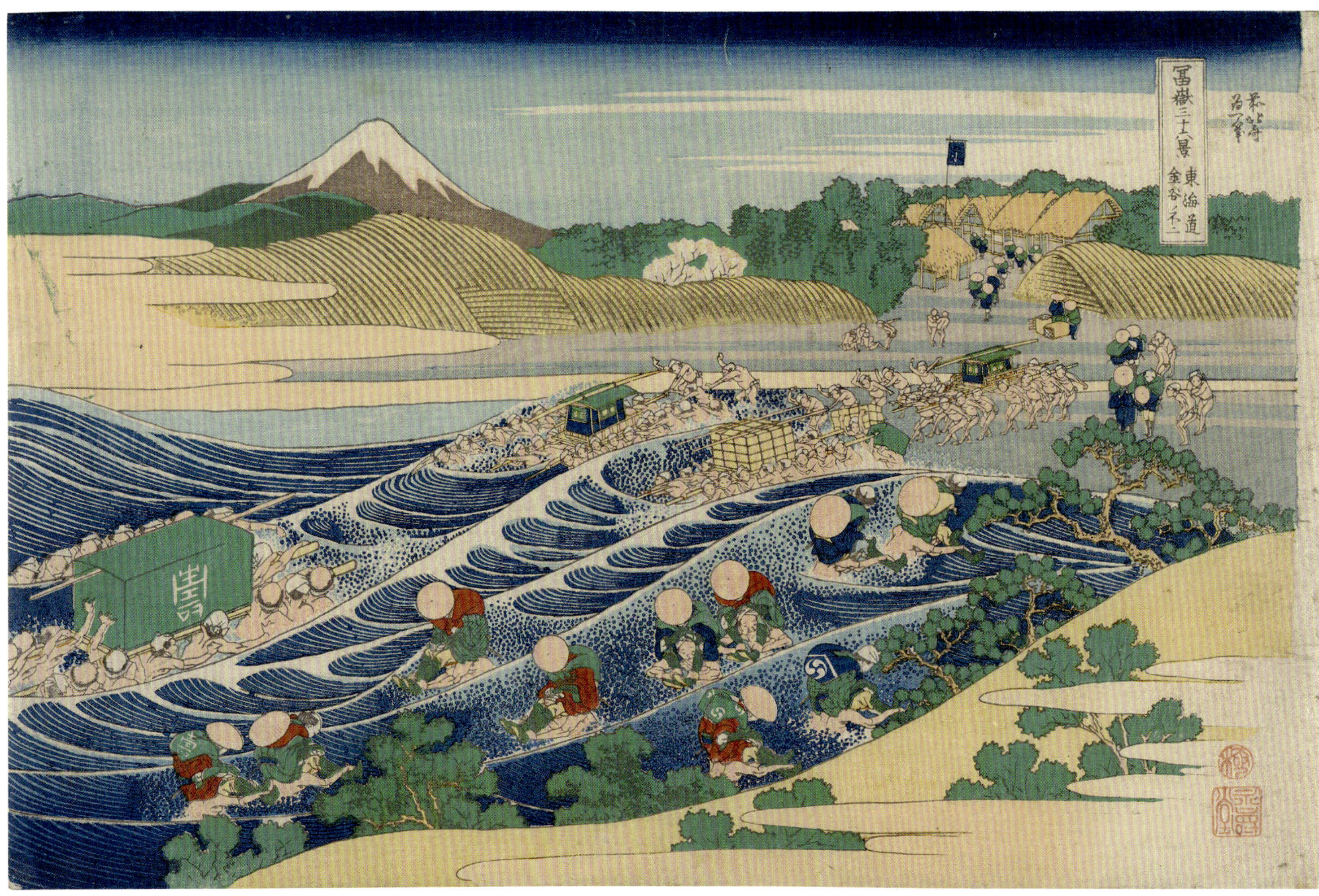

64

Fuji from Kanaya, Tōkaidō highway

About 1833
Signature: Saki no Hokusai Iitsu hitsu ('Brush of Iitsu, the former Hokusai')
Colour woodblock, published by Nishimuraya Yohachi, 25.5 × 37.5 cm
Provenance: Charles Ricketts & Charles Shannon
Literature: MSU 1991, no. 37; Clark 2001, no. 69; Keyes & Morse 2015, no. 641
British Museum, 1937,0710,0.149, bequeathed by Charles Shannon RA
Osaka only

Kanaya is a village situated on the east shore of the broad, shallow Ōi river where it cut across the Tōkaidō highway. Travellers hired porters to carry them and their luggage and goods across – either seated directly on the porters' shoulders, or by having their palanquins transported on rafts. Hokusai uses a close-packed, repeating pattern of swell and foam to suggest a treacherous current. The large box, left, and two of the packs are marked with the emblem of the publisher, Nishimuraya. RK/TC

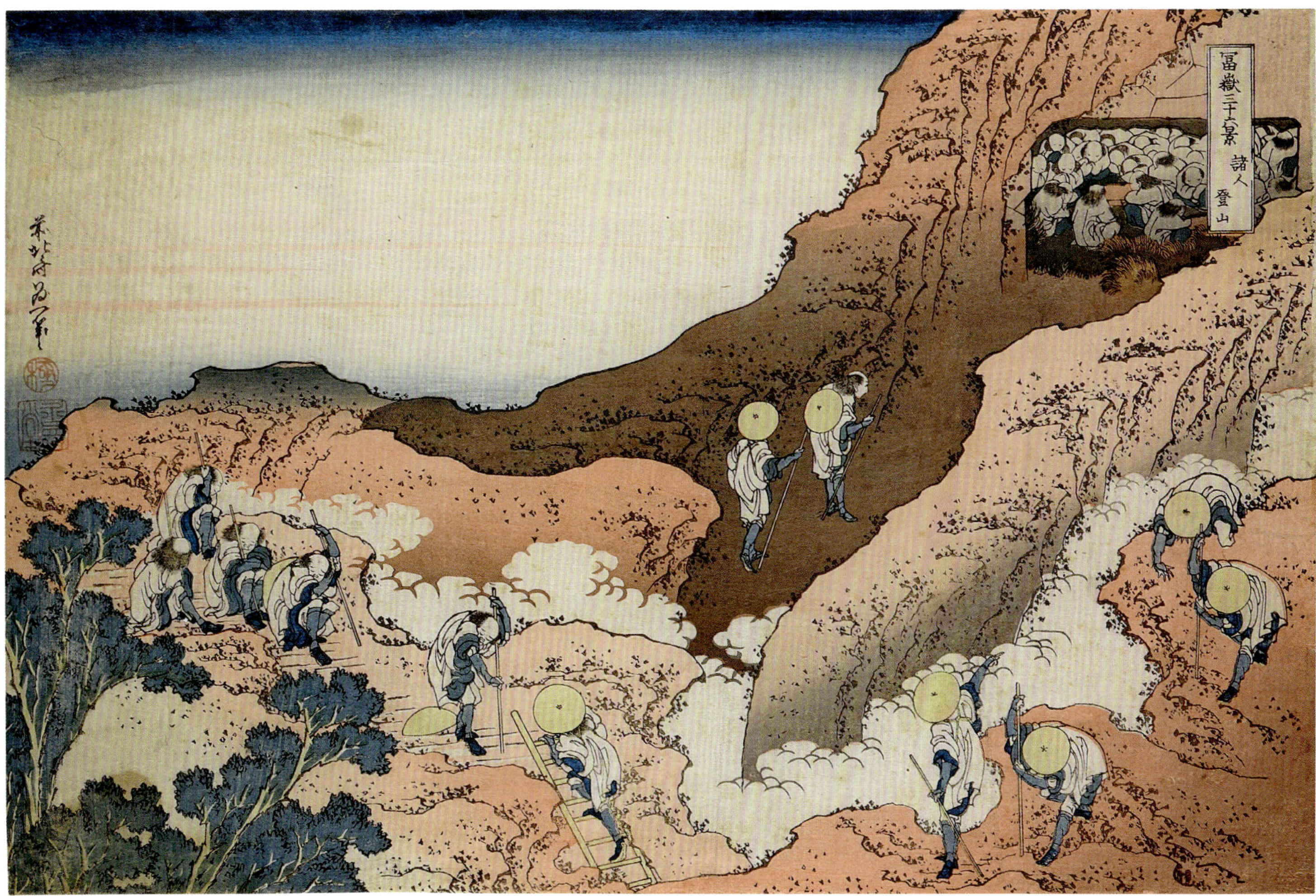

65
Various people climbing the mountain

About 1833
Signature: Saki no Hokusai Iitsu hitsu ('Brush of Iitsu, the former Hokusai')
Colour woodblock, published by Nishimuraya Yohachi, 25.8 × 37.7 cm
Provenance: Charles Ricketts & Charles Shannon
Literature: MSU 1991, no. 34; Clark 2001, no. 70; Keyes & Morse 2015, no. 638
British Museum, 1937,0710,0.167, bequeathed by Charles Shannon RA

Male pilgrims with matching white robes, travelling hats and poles clamber over rocks and climb a ladder towards a cave where others are already huddled at rest. A pink glow in the sky suggests they are about to make their final ascent to greet the sunrise from the peak. The cave may evoke Eboshi-iwa, where the charismatic preacher Jikigyō Miroku fasted himself to death in 1733, leading to a rapid expansion of the 'Fuji cult' (*Fuji-kō*) among his followers. This is the only design showing the experience of being on Mt Fuji, and perhaps it was intended to complete the series. RK/TC

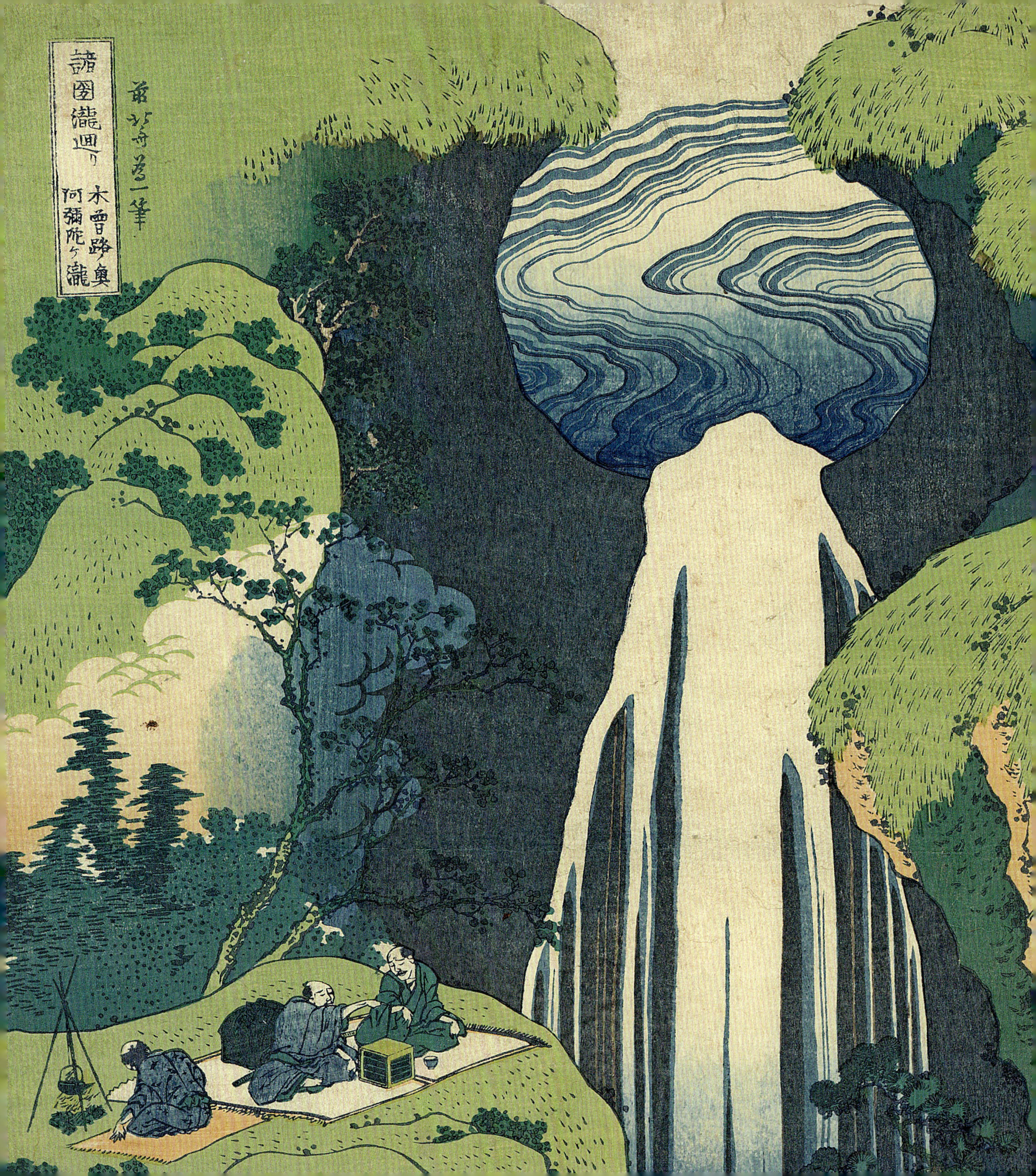

諸国瀧廻り
木曾路ノ奥阿彌陀ヶ瀧
前北斎為一筆

Worlds seen

Hokusai was a meticulous observer of the social and natural worlds. He started as an artist of the 'floating world' (ukiyo-e) (cat. 1), and he continued to depict figure subjects throughout his career (e.g. cats 113, 114, 148). By the time he turned sixty, though, they were just part of an encyclopaedic account of the visible world. Hokusai worked tirelessly to capture what he called the 'form of things': physiological differences (e.g. cat. 61) and affective states (e.g. cat. 114); the skilled motions of a craftsman (cat. 55) or the coordination of labour (cat. 75); botanical and zoological minutiae (cats 82 ff.); and the way in which land, light and water combine (*Thirty-Six Views of Mt Fuji*, cats 41–65). A subject or composition that had appeared in one medium might well reappear in another, travelling from brush drawing manuals to prints (cats 82 ff.), for example, or vice versa (cats 103, 104).

These pictures were often the result of close observation, but Hokusai's ambition was not merely realistic depiction. First, he was both drawing on and breaking with long pictorial traditions, of bird-and-flower painting and of 'famous places', wherein nature was over-written with literary reference and cultural meaning (e.g. cats 78, 115). He also looked to his own, immediate artistic predecessors, who provided models for compositions that could be used to reveal the beauty and wonder of this world (for example Utamaro, cat. 88).

In addition, Hokusai lived at a time when horizons were generally local. Travel was only possible on foot or by horse. But Hokusai did not need to see something to depict it. He had access to a wealth of information and illustrations about life in the Japanese archipelago and beyond. He was anyway not trying to produce a simple documentary record. A 'tour' of famous waterfalls could include both places he knew well (cat. 66) and imaginative evocations of famous but inaccessible places he may never have visited (cat. 67). A landscape could be the result of a vision (cat. 74).

Finally, Hokusai's designs were less about observed phenomena than making his subjects speak a larger truth about the connectedness of things: male and female (cat. 100), for example, or larger groups (cat. 108); animal and vegetable (cat. 87); the physical and the immaterial (cat. 83); micro and macro (cat. 67), and therefore, ultimately, the human and the divine. Hokusai's brush sought to provide a way for the viewer to see the mystery in the everyday (cat. 117), to enter communion with, for example, a cormorant (cat. 101) and thereby a world beyond the surface of things. AL

Tour of Waterfalls in Various Provinces (*Shokoku taki-meguri*)

Throughout his life, Hokusai strove to explore and express transformation in nature, particularly the varied appearances of water. Waves, currents, waterfalls, rain and snow formed an important subject for him, as is clear from *Hokusai's Sketches* (*Hokusai manga*, cats 164, 165) and other works. This series, featuring eight different waterfalls in various provinces in Japan, is a major product of this interest. Some compositions apparently derive from Hokusai's own observations, others from the pages of illustrated gazetteers (*meisho zue*). In all the prints the artist emphasizes the contrasting forms of the eight waterfalls (six of which are seen here, cats 66–71); we savour his powers of formal invention, allowing each waterfall its distinctive personality. The signatures on the eight prints can be divided into two types according to the way in which the character 'i' (of Iitsu) is written: a first group comprises the designs for the falls of Aoigaoka, Yōrō, Kirifuri and Kiyotaki, where it is written in formal *kaisho* script; and a second, comprising those for Ono, Uma-arai, Amida and Roben, where it is written in cursive *sōsho* script. Considering the way in which Hokusai's signature changed in the course of other series at this time, such as *Thirty-Six Views of Mt Fuji* (cats 41–65), the first group was probably published a little earlier than the second, likely around the New Year of 1833. At the back of *Iroage Danshichi-jima*, a book published at the same time, is an advert that reads, '*Tour of Waterfalls in Various Provinces*, designed by the same artist.... Like his previous work, these will be highly unusual pictures.' AS

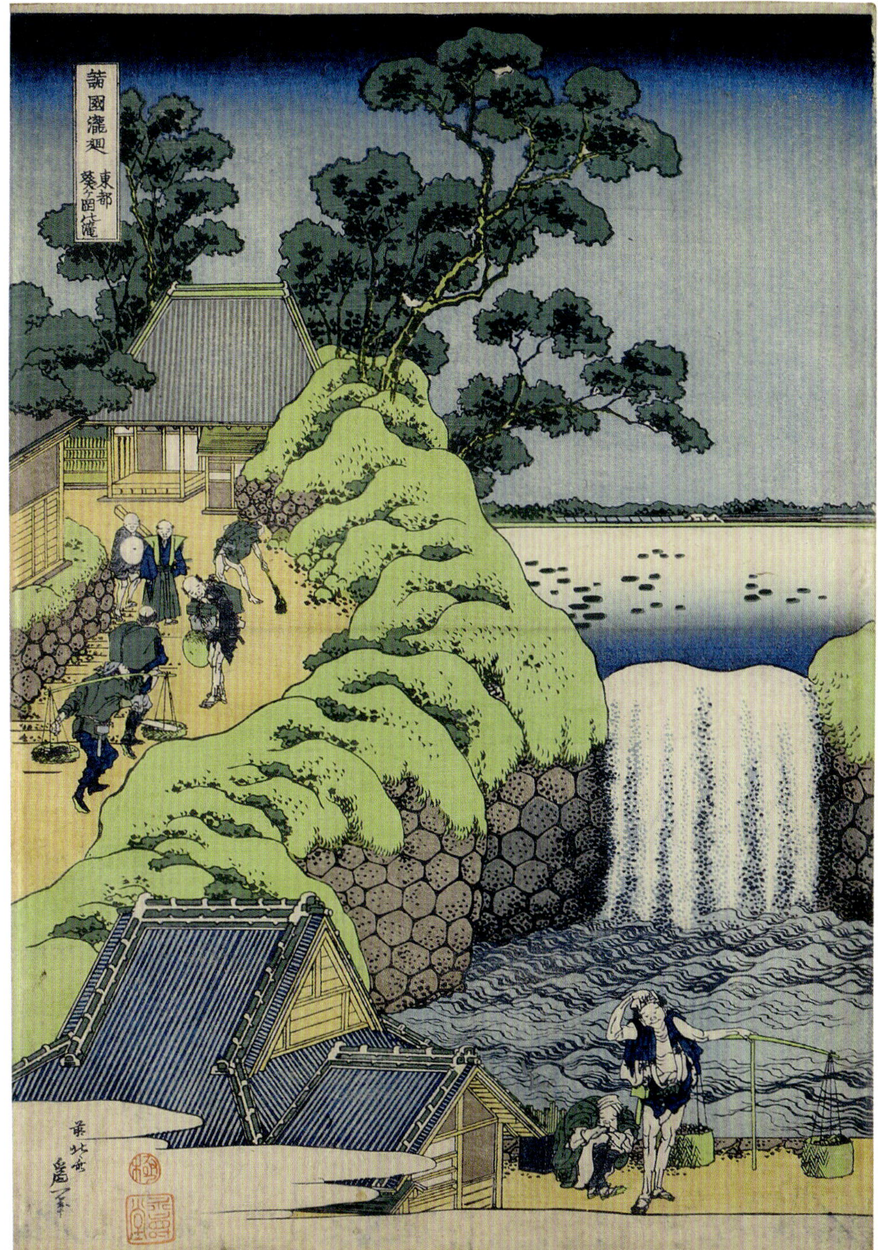

66

Aoigaoka waterfall, Edo

About 1833
Signature: Saki no Hokusai Iitsu hitsu ('Brush of Iitsu, the former Hokusai')
Colour woodblock, published by Nishimuraya Yohachi, 38.0 × 26.0 cm
Provenance: Charles Ricketts & Charles Shannon
Literature: MSU 1991, no. 74; RA 1991, no. 43; TNM 2005, no. 313; Keyes & Morse 2015, no. 688
British Museum, 1937,0710,0.197, bequeathed by Charles Shannon RA
Osaka only

What Hokusai here calls a waterfall was in fact a weir at the north end of the Akasaka reservoir at Aoigaoka, in Edo. The view is from in front of the upper residence of the Marugame fief looking west towards Aoizaka. A constant stream of worshippers came to the Kompira shrine in the precincts of the residence. The buildings at the top of the slope and in the bottom left corner are guard posts. There is no record of this weir having been called a waterfall before Hokusai's time, and doing so seems to have been his idea (Hinohara 2013, p. 44). With this print, therefore, Hokusai has coined a new 'famous place' (*meisho*) for the city of Edo. Certainly, many later artists such as Utagawa Hiroshige (1797–1858) would go on to design their own views of Aoi slope and the weir. AS

67

Yōrō waterfall, Mino province

About 1833
Signature: Saki no Hokusai Iitsu hitsu ('Brush of Iitsu, the former Hokusai')
Colour woodblock, published by Nishimuraya Yohachi, 37.0 × 25.0 cm
Provenance: Hayashi Tadamasa; Charles Ricketts & Charles Shannon
Literature: MSU 1991, no. 75; RA 1991, no. 41; Keyes & Morse 2015, no. 690
British Museum, 1937,0710,0.199, bequeathed by Charles Shannon RA
Osaka only

This waterfall in the town of Yōrō, in modern Gifu prefecture, is mentioned in a legend about the filial piety of a son who offered some of its water to his ailing father. Upon drinking it, his father revived. The real falls are some 30 metres (100 ft) in height, but here seem to have been deliberately abbreviated, since depicting the waterfall to scale would mean making the human figures tiny. It is not known whether Hokusai actually visited these falls. The illustration of the same waterfall in the gazetteer *Famous Places on the Kiso Highway* of 1805 suggests that the small building in the bottom right must be a simple rest house for travellers. AS

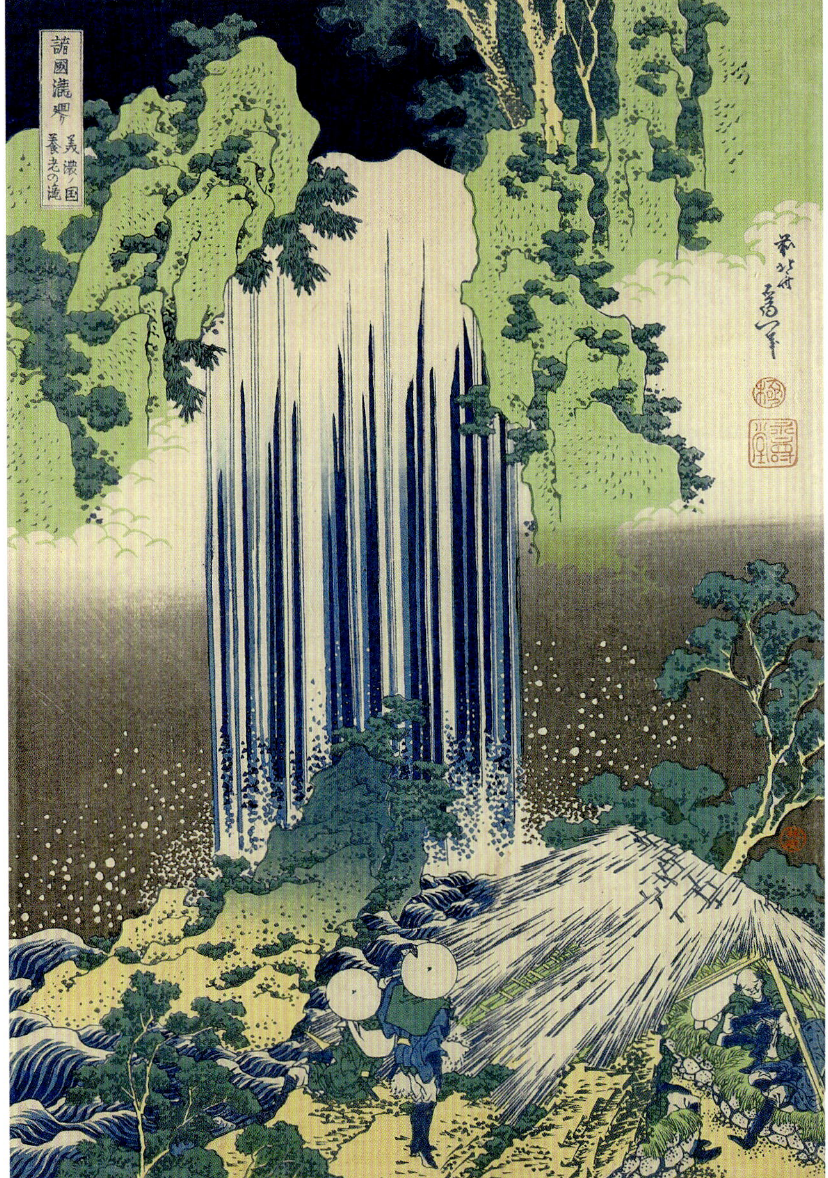

68

Kirifuri waterfall, Mt Kurokami, Shimotsuke province

About 1833
Signature: Saki no Hokusai Iitsu hitsu ('Brush of Iitsu, the former Hokusai')
Colour woodblock, published by Nishimuraya Yohachi, 37.0 × 24.5 cm
Literature: MSU 1991, no. 73; RA 1991, no. 39; TNM 2005, no. 310; Keyes & Morse 2015, no. 683
Tōyō Bunko (The Oriental Library), Tokyo
London only

The Kirifuri falls, a famous waterfall in the mountains of Nikkō, are not actually on Mt Kurokami (also known as Mt Nantai), but about 10 kilometres (6 miles) to the east. Hokusai draws the streams of water as if alive, spreading out like the flow of blood in the human body. In 1837, about four years after this print was issued, Hokusai designed two illustrations of the 'Dragon's Head waterfall' for the gazetteer *Nikkōzan shi* (cat. 72), one of which includes the signature 'Brush of Manji, old man crazy to paint, aged seventy-two', implying that it was drawn in 1831. If sketched from life, this suggests that Hokusai actually visited Nikkō in 1831. This print of the Kirifuri falls may therefore also be based on a sketch made at that time. **AS**

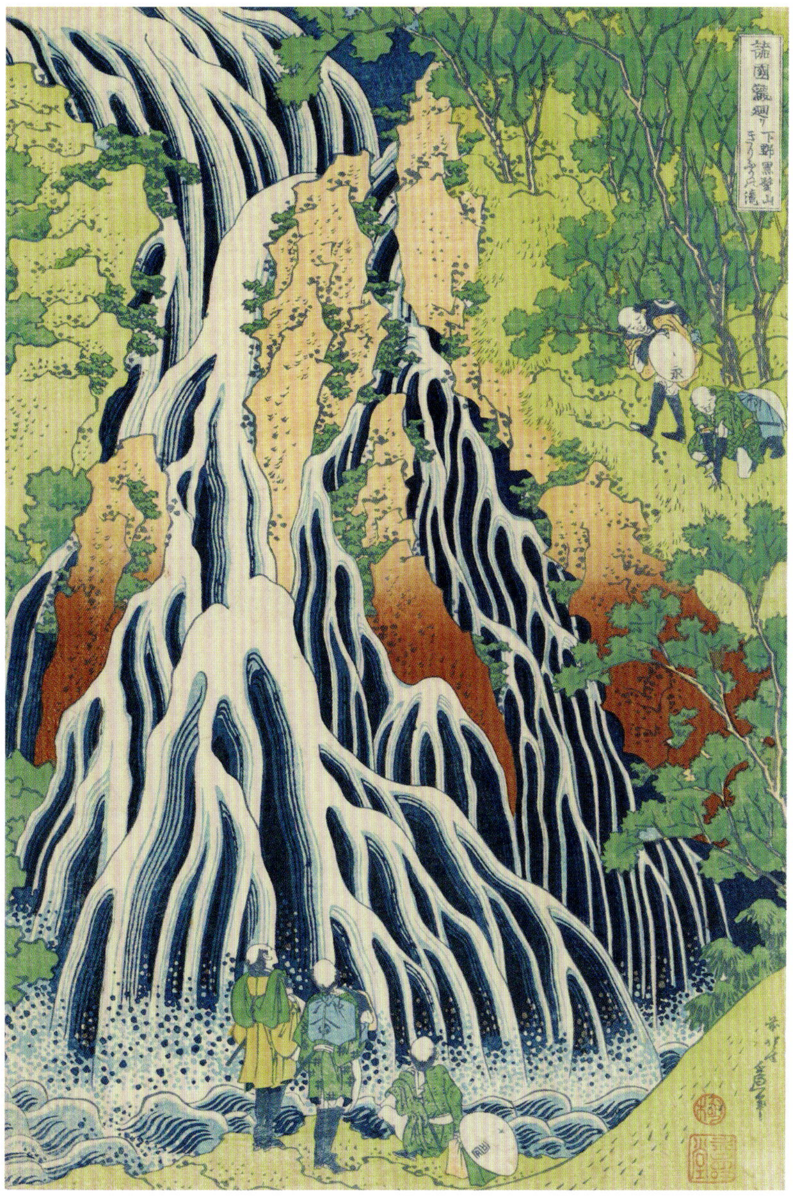

69

Ono waterfall, Kiso highway

About 1833

Signature: Saki no Hokusai Iitsu hitsu ('Brush of Iitsu, the former Hokusai')

Colour woodblock, published by Nishimuraya Yohachi, 38.3 × 25.7 cm

Provenance: Arthur Morrison

Literature: MSU 1991, no. 78; RA 1991, no. 40; TNM 2005, no. 309; Keyes & Morse 2015, no. 684

British Museum, 1906,1220,0.553

This famous waterfall is located near the post-station of Agematsu on the Kiso highway, in Shinano province (modern Nagano prefecture). In volume 7 of *Hokusai's Sketches* (*Hokusai manga*, 1817), Hokusai includes an illustration entitled 'Ono waterfall, Shinano province', suggesting he may have actually visited the spot. The view is from the left side of the falls, so the water appears to bubble upwards at the top, before dropping down. Hokusai and his printer have created a fantastical atmosphere by linking the gradated band of black from above the falls to the coil of pale blue clouds rising from below. The gazetteer *Famous Places on the Kiso Highway* (1805) has an illustration of this waterfall, which allows us to identify the 'Ono teahouse', here in the bottom left (Hinohara 2013), and the shrine to Fudō, projecting towards the waterfall in the centre. In the gazetteer, though, it stands to the left of the small bridge. AS

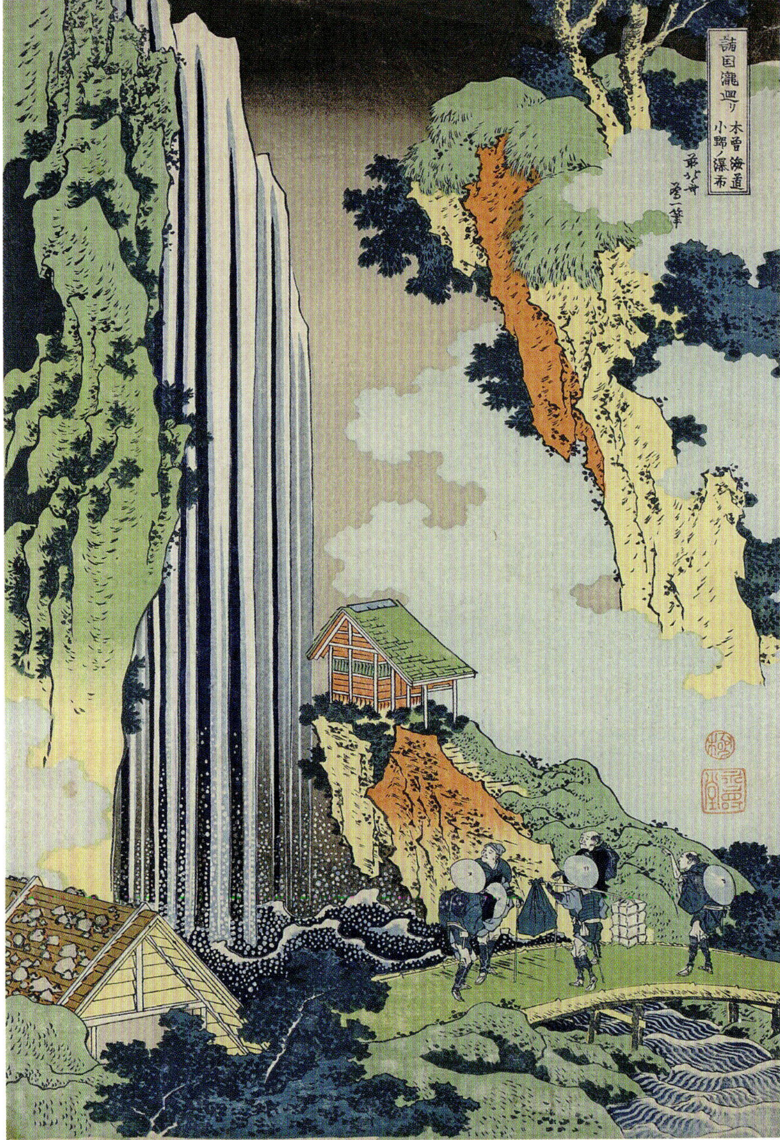

The waterfall where Yoshitsune washed his horse in Yoshino, Yamato province

About 1833
Signature: Saki no Hokusai Iitsu hitsu ('Brush of Iitsu, the former Hokusai')
Colour woodblock, published by Nishimuraya Yohachi, 37.5 × 25.5 cm
Provenance: Charles Ricketts & Charles Shannon
Literature: MSU 1991, no. 71; RA 1991, no. 46; TNM 2005, no. 308; Keyes & Morse 2015, no. 686
British Museum, 1937,0710,0.195, bequeathed by Charles Shannon RA

The print shows a small waterfall in Yoshino where, according to legend, the warrior Minamoto no Yoshitsune (1159–1189) washed his horse (*uma-arai*). There is no direct evidence for this event, although several Yoshino gazetteers contain related accounts. For example, *Yoshino-gun meizan zushi*, in the early 1800s, notes that 'there are still horses [descended from] the one ridden by Yoshitsune in the Ōdai mountains'. Evidently, by the early 1800s, there were legends about Yoshitsune coming to Yoshino on horseback. Perhaps Hokusai visited Yoshino, saw the falls, heard the legends and drew the picture? Alternatively, he may simply have fabricated the story (Hinohara 2013, p. 58). The falls zigzag down the picture, flowing to the left in the centre, then switching to the right where the two men are washing the horse, and then finally back to left and out of the image. AS

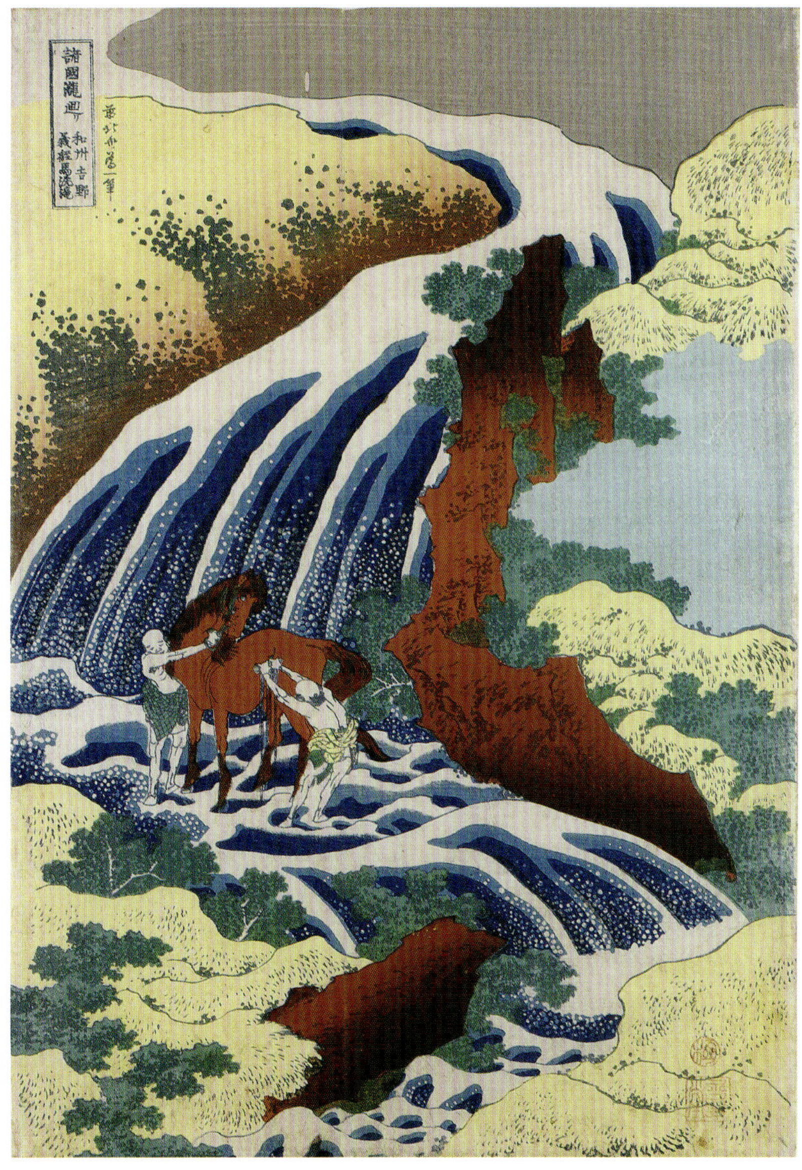

Amida waterfall, deep beyond the Kiso highway

About 1833
Signature: Saki no Hokusai Iitsu hitsu ('Brush of Iitsu, the former Hokusai')
Colour woodblock, published by Nishimuraya Yohachi, 37.0 × 24.5 cm
Literature: MSU 1991, no. 76; RA 1991, no. 42; Keyes & Morse 2015, no. 687
Tōyō Bunko (The Oriental Library), Tokyo
London only

This large waterfall, some 60 metres (almost 200 ft) in height, is located deep in the mountains near Gujō city, in modern Gifu prefecture. Originally named Long waterfall, it was renamed Amida waterfall in the early 1500s by a monk who experienced a vision of Amida while practising asceticism in a cavern nearby. Hokusai creates a striking contrast between the meandering currents of water, like marbling, in the round opening at the head of the falls and the sudden perpendicular drop of the falls themselves. Three men are shown warming saké over a fire and calmly enjoying the view down into the waterfall from a high ledge. Hokusai probably composed this design without seeing the waterfall or having a reference to a published source – the falls are quite a long way from the Kiso highway. His imagination thus freed, he produced a strikingly idiosyncratic design. The Amida waterfall and the Kirifuri falls (cat. 68) are the two most admired designs in the series. AS

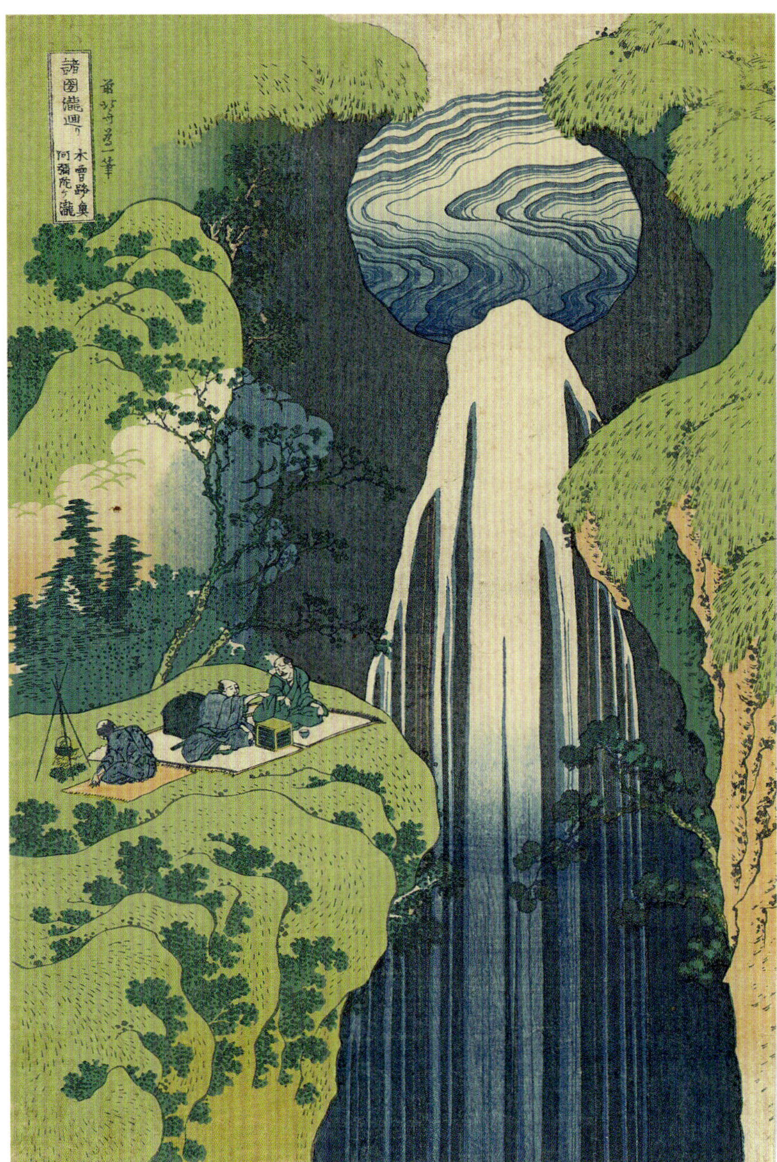

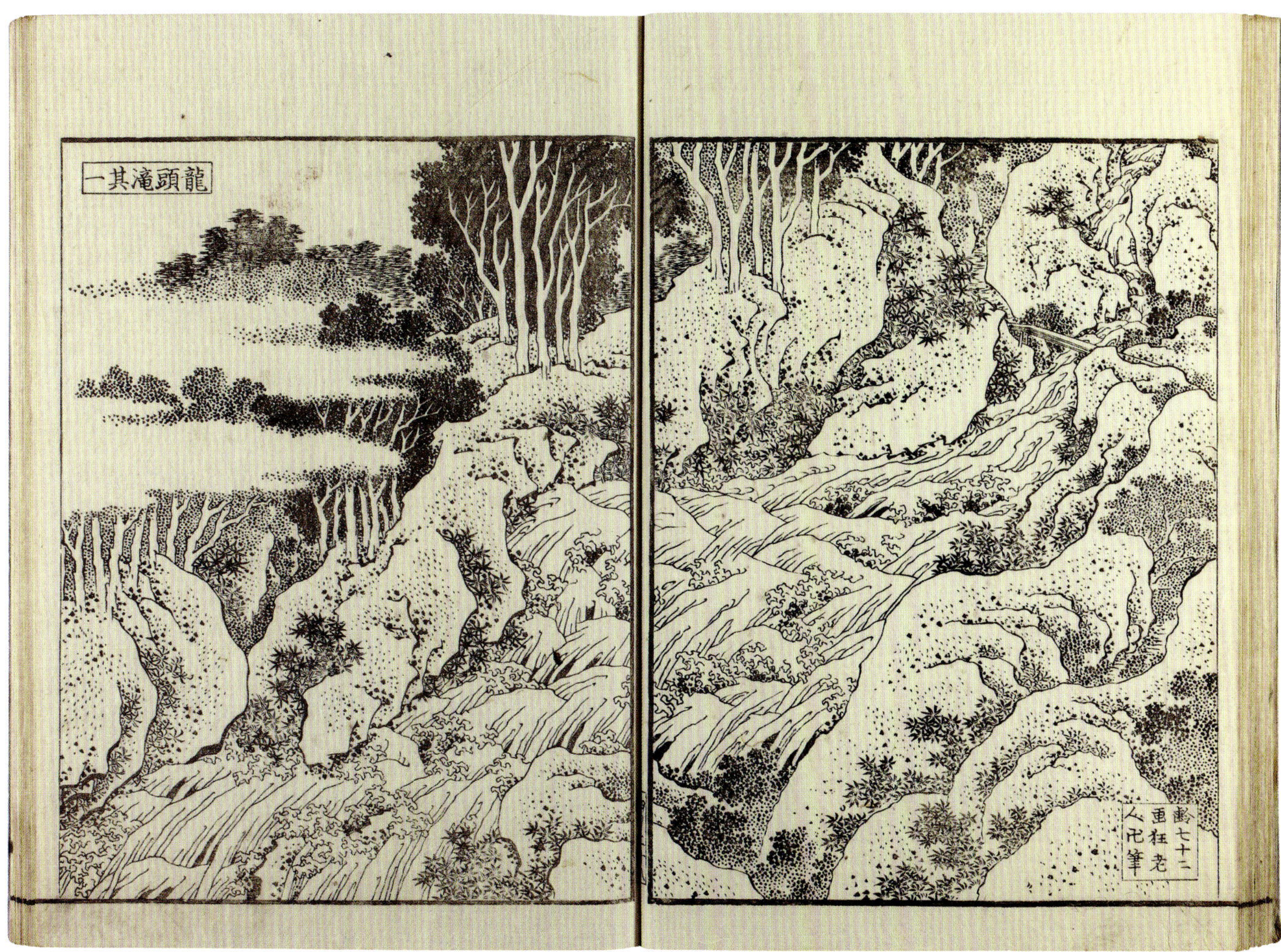

Dragon's Head waterfall, no. 1, from *Record of Mt Nikkō (Nikkōzan shi)*

1837

Signature: Yowai nanajūni / gakyō rō / jin Manji hitsu ('Brush of Manji, old man crazy to paint, aged seventy-two')

Woodblock illustrated book, vol. 4 (of 5), published by Suharaya Ihachi and others, 26.0 × 18.5 cm (covers)

Literature: Paris 2014, no. 531

Ebi collection, UK, Ebi0562

Record of Mt Nikkō (Nikkōzan shi) is a gazetteer explaining the history, geography and sacred festivals of the Mt Nikkō area, which was published jointly by ten Edo firms at the New Year of 1837; however, the preface is dated 1825. The illustrations are by a large number of different artists. Hokusai contributed two illustrations to volume 4, 'Dragon's Head waterfall, no. 1' and 'no. 2', showing the famous falls at Yukawa. The signatures are, respectively, 'Brush of Manji, old man crazy to paint, aged seventy-two' (no. 1) and 'Painting the essence, Manji, old man crazy to paint, at special request' (no. 2). Hokusai was seventy-two in 1831 and the views are drawn quite naturalistically, raising the strong possibility that he visited Nikkō in that year and sketched the scenes from life. Both illustrations capture brilliantly the torrents of water rushing down gorges in the mountains. AS

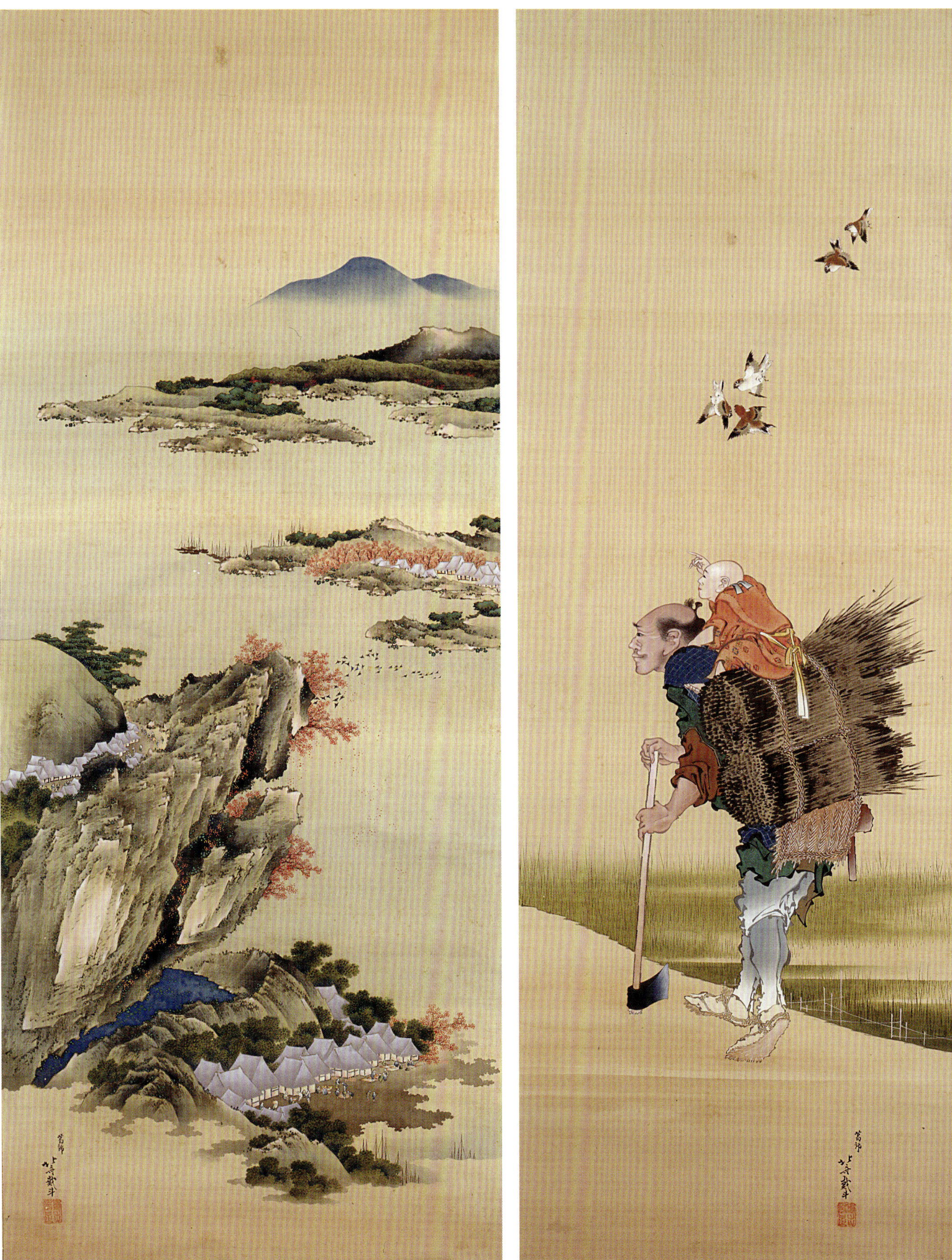

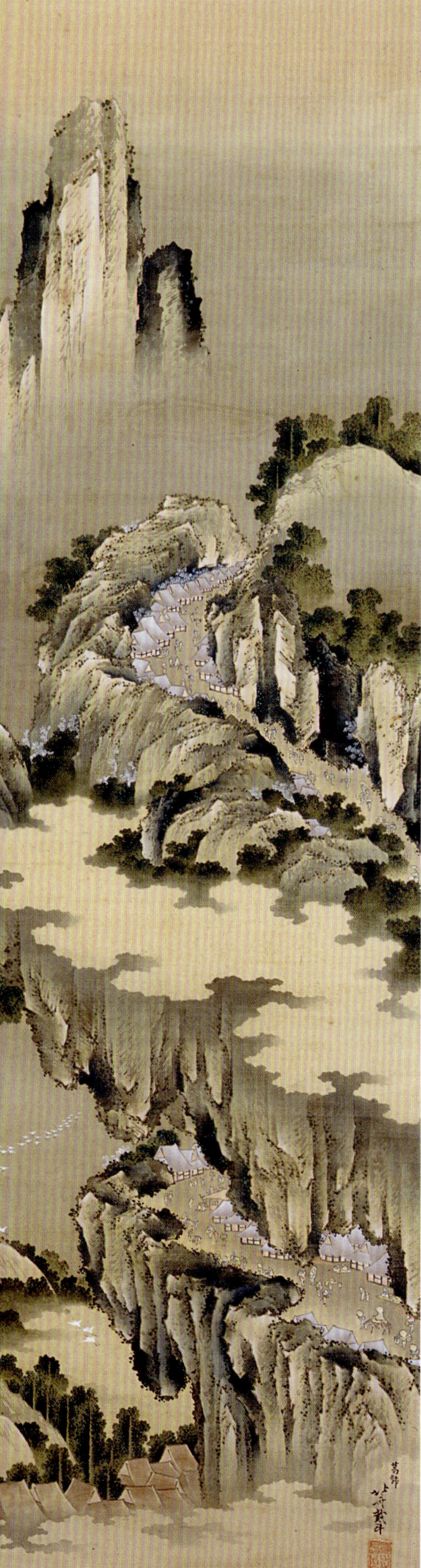

Woodcutter, spring and autumn landscapes

Early 1810s
Signature: Katsushika / Hokusai Taito
Seal: Kimō dasoku ('Hair on the turtle, legs on the snake')
Triptych of hanging scrolls, ink and colour on silk, each about 99.0 × 38.9 cm
Provenance: Yanagihara Shinjūrō (1974)
Literature: Ozaki 1967, nos 13–17; Edo Tokyo 2007, no. 194; Asano 2010, p. 53
Fukui Prefectural Museum of Fine Arts
Osaka only

In the central painting of the triptych, a woodcutter is returning home, carrying firewood as well as his son on his back; the right scroll shows a spring landscape; the left, an autumn landscape. The woodcutter's clothing is outlined with forceful, wrinkled brushstrokes that taper and swell – a characteristic of Hokusai's style from the middle of the Bunka era (1804–1818). In the spring picture, a steep massif spirals upwards above the clouds, with a road also winding upwards, closely hugging the mountainside. Some flowering trees, perhaps cherries, are picked out in white. Clusters of houses look like toys and the road is full of people. The autumn picture, in complete contrast, shows a coastal road dotted with brilliant red foliage. Numerous travellers are coming and going between the mauve-coloured houses, while village people are working on the shore below. The overall landscape style is Chinese in appearance, but the people seem to be Japanese, making for a fantastical, illusory scene. Hokusai clearly studied the Chinese illustrated book *Mustard Seed Garden Painting Manual*, as well as paintings by the Nagasaki school of Qing dynasty painter Shen Nanpin (1682–1760). It has also been argued that certain Hokusai works show the influence of other Qing painters, such as Giuseppe Castiglione (1688–1766) and Yuan Yao (worked mid-1700s). AS

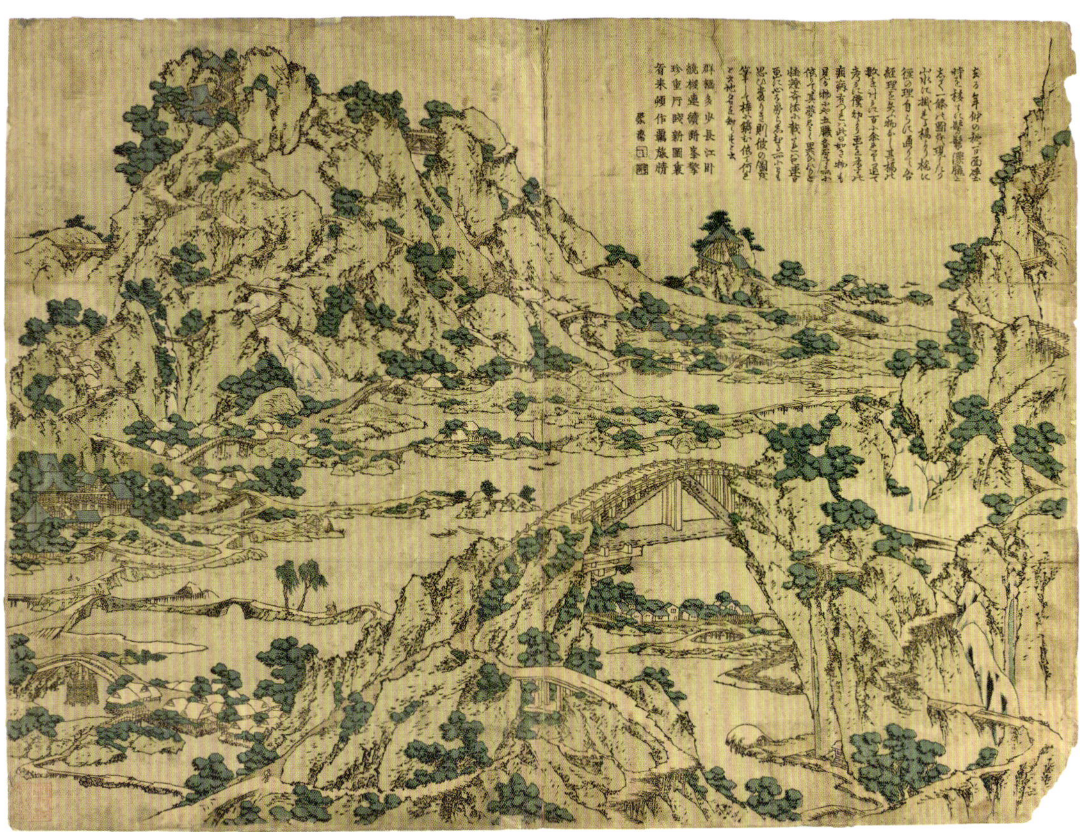

74
One hundred bridges at a glance

About 1823
Seal: Hokusai aratame Iitsu / Eijudō / Nishimura
no in ('Hokusai changed to Iitsu, Seal of Nishimura,
Eijudō')
Extra-large colour woodblock, published by
Nishimuraya Yohachi, 41.7 × 56.4 cm
Literature: RA 1991, no. 33; Sumida 2009, no. 258;
Keyes & Morse 2015, no. 969
Ōta Memorial Museum of Art, Tokyo

The inscription above the image, thought to be by
Hokusai himself, explains the genesis of this print: 'Last
autumn, as I spent a day in meditation seated before a
wall, a picture materialized, obscurely, as out of a mist.
The landscape had bridges that led from one to another
in a logical order that was never lost; there were over
a hundred when I counted them. Later I pondered this
vision, since I have drawn and painted ever since my
youth [and this has never happened]. Was I suffering
a temporary illness or the fatigue of my five internal
organs? I was quite at a loss to explain it, but concluded
that the strange dream-like phenomenon must have
occurred because every day recently I have been putting
so much of myself into my work. I made a drawing of
the image that has been cut and printed. The landscape
is nowhere in particular.' (Trans. Roger Keyes.)

This is surely one of the most extraordinary of
Hokusai's 'wondrous views' (*kiran*), even though there
are actually about fifty bridges in the image rather than
the promised one hundred. Hokusai's inscription is
followed by a Chinese-style poem, whose author remains
unidentified (perhaps also Hokusai?). A printed wrapper
(National Diet Library, Tokyo) includes the title
'One hundred bridges at a glance' (*Hyakkyō ichiran*)
and the date 1823. A later edition was given the revised
title 'Famous bridges in various provinces at a glance',
with the names of the fifty or so bridges inserted into
the image. The name 'Boat bridge at Sano', which
relates to a later print (cat. 79), was inserted in the
wrong place. It seems Hokusai was not involved in
the production of the later edition. AS

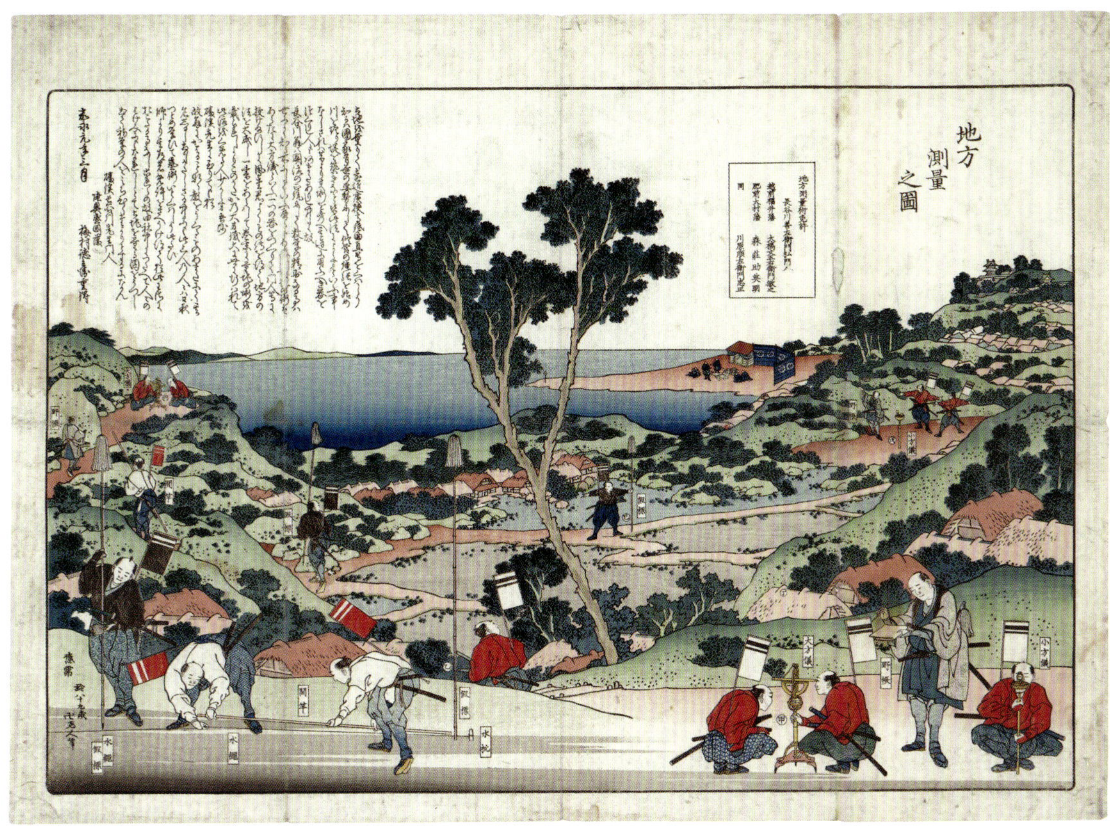

75
Picture of land surveyors

Third month, 1848
Signature: Ōju / yowai hachijūkyū sai / Manji rōjin hitsu ('Brush of old man Manji, aged eighty-nine years, at special request')
Extra-large colour woodblock, publisher unknown,
39.5 × 53.2 cm
Provenance: Purchased from K. Murakami
Literature: RA 1991, no. 84; Paris 2014, no. 494
British Museum, 1925,1016,0.2

The print shows samurai officials surveying land along a coast. Some are measuring with rulers between marker posts, others are using large and small theodolites. The signature tells us that Hokusai is eighty-nine and the text, signed by Umemura Tokubei Shigeyoshi, 'pupil of Professor Hankei Hasegawa', is dated third month, 1848. This is thus one of the last known dated single-sheet prints by Hokusai. The text celebrates the achievements of master surveyor Hasegawa Zenzaemon II (Hankei, 1810–1887) and his adoptive father, the late Hasegawa Zenzaemon I (1782–1839), a famous mathematician. It also gives instructions for beginners on the basics of surveying. The print was apparently distributed to celebrate the qualification of three new surveyors, from three different fiefs, all pupils of Zenzaemon II. A printed wrapper survives, with the title 'Picture of surveying' (*Ryōchi no zu*). AS

Wondrous Views of Famous Bridges in Various Provinces (*Shokoku meikyō kiran*)

Hokusai was generally interested in the structure and shape of bridges. He drew many different types in volumes 4 and 7 of *Hokusai's Sketches* (*Hokusai manga*, 1816 and 1817), as well as the large-format print 'One hundred bridges at a glance' (cat. 74). The publisher Nishimuraya Yohachi commissioned this series from Hokusai following their collaboration on the 'Waterfalls' (cats 66–71). It can be dated to about the spring of 1834, on the basis of both the artist's signature and its mention in an advert that appeared in a book published that same New Year. There are five other known designs in addition to the six illustrated here (cats 76–81). Eleven is a curious number for a print series. Perhaps twelve were originally intended and for some reason only eleven were produced. Or possibly ten were planned and then an extra one was added. If the latter, the most likely candidate for the additional print is 'Mt Tenpō, mouth of the Aji river, Settsu province' (cat. 81), which does not feature a prominent bridge but did have topical value – Mt Tenpō park had only recently been constructed in Osaka, in 1832. Two of the designs presented pictures of bridges no longer extant, underlining the title's emphasis not just on actual bridges but also on 'wondrous views'. AS

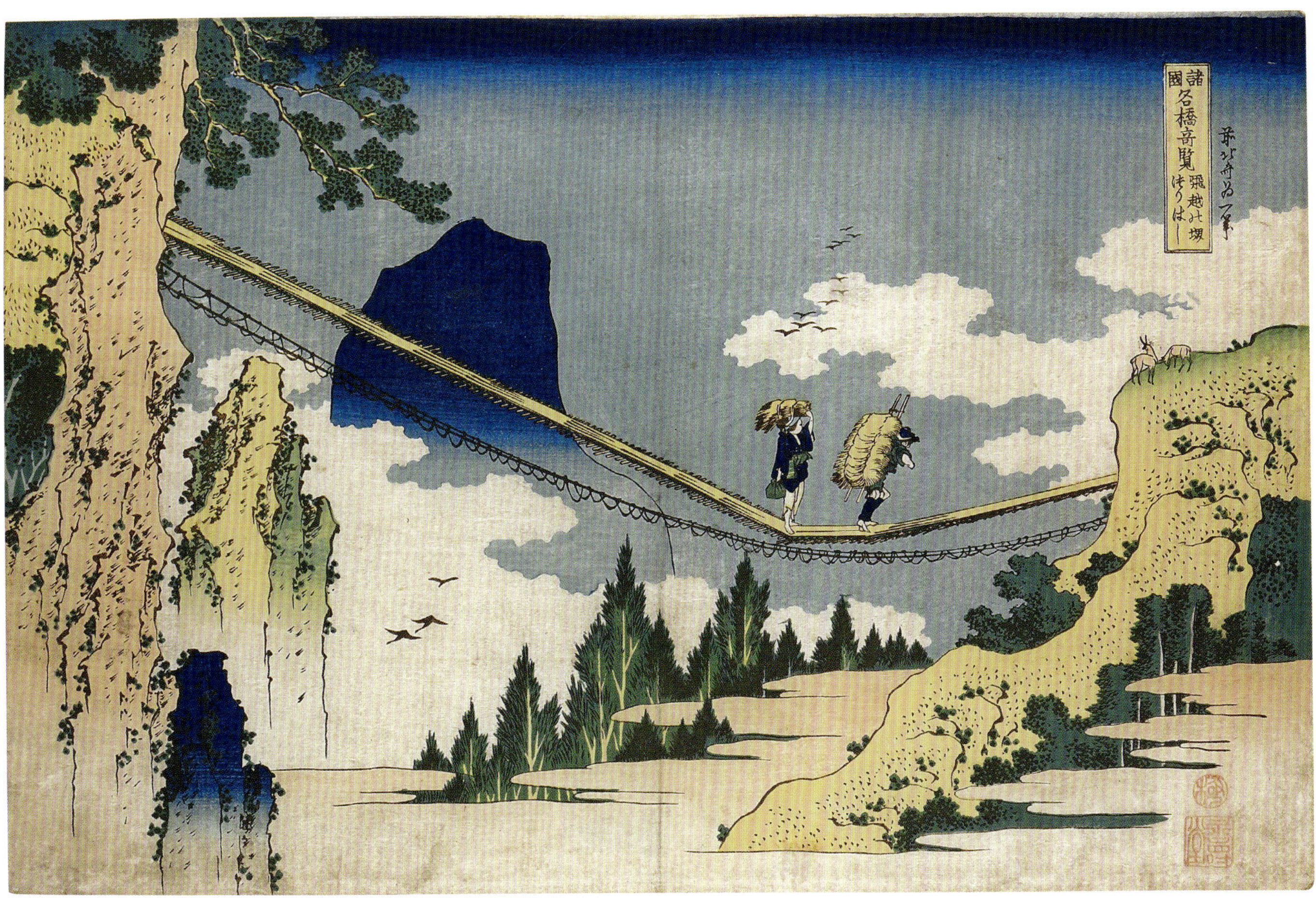

76

Suspension bridge on the border between Hida and Etchū provinces

About 1834
Signature: Saki no Hokusai Iitsu hitsu ('Brush of Iitsu, the former Hokusai')
Colour woodblock, published by Nishimuraya Yohachi, 25.7 × 37.9 cm
Provenance: Charles Ricketts & Charles Shannon
Literature: MSU 1991, no. 60; RA 1991, no. 38; Keyes & Morse 2015, no. 597
British Museum, 1937,0710,0.181, bequeathed by Charles Shannon RA

A couple returning home from their work in the mountains cross a suspension bridge with no handrail; the man is carrying a load of brushwood on his back and his wife has a small stack on her head. The image evokes conflicting sensations: on the one hand the figures proceed calmly through the deep mountain valley, where geese fly and deer graze; on the other, they seem to inhabit a space far beyond normal reality. The title suggests that there really may have been such a bridge on the border between Hida and Etchū (or Echizen) provinces. More likely, Hokusai used his imagination to exaggerate the form of a typical suspension bridge, which could surely be found all over Japan at the time. AS

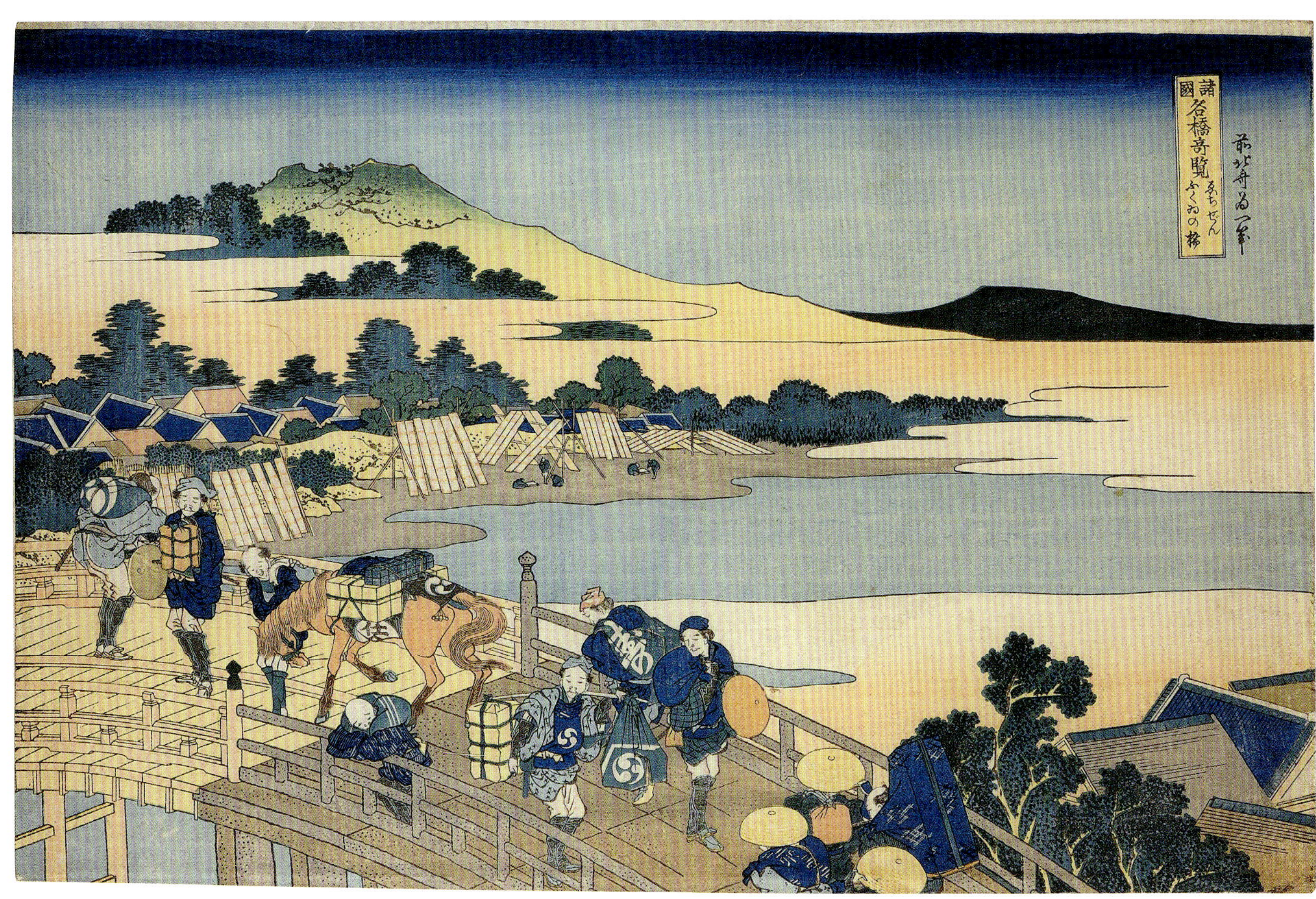

77

Fukui bridge, Echizen

About 1834
Signature: Saki no Hokusai Iitsu hitsu ('Brush of Iitsu, the former Hokusai')
Colour woodblock, published by Nishimuraya Yohachi, 25.8 × 38.4 cm
Provenance: Charles Ricketts & Charles Shannon
Literature: MSU 1991, no. 66; Keyes & Morse 2015, no. 603
British Museum, 1937,0710,0.190, bequeathed by Charles Shannon RA
Osaka only

Tsukumo bridge, constructed in 1575, was famous for having a wooden northern half, closer to Fukui castle, and a stone southern half. The idea was that the wooden part could be destroyed to prevent an enemy's advance, while the surviving stone part would then make repair easier. Hokusai was clearly fascinated by the bridge, and prominently contrasts the two materials in the foreground. In reality, there is a town rather than mountains on the far bank of the river, so it seems unlikely that Hokusai actually visited Fukui. It is more probable that he used a gazetteer, perhaps *Nihon sankai meibutsu zue* (*Famous Products of Land and Sea in Japan*, 1754). Volume 3 features an illustration of Tsukumo bridge, followed by one of 'Echizen *hōsho* paper', a renowned local product, sheets of which are here shown drying on the far bank. Each traveller on the bridge is carrying a bundle featuring the trademark of the publisher, Nishimuraya. AS

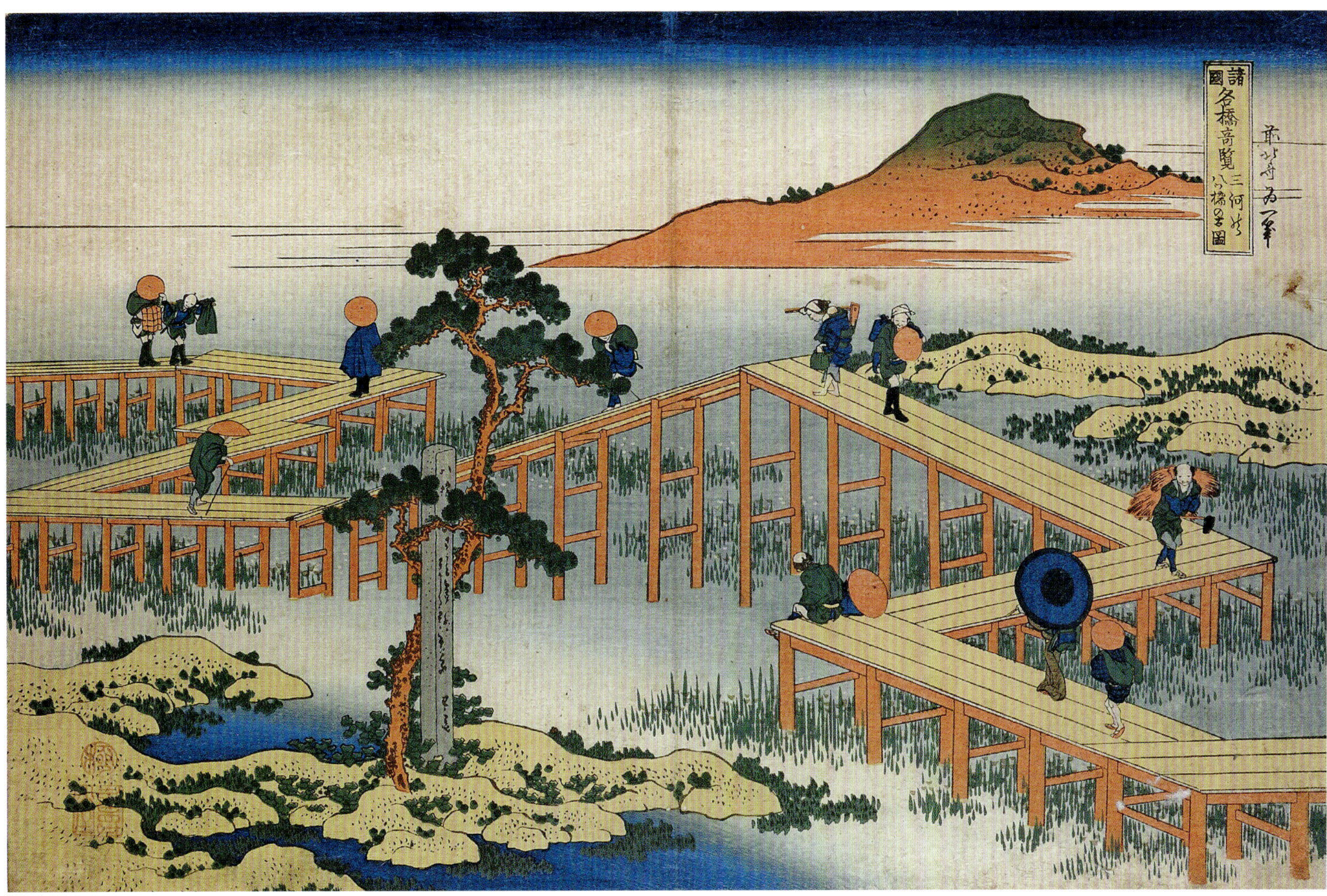

78

Old picture of Eight-plank bridge in Mikawa

About 1834
Signature: Saki no Hokusai Iitsu hitsu ('Brush of Iitsu, the former Hokusai')
Colour woodblock, published by Nishimuraya Yohachi, 25.8 × 38.1 cm
Provenance: Charles Ricketts & Charles Shannon
Literature: MSU 1991, no. 67; RA 1991, no. 36; Keyes & Morse 2015, no. 604
British Museum, 1937,0710,0.191, bequeathed by Charles Shannon RA

Yatsuhashi ('Eight-plank bridge') in Mikawa province became celebrated for its poetic associations after it was featured in the literary classic *Tales of Ise* in the AD 800s. The site is now in modern Chiryū city, Aichi prefecture. The original eight-plank bridge over the iris pool was already in ruins by the 1000s, but it continued to appear as a subject in the visual and decorative arts. If 'parody pictures' (*yatsushi-e*) of the later Edo period are included, then the total number of such works is enormous. Hokusai surely had these in mind when he drew this print, titling it an 'old picture'. Nevertheless, he added some distinctive extra flourishes, such as dressing the figures in the fashions of the day and making the centre of the bridge rise and fall. AS

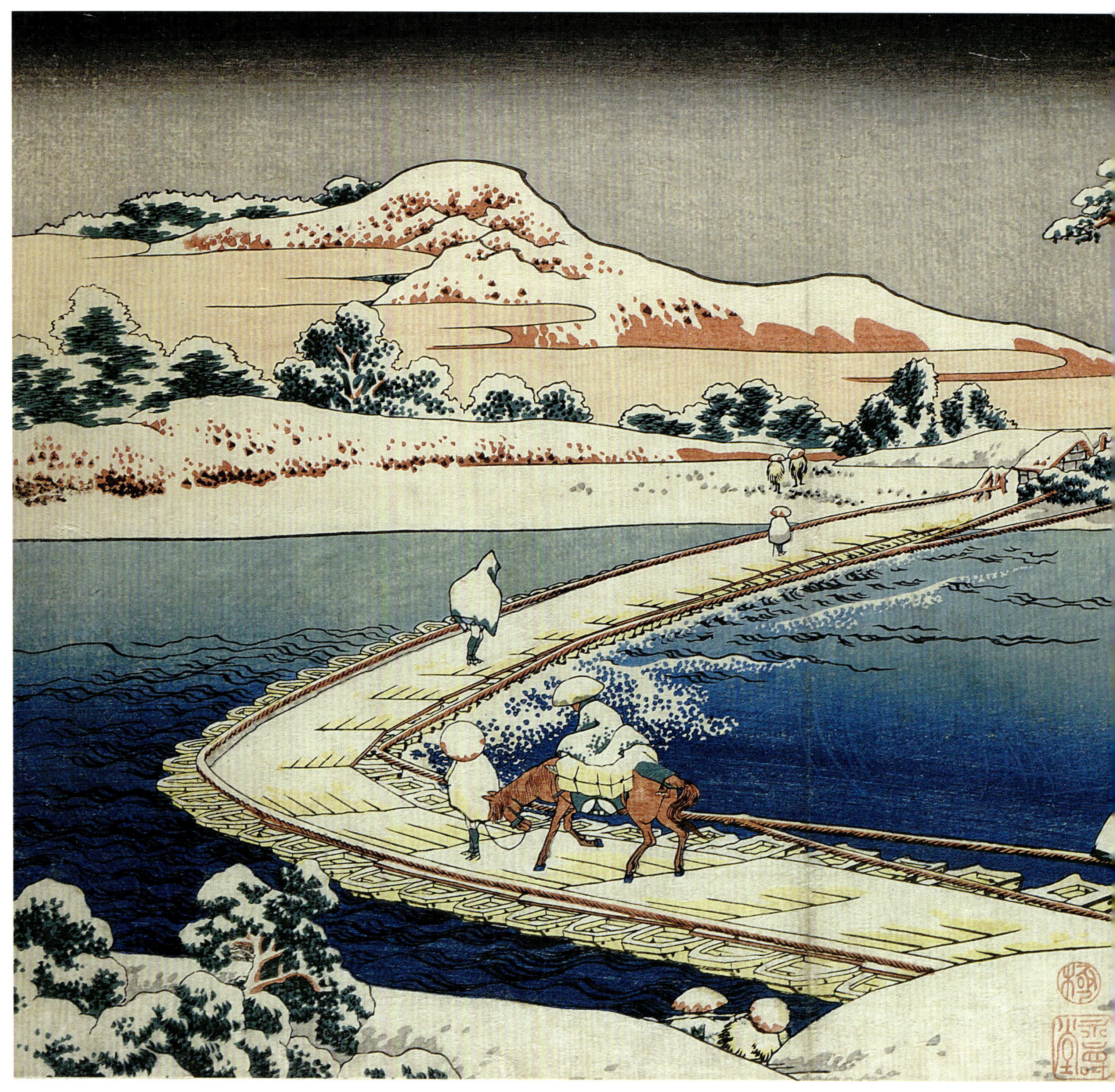

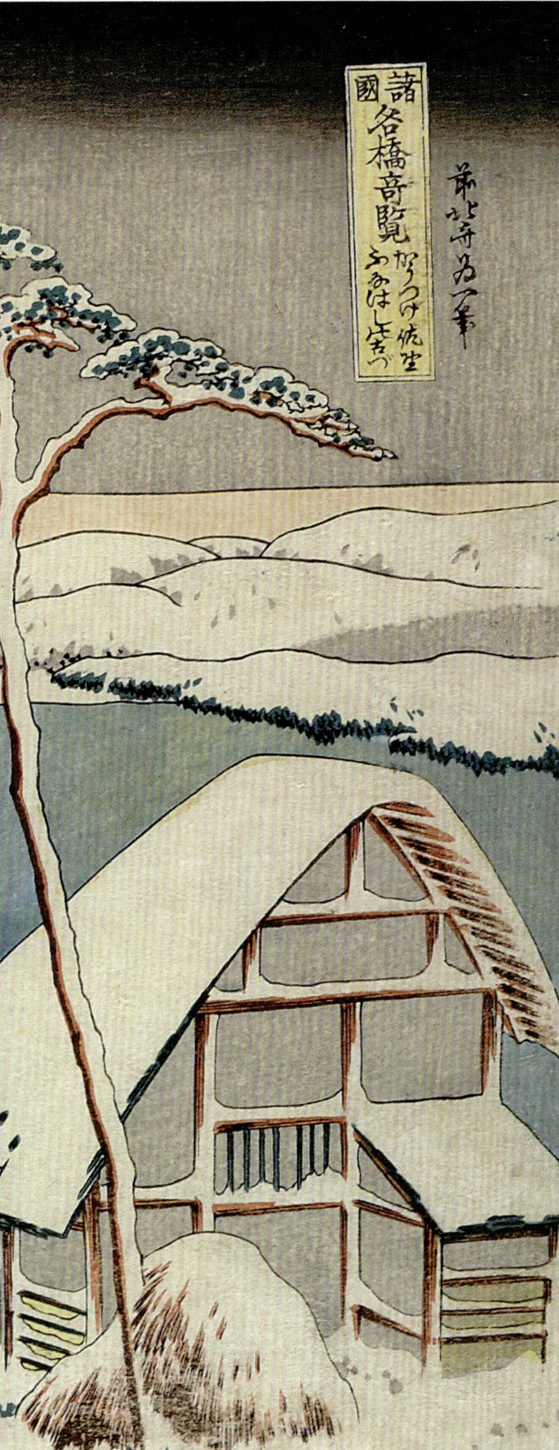

79
Old picture of Boat bridge, Sano, Kōzuke

About 1834
Signature: Saki no Hokusai Iitsu hitsu ('Brush of Iitsu, the former Hokusai')
Colour woodblock, published by Nishimuraya Yohachi, 24.9 × 36.8 cm
Provenance: Arthur Morrison
Literature: MSU 1991, no. 58; RA 1991, no. 34; Keyes & Morse 2015, no. 595
British Museum, 1906,1220,0.560

A boat bridge is constructed by fixing a line of boats together with planks. They existed in many places, but the boat bridge at Sano in Kōzuke province (modern Takazaki city, Gunma prefecture) was particularly well known. The bridge was made famous in the medieval Noh play *Funabashi* (*Boat Bridge*), which in turn took its inspiration from a poem in the ancient *Manyōshū* collection of the late AD 700s. In creating this scene, Hokusai may have been influenced by a poem by Fujiwara no Teika (1162–1241) about a completely different place, the ferry crossing at Sano (modern Shinmiya city, Wakayama prefecture). The large print 'One hundred bridges at a glance' (1823, cat. 74) includes at bottom right a similar image of a boat bridge, which Hokusai apparently enlarged to create the present print. AS

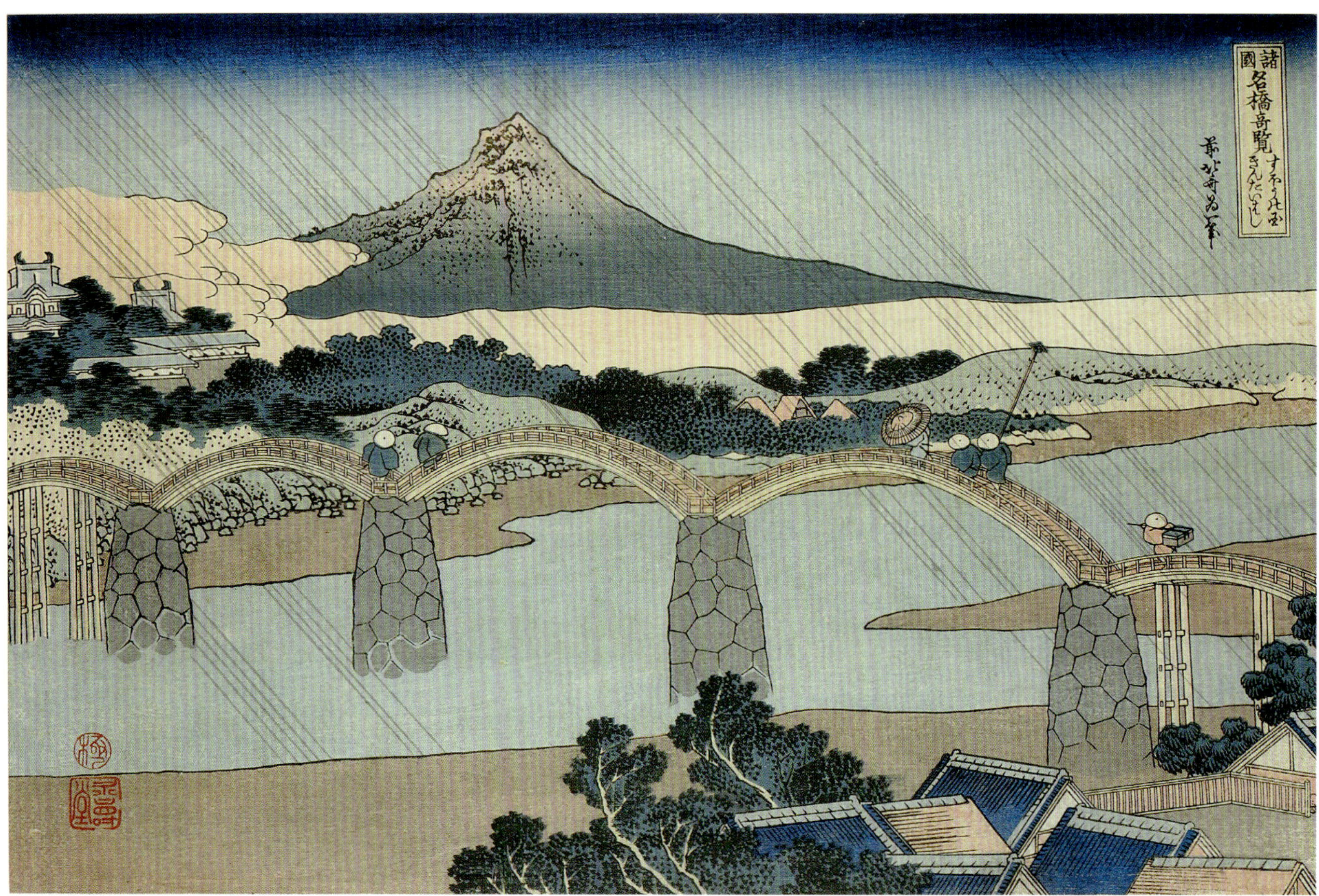

80

Kintai bridge, Suō province

About 1834
Signature: Saki no Hokusai Iitsu hitsu ('Brush of Iitsu, the former Hokusai')
Colour woodblock, published by Nishimuraya Yohachi, 25.0 × 36.9 cm
Provenance: Arthur Morrison
Literature: MSU 1991, no. 61; TNM 2005, no. 316; Keyes & Morse 2015, no. 598
British Museum, 1906,1220,0.565

Kintai ('Brocade Sash') bridge, with its striking five arched spans, crosses the Nishiki river in Suō province (modern Iwakuni city, Yamaguchi prefecture) in western Japan. The bridge was built in 1673 by order of Kikkawa Hiroyoshi (1621–1679), the third generation samurai lord of the Iwakuni fief. As shown in this print, the three central wooden arches over the river rest on stone pillars, with an arched wooden span at either end. Hokusai surely used local pictures and gazetteers as reference, but even making allowance for this, the depiction of the stone pillars is rather rough. In later printings, the atmospheric slanting rain is omitted. AS

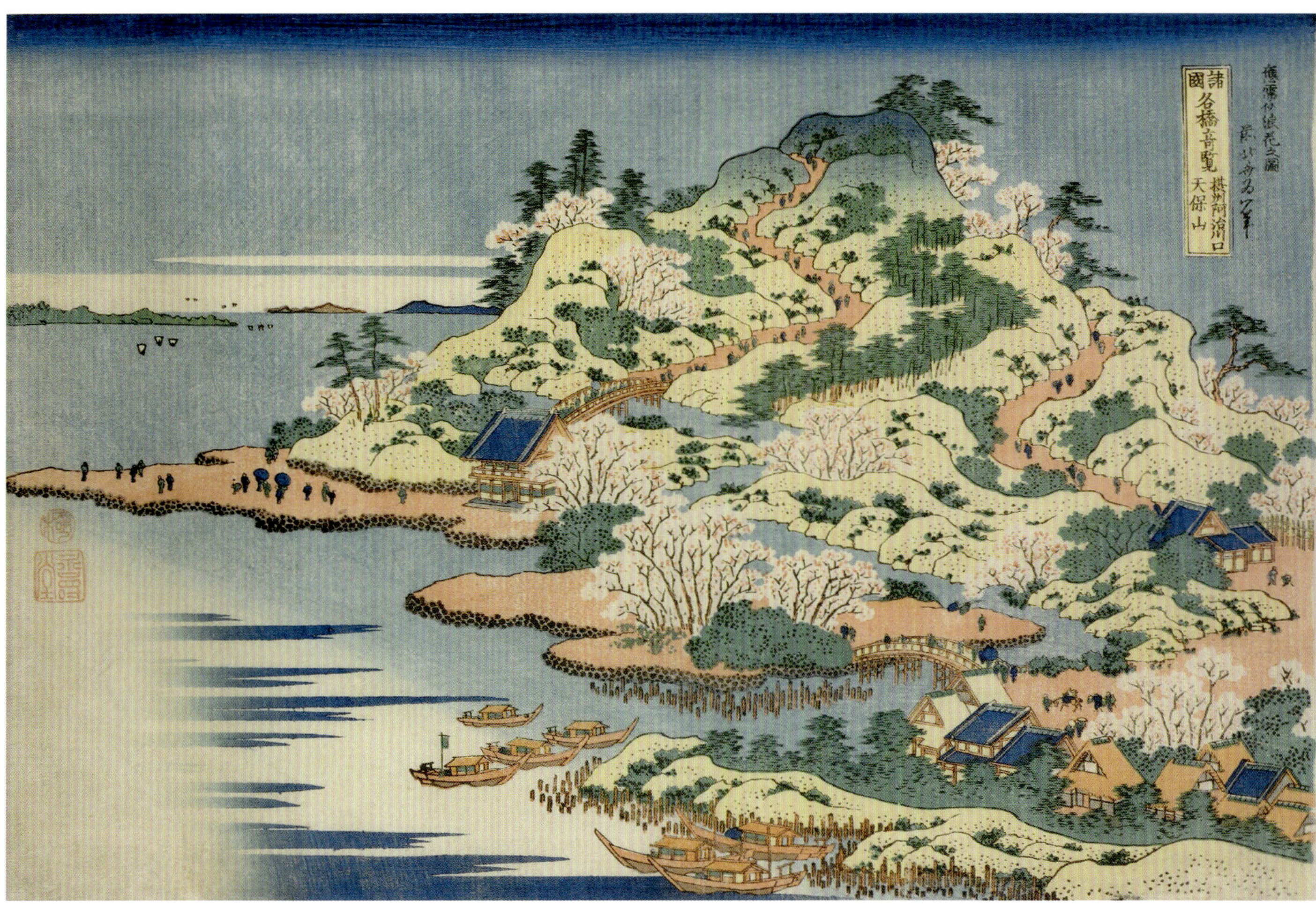

81

Mt Tenpō, mouth of the Aji river, Settsu province

About 1834
Signature: Ōju Naniwa no zu [o] motte / Saki
no Hokusai Iitsu hitsu ('Brush of Iitsu, the former
Hokusai, using a picture of Osaka, at special request')
Colour woodblock, published by Nishimuraya Yohachi,
25.9 × 38.0 cm
Provenance: Arthur Morrison
Literature: MSU 1991, no. 64; TNM 2005, no. 315;
Keyes & Morse 2015, no. 601
British Museum, 1906,1220,0.567
Osaka only

Mt Tenpō was an artificial hill constructed in 1832
from the silt generated by a major dredging of the
mouth of the Aji river in Osaka. Boasting fine views,
it immediately became a bustling tourist attraction.
Unusually, Hokusai added the notation 'using a picture
of Osaka, at special request'. This made it clear that
his design was based on a picture drawn in Osaka,
but he may also have been concerned that the print
does not feature a famous bridge and that his originality
would not be evident. The request surely came from
the publisher, Nishimuraya Yohachi, who was also
involved in the spring of 1834 in the publication of an
album by Yashima Gakutei (?1786–1868) of famous
places in Osaka, including views of Mt Tenpō. He must
have hoped for cross-sales between the two works. AS

Large flowers

Hokusai designed two different flower series for the publisher Nishimuraya Yohachi: the so-called *Large flowers* (cats 82–88) and *Small flowers* (cats 90–99). The former was published about 1831–1832 and can be divided stylistically into two groups of five. The first group have a limited colour palette and the brush style is deliberately rough and forceful: 'Poppy', 'Lily', 'Leopard lily [*hiōgi*]', 'Hibiscus and sparrow' and 'Hydrangea and swallow'. The second group are more delicate and detailed, featuring combinations with insects and stronger colour contrasts: 'Peony and butterfly', 'Chrysanthemum and bee', 'Chinese bellflower and dragonfly', 'Morning glory and frog' and 'Iris and grasshopper'. The slightly different signatures suggest that the first five were probably issued before the second. In the latter, in particular, the artist seems to be striving to express a vibrant sense of life-force. In adding the insects and frog, Hokusai must have been influenced by *Mushi erabi* (*Selected Insects*, 1788) by Kitagawa Utamaro (died 1806) – the blocks for which his publisher had purchased in 1823 and used to issue a reprint edition.

There is a sense that in this series Hokusai is developing further in the format of the single-sheet colour print ideas that were first published as illustrations in his printed brush drawing manuals of the 1810s and 1820s: *Hokusai shashin gafu* (cat. 89), *Santai gafu*, *Hokusai gashiki* and *Ryōbi shahitsu*. *Santai gafu*, in particular, showed how the same motif could be represented differently in the three traditional brush styles: formal, semi-cursive and cursive (*shin*, *gyō*, *sō*). The first group of *Large flowers*, therefore, with its rough and forceful brushwork, corresponds to 'cursive'; while the second, with its delicate and detailed style, corresponds to 'formal'. **AS**

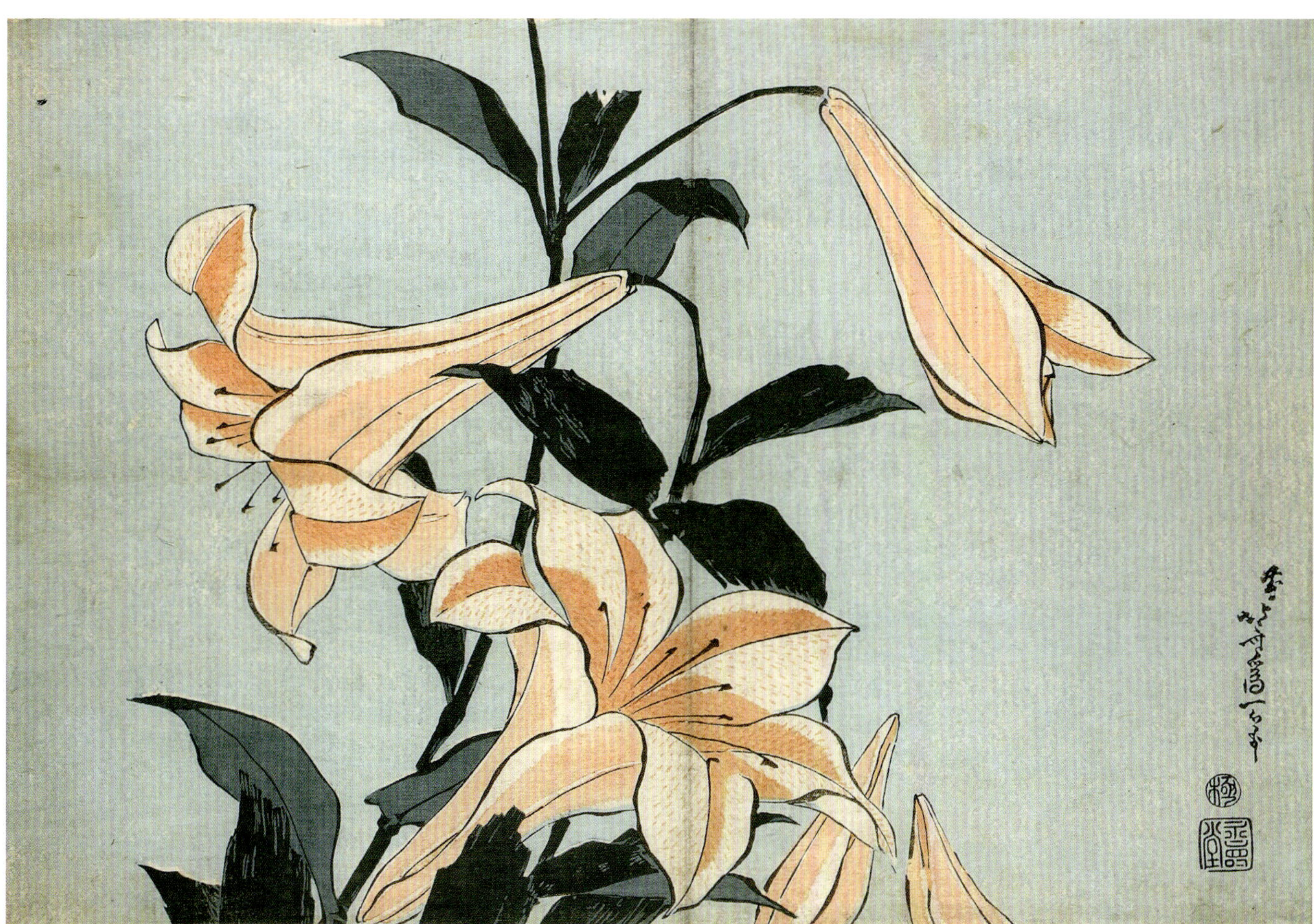

82

Lily

About 1831–1832
Signature: Saki no Hokusai Iitsu hitsu ('Brush of Iitsu, the former Hokusai')
Colour woodblock, published by Nishimuraya Yohachi, 25.4 × 36.3 cm
Literature: RA 1991, no. 59; TNM 2005, no. 366; Keyes & Morse 2015, no. 888
British Museum, 1924,0327,0.17, given by R. N. Shaw

Lilies loom in close-up against a pale blue background. Two open flowers, two buds and one half-open flower are all drawn with the same, somewhat ragged outline. Even the finest lines taper and swell and, almost imperceptibly, tremble and (occasionally) fragment. This rejection of smoothly flowing lines is certainly a deliberate strategy on Hokusai's part. The delicate stamens reflect directly the traces of the brush. As in 'Leopard lily [*hiōgi*]' and 'Poppy' (cat. 83), the leaves are expressed, unusually, only in green and black ink, with the green printed flat, but the black deliberately preserving the traces of the brush. The darker and lighter areas of pink are achieved by abrading the edges of the block to achieve a gradated effect (*ita-bokashi*), which is carefully overprinted with fine, fragmented coloured lines. The overall impression is of an abbreviated brush style, but it is actually the product of the most careful calculation. Hokusai had already drawn lilies in volume 1 of *Hokusai's Sketches* (*Hokusai manga*, 1814) and again in volume 4 (1816); the latter, also in 'cursive' (*sō*) style, is very similar to the image here. 'Lily', 'Poppy' (cat. 83) and 'Leopard lily [*hiōgi*]' are the only three designs that present the flower alone, without an insect or a bird. AS

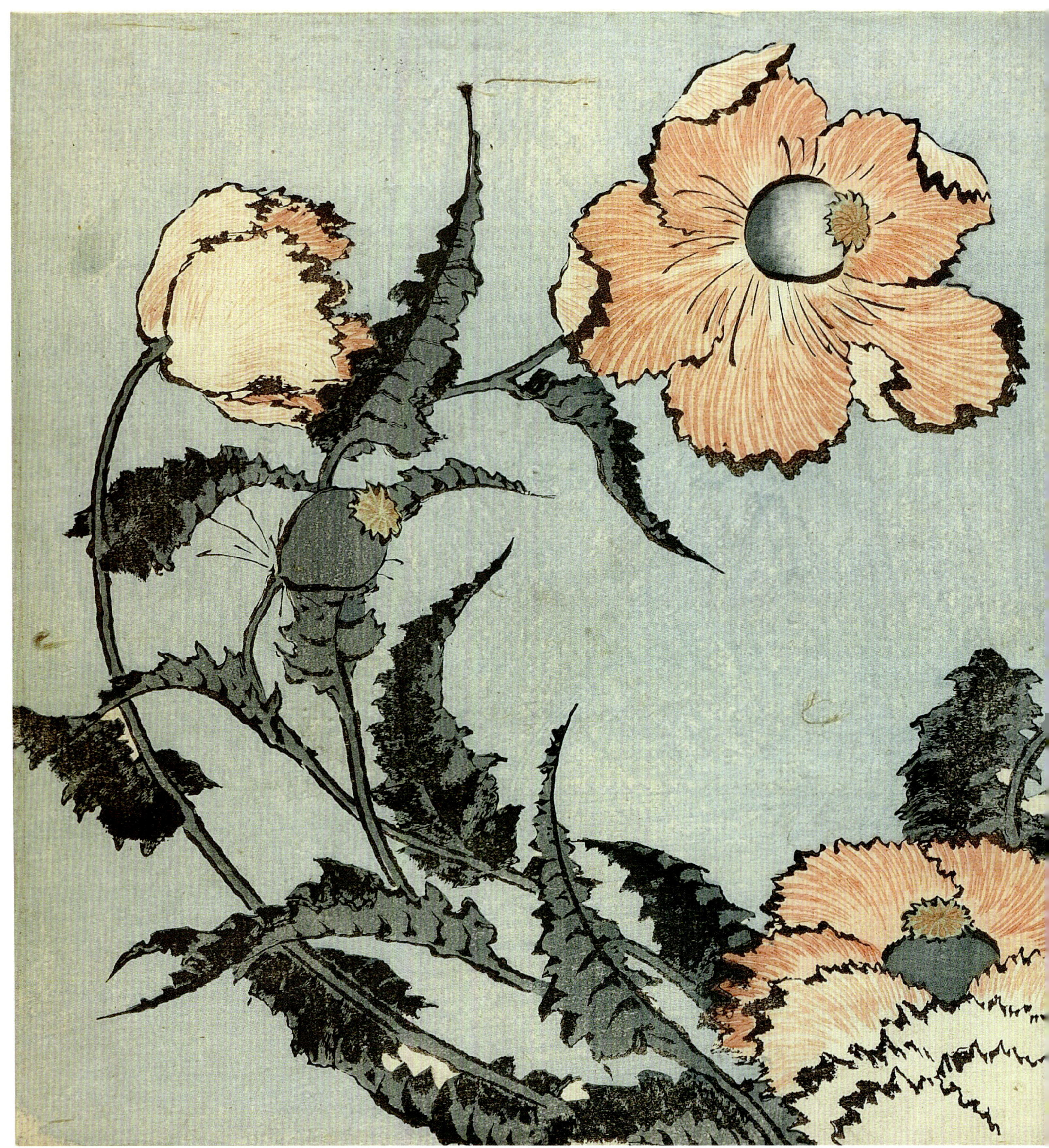

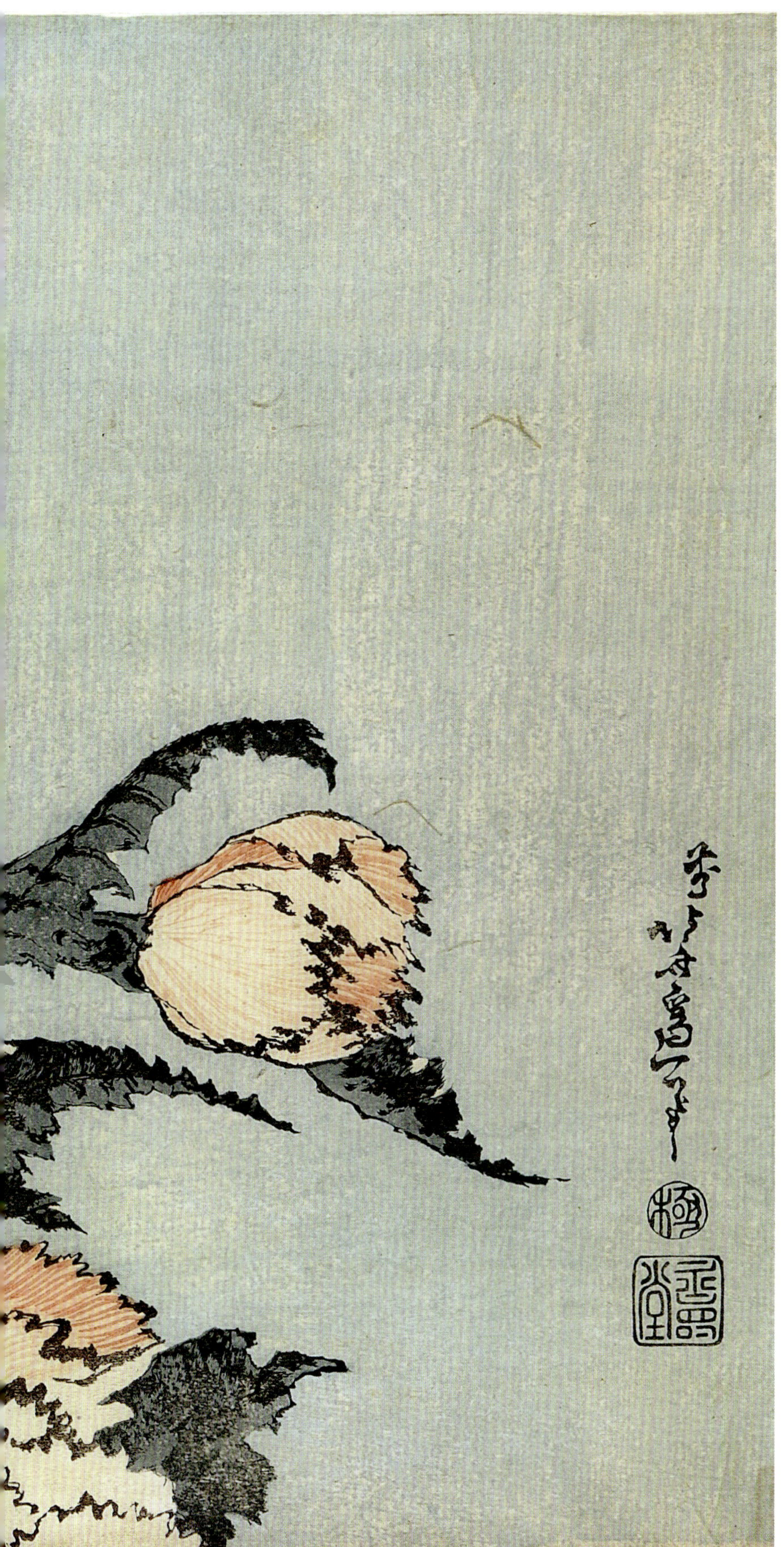

83
Poppy

About 1831–1832
Signature: Saki no Hokusai Iitsu hitsu ('Brush of Iitsu, the former Hokusai')
Colour woodblock, published by Nishimuraya Yohachi, 25.5 × 37.1 cm
Literature: RA 1991, no. 57; TNM 2005, no. 357; Keyes & Morse 2015, no. 887
British Museum, 1960,0716,0.10, bequeathed by Morton Harcourt Sands

A strong wind blows from the left, but the poppy plant seems stoically to resist. This is achieved by orchestrating the stalks of the poppies so that they lean first to the left and then to the right, bent firmly back by the wind. The open flower appears almost to be snarling at something. It is outlined with a rough touch in what looks like a single stroke; the writhing brush has a life-force of its own. In contrast, the patterning of the petals is delicate, imbuing the poppies with a wonderful sense of presence. As with 'Lily' (cat. 82), the leaves are printed in green and black only, but the brushwork is quite different. Significantly, volume 4 of *Hokusai's Sketches* (*Hokusai manga*, 1816) includes an image of a poppy which, like 'Lily', is similarly drawn in 'cursive' (*sō*) style. The design is a masterpiece among Hokusai's prints. AS

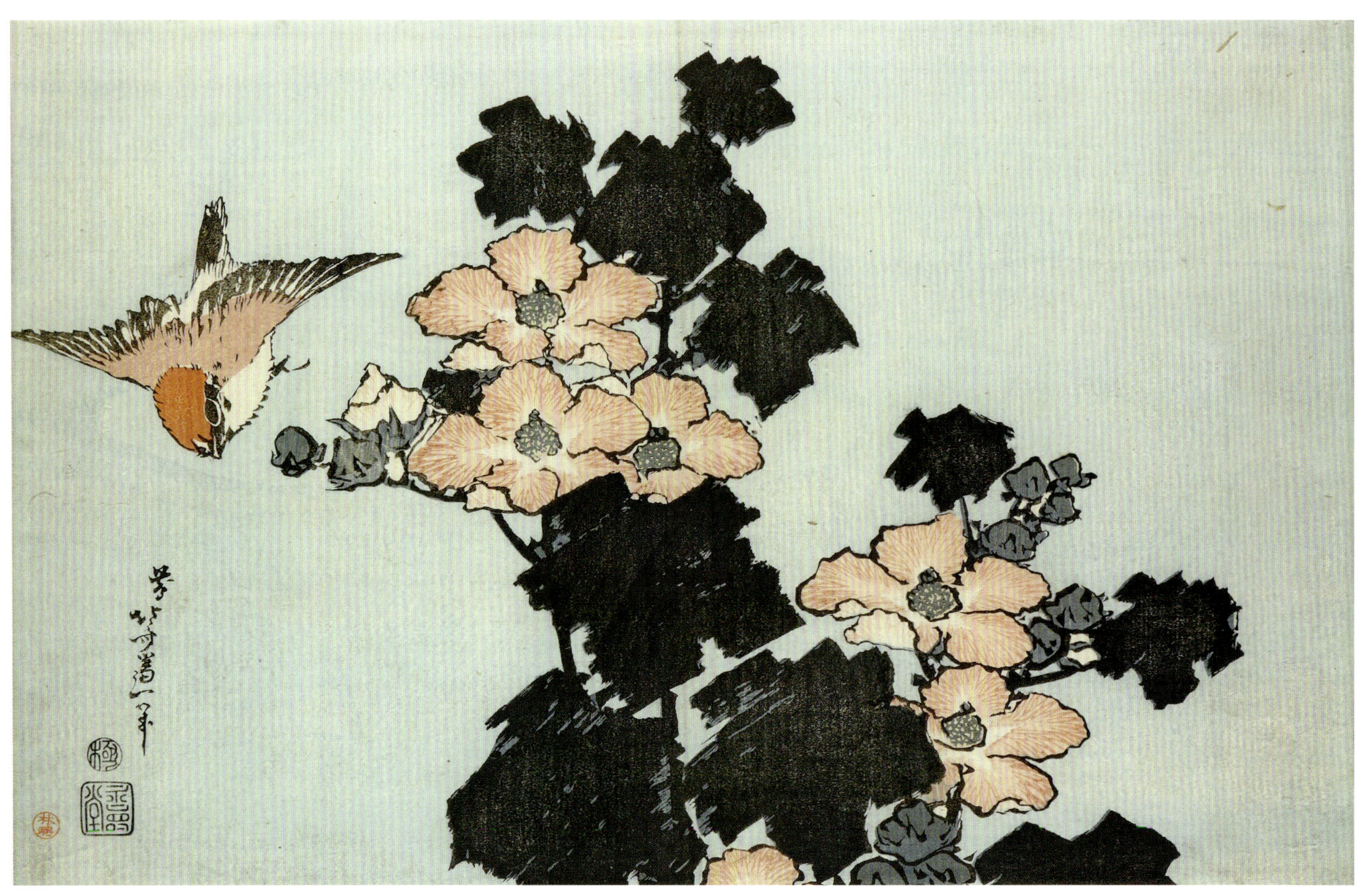

84

Hibiscus and sparrow

About 1831–1832
Signature: Saki no Hokusai Iitsu hitsu ('Brush of Iitsu, the former Hokusai')
Colour woodblock, published by Nishimuraya Yohachi, 24.7 × 37.2 cm
Provenance: Hayashi Tadamasa
Literature: RA 1991, no. 61 (blue ground); TNM 2005, no. 358 (yellow ground); Keyes & Morse 2015, no. 881
British Museum, 1926,0714,0.2

A single sparrow flies to the left of a hibiscus. The flowers are outlined with a rough touch, similar to 'Poppy' (cat. 83), but the depiction of the leaves is even more daring – they seem to have been drawn quickly with flat strokes of a wide brush. This wonderfully evokes both the shape of hibiscus leaves and a unique sense of presence that surely only Hokusai could have achieved. Still, one wonders what the public at the time thought of such eccentricity. This impression has a pale blue background, but others have yellow (TNM 2005, no. 358). 'Chrysanthemum and bee' has the same two variants. AS

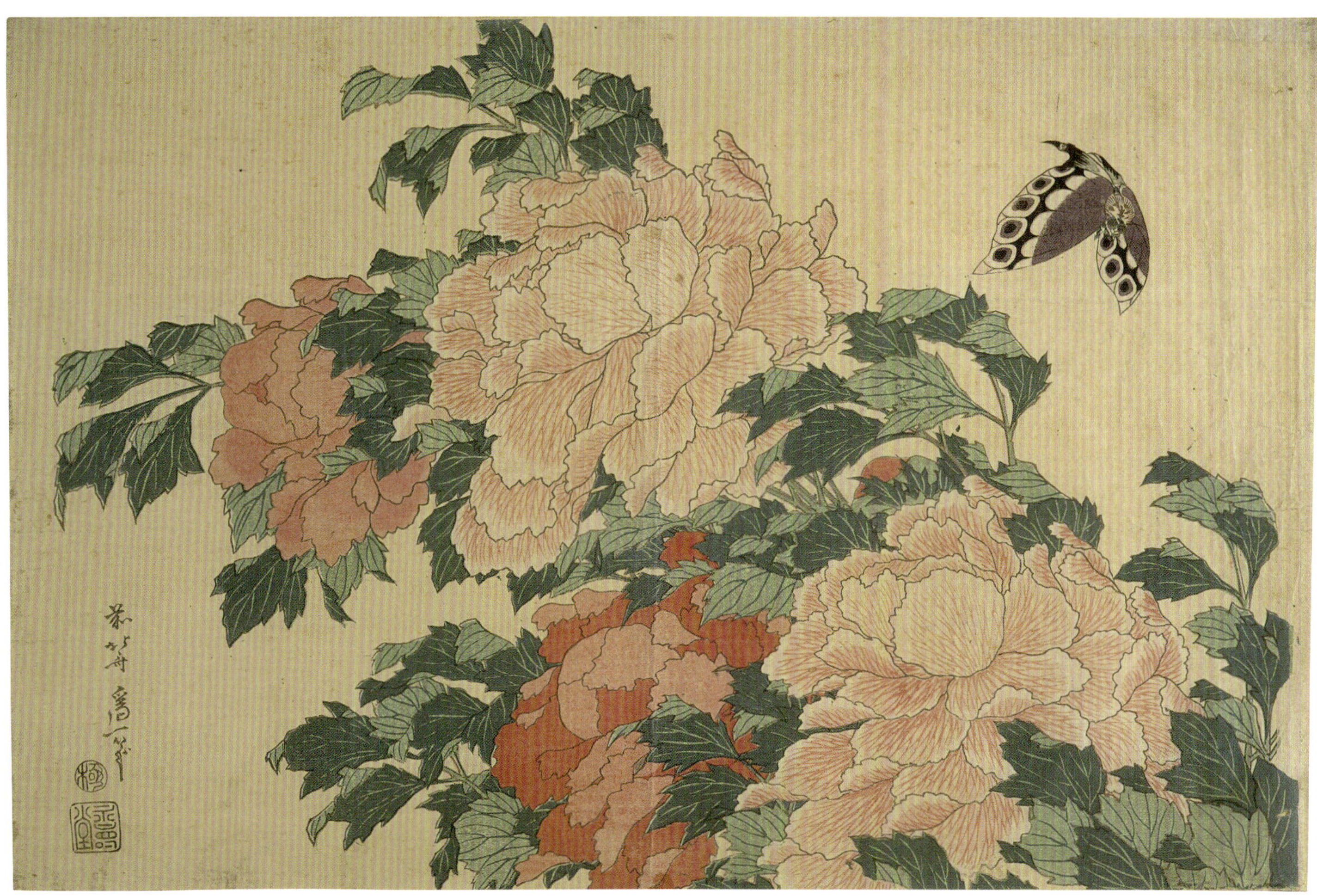

Peony and butterfly

About 1831–1832

Signature: Saki no Hokusai Iitsu hitsu ('Brush of Iitsu, the former Hokusai')

Colour woodblock, published by Nishimuraya Yohachi, 26.0 × 38.8 cm

Literature: RA 1991, no. 56; TNM 2005, no. 363; Keyes & Morse 2015, no. 885

Tokyo National Museum, A-11120

Osaka only

Fine, intricate lines trace the blossoms and foliage of a peony. The petals and leaves overlay one another rhythmically. The final addition of the butterfly creates an almost musical atmosphere of lightness. The transitions are so subtle that it is not immediately clear which petals and leaves are being blown by the wind and which not; overall, however, there is an impression of fluttering movement. In *Santai gafu*, published in about 1816, there is a similar image of a peony drawn, significantly, in the 'formal' (*shin*) style. The same book includes studies of butterflies and dragonflies (which relate to cat. 86). AS

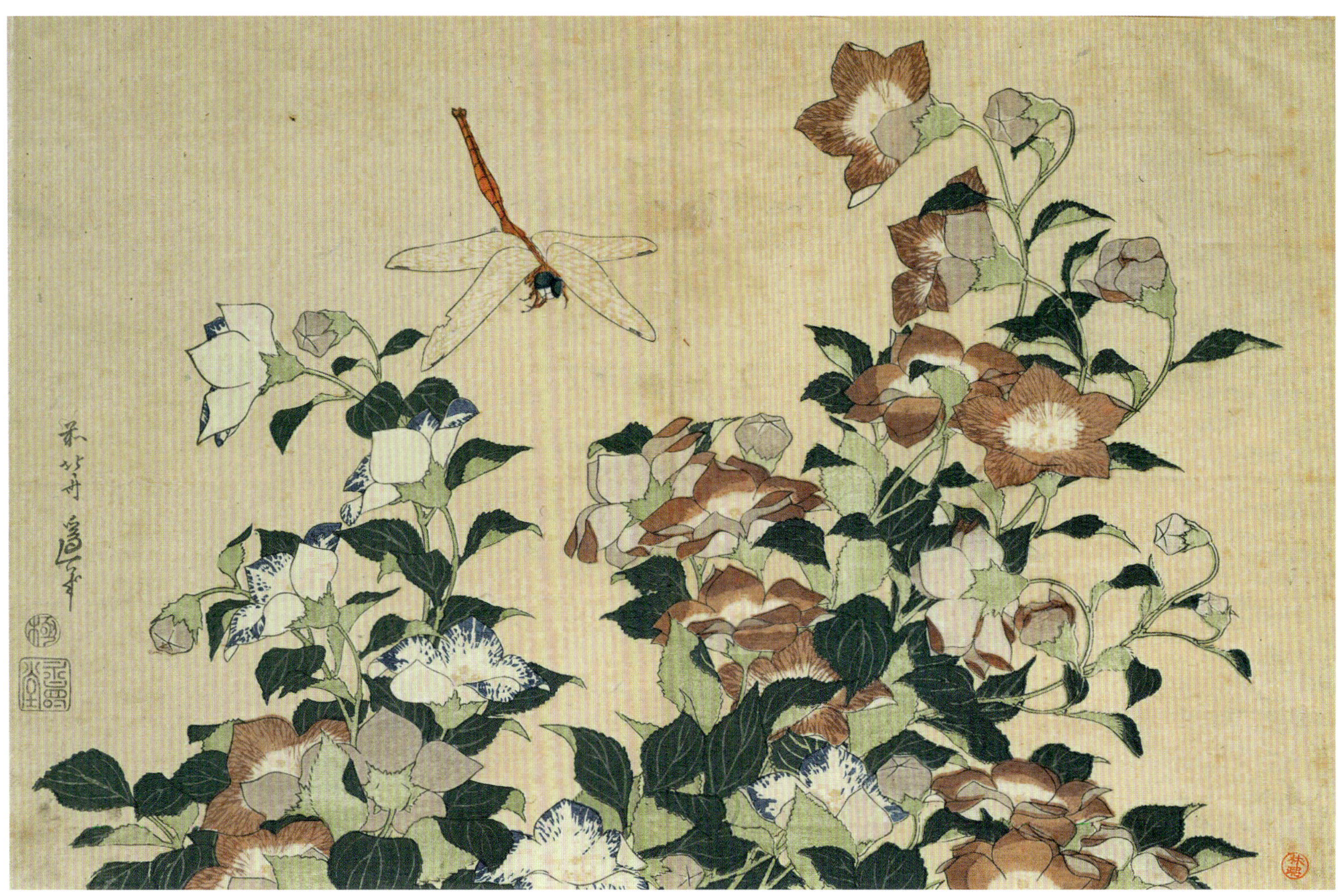

86

Chinese bellflower and dragonfly

About 1831–1832
Signature: Saki no Hokusai Iitsu hitsu ('Brush of Iitsu, the former Hokusai')
Colour woodblock, published by Nishimuraya Yohachi, 25.1 × 37.6 cm
Literature: RA 1991, no. 54; TNM 2005, no. 359; Keyes & Morse 2015, no. 886
Tokyo National Museum, A-10569-2782
Osaka only

Purple and blue Chinese bellflowers (*kikkyō*) are accompanied by a single dragonfly. This pairing of a bellflower and dragonfly had already appeared in the illustration 'Red dragonfly and grasshopper' in the poetry anthology *Mushi erabi* (*Selected Insects*) of 1788 by Kitagawa Utamaro (died 1806). Hokusai was perhaps inspired here by his knowledge of this earlier image. AS

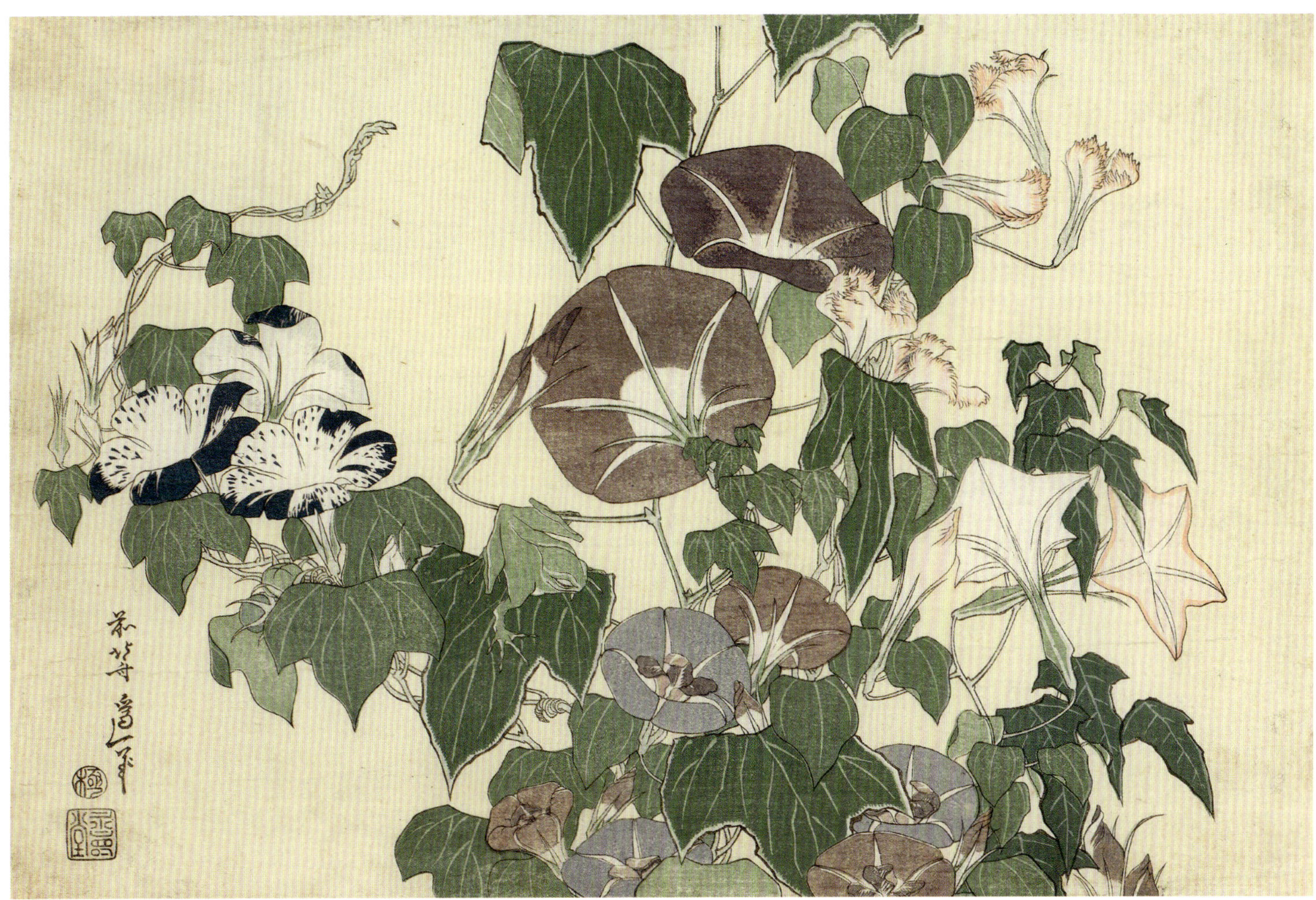

87

Morning glory and frog

About 1831–1832
Signature: Saki no Hokusai Iitsu hitsu ('Brush of Iitsu, the former Hokusai')
Colour woodblock, published by Nishimuraya Yohachi, 26.2 × 38.5 cm
Provenance: Erwin and Irma Grabhorn
Literature: RA 1991, no. 55; TNM 2005, no. 365; Keyes & Morse 2015, no. 882
Fitzwilliam Museum, Cambridge, P.10-2006

Multicoloured morning glories are delicately and finely depicted. It takes the viewer a while to spot the small tree frog perched on one of the leaves, camouflaged by its colour. There is a similar image of a frog with lotus and water lily, entitled 'Frog and scarabaeid beetle [*koganemushi*]' in Utamaro's *Mushi erabi* (*Selected Insects*) of 1788. AS

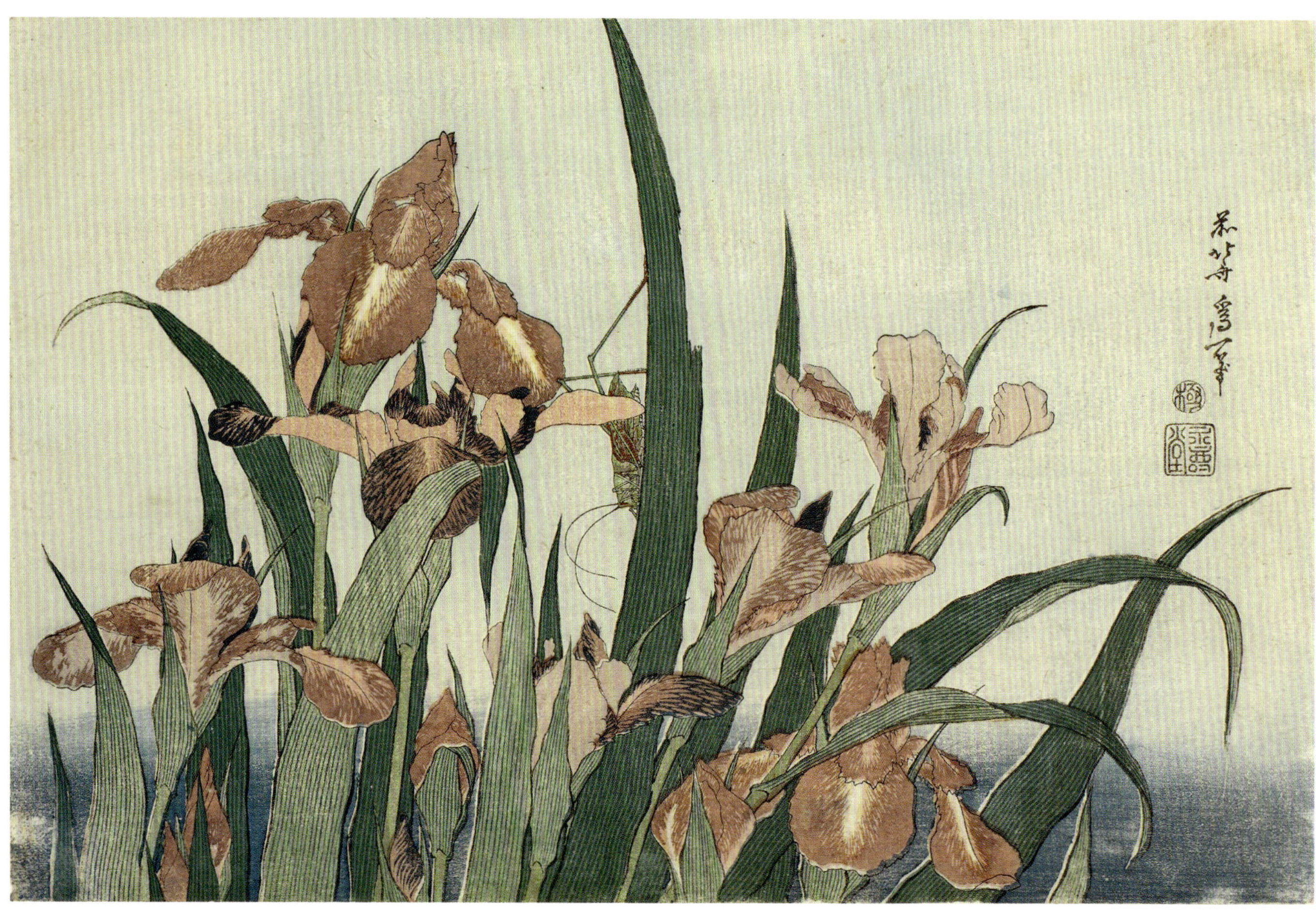

88

Iris and grasshopper

About 1831–1832
Signature: Saki no Hokusai Iitsu hitsu ('Brush of Iitsu, the former Hokusai')
Colour woodblock, published by Nishimuraya Yohachi, 25.8 × 38.0 cm
Literature: RA 1991, no. 60; TNM 2005, no. 364; Keyes & Morse 2015, no. 886A
Fitzwilliam Museum, Cambridge, P.191-1946

The print features a clump of iris growing in water and a lone grasshopper. Hokusai drew many irises during his career; this is close in feeling to a page in *Hokusai shashin gafu* (1819, cat. 89), although that does not include the grasshopper. The addition of the insect was surely suggested by the example of Utamaro's album *Mushi erabi* (*Selected Insects*, 1788). This print also echoes the image of an iris in 'formal' (*shin*) style in *Santai gafu* (about 1816), and an unpublished block-ready drawing of iris in *Drawings for a three-volume picture book*, volume 2 (1823–1835, cats 30, 168). With the exception of this print, the backgrounds of the *Large flowers* series are all printed in uniform pale blue or yellow. Here, in addition to the pale blue background, there is a gradated band of deep Prussian blue rising from the bottom – presumably indicating the water in which the iris are growing. **AS**

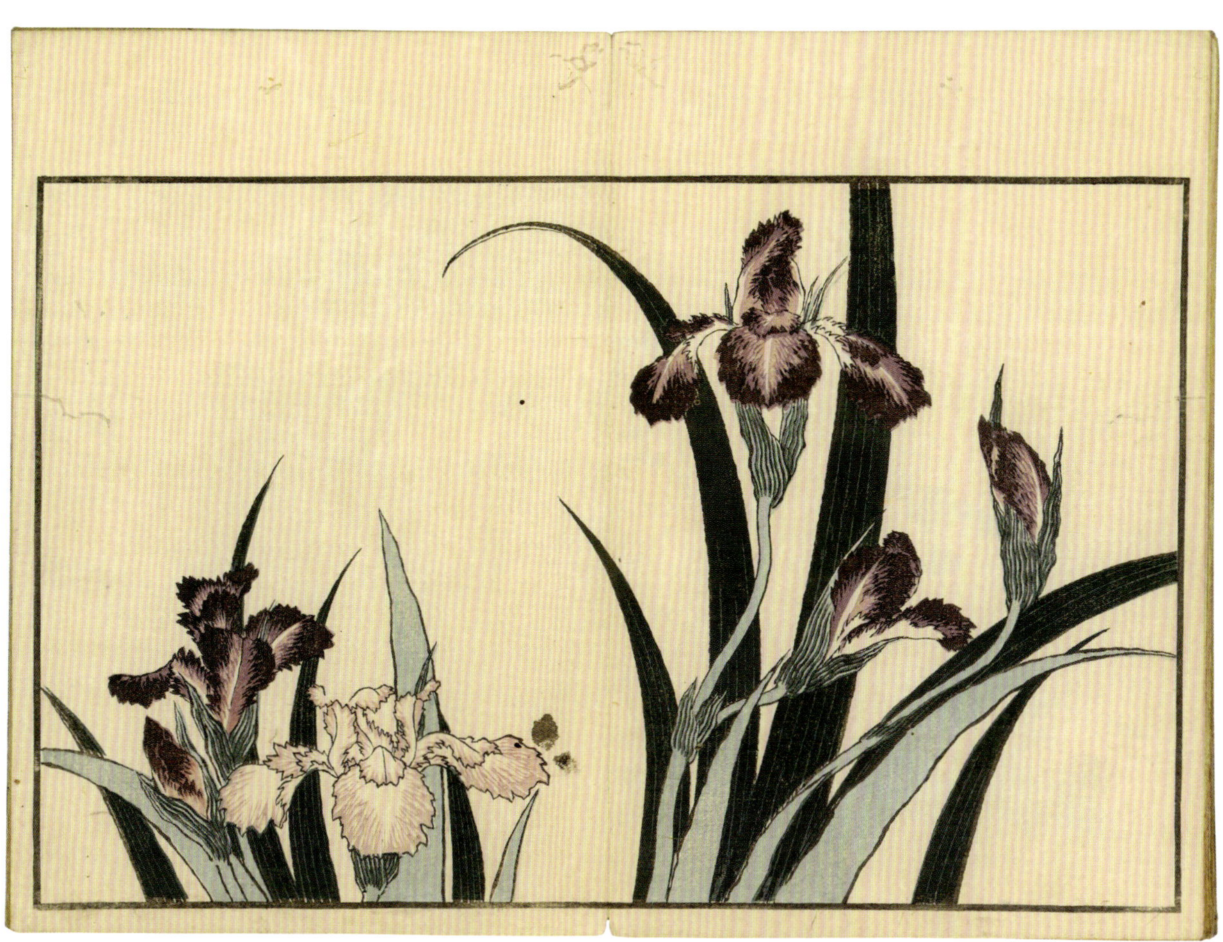

Iris, from *Hokusai's Album Drawn True to Life* (*Hokusai shashin gafu*)

1819
Unsigned (attributed to Hokusai)
Illustrated album, colour woodblock, published
by Tsuruya Kiemon, 25.7 × 16.9 cm (covers)
Provenance: Hayashi Tadamasa; Henri Vever;
M. Baudoin
Literature: Hillier 1980, pp. 89–95; RA 1991,
nos 122, 123
British Museum, 1948,0508,0.35

The album has seventeen openings, consisting of
a preface by the nativist scholar Kishimoto Yuzuru
(1788–1846), fifteen double-page, lightly coloured
pictures, and a colophon. The subjects of the pictures
vary, ranging from the deities Hotei and Kannon to
landscapes, flowers, birds and animals. Many are

drawn meticulously in formal brush style (*shintai*).
Among Hokusai's illustrated books, this album is
appreciated for its distinctive style and high production
values, very different from, say, *Hokusai's Sketches*
(*Hokusai manga*, cats 164, 165). The last line of the preface
gives a date of Bunka 11 (1814), but the colophon here
records the publisher as Tsuruya Kiemon and a date of
Bunsei 2 (1819). Some surviving copies lack the colophon,
and it may be that they were published earlier and
privately – so as to avoid punishment by the authorities,
who in 1804 had prohibited the publication of luxurious
colour illustrations. Once the possibility of being
penalized had decreased, however, copies such as this
could be issued openly, with the publisher's name
and the date included. The iris pictured here were
later reworked as a single-sheet print (cat. 88) in the
Large flowers series of about 1831–1832. AS

Small flowers

This series of ten medium-format (*chūban*) prints published by Nishimuraya Yohachi, known as the *Small flowers* (cats 90–99), is similar in theme to the *Large flowers* issued by the same publisher (cats 82–88). *Small flowers* should be dated to about the New Year, 1834, since they are advertised by Nishimuraya at the end of a serialized novel (*gōkan*) he published at that date, as follows: 'Bird-and-flower pictures in poetry-card [*shikishi*] format, brightly coloured'. The prints can be linked in five pairs by their similar backgrounds. Rare examples of unseparated pairs, and of prints whose trimming guidelines remain intact, indicate that each pair was carved on a single printing block, side by side. The term 'brightly coloured' in Nishimuraya's advertisement indicates that Hokusai had an entirely different purpose in mind when designing this series, in contrast to the *Large flowers*. Here he has used thin, precise lines to define the forms, and colours that are fresh and vibrant, in a style like formally written Chinese characters (*kaisho*). The idiosyncratic forms of his birds and flowers, with their superabundance of colour, can even seem somewhat stiff. They produce an impression like the meticulous, colourful bird-and-flower paintings of Itō Jakuchū (1716–1800). As with the *Large flowers*, the *Small flowers* are in some respects colour print versions of images from the brush drawing manuals that Hokusai produced during the 1810s–1820s. They relate even more closely to unpublished block-ready drawings of birds and flowers in volume 2 of *Drawings for a three-volume picture book* (1823–1835, cats 30, 168). It could be that when he was commissioned to create the present series, Hokusai decided to reuse the designs from that unpublished manual. **AS**

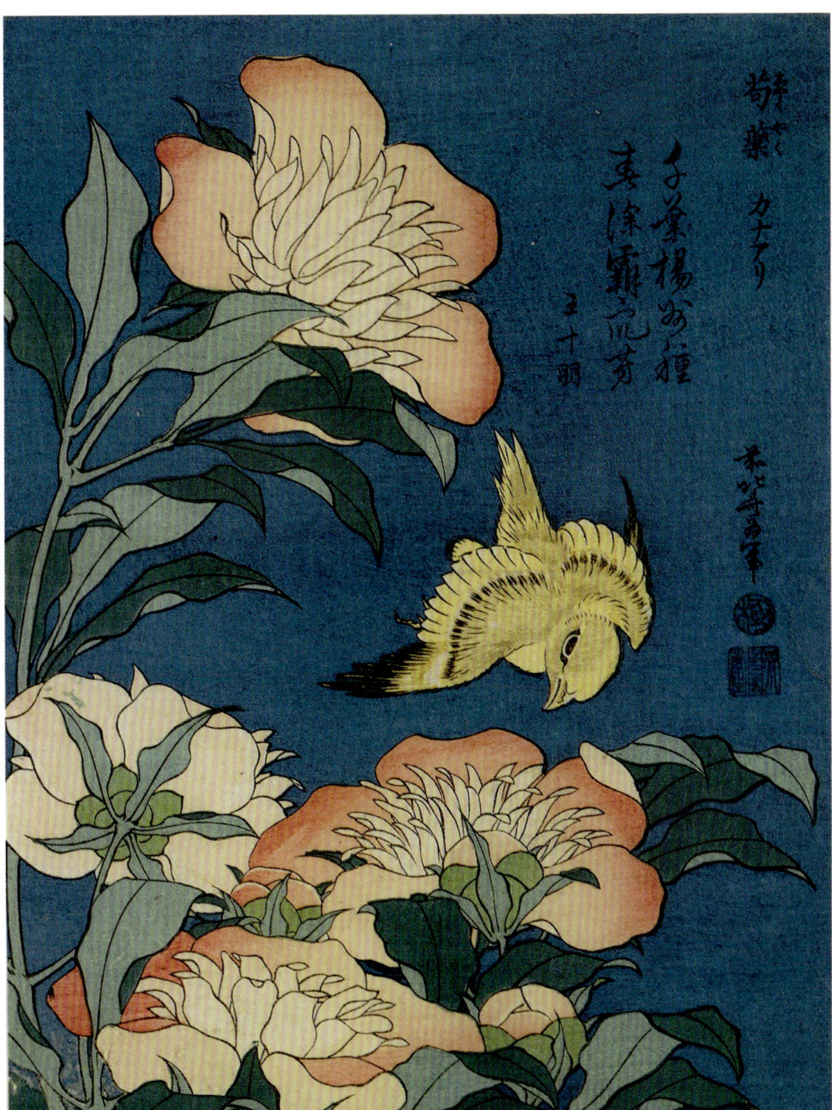

Herbaceous peony and canary

About 1834
Signature: Saki no Hokusai Iitsu hitsu ('Brush of Iitsu, the former Hokusai')
Colour woodblock, published by Nishimuraya Yohachi, 25.4 × 18.6 cm
Provenance: Fine Art Society
Literature: TNM 2005, no. 368; Keyes & Morse 2015, no. 899
British Museum, 1910,0614,0.20

As with 'Weeping cherry and bullfinch' from the same series (cat. 91), the background of solid Prussian blue sets in relief the featured bird and flower. Hokusai is known to have depicted a herbaceous peony on only one other occasion, in volume 3 of *Hokusai's Sketches* (*Hokusai manga*, 1815). In this print, he shows the flowers from various viewpoints, lending variety to the design. Hokusai discussed his methods of drawing and colouring canaries twice in his painting manual, *Picture Book: Essence of Colouring* (1848, cat. 211). Inscribed at top right are the first two lines from a Chinese poem on the herbaceous peony by the Song dynasty politician and scholar Wang Shipeng (1112–1171), whose writings are collected in the *Plum Creek Collection* (*Meiqiji*): 'The many-leaved Yangzhou variety / at spring's height reigns supreme over the multitude of aromas.' AS

Weeping cherry and bullfinch

About 1834
Signature: Saki no Hokusai Iitsu hitsu ('Brush of Iitsu, the former Hokusai')
Colour woodblock, published by Nishimuraya Yohachi, 25.4 × 18.6 cm
Provenance: Fine Art Society
Literature: TNM 2005, no. 367; Keyes & Morse 2015, no. 900
British Museum, 1910,0614,0.29

The bullfinch (*uso*) is featured in a ceremony conducted at the New Year at Tenjin shrines all over Japan. A wooden bullfinch acquired the previous year is exchanged for a new one, which is blessed so as to protect against misfortune in the coming year. The actual bird is slightly larger than a sparrow and has a call like a whistle. Hokusai here depicts the male, distinguished by its pink marking from cheek to throat. His painting manual *Picture Book: Essence of Colouring* (1848, cat. 211) includes a detailed discussion of how to draw and colour a bullfinch. An illustration of a weeping cherry appears in *Santai gafu* (about 1816). In this print, Hokusai rhythmically mixes buds with blossoms, highlighting the buds with a cheerful red. Inscribed top right is a short verse of seventeen syllables (*hokku*) by Bunrai'an Setsuman (worked late 1700s–early 1800s), a haiku poet of the Setsumon school that Hokusai was associated with: 'A single bird wets / its feathers and flits away: / morning cherry' (*Tori hitotsu / nurete dekakeri / asazakura*). 'Morning cherry' refers to a flowering cherry tree wet with dew. Another inscription by Setsuman appears on the Hokusai painting *Pines and Mt Fuji* (Japan Ukiyo-e Museum, Matsumoto; Nagata 2000, no. 25). AS

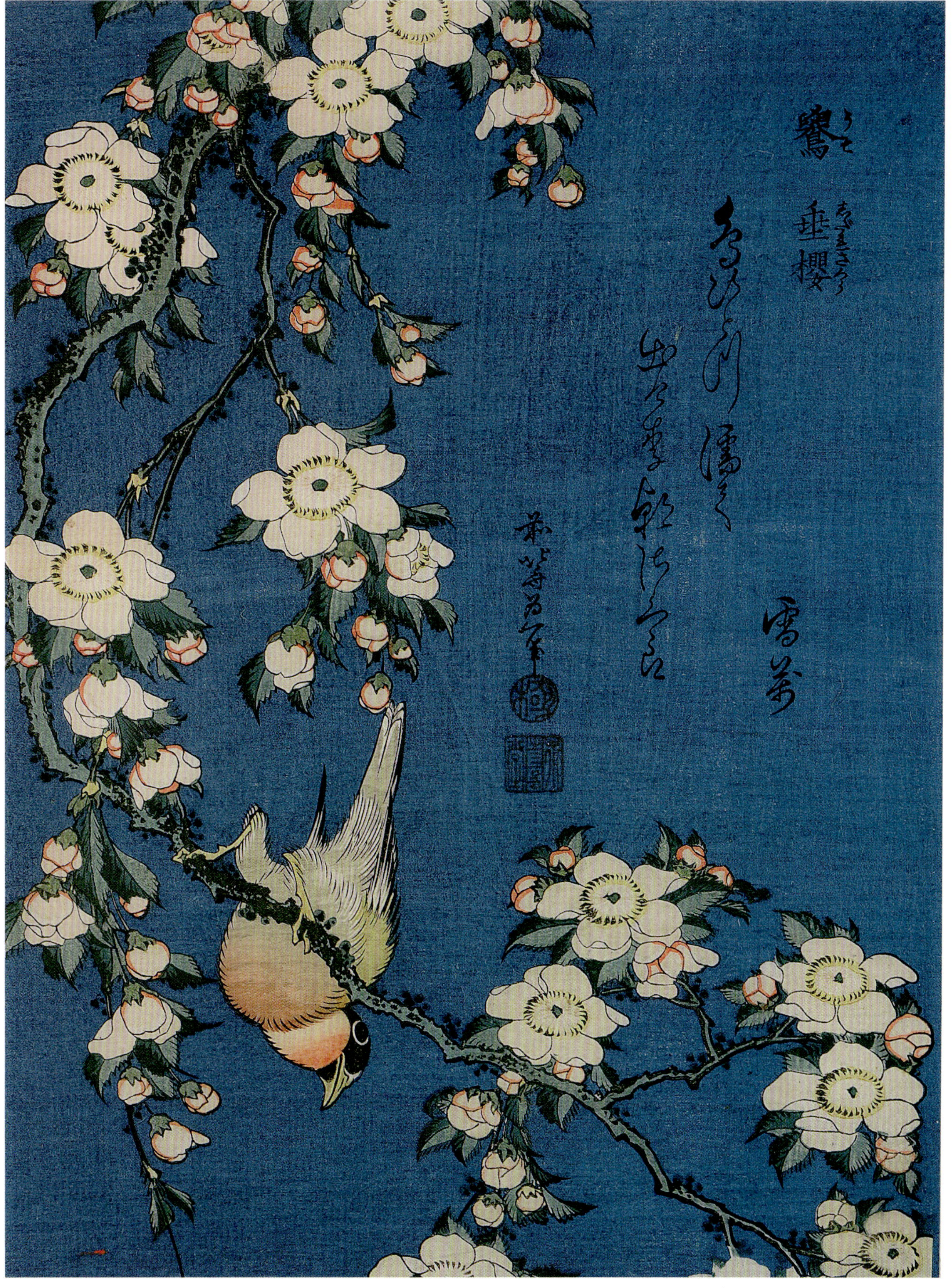
鶯
垂櫻

Magnolia and Java sparrow

About 1834

Signature: Saki no Hokusai Iitsu hitsu ('Brush of Iitsu, the former Hokusai')

Colour woodblock, published by Nishimuraya Yohachi, 25.4 × 18.6 cm

Provenance: Fine Art Society

Literature: TNM 2005, no. 374; Keyes & Morse 2015, no. 898

British Museum, 1910,0614,0.24

Osaka only

Both this print and cat. 93 have gradated crimson from the top, with purple flowers featured in the design. The winding, S-shaped branch that gives this composition its dancing movement has an almost exact counterpart in an illustration of a kerria plant and sparrow in Hokusai's book *Ryōbi shahitsu* (1820). Hokusai here replaces the kerria with a magnolia and the sparrow with a Java sparrow, an ornamental bird kept as a pet. Inscribed at top right is a poem about magnolia by the Ming dynasty literati painter Chen Daofu (or Chen Chun, 1483–1544): 'The east wind rises day and night. / Peach and plum blossoms cannot help being ruffled. / I study the dewdrops drenching the flowers. / The magnolia falls comparatively later.' AS

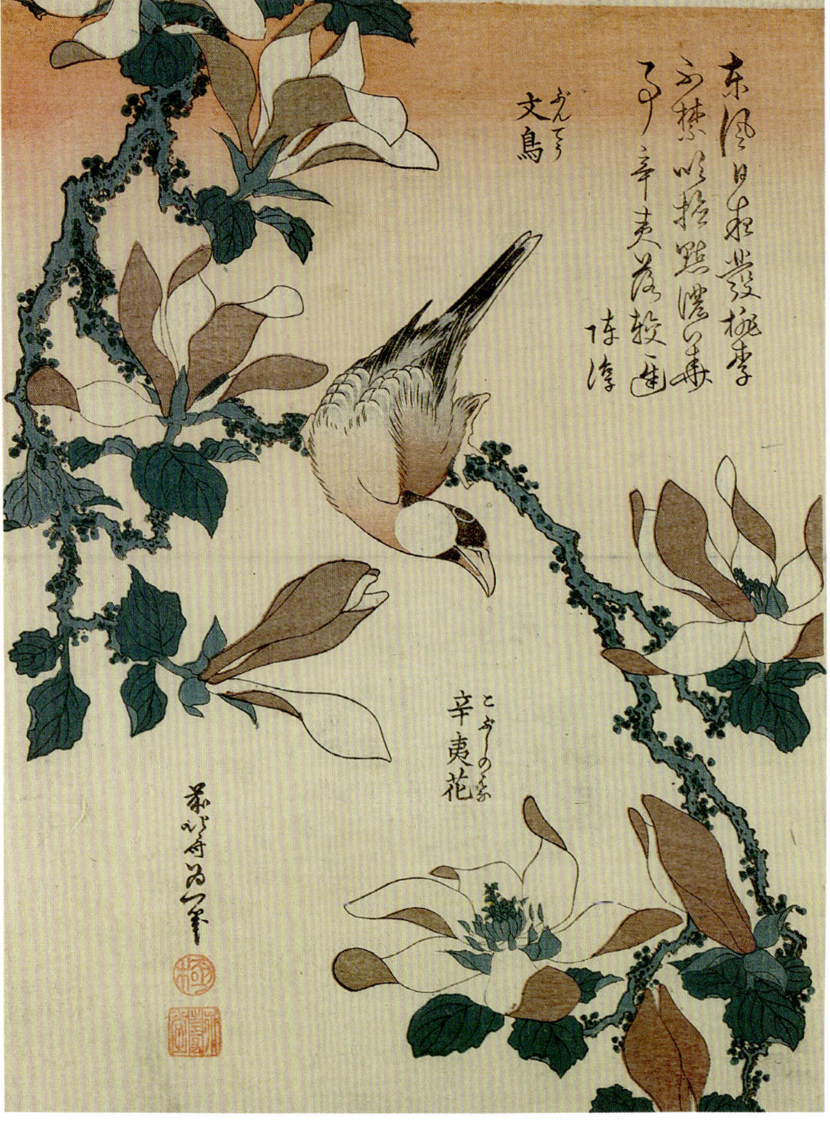

93
Wisteria and wagtail

About 1834
Signature: Saki no Hokusai Iitsu hitsu ('Brush of Iitsu,
the former Hokusai')
Colour woodblock, published by Nishimuraya Yohachi,
25.4 × 18.4 cm
Provenance: Fine Art Society
Literature: TNM 2005, no. 375; Keyes & Morse 2015,
no. 893
British Museum, 1910,0614,0.21
Osaka only

This novel composition positions a wagtail at the
end of a tendril of wisteria just coming into leaf.
The wagtail is so-named for the way it wags its long tail
feathers up and down. An almost identical illustration
of the bird is found among the formal style (*shintai*)
drawings in Hokusai's book *Santai gafu* (about 1816).
Inscribed at centre are the first two lines from a poem
entitled 'Aged Wisteria' by the Tang dynasty poet Qian
Qi (AD 710?–780?): 'Reaching tendrils emerge from
the towering trees. / Dangling threads cover the nesting
crane.' The poem appears in volume 10 of the poet's
collected writings, *Qian kao gong ji*. AS

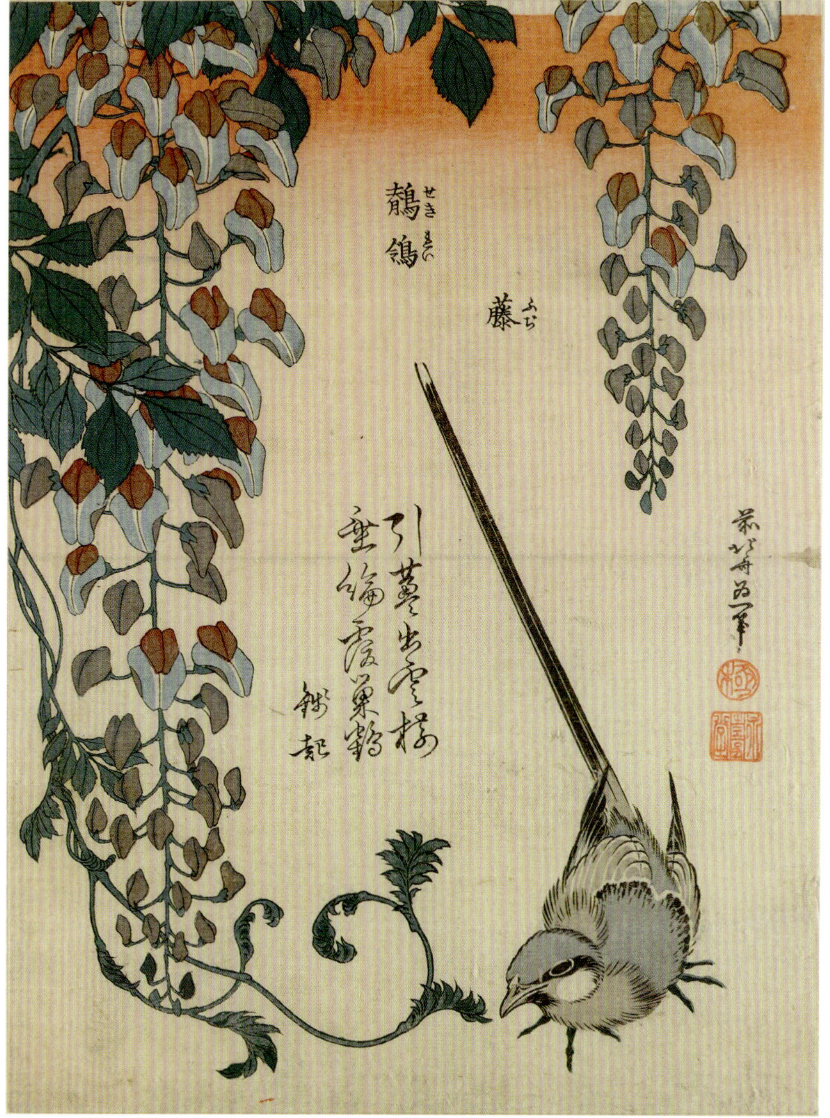

Azalea and lesser cuckoo

About 1834
Signature: Saki no Hokusai Iitsu hitsu ('Brush of Iitsu, the former Hokusai')
Colour woodblock, published by Nishimuraya Yohachi, 25.4 × 18.6 cm
Provenance: Fine Art Society
Literature: TNM 2005, no. 373; Keyes & Morse 2015, no. 897
British Museum, 1910,0614,0.25

Both this print and cat. 95 have backgrounds which feature light Prussian blue. An undivided pair of these two prints (lesser cuckoo on the left and bush warbler on the right) is in the collection of the Museum of Fine Arts, Boston. Hokusai's book *Santai gafu* (about 1816) includes illustrations of the lesser cuckoo, and most similar to the bird here is the example drawn in semi-cursive style (*gyōtai*). Inscribed at top left are two lines from a poem by the Southern Song dynasty poet Yang Wanli (studio name Yang Chengzhai, 1127–1206): 'A single cuckoo by day splits the mountain bamboo / with an initial cry upon first hearing about Du Yu.' Du Yu (AD 222–285) was a Chinese general of the Three Kingdoms period; according to legend a cuckoo cried out at the time of his death. AS

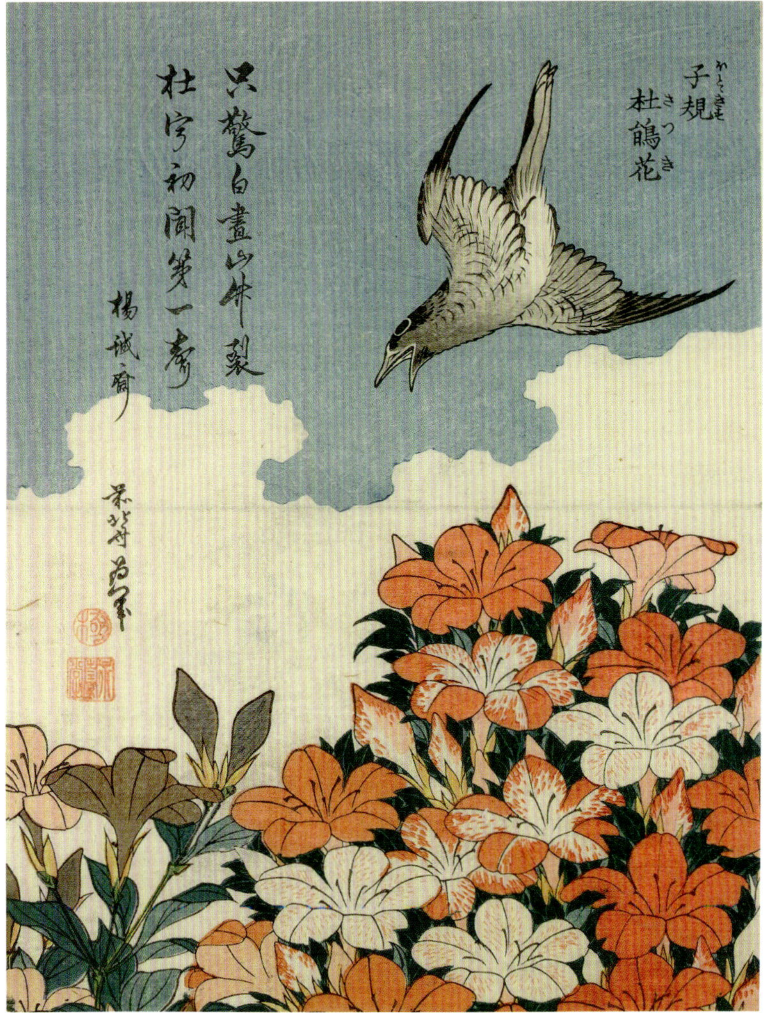

95

Rose and bush warbler

About 1834
Signature: Saki no Hokusai Iitsu hitsu ('Brush of Iitsu, the former Hokusai')
Colour woodblock, published by Nishimuraya Yohachi, 25.3 × 18.5 cm
Provenance: Fine Art Society
Literature: TNM 2005, no. 376; Keyes & Morse 2015, no. 896
British Museum, 1910,0614,0.22
Osaka only

The inscription refers to a 'yellow bird' (*kōchō*), another name for the bush warbler. Warblers are almost always depicted with a plum tree, but here it is paired with the rose. An illustration in Hokusai's book *Santai gafu* (about 1816) shows the bird on a plum branch. Inscribed at top left is a short verse (*hokku*) by Iwama Otsuni (1756–1823), one of the four leading haiku masters of northeast Japan: 'So now's the season / when roses droop and fall? / Home on a hill' (*Bara no hana / chiri nuru ori ka / oka no ie*) (trans. Alfred Haft). The immediate source of this poem is uncertain, but the *Collected Short Poems of Shōsō Otsuni* (*Shōsō Otsuni hokku shū*, 1835), includes a similar verse: 'The briar roses / have drooped and fallen at our / home on a hill' (*Kaya no hana / chiri nuru o waga / oka no ie*) (trans. Alfred Haft). AS

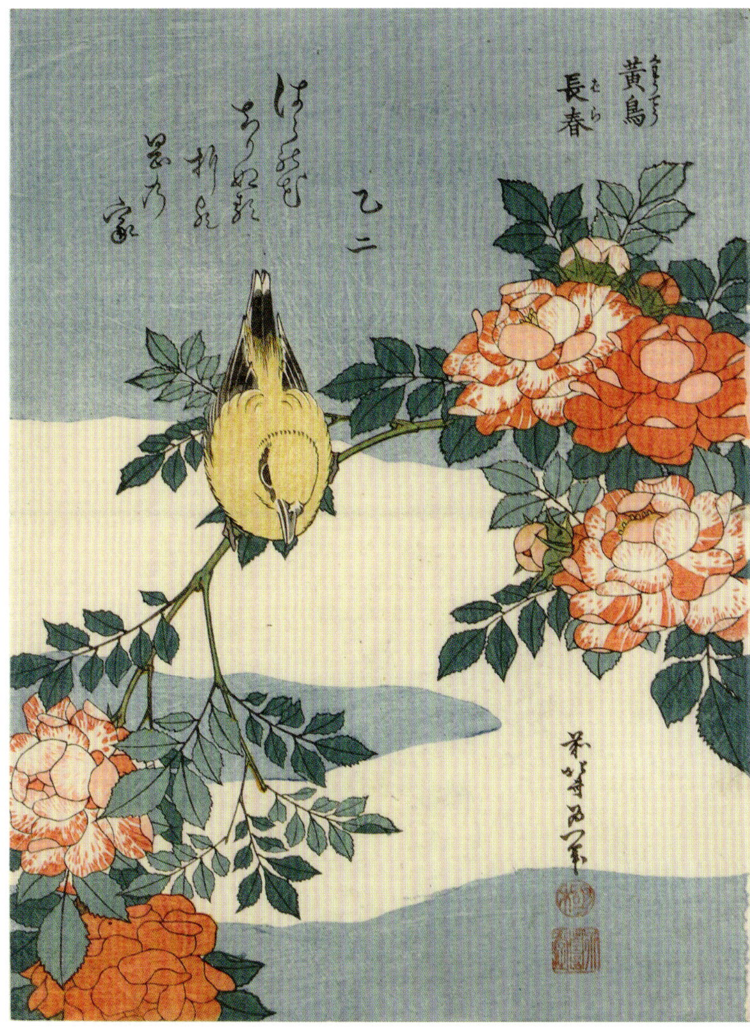

96
Mirabilis jalapa and grosbeak

About 1834

Signature: Saki no Hokusai Iitsu hitsu ('Brush of Iitsu, the former Hokusai')

Colour woodblock, published by Nishimuraya Yohachi, 25.4 × 18.5 cm

Provenance: Fine Art Society

Literature: TNM 2005, no. 372; Keyes & Morse 2015, no. 892

British Museum, 1910,0614,0.23

Both this print and cat. 97 have gradated crimson shading from the top, with red flowers featured at the bottom. Examples are known with and without a very light Prussian blue ground in the lower half of the design. The grosbeak is quite a large bird, with a distinctive yellow beak. It appears also in volume 3 of *Hokusai's Sketches* (*Hokusai manga*, 1815). *Mirabilis jalapa* (also called four o'clock flower, or marvel of Peru) is native to the Americas. It is thought to have reached Japan via Holland, entering the country through the port of Nagasaki. As Hokusai shows here, the flowers come in a variety of colours with different patterning. This plant appears again among Hokusai's *Drawings for a three-volume picture book* (1823–1835, cats 30, 168). At top right is a short verse (*hokku*) by a female poet named Yōdai: 'Four o'clock flowers / thrive on the far side of fences, / behind the peonies' (*Oshiroi no / hana ya botan no / ushirogaki*) (the source of the poem is unknown). **AS**

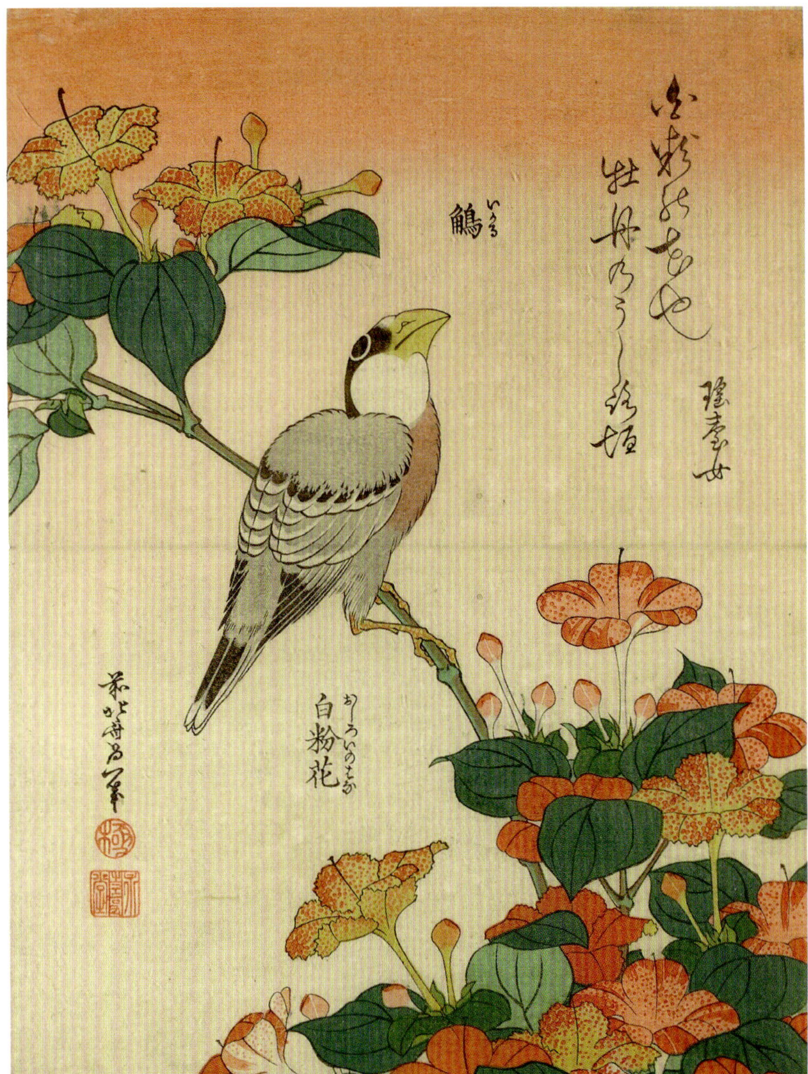

97
Fringed iris, dianthus and kingfisher

About 1834

Signature: Saki no Hokusai Iitsu hitsu ('Brush of Iitsu, the former Hokusai')

Colour woodblock, published by Nishimuraya Yohachi, 25.3 × 18.5 cm

Provenance: Fine Art Society

Literature: TNM 2005, no. 371; Keyes & Morse 2015, no. 895

British Museum, 1910,0614,0.28

Osaka only

A beautiful bird known also as the 'flying jewel' (*tobu hōseki*), the kingfisher has been depicted in paintings and the decorative arts since ancient times. Hokusai illustrated the bird in both volume 3 of *Hokusai's Sketches* (*Hokusai manga*, 1815) and *Santai gafu* (about 1816). Fringed iris (*shaga*) have serrated petals, complicated patterning and, as here, a brilliant appearance. They also feature in Hokusai's *Drawings for a three-volume picture book* (1823–1835, cats 30, 168), as well as the later books *Manji-ō sōhitsu gafu* (1843) and *Picture Book: Essence of Colouring* (1848, cat. 211). Chinese dianthus (*kara-nadeshiko*) appears in both Hokusai's book *Ryōbi shahitsu* (1820) and cat. 168. Here, the fringed iris's sinuous stems combine with the kingfisher's twisting body to create an appealing composition. Inscribed top right are two lines from a Chinese poem on the kingfisher by the Later Han dynasty Confucian scholar and calligrapher Cai Yong (AD 132/133–192): 'I look back to see the water generating emerald greens, / the rippling current producing pale blues.' The poem appears in the fourteen-volume collection, *Gu shi yuan* (Japanese: *Koshigen, A Fountain of Ancient Poetry*, 1719). **AS**

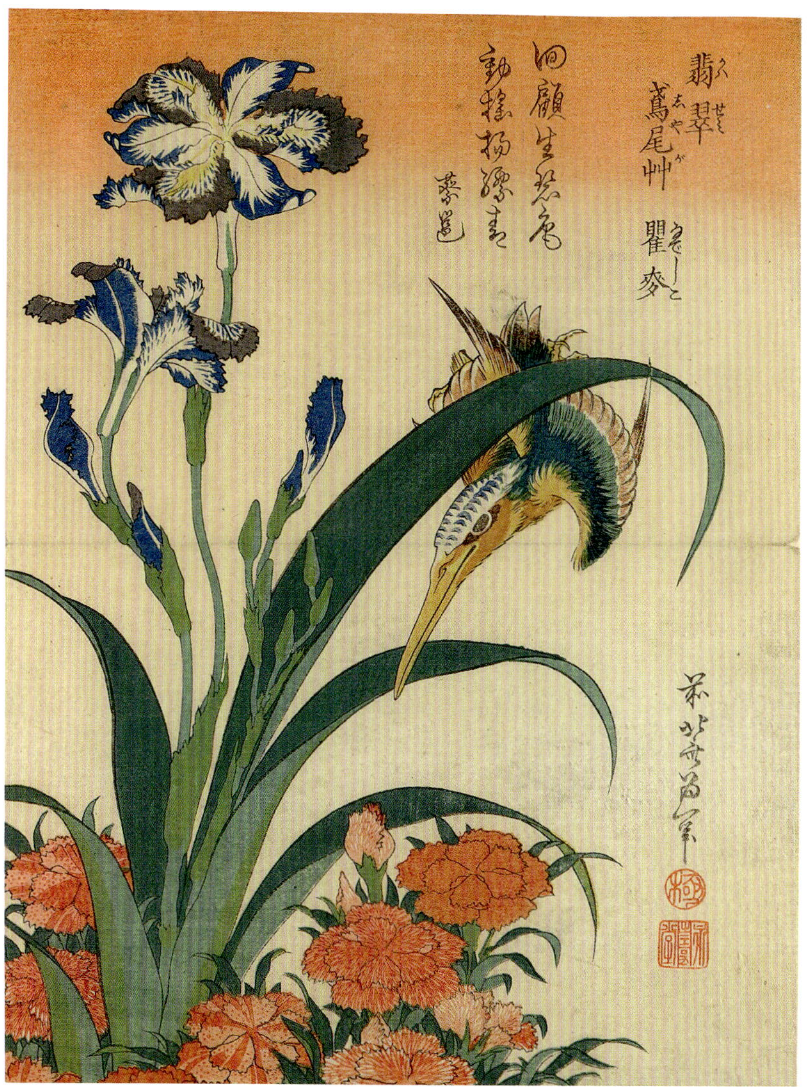

Thistle and crossbill

About 1834

Signature: Saki no Hokusai Iitsu hitsu ('Brush of Iitsu, the former Hokusai')

Colour woodblock, published by Nishimuraya Yohachi, 25.4 × 18.6 cm

Provenance: Fine Art Society

Literature: TNM 2005, no. 370; Keyes & Morse 2015, no. 894

British Museum, 1910,0614,0.27

Osaka only

Both this print and cat. 99 present the birds and flowers against a background of Prussian blue that gradates from dark to light from the top of the image. The crossbill is a small bird, somewhat larger than a sparrow, with a beak that crosses over at the tip, as clearly seen in the print. This adaptation allows the bird to prise open pine cones to retrieve the seeds. The flowering plant is identified as a 'plumed thistle' (*oniazami*). It appears also among Hokusai's *Drawings for a three-volume picture book* (1823–1835, cats 30, 168). Inscribed at top left is a short verse (*hokku*) by a poet named Tōha: 'The thistle grows / on banks bathed in sunshine / right until dusk' (*Kureru made / hi ataru kishi ya / hana azami*) (the source of the poem is unknown). AS

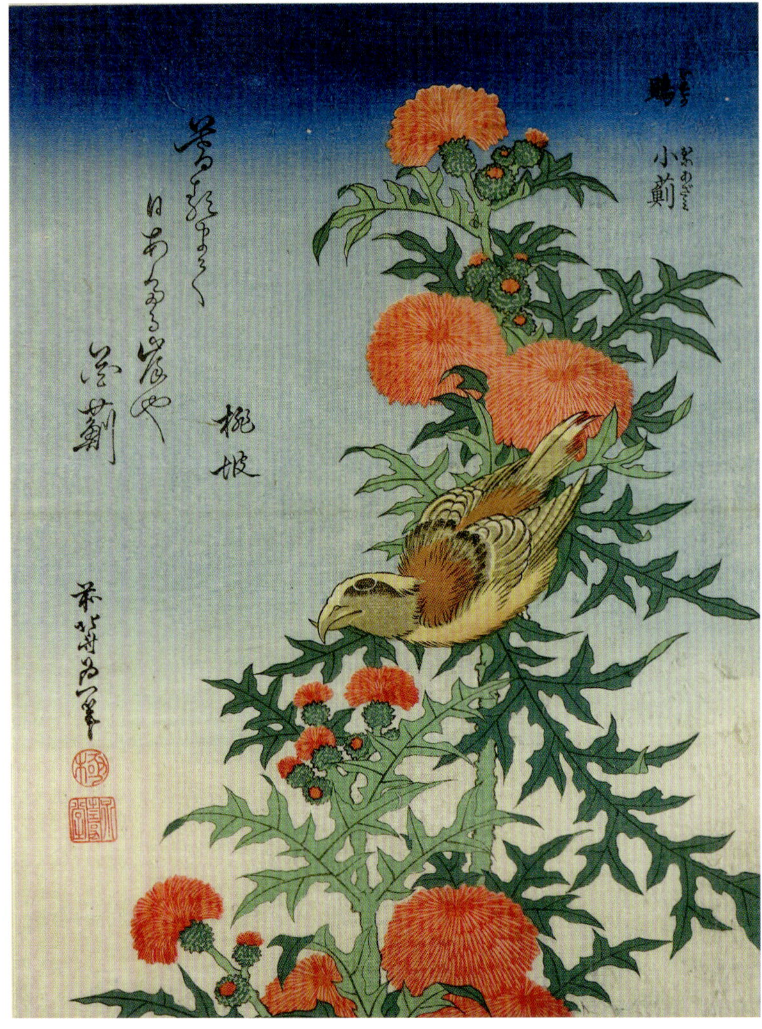

99

Saxifrage and wild strawberry, shrike and red-flanked bluetail

About 1834
Signature: Saki no Hokusai Iitsu hitsu ('Brush of Iitsu, the former Hokusai')
Colour woodblock, published by Nishimuraya Yohachi, 25.4 × 18.6 cm
Provenance: Fine Art Society
Literature: TNM 2005, no. 369; Keyes & Morse 2015, no. 891
British Museum, 1910,0614,0.26
Osaka only

The shrike (*mozu*), at the top, eats both insects and frogs, and in autumn it is known to leave its dead prey skewered on tree branches for later consumption. In *Picture Book: Essence of Colouring* (1848, cat. 211), Hokusai provides a detailed account of methods for drawing and colouring this type of bird. The red-flanked bluetail, lower down, seems to be a male, with some lapis lazuli colouring. Saxifrage, bottom left, has distinctive patterned leaves, as its Chinese name, 'Tiger's-ear plant' (*huercao*), also suggests. Once again, Hokusai provides a detailed discussion of this plant's form and coloration in his book *Picture Book: Essence of Colouring*, and saxifrage and wild strawberry both appear in *Drawings for a three-volume picture book* (1823–1835, cats 30, 168). Inscribed at upper left is a short verse (*hokku*) by a poet named Ra'un: 'It's been decided: / those hordes of shrike have vanished / into the grass' (*Mozu-dori ya / bunbetsu wa mina / kusa ni aru*). The poem recalls the shrike's springtime habit of suddenly disappearing from lowlands up into the mountains, as though the flocks have vanished into the grass. The source of the poem is unknown. AS

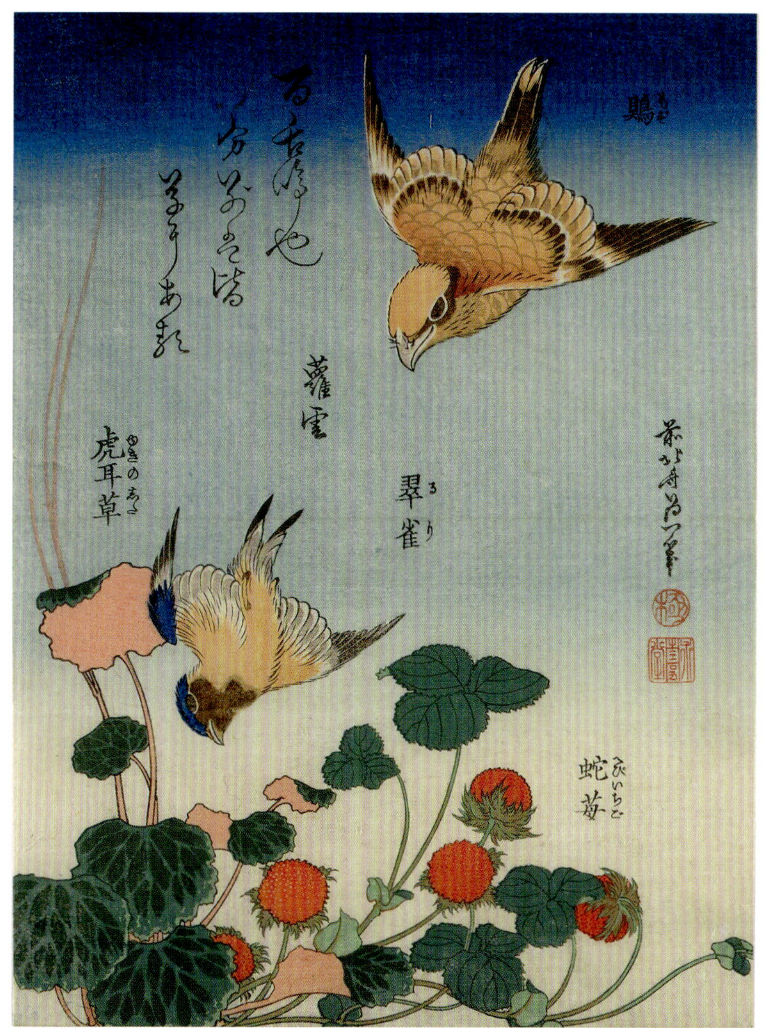

Gamecock and hen

1826–1834
Signature: Saki no Hokusai / Iitsu hitsu ('Brush of
Iitsu, the former Hokusai')
Seal: Katsushika (1)
Hanging scroll, ink and colour on silk, 133.9 × 46.4 cm
Literature: UT 1931, no. 14; NU 1982, no. 24; Nagata
2000, no. 76; TNM 2005, no. 433; Paris 2014, no. 470
MOA Museum of Art, Atami
London only

A male gamecock poses heroically, looking up at the sky,
while a female stands behind him. The bodies have been
drawn and coloured with great care, from the dots on
the cockscomb and neck to the scales on the legs and
talons and feathers. The large tail feathers give an
impression of roughness, the flight feathers of precision,
and the back and breast feathers of softness – while
brush-shading serves to distinguish between them.
Thus depicted, the birds are endowed with the gravity
and dignity of the king of the birds, but also raised to
a kind of hyper-real, fantastical form. The leaves of
bamboo grass at the top serve to maintain the balance
of the picture, which is considered a masterpiece
among Hokusai's later paintings. AS

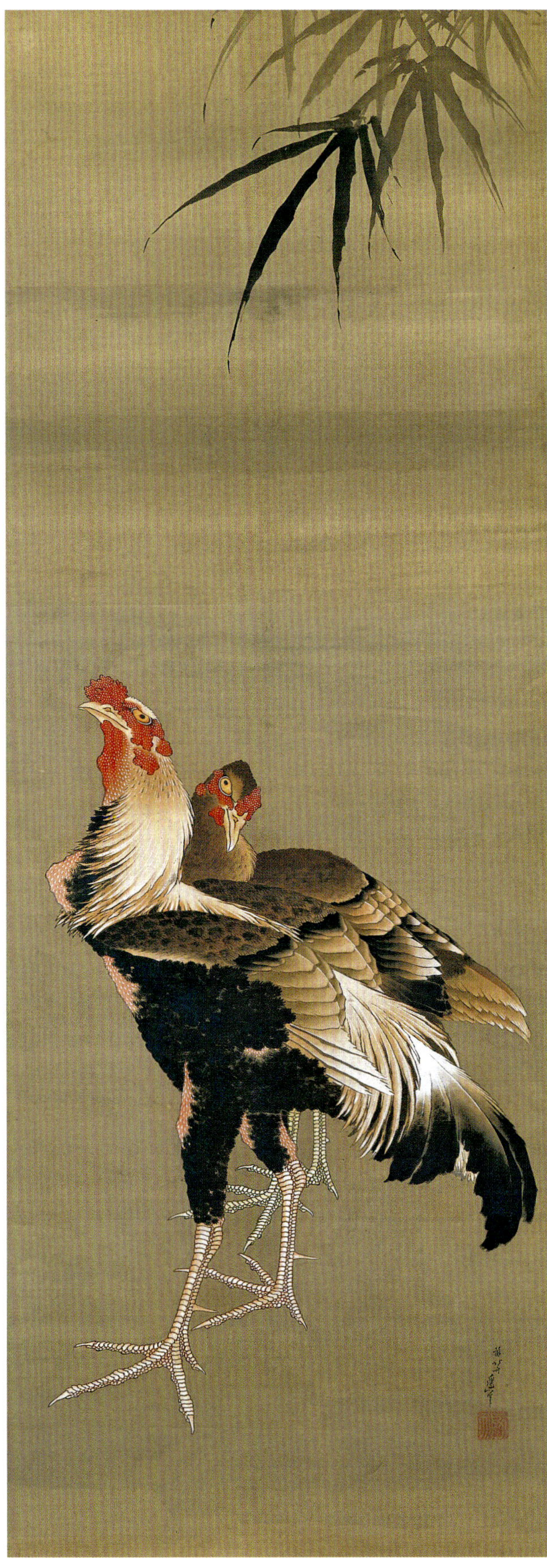

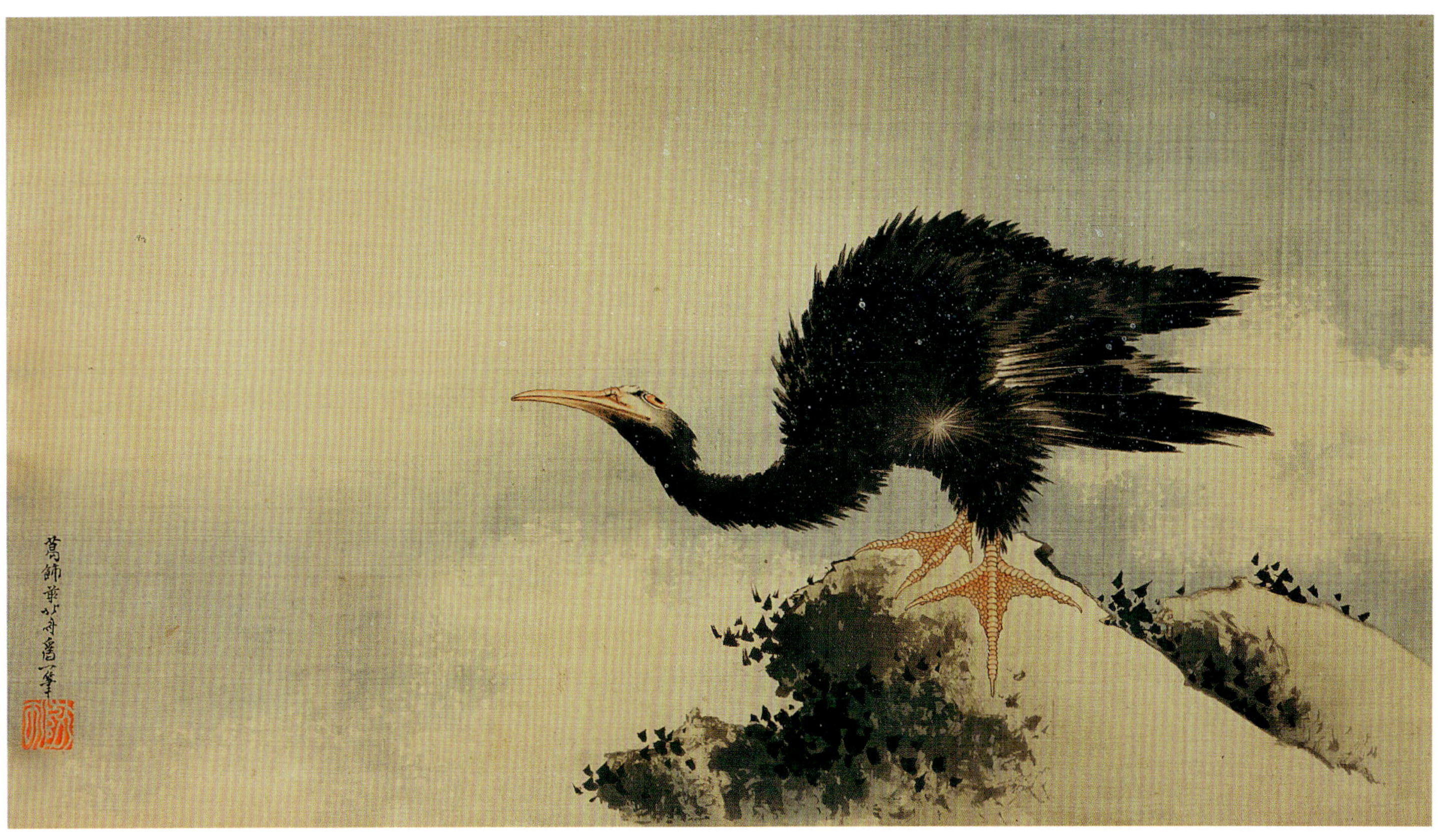

101

Cormorant on a rock

1823–1826
Signature: Katsushika saki no Hokusai Iitsu hitsu
('Brush of Iitsu, the former Hokusai [of] Katsushika')
Seal: Katsushika (1)
Hanging scroll, ink and colour on silk, 41.3 × 71.3 cm
Literature: UT 1931, no. 9; Ōta 1985, no. 556; Nagata
2000, no. 77; TNM 2005, no. 434; Paris 2014, no. 471
Hayashibara Museum of Art, Okayama
Osaka only

A cormorant perches on a rock and stares at the sky.
The fine detail in the depiction of the bird – for example,
the meticulously webbed feet – means we can classify
this as a work in 'formal' (*shin*) painting style. The tiny
spots of white, like splashes of water, and the fine
plumage that radiates from the centre of the body are
impressive. *Cormorant and morning glory* (cat. 102), painted
slightly later, is also compelling in its brushwork,
but lacks the imposing presence. Here the cormorant,
whipped by the wind and splashed by spray, stands
on a rock, but ignores the water beneath and stares
instead up into the sky. It embodies some great spirit
– a projection by Hokusai himself, a state towards
which he aspired. Transformed from a this-worldly
cormorant to a universal life-form, with a will of its
own, it emanates the brilliant intensity of an other-
worldly being. AS

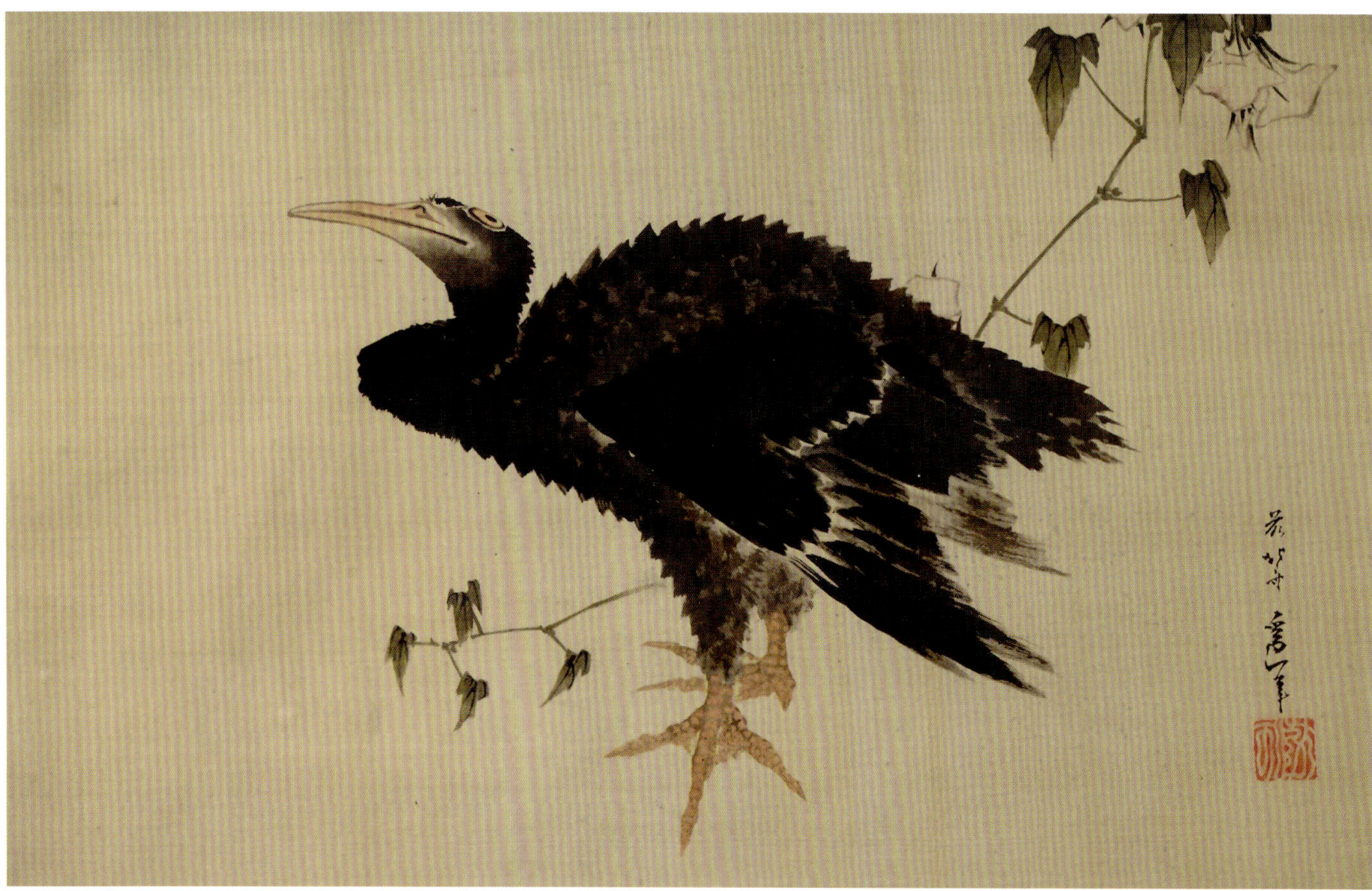

Cormorant and morning glory

1830–1832
Signature: Saki no Hokusai Iitsu hitsu ('Brush of Iitsu, the former Hokusai')
Seal: Katsushika (1)
Hanging scroll, ink and colour on silk, 36.5 × 55.8 cm
Provenance: William Anderson
Literature: Clark 1992, no. 98; Nagata 2000, BW no. 140; TNM 2005, no. 435
British Museum, 1881,1210,0.1899
Osaka only

The work is light in tone: a quizzical cormorant stands in front of a delicate morning glory. Hokusai's use of his brush to build up the layers of darker and lighter ink is remarkable. *Cormorant on a rock* (cat. 101) was done in formal (*shin*) painting style, but here the bird combines semi-cursive (*gyō*) and cursive (*sō*) elements of brush styles. In the cursive style, the subject is represented as much as possible by building up planes of colour, avoiding outline. Here, Hokusai does use lines for the face, for the webbing on the cormorant's feet and for the veins of the morning glory leaves – so strictly speaking this should be classified as semi-cursive style. From the form of the signature, the painting can be dated to about 1830–1832. It bears interesting comparison to the cormorant drawn in cursive style in *Manji-ō sōhitsu gafu* (1843). AS

Eagle and cherry

1843
Signature: Hachijūyon rō / Manji hitsu ('Brush of
Manji, old man of eighty-four')
Seal: Katsushika (3)
Hanging scroll, ink and colour on silk, 97.2 × 45.7 cm
Literature: Kaneko 1964, no. 7; Ozaki 1967, no. 32; NU
1982, no. 33; Nagata 2000, no. 113; TNM 2005, no. 475
Ujiie Ukiyo-e Collection, Kamakura

An eagle, looking up at the sky, grips a rock with its
talons, with a small waterfall beneath. The modulation
of the rocks – alternating dots and planes – resembles
the treatment of the woods in the print 'Clear day with
a southern breeze' (cats 52, 53). In the background, a
cherry tree is in full bloom, its trunk twisting and its
colour and hue changing as it rises mysteriously. The
flowers are pink at the bottom, then white, then pink
again, ornamenting the eagle and emphasizing its
heroic qualities. Hokusai gives instructions for drawing
and colouring eagles and hawks in *Picture Book: Essence
of Colouring* (1848, cat. 211). Here, the way in which he
has applied the black ink for the breast using the
middle rather than the tip of the brush, the depiction
of the hair-like feathers on the beak, and, above all,
the form as a whole, are exactly as in the picture of an
'eagle' in volume 1 of that book. AS

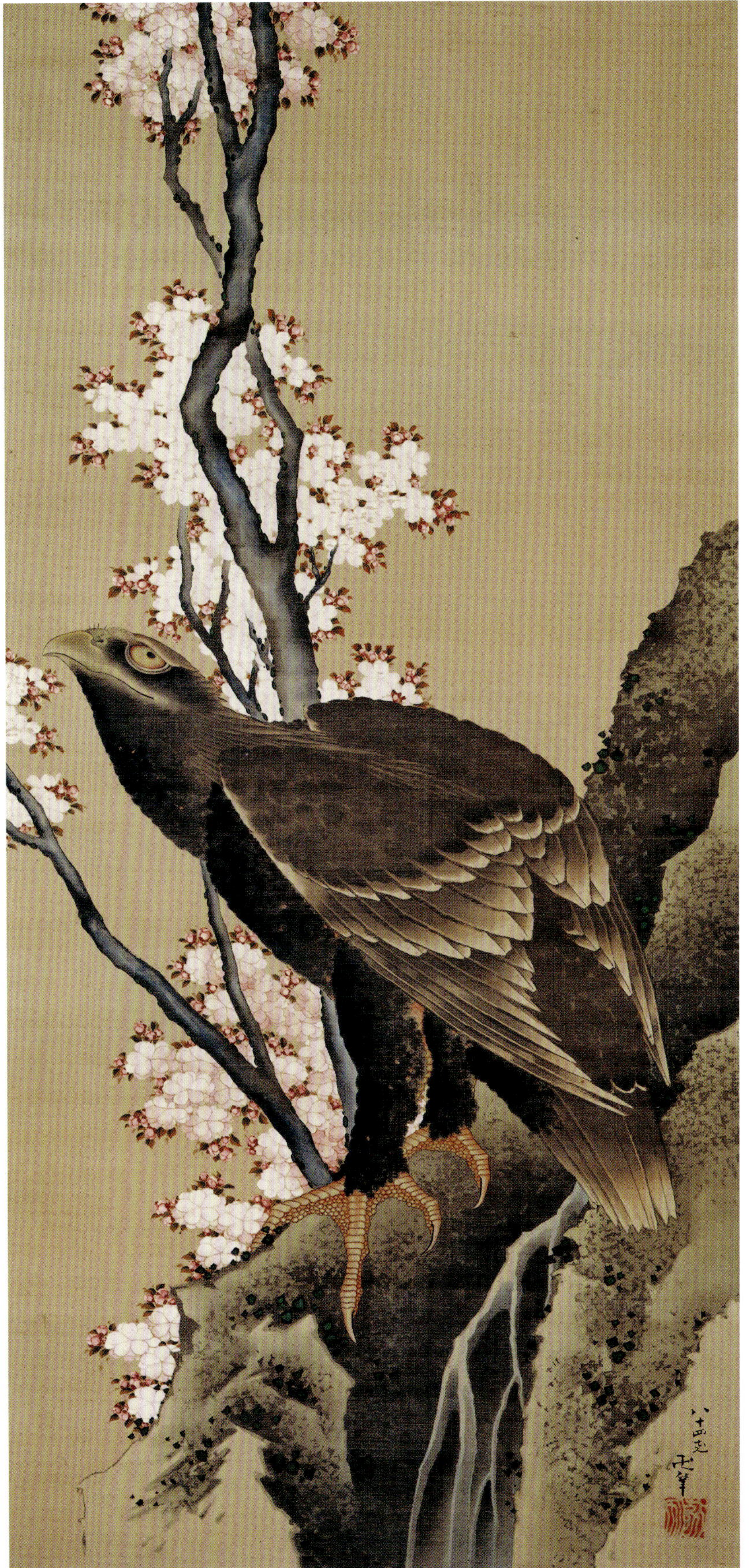

Hawk and cherry

About 1833–1834
Signature: Saki no Hokusai Iitsu hitsu ('Brush of Iitsu, the former Hokusai')
Colour woodblock, published by Moriya Jihei, 52.0 × 23.1 cm
Provenance: Henri Vever
Literature: TNM 2005, no. 380; Keyes & Morse 2015, no. 1797
Tokyo National Museum, A-10569-697
London only

A hawk perches on a splendidly decorated stand (*takahoko*). There are many similar pictures by painters working in various Chinese-influenced styles (*kanga*). Hokusai drew one in the first volume of *Hokusai's Sketches* (*Hokusai manga*, 1814), but the figure of the hawk here most closely resembles one in *One Hundred Views of Mt Fuji* (1834, cat. 176), while the stand is very similar to one included in *Album of model paintings* (cat. 175). This work and 'Carp in waterfall' (cat. 105) are from a set of five large vertical prints by Hokusai of animals, birds and fish. The others are 'Horses in pasture', 'Turtles in water' and 'Cranes on a branch of snow-covered pine'. The tall *nagaōban* format imitates a hanging scroll painting. All five are auspicious subjects, and they may have been produced to celebrate the New Year. The inclusion of 'Horses in pasture' suggests 1834, a horse year. **AS**

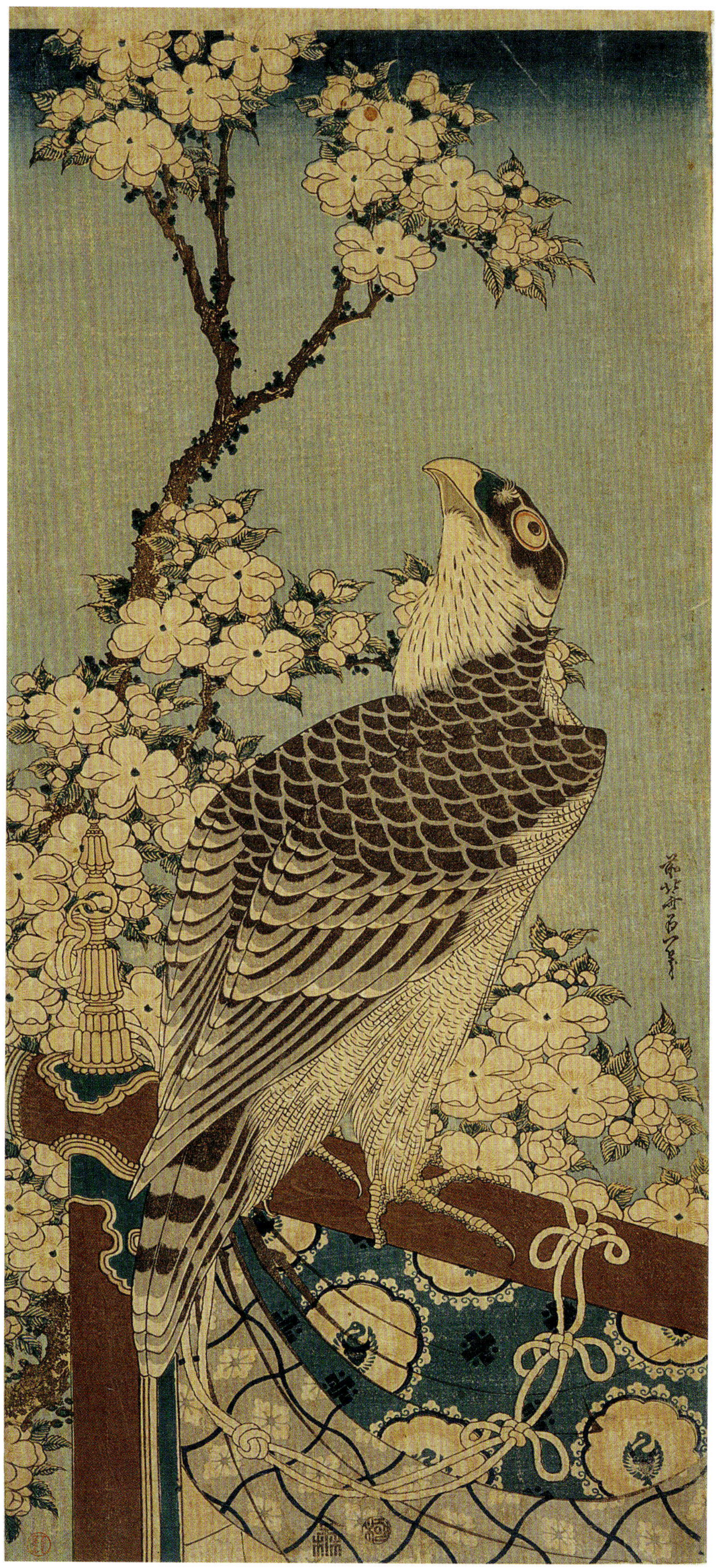

105
Carp in waterfall

About 1833–1834

Signature: Saki no Hokusai Iitsu hitsu ('Brush of Iitsu, the former Hokusai')

Colour woodblock, publisher unknown (Moriya Jihei?), 52.2 × 23.2 cm

Provenance: Katō Shōzō

Literature: HUT 1987–1990, vol. 3, no. 60; RA 1991, no. 66; Paris 2014, no. 414; Keyes & Morse 2015, no. 984

British Museum, 1927,0413,0.14

The phrase 'ascending dragon gate' (*tōryūmon*) denotes the gateway to success in life. The name comes from a legend about carp gathering below the rapids known as 'Dragon Gate' (Chinese: *longmen*; Japanese: *ryūmon*) in the upper reaches of the Yellow River in China. Many of the fish cannot continue any further, but if a carp can climb the rapids, it becomes a dragon. Numerous pictures were therefore produced of carp climbing waterfalls, as a way of signifying success in life. This image may be one of them, but Hokusai's main focus seems to be not the ascending carp, but rather the one down below looking out at us. The continuity in the treatment of the white spray – at the bottom of the waterfall, on the body of the carp and on the yellowish rocks to the right of the picture – demonstrates the attention to fine detail characteristic of Hokusai. AS

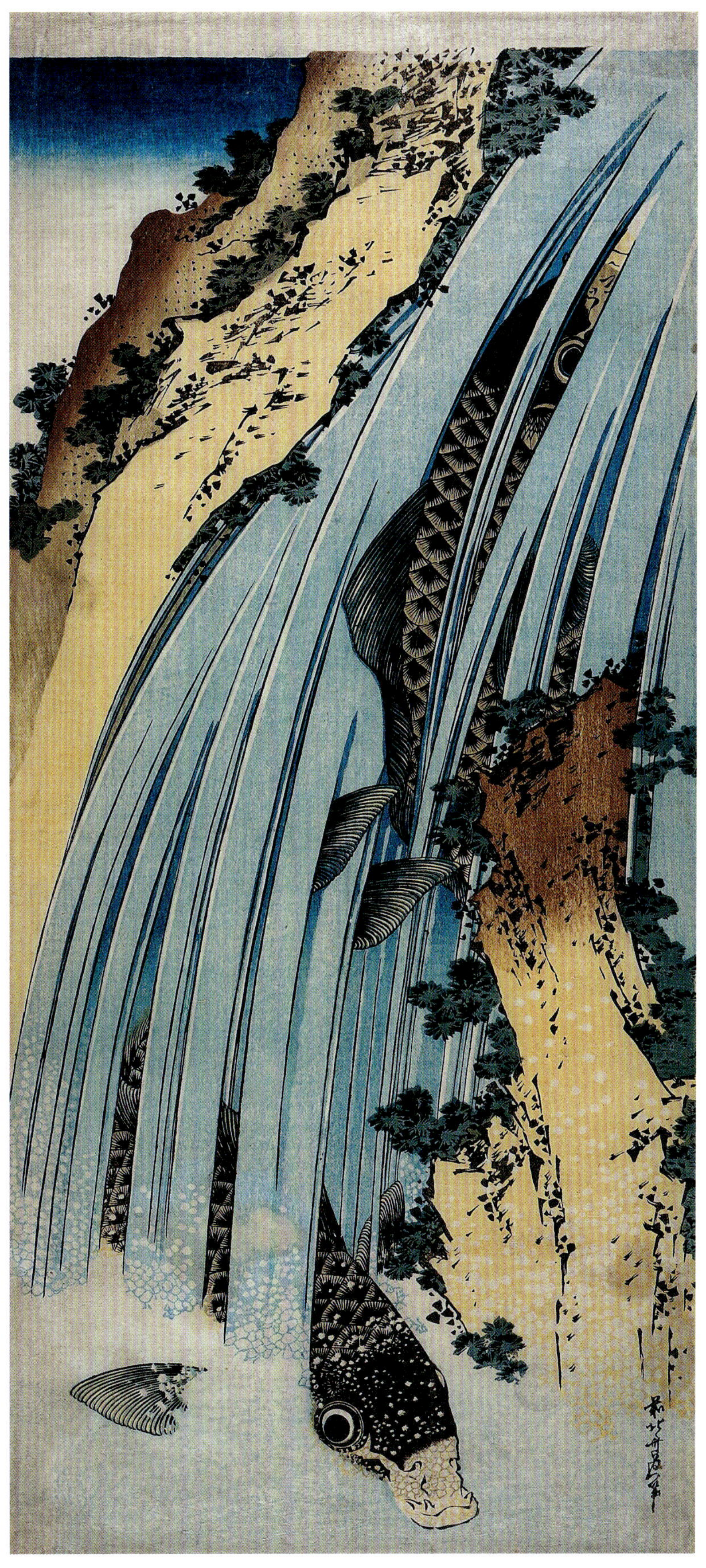

Cockerel, hen and chick with spiderwort (proof print)

1832
Signature: Saki no Hokusai / Iitsu hitsu ('Brush of
Iitsu, the former Hokusai')
Fan print mounted in a folding album, woodblock
proof with red ink, 24.4 × 30.0 cm
Provenance: W. G. Alexander
Literature: HUT 1987–1990, vol. 4, BW no. 147; Paris
2014, no. 419; Keyes & Morse 2015, no. 930
Victoria and Albert Museum, London, E.1361-1916,
given by the Misses Alexander

Cockerel, hen and chick with spiderwort

About 1832
Signature: Saki no Hokusai / Iitsu hitsu ('Brush of
Iitsu, the former Hokusai')
Fan print, colour woodblock, publisher 'Ta'
unidentified, 22.9 × 29.2 cm
Literature: Keyes & Morse 2015, no. 930
Metropolitan Museum of Art, New York, JP745,
Francis Lathrop collection, Purchase, Frederick
C. Hewitt Fund, 1911

The fan print features a cockerel, hen and chick – a
family of chickens. Hokusai frequently drew pictures
of chickens, but these resemble most closely the cockerel
and hen he drew in *Picture Book: Essence of Colouring*,
volume 2 (1848, cat. 211). The spiderwort in the
background resembles one of the block-ready sketches
in *Drawings for a three-volume picture book* (cats 30, 168) in
the collection of the Museum of Fine Arts, Boston.
The monochrome proof print has survived by chance,
and the red ink was probably added by a later owner.
There are two notable differences between the proof
and the finished colour print. First, the 'dragon' (*tatsu*)
date seal for 1832 on the proof print is absent on the
colour woodblock. Perhaps this was removed because
the print was still being offered for sale after the dragon
year of 1832 and the publisher did not want it to seem
out of date. Second, the pattern on the hen's breast is
different. This must also have been changed before the
print was put on sale, although it is not clear when. AS

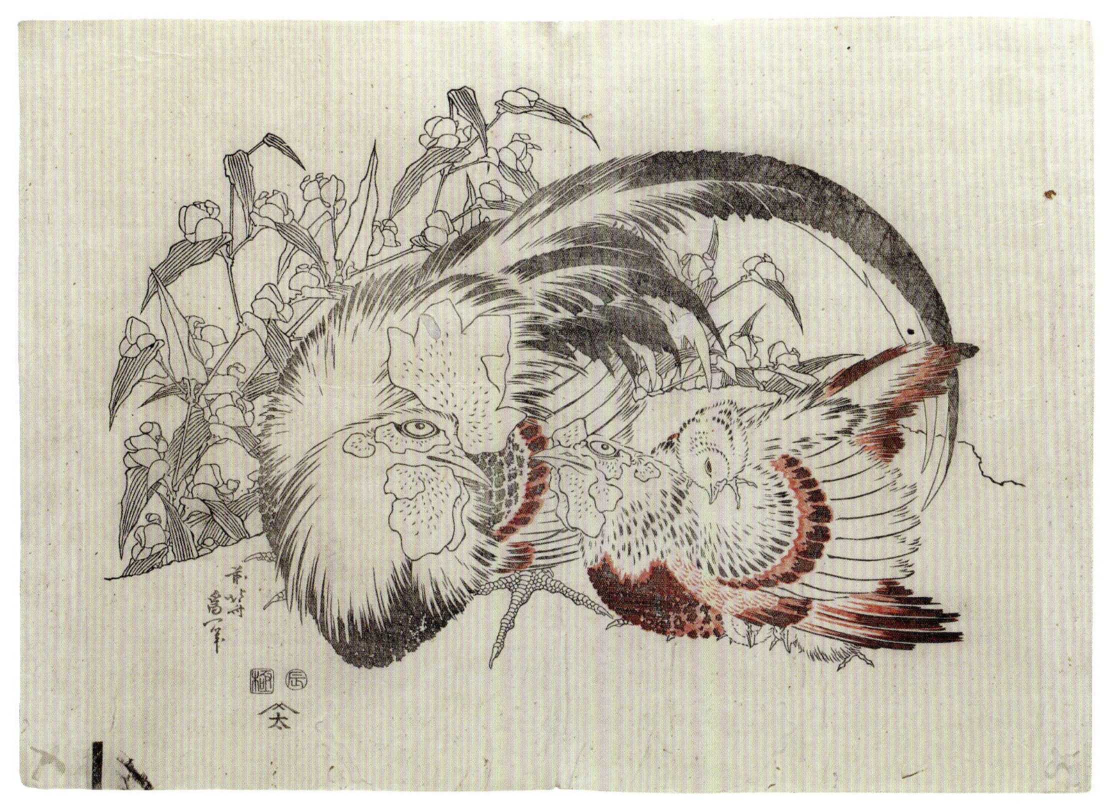

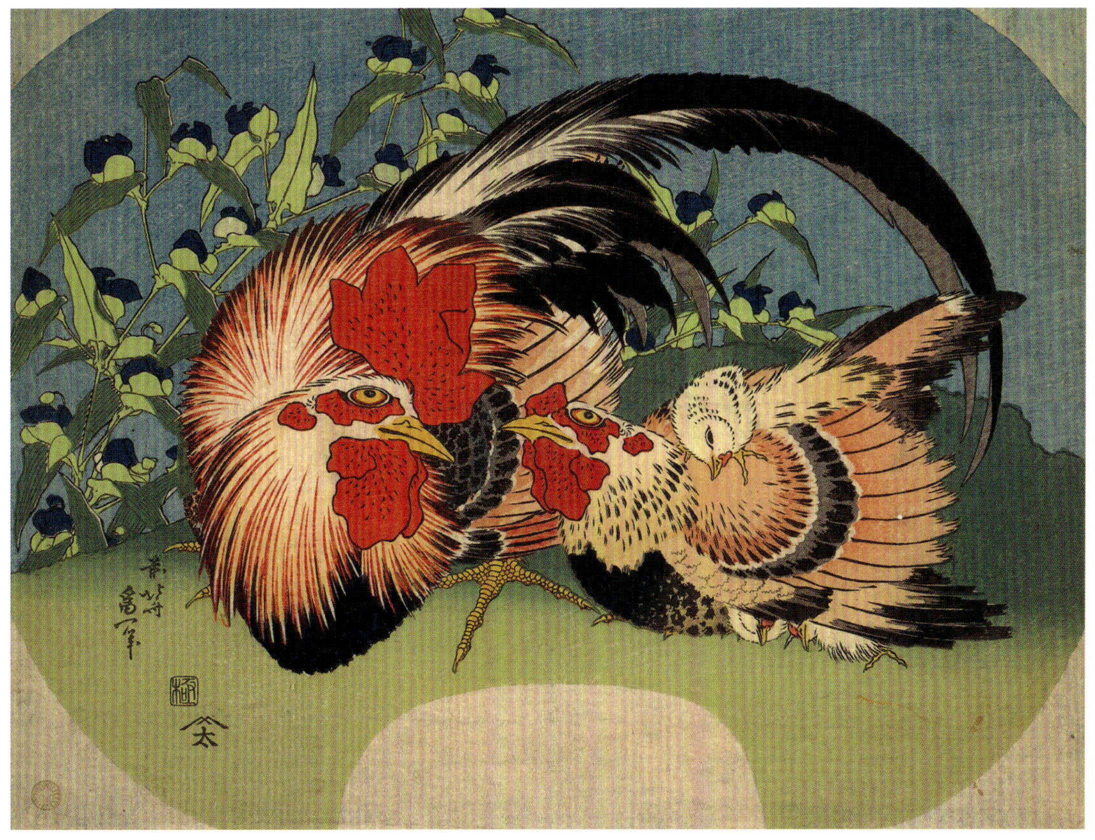

Cockerels and hens

About 1833–1834 (date/censorship seal, 1835)
Signature: Saki no Hokusai / Iitsu hitsu ('Brush of
Iitsu, the former Hokusai')
Fan print, colour woodblock, published by Iseya
Ichiemon, 22.5 × 29.0 cm
Literature: TNM 2005, no. 356; Keyes & Morse 2015,
no. 931
Tokyo National Museum, A-10569-691
Osaka only

Abandoning perspective, Hokusai has here captured
seven chickens as a single, solid mass, producing an
image of almost overpowering intensity. The strange,
almost uncanny charm is characteristic of his work at
the time. The background is Prussian blue, with which
Hokusai was experimenting in the early 1830s and
which also appears in his medium-format (*chūban*)
prints of birds and flowers (cats 90, 91) and his
large-format (*ōban*) warrior prints (cat. 131). Hokusai
used the art name Iitsu until the end of 1833, but this
seems to be contradicted here by the censorship seal of
1835. This gap can be explained by a lag between the
completion of the block-ready drawing and its finally
receiving the censor's approval. There is another
impression of the design in the Museum of Fine Arts,
Boston (21.10192), but with a number of printing
differences – most notably, the background has
gradated bands of purple (top) and green (bottom),
rather than just uniform blue. AS

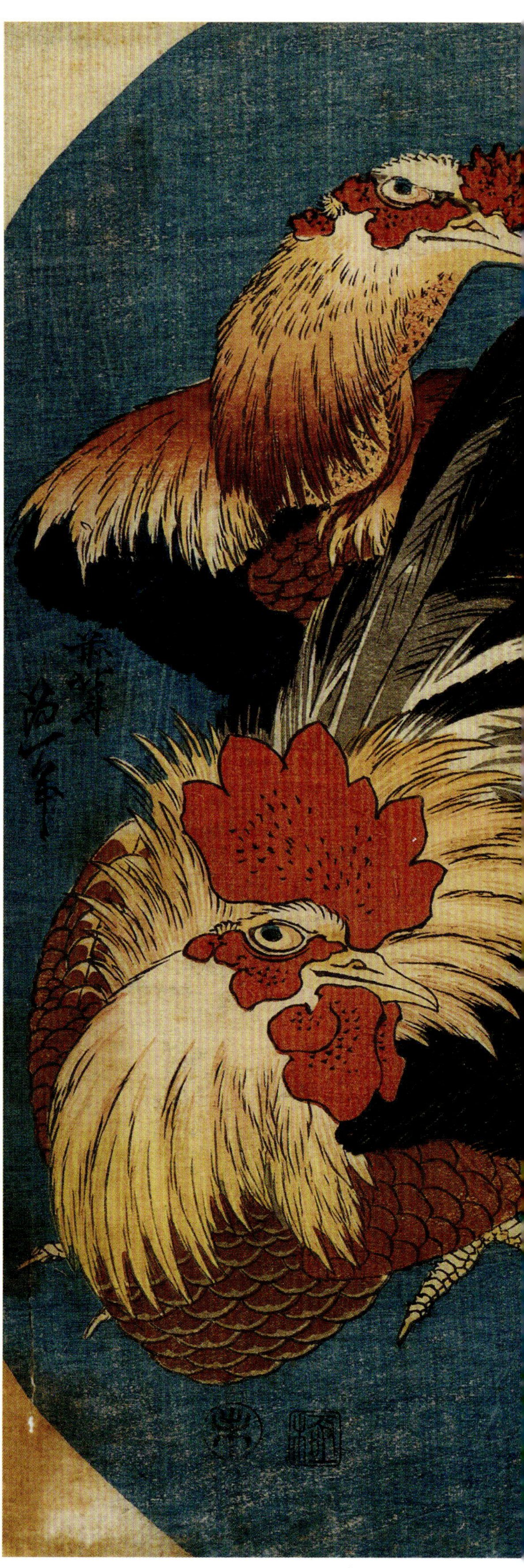

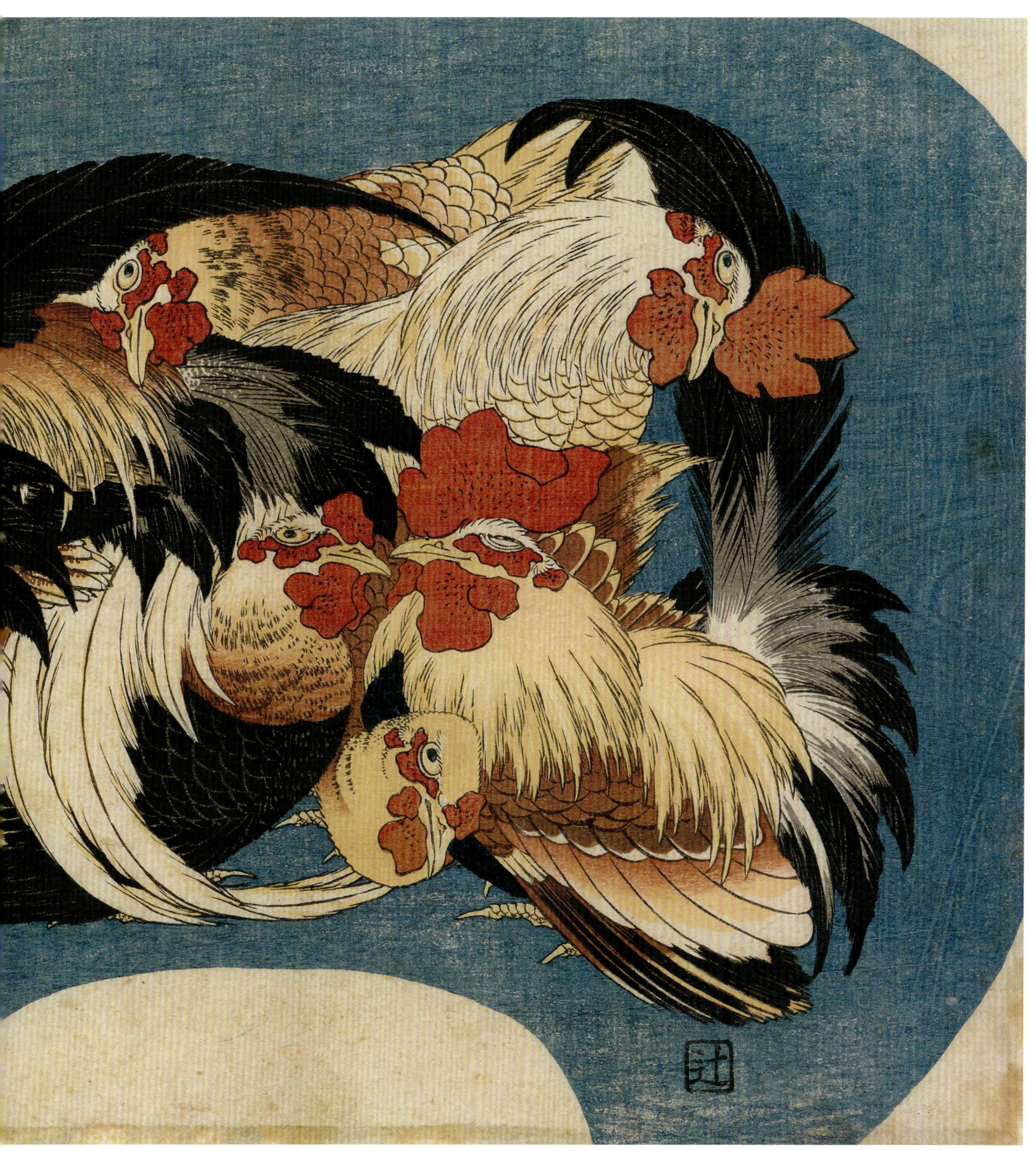

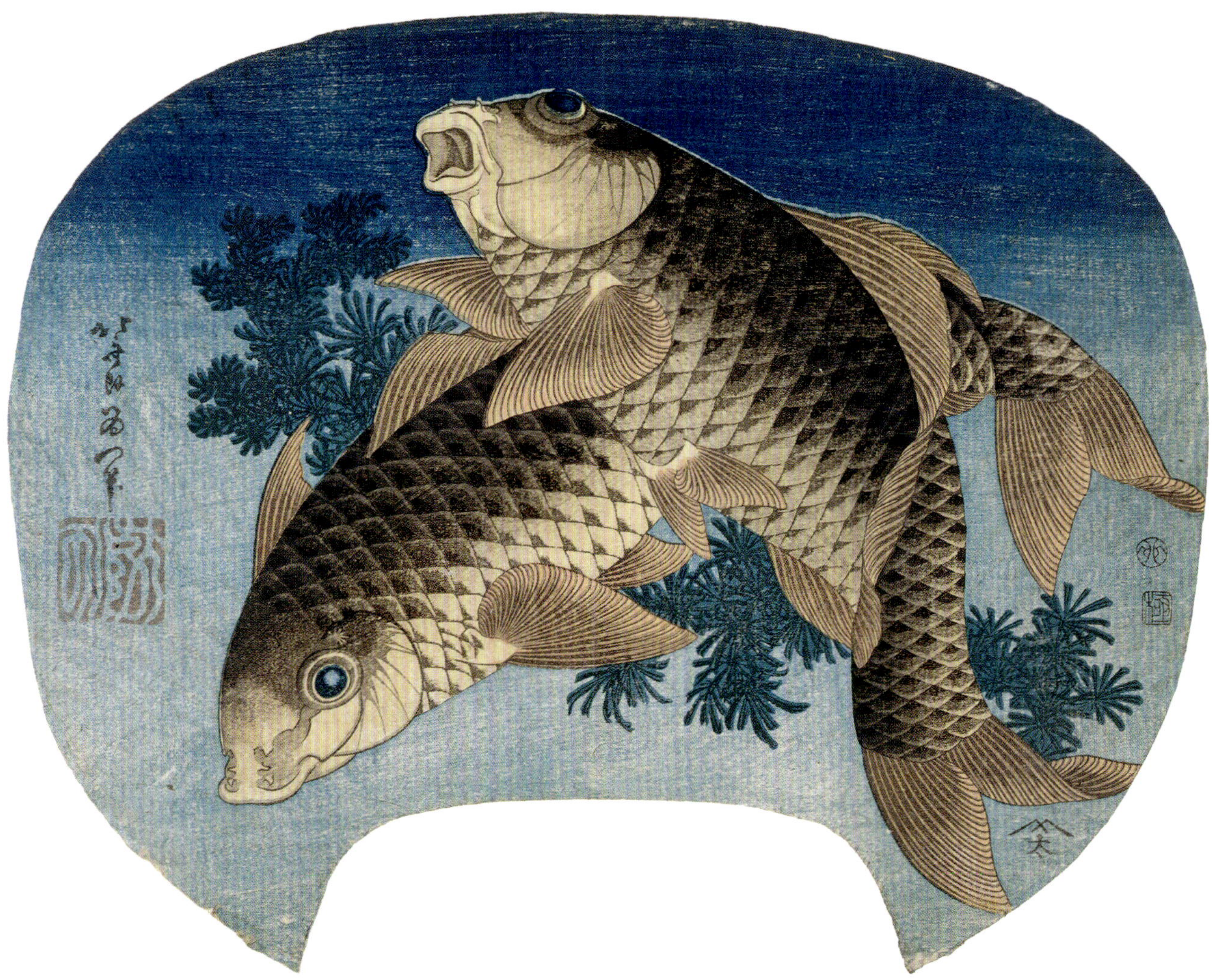

109

Carp

1831

Signature: Saki no Hokusai / Iitsu hitsu ('Brush of Iitsu, the former Hokusai')

Seal: Katsushika

Fan print, colour woodblock, publisher 'Ta' unidentified, 23.2 × 28.7 cm

Literature: HUT 1987–1990, vol. 7, no. 134; RA 1991, no. 67; TNM 2005, no. 354; Guimet 2008, no. 72; Paris 2014, no. 417; Keyes & Morse 2015, no. 1862

Musée national des arts asiatiques Guimet, Paris, EO.1901, bequeathed by Issac de Camondo, 1911

Osaka only

Two carp are swimming against a background of river weed. The carp are very similar to those in a painting Hokusai gave to his student Katsushika Hokumei (worked about 1804–1830) in 1813 (Saitama Prefectural Museum). In the painting, though, the carp are depicted together with ripples of water, whereas here those ripples are absent. Hokusai has avoided making the picture overly complex, the water being adequately represented by the gradated Prussian blue background. The printed 'Katsushika' seal here is similar to the first type of 'Katsushika' seal that Hokusai used on his paintings (for instance cat. 100), and it is rare to find it on a colour woodblock print. Three other examples are known of Hokusai fan prints bearing the otherwise unidentified publisher's mark 'Ta', including 'Cockerel, hen and chick with spiderwort' (cat. 107). AS

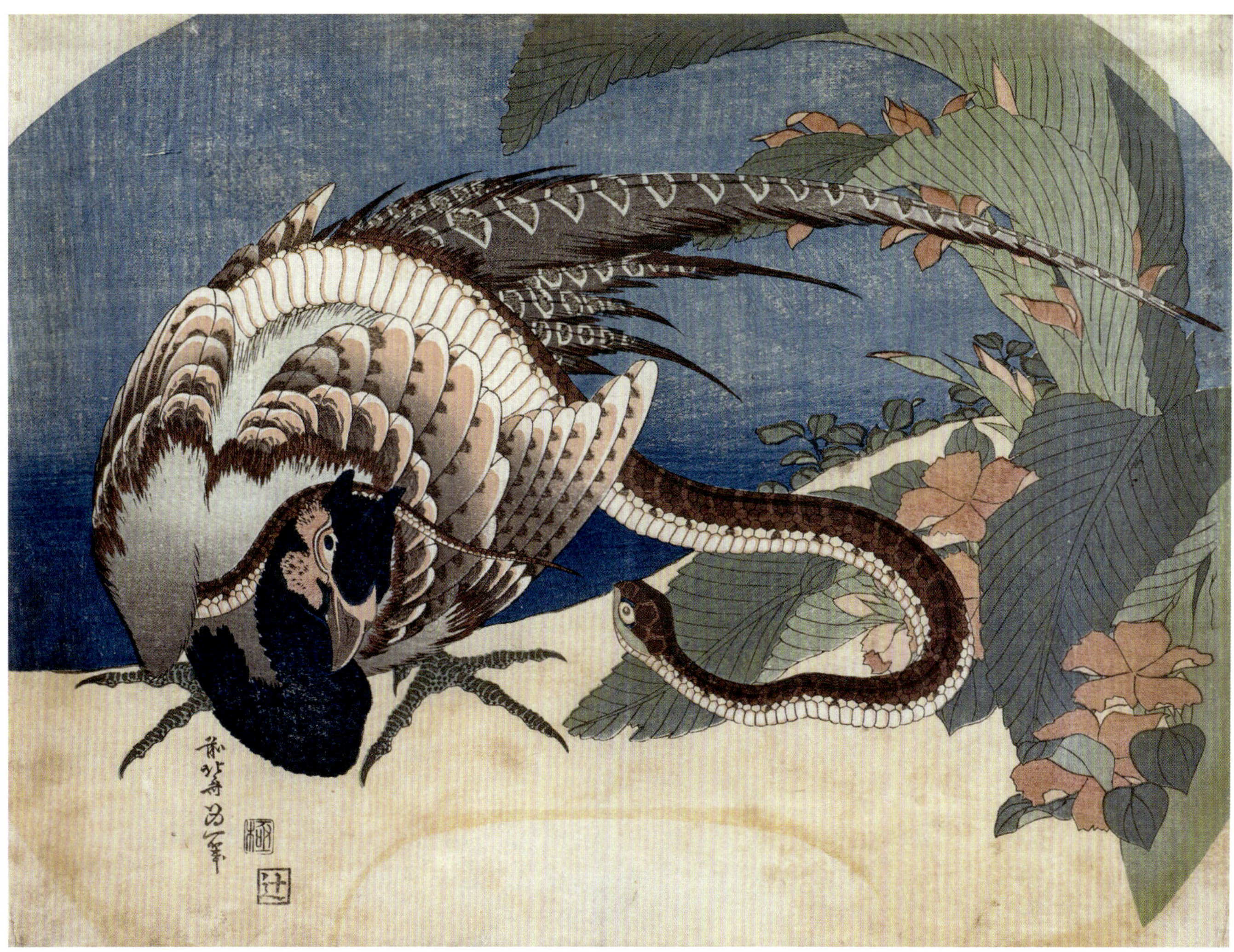

Pheasant and snake

About 1833
Signature: Saki no Hokusai Iitsu hitsu ('Brush of Iitsu,
the former Hokusai')
Seal: Katsushika
Fan print, colour woodblock, published by Iseya
Ichiemon, 22.6 × 29.1 cm
Literature: HUT 1987–1990, vol. 7, no. 131; Guimet
2008, no. 73; Paris 2014, no. 418; Keyes & Morse 2015,
no. 932
Musée national des arts asiatiques Guimet, Paris,
EO.1670, bequeathed by Issac de Camondo, 1911
Osaka only

A pheasant and a snake fight to the death. It is not
clear if this was drawn from life, but Hokusai was
attracted to such scenes of intertwined pheasants and
snakes, with other examples in the illustrated books
Ryōbi shahitsu (1820) and *Picture Book: Essence of Colouring*,
volume 2 (1848, cat. 211). Typically the pheasant was
depicted attacking and eating the snake, but here
Hokusai designs something more ambiguous: the snake
coils around the pheasant and each beast glares at
the other. The identity of the publisher 'Tsuji' was
formerly unknown, but has recently been identified as
Iseya Ichiemon, a fan dealer, also known as 'Kaku Tsuji'
(Iwakiri 2009, p. 42). Two other examples of Hokusai
fan prints are known with this 'Tsuji' seal, including
'Cockerels and hens' (cat. 108). AS

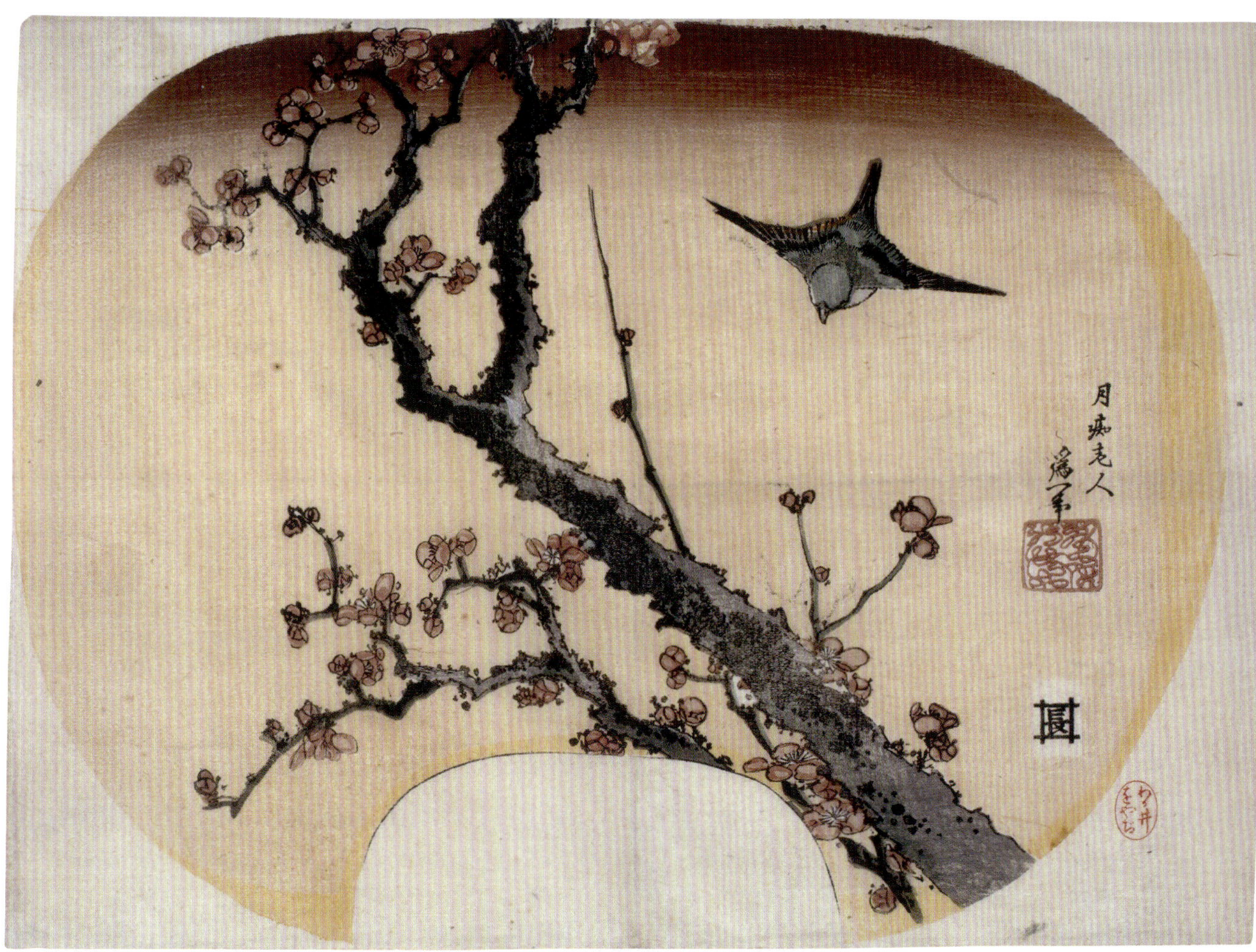

Plum and warbler

About 1821
Signature: Getchi rōjin / Iitsu hitsu ('Brush of Iitsu,
moon-crazed old man')
Seal: [unread]
Fan print, colour woodblock, published by Aritaya
Sei'emon, 23.5 × 31.5 cm
Provenance: Wakai Kensaburō
Literature: HUT 1987–1990, vol. 7, no. 132; Guimet
2008, no. 71; Keyes & Morse 2015, no. 1865
Musée national des arts asiatiques Guimet, Paris,
EO.1667, bequeathed by Isaac de Camondo, 1911
London only

A warbler has flown into the picture, as if invited by
the just-opening plum flowers. The scene is early
spring – perhaps not so suitable for a summer fan, yet
the design has a bright, festive charm. The rough,
Chinese-style branches of the plum and the accurate
warbler are drawn in formal style (*shintai*), like the
plum in *Hokusai shashin gafu* (1819, cat. 89) and
the plum and warbler in *Santai gafu* (about 1816).
As Ōta Nanpo (1749–1823) writes in the latter book's
preface, 'A blossom is truest just when it opens.'
So a flower on the point of blossoming was indeed
best depicted in 'true', formal style. Though there are
no other examples of Hokusai fan prints from this
publisher or with this signature, the signature and style
match those of the *surimono* series *Genroku kasen kai awase*
(*Genroku Shell Competition*, 1821), suggesting that it was
produced around the same time. AS

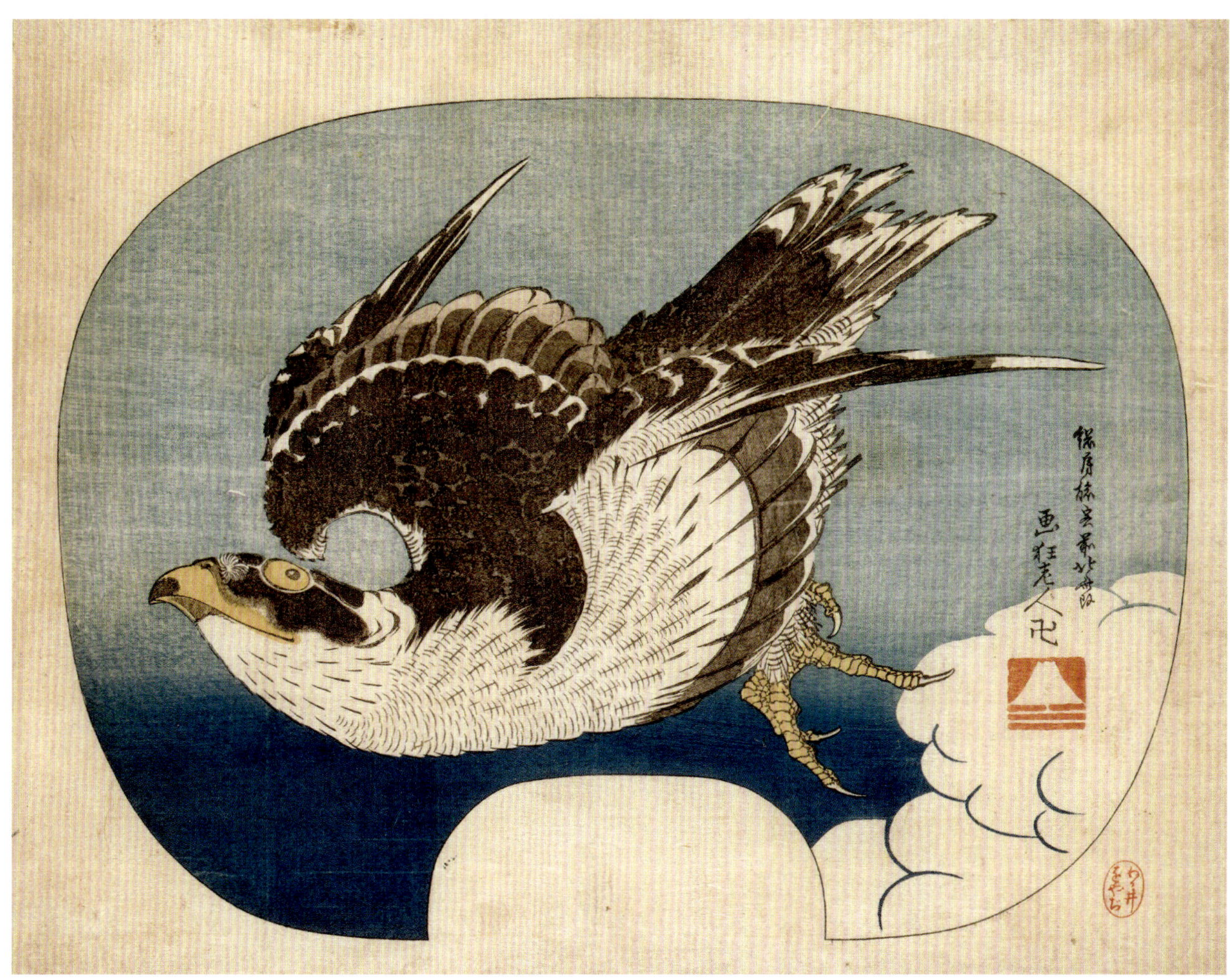

112

Hawk

1840 (or earlier)
Signature: Sōbō ryokyaku saki no Hokusai aratame /
Gakyō rōjin Manji ('Manji, old man crazy to paint,
changed from the former Hokusai, traveller in Kazusa
and Awa provinces')
Seal: Mt Fuji above trigram
Fan print, colour woodblock, publisher unknown,
25.2 × 32.0
Provenance: Wakai Kensaburō
Literature: HUT 1987–1990, vol. 7, no. 133; TNM
2005, no. 453; Guimet 2008, no. 74; Paris 2014, no. 489;
Keyes & Morse 2015, no. 933
Musée national des arts asiatiques Guimet, Paris,
EO.1662, bequeathed by Issac de Camondo, 1911
Osaka only

A hawk flies through the sky. Hokusai's pictures of
hawks are characterized, as here, by the white of the
breast and a small whorl of feathers under the eye.
There are about ten known fan prints by Hokusai,
but this is the only one from his Manji period.
The signature reveals that he produced the preliminary
drawing while travelling in the Bōsō peninsula
(present-day Chiba). The signature on 'Picture of famous
places in China' (cat. 119) also mentions travelling in
Bōsō, but adds that Hokusai was eighty-one, giving
a date of 1840. If he produced the preliminary drawing
for this picture during the same trip, then we could
date it to the same year; however, given the form of
the signature and the use of the Fuji seal, it may have
been produced somewhat earlier. AS

113
Young man composing a letter

1840
Signature: Gakyō rōjin / Manji hitsu / yowai
hachijūichi ('Brush of Manji, old man crazy to paint,
aged eighty-one')
Seal: Katsushika (3)
Hanging scroll, ink and colour on silk, 73.3 × 32.7 cm
Literature: Kaneko 1964, no. 6; Nagata 2000, no. 108;
TNM 2005, no. 470
Ujiie Ukiyo-e Collection, Kamakura

The subject, composition, size, signature and seal all
suggest that this must have formed a pair with *Young
man seated on a bench* (cat. 114). A young townsman wears
a kimono with long, hanging sleeves (*furisode*). His clothes
seem subdued in comparison to the other painting, but
the cracked ice and plum flower pattern on the topmost
layer is delicately painted in fine detail. The writing
box, wrapping paper and small stationery knife in the
foreground suggest that he is troubled about how to
compose a letter (maybe a love letter). In the background
are books wrapped in a decorative carrying cloth.
At first glance, this looks like a shop boy, or apprentice
– but if so he would be unlikely to wear the kimono
with long, hanging sleeves, which suggests, rather,
a young male sex worker (*kagema*). He may even be an
itinerant book-lender (*kashihonya*), who also offers casual
sexual favours to his clients. **AS**

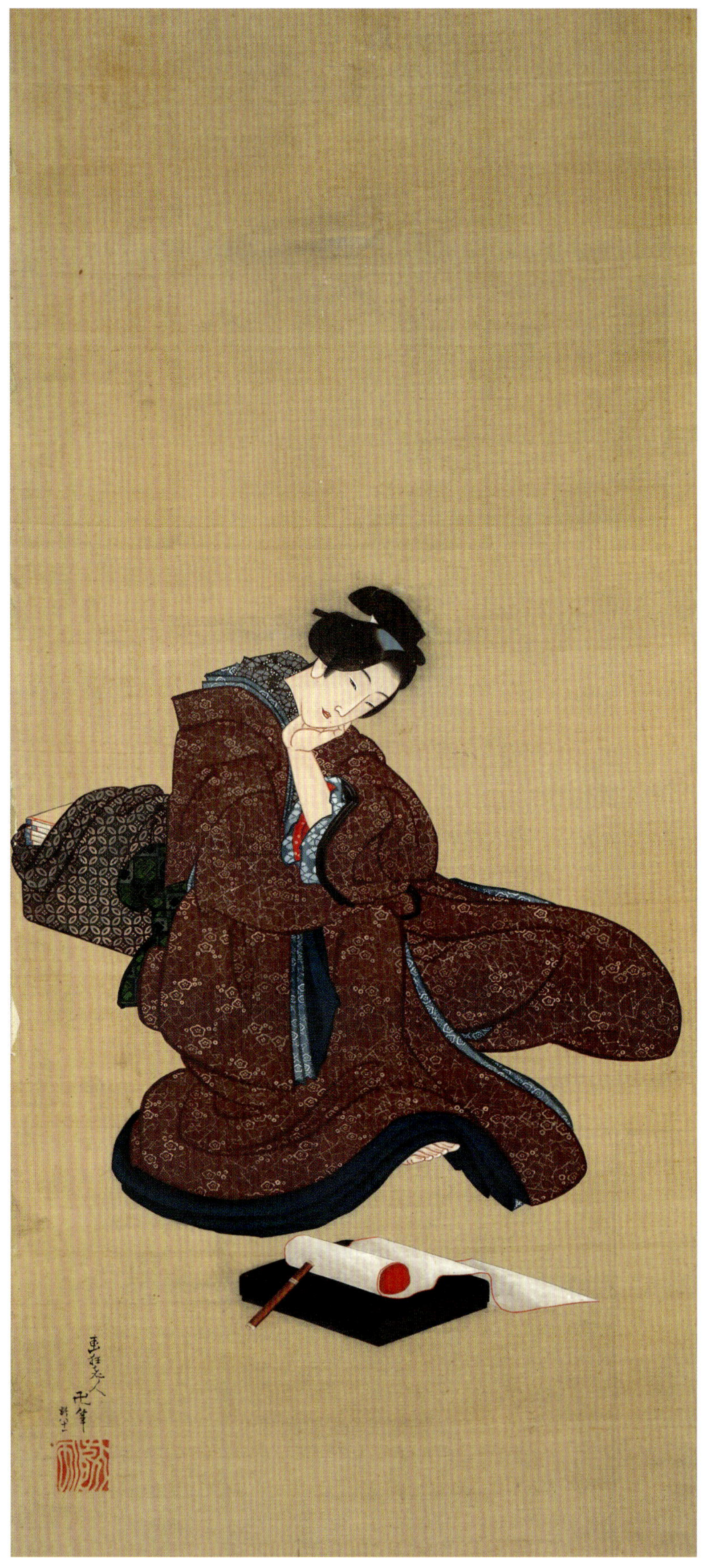

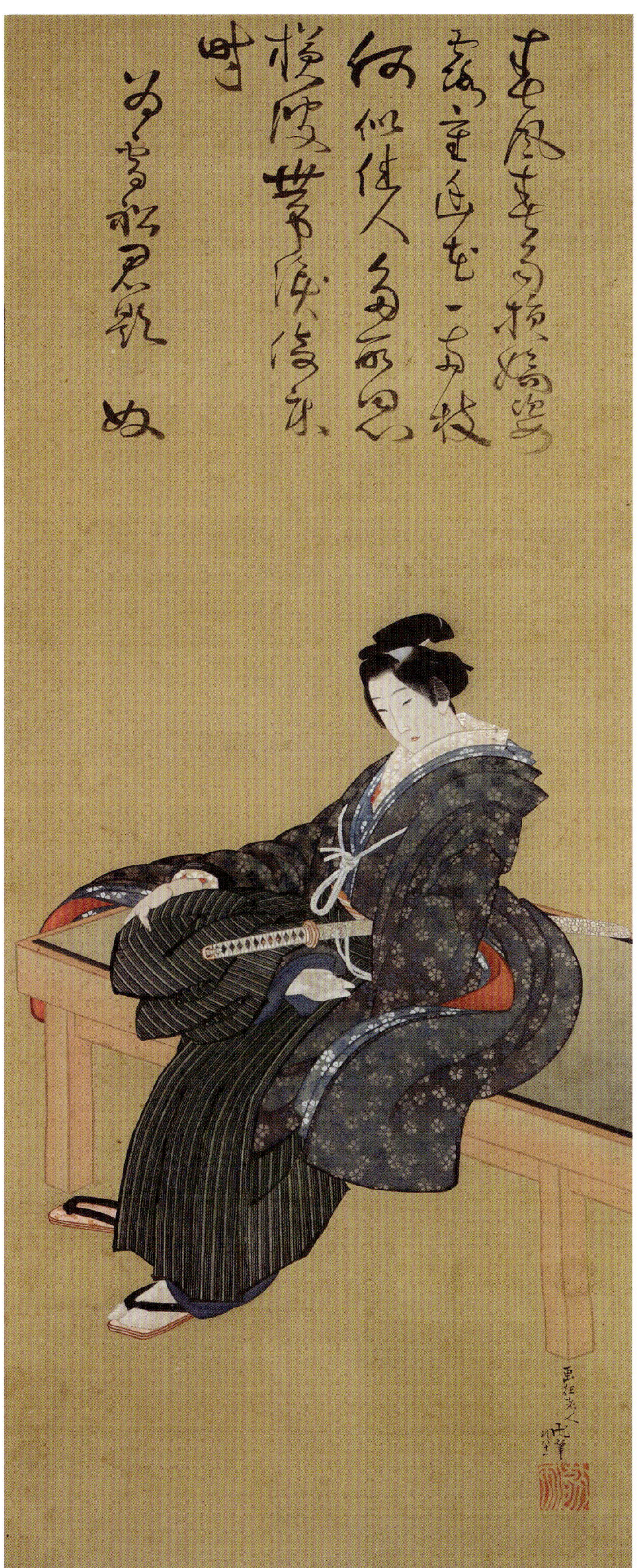

114

Young man seated on a bench

1840
Signature: Gakyō rōjin / Manji hitsu / yowai hachijūichi ('Brush of Manji, old man crazy to paint, aged eighty-one')
Seal: Katsushika (3)
Inscription by 'Yakko'
Hanging scroll, ink and colour on silk, 80.4 × 32.7 cm
Provenance: Arthur Morrison
Literature: Clark 1992, no. 101; Nagata 2000, no. 107; TNM 2005, no. 469
British Museum, 1913,0501,0.318, given by Sir W. Gwynne-Evans, Bt

A beautiful young man is seated on a bench, seemingly sunk in thought. He is dressed in gorgeous fabrics – multiple layers decorated with patterns of blossoming cherry. He sits somewhat awkwardly on the large bench, but the composition is balanced by the long, sharkskin-covered scabbard of his sword (*wakizashi*). Hokusai created other depictions of sexually alluring young men, for example in volume 9 of *Hokusai's Sketches* (*Hokusai manga*, 1819, cats 164, 165). Determining the social status of this particular young man is difficult. He may look like a young samurai, but it would be unlikely for the warrior class to wear fashions like these in the 1800s. Alternatively, perhaps he is an *onnagata*, a kabuki actor specializing in female roles, young enough still to have his adolescent forelocks – and therefore likely also an *iroko*, or young male sex worker. But it may simply be a nostalgic image of a beautiful young man from times long past. The inscription, a Chinese-style verse, may be tentatively translated: 'Spring breezes and spring rains assail his lovely form / the dew is heavy on a branch or two of fleeting blossom / like a beautiful woman, lost in thought / brimming with tears, resting on the bench. / Poem for young Sessen by Yakko (your servant)' (trans. Kobayashi Tadashi, Robert Campbell and Timothy Clark). AS

Horses: Stockade

1822

Signature: Fusenkyo Iitsu hitsu ('Brush of Fusenkyo Iitsu')
Printed inscription by Sanseitei Marumi
Surimono, colour woodblock with metallic pigments and embossing, 20.1 × 17.6 cm
Provenance: Charles Ricketts & Charles Shannon
Literature: RA 1991, no. 98; Roger Keyes, *The Art of Surimono*, London, 1985, no. 200; TNM 2005, no. 418; Keyes & Morse 2015, no. 1506
British Museum, 1937,0710,0.212, bequeathed by Charles Shannon RA

Horses was a series of thirty luxuriously produced *surimono* prints specially commissioned by the Yomo group to carry their poems celebrating the spring, published in 1822, a horse year. Each print was given a title relating in some way to horses, from which a concept was devised, poems composed and a picture created. Most of the scenes are still lifes, but they also include landscapes and genre scenes. Compared to the series *Genroku kasen kai awase* (*Genroku Shell Competition*) of the previous year, the originality of conception and composition in this series is even more fully realized.

This image features equipment for face-washing – water pitcher, basin, towel and towel rack – as well as a potted pine and Adonis flower. The inscription on the plant pot – 'Mii, Ishiyama, and Hira – three views' – indicates the picture playfully incorporates references associating particular objects with the canonical *Eight Views of Lake Biwa*, as follows: the plant pot with Miidera, Ishiyama and Hira; the miniature pine with Karasaki; the lacquer design on the pitcher with Seta; the basin, which depicts Ukimidō temple, with Katada; and the pictures on the towel with Awazu and Yabase. (The towel on the rack may stand for 'Returning sails at Yabase'.) The poem reads: 'In the first rays / of the spring sun / on Lake Biwa / Mirror mountain / also glitters. Sanseitei Marumi' (trans. Roger Keyes). The print's title, *Mayoke*, can mean 'stockade' (for keeping out people and animals); if so it could be connected to the legend of Akechi Mitsuharu. Having crossed Lake Biwa after the Battle of Yamazaki riding Okage, his much-loved horse, Mitsuharu then tethered the animal and entered Sakamoto castle alone, on foot. **AS**

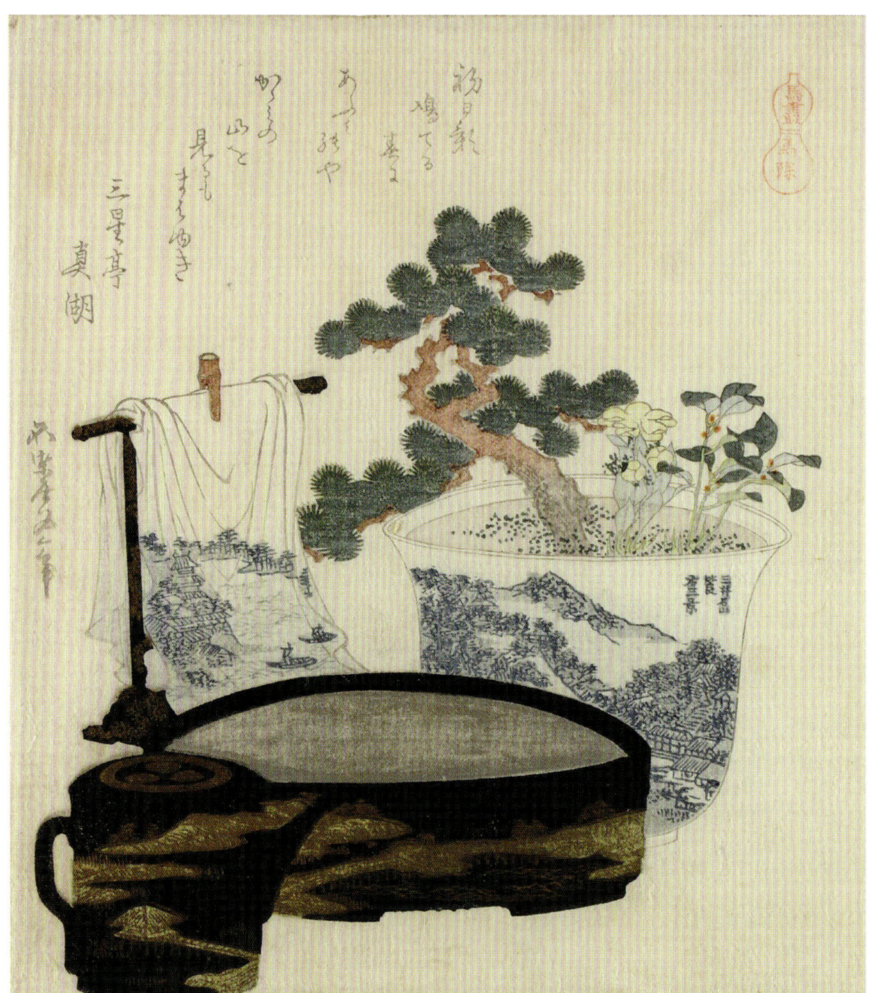

Horses: Bamboo horse

1822
Signature: Fusenkyo Iitsu hitsu ('Brush of Fusenkyo Iitsu')
Printed inscriptions by Shinkōtei Nakagaki and Shinratei Manzō
Surimono, colour woodblock with metallic pigments and embossing, 19.7 × 17.1 cm
Provenance: Ernest Hart
Literature: Keyes & Morse 2015, no. 1523
British Museum, 1902,0212,0.366

The 'Bamboo horse' of the title is a frame made of bamboo carried on the shoulders to transport loads. Judging from the poems and picture, the one depicted here seems to be for carrying food and drink for a plum blossom viewing. Also depicted are a tobacco pipe, pouch and tray, with what seems to be a specially made arm rest at bottom left. The swastika on the covering of the bamboo horse is the mark of the poetry group led by Shinratei Manzō (1760–1831). The poems may be translated: 'In a spring garden / riding tall on bamboo stilts / in easy harmony with friends / and the long sweet chorus / of the warblers. Shinkōtei Nakagaki'; 'The sweet song / of the warbler / calls to mind / the smouldering scent / of the plum at night. Shinratei Manzō' (trans. Alfred Haft). **AS**

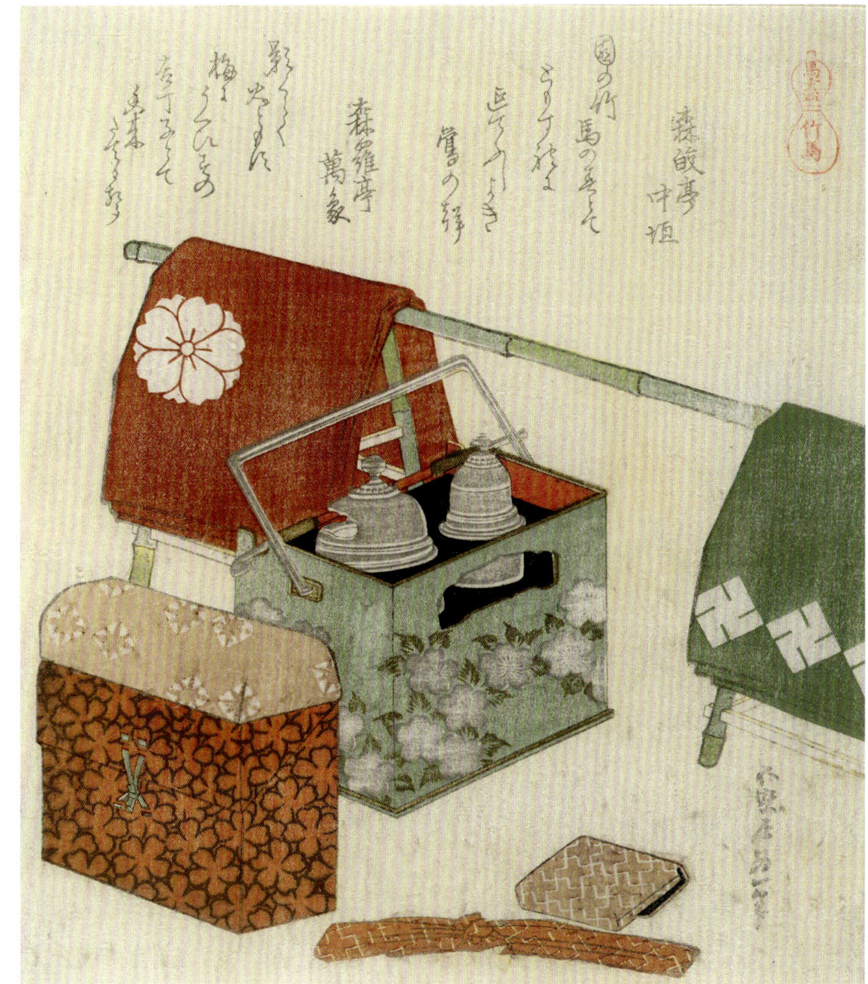

Watermelon and knife

1839

Signature: Gakyō rōjin Manji hitsu / yowai hachijū
('Brush of Manji, old man crazy to paint, aged eighty')
Seal: Katsushika (2)
Hanging scroll, ink and colour on silk, 86.1 × 29.9 cm
Literature: NU 1982, no. 31; Imahashi 1996; Nagata
2000, no. 103; TNM 2005, 471
The Museum of the Imperial Collections, Sannomaru
Shōzōkan, Tokyo
London only

The painting features a cut watermelon covered by
a piece of thin paper, with a kitchen knife placed on
top of that. Above them is suspended a rope, from
which hang down two long strips of the finely sliced
skin of the watermelon, pale pink on the left and white
on the right. Ōju ('at special request') is engraved near
the handle of the knife. Various interpretations have
been put forward to account for the painting's
unprecedented composition. Scholar Imahashi Riko
has proposed that each element stands in place of the
paraphernalia and decorations used for 'Kikkōden',
the precursor of Tanabata, the star festival, at the
Imperial Court. The hanging strips of watermelon
represent five-coloured silk cords, the knife and paper
refer to decorative mulberry branches, and the
watermelon to a four-handled washing basin (*tsuno-
darai*). Whatever the correct interpretation, the
mysterious effect of the watermelon glimpsed through
the paper, the extraordinary materiality of the knife
and the complex twisting of the melon rind all
combine into a veritable tour de force. AS

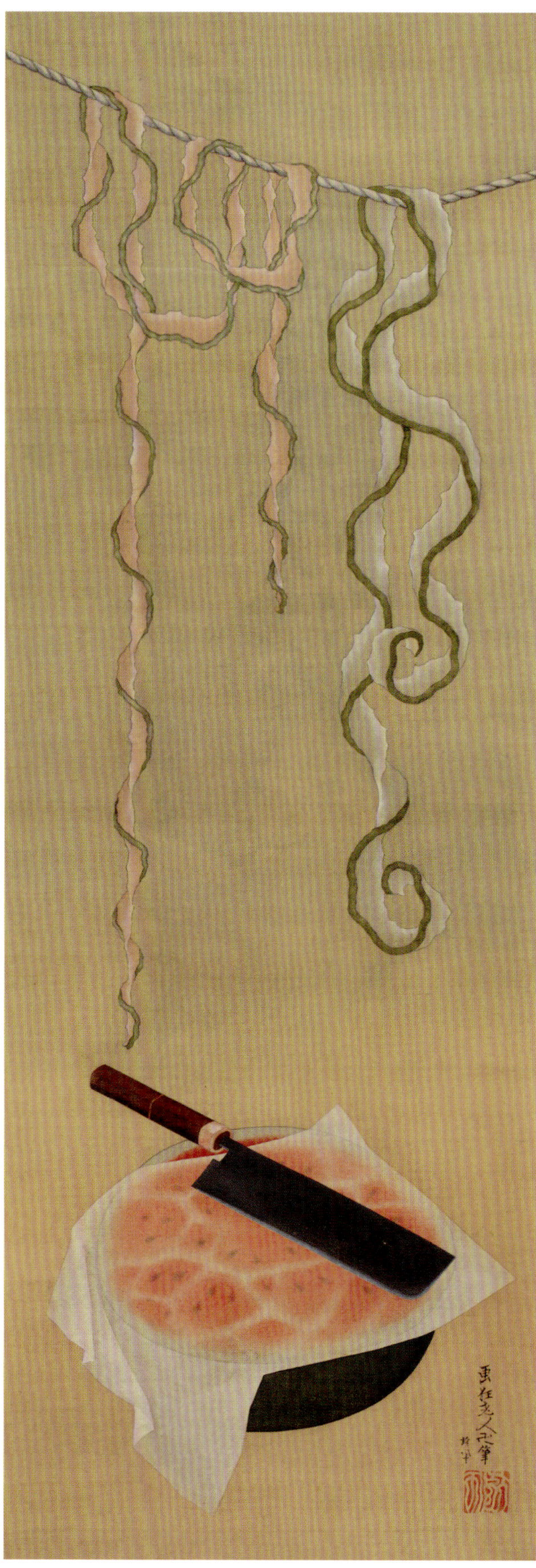

Boys' Festival decorations

1844
Signature: Gakyō rōjin / Manji hitsu / yowai
hachijūgo sai ('Brush of Manji, old man crazy to paint,
aged eighty-five years')
Seal: Katsushika (3)
Hanging scroll, ink and colour on silk, 90.4 × 33.2 cm
Literature: Edo Tokyo 2007, no. 211; Kobayashi 2008;
Itabashi 2008, no. 18; Asano 2010, p. 143
Fukada Art Museum, Kyoto

This decorative ensemble for the annual Boys' Festival
on the 5th day of the fifth month consists of a samurai
helmet on a stand with a plum design in *makie* lacquer,
to which has been attached a bunch of iris. The flowers
are presented in a ceremonial 'iris wrapper' (*shōbu-
zutsumi*), while the helmet may be a decorative model
created especially for the festival. Hokusai's still life
paintings contain some of the most intricate passages
of his entire oeuvre. The fine detail of the stand
and helmet, the softness of the textile, the vibrancy
of the iris and the contrasts between these very different
elements are what create such a satisfying sense of
tension in this work. AS

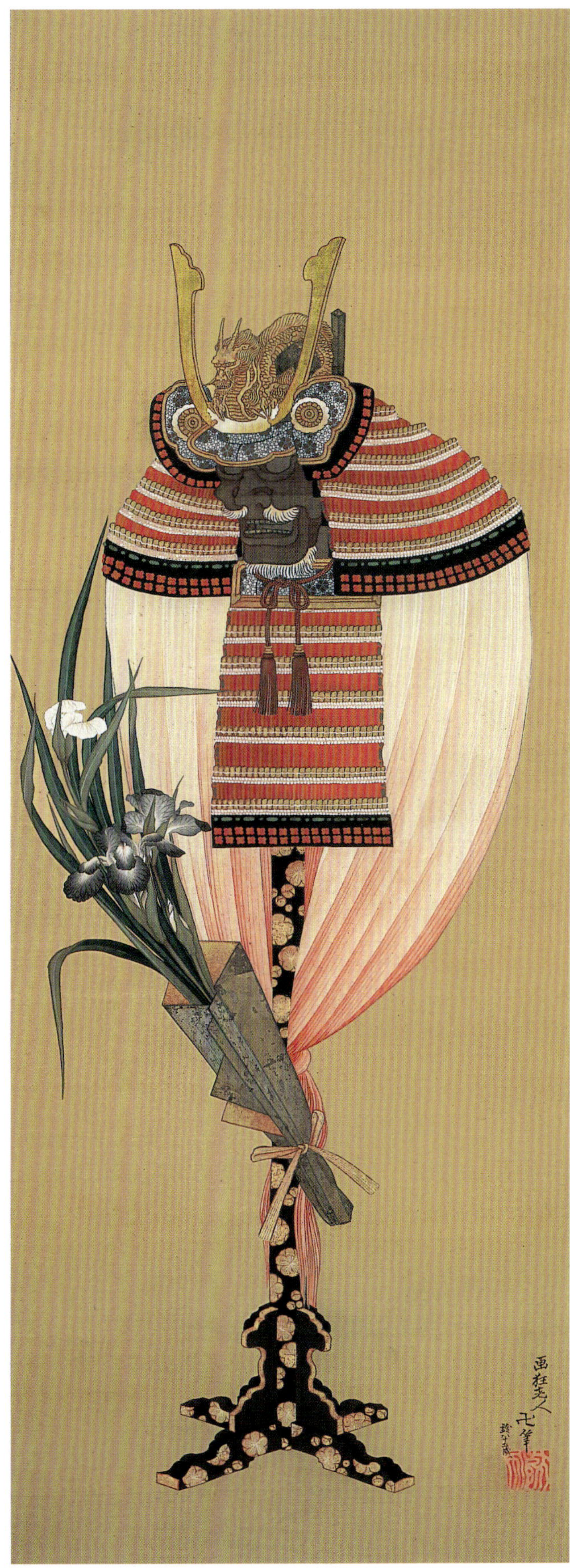

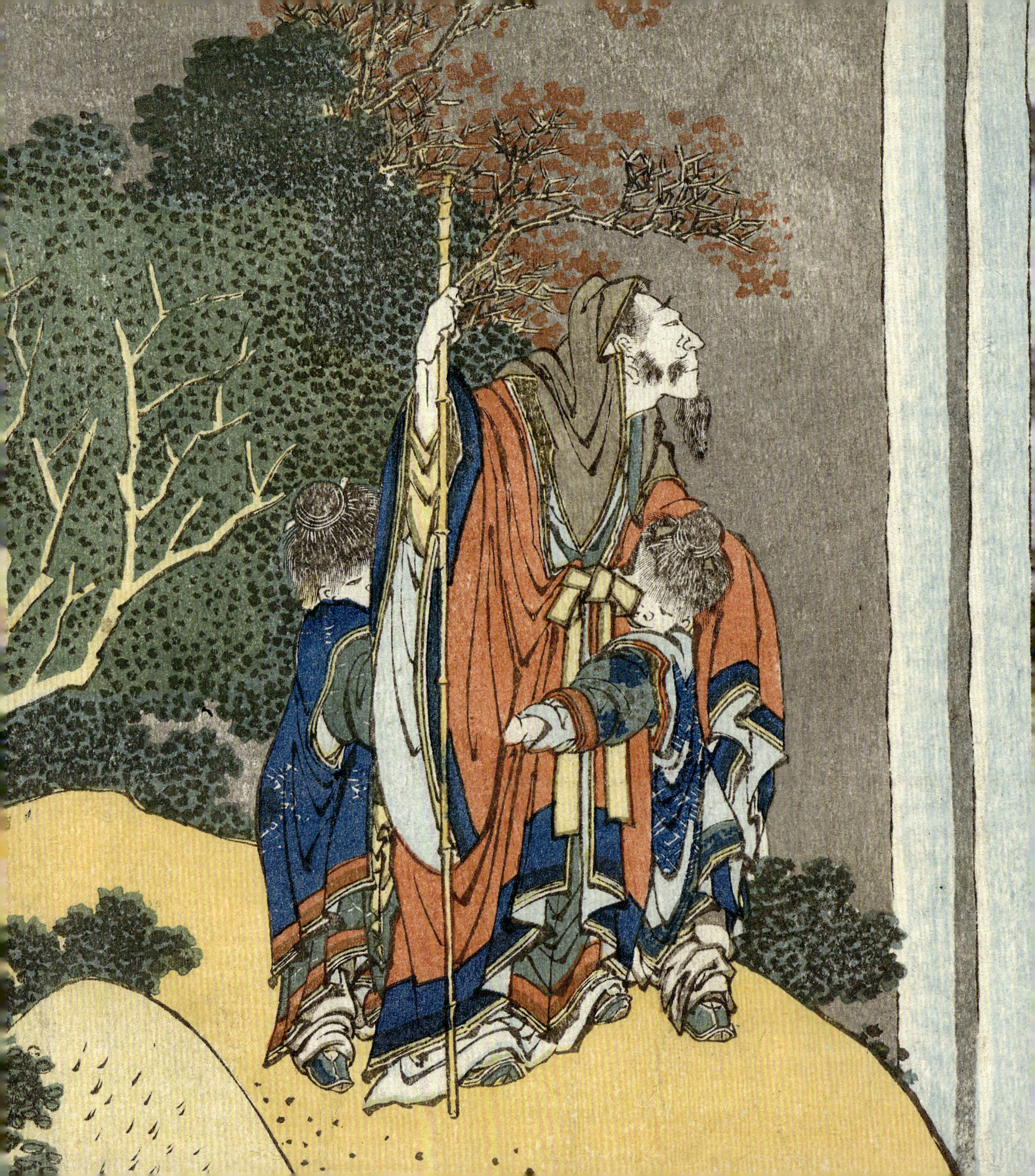

Worlds imagined

Hokusai moved easily between the worlds of observation and imagination. His vision of one hundred Japanese bridges (cat. 74), his distorted view of the Tōkaidō highway (cat. 37) and his topographically accurate map of China (cat. 119) blur the distinction between the world as it is and a world of make-believe.

China was everywhere in Tokugawa Japan. It had furnished the painting medium within which Hokusai worked, the stylistic foundations on which he built and many of the subjects and themes which he used to capture an audience. Most popular were the 108 bandits of *Outlaws of the Marsh*, a serialized novel that appeared in ninety-one printed volumes over more than three decades (cats 120–122). But China also provided literary figures and poetic models (cat. 220), as well as various deities to help ward off the perils of the present (cats 159–161). Japan had its own indigenous canon, of course, of both literary accomplishment (cat. 132 ff.) and military achievement (cat. 150). The landscape was known through its historical associations, as imagined over the centuries in literature and art (cat. 115). But Japan took its place within a China-centric paradigm. Japanese and Chinese warriors could combine to reassure in an age of anxiety (cats 151, 169). Great poets of the past could easily be transplanted – a Japanese poet depicted in China and a Chinese poet in Japan (cat. 127 and p. 212).

Nowhere was more real, ultimately, than the unseen worlds of fantasy and faith. Hokusai conjured demons that had long haunted the Japanese imagination but were rarely as effectively depicted (cats 153–155). He also provided powerful talismans with which to ward off the life-threatening diseases that swept through his city at regular intervals (cats 159–161). Hokusai's art, though, was not simply calibrated to the market, but was anchored in belief. His ambition and achievement were underpinned by devotion to the North Star (e.g. cats 2, 3) and his belief in Nichiren Buddhism (cats 157, 193, 194). At times, his depictions of monk Nichiren (cat. 215) and of the historical Buddha (cat. 158) demonstrated the extraordinary forces to which such faith provided access. At others, the Buddha seems not so far from us (cat. 156), and comparable with other figures with whom we might identify (cat. 214). As he grew older, Hokusai seems to have formed an ever closer connection to this world of supernatural authority – which prompted both fearful awe and quiet communion – and to have felt ever more keenly a need to depict it. AL

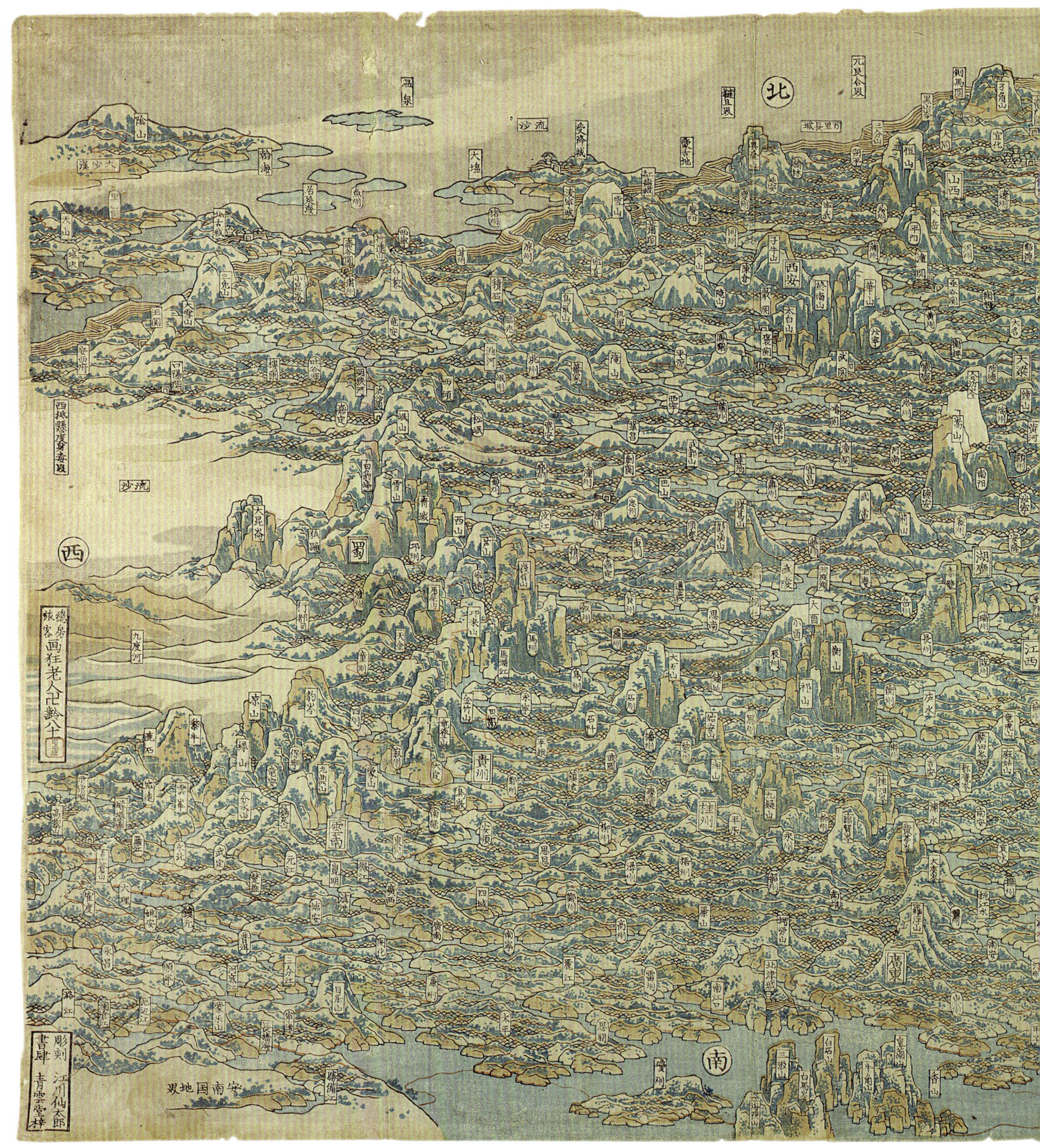

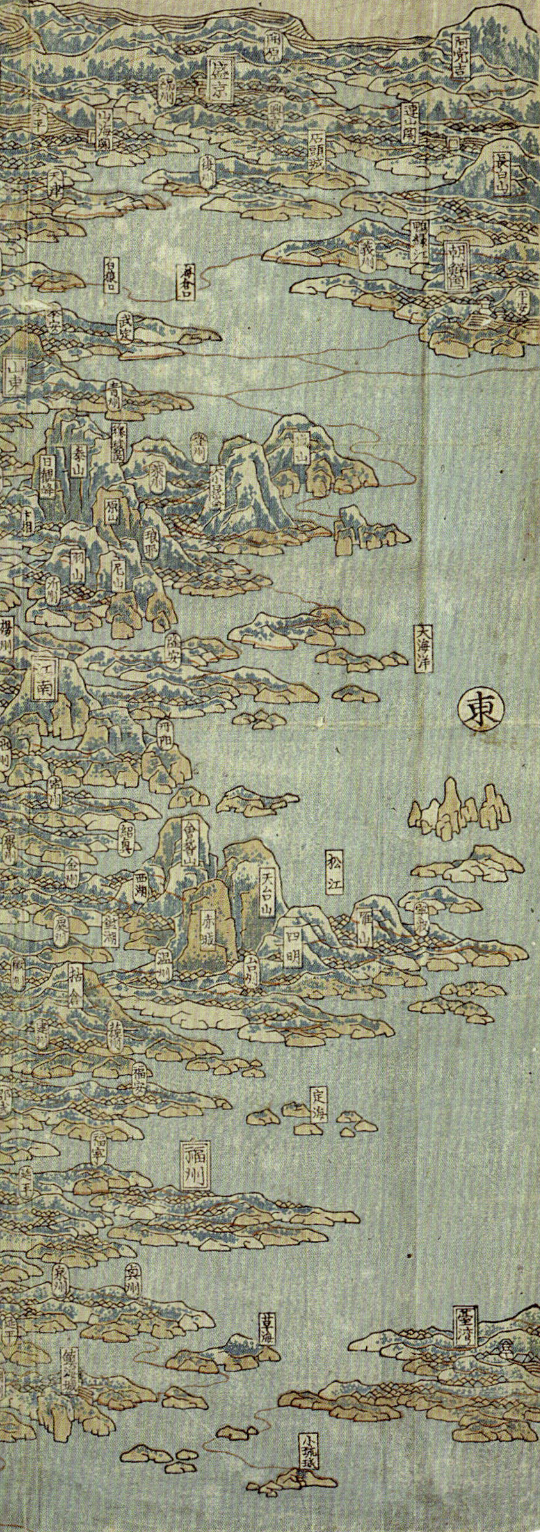

Picture of famous places in China

1840
Signature: Sōbō ryokyaku / Gakyō rōjin Manji yowai hachijūichi ('Manji, old man crazy to paint, aged eighty-one, traveller in Kazusa and Awa provinces')
Seal: No in ('Seal of')
Block cutter: Egawa Sentarō
Extra-large colour woodblock, published by Hanabusaya Bunzō (Seiundō), 41.9 × 54.2 cm
Provenance: purchased 1958
Literature: Asano 2010, p. 62; Paris 2014, no. 490; Keyes & Morse 2015, no. 968
The British Library, London, Maps 188.v.3
London only

For most Japanese of the Edo period (1615–1868), China remained a realm of the imagination, a distant source of ancient culture and wisdom. The country emerged as a more concrete reality, however, with the publication of practical multi-volume guides such as *Illustrations of Famous Places in China* (about 1806). Hokusai may have referred to one of these earlier publications when designing this map, but here created a rich impression of the region's topography by drawing mountains and coastlines to relative scale. The map identifies China's districts and smaller cities (oval cartouches), geographic features (single-border rectangles), and major cities and provinces (double-border rectangles). The brown ribbon of the Great Wall marks China's northern boundary. Packing the valleys and ravines are small triangles that represent the roofs of houses and suggest China to be densely populated. This is the last of five grand bird's-eye views that Hokusai produced between 1818 and 1840; the others depict places in Japan (cat. 37). Hokusai designed this print while travelling in the provinces east of Edo. The talented block cutter Egawa Sentarō helped to realize this and a number of other important works by Hokusai. AH

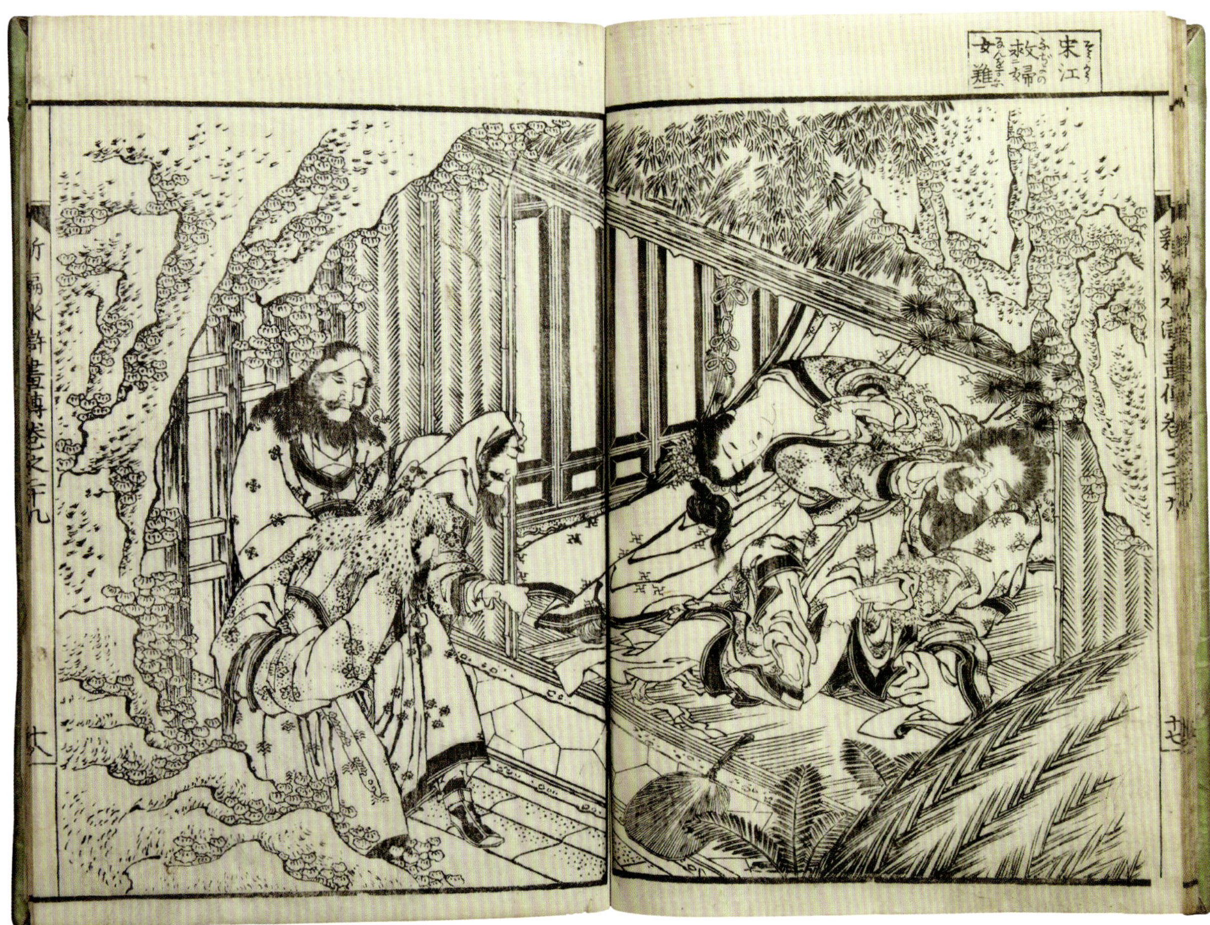

120

Song Jiang rescues a woman, from *New Illustrated 'Outlaws of the Marsh'* (*Shinpen suiko gaden*)

1835
Signature: Saki no Hokusai Iitsu rōjin ga ('Drawn by old man Iitsu, the former Hokusai')
Illustrated book, vol. 29 (of 91), woodblock, published by Hanabusa Heikichi (Mankyūdō) and Chōjiya Heibei (Bunkeidō), 22.3 × 15.7 cm (covers)
Literature: Hillier 1980, pp. 76–77; Calza 2003, no. V.30A
Uragami Mitsuru collection, Japan

Set during the late Song dynasty (960–1279), the Chinese historical novel *Outlaws of the Marsh* (*Shui hu zhuan*, 1300s) relates the adventures of 108 rebellious warriors based in Liangshan marsh. The brigands specialize in vigilante justice, punishing evil bureaucrats and assisting the poor. The novel reached Japan in the early 1600s and soon became a favourite with scholars. An annotated Japanese edition and a simplified translation appeared in instalments over the 1700s, sparking wider interest and leading to this edition (published 1805–after 1839) – the first in vernacular Japanese and the first produced in Japan with illustrations. The subject seems to have captured Hokusai's imagination, since he illustrated all of this edition's 91 volumes, as well as a companion volume with portraits of the 108 heroes (published in 1829). The original translator of this edition, Kyokutei Bakin (1767–1848), moved on to other projects after completing part I (volumes 1–11) of this translation, but continued to think highly of Hokusai's visualizations of the narrative. He was succeeded as translator by Takai Ranzan (1762–1838). AH

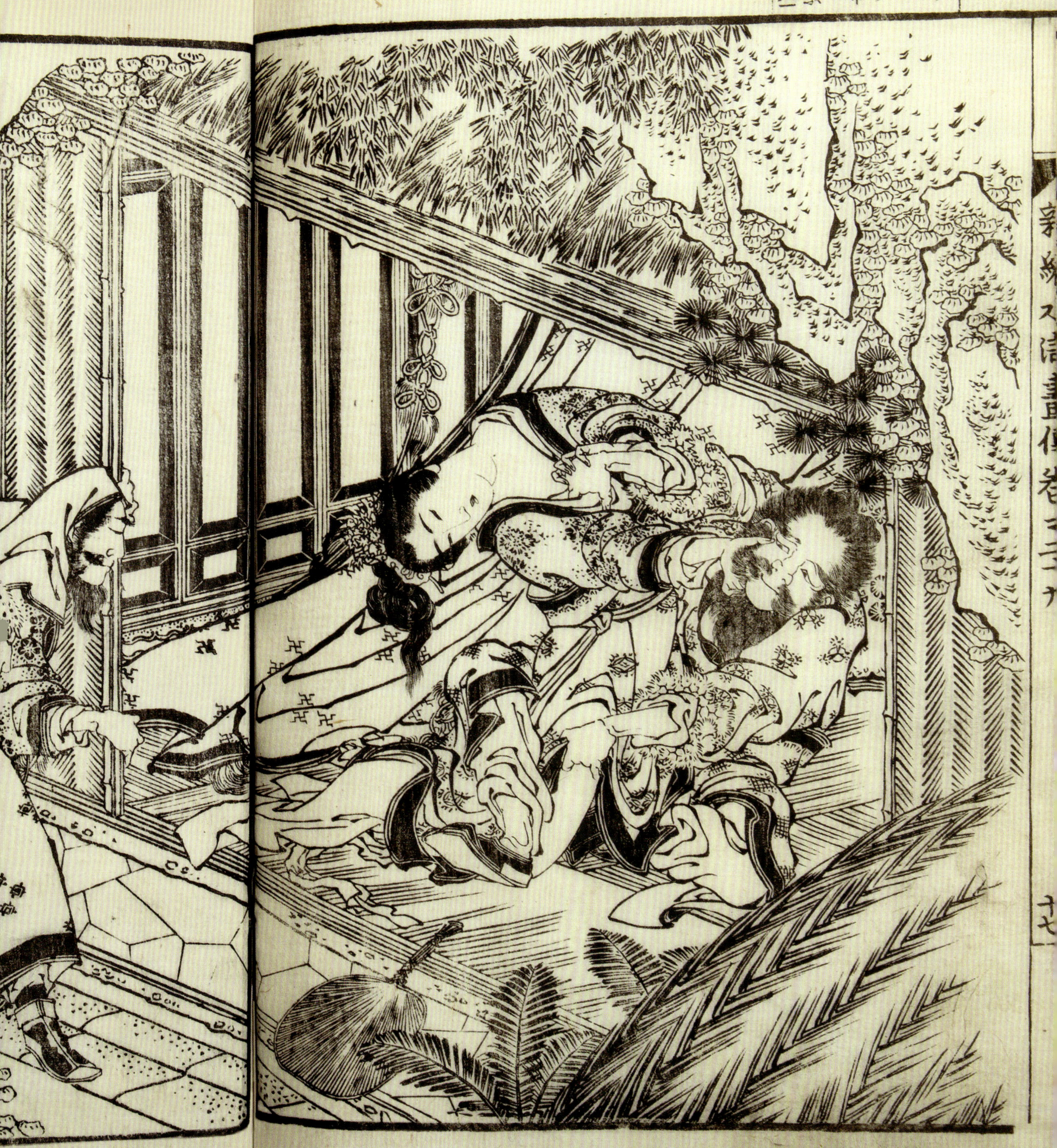

江婦の難
孝経又信畫傳卷二二丁

Chinese hero Lu Zhishen

1823–1826
Signature: Katsushika / Hokusai Iitsu hitsu ('Brush of
Hokusai Iitsu [of] Katsushika')
Seal: Katsushika (1)
Hanging scroll, ink and colour on silk, 105.5 × 42.4 cm
Provenance: Ozu family, Ise Matsuzaka
Literature: Kobayashi Tadashi, 'Katsushika Hokusai
hitsu *Kaoshō* zu', *Kokka* 1213, Dec. 1996, p. 27; Edo
Tokyo 2007, no. 202; Asano 2010, p. 152
Private collection, Japan

The monk Lu Zhishen numbers among the 108 heroic
bandits of the Chinese novel *Outlaws of the Marsh* (1300s).
Lu is a volatile character described in Chinese editions
as 'the old monk who loved to kill'. Early in the novel,
he returns drunk to his temple and, thinking that a
wooden guardian statue has reprimanded him, destroys
the temple gate. Later, in chapter 8, to intimidate two
corrupt guards plotting to kill his friend Lin Zhong,
he fells a giant pine tree with a single blow of his iron
monk's staff. Here, flying pine needles hint at the episode,
with the fleeing sparrows a humorous reference to Lu's
opponents. Hokusai's vigorous calligraphic brushstrokes
convey the monk's raw energy. The dynamic composition
is an inventive development of a standard portrait of
Lu Zhishen found in Chinese editions of the novel. AH

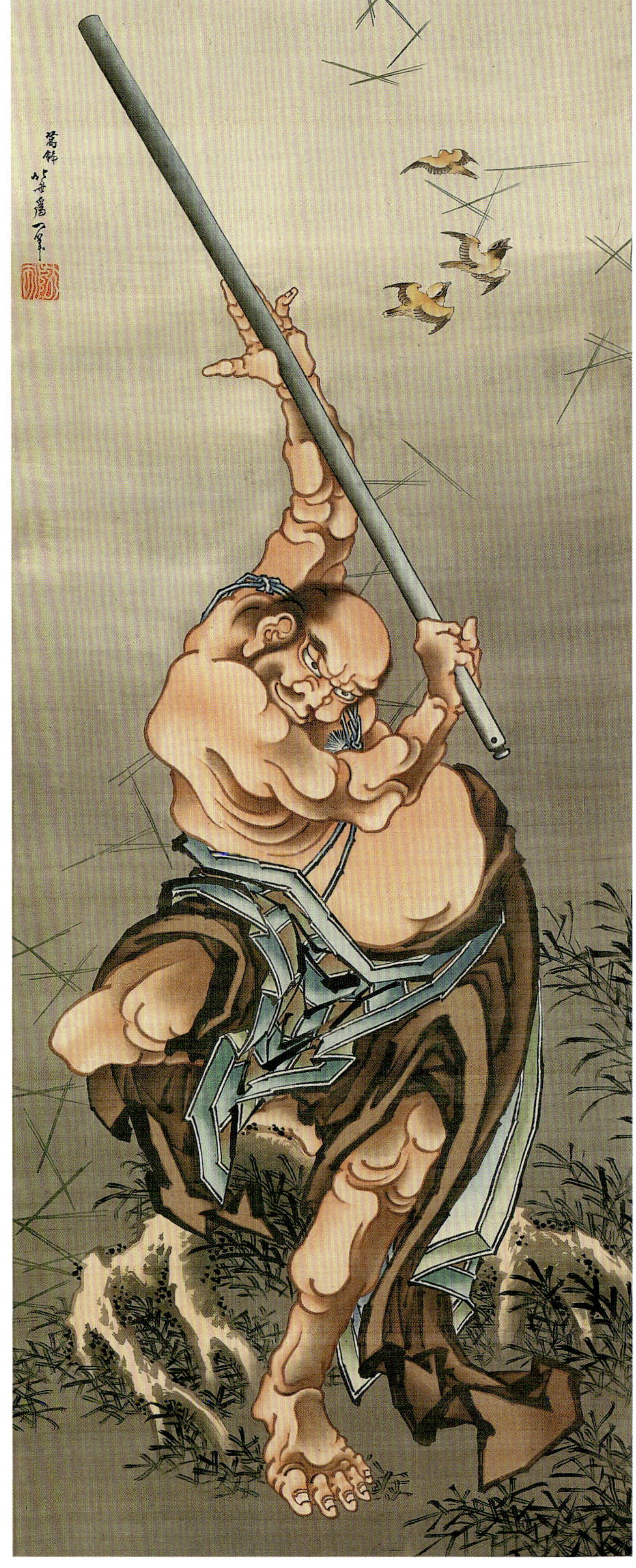

Chinese hero in the snow

1843
Signature: Yowai hachijūyon sai / Gakyō rōjin Manji
hitsu ('Brush of Manji, old man crazy to paint, aged
eighty-four years')
Seal: Katsushika (3)
Hanging scroll, ink and colour on silk, 132.6 × 43.9 cm
Literature: Kaneko 1964, no. 12; Nagata 1990, vol. 5,
nos 111–112; Nagata 2000, no. 114
Ujiie Ukiyo-e Collection, Kamakura

In the Chinese historical novel *Romance of the Three
Kingdoms* (1300s), generals Liu Bei (AD 161–223), Guan
Yu (died AD 220) and Zhang Fei (died AD 221) halt the
advance of General Cao Cao from the north and
inaugurate the Three Kingdoms period (AD 220–280).
Early in the novel, the three allies trek through heavy
snow to consult with the military strategist Kongming
(the 'Sleeping Dragon'), and this painting is sometimes
said to show Zhang Fei (the fiercest and most sceptical
of the three generals) checking for a break in the weather.
Alternatively, however, the dusky sky, comparison with
Hokusai's illustrations for the Chinese novel, *Outlaws
of the Marsh* (cat. 120), and a portrait in his companion
volume to that novel suggest that this warrior may be
Lin 'Panther Head' Zhong, trekking at night to join
the other outlaws after having slaughtered the guards
who held him in snow-bound captivity. In either case,
Hokusai's masterfully controlled, European-influenced
shading and use of lines of varying thickness lend the face
and robes a powerful three-dimensionality, in keeping
with the warrior's heroic stance and intense gaze. AH

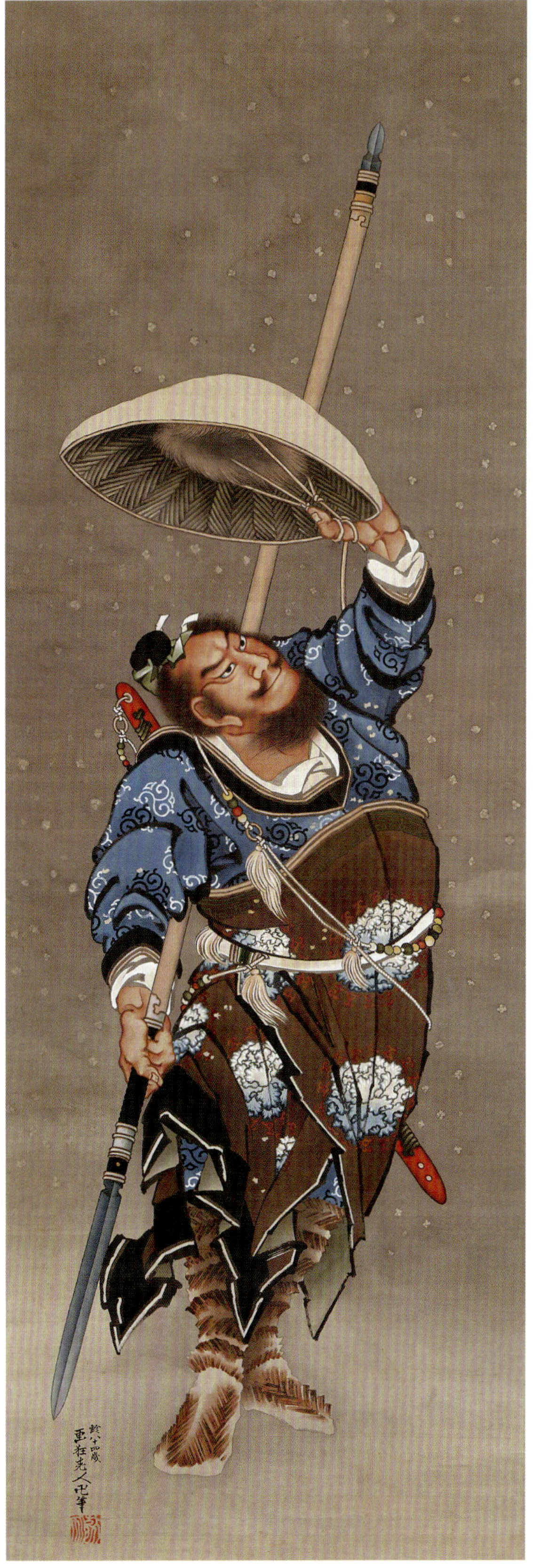

True Mirror of Chinese and Japanese Poems (*Shiika shashin kyō*)

This series of tall-format (*nagaōban*) prints depicts subjects from classical Chinese and Japanese poetry. Many cultivated people during the Edo period could read Chinese and Japanese with equal fluency, and admired the poetry of both civilizations. The prints have no inscribed poem, suggesting that they were aimed at an audience familiar enough with the classics to interpret the subjects. For several decades before this, Hokusai had been designing privately commissioned prints (*surimono*) for poetry clubs that specialized in humorous verses (*kyōka*) about modern life. This series, however, seems to have been the artist's first foray into designing single-sheet prints related to classical literature. Presenting the Japanese poets in court costume and the Chinese poets in foreign garb, he conjures up a distant age of high culture. The past notwithstanding, the modern synthetic pigment Prussian blue (*bero-ai*) features prominently in the designs. Publisher Moriya Jihei may have hoped to capitalize on the popularity of that newly adopted pigment around the time of publication (about 1833–1834, based on the artist's signature). However, knowing the artist and perhaps gauging the likely audience for the series, Moriya also had the prints crafted to an exceptionally high standard.

A general inspiration for the series may have been the anthology, *Japanese and Chinese Poems to Sing* (*Wakan rōei shū*, around 1013), in which Japanese poems are paired with Chinese poems on a similar topic. The particular selections in the *True Mirror* series, though, reflect also the popularity of Noh theatre (developed late 1300s) and a late Edo preference for Chinese poets of the High rather than Late Tang dynasty (AD 618–907). Ten designs are known – five on a Chinese theme, five on a Japanese theme – but the China/Japan divide is not rigid. For while the poems by four Japanese poets are set in Japan, and the poems by three Chinese poets are set in China, one Chinese poet is shown writing in Japan, one Japanese poet is writing in China, and another Japanese poet is writing about China. A study of the publisher's and censor's seals suggests that the first three prints issued were 'Ariwara no Narihira' (not illustrated), 'Li Bo' (cat. 123) and an untitled winter scene associated with a poem by Du Fu (cat. 124). This catalogue illustrates seven designs (cats 123, 124, 126–130), grouped by the nationality of the related poet or likely source of the image. AH

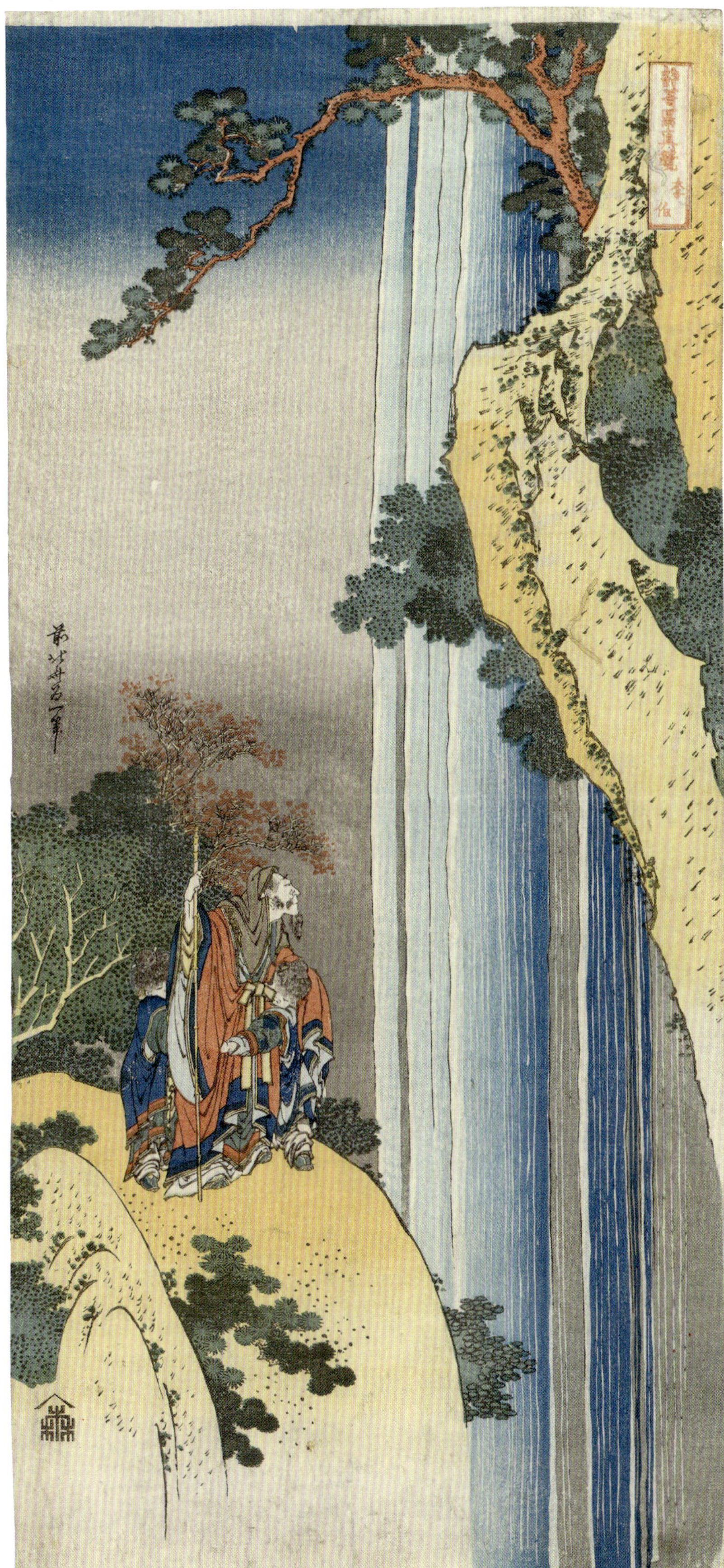

Poet Li Bo

About 1833–1834
Signature: Saki no Hokusai Iitsu hitsu ('Brush of Iitsu, the former Hokusai')
Colour woodblock, published by Moriya Jihei, 50.9 × 22.9 cm
Provenance: Katō Shōzō
Literature: MSU 1991, no. 81; RA 1991, no. 70; Iwakiri 2012, p. 14; Keyes & Morse 2015, no. 978
British Museum, 1927,0413,0.15

The Chinese poet Li Bo (AD 701–762) gazes in rapture at a waterfall, while two young servants steady him at the edge of the chasm. Renowned for his intensity and fondness for alcohol, Li Bo ranks among China's greatest poets. He composed two celebrated poems while viewing Horsetail fall at Mt Lu (Lushan), in southeastern China. Hokusai probably had in mind the second poem of four lines: 'Censer Peak in the sunlight puffs clouds of purple haze, / as, seen afar, the waterfall hangs before the river. / The current leaps and tumbles sheer for three-thousand feet. / Or is that the Milky Way pouring from the heights of heaven?' (trans. Alfred Haft). Rarely had this popular subject been depicted with the boldness of the present design, which makes striking use of the tall format by splitting the composition into vertical halves. Hokusai may have borrowed the motif of the young servants from an illustration of the same subject in *Treasures of Pithy Instruction* (*Ehon nezashi takara*, 1745), by Tachibana Morikuni (1679–1748). AH

Untitled (Poet Du Fu)

About 1833–1834

Signature: Saki no Hokusai Iitsu hitsu ('Brush of Iitsu, the former Hokusai')

Colour woodblock, published by Moriya Jihei, 50.9 × 22.1 cm

Literature: MSU 1991, no. 88; RA 1991, no. 72; Iwakiri 2012, pp. 10–11; Keyes & Morse 2015, no. 980

Fitzwilliam Museum, Cambridge, P.14-1997

This design is a revised version of an illustration that Hokusai produced for *Illustrated Anthology of Tang Poetry*, part 6, volume 3 (1833, cat. 125). The scene relates to a farewell poem that the great Du Fu (AD 712–770) sent to a friend who had departed for war in winter. Here, the friend (an officer) appears to have ridden part of the way up a rocky promontory in order to obtain a last view of the poet's hut. The new composition moves the scene closer to the personal tone of the poem, but at the same time lightens the wintry mood through a play of triangular forms – associating the hut's pitched roof with the tree branch framing the departing friend and the horse's straining neck. AH

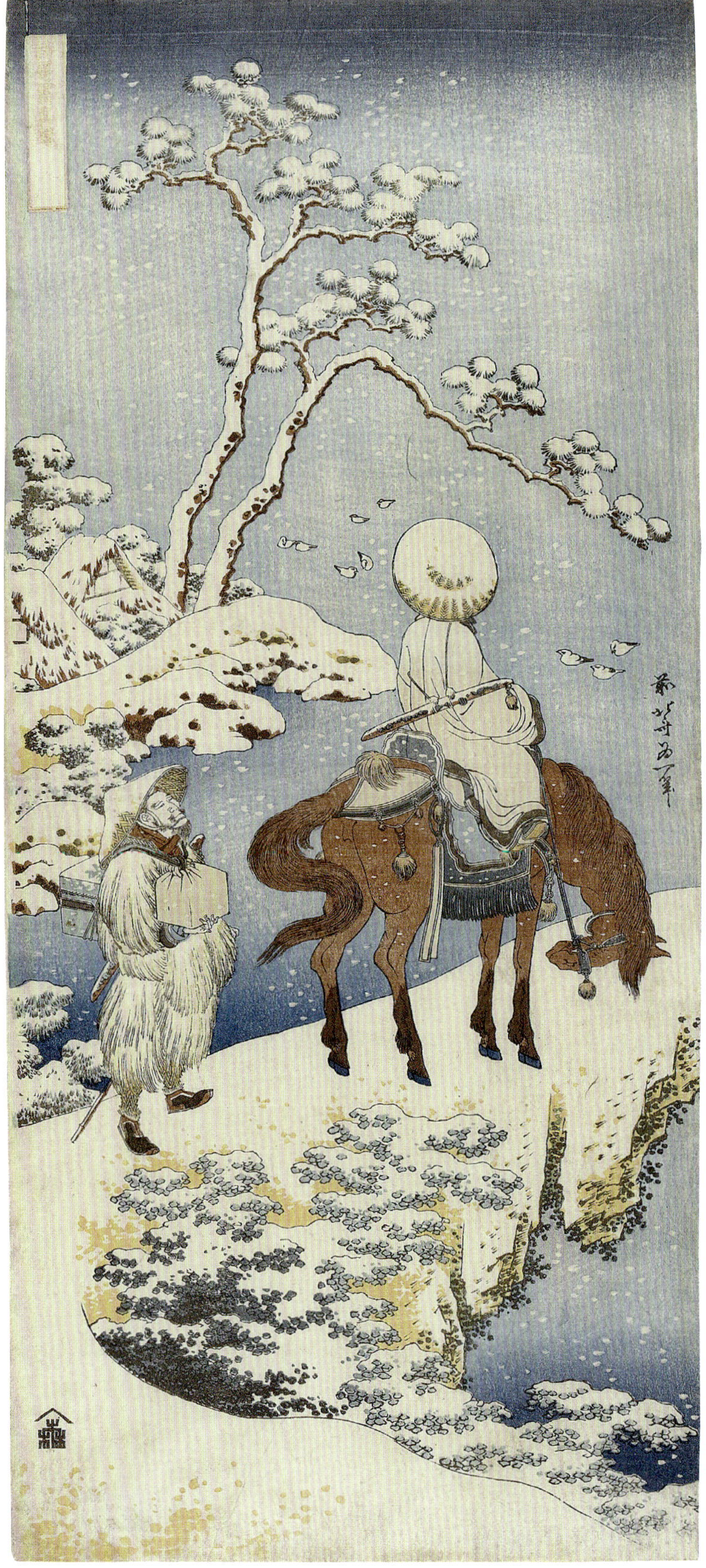

Poet Du Fu, from *Illustrated Anthology of Tang Poetry* (*Tōshisen ehon*), part 6, vol. 3

1833
Signature: Saki no Hokusai Iitsu rōjin ga ('Drawn by old man Iitsu, the former Hokusai')
Illustrated book, woodblock, published by Kobayashi Shinbei (Sūzanbō), 22.7 × 15.8 cm (covers)
Literature: Nagata *Ehon sashi-e* 1987, vol. 2, p. 54; Iwakiri 2012, pp. 10–11
Ebi collection, UK, Ebi0127

Following the example of Ogyū Sorai (1666–1728), a philosopher and aficionado of Chinese culture, late Edo scholars of China studied the poetry of the High Tang dynasty (*c*. AD 713–766), especially as collected in *Anthology of Tang Poetry* (*Tang shi xuan*, mid-1500s). By the late 1700s an illustrated Japanese edition was planned, although the scale of the project resulted in a long-term publishing effort spanning many decades (1788–1836) and multiple illustrators. Hokusai illustrated parts 6 (five volumes, 1833) and 7 (five volumes, 1836), and so brought the book to completion. The volumes are laid out so that an illustration follows each poem. In this illustration, an officer studies a snow-bound landscape while his servant trudges behind him. The scene relates to a desolate farewell poem that Du Fu (AD 712–770) sent to a friend who had ridden off to war in winter. Hokusai seems to have used this illustration as the starting point for a print in the contemporaneous series *True Mirror of Chinese and Japanese Poems* (cat. 124). AH

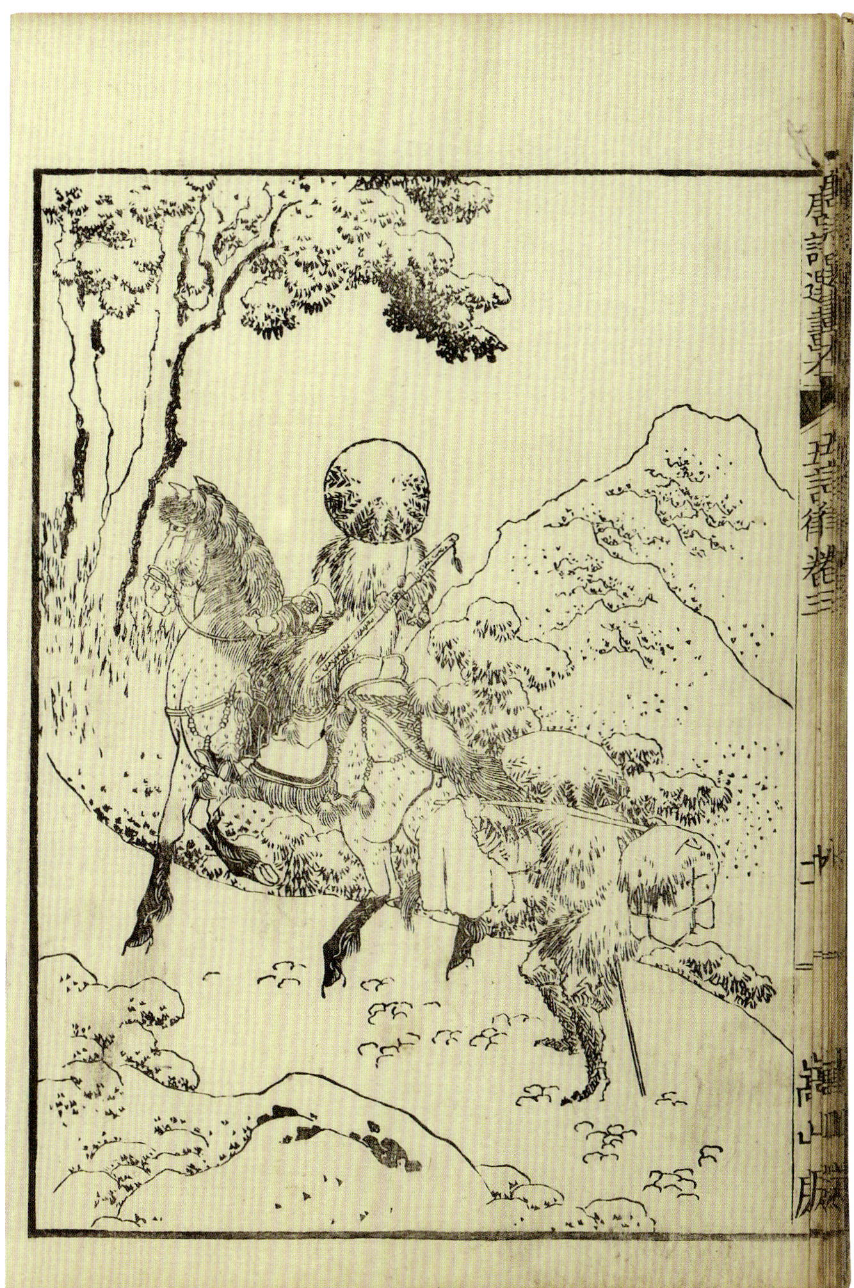

The Youth's Song (by Poet Cui Guofu)

About 1833–1834

Signature: Saki no Hokusai Iitsu hitsu ('Brush of Iitsu, the former Hokusai')

Colour woodblock, published by Moriya Jihei,

50.3 × 22.7 cm

Provenance: Arthur Morrison

Literature: MSU 1991, no. 79; RA 1991, no. 71; Iwakiri 2012, p. 15; Keyes & Morse 2015, no. 976

British Museum, 1906,1220,0.571

Osaka only

Classical Chinese poets occasionally composed verses inspired by ancient folk songs (*yuefu*). Cui Guofu's (active early AD 700s) version of the 'Youth's Song' has a wealthy young man recalling a misadventure in the brothel district of Zhangtai, when on his way home he had to substitute a willow branch for his lost riding crop. 'Roadside' in the poem refers to the brothels and their courtesans: 'I'd lost my coral riding crop, / and my white horse tossed his head and balked / so I plucked a strand of Zhangtai willow: / the roadside in the spring sun has its charm' (trans. Alfred Haft). The poem appears in *Illustrated Anthology of Tang Poetry*, part 1, volume 2 (1788). Hokusai shows the stubborn horse, the youth brandishing a willow branch, his servant, and a local fisherman who has surely seen it all before. The winding waterside path leads the eye through the design. AH

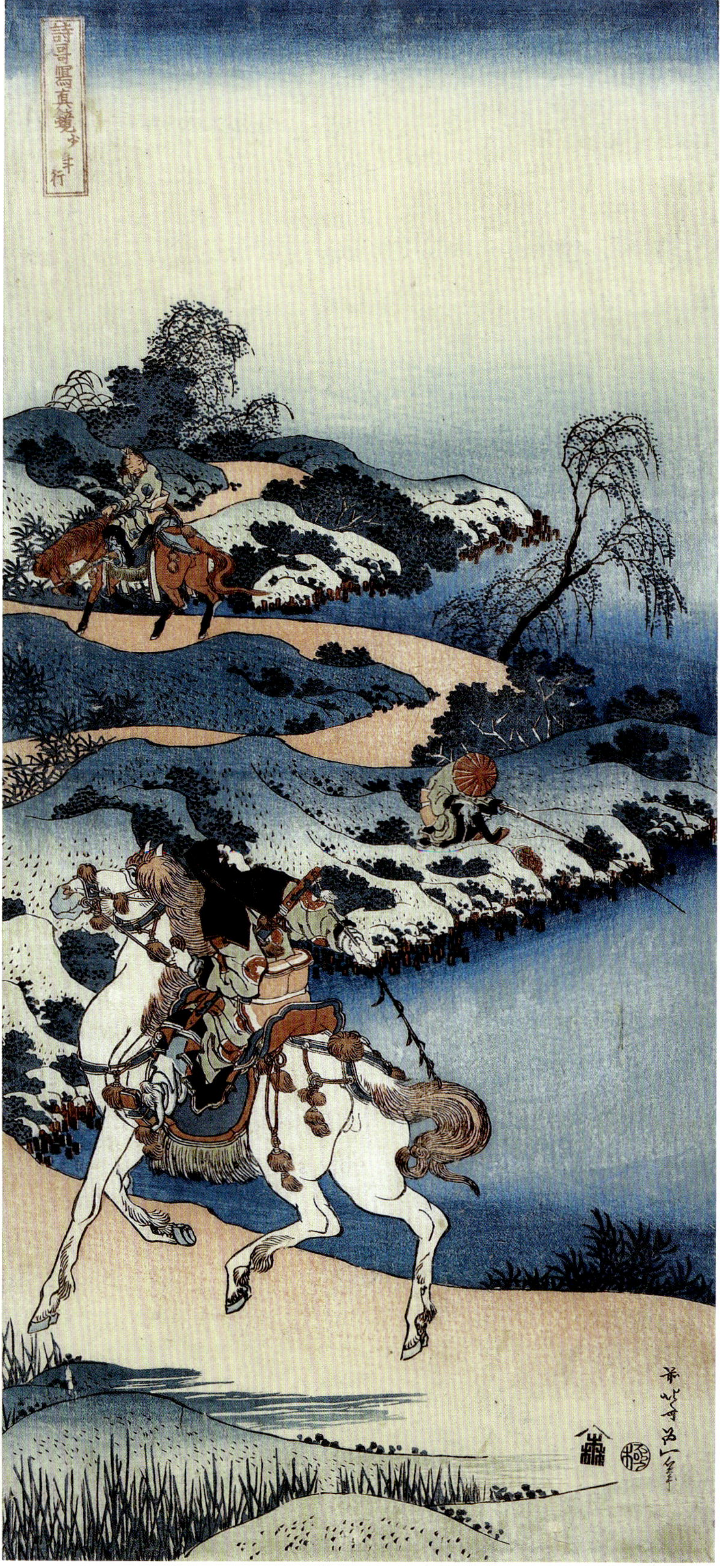

Poet Abe no Nakamaro

About 1833–1834
Signature: Saki no Hokusai Iitsu hitsu ('Brush of Iitsu, the former Hokusai')
Colour woodblock, published by Moriya Jihei,
50.8 × 22.5 cm
Provenance: W. B. Paterson
Literature: MSU 1991, no. 84; RA 1991, no. 69;
McMillan 2008, p. 16; Keyes & Morse 2015, no. 972
British Museum, 1910,0418,0.190

Abe no Nakamaro (AD 698–770) was appointed to
the Japanese embassy to Tang China in AD 717.
Before departure, he followed the custom of making
a pilgrimage to Kasuga shrine on Mt Mikasa in order
to pray for a safe return. In China he had a successful
career, passing the civil service exam and receiving
positions in the Tang administration, but by 734 he
was ready to return home. Just as he set sail, a storm
arose and his ship foundered, forcing him back to land.
Around this time he composed a celebrated Japanese
poem expressing nostalgia for his home country:
'When I look up / into the vast sky tonight, / is it the
same moon / that I saw rising / from behind Mt Mikasa
/ at Kasuga shrine / all those years ago?' (trans. Peter
McMillan). Here the architecture and the foreground
Taihu stones (a particular type of porous limestone)
indicate the setting to be China. Hokusai captured
the mood of the poem by showing the poet seated apart,
wearing Japanese court robes, and gazing thoughtfully
at the moon. AH

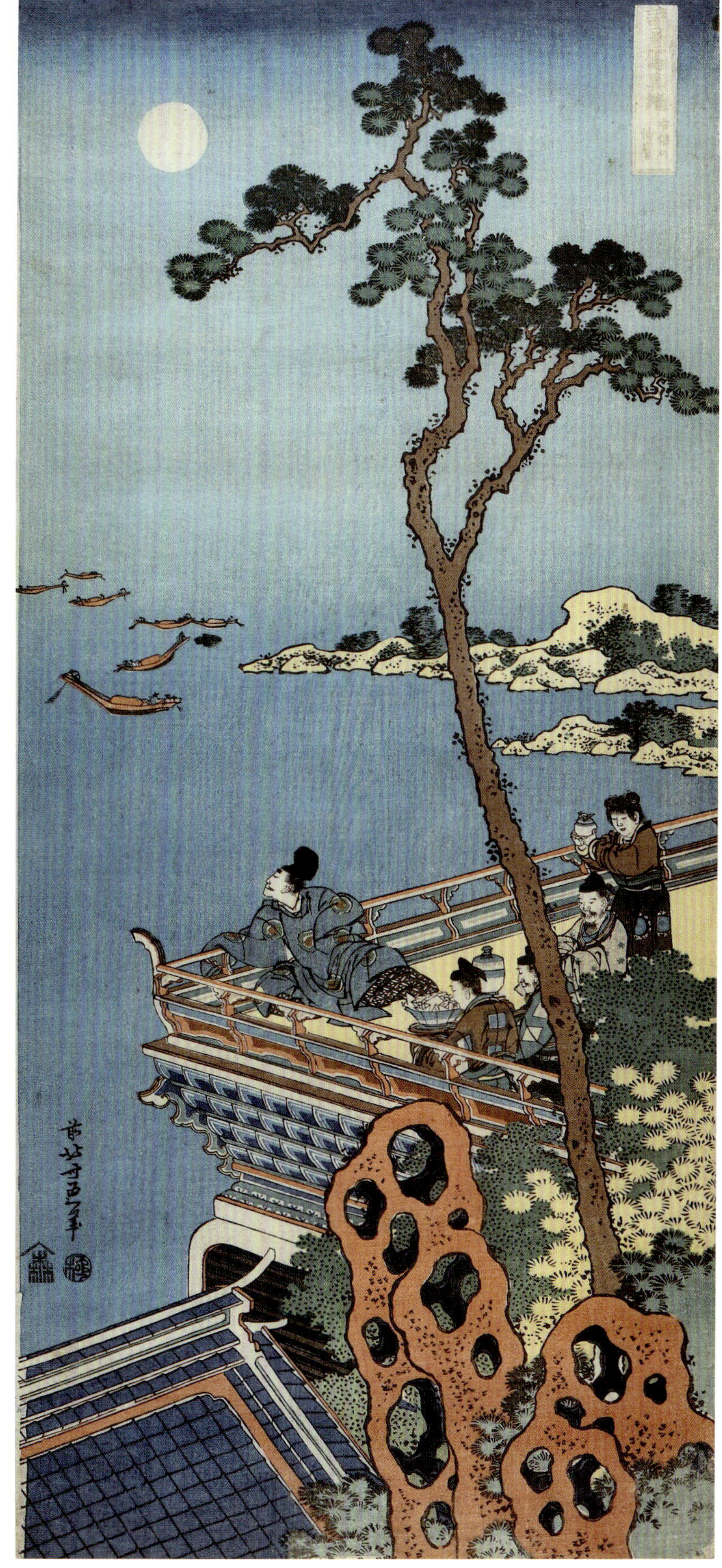

Poet Minister Tōru

About 1833–1834
Signature: Saki no Hokusai Iitsu hitsu ('Brush of Iitsu,
the former Hokusai')
Colour woodblock, published by Moriya Jihei,
49.8 × 23.1 cm
Provenance: W. B. Paterson
Literature: MSU 1991, no. 86; RA 1991, no. 68;
Iwakiri 2012, pp. 11–12; Keyes & Morse 2015, no. 974
British Museum, 1910,0418,0.193

In the garden of his Kyoto villa, Minister of the Left
Minamoto no Tōru (AD 822–895) famously recreated
the seaside landscape of northern Japan, daily
introducing fresh seawater so that marine fish and
shellfish could thrive there. In one area he even installed
working salt-kilns, a well-known feature of that region.
Hokusai's print relates not to a poem but to the Noh
play *Tōru* by Zeami (1363?–1443?), which dramatizes
the story of the garden. Motifs in the print derive from
various lines in the play. For example, Zeami quotes a
poem by Jia Dao (AD 779–843) describing birds nesting
in the branches of a tree found in the middle of a pond.
These appear towards the bottom of the design. Later
in the play, Zeami associates the shape of the crescent
moon with that of boats. In selecting these motifs,
Hokusai may have been guided by illustrations related
to the play in *Illustrated Book of Noh* (*Utai ehon*, 1735),
by Tachibana Morikuni (1679–1748). AH

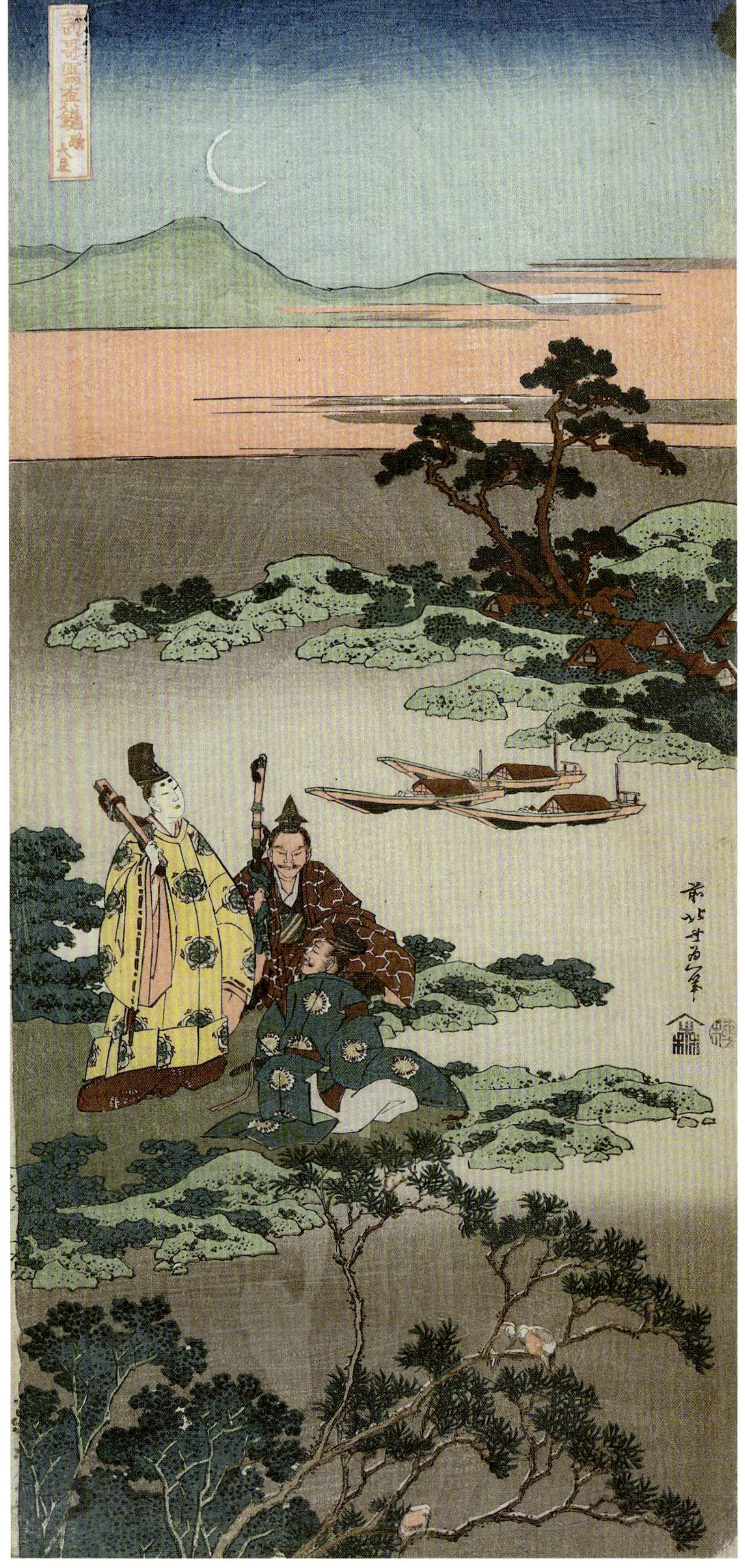

Poet Harumichi no Tsuraki

About 1833–1834
Signature: Saki no Hokusai Iitsu hitsu ('Brush of Iitsu, the former Hokusai')
Colour woodblock, published by Moriya Jihei,
50.3 × 23.0 cm
Provenance: W. B. Paterson
Literature: MSU 1991, no. 83; Iwakiri 2012, p. 16;
Keyes & Morse 2015, no. 971
British Museum, 1910,0418,0.189
Osaka only

Poet Harumichi no Tsuraki (died AD 920) pauses on a footbridge to study a fast-flowing mountain stream. This moment inspired a poem composed by him at year's end and anthologized in *Collection of Ancient and Modern Poems* (*Kokin waka shū*, about AD 920): 'Speaking of yesterday / we live today flowing on / like Tomorrow river, / and so the days and months pass / swiftly one into another' (*Kinō to ii / kyō to kurashite / Asukagawa / nagarete hayaki / tsuki hi nari keri*) (trans. Alfred Haft). Hokusai offsets the melancholy of the verse by evoking the idyllic beauty of the classical past, with a view of the crystalline Tomorrow river (Asukagawa), a prosperous village and mountains rising – as if eternally – in the distance. AH

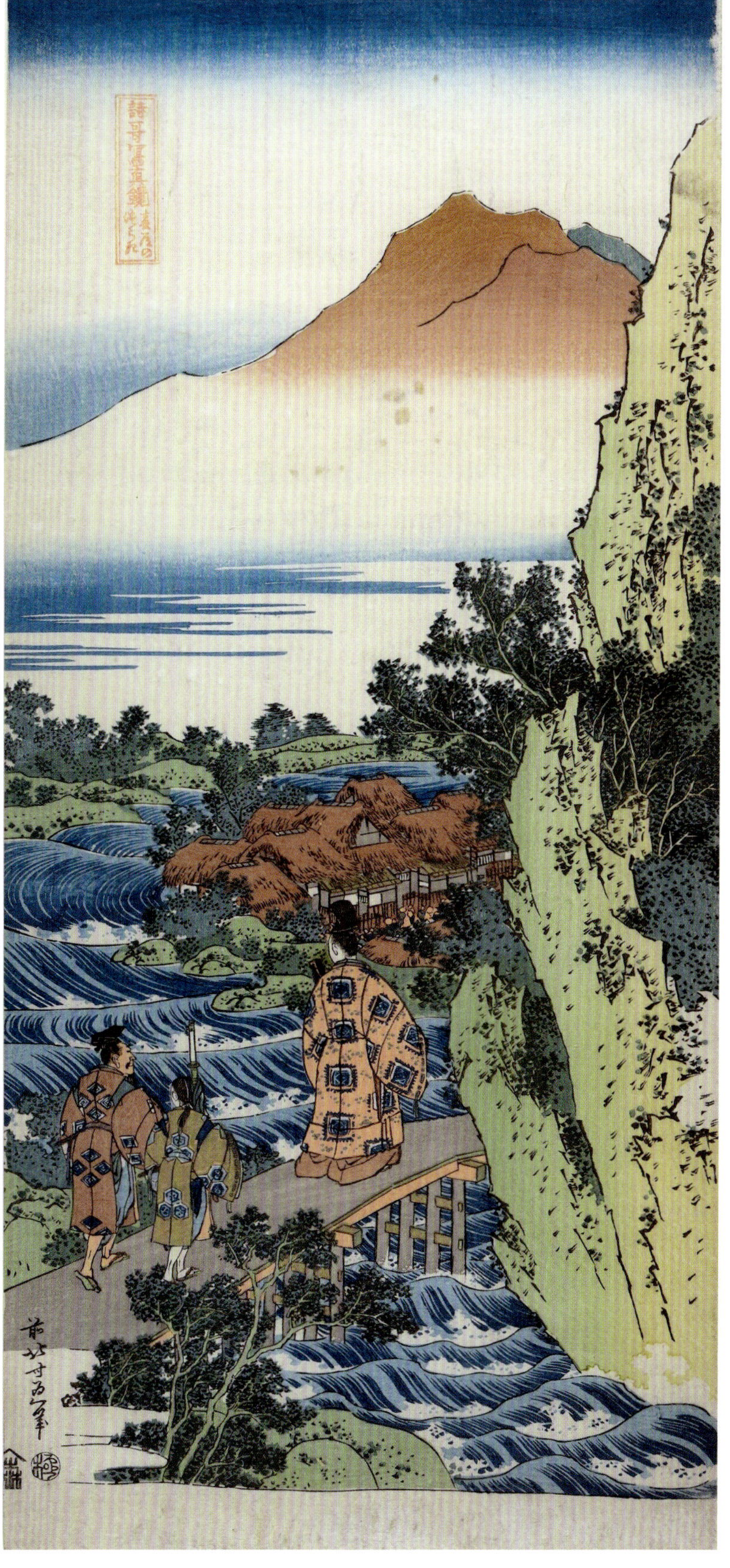

130
The Reed Gatherer (Tokusa-gari)

About 1833–1834
Signature: Saki no Hokusai Iitsu hitsu ('Brush of Iitsu, the former Hokusai')
Colour woodblock, published by Moriya Jihei, 50.5 × 23.0 cm
Provenance: W. B. Paterson
Literature: MSU 1991, no. 87; RA 1991, no. 73; Iwakiri 2012, p. 13; Keyes & Morse 2015, no. 975
British Museum, 1910,0418,0.194
Osaka only

An old man heads home alone carrying the day's harvest of reeds, with a rising full moon lighting his way. As the title indicates, this print relates to the Noh drama *Tokusa* (*Reeds*), in which an old reed gatherer in remote Shinano province (present-day Nagano prefecture) is reunited with his long-lost son. After the man has performed a mad dance to expel his years of grief, the two vow to enter the Buddhist clergy together. In preparing this design, Hokusai may have had in mind a poem by Minamoto no Nakamasa (active late 1000s – early 1100s) quoted in the play: 'Through the trees / on Mt Engen / where they gather reeds / appears the polished full moon / of an autumn night' (*Tokusa karu / Engenyama no / ki no ma yori / migakare izuru / aki no yo no tsuki*) (trans. Alfred Haft). This is perhaps the most atmospheric print in the series, with low evening mist, a running stream and a pair of water birds to emphasize the old man's quiet isolation. AH

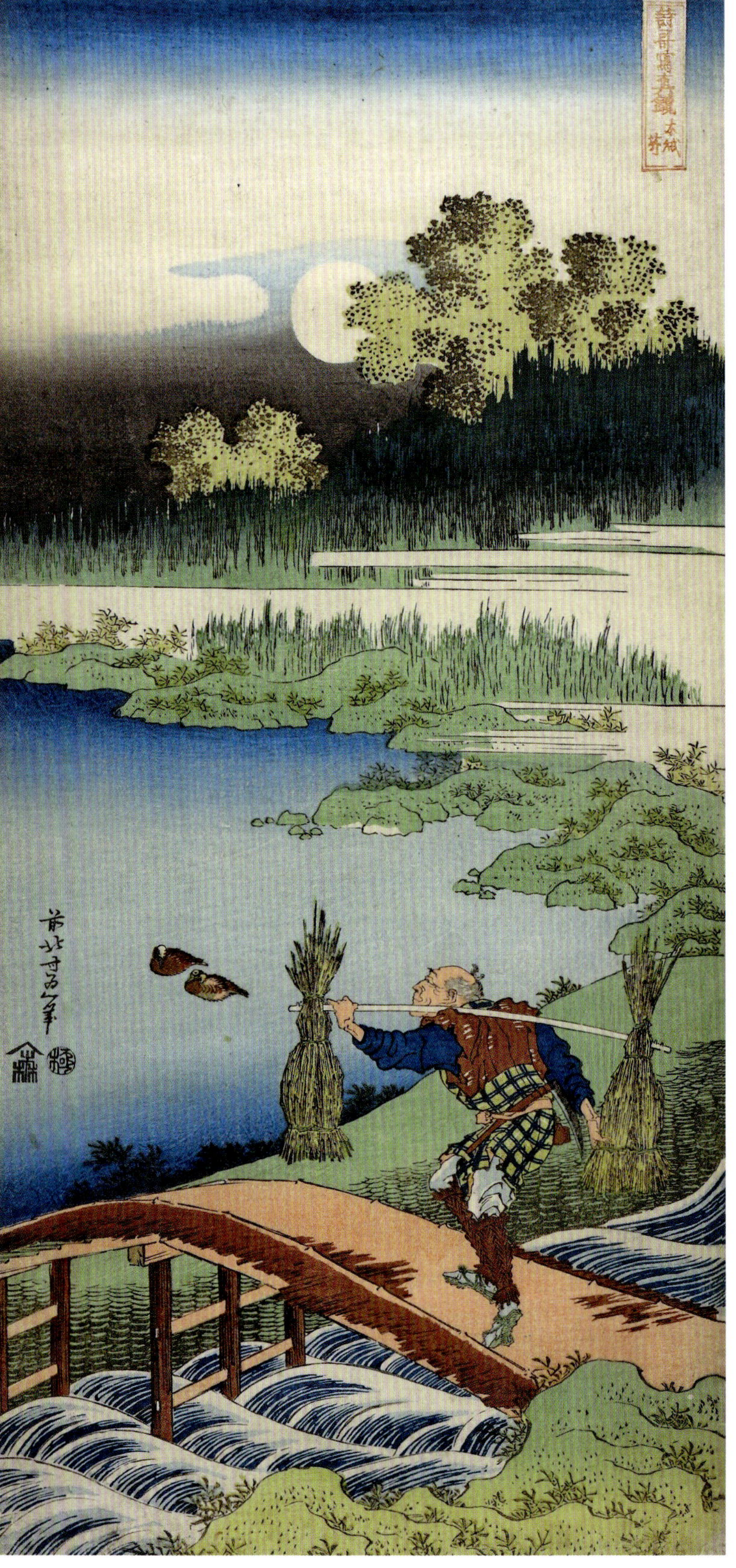

131

Warriors Kojima Yatarō and Saihōin Akabōzu

1833–1835
Signature: Saki no Hokusai Iitsu hitsu ('Brush of Iitsu, the former Hokusai')
Colour woodblock, published by Yamamotoya Heikichi (Eikyūdō), 38.1 × 26 cm
Literature: Asano 2010, p. 149; Osaka 2012, no. 267; Boston 2013, no. 95; Keyes & Morse 2015, no. 1880
Museum of Fine Arts, Boston, 11.39701, William Sturgis Bigelow collection
Osaka only

Hand-to-hand combat is the theme of five bold prints that Hokusai designed in the early 1830s. Warriors first appeared as an independent subject in popular prints around the mid-1700s, and the young Hokusai had explored the idea of warrior valour during the 1790s. In this series, however, he took advantage of the brilliant new pigment Prussian blue as an atmospheric background colour to show pairs of combatants in the heat of battle. Here Kojima 'The Demon' Yatarō (active late 1500s, top left) prevents the mischievous monk Saihōin Akabōzu from stealing the bell of Rinsenji, a temple patronized by Yatarō's lord, Uesugi Kenshin (1530–1578). The juxtaposition of pure red, white and green pigments and the tonal gradation in the bell make this one of the set's liveliest prints. A stylized demon's head serves as a prominent decoration on Yatarō's arm guard. AH

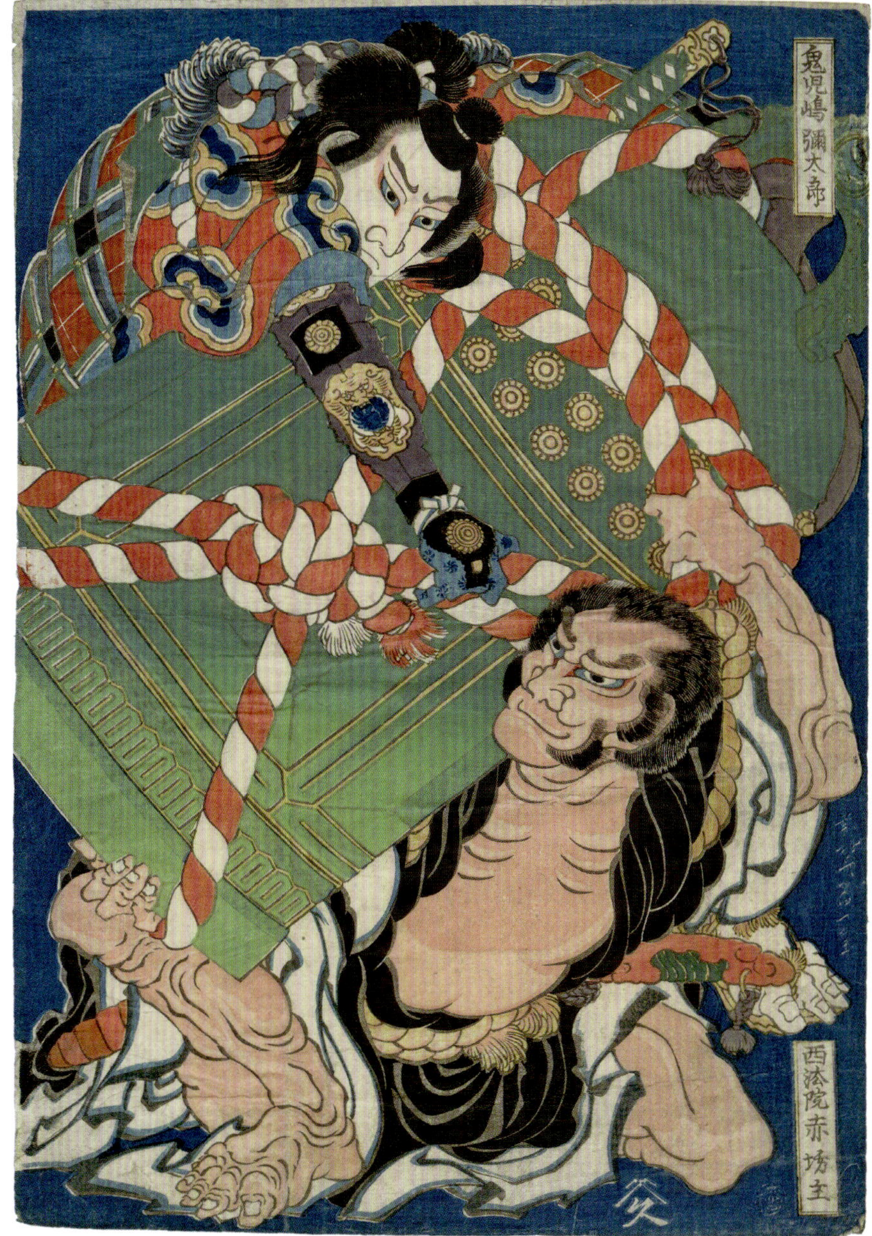

One Hundred Poems by One Hundred Poets, Explained by the Nurse (*Hyakunin isshu uba ga etoki*)

Courtier and poet Fujiwara no Teika (1162–1241) assembled the 'One Hundred Poems' anthology around 1235 at the request of Utsunomiya Yoritsuna (1172–1259), a fellow poet and his son's father-in-law. Yoritsuna wanted to give his villa in Ogura (near Kyoto) a literary ambience by decorating it with cards inscribed with classical verses. Teika searched through eight imperial poetry anthologies (*hachidaishū*), and selected one hundred exemplary verses, each by a different author, which he arranged in chronological order, commencing with a poem by benevolent Emperor Tenji (AD 626–672). Sometime later, it was perhaps Teika's son who revised the selection to end with Retired Emperor Juntoku (1197–1242), whom Teika had tutored and whose poem suitably begins with the number one hundred. The verses vary in subject. Some are charming nature studies; many others are mature in content, offering personal observations on human relationships. For centuries thereafter, educated Japanese memorized the One Hundred Poems and studied the commentaries of Teika's literary heirs. Not until the early Edo period, however, did artists have an opportunity to treat the anthology as a pictorial subject. From that point, reprinted in general references, reproduced in books with new illustrations and reformatted into games, the One Hundred Poems evolved into one of the most familiar and treasured works of Japanese literature. Still, even by the mid-1830s, never had the anthology appeared complete in a series of colour woodblock prints.

This challenge alone may have sparked Hokusai's interest in the subject. In a letter dated the second month of 1835, he indicates that he has taken over as illustrator of a mid-size book (*chūbon*) about the One Hundred Poems from his daughter Ōi, who had been commissioned for it (Machotka 2009, p. 17). Perhaps it was Hokusai who then reconceived the project for single-sheet prints and suggested that the 'narrator' of the series be not a scholar but a nurse (*uba*), that is, someone of wide and down-to-earth experience of the world. Hokusai then produced ninety-one known designs, taking full advantage of the possibilities that the 'nurse' guise would offer him. Thirteen designs are respectful illustrations of the classical past. The vast remainder depict ordinary people of Hokusai's own day: farmers, labourers, travellers, tradesmen and an occasional low-ranking samurai – people from the same walks of life that the artist had celebrated in prior series and throughout the illustrated book *Hokusai's Sketches* (*Hokusai manga*, cats 164, 165). Similarly, while a few designs illustrate the contents of a particular poem, many others take the poem in a new direction.

In the end, despite his enthusiasm for the project, Hokusai saw just twenty-seven of his designs realized as finished prints. Not long after issuing five prints (poem nos 1, 2, 3, 6 and 9), the initial publisher, Nishimuraya Yohachi, filed for bankruptcy, perhaps due to the harsh economic conditions associated with the famine occurring in the mid-Tenpō era (1830–1844). The publisher Iseya Sanjirō then managed to produce another twenty-two prints, with an additional one as a key-block print. Most of Hokusai's other proposed designs have fortunately survived in the form of his superb block-ready drawings, of which sixty-three are known. Art dealer Hayashi Tadamasa (1853–1906) acquired sixty in Japan around 1885, and sold them that year to Ernest Hart (1835–1898), a London surgeon. A decade later Hart sold to London collector Michael Tomkinson (1841–1921) a group of thirty-three drawings, which American industrialist and collector Charles Lang Freer (1854–1919) acquired in 1902 and later donated with an additional drawing to the Smithsonian Institution in Washington, DC (which now holds a total of forty). The locations of seventeen other drawings are known in public and private collections in the West and Japan. The small, square collector's seal, apparently reading 'Gyōzan-shujin', is impressed on the back of many of the drawings, but remains to be identified conclusively. Together the drawings and finished prints show how, by his late years, Hokusai had moved away from traditional Japanese-style painting methods and embraced the 'Chinese mode' (*karayō*) for which he is popularly known. Especially in the landscapes, every dot and line seems to express the artist's engagement with Chinese painting, in particular the methods of the Ming literati (Chinese: *nanhua* or *wenren*; Japanese: *nanga* or *bunjin*) style. In its subject-matter, however, Hokusai's series is both ancient and Japanese, and the interpretations are characteristically his own. This catalogue presents a selection of fifteen designs from the series (cats 132–146), arranged in the sequence of Teika's anthology. AH

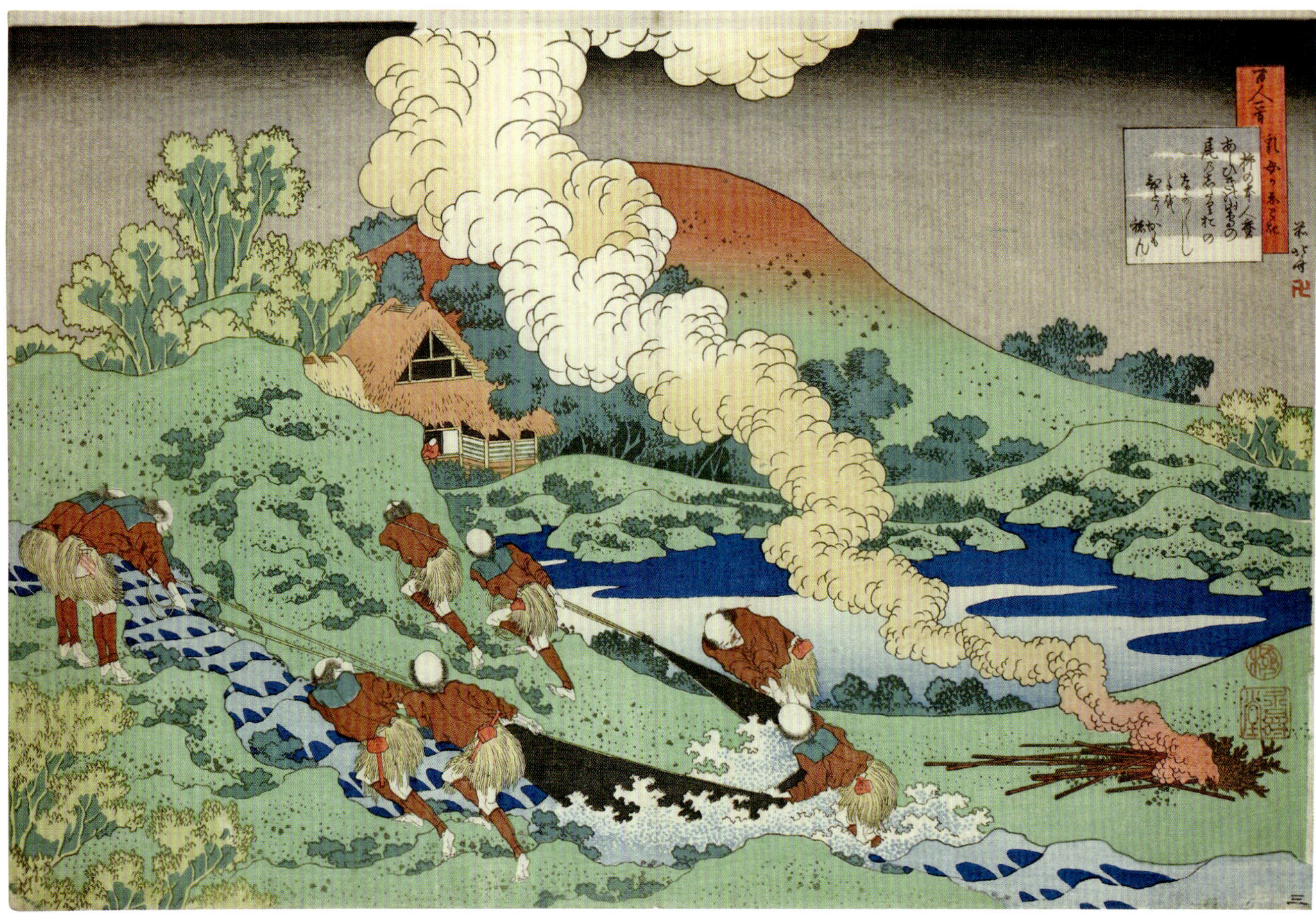

132

Poet Kakinomoto no Hitomaro

About 1835–1836
Signature: Saki no Hokusai Manji ('Manji, the former Hokusai')
Colour woodblock, published by Nishimuraya Yohachi,
26.2 × 37.7 cm
Literature: Morse 1989, no. 3; MSU 1992, no. 3;
Mostow 1996, pp. 149–151; Keyes & Morse 2015,
no. 653
British Museum, 1919,0715,0.2

Poem 3: *Ashibiki no / yamadori no o no / shidari-o no / naganagashi yo o / hitori kamo nemu* (Must I sleep alone / through the long autumn nights, / long like the dragging tail / of the mountain pheasant / separated from his dove?) (Trans. Joshua Mostow.)

Hokusai conveyed the dragging feeling of a long night spent alone through a composition of fishermen hauling a dragnet upstream as night descends. Carried by a steady breeze and mirroring the path of the stream (as well as perhaps suggesting the tail of Hitomaro's pheasant), a plume of campfire smoke traverses the scene from right to left, leading the eye to a tiny figure who reclines at the window of a rustic mountain villa, like a scholar or nobleman expecting a visitor. AH

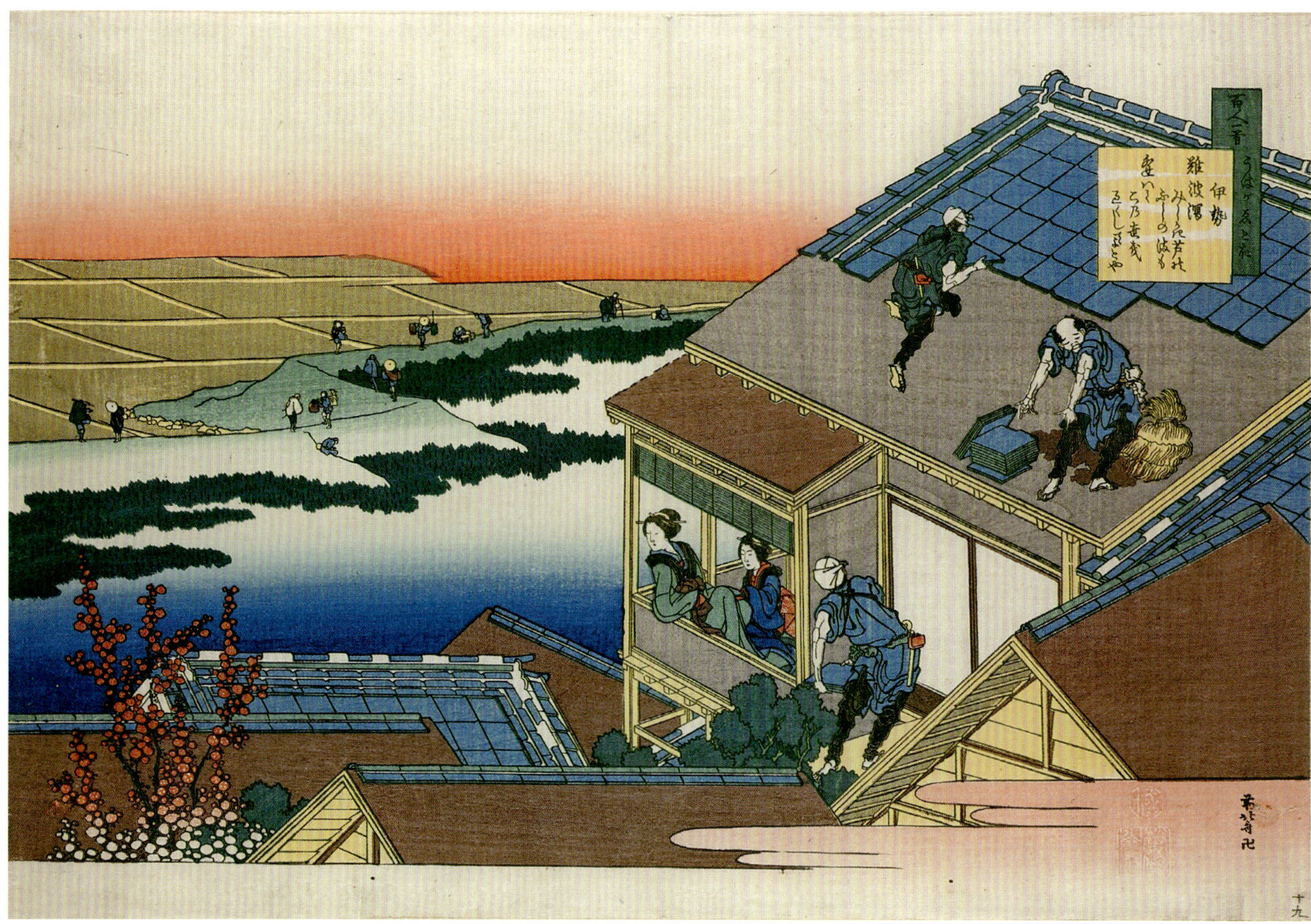

¹³³

Poet Ise

About 1835–1836
Signature: Saki no Hokusai Manji ('Manji, the former Hokusai')
Colour woodblock, published by Iseya Sanjirō,
26.3 × 37.7 cm
Literature: Morse 1989, no. 19; MSU 1992, no. 13;
Mostow 1996, pp. 198–199; Keyes & Morse 2015,
no. 663
British Museum, 1919,0715,0.3
Osaka only

Poem 19: *Naniwagata / mijikaki ashi no / fushi no ma no / awade kono yo o / sugushite yo to ya* (To go through this life, not meeting / for even as short a time as the space / between two nodes of a reed / in Naniwa inlet – / is that what you are telling me?) (Trans. Joshua Mostow.)

A courtesan of Yoshiwara pleasure quarter sits at the upper-storey window of a teahouse, accompanied by her young attendant (*kamuro*). She appears unconcerned by the workmen repairing the restaurant's tile roof, but gazes longingly towards the Embankment of Japan (Nihon-tsutsumi), the path that led Yoshiwara patrons from the Sumida river through rice fields to the pleasure quarter. A flowering plum tree at lower left suggests that the season is the New Year or early spring, ordinarily one of Yoshiwara's busiest periods. Hokusai's illustration transfers the poet Ise's verse to Edo, and interprets it as a lament of the pleasure quarters, with the courtesan disappointed to learn that she has lost a client. Perhaps Hokusai imagined her having to rebuild her client-base with new lovers. More concretely, in the second month of 1835 Yoshiwara burned to the ground, and the roof repairs might allude to the rebuilding, helping to date the publication of the series. AH

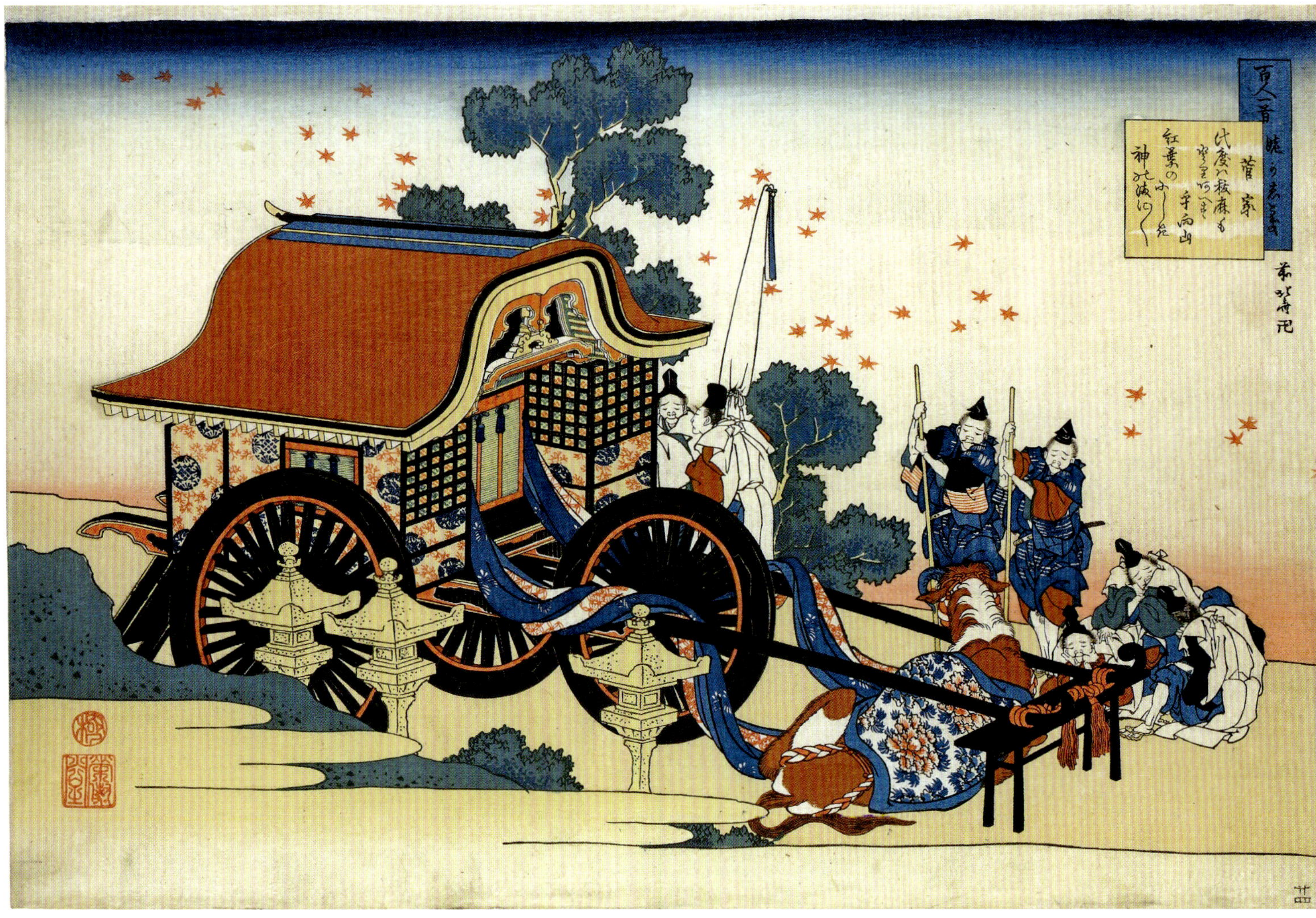

134

Poet Kan Ke (Sugawara no Michizane)

About 1835–1836
Signature: Saki no Hokusai Manji ('Manji, the former Hokusai')
Colour woodblock, published by Iseya Sanjirō,
25.7 × 37.0 cm
Literature: Morse 1989, no. 24; MSU 1992, no. 15; Mostow 1996, pp. 213–214; Keyes & Morse 2015, no. 665
British Museum, 1919,0715,0.4

Poem 24: *Kono tabi wa / nusa mo tariaezu / Tamukeyama / momiji no nishiki / kami no manimani* (This time around / I couldn't even bring sacred streamers / – Offering Hill – / but if this brocade of autumn leaves / is to the gods' liking….) (Trans. Joshua Mostow.)

One of the few designs in the series to give the ancient poem a courtly setting, this print shows an imperial carriage parked outside a shrine, with servants, guards and decorated oxen patiently awaiting the return of their passenger, as autumn leaves start to fall. The scene appears to be based on the circumstances behind the poem's composition. In AD 898, Kan Ke (Sugawara no Michizane, AD 845–903) accompanied Emperor Uda (AD 887–897) on an autumn excursion to Offering Hill in Nara, and recognizing the beauty of the surrounding foliage, imagined that a 'brocade of autumn leaves' might serve as a suitable gift for the gods. AH

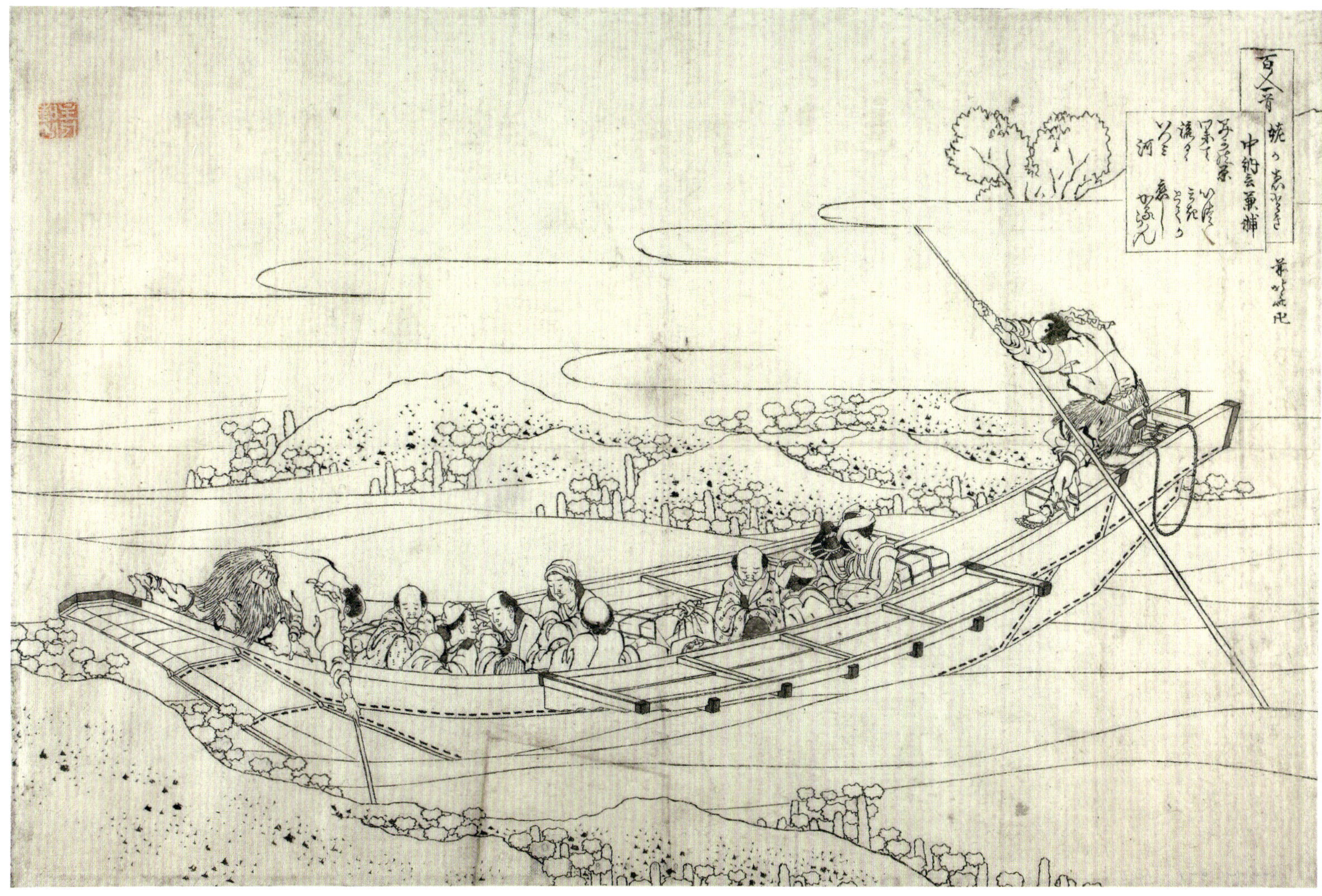

135

Poet Chūnagon Kanesuke

About 1835–1838
Signature: Saki no Hokusai Manji ('Manji, the former Hokusai')
Block-ready drawing, ink on paper, with pentimenti, 24.8 × 36.6 cm
Provenance: William Pitcairn Knowles
Literature: HUT 1987–1990, vol. 3, BW no. 53; Morse 1989, no. 27; Mostow 1996, pp. 223–224
British Museum, 1905,0608,0.1

Poem 27: *Mikanohara / wakite nagaruru / Izumigawa / itsu miki tote ka / koishikaruramu* (Like Izumi river / that wells up and flows, / dividing the Moor of Urns – / when did I see her, I wonder, that I should yearn for her so?) (Trans. Joshua Mostow.)

Two pole-men steer a passenger ferry along a river channel. Platforms extending from the gunwales steady the boat on its course. Towards the stern sits a young samurai lady with her maids and a servant; towards the bow sits a young samurai gentleman with his servants. The two groups appear unaware of each other and absorbed in separate conversations. Hokusai in this way presented the everyday circumstances that the gentleman (like the poet Kanesuke) would later be unable to recall as he found himself yearning for the lady. The river setting follows from the Izumi river of the poem, a metaphor for a welling sense of longing. AH

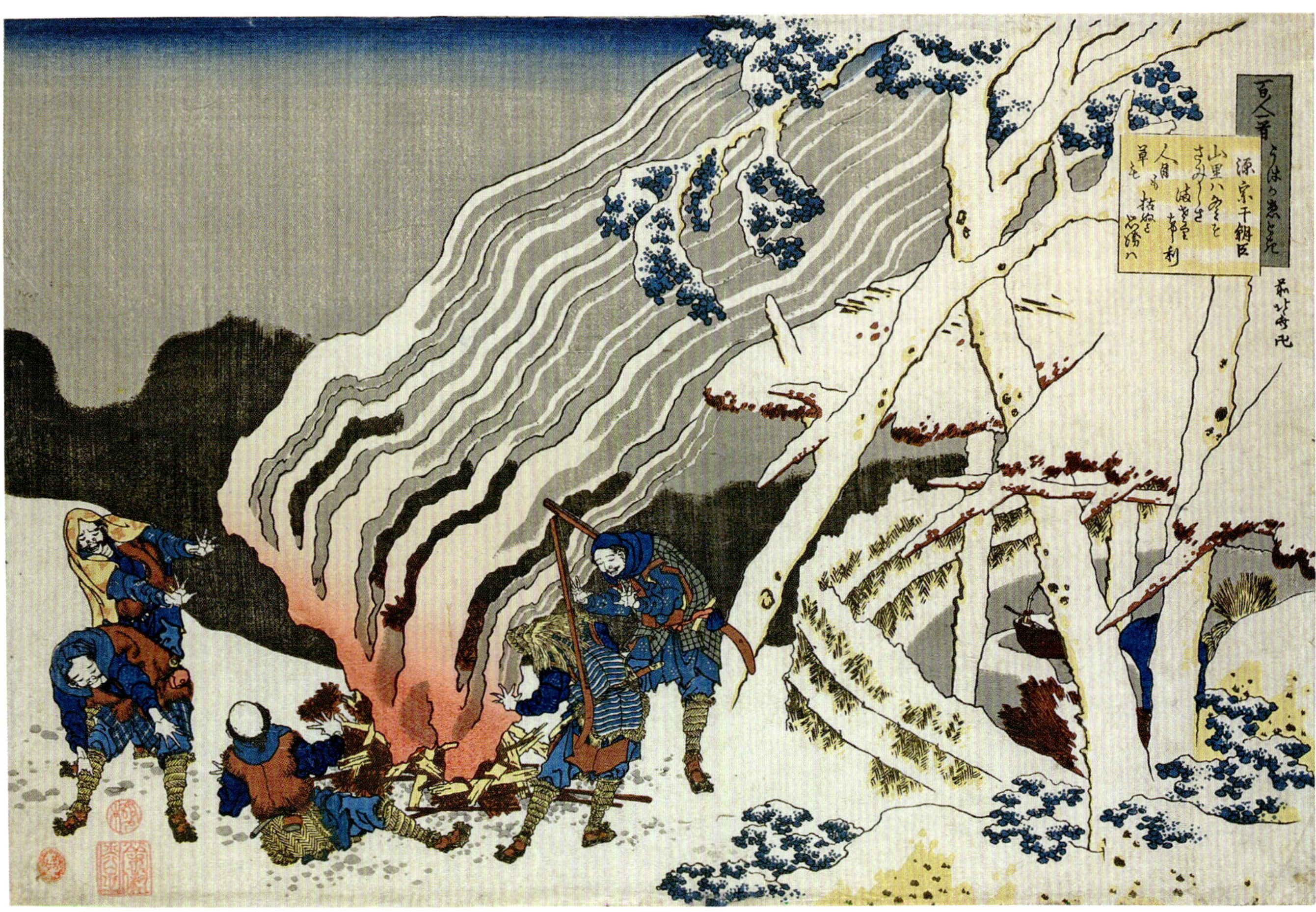

136

Poet Minamoto no Muneyuki Ason

About 1835–1836
Signature: Saki no Hokusai Manji ('Manji, the former Hokusai')
Colour woodblock, published by Iseya Sanjirō,
25.0 × 36.5 cm
Provenance: James Tregaskis
Literature: Morse 1989, no. 28; MSU 1992, no. 17;
Mostow 1996, pp. 226–227; Keyes & Morse 2015,
no. 667
British Museum, 1920,0514,0.10

Poem 28: *Yamazato wa / fuyu zo sabishisa / masarikeru / hitome mo kusa mo / karenu to omoeba* (In the mountain village, / it is in winter that my loneliness / increases most, / when I think how both have dried up, / the grasses and people's visits.) (Trans. Joshua Mostow.)

Disregarding the heavy mood of the poem, Hokusai shows a group of jolly hunters enjoying the warmth of a bonfire after a day in the woods. The soaring flames seem to echo their high spirits. As part of their outdoor winter gear, the hunters wear straw sandals (*waraji*) and straw leggings (*habaki*) to ward off the cold. At the right, protected by a brushwood fence, is the snow-encrusted mountain hut where they will spend the night. Among all the designs in the series, this one in particular seems to reflect the artist's customary exuberance. **AH**

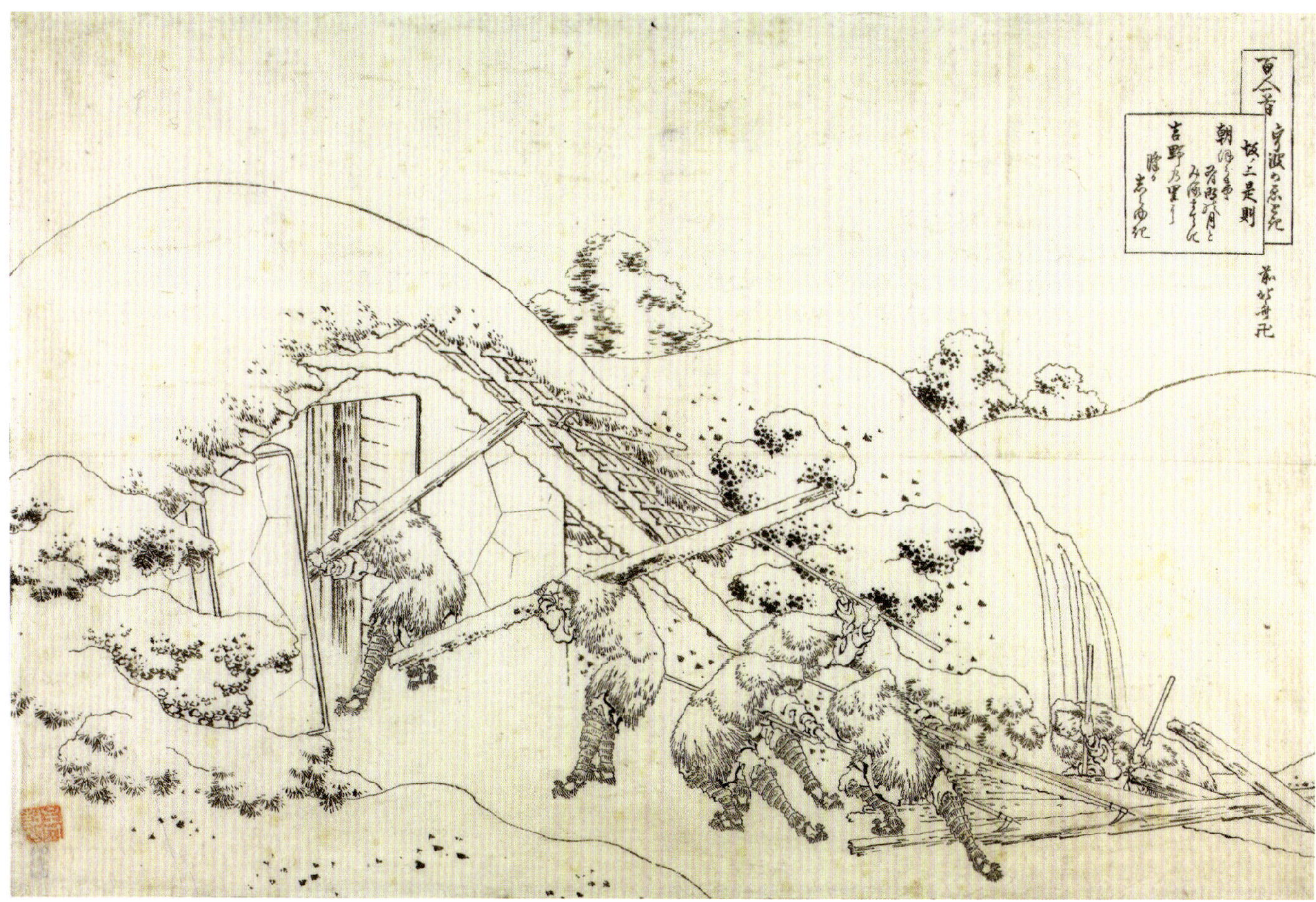

137
Poet Sakanoue Korenori

About 1835–1838
Signature: Saki no Hokusai Manji ('Manji, the former Hokusai')
Block-ready drawing, ink on paper, 25.2 × 36.7 cm
Provenance: Arthur Morrison
Literature: HUT 1987–1990, vol. 3, BW no. 54;
Morse 1989, no. 31; Mostow 1996, pp. 235–236
British Museum, 1913,0501,0.345, given by Sir
W. Gwynne-Evans, Bt
Osaka only

Poem 31: *Asaborake / ariake no tsuki to / miru made ni / Yoshino no sato ni / fureru shirayuki* (So that I thought it / the light of the lingering moon / at dawn – / the white snow that has fallen on the village of Yoshino.) (Trans. Joshua Mostow.)

Workmen haul logs from a stream and load them into a storehouse constructed of dressed stones in good repair. This building epitomizes a domain lord (*daimyō*) managing a successful local industry. The composition moves from right to left, tying the ascent from the river into the line of the storehouse's low roof, which consists of a lattice frame covered in thatch. Piled with snow, the roof acquires a rounded profile that continues into the hilly landscape and is representative of the mountains of Yoshino, traditionally depicted as lines of low, rolling hills. Whereas the poet offered a general, idealized description of a village, Hokusai focused on the people hard at work there – people hardly known to those in Edo, who were the main audience for his prints. AH

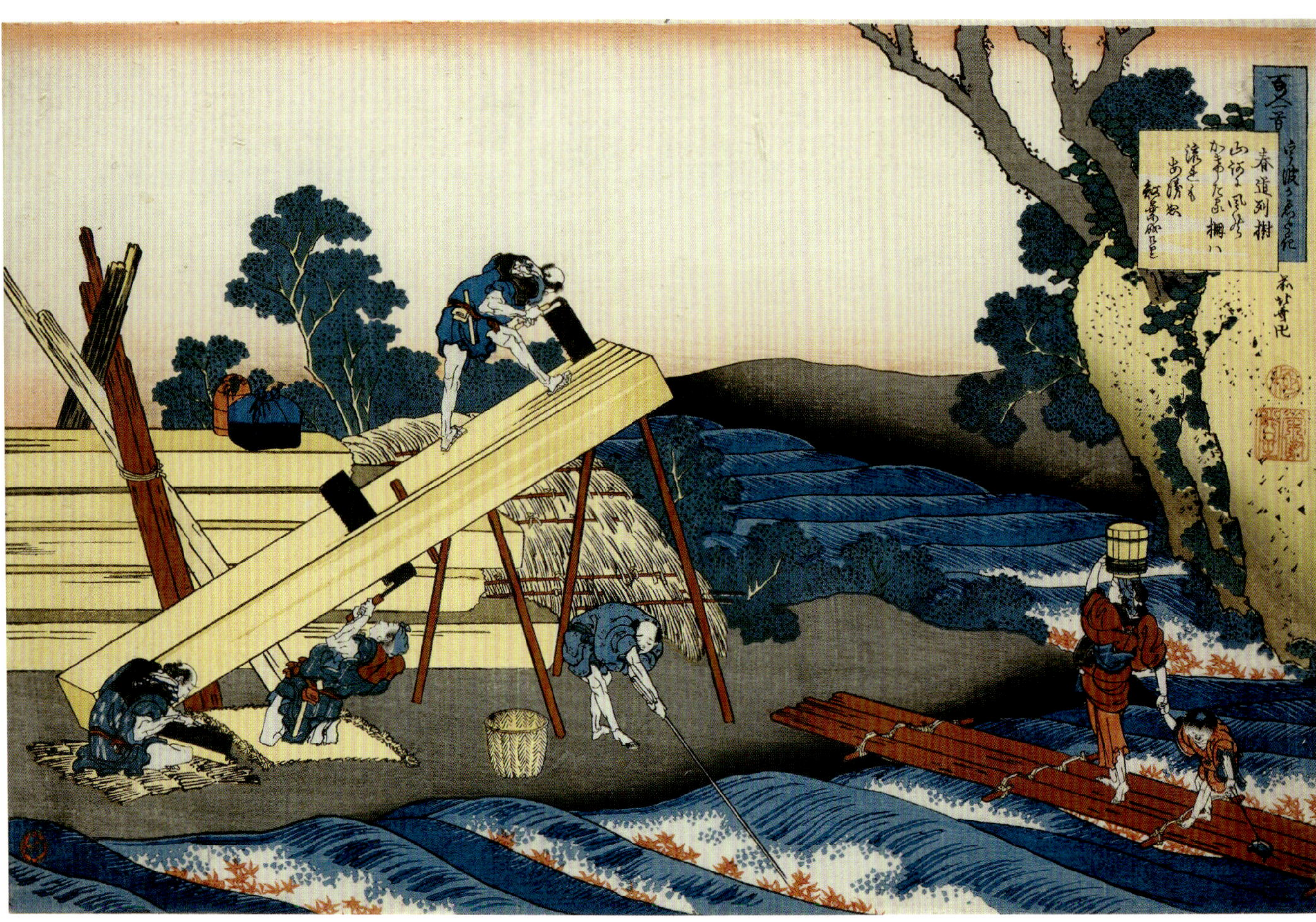

138

Poet Harumichi no Tsuraki

About 1835–1836

Signature: Saki no Hokusai Manji ('Manji, the former Hokusai')

Colour woodblock, published by Iseya Sanjirō,

25.1 × 36.6 cm

Literature: Morse 1989, no. 32; MSU 1992, no. 18; Mostow 1996, pp. 238–239; Keyes & Morse 2015, no. 669

British Museum, 1922,0719,0.4

Osaka only

Poem 32: *Yamagawa ni / kaze no kaketaru / shigarami wa / nagare mo aenu / momiji narikeri* (Ah, the weir / that the wind has flung / across the mountain stream / is the autumn foliage that / cannot flow on, even though it would.) (Trans. Joshua Mostow.)

The previous drawing (cat. 137) and this print form a pair of genre scenes illustrating aspects of the timber industry and rural life. From the right, a doughty farmwoman arrives balancing a bucket of lunch-rice on her head and leading her young son, who in turn leads a pet terrapin by a string. Downstream to the left, perhaps suggested by the poem, a man clears maple leaves from a watercourse that probably serves as the area's transportation lifeline. At far left a workman files the teeth of a saw blade, as two others cut timber into planks. Hokusai illustrated a similar subject and farmwoman in the 'Tōtōmi' print from *Thirty-Six Views of Mt Fuji*. He seems to have particularly liked this farmwoman, as she appears yet again bringing lunch in *One Hundred Views of Mt Fuji*, volume 2. AH

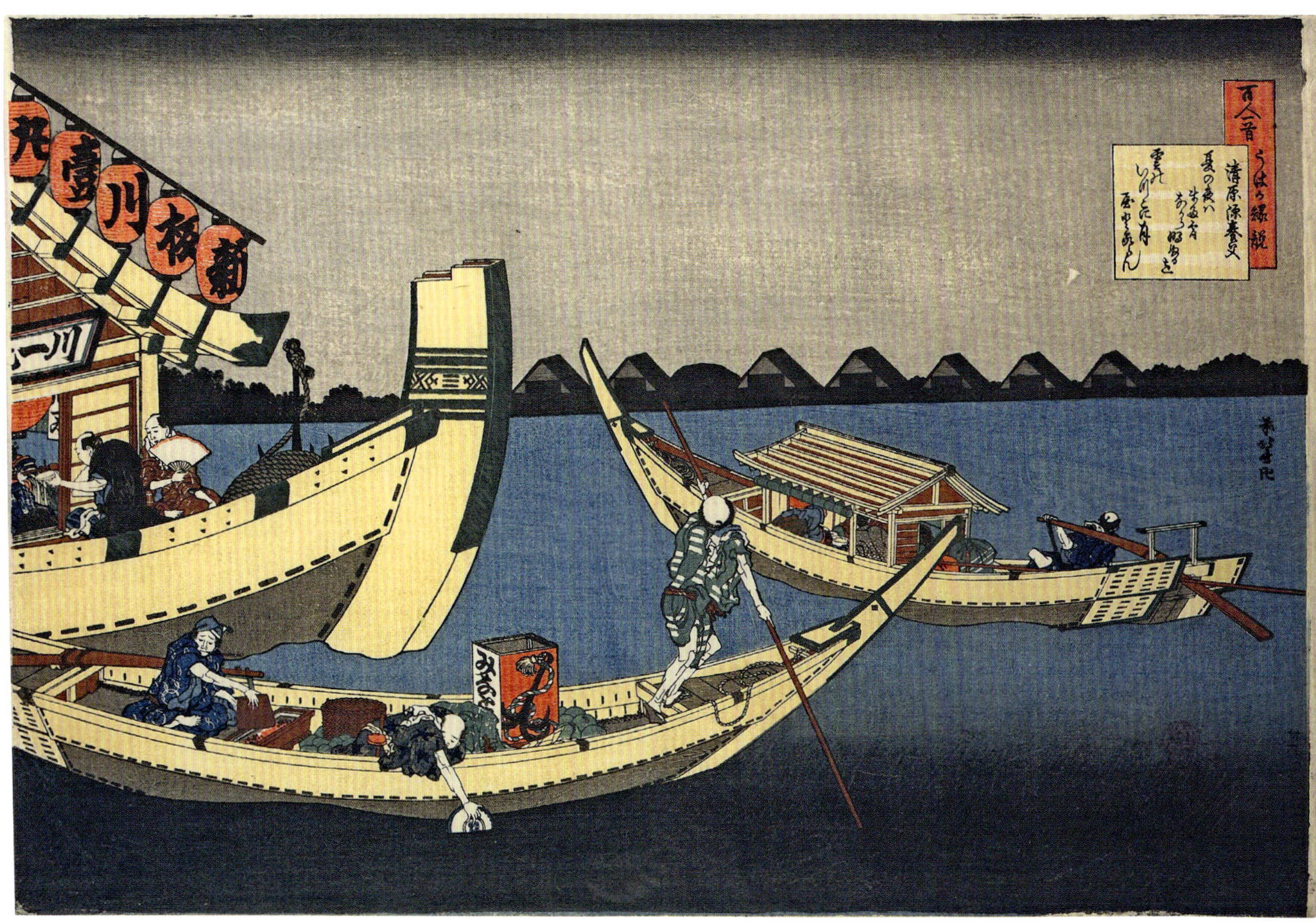

139

Poet Kiyowara no Fukayabu

About 1835–1836
Signature: Saki no Hokusai Manji ('Manji, the former Hokusai')
Colour woodblock, published by Iseya Sanjirō,
26.0 × 37.7 cm
Literature: Morse 1989, no. 36; MSU 1992, no. 19;
Mostow 1996, pp. 249–250; Keyes & Morse 2015,
no. 670
British Museum, 1919,0715,0.5
Osaka only

Poem 36: *Natsu no yo wa / mada yoi nagara / akenuru o / kumo no izuko ni / tsuki yadoruramu* (The short summer nights: / while it seems yet early evening, / it has already dawned, but / where in the clouds, then, / does the moon lodge, I wonder?) (Trans. Joshua Mostow.)

Summer nights in Edo were a time for boating on the Sumida river. The imposing roofed vessel (*yagatabune*) at the left is the *Kawa-ichimaru* ('Best-on-the-River'). Frequently shown in prints, this was one of the Sumida river's largest, most luxurious and most expensive rental pleasure barges. The two lanterns at the right end of the roof suggest that the craft may have been recently renovated. Towards the right, a party of commoners has hired a more modest type of *yagatabune*. Approaching them is one of the river's many floating vendors, offering fresh watermelon, grilled fish and other foods. The pole-man, like the poet Fukayabu, appears to be searching the sky for the moon hidden behind clouds. The buildings lining the riverbank might be shogunal boathouses in Honjo (east bank) or rice granaries at Kuramae (west bank). AH

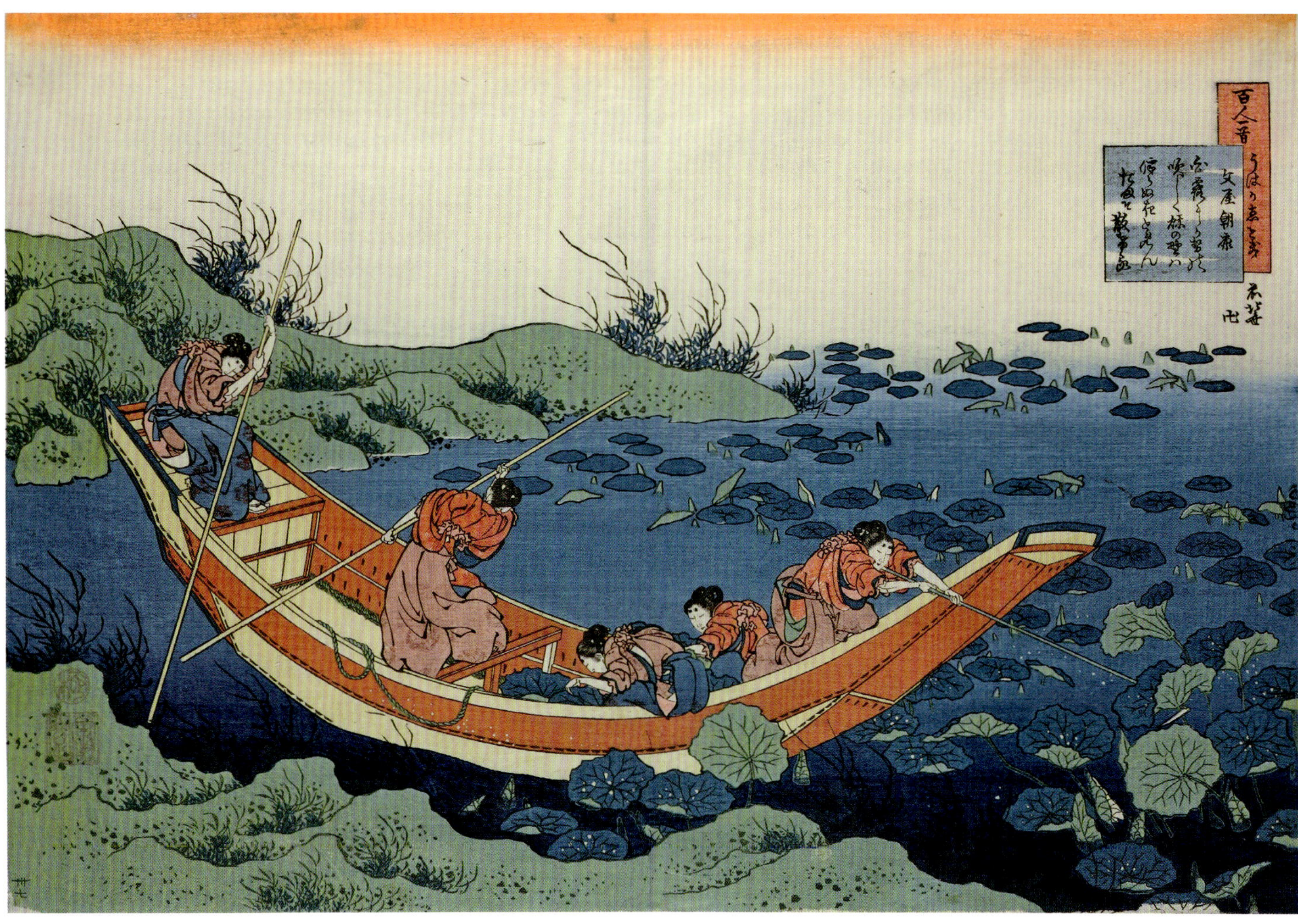

Poet Bunya no Asayasu

About 1835–1836
Signature: Saki no Hokusai Manji ('Manji, the former
Hokusai')
Colour woodblock, published by Iseya Sanjirō,
26.1 × 37.1 cm
Provenance: James Tregaskis
Literature: Morse 1989, no. 37; MSU 1992, no. 20;
Mostow 1996, pp. 252–253; Keyes & Morse 2015,
no. 671
British Museum, 1920,0514,0.1
Osaka only

Poem 37: *Shira-tsuyu ni / kaze no fuki-shiku / aki no ta wa /
tsuranuki tomenu / tama zo chirikeru* (In the autumn fields /
where the wind blows repeatedly / on the white
dewdrops, / the gems, not strung together, / do scatter
about indeed.) (Trans. Joshua Mostow.)

Five court page-boys harvest lotus leaves from a pond.
As two of them sort the harvest, another one strains to
hook a final leaf before the wind carries their boat away,
defeating the two inexperienced pole-men at the stern,
who seem to be fighting each other more than the wind.
Asayasu's poem revises the ancient association between
dew and gems by imagining the 'dew/gems' in their
natural state, 'not strung together', as yet untouched
by human hands. Following the poem, Hokusai shows
dewdrops on leaves, but transfers the scene from fields
to a pond and employs light comedy to convey the
strength of the wind. This and the previous print
(cat. 139) seem to form a pair of boating scenes. AH

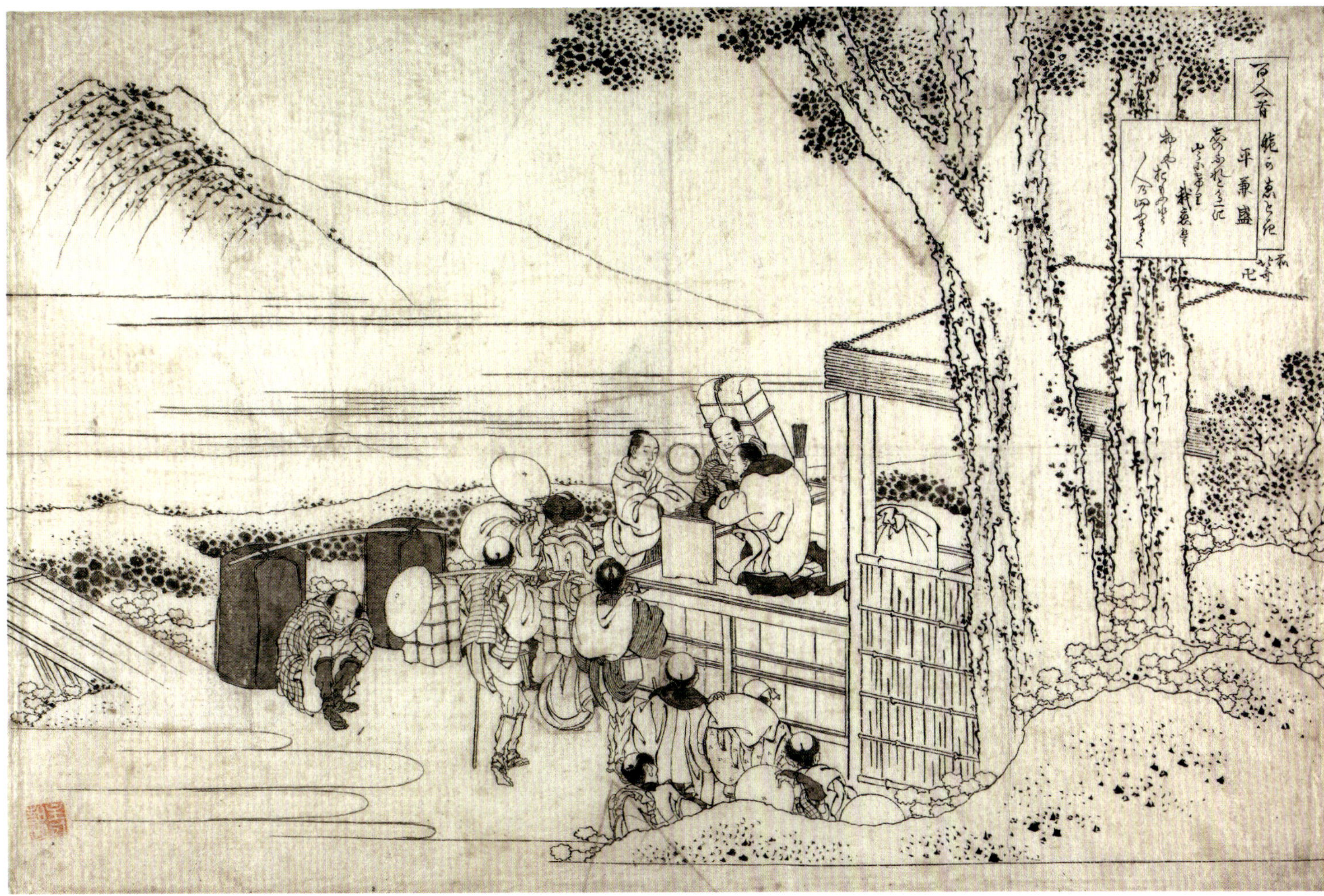

141

Poet Taira no Kanemori

About 1835–1838
Signature: Saki no Hokusai Manji ('Manji, the former Hokusai')
Block-ready drawing, ink on paper, with pentimenti, 25.1 × 37.0 cm
Provenance: William Anderson; Stephen D. Winkworth
Literature: HUT 1987–1990, vol. 3, BW no. 51; Morse 1989, no. 40; Mostow 1996, pp. 260–261
British Museum, 1951,0714,0.40
Osaka only

Poem 40: *Shinoburedo / iro ni ide ni keri / wa ga koi wa / mono ya omou to / hito no tou made* (Even though I hide it, / it shows all over my face, / such is my longing, / so that people ask me / 'What *are* you thinking about?') (Trans. Joshua Mostow.)

Kanemori's poem was awarded first place in a poetry contest in AD 960, and it remained a favourite because of the colloquial question introduced towards the end. In considering this poem, Hokusai seems to have recalled the popular belief that faces could reveal both states of mind and the future, if discerned by a practitioner of the art of physiognomy, or reading faces. Physiognomists (*ninsōmi*) set up booths where travellers could have their fortune told, and here a young samurai presents himself for inspection by an expert, who holds up a large magnifying glass. The samurai's entourage – baggage-handlers, retainers and others – stretch along the road, awaiting the expert's verdict. Hokusai treated this potentially humorous subject with empathy. AH

Poet Fujiwara no Yoshitaka

About 1835–1836
Signature: Saki no Hokusai Manji ('Manji, the former
Hokusai')
Colour woodblock, published by Iseya Sanjirō,
24.0 × 35.6 cm
Provenance: Arthur Morrison
Literature: Morse 1989, no. 50; MSU 1992, no. 23;
Mostow 1996, pp. 290–291; Keyes & Morse 2015,
no. 674
British Museum, 1906,1220,0.580
Osaka only

Poem 50: *Kimi ga tame / oshikarazarishi / inochi sae /
nagaku mogana to / omoinuru kana* (Even the life that /
I'd not have been sorry to lose / just to meet you once,
/ now, having met, I think: / 'I want it to last forever!')
(Trans. Joshua Mostow.)

Yoshitaka's poem is a 'morning-after' (*kinuginu*) verse,
sent to a woman after a man has spent the night with
her for the first time. The poem implies a night of
heat, languor and rejuvenation, like the feeling after
a soak in a hot bath – or so the practical 'nurse' of
the series title might have explained sexual passion to
one of her young charges. Hokusai conveyed the mood
with a view of men and women relaxing on a veranda,
dressed in loosely tied robes, and taking in the sight
of quiet, open water. Seen from behind and at a distance,
they retain a sense of privacy, of being left content with
their own thoughts. AH

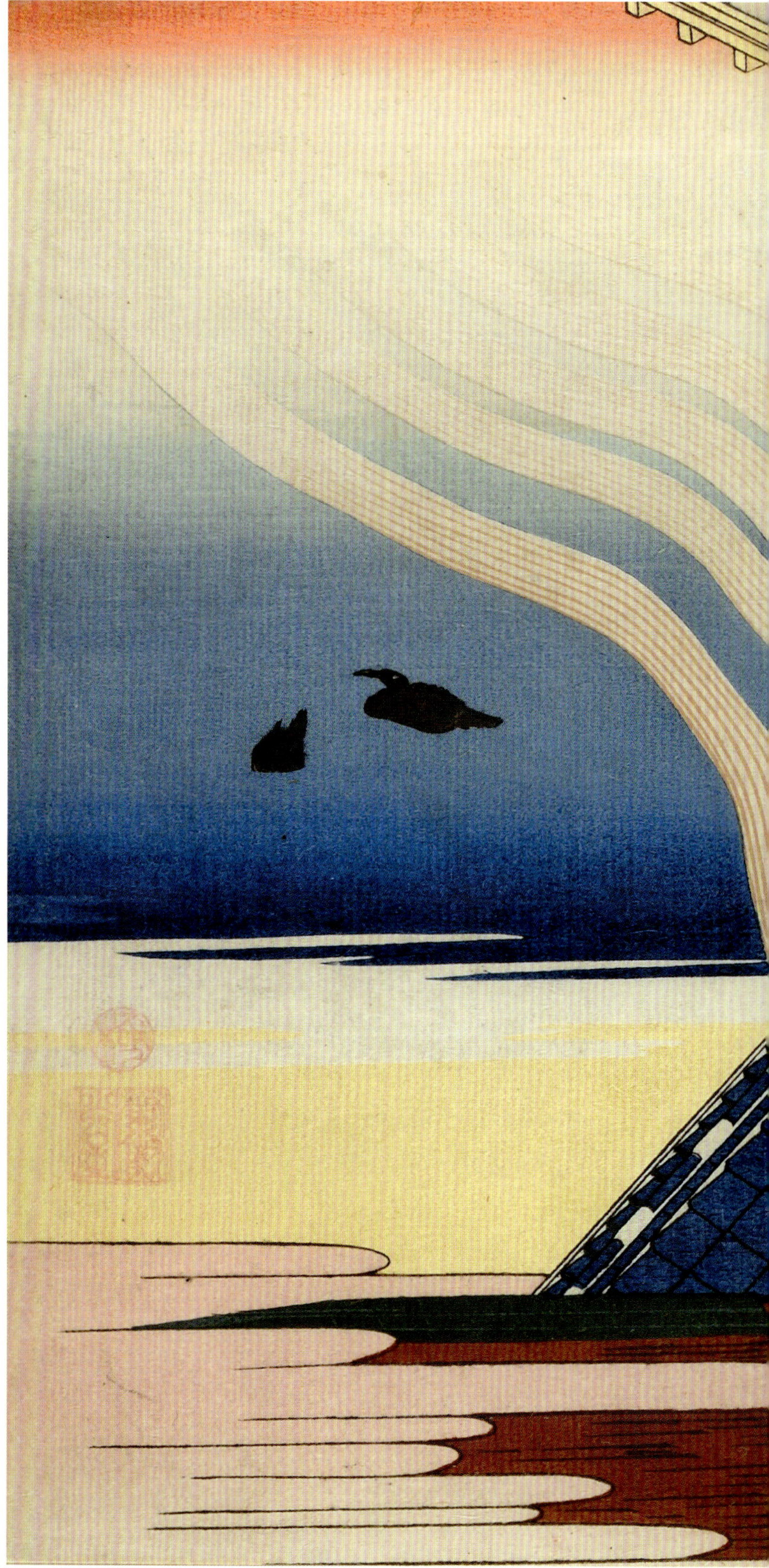

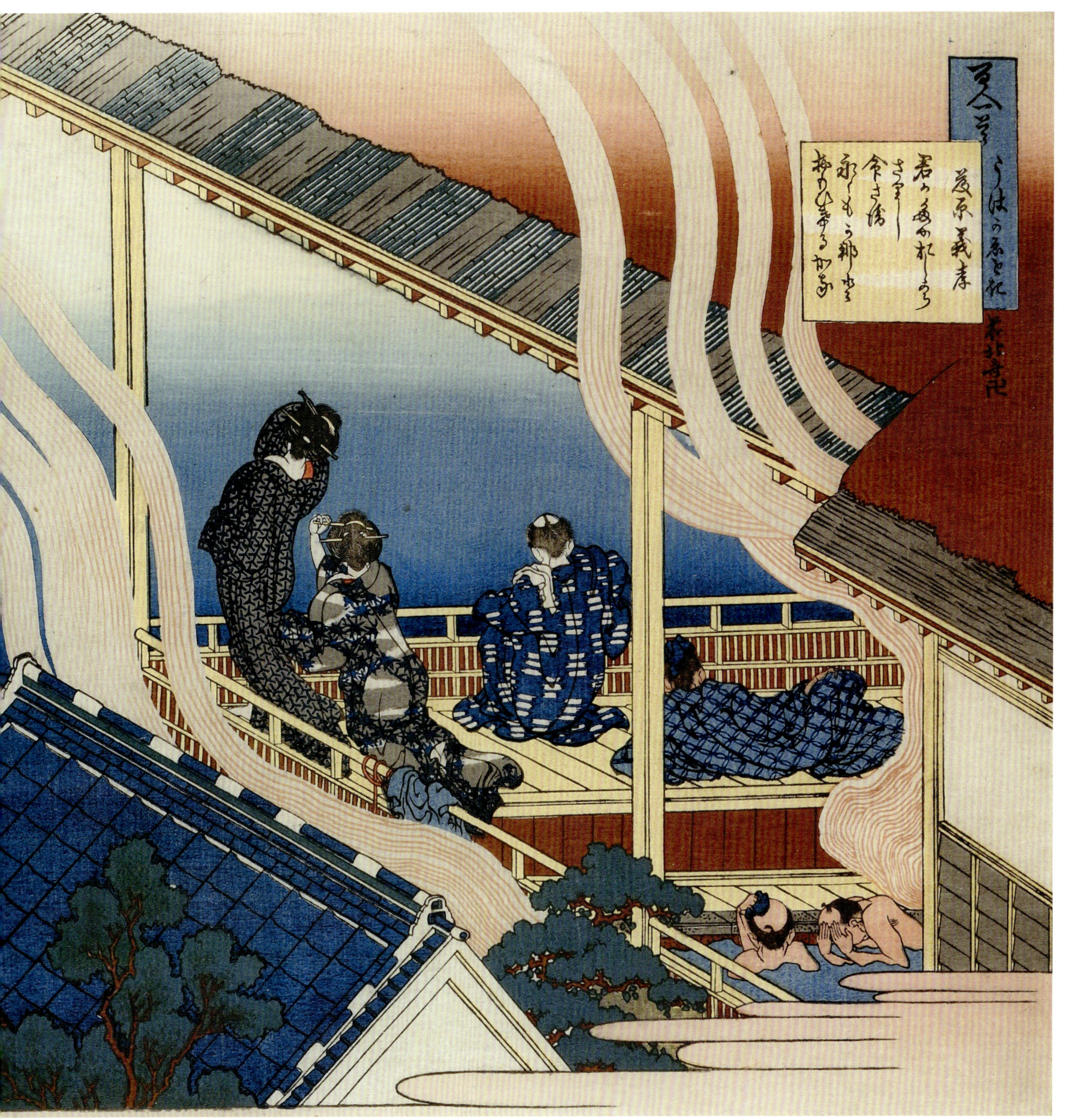

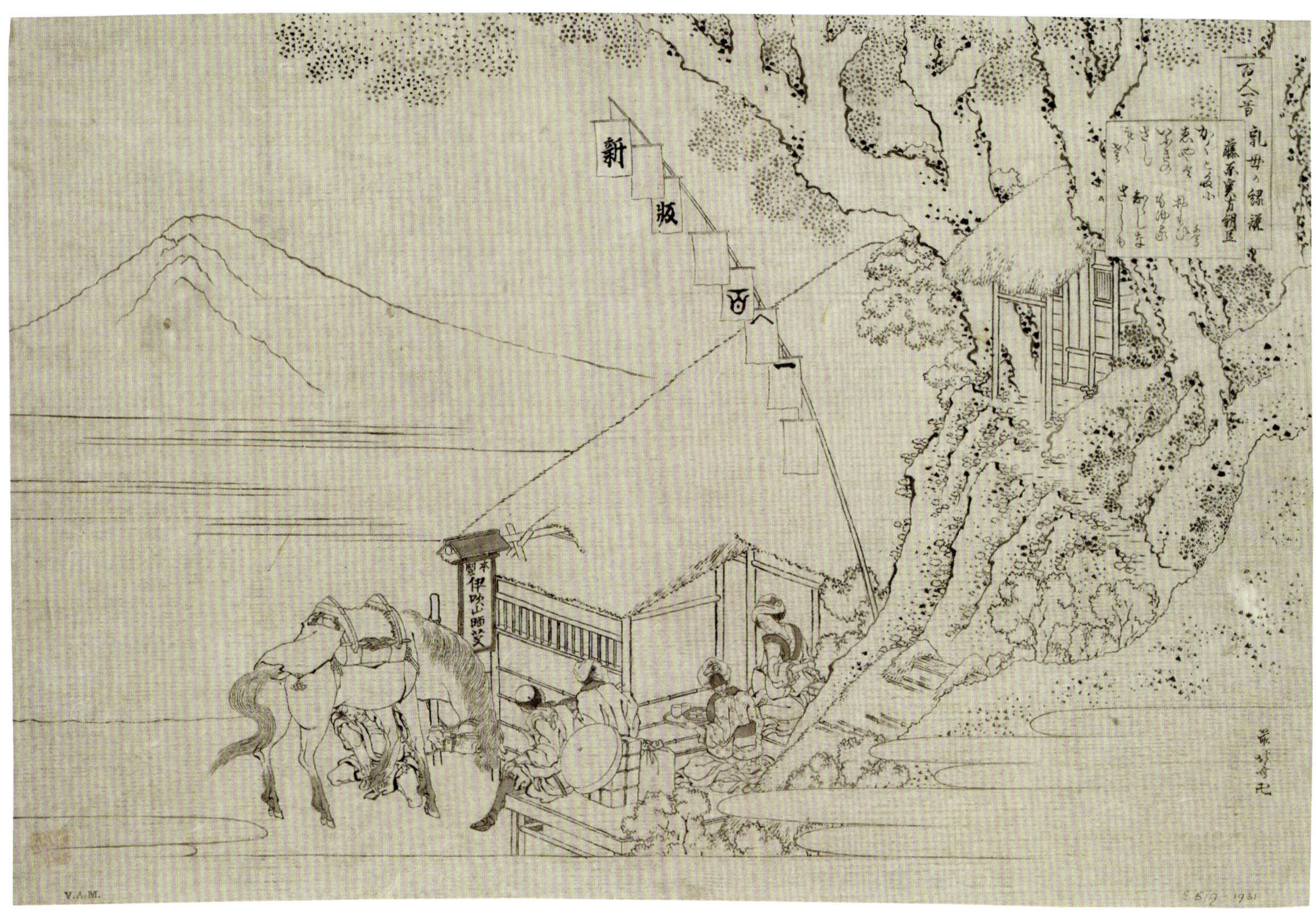

143

Poet Fujiwara no Sanekata Ason

About 1835–1838
Signature: Saki no Hokusai Manji ('Manji, the former Hokusai')
Block-ready drawing, ink on paper, 25.4 × 36.7 cm
Literature: HUT 1987–1990, vol. 4, no. 17; Morse 1989, no. 51; Mostow 1996, pp. 293–294
Victoria and Albert Museum, London, E.519-1931

Poem 51: *Kaku to dani / e ya wa Ibuki no / sashimogusa / sa shimo shiraji no / moyuru omoi o* (Can I even say / 'I love you this much'? – No, and so / you do not know of it / any more than of the *sashimo* grasses of Ibuki, / my burning love for you!) (Trans. Joshua Mostow.)

The fields around Mt Ibuki were famous for producing *sashimo* grass, the main component of *moxa*, a medicinal cone burned on the skin to heal ailments. Hokusai situated Sanekata's metaphorical verse about unrequited love at the entrance to a roadside shop selling *moxa* and snacks, within view of the mountain itself. The mountain's profile resembles that of Mt Ibuki when viewed from the east, for example from the Tōkaidō highway. The verse here appears to express the feelings of a travelling vendor as he exchanges glances with a waitress. Perhaps for variety's sake, the first part of the poem was inscribed from right to left and the second part below it from left to right. This configuration occurs five other times in the series. The series title is repeated in the banner above the shop. AH

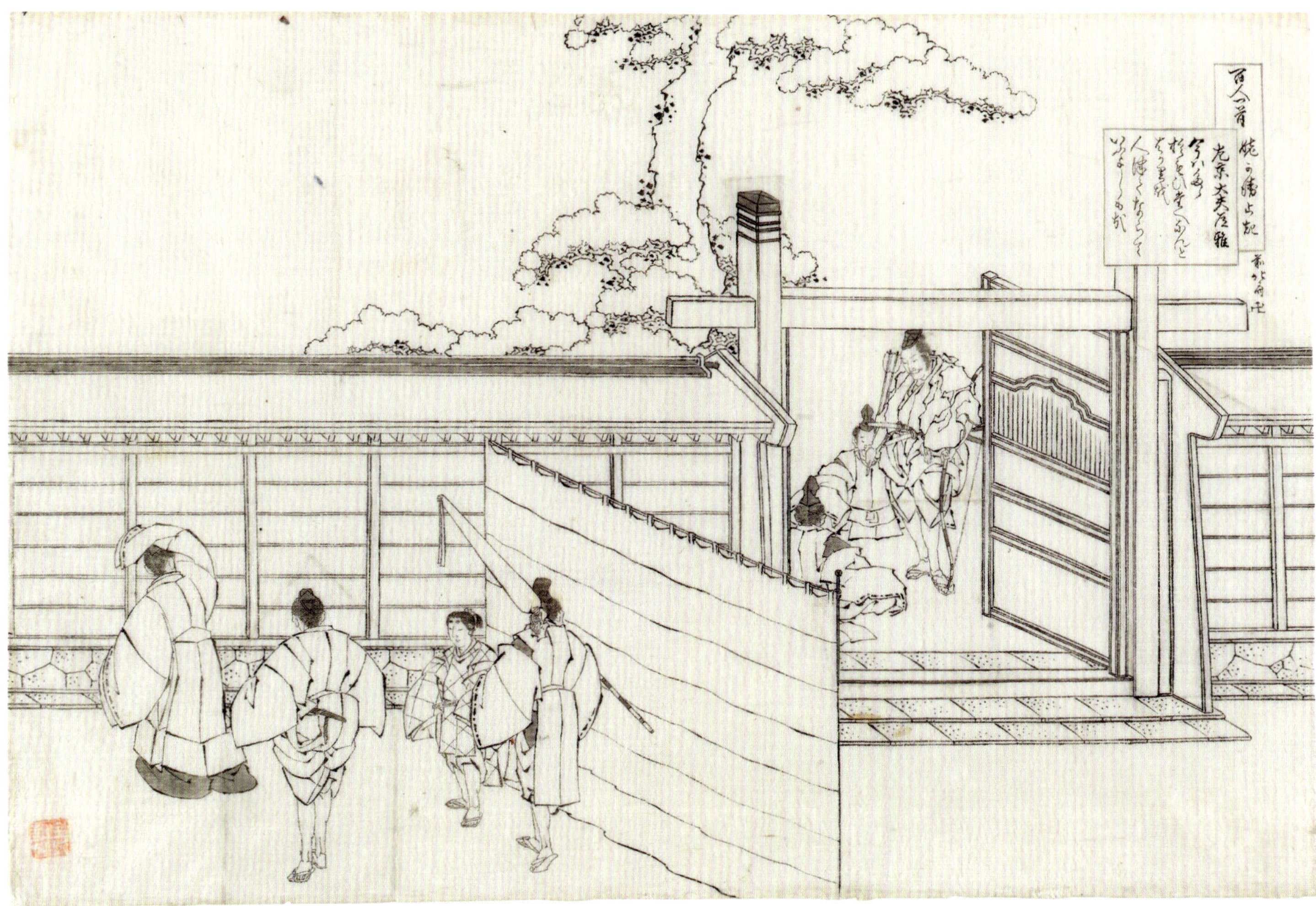

144

Poet Sakyō Dayū Michimasa

About 1835–1838
Signature: Saki no Hokusai Manji ('Manji, the former Hokusai')
Block-ready drawing, ink on paper, with pentimenti, 25.8 × 37.2 cm
Provenance: Charles Ricketts & Charles Shannon
Literature: Morse 1989, no. 63; Morse 1992; Mostow 1996, pp. 328–329; Machotka 2009, pp. 112–113; Keyes & Morse 2015, no. 678
Fitzwilliam Museum, Cambridge, PD.3942-1937, Ricketts and Shannon bequest

Poem 63: *Ima wa tada / omoi-taenamu / to bakari o / hitozute narade / iu yoshi mogana* (Now, the only thing / I wish for is a way to say/ to you directly / – not through another – / 'I will think of you no longer!') (Trans. Joshua Mostow.)

Poet Michimasa was secretly seeing a woman who was formerly high priestess of Ise shrine. When her father, the retired emperor, learned of their relationship, he posted guards at her gate to prevent the two from ever meeting again. Hokusai illustrated the well-documented circumstances behind Michimasa's poem, but organized the composition in an expressive way not seen in other artists' illustrations of the subject. The gate to the right solidly frames the guards blocking the poet's way; the rigid geometry of the wall and curtain to the left imply the finality of the separation. The location of this drawing had long eluded scholars. AH

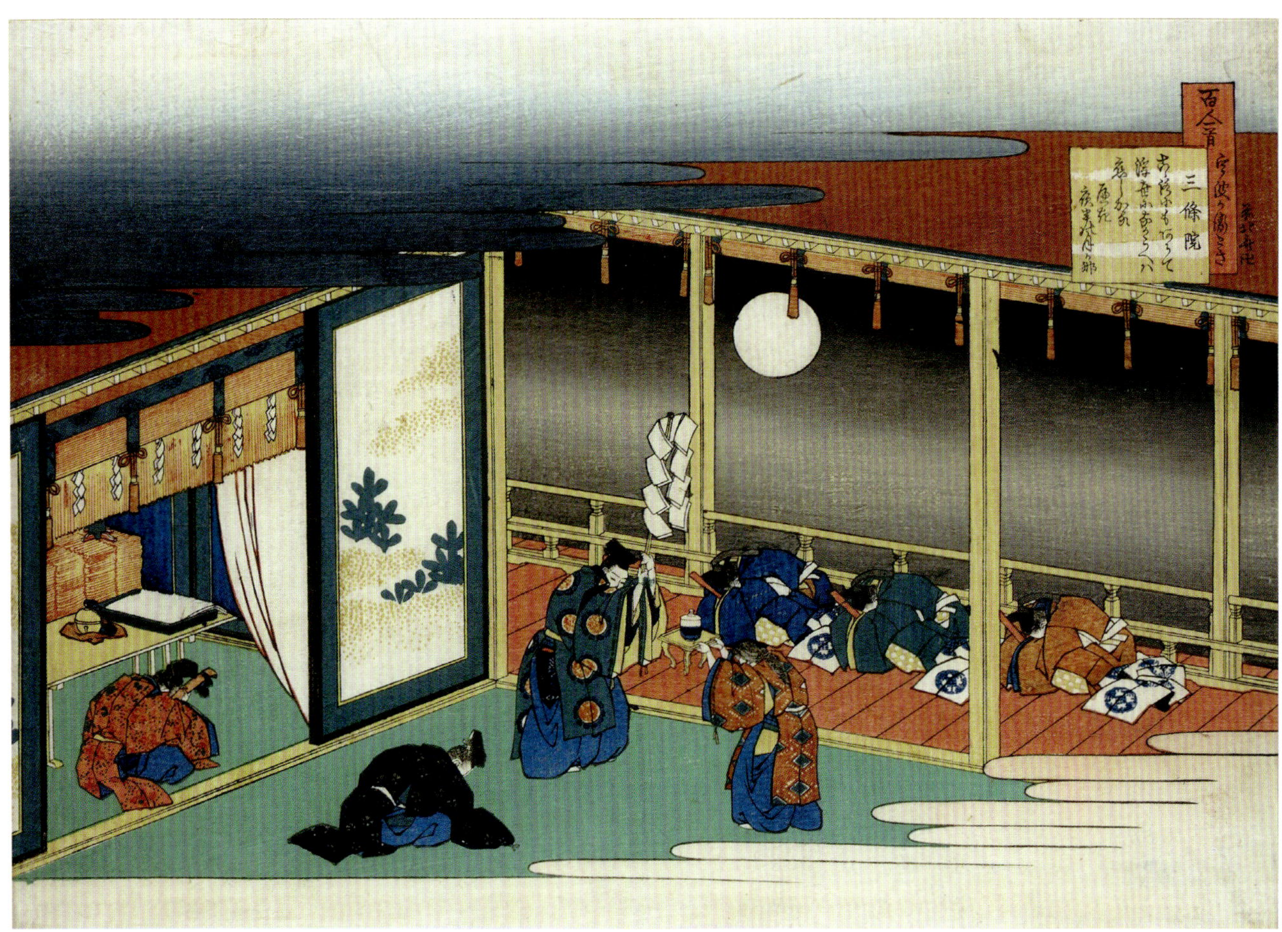

145

Poet Sanjō'in

About 1835–1836
Signature: Saki no Hokusai Manji ('Manji, the former Hokusai')
Colour woodblock, published by Iseya Sanjirō,
24.8 × 36.3 cm
Provenance: Arthur Morrison
Literature: Morse 1989, no. 68; MSU 1992, no. 25; Mostow 1996, pp. 343–344; Keyes & Morse 2015, no. 676
British Museum, 1906,1220,0.582

Poem 68: *Kokoro ni mo / arade uki yo ni / nagaraeba / koishikarubeki / yowa no tsuki kana* (Though it is not what's in my heart, / if in this world of pain / I should linger, then / no doubt I shall remember fondly / the bright moon of this dark night.) (Trans. Joshua Mostow.)

Emperor Sanjō (976–1017) composed this verse when he was ill and contemplating retirement in the winter of 1015. Hokusai here depicts high-ranking members of the court holding a ceremony on the night of a full moon to honour Sanjō'in's memory after his death. They bow in reverence as a priest blesses with sacred paper streamers (*gohei*) a funeral urn containing the imperial ashes. A courtier at left holds wrapped in cloth a rectangular poem card (*tanzaku*), perhaps inscribed with Sanjō'in's verse. At far left, the mirror stand (just visible) calls to mind the imperial regalia – mirror, sword and jewel – with the sword perhaps wrapped in white silk cloth in the nearby tray. This is arguably the most solemn and moving design in the series. AH

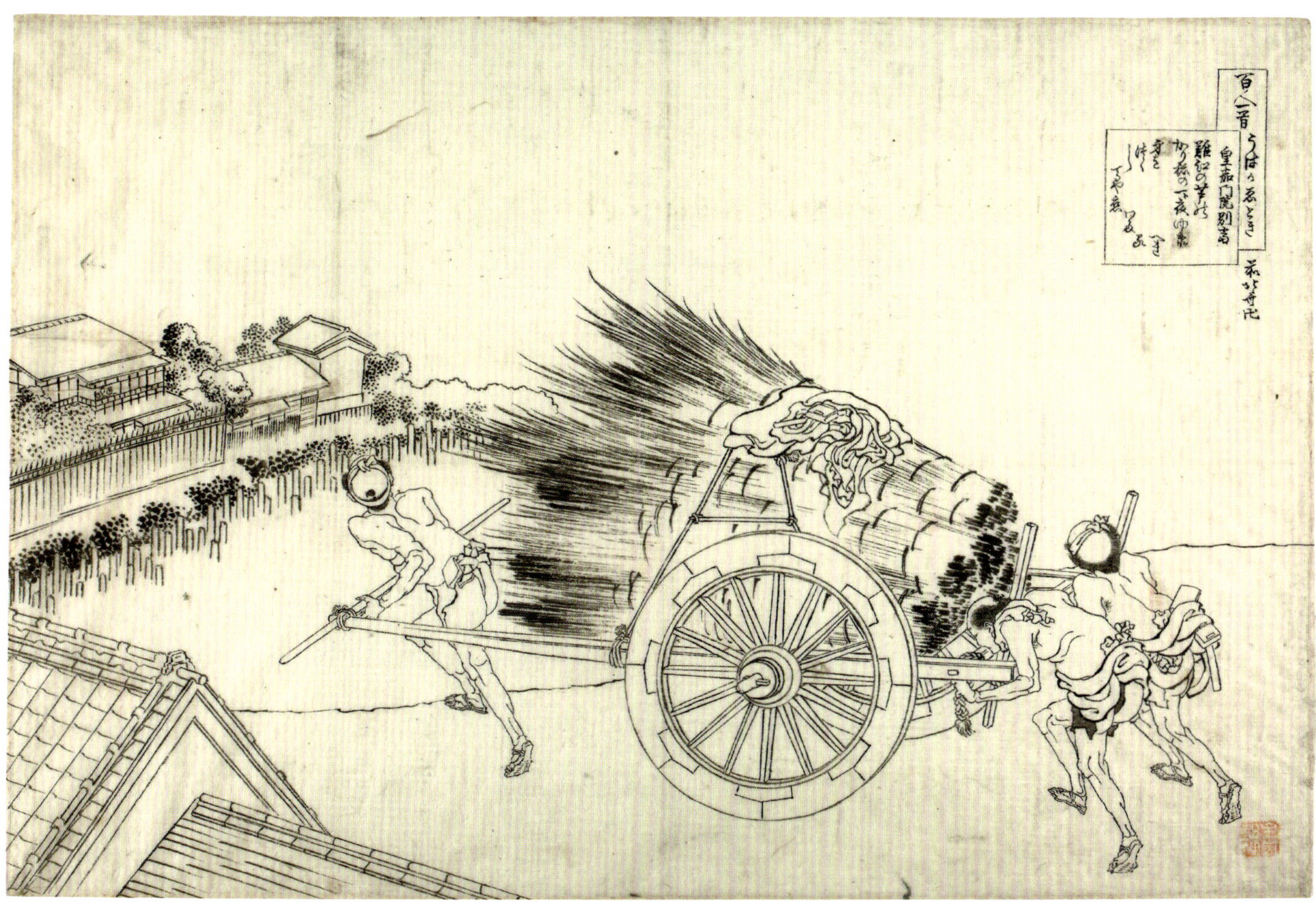

146

Poet Kōka Mon'in no Bettō

About 1835–1838
Signature: Saki no Hokusai Manji ('Manji, the former Hokusai')
Block-ready drawing, ink on paper, with pentimenti, 25.0 × 37.1 cm
Provenance: Charles Ricketts & Charles Shannon
Literature: HUT 1987–1990, vol. 3, BW no. 52; Morse 1989, no. 88; Mostow 1996, pp. 400–401
British Museum, 1937,0710,0.286, bequeathed by Charles Shannon RA

Poem 88: *Naniwa-e no / ashi no karine no / hito yo yue / mi o tsukushite ya / koi wataru beki* (Due to that single night / of fitful sleep, short as a reed's joint cut at the root / from Naniwa Bay, / am I to exhaust myself, like the channel-markers, / passing my days in longing?) (Trans. Joshua Mostow.)

Exhausted workmen haul a cart loaded with a harvest of *igusa* reeds towards a seaside inn, where perhaps the reeds will be woven into tatami mats. Hokusai expanded on the poem's key motif, but inverted the background social hierarchy by prioritizing labour over courtly leisure. The inn suggests that Hokusai knew the poem had been composed on the topic 'love meeting at travel lodgings'. The illustration additionally recognizes a pun central to the poem: the phrase *mi o tsukushi* means 'exhausting oneself', while the word *miotsukushi* means 'channel-marker' (or 'tide-marker'), as found here along the shore below the inn. In the cartouche, the poem trails into a closed circle, perhaps to suggest a bundle of reeds. A similar team of workmen appears in volume 2 of *Hokusai's Sketches* (*Hokusai manga*, 1815). AH

Poem-diviner

2nd day, first month, 1827
Signature: Bunsei jū hinoto i nen / shōgatsu futsuka
fude-hajime / Hokusai Iitsu keiga ('Respectfully drawn
by Hokusai Iitsu, first use of the brush on the 2nd day
of the first month, Bunsei 10 [1827]')
Seal: Katsushika (1)
Hanging scroll, ink and colour on paper,
124.2 × 50.5 cm
Provenance: Arthur Morrison
Literature: UT 1931, no. 77; NU 1982, no. 32;
Clark 1992, no. 100
British Museum, 1913,0513,0.317, given by
Sir W. Gwynne-Evans, Bt

A poem-diviner (*uta-uranai-shi*) told fortunes by
interpreting a verse that a customer selected apparently
at random from those attached to the diviner's bow
(an ancient tool of Shinto shamanism). An illustration
of the subject in volume 11 of *Hokusai's Sketches* (*Hokusai
manga*, 1834) credits the soothsayer Watarai Ietsugu with
initiating the practice. Watarai's story is told in the
medieval Noh drama *Utaura* (*Divination by Poem*, early
1400s), in which he is reunited with his son after a
three-day sojourn in hell and a long period of travelling.
Hokusai's painting shows Watarai on the road, dressed
in the white robes of a Shinto priest, and with a
pensive expression, as though he is contemplating
the vicissitudes of human fortune. Perhaps Hokusai
blended something of his own worldview into his
portrayal of the character. Both the abbreviated but
expertly controlled brush technique, and the terms
in the signature 'respectfully drawn' and 'first use
of the brush' at the beginning of the year, suggest
that Hokusai may have produced this work as an
'impromptu painting' (*sekiga*) for a patron of rank
during a New Year gathering. New Year was a time
for both social events and fortune-telling. AH

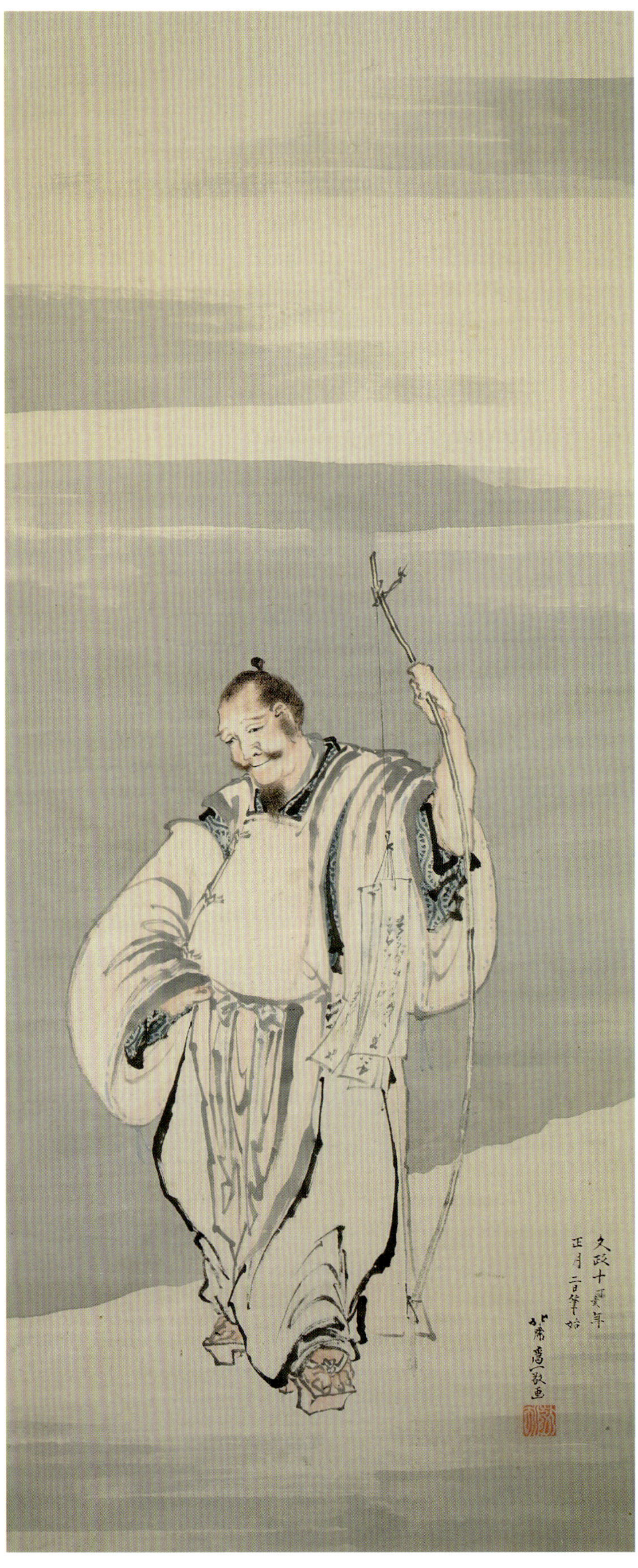

148

The Third Princess and her cat

1823–1826

Signature: Hokusai aratame / Iitsu hitsu ('Brush of
Iitsu, changed from Hokusai')

Seal: Katsushika (1)

Hanging scroll, ink and colour on silk, 98.4 × 36.9 cm

Literature: Nagata Seiji, 'Nyosan no miya zu ippuku',
Kobijutsu 82, April 1987, pp. 126–127; Nagoya 1991,
no. 211; Nagata 2000, no. 73

Private collection, Japan

The Third Princess was a favourite theme in pictures
of beautiful women (*bijin-ga*). As told in the *Tale of Genji*,
'New Herbs, Part I', the princess's ladies were behind
their bamboo curtains one spring day, enjoying a view
of courtiers playing kickball, when a Chinese kitten
darted out, pursued by a large cat. The kitten's leash
whipped around, wreaking havoc. As curtains shifted
during the scuffle, the courtier Kashiwagi saw the
princess and, captivated by her cool charm amid
the confusion, resolved to pursue her – with tragic
consequences for them both. Hokusai followed artistic
convention by showing the princess close to a veranda,
half-hidden by a curtain and restraining her kitten on
a leash, but he rendered the young lady in lavish detail,
wearing refined robes suited to a lovely woman from
the classics, even offering a glimpse of her kimono
through the bamboo scrim. The composition skilfully
contrasts the princess's elegance with the kitten's
ferocity. The flowering cherry tree lower right indicates
the season of the episode. **AH**

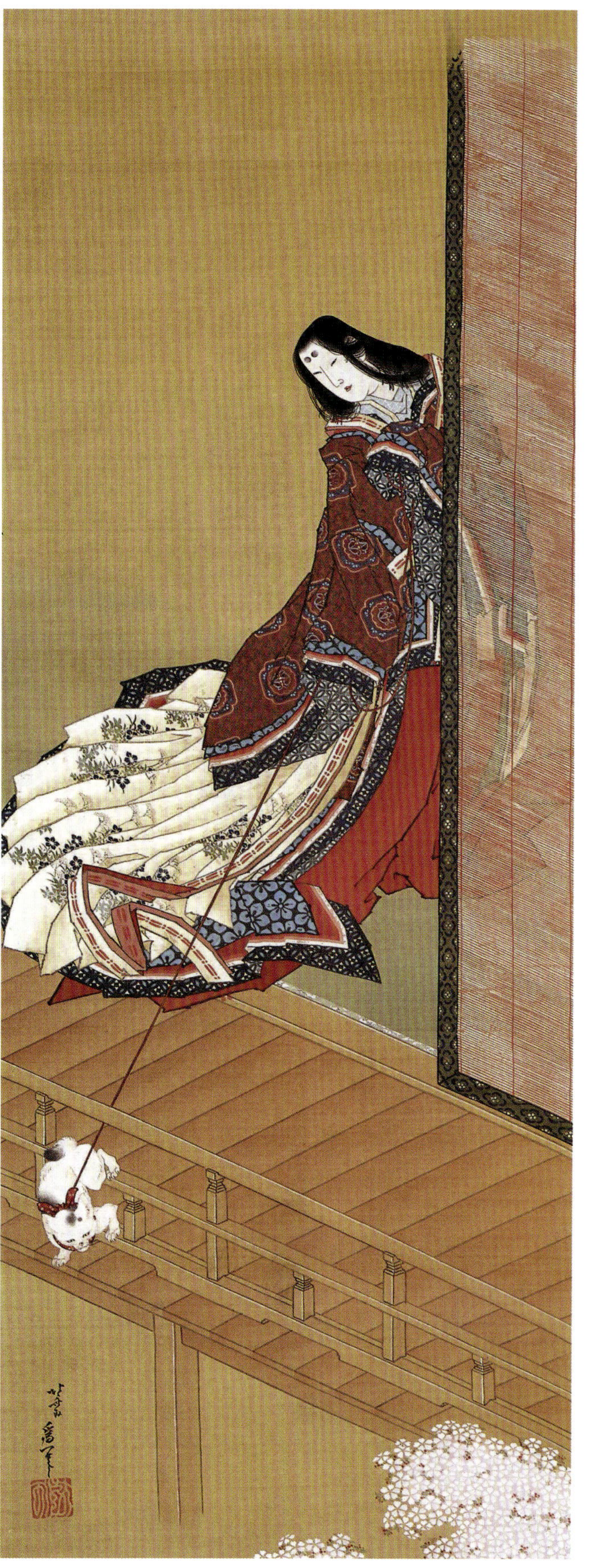

Shirabyōshi dancer

About 1820
Signature: Hokusai Taito aratame / Iitsu hitsu ('Brush
of Iitsu, changed from Hokusai Taito')
Seal: Katsushika (1)
Hanging scroll, ink and colour on silk, 98.0 × 41.9 cm
Literature: Sankei Shinbun 1977 [pages not numbered];
Marais 1980, no. 241; Calza 2003, no. V.1; Hokusaikan
2015, pp. 48–49
Hokusai Museum, Obuse

Shirabyōshi were female entertainers trained in song and
dance. Their costume combined different elements
of men's court attire, including a long sword (*tachi*),
man's folding fan (*kawahori-ōgi*), Shinto priest's white
jacket (*suikan*) and an upright ceremonial hat (*tate-eboshi*)
covered in gold. The most famous *shirabyōshi* is Shizuka
Gozen (1165–1211), the lover of warrior Minamoto no
Yoshitsune (1159–1189). This composition develops an
illustration of a 'courtesan, female performer' found
in volume 9 of *Hokusai's Sketches* (*Hokusai manga*, 1819).
The figure's commanding pose – with left arm raised
and right arm lowered, holding an open fan inwards
– may correspond to the climax of Shizuka Gozen's
dance before Yoshitsune in the first part of the Noh
drama *Funa Benkei* (*Benkei on the Boat*). Distinctive
to Hokusai's portrayal are the agitated, segmented
outlines of the robes – an inventive way of animating
the costume and lending the figure a sense of movement.
Female subjects appear only occasionally in Hokusai's
later paintings. AH

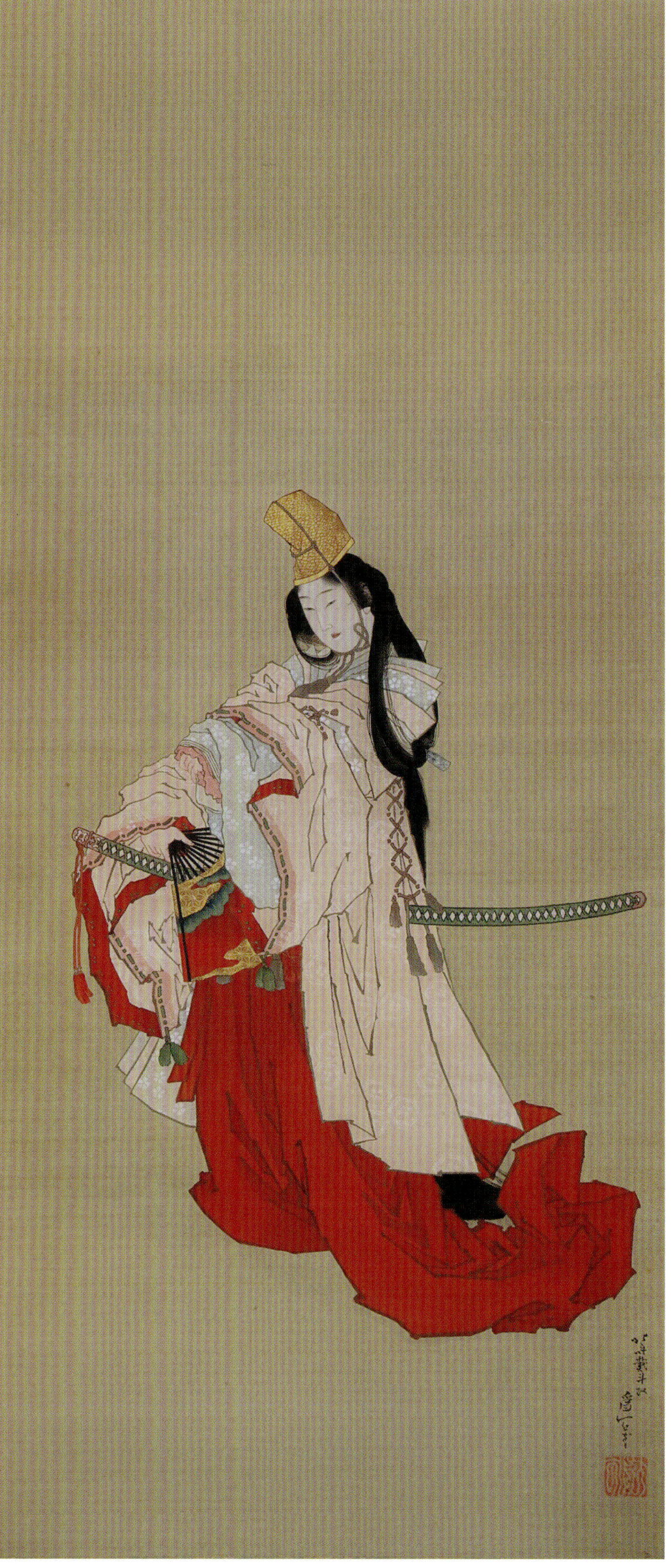

Night attack on the Horikawa palace

1823–1826
Signature: Hokusai aratame / Iitsu hitsu ('Brush of Iitsu, changed from Hokusai')
Seal: Katsushika (1)
Inscription signed Ōhira
Hanging scroll, ink and colour on silk, 106.3 × 37.6 cm
Provenance: Tamura Ichirō (1919); Manno Art Museum
Literature: UT 1931, no. 88; Nagata 1990, vol. 5, nos 15–16; NUT 1994–1996, vol. 7, no. 51; Freer-Sackler 2006, vol. 2, no. 82
Okada Museum of Art, Hakone
Osaka only

Soon after founding his military government in Kamakura in 1185, Minamoto no Yoritomo (1147–1199) began eliminating potential rivals. Most dangerous in his mind was his younger brother, Yoshitsune (1159–1189), who over the previous four years had handed him important victories. Yoritomo sent assassins to attack Yoshitsune's residence on Horikawa-dōri, in Kyoto. Here Yoshitsune prepares for the attack, as his lover Shizuka Gozen (1165–1211) presents his battle sword to him. The third figure, wearing a robe decorated with Buddhist wheels-of-the-law (*dharma-chakra*, Japanese: *hōrin*), is Yoshitsune's loyal ally, priest Benkei, on the lookout for the enemy (volume 10 of *Hokusai's Sketches* [*Hokusai manga*, 1819], includes a similarly posed and dressed figure identified as Benkei). From bottom to top the figures suggest ascending nobility of character. Yoshitsune was the youngest in his family, hence the inscribed poem by Motoori Ōhira (1756–1833) describes him as a 'terminal branch', and calls for 'mountain winds' (i.e., supporting troops) to hasten from Ichinotani, site of one of Yoshitsune's victories: 'Hie, you mountain winds / serving the terminal branch / of Kamakura's pine, / depart with all due speed, make / haste from Ichinotani!' (*Kamakura no / matsu no matsue no / yama-kaze zo / Ichinotani yori / ichihayaku shite*). AH

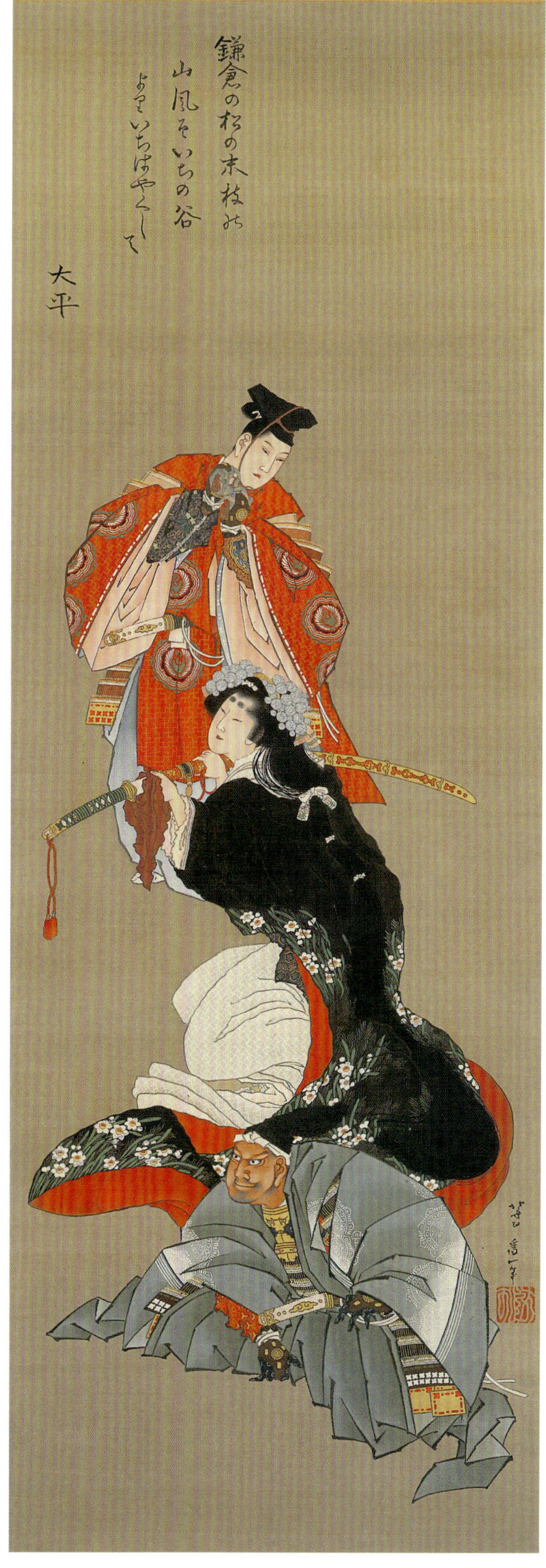

151

Priest Mongaku beneath a waterfall, from *Picture Book of the Warrior Vanguard in Japan and China* (*Wakan ehon sakigake*)

1836
Signature: Nanajūnana rei saki no Hokusai aratame
Gakyō rōjin Manji hitsu ('Brush of Manji, old
man crazy to paint, changed from Hokusai, aged
seventy-seven')
Seal: Mt Fuji above trigram
Illustrated book, woodblock, published by Okadaya
Kashichi, 22.6 × 16.0 cm (covers)
Provenance: E. W. Tuke
Literature: Calza 2003, no. VI.8
British Museum, 1939,0524,0.26

In addition to brush drawing manuals of genre and
nature subjects, such as *Hokusai's Sketches* (*Hokusai manga*,
cats 164, 165), Hokusai also produced four manuals
depicting military heroes of ancient Japan and China.
The volumes are filled with dynamic, double-page
tableaus of warriors engaged in deeds of valour.
Hokusai presented most of the narratives in horizontal
format, but here in novel vertical format he depicted
priest Mongaku (1139–1203), formerly the warrior
Endō Moritō, who mistakenly killed a married woman
he loved, and afterwards endured penance beneath
the icy waters of Nachi waterfall. Mongaku stands
resolutely at the centre of the fall, his fingers locked
in the type of ritual gesture (*mudra*) associated with
Esoteric Buddhist practice. This is the second of a
two-part sequence; the previous illustration shows the
Buddhist deities who watched over Mongaku during
the ritual. Hokusai noted that he drew these figures not
in the manner of a Buddhist painting but in proportion
with the human physique. AH

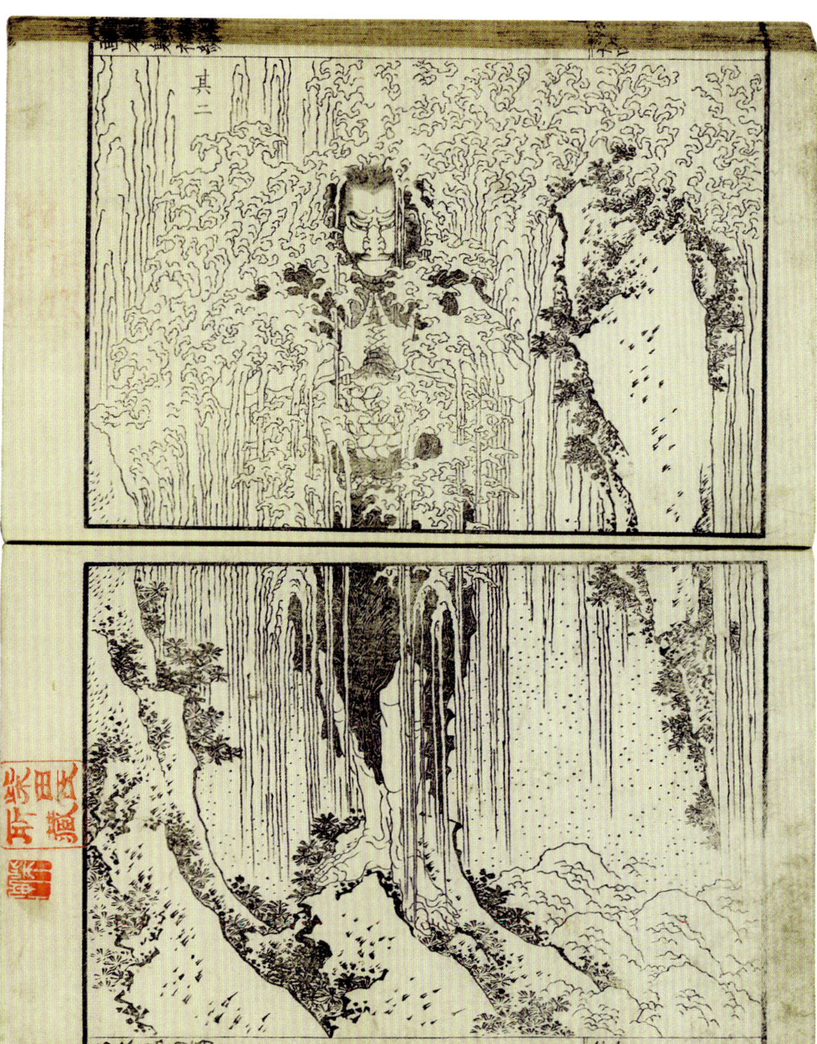

Netsuke of Priest Mongaku beneath a waterfall

After 1836
Signature: Shunkōsai Chōgetsu
Netsuke (toggle, *manjū*), ivory, 5.3 cm (diameter)
Literature: Richard Barker and Lawrence Smith,
Netsuke: The Miniature Sculpture of Japan, London, BMP,
1976, no. 135; Noriko Tsuchiya, *Netsuke: 100 Miniature
Masterpieces from Japan*, London, BMP, 2014, pp. 184–185
British Museum, 1945,1017.638, bequeathed by Oscar
Charles Raphael

Craftspeople in many fields turned to Hokusai's
published manuals for inspiration. Netsuke were
toggles that fastened cords supporting pouches hanging
from the sash. Working in three dimensions, netsuke
carvers could develop Hokusai's illustrations in ways
not possible for other craftspeople. This *manjū* netsuke,
for example, is carved on both sides. The front shows
priest Mongaku enduring penance beneath a waterfall,
based on the illustration discussed opposite (cat 151).
The reverse shows the two Buddhist deities who saved
Mongaku at the point of death, based on the previous
illustration in the same book. The carver successfully
captured Hokusai's drawing style and composition,
and then added an important detail: here Mongaku
holds an esoteric ritual bell (*kongōrei*) clenched in his
teeth. Further research may uncover the significance
of this detail. AH

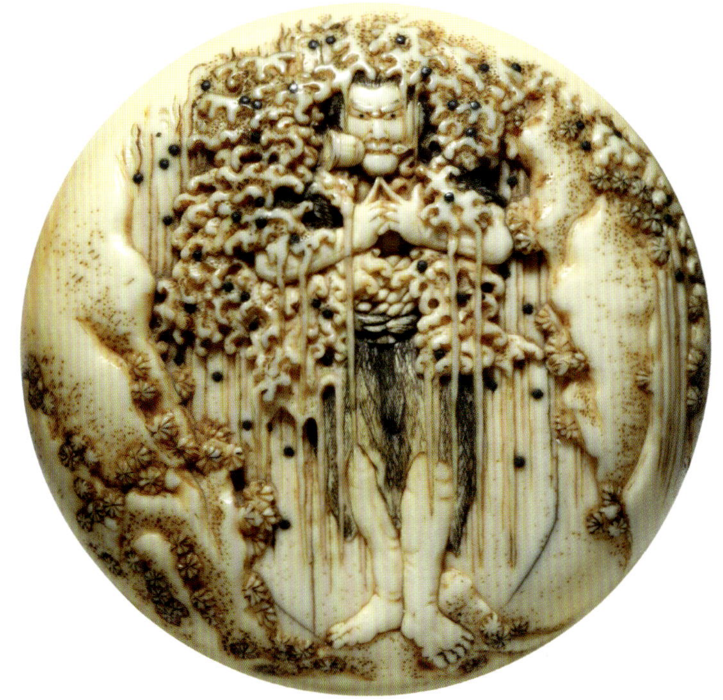

One Hundred Ghost Tales (*Hyaku monogatari*)

This series of medium-format prints refers to the popular practice of people gathering together to tell ghost stories, and blowing out a lamp wick after each, in the hope – or fear – that a ghost would appear when the final wick had been extinguished. Forty years earlier, Hokusai had designed a perspective print of a haunted house, incorporating ten famous ghosts. Here he focuses on individual spooks, although only five of the projected hundred designs were published. The modest format allows Hokusai to demonstrate his mastery of composition, excluding the inessential in order to capture the horror – and humour – of the uncanny. AL

153
Kohada Koheiji

About 1833
Signature: Saki no Hokusai hitsu ('Brush of the former Hokusai')
Colour woodblock, published by Tsuruya Kiemon,
26.1 × 18.6 cm
Provenance: Henri Rivière
Literature: TNM 2005, no. 389; Boston 2013, no. 99;
Keyes & Morse 2015, no. 904
British Museum, 2016,3015.2, purchase funded by
the Theresia Gerda Buch bequest in memory of her
parents Rudolph and Julie Buch

The skeletal ghost of Kohada Koheiji, with eerie
flames flickering around him, pulls down the edge
of a mosquito net. The viewer should know that he
is haunting his sleeping wife, who, with her lover,
had drowned him in Asaka swamp. The story seems
to have circulated for much of the eighteenth century,
before being written up as a novel by Santō Kyōden
(1761–1816) in 1803. Kohada's reddish muscles and
green-tinged tendons echo the unearthly net and its
cloth border. Given his rictus grin, his victim is in for
a shock. AL

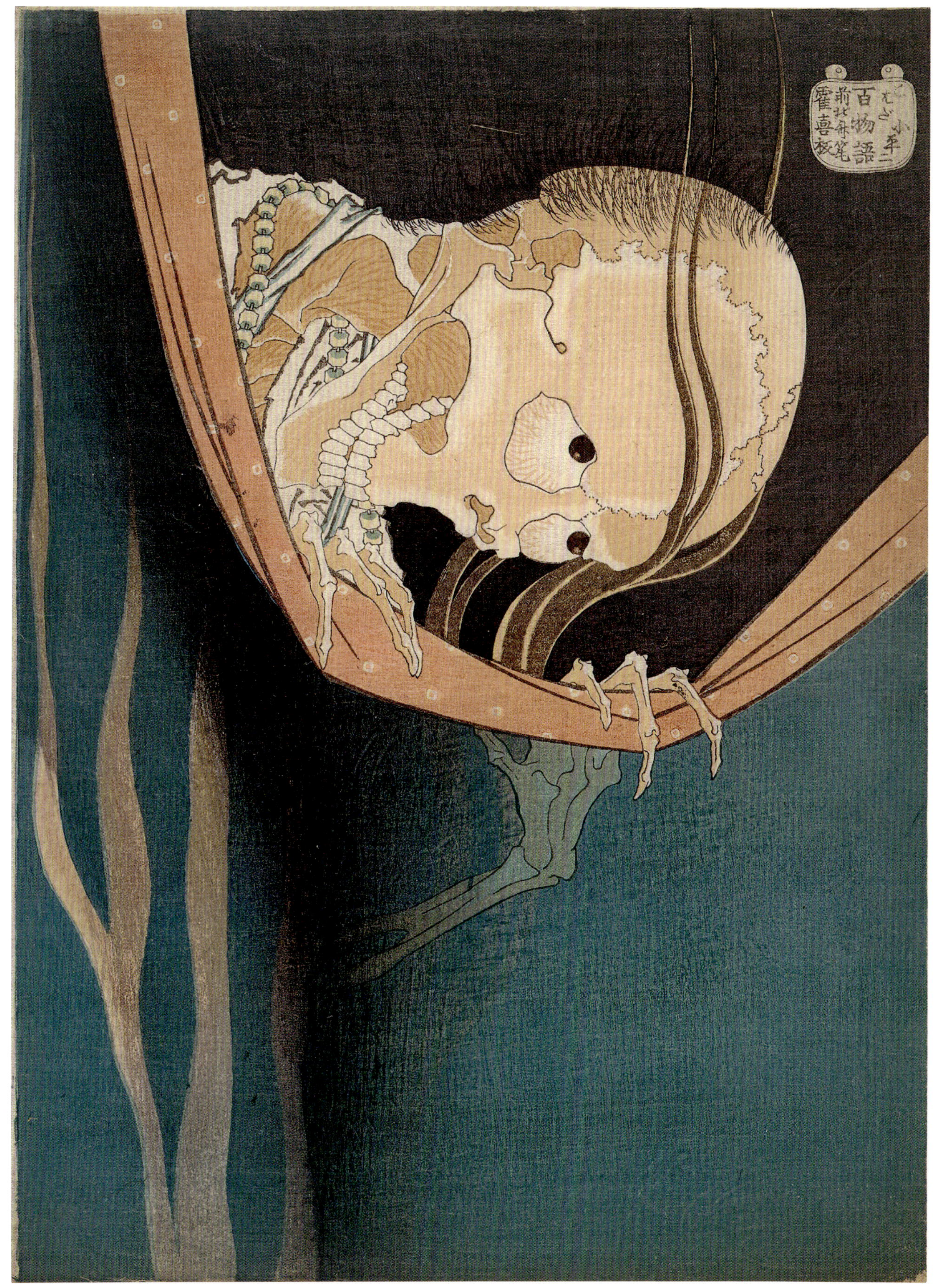
こはだ小平二
百物語
前北斎筆
霍喜板

Oiwa-san

About 1833
Signature: Saki no Hokusai hitsu ('Brush of the former Hokusai')
Colour woodblock, published by Tsuruya Kiemon, 26.2 × 18.7 cm
Provenance: Henri Vever
Literature: TNM 2005, no. 390; Guimet 2008, no. 63a; Boston 2013, no. 97; Keyes & Morse 2015, no. 902
Musée national des arts asiatiques Guimet, Paris, EO.172, given by Henri Vever 1894
London only

Oiwa-san first appeared in 1825, as the tragic heroine of *Yotsuya kaidan*, a kabuki play that would go on to become one of the most famous Japanese ghost stories of all time. Tricked by a rival into using a disfiguring face cream and abandoned by her husband, Oiwa accidentally kills herself, then dedicates herself in the afterlife to exacting her revenge. Here her face merges with a Bon festival lantern, the burnt paper forming a gaping mouth and corrugated wrinkles framing bloodshot eyes. On the lantern's side is a Buddhist prayer for her soul, *Namu Amida butsu*. AL

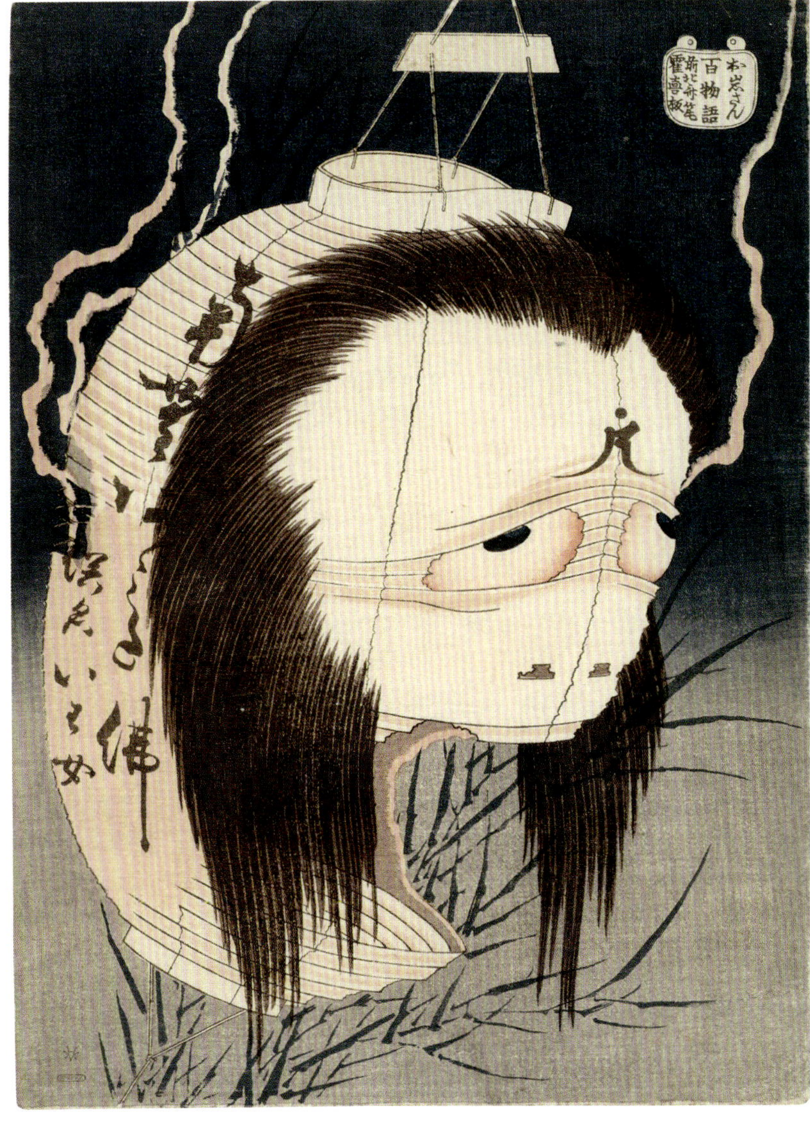

Laughing demoness

About 1833
Signature: Saki no Hokusai hitsu ('Brush of the former
Hokusai')
Colour woodblock, published by Tsuruya Kiemon,
25.6 × 18.8 cm
Provenance: Henri Rivière
Literature: TNM 2005, no. 387; Boston 2013, no. 98;
Keyes & Morse 2015, no. 903
British Museum, 2016,3015.1, purchase funded by
the Theresia Gerda Buch bequest in memory of her
parents Rudolph and Julie Buch

A grinning, horned female demon (*hannya*) appears in
a round window, pointing to the severed, bloody head
of an infant, gripped in her talons. Hokusai seems
to have combined two demonic strains here. Hannya
was originally an Indian smallpox deity, who came to
represent the ghost of a jealous lover in the Noh
theatre, often with a horned mask. To heighten
the horror, he has also given her the attributes of a
'mountain woman' (*yamauba*), who by the eighteenth
century usually nurtured infants, but earlier had often
devoured them. AL

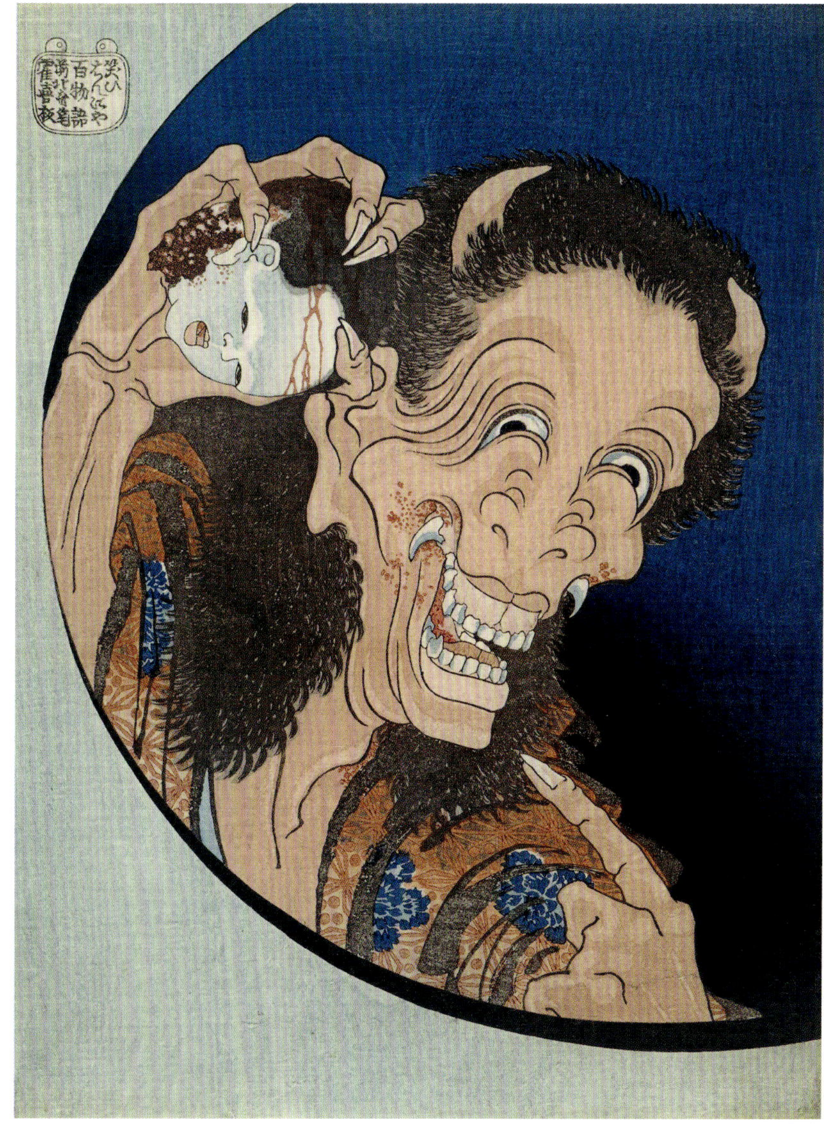

Shakyamuni on a lotus

1823–1826
Signature: Dokuryū Hokusai aratame Iitsu haisha
('Respectfully drawn by Iitsu, changed from Hokusai,
independent school')
Seal: Katsushika (1)
Hanging scroll, ink and colour on paper,
118.1 × 52.5 cm
Literature: Nagata 2000, no. 145; Carpenter 2005,
p. 126; Hokusaikan 2015, pp. 132–133
Private collection, Japan

Shakyamuni Buddha, the founder of Buddhism, sits
on a lotus pedestal and holds a burning incense stick,
presumably left by worshippers, as though preparing
to light a *moxa* preparation on his raised leg. The incense
burner before him is inscribed 'Shakyamuni on a
lotus' (*renjō Shaka*). Moxibustion is an ancient Chinese
medicinal treatment in which *moxa* is burned against
the skin. The painting humanizes the Buddha by
depicting him in such a playful way. Indeed, with its
equally informal technique, the work may have been
painted as an 'impromptu painting' (*sekiga*), done to
request on the spot at a banquet. The subject alone
is unusual and humorous, but the variety and skill of
Hokusai's handling of the brush – fine wrinkles in the
robes, contrastingly bold presentation of the lotus
pedestal, and delicate yet vigorous lines throughout –
all combine into a uniquely individual manner of
expression. Hokusai's signature confidently declares
that he represents an 'independent school'. MR

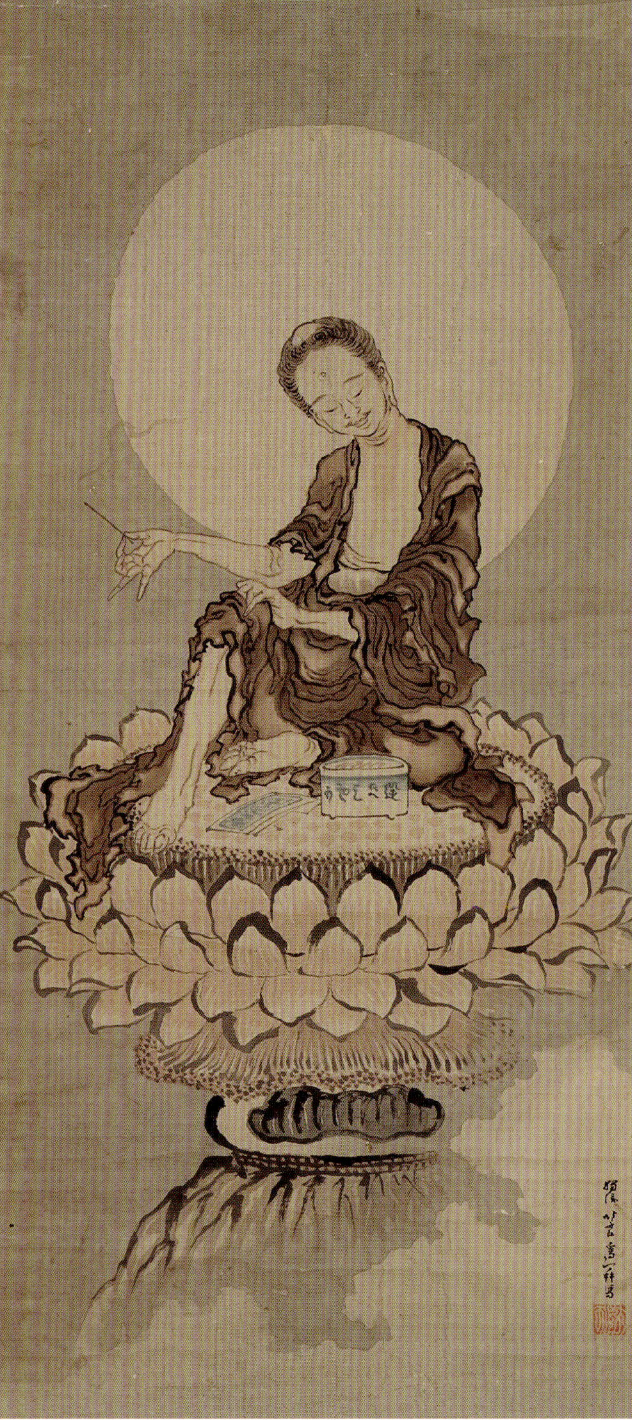

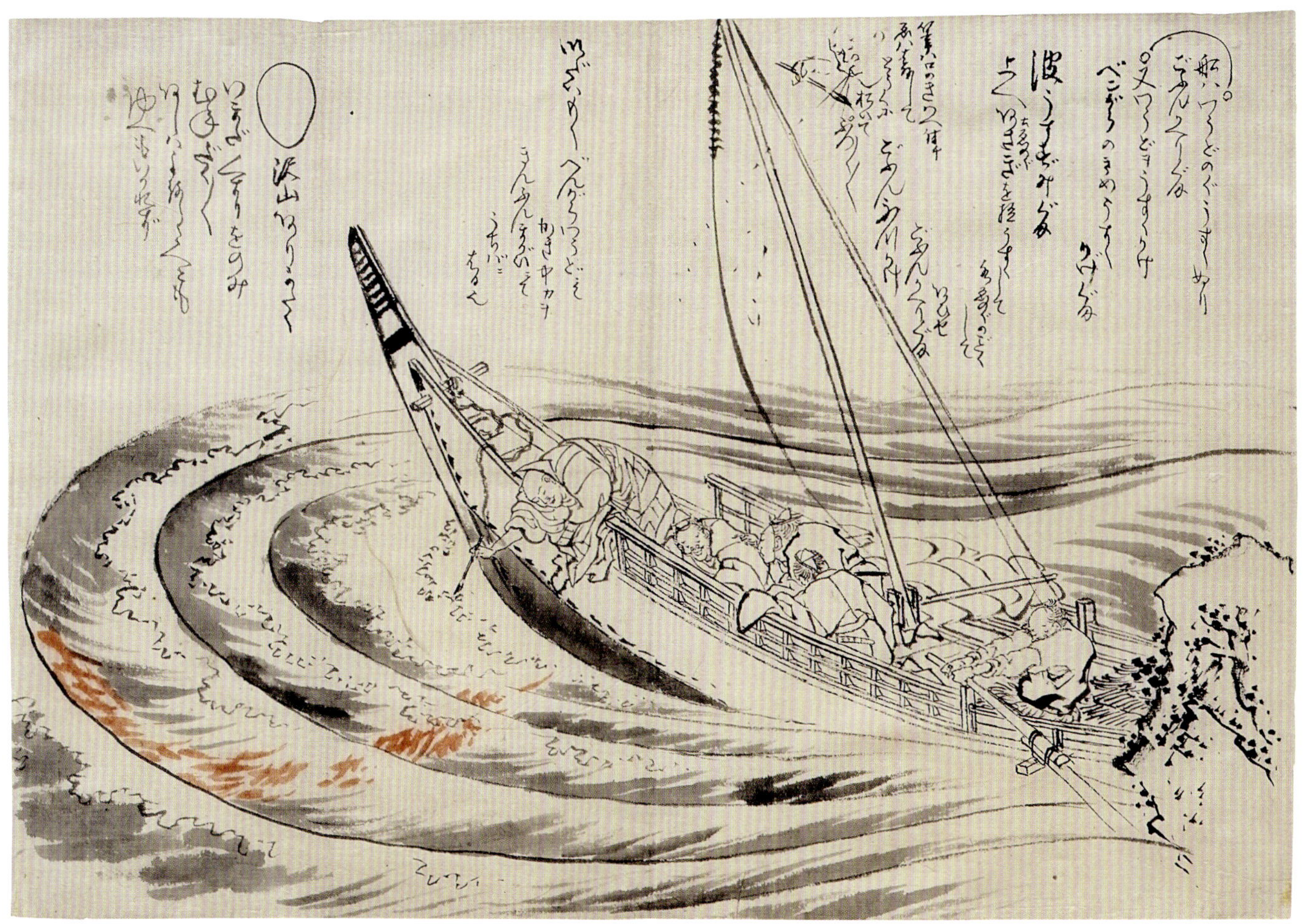

157

Monk Nichiren writing on the waves

About 1830–1844
Unsigned (attributed to Hokusai)
Preparatory drawing, ink and red colour on paper,
27.7 × 39.2 cm
Literature: Boston 2000, no. 72; Guth 2015, p. 50
Museum of Fine Arts, Boston, 11.9363, William Sturgis
Bigelow collection
Osaka only

As a lifelong follower of Nichiren Buddhism, Hokusai
draws on the holy man's life, as elsewhere in his
work (cat. 215), to reveal the dramatic influence of
supernatural forces in this world. Annotated with
detailed directions on how to colour the design ('pale
ochre for the boat') – instructions, perhaps, for a
painting student – the sketch depicts the climactic
moment in Nichiren's crossing of the stormy Sea of
Japan on his way into exile on Sado island. The monk
calms the waves by writing the mantra of the *Lotus
Sutra* on the water, while his followers cower behind
him. In a version by Utagawa Kuniyoshi (1797–1861),
published around the same time, Nichiren intones the
mantra while the waves tower over the boat, as they do
elsewhere in Hokusai's oeuvre (cats 18, 19). Here, by
contrast, the monk writes directly on the water with a
brush, and the waves have calmed, encircling the boat.
Red ink, elsewhere used for preliminary underdrawing
in a design for a print (for example, cat. 178 ff.), is here
reserved for the holy scripture. AL

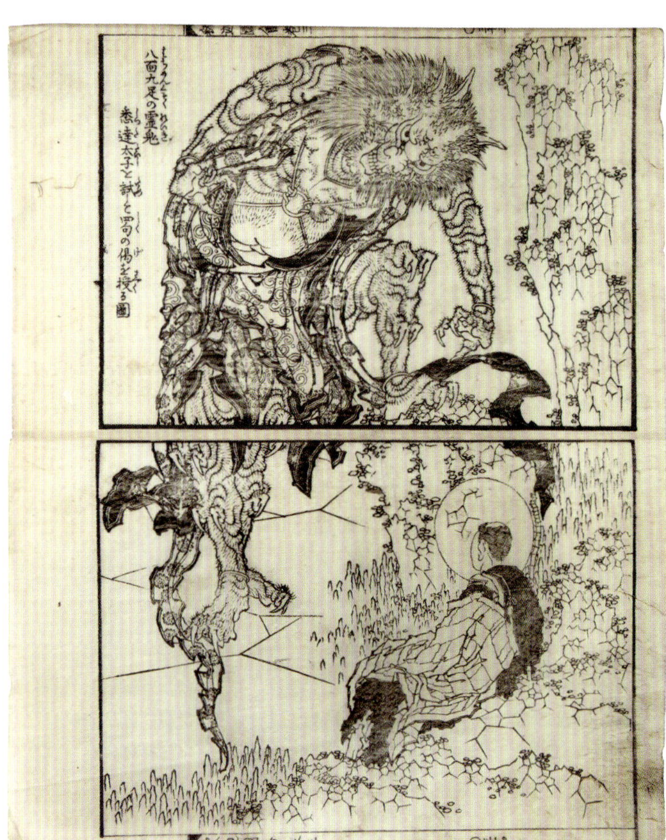
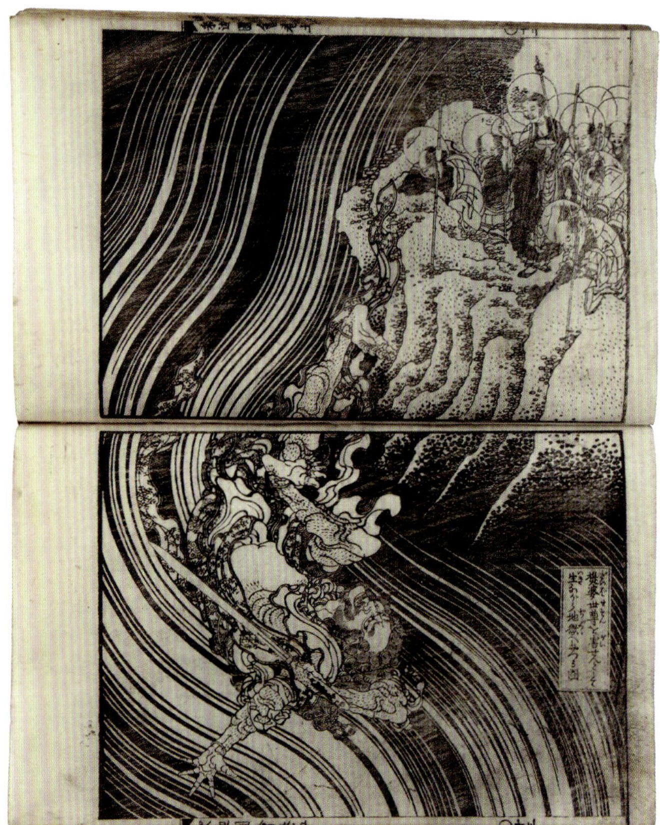

158

Prince Siddhartha tested by a demon, from *Illustrated Life of Shakyamuni* (*Shaka go-ichidaiki zue*)

1845
Signature: Saki no Hokusai Manji rōjin shūzō
('Illustrations by old man Manji, the former Hokusai')
Illustrated book, woodblock, vol. 3 (of 6), published
by Kawachiya Mohei, Yamashiroya Sahei and others,
25.2 × 17.5 cm (covers)
Literature: Edo Tokyo 2007, no. 224; Asano 2010,
pp. 72–73; Osaka 2012, no. 241
Uragami Mitsuru collection, Japan

In his eighties, Hokusai briefly returned to illustrating
adventure stories in the *yomihon* genre. This particular
project originated in Osaka, with a text by Yamada Isai
(1788–1846), a prolific author of 'illustrated things'
(*zue-mono*). The six volumes comprised fifty-five stories
and twenty-nine illustrations, imparting the educational
precepts afforded by the life of Shakyamuni, the
historical Buddha. Hokusai seems to have revelled
especially in the opportunity to depict the awesome
power of supernatural forces, which intervene here
at a pivotal moment in the young Prince Siddhartha's
search for enlightenment (left). Having undertaken
austerities in the mountains for six years, he is
confronted by a huge demon with eight faces and
nine limbs, who recites the first two lines of a four-line
verse (*shiku no ge*). Siddhartha agrees to sacrifice his
body in exchange for the remaining two lines, which
will complete the revelation he had been seeking.
The demon thereupon transforms into Vairocana,
the universal Buddha, and Siddhartha leaves the
mountains, taking up his mantle as Shakyamuni. AL

Shōki

About 1826

Signature: Saki no Hokusai Iitsu hitsu ('Brush of Iitsu, the former Hokusai')

Seal: Katsushika (1)

Hanging scroll, ink on silk, 102.2 × 30.4 cm

Provenance: Tozuka Yakichi IV (fifth month, 1826, inscription on verso of mounting); Imanishi Kikumatsu (1954)

Literature: Kumamoto Kenritsu Bijutsukan, eds, *Imanishi korekushon mehin ten* I, 1989, no. 50; TNM 2005, no. 432; Carpenter 2005, pp. 88–90; Freer-Sackler 2006, no. 152

Kumamoto Prefectural Museum of Art

Osaka only

Shōki began life as Zhong Kui, in seventh-century China. On failing the imperial examinations he committed suicide, but nonetheless was given an honourable burial by imperial command. In gratitude, he vowed to chase away demons and banish disease. Over the centuries, dishevelled and hirsute, Shōki became a popular figure throughout East Asia. In Japan, when depicted in red, he was believed to be effective against smallpox. Images of him, often on banners, were displayed at both New Year and the Boys' Festival (cat. 24).

Hokusai painted Shōki throughout his career, in varied poses (cats 160, 161). From the 1820s, as here, the demon he is chasing is generally 'offstage', and Shōki's movement is menacingly stilled and his sword half-concealed. Using powerful, articulated lines and rich ink shading, Hokusai draws the energy inwards, suggesting the latent strength of a body that could attack at any moment. Two bands at the top of the painting imitate a banner. AL

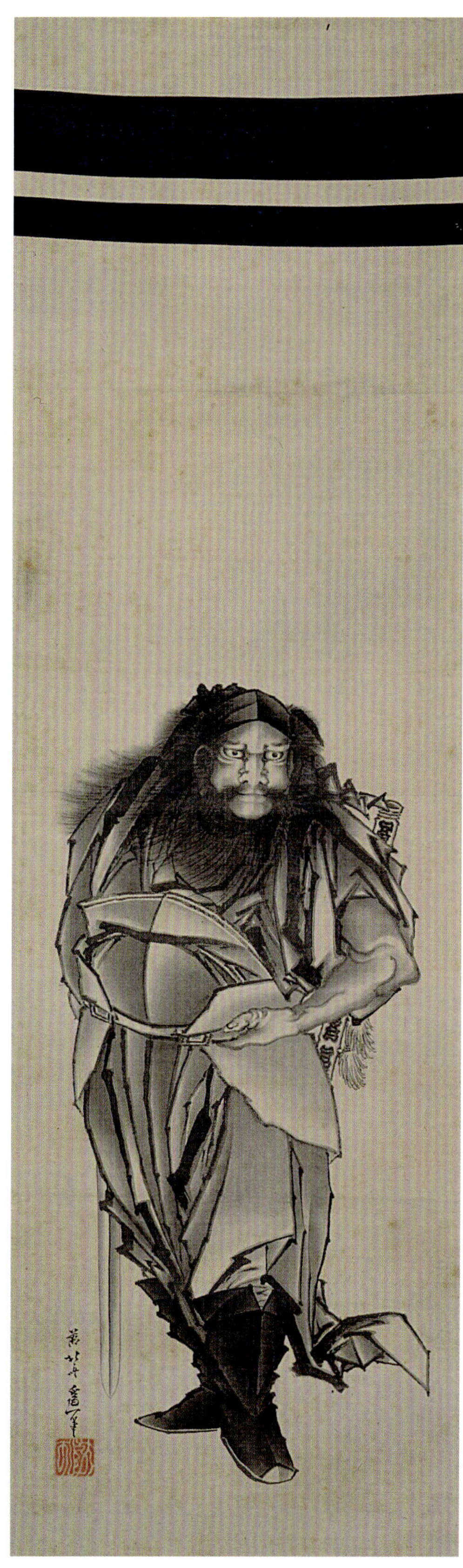

Shōki painted in red

1846
Signature: Hachijūnana rō / Manji hitsu ('Brush of
Manji, old man of eighty-seven')
Seal: Mt Fuji above trigram
Hanging scroll, ink and red pigment on silk,
59.1 × 30.2 cm
Provenance: Charles Stewart Smith
Literature: Calza & Carpenter 1994, no. 11.4; Freer-
Sackler 2006, no. 132; Paris 2014, no. 506
Metropolitan Museum of Art, New York, 14.76.37,
Gift of Mrs Charles Stewart Smith, Charles Stewart
Smith Jr. and Howard Caswell Smith

This is the most extraordinary of the many Shōki that
Hokusai painted during his lifetime (see also cats 159,
161). The demon-queller stands in three-quarter pose,
his body veiled by robes, sword obscured and face
turned towards the viewer. The bravura outlines
underscore Shōki's power and poise, while the
sophisticated shading allows him to fill the space.
Our attention is drawn to his face, framed by a
cloud of hair and beard, and we notice the alert,
determined, but still tender gaze. Both artist and
subject here seem immersed in the moment, but
also contemplating the infinite. AL

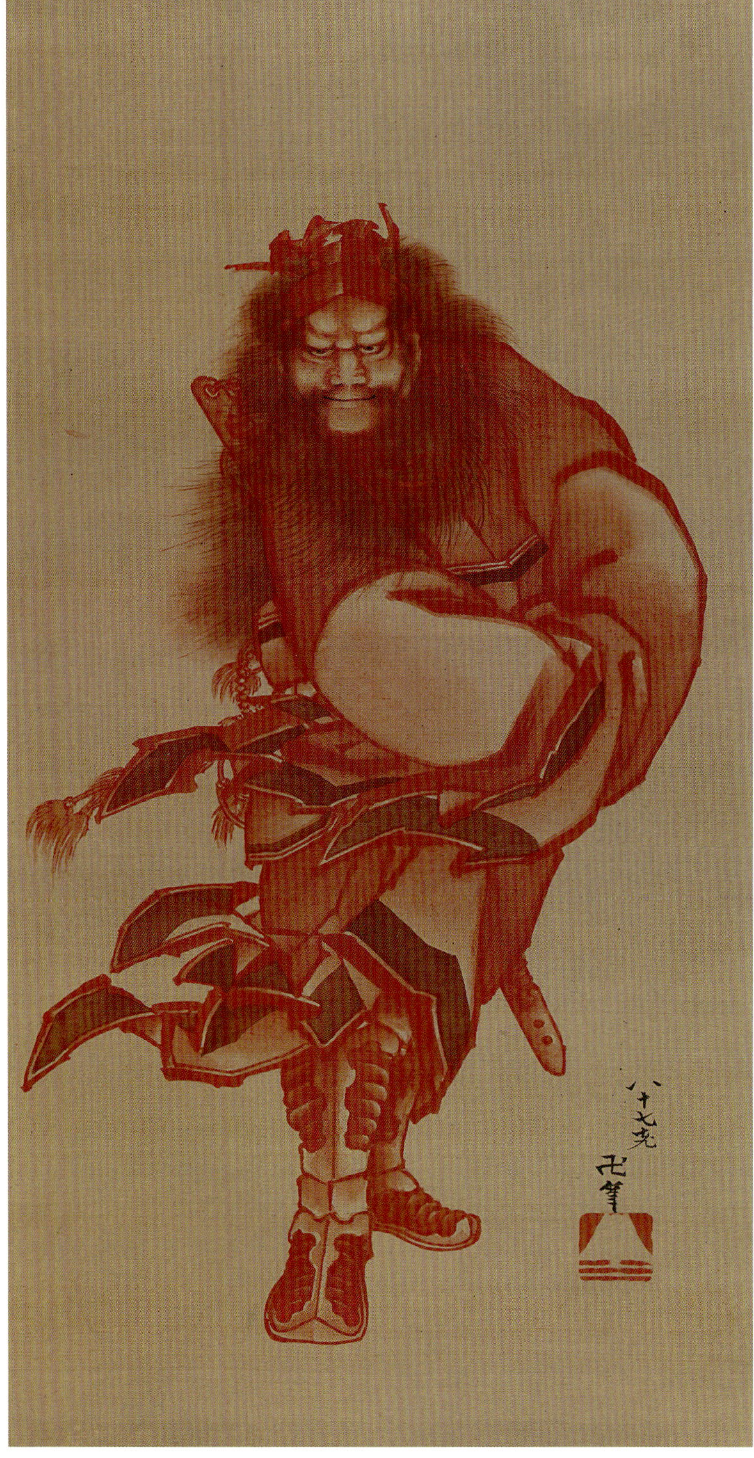

161

Shōki painted in red

1846
Signature: Fuzui rōjin Manji hitsu / yowai hachijūnana
sai ('Brush of Manji, old man without peer, aged
eighty-seven years')
Seal: Katsushika (3)
Hanging scroll, ink and red pigment on silk,
108.0 × 38.5 cm
Literature: Ozaki 1967, no. 36; Nagata 2000, no. 124;
Berlin 2011, no. 365; Paris 2014, no. 507; Sumida 2016,
no. 122
The Sumida Hokusai Museum, Tokyo
Osaka only

Painted in the same year as cat. 160, this Shōki is
a kindred spirit. In 1846 there was an outbreak of
smallpox in Edo (*Edogaku jiten* 1984, p. 837), and images
of the demon-queller painted in red were thought to
offer protection against the disease. Both paintings
were probably specially commissioned works, with the
vigorous outlines and nuanced shading giving Shōki
substance and presence. In cat. 160 he stands straight,
his arms forming a bow that suggests power held in
check. Here, his whole body bows, as if drawn taut,
his arm is exposed and his gaze is stern. Shōki teeters
on the verge of springing into action. AL

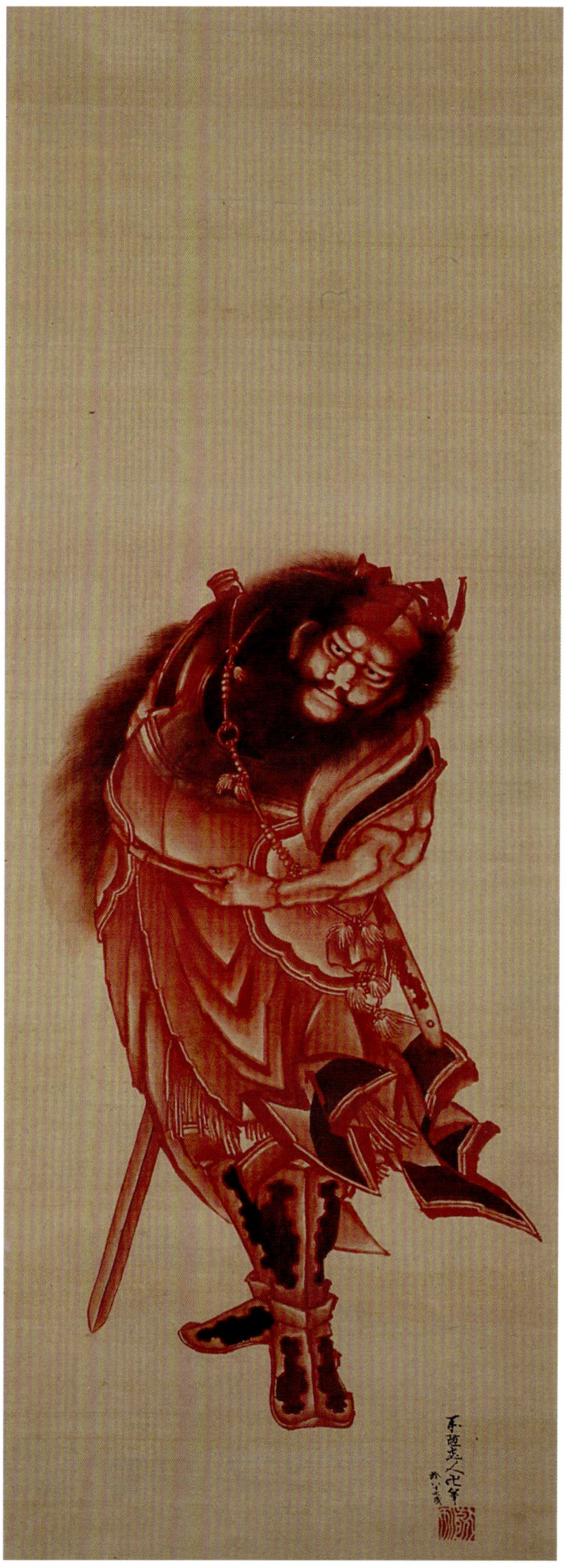

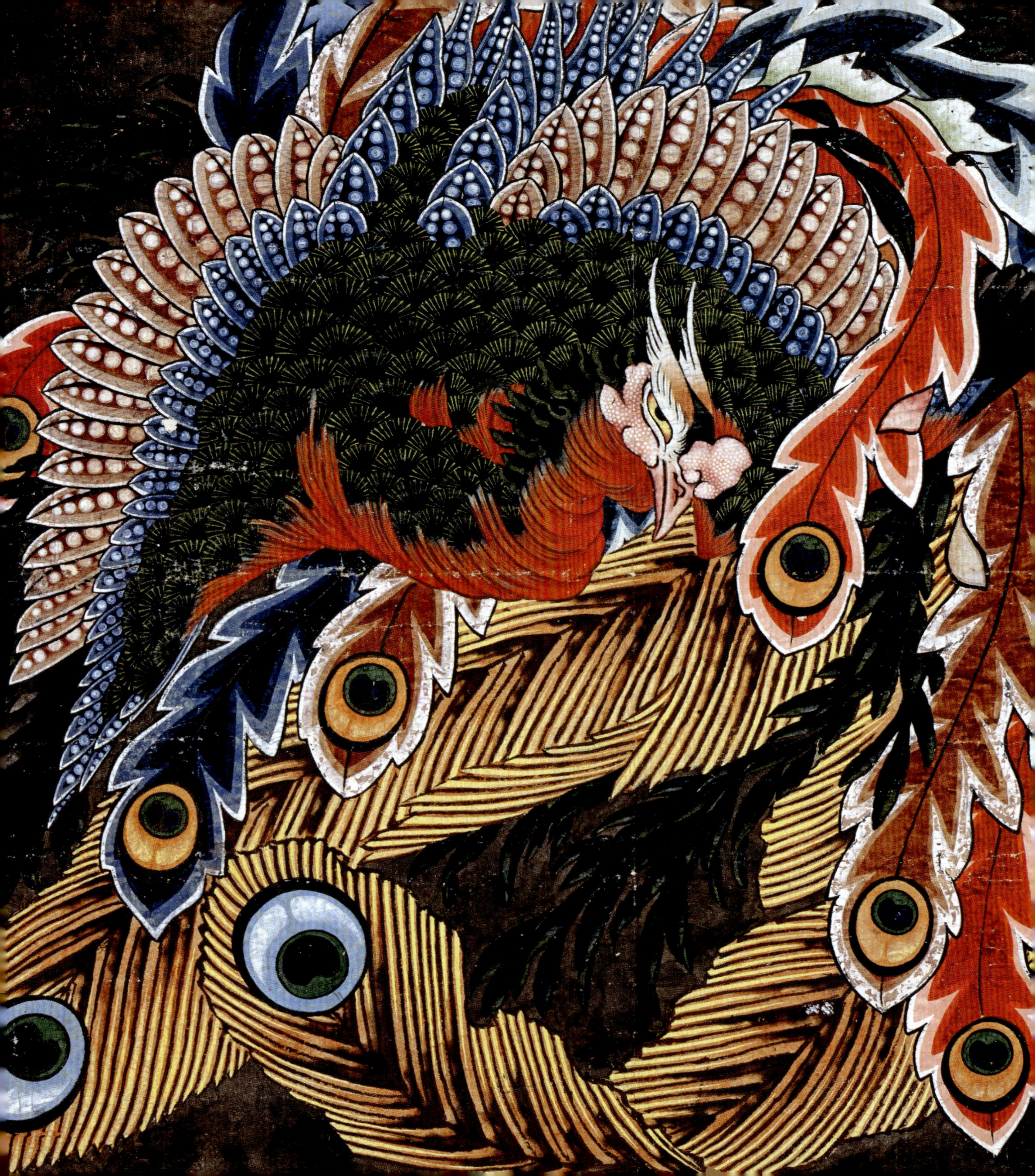

Hokusai's world

Hokusai rarely worked alone. His achievement was rooted in his need to learn from and work with others. It was sustained by the liberality with which he handed on what he had learned. Art was not exclusive, but a way of connecting to the world, open to all.

In part, this was simply how things were done at the time. An artist was apprenticed to a teacher in a school. In time he would acquire his own students, with whom he might produce joint works (cat. 162) and to whom he might pass on his name. Woodblock printing required a well-practised quartet – publisher, artist, block cutter and printer (cat. 166). Artists like Hokusai also worked with craftspeople, providing designs for a variety of objects (cats 172, 173). Hokusai was unusual in the range of his collaboration, especially with writers, and the frequency with which he distributed names and seals among his students, though both were common practice.

By sixty, he had begun to pull back from the social world and the public performances that had characterized his younger days (cat. 163). Collaboration continued, not least for printed work. Hokusai remained in demand from publishers (cat. 176), and he knew the cutters he wanted to transfer his designs to the blocks. He worked closely with his own daughter Eijo (art name Ōi, about 1800–after 1857), whose helping hand can perhaps be detected in a number of works by 'Hokusai' (cats 20, 200). Hokusai's reputation and network also allowed him to travel – leaving behind the demands of life in Edo – and generated commissions, for which he produced some of his most extraordinary paintings (cat. 203 ff.).

Hokusai was distinctive in his determination to share his technique and vision with the world. Many contemporary artists produced albums, sometimes printed, to serve as models for students and primers of style. Hokusai's equivalents were more comprehensive and detailed (cats 89, 174, 175), not just encouraging students to copy, but also showing them how they could master different styles and so produce their own account of the world (cat. 30). In one of his last books, *Picture Book: Essence of Colouring* (cat. 211), he gave step-by-step instructions on how to prepare pigments (see also cat. 199) and then to colour, for example, a canary (cat. 90), chickens (cat. 107) and a cuckoo (cat. 218). Underpinning Hokusai's work and thought was the desire expressed in the subtitle for a number of his teaching manuals, *denshin kaishu*, to convey the spirit. AL

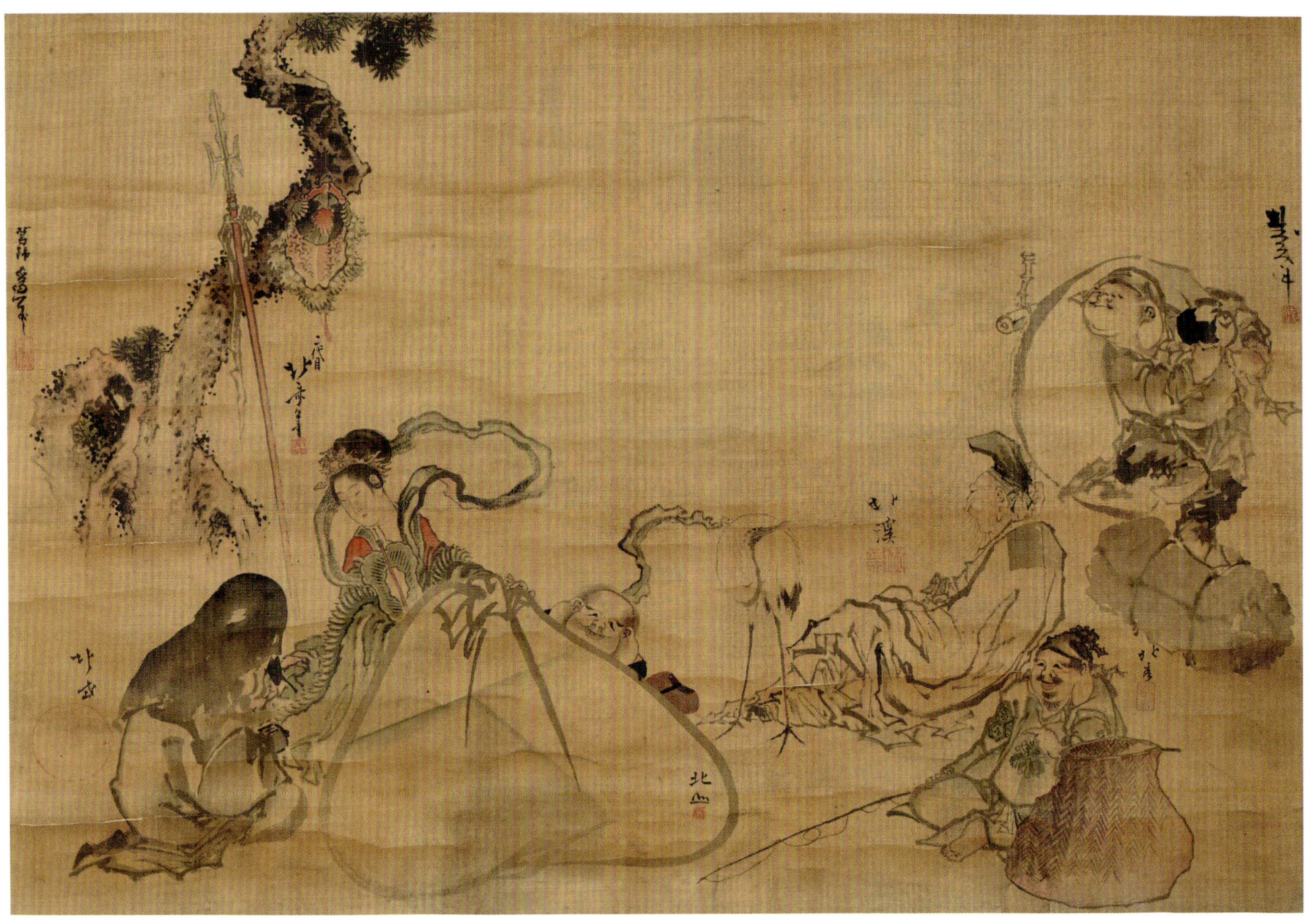

162

Hokusai and six pupils
The Seven Lucky Gods

1823–1826
Signature: Katsushika Iitsu hitsu ('Brush of Iitsu of
Katsushika')
Seal: [single human figure]
Hanging scroll, ink and colour on silk, 49.9 × 71.3 cm
Literature: Nihon Ukiyo-e Hakubutsukan, eds,
Nikuhitsu ukiyo-e senshū, Tokyo, Gakken, 1985, vol. 2, no.
176; Nagata 2000, no. 148; Carpenter 2005, pp. 77, 79;
Itabashi 2008, no. 87
Japan Ukiyo-e Museum, Matsumoto

Hokusai and six pupils collaborated here to depict
the Seven Lucky Gods. From the right are Daikoku
by Taito II, Ebisu by Hokushū, Fukurokuju by Hokkei,
Hotei by Hokuzan, Benzaiten by Hokusai II and Jurōjin
by Hokutai. Hokusai painted Bishamon, but not in
human form. Instead, the god is represented by a helmet
and spear resting on a pine tree, overlooking the scene
like a teacher supervising his pupils. The compositional
flow and the application of colours suggest that the work
was an impromptu product of a gathering of the seven
artists. The painting reveals both their individual styles
and their connection to each other as part of a school.
Hokkei and Taito II were probably the senior pupils.
Taito II and Hokusai II both received one of their
master's former names. MR

163

Hokusai & Ryōdonsai Hōzan (dates unknown)
Record of a giant Bodhidharma painting in Edo

13th day, fourth month, 1804
Signature: Gakyōjin / Hokusai ga ('Drawn by Hokusai, man crazy to paint')
Inscription signed Ryōdonsai Hōzan
Hanging scroll, ink on paper, 84.6 × 27.2 cm
Literature: Iijima 1999, pp. 67–69; Boston 2000, no. 59; Thompson 2015, no. 38
Museum of Fine Arts, Boston, 11.7438, William Sturgis Bigelow collection
Osaka only

In 1804 crowds flocked to Gokokuji temple at Otowayama in Edo to see a special public display of a sculpture of Kannon. While the image was on display, Hokusai staged a public performance, painting a giant portrait of the Buddhist monk Bodhidharma (Japanese: Daruma). The central image here is Hokusai's miniature record of what he had painted. Ryōdonsai Hōzan, apparently an eyewitness, adds an inscription which vividly describes the event: 'In the fourth month of 1804, in the garden of Gokoku temple, he brushed a Buddhist painting 170 tatami mats in area. It was as though [Bodhidharma's] spirit had crossed the ocean… Height 11 *ken* [20 metres/66 feet], width 8 *ken* [14.5 metres/48 feet], around 176 tatami mats [in area]. Done with a brush made from 3 bales of straw, more than 3 *to* [54 litres/14 gallons] of *sumi* ink, and a broom made of hemp palm for shading.' After changing his art name to Hokusai in 1798 – and particularly during the Bunka era (1804–1818) – the artist made various efforts to promote himself. These included improvising paintings at public banquets, live painting performances, as at Gokokuji, drawing sparrows on grains of rice and showcasing his talents before shogun Tokugawa Ienari (1773–1841), by special invitation, in a painting contest with the Edo artist Tani Bunchō (1763–1840). MR

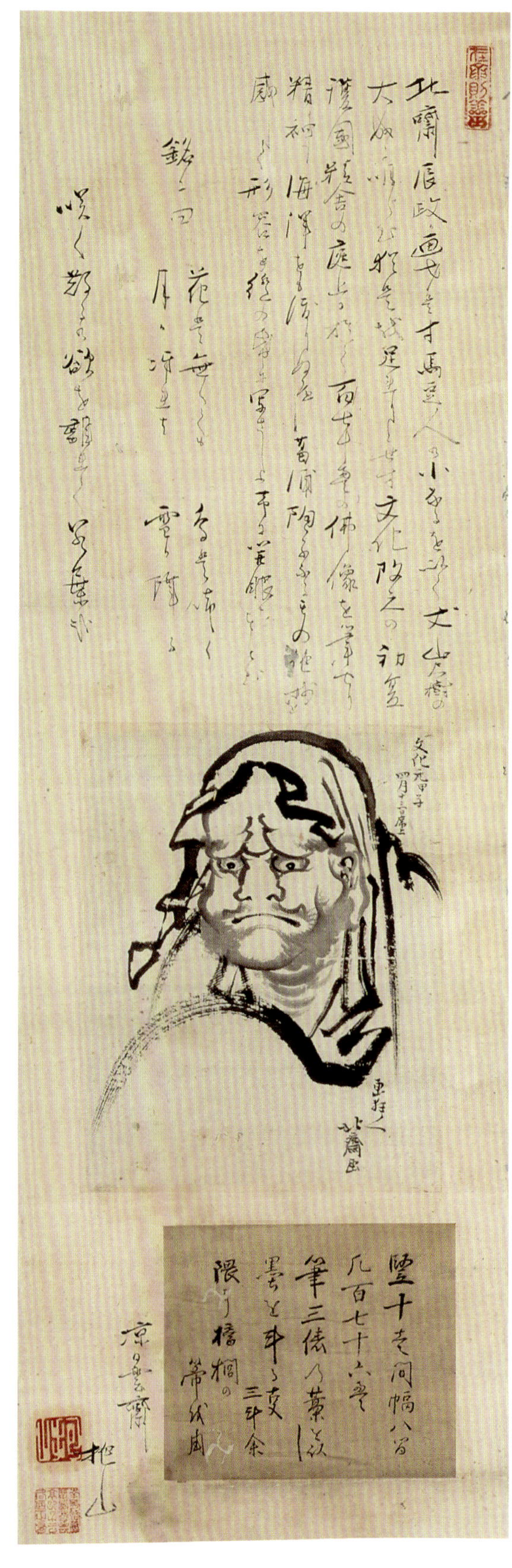

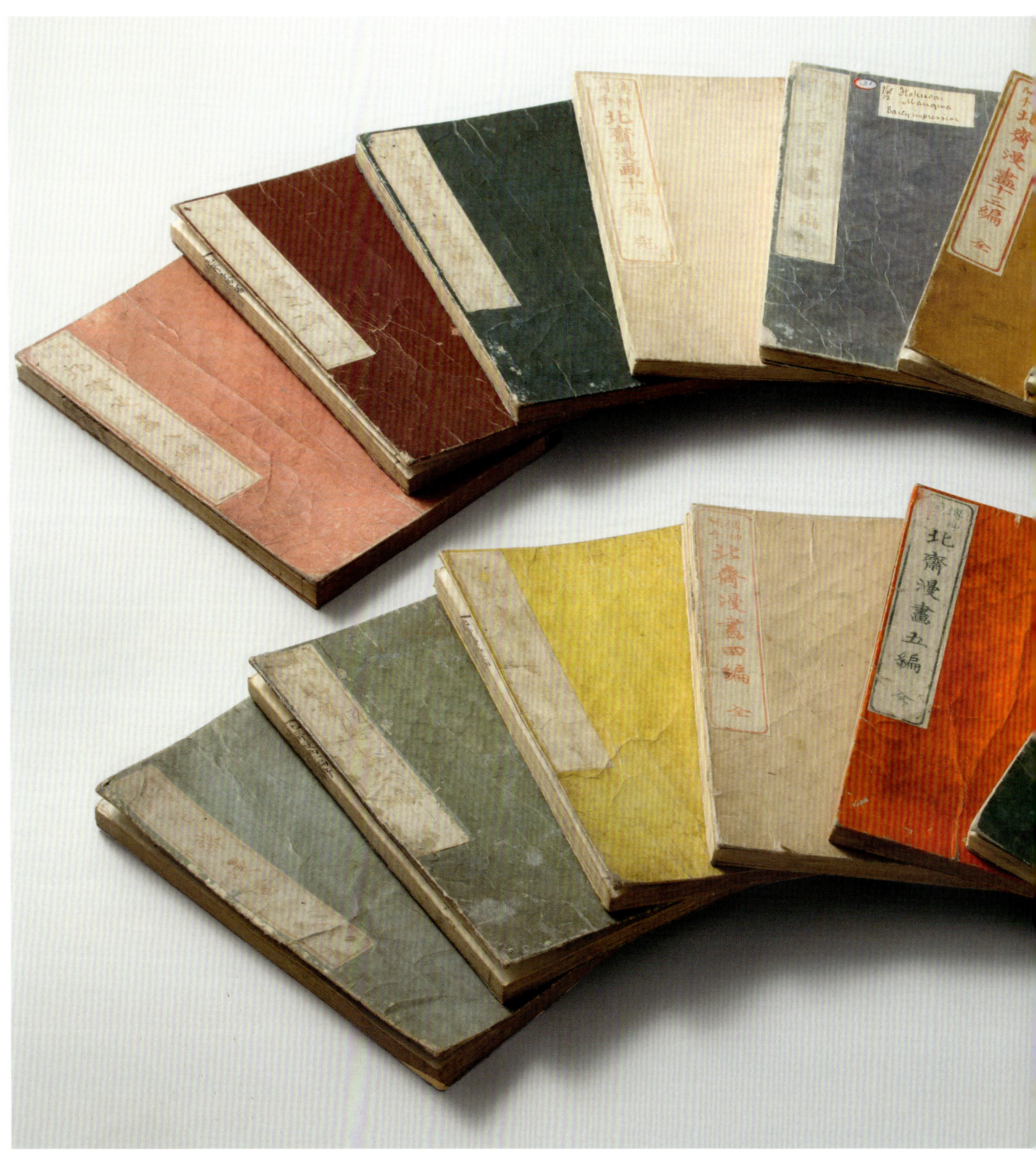

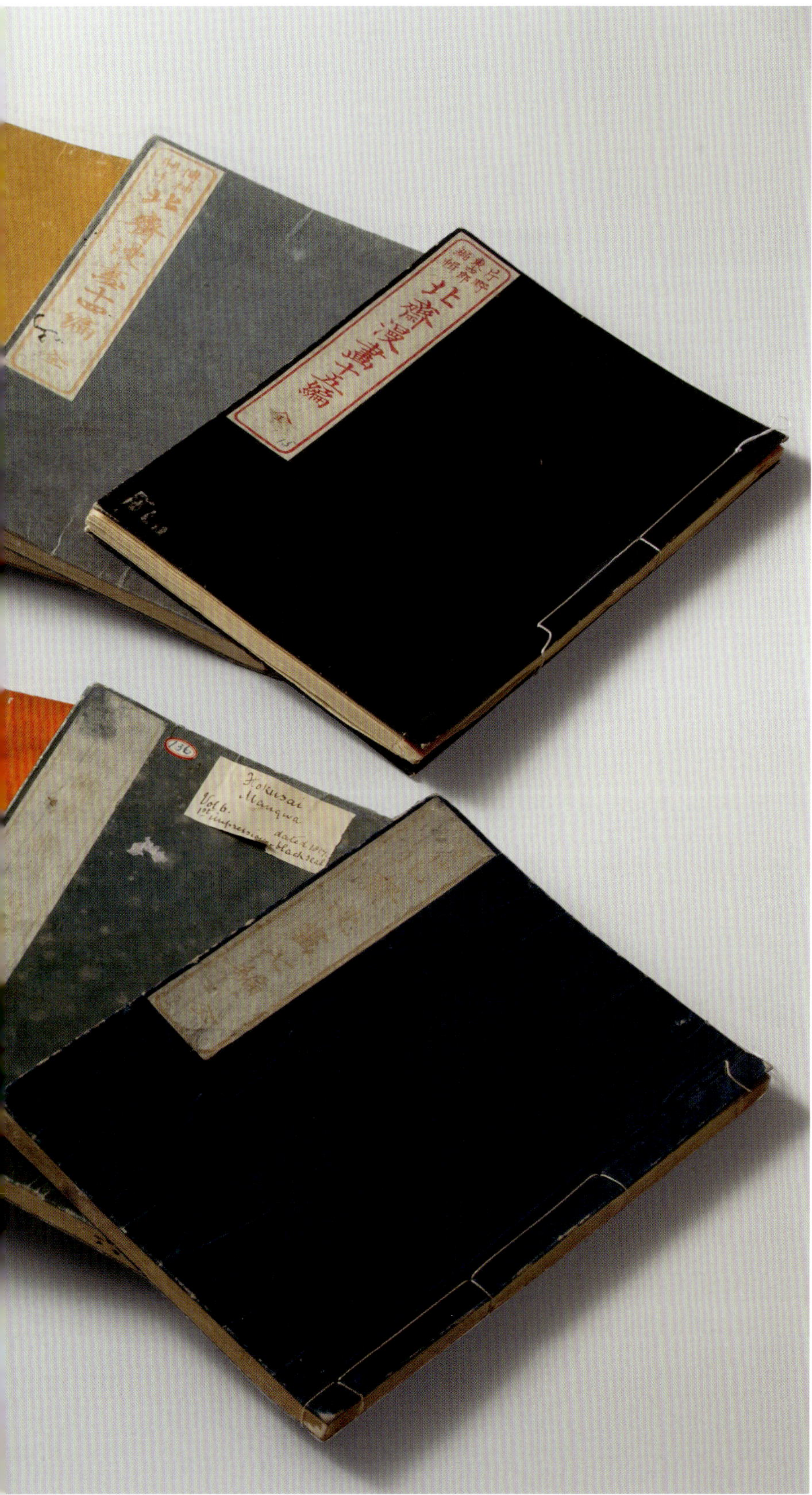

Covers of *Hokusai's Sketches* (*Hokusai manga*), vols 1–15

1814–1878
Illustrated book, 15 vols, colour woodblock,
published by Eirakuya Tōshirō, Nagoya, and others,
22.8 × 15.8 cm (covers)
Literature: Michener 1958; Nagata *Manga* 1986–1987;
Hashimoto 2005; Paris 2014, nos 226–295
Uragami Mitsuru collection, Japan

Hokusai's Sketches (*Hokusai manga*) is a series of fifteen
volumes of brush drawing manuals aimed at students.
They contain myriad pictures by Hokusai in his
personal, Katsushika style, as it was known in his day.
The preface to volume 1 indicates that Hokusai himself
chose the term *manga* for the title, but his *manga* differ
from the manga of today. In Hokusai's case, *manga*
suggests drawings done in a freely associative manner,
as ideas came into his head. The sketches in the series
display just that kind of spontaneity. The colophons
to *Manga* volumes 1 to 10 (1814–1819) identify various
pupils of Hokusai as the volumes' 'pupil compilers'
(*kyōgō monjin*, see cat. 184). Volume 1 was planned in
Nagoya after Hokusai had stayed with his pupil Maki
Bokusen (1775–1824; see also cat. 18) in 1812. The
preface describes how Hokusai produced more than
300 sketches at Maki Bokusen's home. These sketches
were then collated (*kyōgō*) by Bokusen and another
pupil, Katsushika Hoku'un (worked early 1800s), and
published by Eirakuya in 1814. It would seem that
Hokusai's pupils took sketches he had produced
casually, on a whim, and turned them into a series of
page designs suitable for a brush drawing manual. MR

Hokusai's Sketches (*Hokusai manga*), vols 1 & 12

First month, 1814 (vol. 1); first month, 1834 (vol. 12)
Signature: Tōto gakō Katsushika Hokusai hitsu
('Brush of Katsushika Hokusai, artist of the Eastern
capital [Edo]') (vol. 1)
Seal: Raishin ('Thunder tremor') (vol. 1)
Preface signed Hanshū sanjin dai (vol. 1)
Signature (frontispiece): Saki no Hokusai Iitsu
('Iitsu, the former Hokusai') (vol. 12)
Preface signed Shakuyakutei (vol. 12)
Illustrated book, vols 1 & 12 (of 15), colour woodblock
(vol. 1), woodblock (vol. 12), published by Eirakuya
Tōshirō, Nagoya, and others, 22.8 × 15.8 cm (covers)
Literature: Michener 1958; Nagata *Manga* 1986–1987;
Hashimoto 2005; Paris 2014, nos 226–295
Uragami Mitsuru collection, Japan

Throughout volume 1 of *Hokusai manga* the lines and
drawing style appear abbreviated, but they capture
remarkably well the characteristic movements of living
things, as evident for example in the depiction of
insects shown here. After a hiatus of more than ten
years, volumes 11–12 were published in the early 1830s.
The superior quality of production of these later
volumes is apparent in the skilfully cut blocks, credited
in volume 12 to Egawa Tomekichi. Reproduced here
from volume 12 is the spirited composition 'Wind'
(*Kaze*), which matches the high standards applied
around the same time to the production of *One Hundred
Views of Mt Fuji* (cat. 176), also supervised by Egawa.
Hokusai manga did not lose its appeal even after the
artist's death. Volumes 13 and 14 were published in
the late Edo period, and the final volume in 1878.
Thanks to the effective distribution of Hokusai's books
by publishers, the artist's concepts and techniques
became widely known throughout Japan and, after
1860, were already garnering admirers overseas. MR

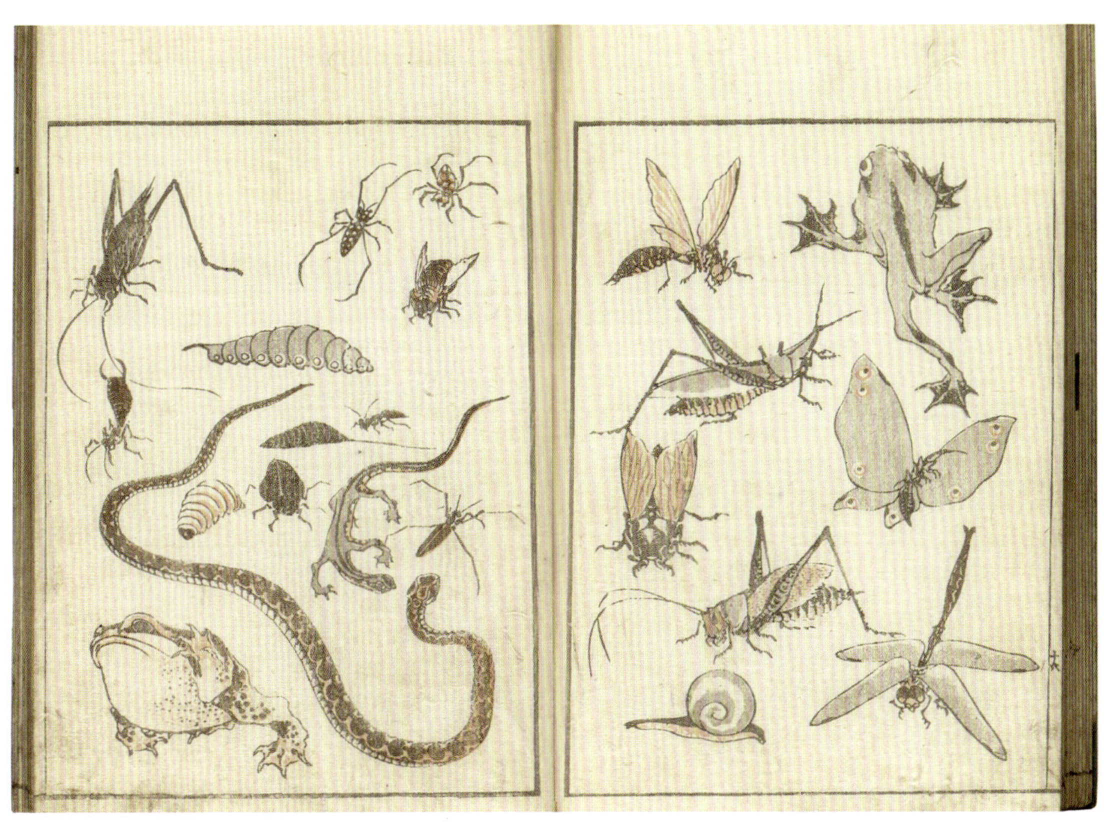

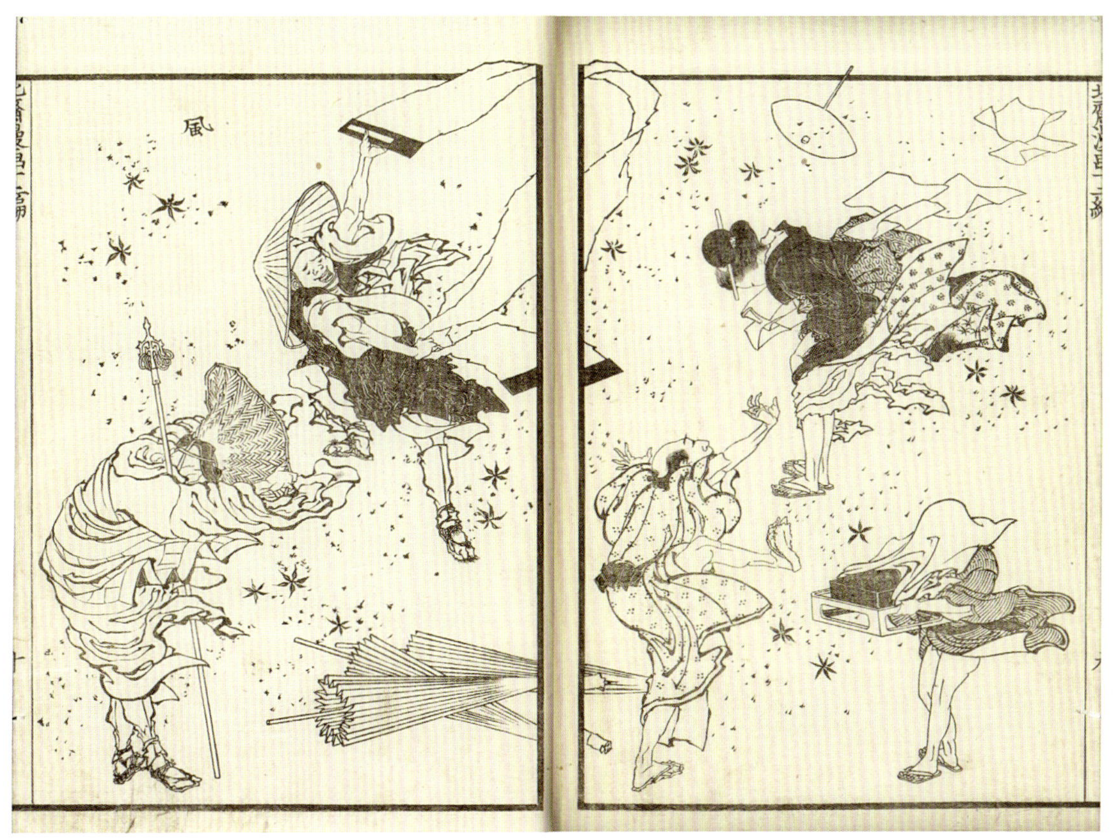
風

Making woodblock prints

1825

Signature: Hokusai aratame / Iitsu hitsu ('Brush of
Iitsu, changed from Hokusai')
Surimono, colour woodblock with metallic pigments
and embossing, 21.2 × 18.7 cm
Provenance: E. Evelyn Barron
Literature: Marais 1980, no. 86; Roger Keyes,
The Art of Surimono, Sotheby's, 1985, p. 24; Keyes
& Morse 2015, no. 1485
Fitzwilliam Museum, Cambridge, P.438-1937

Minamiyama (Nanzan), a poet from the far southwest
of Japan's main island, ordered this privately
commissioned print (*surimono*) from Hokusai to
celebrate the New Year of 1825. The poems read:

Not only is today / the first day of spring, / but this
very morning, / the houses of Musashi Plain stand /
hidden behind veils of mist.

For this jewel / of a blossoming New Year, / the world
carves words / into blocks of cherry wood, / as they do
in Ōtsu province.

Carved into cherry blocks, / this auspicious spring /
surimono will ensure / that the Southern Mountain
(Minamiyama) / will never crumble or fall.

In the foreground a woman is printing green and
red pigments on a large-format (*ōban*) sheet of paper,
pressing down on the burnishing disk (*baren*). In the
background a man is cutting text characters into
a block. Hokusai vividly represents the details of a
contemporary block-cutter's workshop, from the
handling of the knife, to the use of large and small
wooden mallets. Before becoming an artist, Hokusai
had himself worked as a block cutter. Perhaps for
that reason, he was particular about the carving and
printing of his designs (Iijima 1999, pp. 149–150;
Tinios 2015). Hokusai clearly considered the
contributions of the block cutter and printer to
be a vital part of the finished work. MR

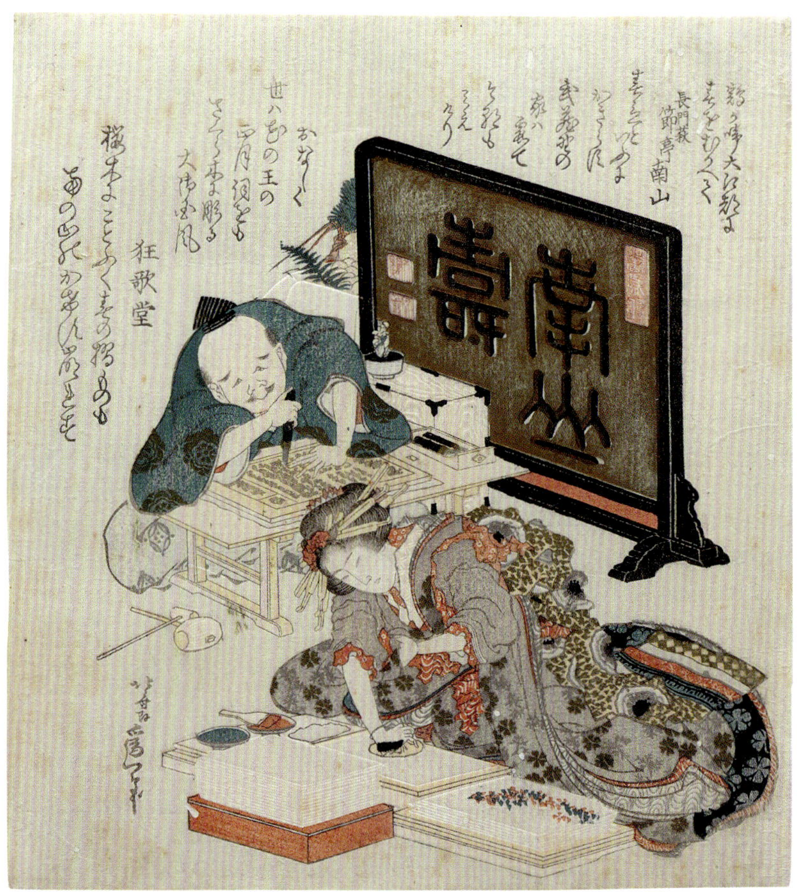

167
Baren (woodblock printer's tool)

Early 1900s
Bamboo, lacquered paper, 11.8 × 1.4 cm
Literature: Yura 1971, pp. 57–58; GUDHJ 1980–1982,
vol. 3, p. 87
British Museum, OA+.7399

Throughout his career, Hokusai was closely involved
in the production of his print designs and therefore
intimately familiar with the *baren*, the woodblock
printer's essential tool. The *baren* consists of a tight coil
of bamboo twine (*shin*) sandwiched between two rigid
disks of lacquered paper wrapped in silk (*ate-kawa*).
The whole is then wrapped in a thin sheet of bamboo
bark (*tsutsumi-kawa*), knotted against one face to form
a handle and leaving the opposite face as a flat surface.
The thickness of the twine at the core determines the
character of the tool. A *baren* made of thick twine lends
itself to heavy pressure and printing large areas of
a design. Thin twine sustains only light pressure and
produces a tool useful for delicate printing effects.
A *baren* may range in diameter from around 8 cm
to around 21 cm (3–8 in.). Having positioned a sheet of
paper on an inked woodblock, the printer uses the *baren*
to burnish the back of the paper, transferring the ink
and producing a print. The bamboo covering of the
baren can last for a few hundred prints before it has to
be replaced. During the Edo period, *baren* were made
by specialist craftsmen. AH

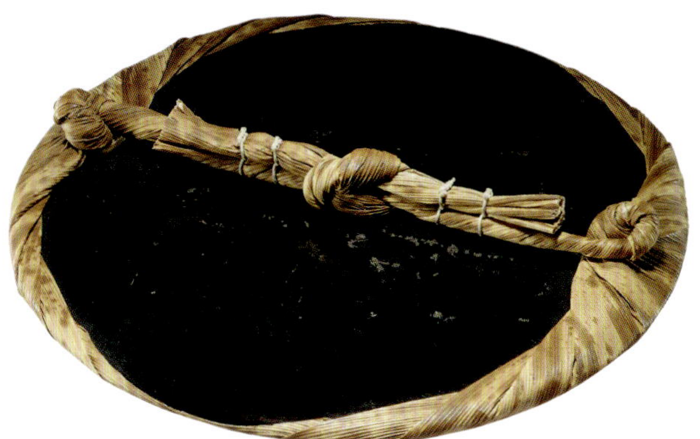

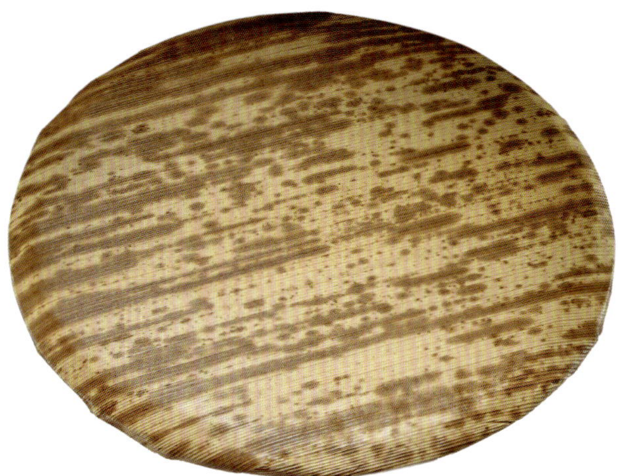

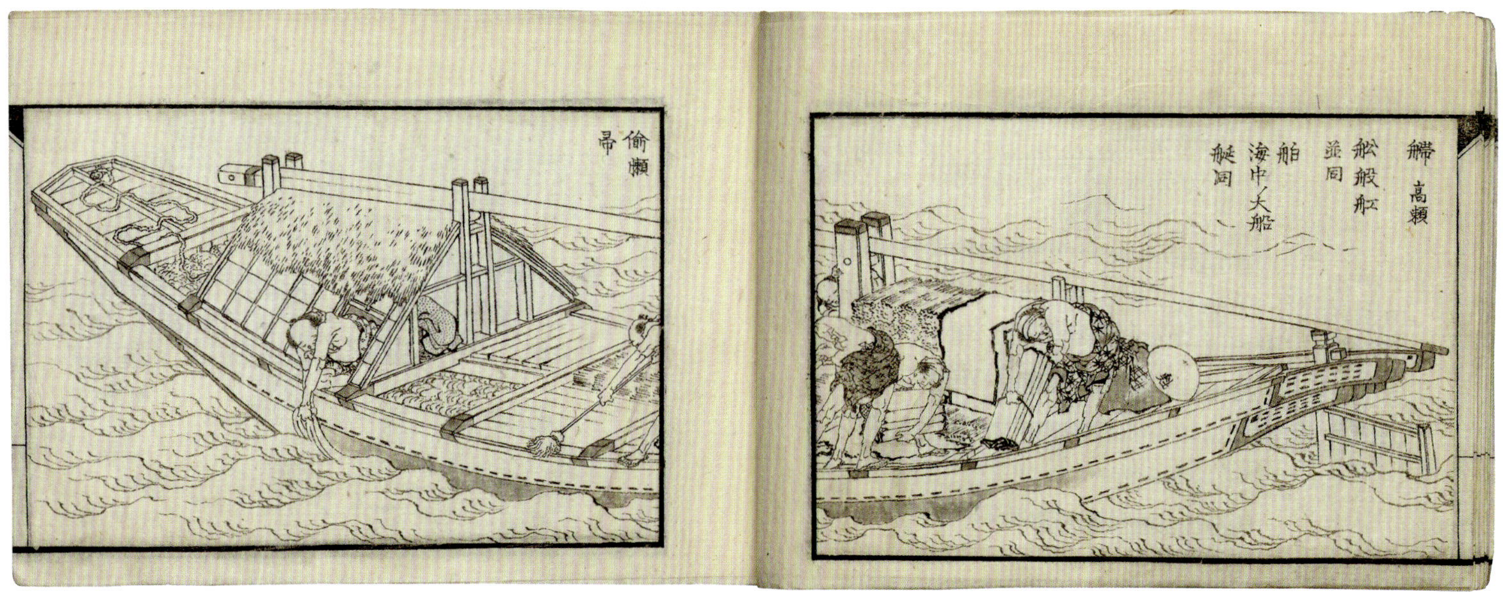

Drawings for a three-volume picture book

1823–1835
Block-ready drawings, ink on paper, vol. 1 (of 3),
13.8 × 20.4 cm (covers)
Literature: Calza 2003, no. III.70.1-3; Boston 2013,
no. 141; Thompson 2016
Museum of Fine Arts, Boston, 1998.670.1, source
unidentified
Osaka only

These block-ready drawings are for an illustrated book that was never published, leaving the manuscript in its present form. The eighty-nine leaves of drawings rival the fifteen volumes of *Hokusai's Sketches* (*Hokusai manga*, cats 164, 165) in the variety of their subject matter. Their format echoes Hokusai's book *Modern Designs for Combs and Tobacco Pipes* (1823, cats 29, 39), published by Nishimuraya, which includes an advertisement for a new Hokusai painting manual (*edehon*), titled *Iitsu sensei keiroku gafu* (*Master Iitsu's Chicken-rib Picture Album*).

No such book was published, but the description in the advertisement mirrors the contents of this set of drawings. It may be, therefore, that production was abandoned after these preparatory drawings had been completed. As the brushwork indicates, the book would have been a tour de force. The carefully drawn lines and dynamic compositions fill the narrow, horizontal pages, demonstrating an artist pouring all his skill into the designs, and providing direct insight into Hokusai's brush drawing style. MR

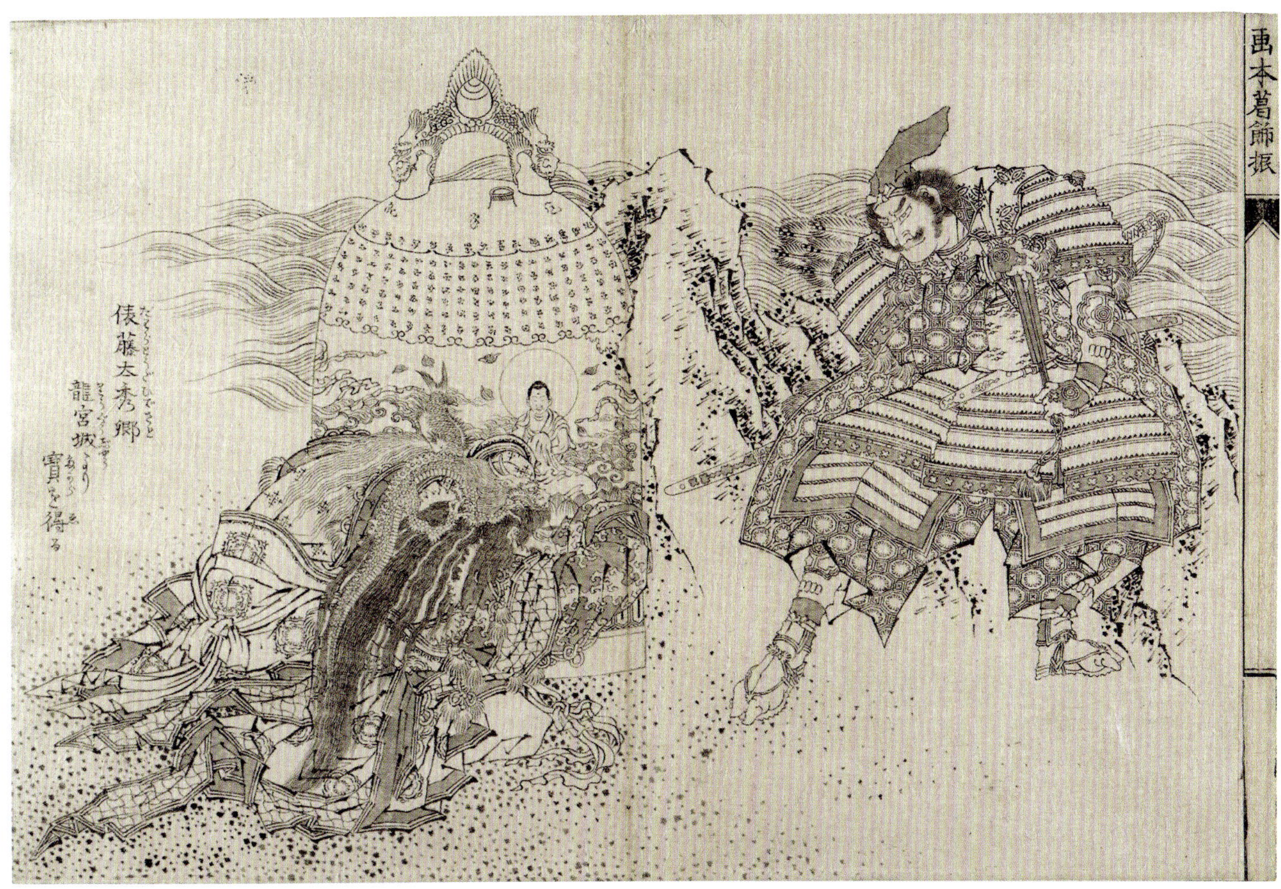

169

Block-ready drawings for *Picture Book: Japan and China in the Katsushika Style* (*Ehon Wakan Katsushika-buri*)

About 1836
Unsigned (attributed to Hokusai)
Folding album pasted with twenty-eight block-ready drawings for an illustrated book, ink on paper, with woodblock-printed borders and title, 25.4 × 39.4 cm
Provenance: Charles Stewart Smith
Literature: HK 18, April 1995, pp. 72–75; Nagata 2000, nos 183–207; Calza 2003, no. VI.10.1–25
Metropolitan Museum of Art, New York, 14.76.58.1–25, Gift of Mrs Charles Stewart Smith, Charles Stewart Smith Jr. and Howard Caswell Smith, in memory of Charles Stewart Smith

This folding album has a total of twenty-eight block-ready drawings for a picture book of warriors. The projected title *Ehon Katsushika-buri* is carved into the block at the edges of the pages (see below), and an alternative title, *Ehon Wakan Katsushika-buri*, is inscribed on the single-page drawing 'Strongman hero Benkei steals the bell'. Although this alternative title includes 'Japan and China' (*Wakan*), all except two of the single-page drawings present figures from historical sources, legends and tales of Japan. The publication that was intended to be created from these block-ready drawings is referred to in adverts in two other warrior books. For some reason, however, the book was never published. The edge-of-page title *Ehon Katsushika-buri* and the border outlines of each page here are printed, so the drawings have been made on specially prepared blank pages. The original format for these block-ready drawings was surely similar to *Record of Shoguns of Great Japan, Collection One* (cat. 171). In the modern period they were cut up and mounted in the present album. This is a rare and precious example of block-ready outline drawings by Hokusai, reading for cutting. AS

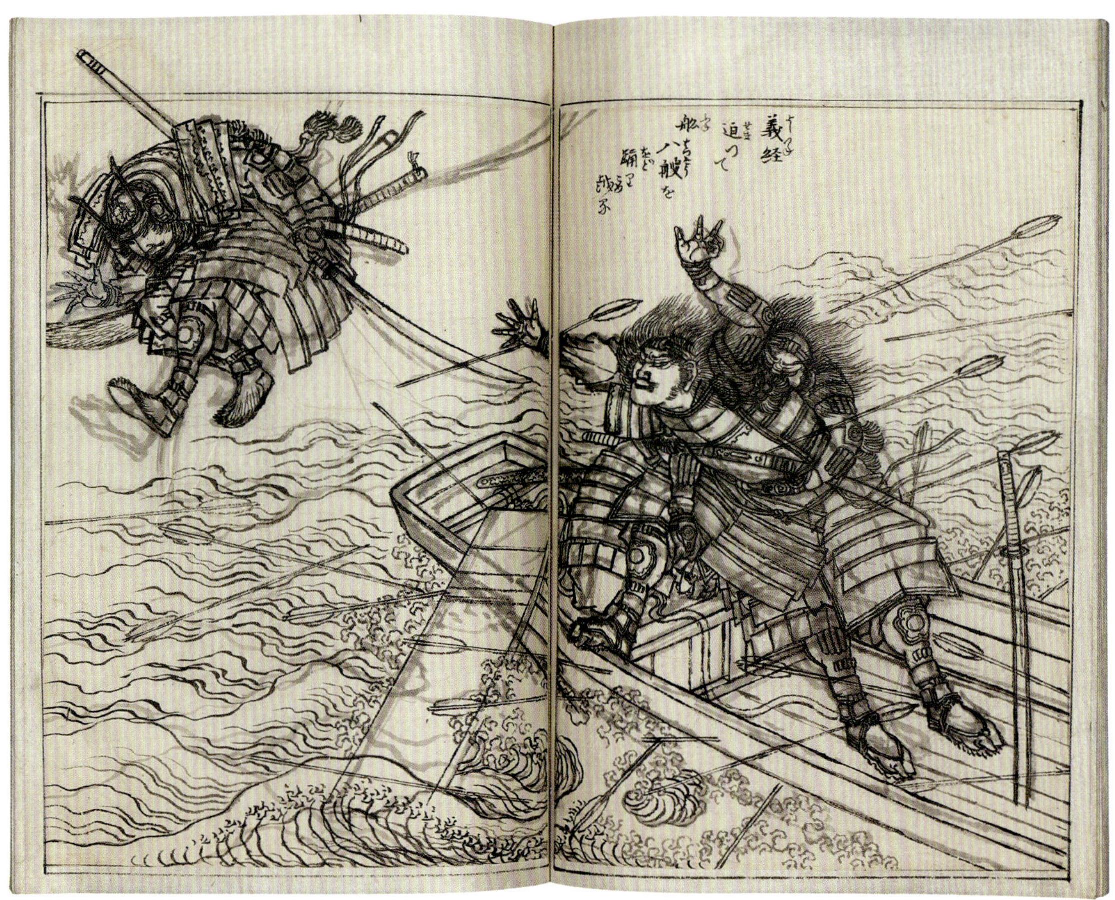

170

Preparatory drawings for a picture book, *Lives of Famous Generals of Japan (Nihon meishō den)*

About 1820–1835
Unsigned (attributed to Hokusai)
Illustrated book, ink on paper, vol. 1 (of 3),
23.5 × 16.4 cm (covers)
Museum of Fine Arts, Boston, 2006.1863.1, source
unidentified
Osaka only

Each of the three volumes for this illustrated book is inscribed 'Drawings by Hokusai' (*Hokusai ga*), and on a sheet pasted inside the cover is written the title *Lives of Famous Generals of Japan*. On the title page of volume 1 is the inscription: 'Preparatory drawings for block-ready drawings by Hokusai / These pictures were never made into blocks. They are a masterpiece for all ages.' The volumes contain a total of thirty-two double-page compositions of drawings, which comparison reveals were prepared for the block-ready drawings *Record of Shoguns of Great Japan, Collection One* (cat. 171), though the latter has one additional composition. The content relates to the Genpei civil wars of the late 1100s, from Minamoto no Yoritomo first raising his armies in 1180 until his final victory in Mutsu province in 1189. However, most of the images are not battle scenes, so the title was clearly provisional. The drawings display wonderful characteristics only found in genuine works by Hokusai, including numerous working corrections and editorial notes written by Hokusai on small slips of thin paper attached to the compositions. Fragmentary groups of preparatory drawings by Hokusai have survived from the Tenpō era (1830–1844). However, this is the only case where both preparatory drawings and his related block-ready drawings are known and is therefore very significant (see also Asano essay, pp. 40–47). AS

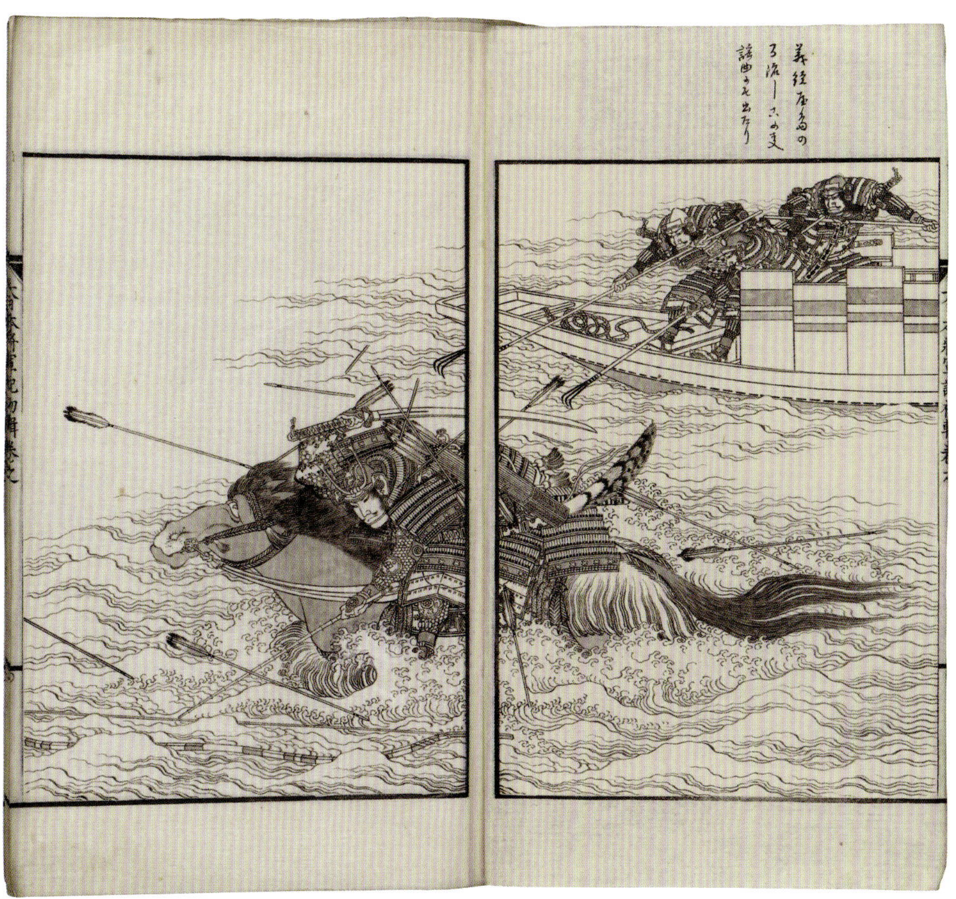

171

Block-ready drawings for a picture book, *Record of Shoguns of Great Japan, Collection One* (*Dai Nihon shōgun ki, shoshū*)

About 1820–1835
Unsigned (attributed to Hokusai)
Illustrated book, ink on paper, vol. 5 (of 6),
28.0 × 20.0 cm (covers)
Literature: Hillier 1980, pp. 78–79; Calza 2003, no. V.31
Museum of Fine Arts, Boston, 1998.669.5, source
unidentified
Osaka only

Thirty-three double pages of block-ready drawings are
contained within rectangular printed page outlines, with
the title *Record of Shoguns of Great Japan, Collection One,
Volume [blank]* at the edge of the page. The block-ready
drawings are interleaved in the six volumes with blank
pages, to make it easier to disassemble them for block

cutting. It is apparent from study that these block-ready
drawings were based on the preparatory drawings for
Lives of Famous Generals of Japan (cat. 170), except that the
present group has one additional composition. The
drawings are unsigned, but comparison with published
picture books of warriors from the Tenpō era (1830–
1844) strongly suggests that they are by Hokusai. Of
particular interest are the artist's comments inscribed
on thin slips of paper attached to the drawings, and his
instructions to the block cutter written in the margins.
As with *Lives of Famous Generals of Japan*, the drawings
illustrate events from the Genpei civil wars of the late
1100s, though since the majority do not depict battle
scenes, the title at the edge of the page, *Record of Shoguns
of Great Japan*, seems inappropriate. Perhaps Hokusai
was commissioned by a publisher to create *Lives of
Famous Generals of Japan*, but instead produced
compositions relating to the Genpei civil wars, and
included scenes that were not battles, so the book was
never produced (see also Asano essay, pp. 40–47). AS

Miniature drawings for craftspeople

1829–1831
Signature: Nanajūichi ō / Hokusai Iitsu utsusu
('Drawn by Hokusai Iitsu, old man of seventy-one'),
and five other variants, giving ages between seventy
and seventy-two
Two albums pasted with 548 drawings, ink and colour
on paper, 19.7 × 13.3 cm (covers)
Provenance: Edgar Walter
Literature: HK 20, April 1996, pp. 136–139; Nagata
2000, pp. 190–193; Paris 2014, no. 472
Metropolitan Museum of Art, New York, JIB 141,
Fletcher Fund 1941

The small preparatory drawings pasted into this album
were intended as a reference for skilled craftspeople
specializing in decorative arts such as metalworking
and netsuke carving. The annotations indicate that
both of the vertical pair of drawings form part of a
single design, demonstrating how two-dimensional
drawings could be used to create a three-dimensional
object. In his illustrated books, Hokusai published
several sets of such drawings for craftspeople, which
were used to make high-quality decorative arts (cats
29, 151, 152). His pupils were also closely involved
with craft production and included a number of
craftspeople. This pair of albums contains designs by
Hokusai and his pupils in no particular order. Pin holes
in some of the drawings show that they have been
used. Evidently, a collection of loose preparatory
drawings was at some point pasted into the albums. MR

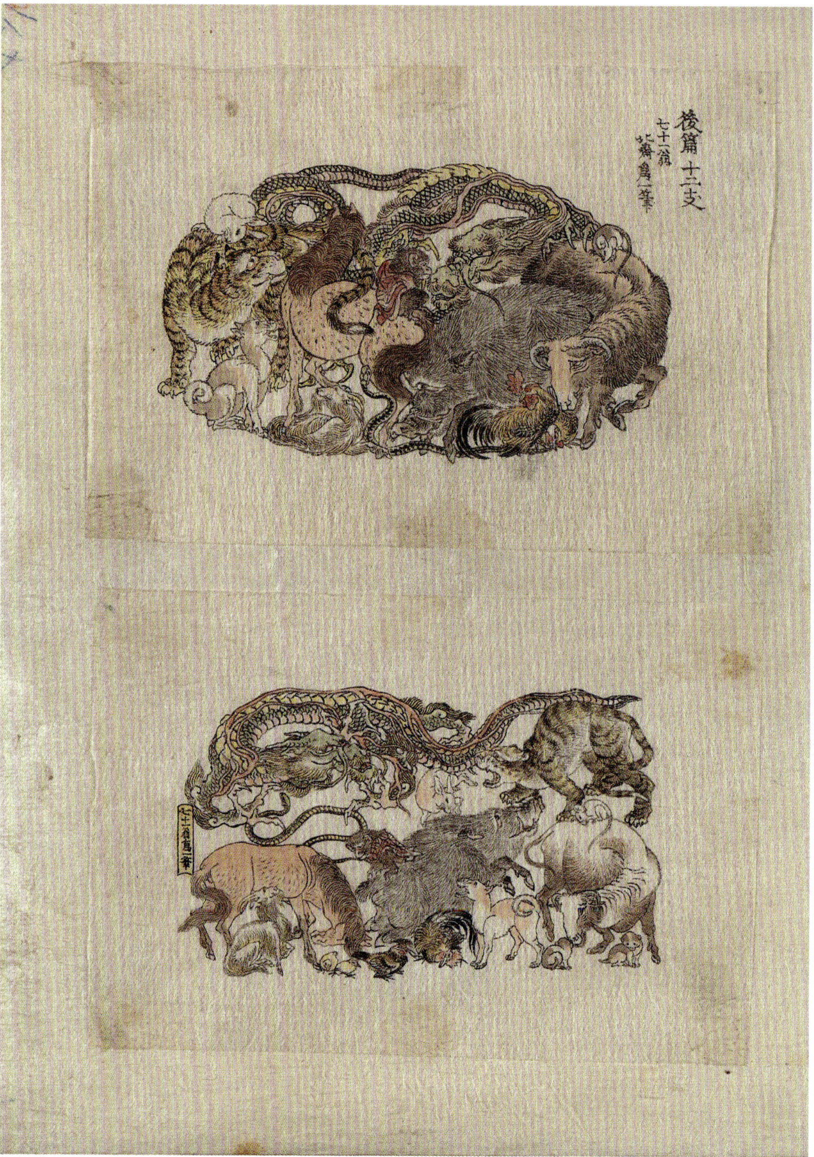

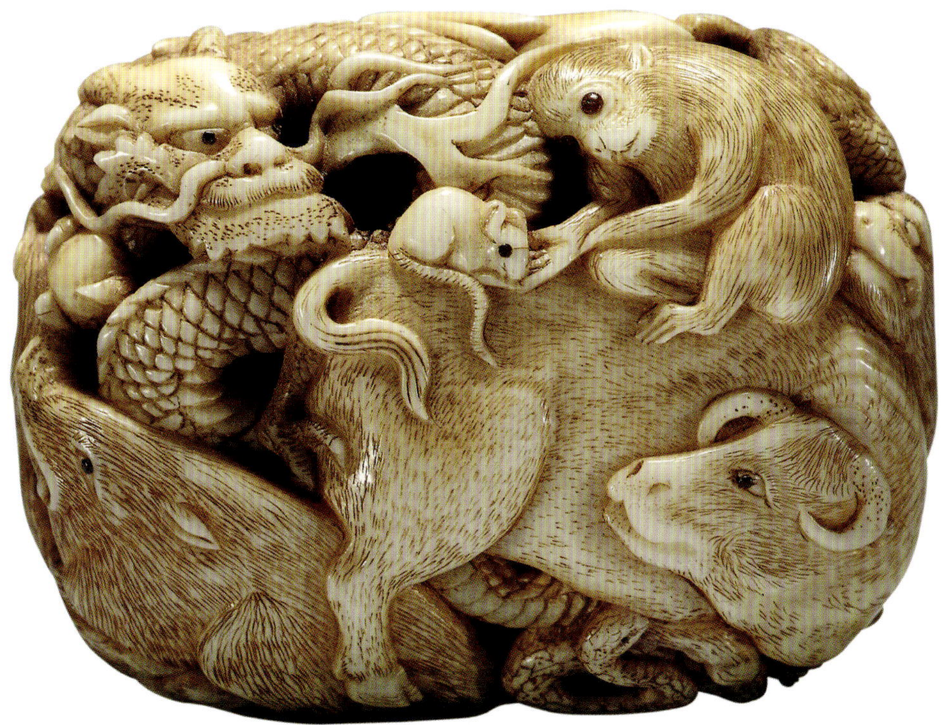

173
Netsuke of twelve zodiac animals

About 1880
Unsigned (style of Kaigyokusai Masatsugu, 1813–1892)
Netsuke, ivory with eyes inlaid in different colours of
horn, 2.8 × 3.4 cm
Literature: Iijima 1999, pp. 131–132; Noriko Tsuchiya,
Netsuke: 100 Miniature Masterpieces from Japan, London,
BMP, 2014, p. 107
British Museum, F.1073, given by Sir Augustus
Wollaston Franks

Netsuke were one of the well-dressed Edo man's key
accessories, and the custom of wearing one with the
kimono continued into the early Meiji era (1868–1912).
As an artist interested in all aspects of daily life,
Hokusai produced model drawings not only for his
students (cats 174, 175), but also for netsuke carvers
and other craftspeople trained in the decorative arts.
When very young, the Osaka netsuke carver Kaigyokusai
Masatsugu (1813–1892) reportedly met Hokusai during
the artist's visit to the city in 1817, evidence perhaps
that Hokusai took time to see at least one of the city's
netsuke-carving studios. Similar in concept to two of
Hokusai's designs (cat. 172) and carved in Kaigyokusai's
style, this netsuke combines the twelve animals of the
East Asian zodiac (Japanese: *jūnishi*), from rat to boar,
in a miniature menagerie. The rat sits on the back of
the ox in a reference to a Buddhist story: as the animals
approached the Buddha for a sermon, the rat riding
the ox leaped ahead and became the first to greet the
master, and is therefore first in the zodiac cycle. AH

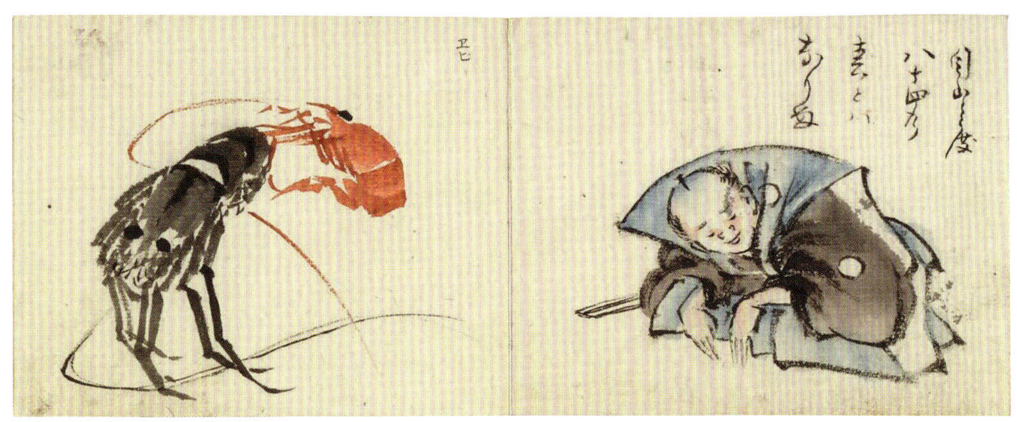

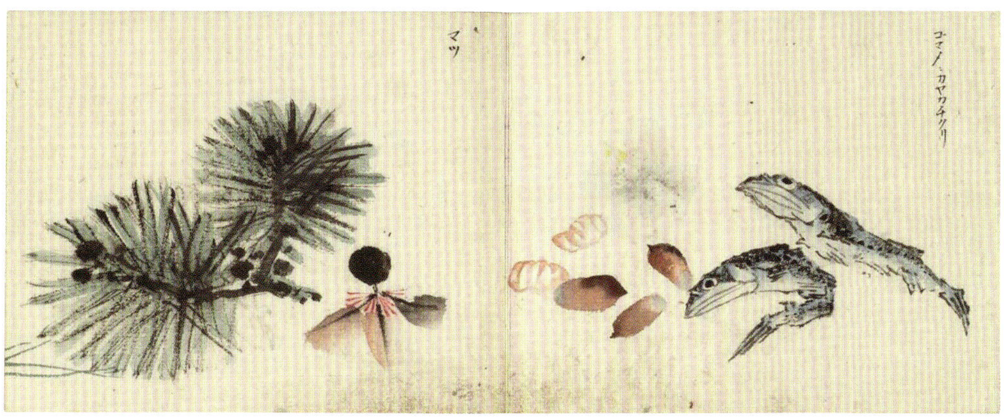

174

Album of model paintings

Spring 1843
Unsigned (attributed to Hokusai)
Folding album, ink and colour on paper, 12.1 × 15.0 cm
(covers)
Literature: Ōta 1985, no. 570; Nagata 2000,
nos 262–276
Ōta Memorial Museum of Art, Tokyo

The paintings in this album are models for students
to copy. Such albums are rare compared to the number
of woodblock-printed brush drawing manuals that
Hokusai designed, notably *Hokusai's Sketches* (*Hokusai
manga*, cats 164, 165). Introducing the album is a
portrait of Hokusai bowing down in gratitude for
having reached the spring of his eighty-fourth year.
The paintings are brushed quickly and spontaneously.
While the scenes are independent of each other, there
is an overall unity to the brushwork, which suggests
that they were done at the same time. The subjects
are familiar from Hokusai's other works: lobster,
dried chestnut, aubergine, iris and so on. The album
demonstrates the master fluently painting examples
at the request of his students. Its purpose is similar
to a handscroll of model paintings in the Freer-Sackler
Gallery, Smithsonian Institution, Washington, DC,
dated 1839 (F1902.42, Freer-Sackler 2006, vol. 2, p. 87). MR

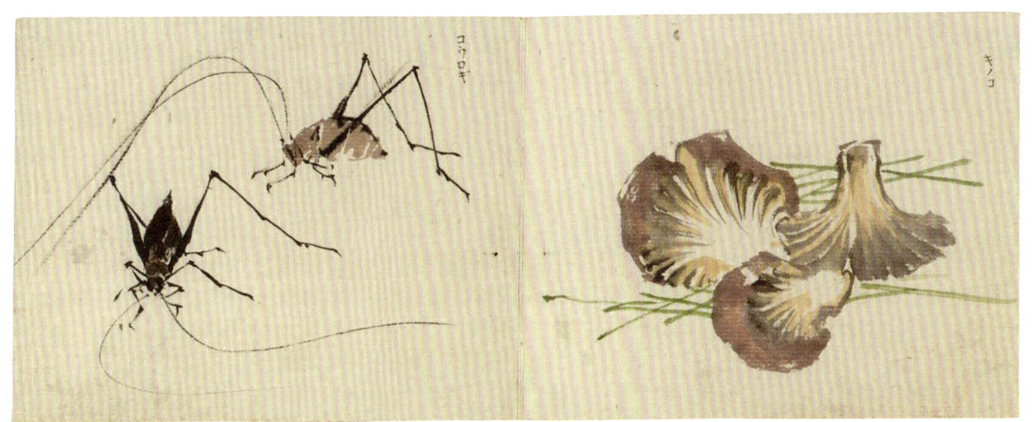
コホロギ
キノコ

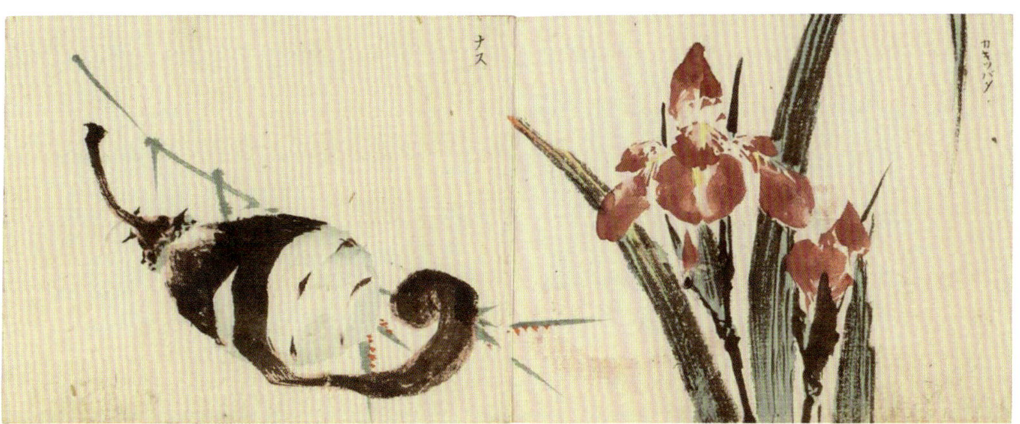
ナス
カキツバタ

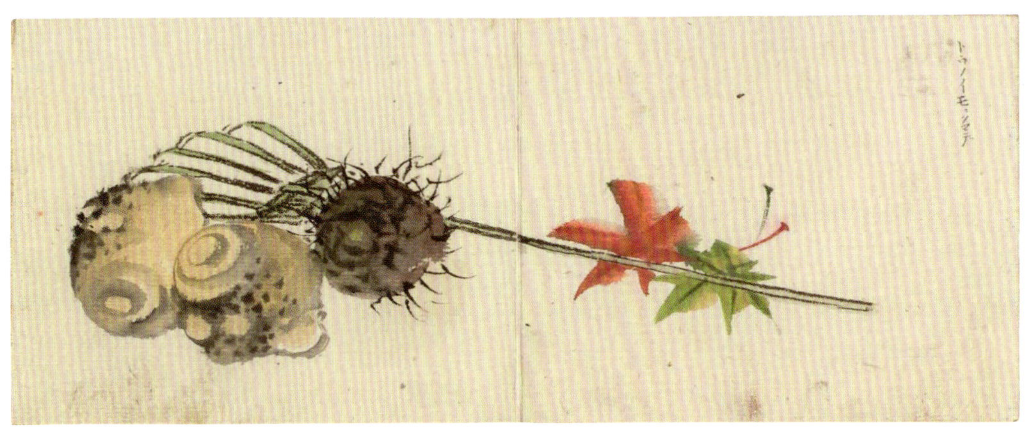
トウノイモ・タケノコ

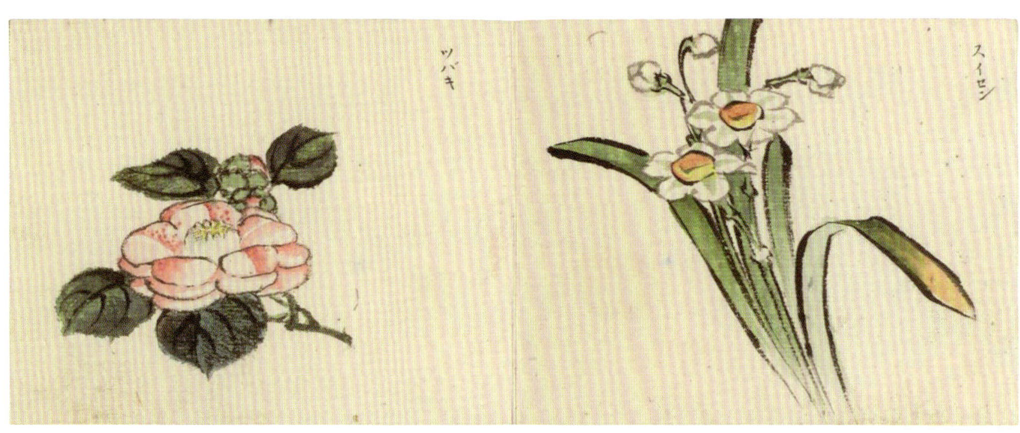
ツバキ
スイセン

Album of model paintings

1835–1836
Signature: Saki no Hokusai Iitsu aratame / Gakyō
rōjin Manji hitsu ('Brush of Manji, old man crazy
to paint, changed from Iitsu, the former Hokusai')
Seal: Mt Fuji above trigram
Folding album, ink and colour on paper,
25.0 × 34.0 cm
Literature: NU 1982, nos 27–30; Tōbu 1993, no. 65;
Itō 2000; Hokusaikan 2015, pp. 106–115
Hokusai Museum, Obuse

In their adverts in printed books, publishers offered
albums of model paintings for students to copy.
According to Hokusai's biographer, in 1835–1836,
during the Tenpō famine, the artist relied on income
from such albums to ensure that he would at least have
enough to eat (Iijima 1999, pp. 163–164; and see Clark
essay, pp. 25–26). Very few have survived, but two other
almost identical examples of this album are known.
The paintings are done on thin paper, raising the
possibility that the three similar versions were traced
from preparatory drawings and then individually
coloured (Itō 2000, pp. 252–253). Certainly, they display
the delicacy of touch that characterized Hokusai's style
in his later years. 'Frog and strawberry geranium'
(above) conveys the glistening texture of frog skin,
while 'Dried salmon and mice' (below) demonstrates
the artist's extraordinary powers of observation. A copy
of the latter painting is known by Hokusai's pupil
Hokkei (1780–1850; Carpenter 2005, p. 143). MR

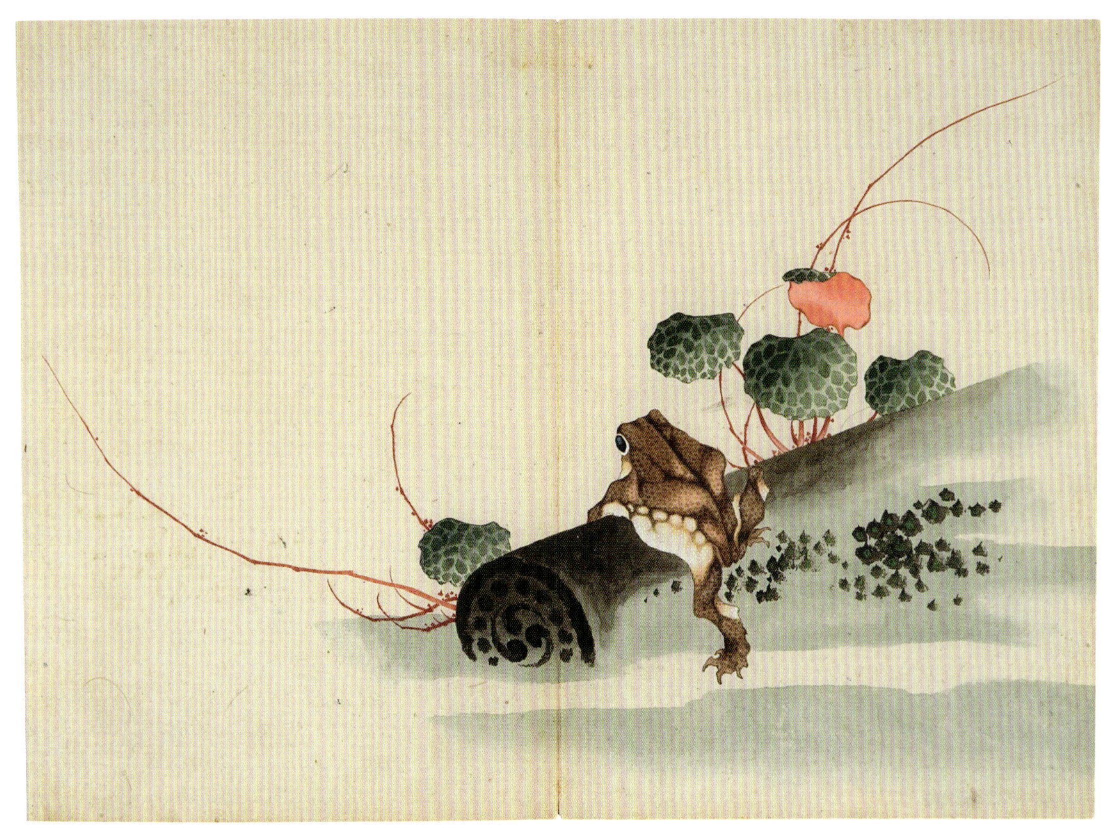

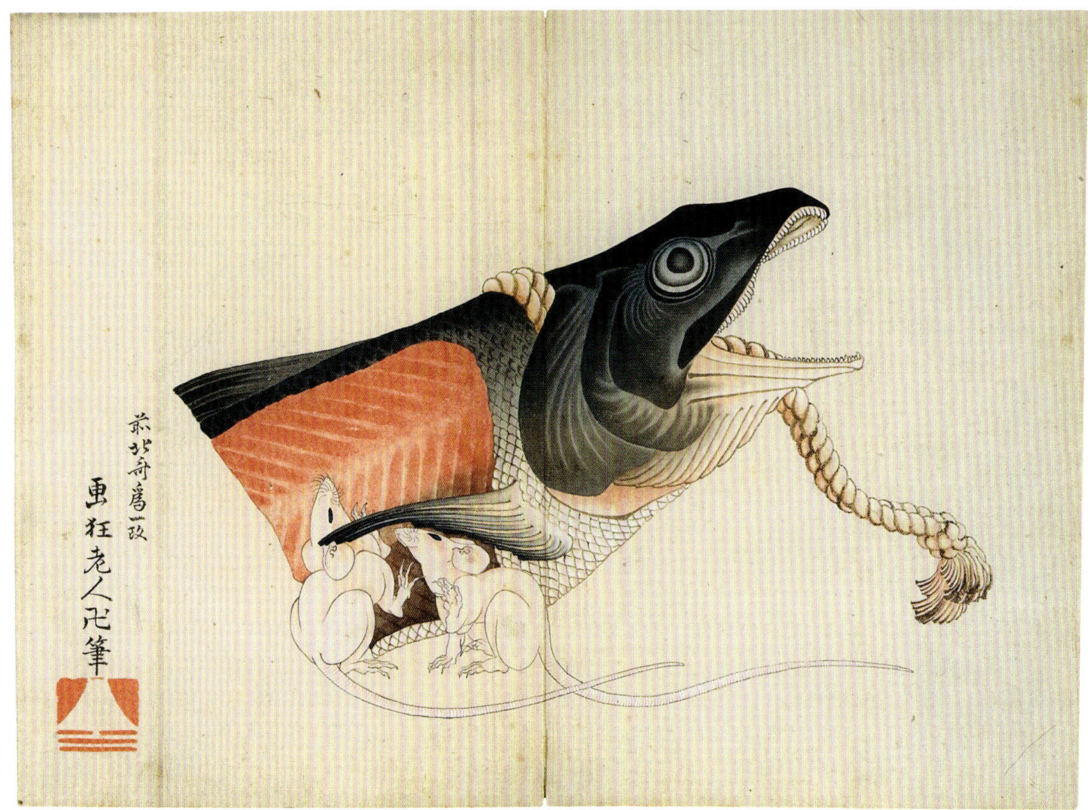

前北齋為一改
画狂老人卍筆

One Hundred Views of Mt Fuji (*Fugaku hyakkei*)

1834, 1835, about 1849 (?)
Signature: Nanajūgo rei / saki no Hokusai Iitsu aratame / Gakyō rōjin Manji hitsu ('Brush of Manji, old man crazy to paint, changed from the former Hokusai Iitsu, aged seventy-five') (vol. 1)
Seal: Mt Fuji above trigram
Illustrated book, woodblock, 3 vols, published by Nishimuraya Yūzō and others, 22.5 × 15.5 cm (covers)
Literature: Suzuki 1986; Smith 1988; HK 42, Oct. 2008, pp. 5–61
Uragami Mitsuru collection, Japan

Hokusai's greatest illustrated book, this three-volume work in fact offers 102 views of Mt Fuji, often in eccentric compositions and contexts that far overstep the limits of conventional representations. Miraculously fine carving of the printing blocks, supervised by Egawa Tomekichi, is matched in early editions by exquisitely subtle printing effects. The sheet print series *Thirty-Six Views of Mt Fuji* (about 1831–1833, cats 41–65) had proved popular and overran to forty-six designs. Indeed, an early advert by publisher Nishimuraya Yohachi in 1831 had already predicted a likely total of more than one hundred Fuji views (pp. 108–109). So there is the sense that *One Hundred Views* is the continuation of the same project, packaged in a new form.

The book also signalled a major relaunch of Hokusai's own life and art. From the colophon of volume 1, published in the third month of 1834 onwards, the artist now regularly uses the new art names Gakyō rōjin ('old man crazy to paint') and Manji ('ten thousand things', that is, 'everything'). He also adopts a new painting seal of Mt Fuji above the ancient Chinese trigram for 'lake' from the *Book of Changes* (the *I Ching*), the combination forming a hexagram which has been interpreted, poignantly, to mean 'decrease' (Chinese: *sun*; Japanese: *son*). 'Fuji' is regularly written in the book using characters meaning 'not two', that is, 'peerless'. Another popular etymology is 'not death'. It is clear that Hokusai regarded Fuji as a powerful potential source of immortality, not necessarily following the beliefs of the religious confraternities known as *Fuji-kō* (Fuji cult), but as one element of a personal collection of powerful talismans of longevity, which also included the North Star.

The *One Hundred Views* is famous for including Hokusai's personal credo, in which he reviews his long career to date (he was seventy-five) and looks forward to an even more artistically accomplished, deeper old age (see fig. 7). This was why he needed to harness the power of Fuji: he was determined to get better and better, even as he grew older and older:

From the age of six I had a penchant for copying the form of things, and from about fifty, my pictures were frequently published; but until the age of seventy, nothing I drew was worthy of notice. At seventy-three years, I was somewhat able to fathom the growth of plants and trees, and the structure of birds, animals, insects and fish. Thus when I reach eighty years, I hope to have made increasing progress, and at ninety to see further into the underlying principles of things, so that at one hundred years I will have achieved a divine state in my art, and at one hundred and ten, every dot and every stroke will be as though alive. Those of you who live long enough, bear witness that these words of mine are not false. (Trans. Henry D. Smith II.)

The exact publication date of volume 3 is debated. Consensus is growing that the key (outline) blocks were already cut by 1835, but that actual publication was delayed until around the death of Hokusai in 1849. The delay arose from the business failure of publisher Nishimuraya Yohachi who was, it seems, unable to weather the social and economic crisis resulting from the widespread famine of the mid-1830s.

Preserved in the Musée Guimet, Paris, is a wonderful group of Hokusai's working brush drawings for six of the double-page illustrations, mainly for volume 2 (cats 177–182). These give a fascinating insight into his method, which seems to have been to rough out in red, before switching to black as the design began to gel. A cleaner and neater tracing could be made by placing a thin sheet of paper over this: the black lines would show through, but not the red. Finally Hokusai would arrive at a line-perfect block-ready drawing (*hanshita-e*; see cat. 31). Hokusai frequently added pentimenti – corrections on small fragments of paper, which could also be used to move figures around within a composition, to see which arrangement worked best (cat. 177). See also the commentaries to cats 35, 38. TC

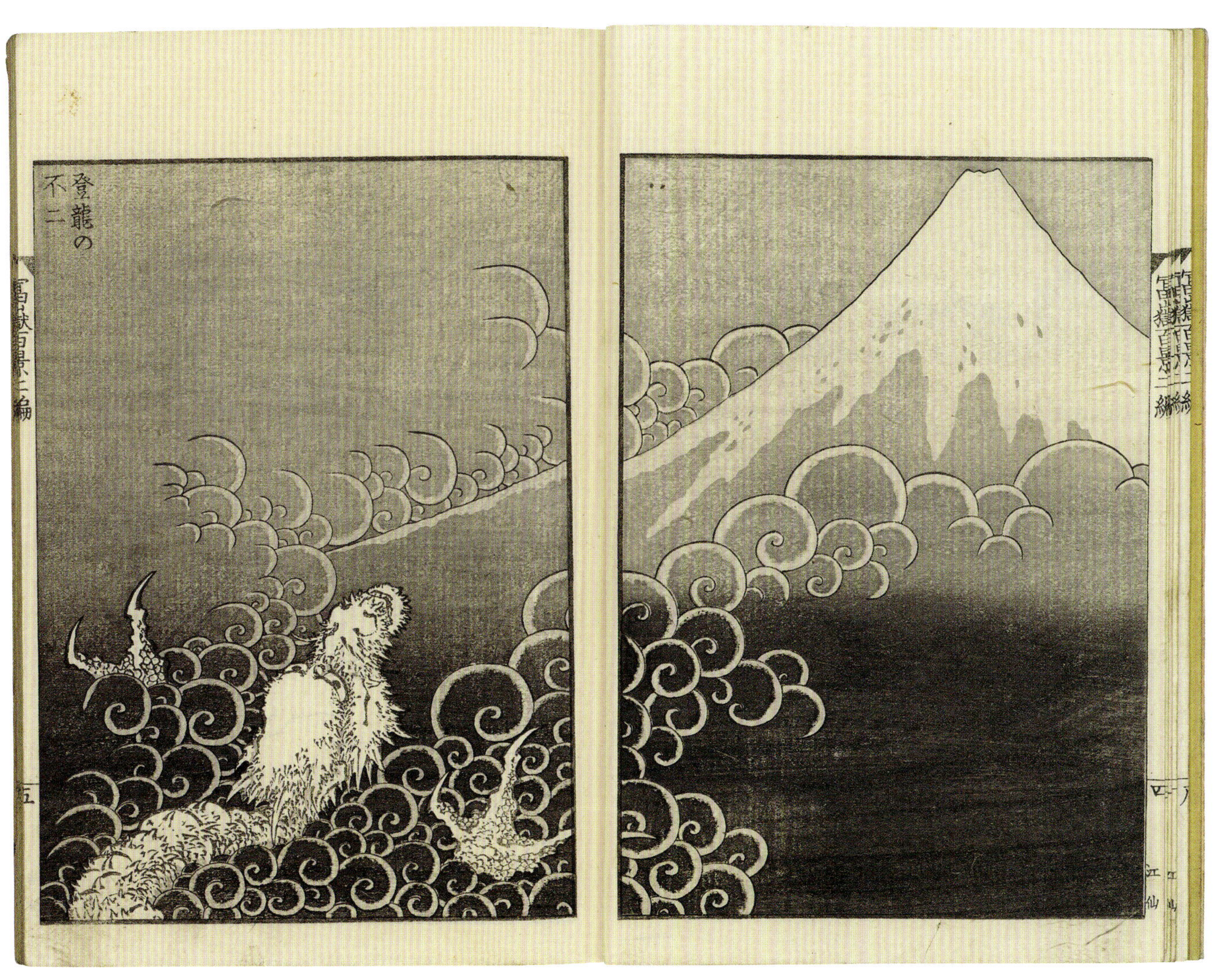
登龍の
不二
冨嶽百景二編
冨嶽百景二編
江仙

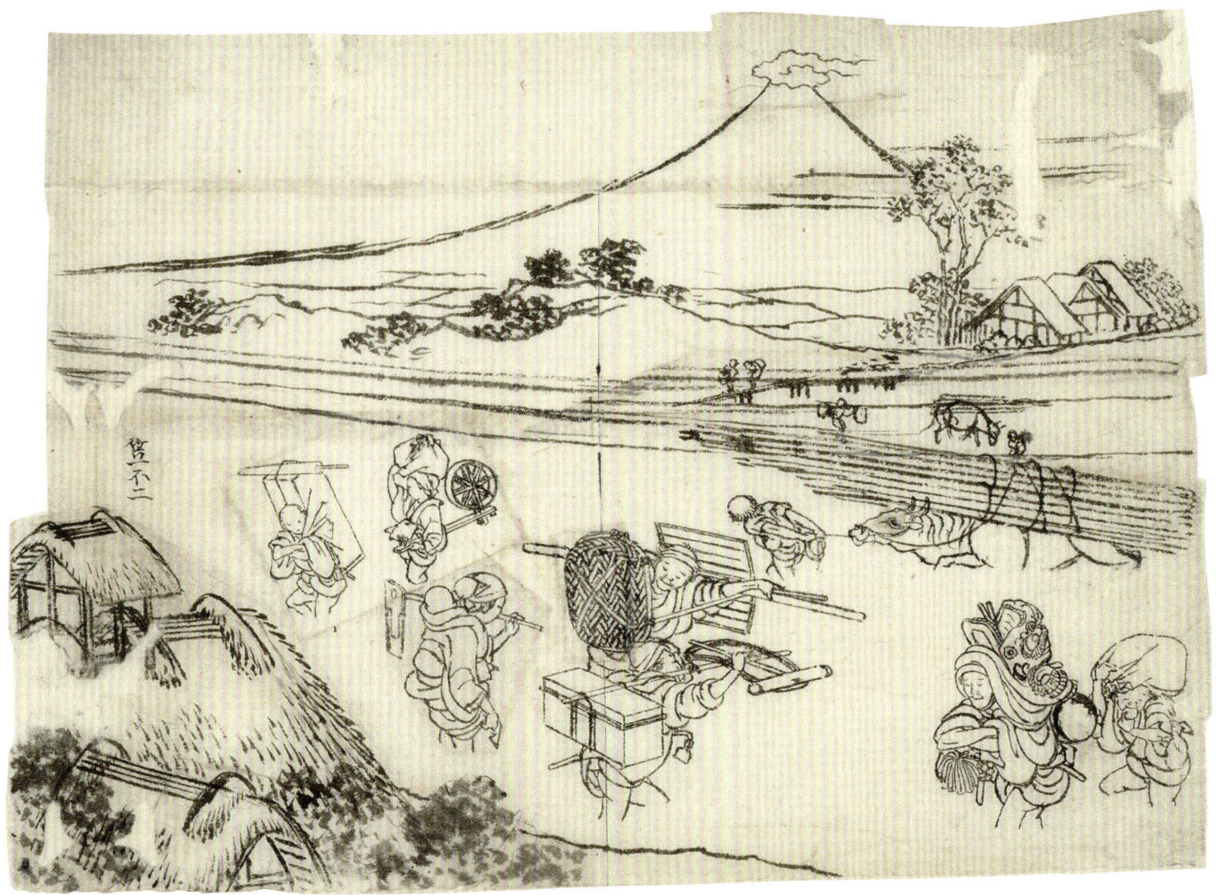

Fuji with a hat

About 1834
Unsigned (attributed to Hokusai)
Preparatory drawing, ink on paper, 17.8 × 24.4 cm
Provenance: Huguette Berès
Literature: Smith 1988, pp. 146–147; Guimet 2008,
nos 95, 101a
Musée national des arts asiatiques Guimet, Paris,
MA. 7061, acquired 2002

The peak of Fuji is shown wearing a 'hat cloud'
(*kasa-gumo*). Country people are fording a wide river,
carrying panniers, hoes and even a spinning wheel;
oxen transport loads of poles. The figure at bottom
right is an itinerant performer of the lion dance,
his mask and costume on his back. As so often,
Hokusai focuses on the working lives of ordinary
people. (Drawing for vol. 1, 21 *verso* & 22 *recto*.) TC

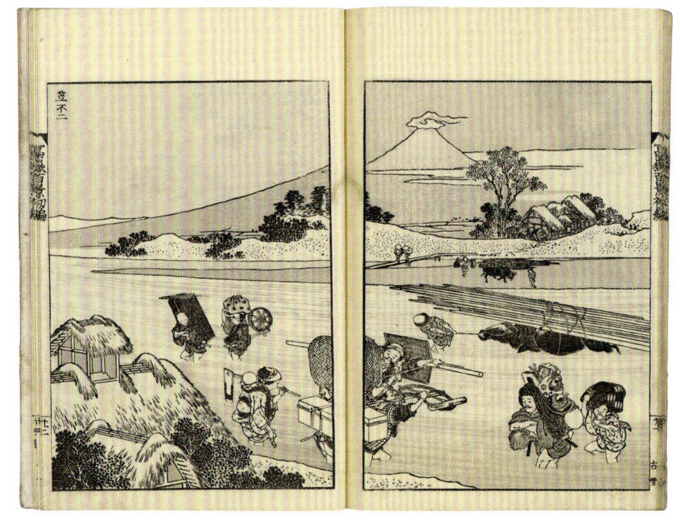

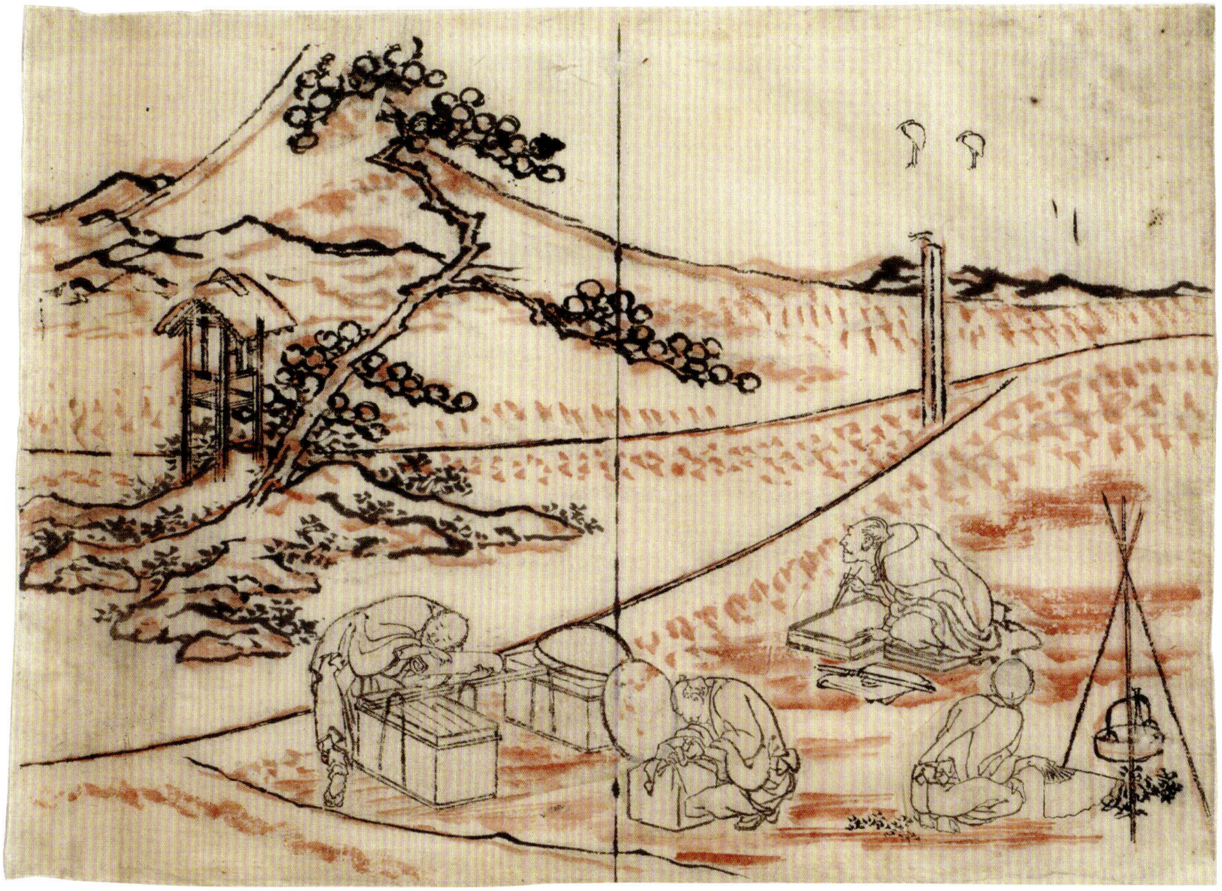

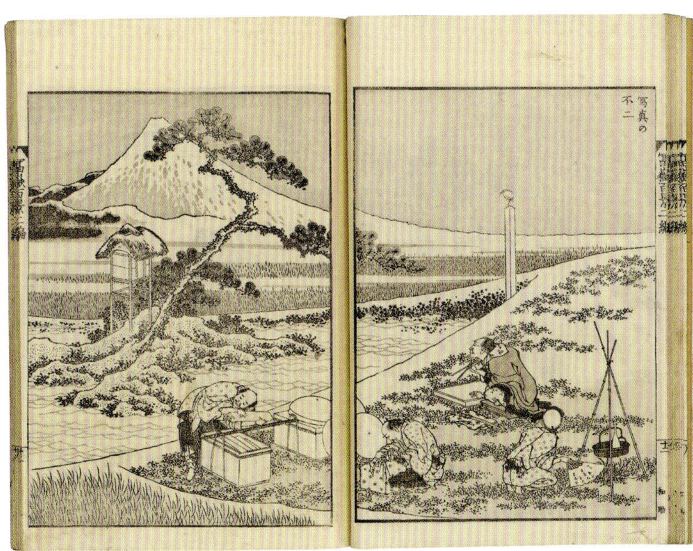

178

Drawing Fuji from life

About 1835
Unsigned (attributed to Hokusai)
Preparatory drawing, red and black ink on paper,
18.0 × 25.1 cm
Provenance: Henri Vever
Literature: Smith 1988, pp. 108–109; Guimet 2008,
nos 100a, 100b
Musée national des arts asiatiques Guimet, Paris,
EO.1455, given by Henri Vever, 1911
Osaka only

An artist of aristocratic demeanour – too grand to
be Hokusai himself – gazes at Mt Fuji, with twin brushes
poised to paint. The title literally means 'copying the
truth [*shashin*] of Fuji'. Three servants attend to luggage,
and heat saké over a fire. Hokusai tries out alternative
poses for the egret, which finally ends up perched on
the post. (Drawing for vol. 2, 12 *verso* & 13 *recto*.) TC

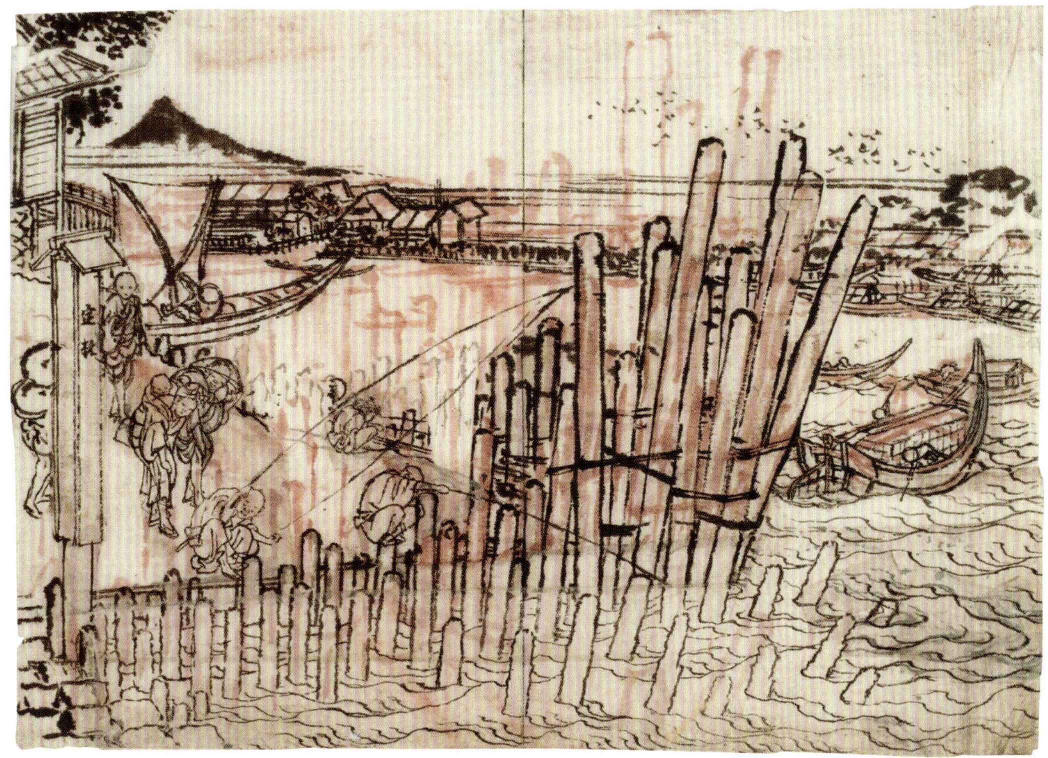

179

Fuji in evening sun, Shimadagahana

About 1835
Unsigned (attributed to Hokusai)
Preparatory drawing, red and black ink on paper,
18.2 × 25.4 cm
Provenance: Léon-Louis Weill; Huguette Berès
Literature: Smith 1988, pp. 102–103; RA 1991, no. 107;
Guimet 2008, nos 96, 101b
Musée national des arts asiatiques Guimet, Paris,
MA.7064, acquired 2002

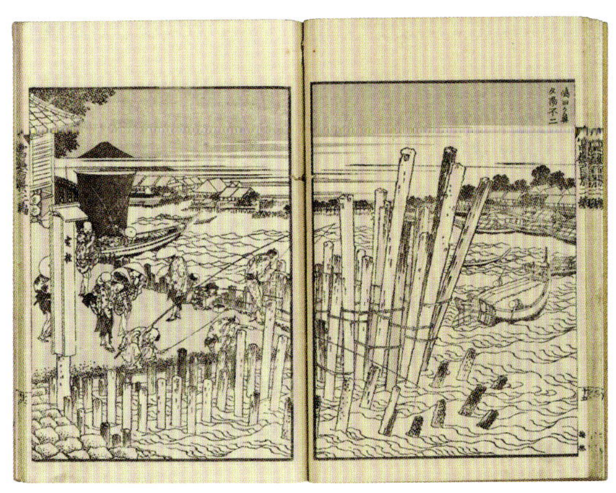

The 'Shimada point' of the title is not known, and
this is actually thought to be Hyappongui ('Hundred
pilings'), just upstream from Ryōgoku bridge, on the
east bank of the Sumida river in central Edo. People
are fishing and going calmly about their evening
business. There are obvious resonances with the
print 'Viewing sunset over Ryōgoku bridge' from
the *Thirty-Six Views* (cat. 56). Hokusai first thought to
make the posts of the breakwater even more prominent.
The variety of his lines and the surety of his touch are
breathtaking. (Drawing for vol. 2, 15 *verso* & 16 *recto*.) TC

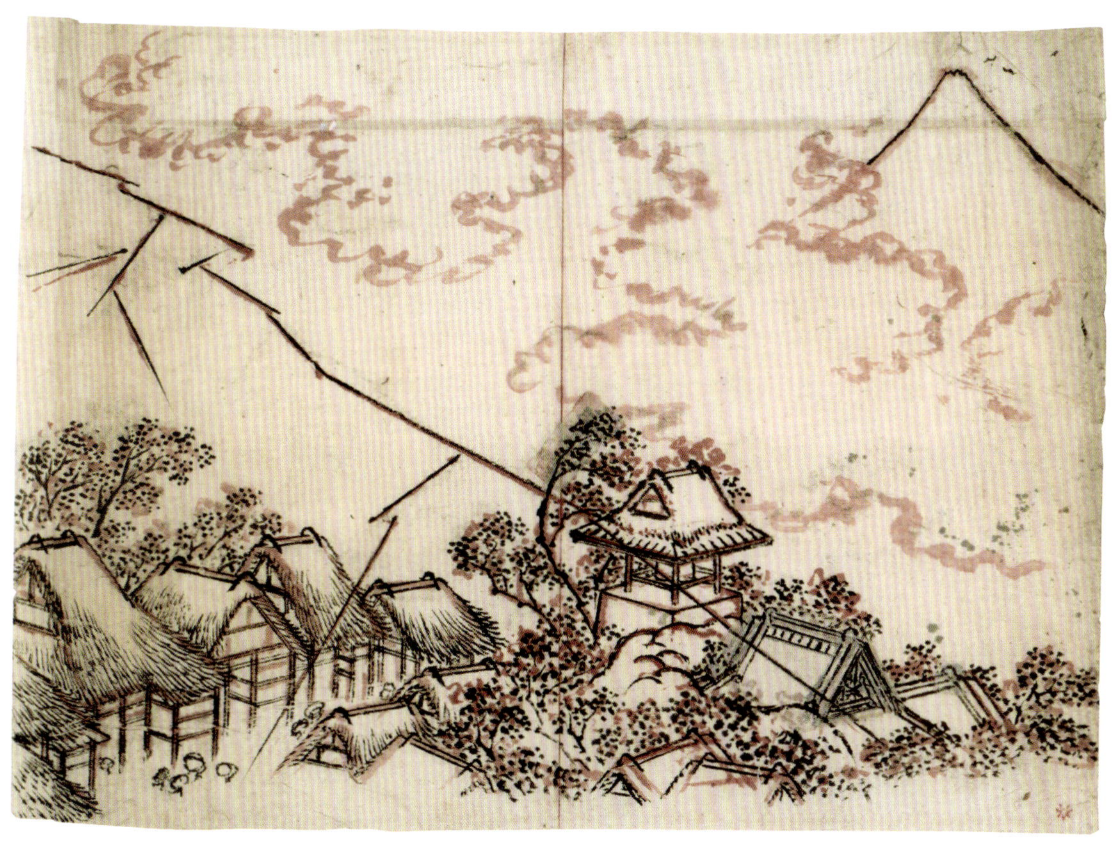

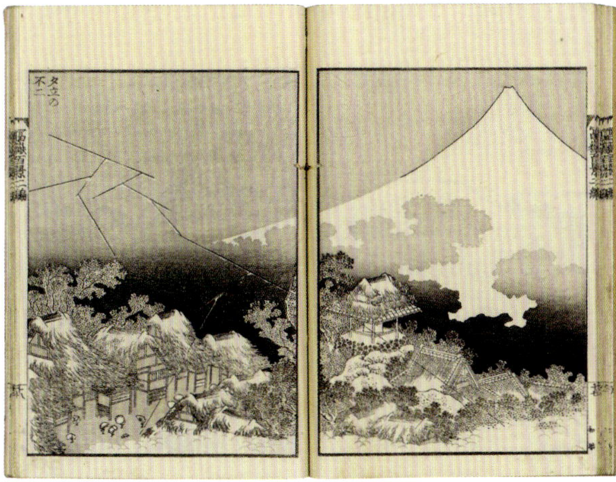

180
Fuji and evening shower

About 1835
Unsigned (attributed to Hokusai)
Preparatory drawing, red and black ink on paper,
18.3 × 24.5 cm
Provenance: Henri Vever; Huguette Berès
Literature: Hillier 1980a, no. 71; Smith 1988,
pp. 98–99; Guimet 2008, no. 97
Musée national des arts asiatiques Guimet, Paris,
MA.7062, acquired 2002

Villagers scatter for shelter during a sudden summer
storm as lightning strikes. Thatched roofs and trees are
buffeted by the squall. Like the print 'Sudden rain
beneath the summit' from the *Thirty-Six Views* (cat. 54),
the peak of Fuji appears impervious to the ragged
lightning on its lower slopes. The cloud formations are
much more extensive in the working drawing than in
the final book illustration. (Drawing for vol. 2, 17 *verso*
& 18 *recto*.) TC

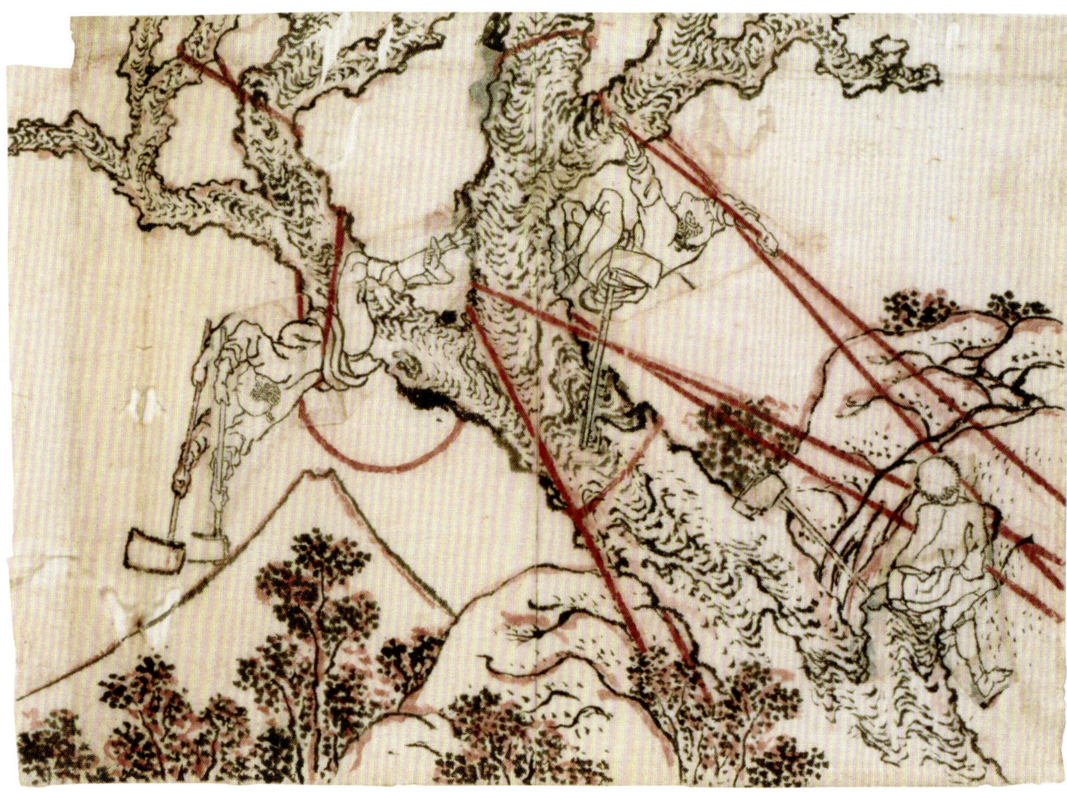

181

Fuji from the mountains of Tōtōmi province

About 1835
Unsigned (attributed to Hokusai)
Preparatory drawing, red and black ink on paper,
18.4 × 25.1 cm
Provenance: Henri Vever; Léon-Louis Weill;
Huguette Berès
Literature: Hillier 1980a, no. 72; Smith 1988,
pp. 96–97; Guimet 2008, nos 98a, 98b
Musée national des arts asiatiques Guimet, Paris,
MA.7065, acquired 2002
Osaka only

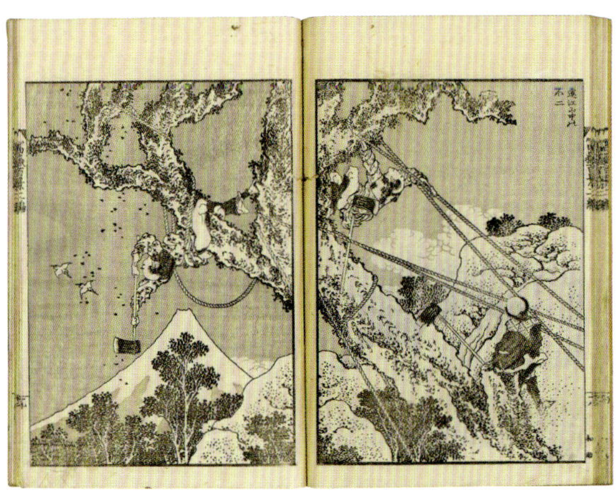

In a virtuoso composition, with Mt Fuji framed by
branches, bodies and ropes, three men with axes are
cutting down a gnarled dead tree, deep in the mountains
of Tōtōmi province (the west part of modern Shizuoka
prefecture). Dense dots and graphic lines spin a rich
texture of leaves, bark and rocks. In the finished book
illustration the acrobatic axeman's strokes send wood
chips flying into the air. (Drawing for vol. 2, 18 *verso*
& 19 *recto*.) TC

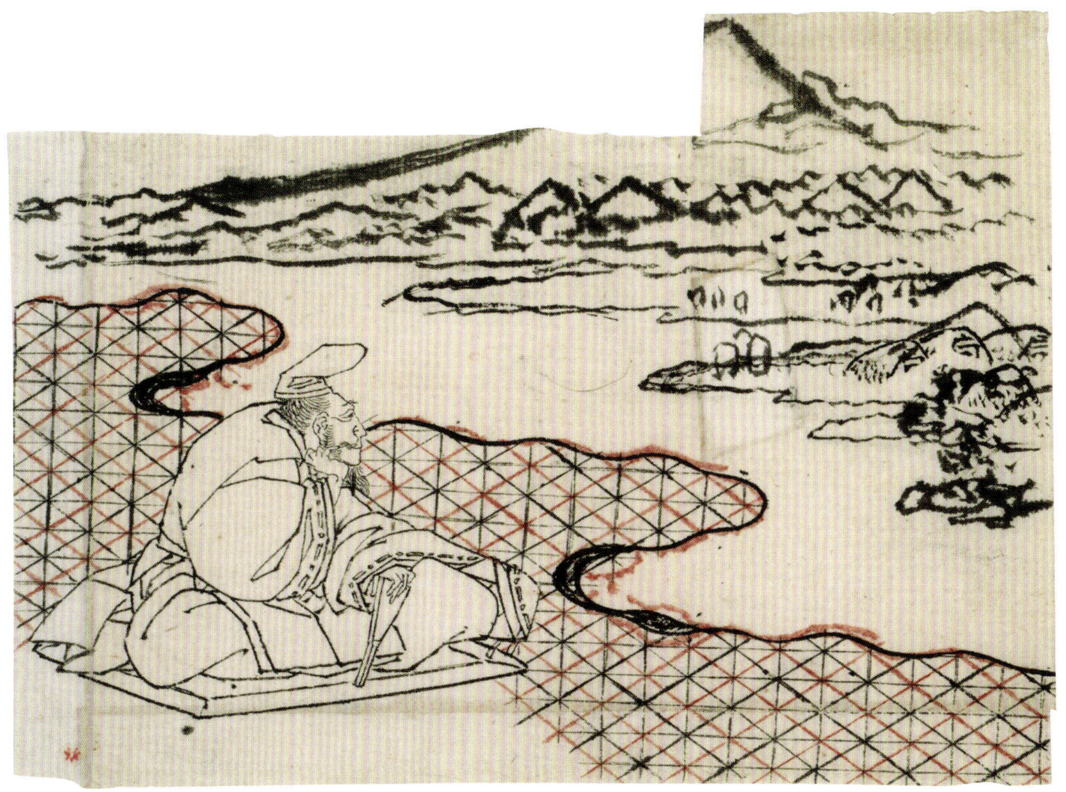

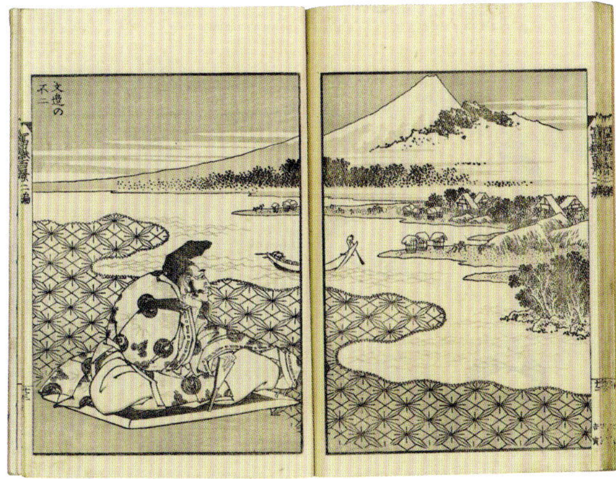

182

Fuji of letters

About 1835
Unsigned (attributed to Hokusai)
Preparatory drawing, red and black ink on paper,
18.7 × 25.3 cm
Provenance: Henri Vever; Huguette Berès
Literature: Smith 1988, pp. 88–89; Guimet 2008,
no. 99
Musée national des arts asiatiques Guimet, Paris,
MA.7060, acquired 2002

The meandering, decorative cloud – more elaborate in
the finished book illustration – emphasizes the historical
disjunction between the courtier poet of old, gazing
raptly at Fuji, and the middle-ground scene of modern
salt-making on Tago beach. The poet is surely Yamabe
no Akahito (active AD 724–736), whose best-known verse
celebrates Fuji: 'As I set out on the beach of Tago, and
look, / I see the snow constantly falling / on the high
peak of Fuji, / white as mulberry cloth' (trans. Joshua
Mostow). (Drawing for vol. 2, 22 *verso* & 23 *recto*.) TC

Portraits of Hokusai

Artists in traditional schools generally did not produce self-portraits, or indeed many portraits of other artists. The 'floating world' (ukiyo-e) school from which Hokusai emerged was in any case particularly low in social prestige. However, illustrated books of 'playful literature' (*gesaku*) of the late 1700s and early 1800s began regularly to include small caricature portraits of the authors and artists integrated into the stories, and there are several of these 'self-portraits' from Hokusai's early career. In the early 1800s, more extensive biographical accounts of authors and artists started to be written, which led to a new interest in recording their appearance. Such are the portraits of Hokusai in old age by fellow floating world artists Utagawa Kuniyoshi (1797–1861, cat. 185) and Keisai Eisen (1790–1848, cats 186, 187). And Roger Keyes has suggested that one of the block-ready drawings created by Hokusai in 1838 for the series *One Hundred Poems by One Hundred Poets, Explained by the Nurse* (Keyes Preface, fig. 2) includes allegorical portraits of three ages of the artist.

In addition to these more formal efforts, we have a number of informal sketches from Hokusai's letters. About forty letters are either extant or were historically recorded, mostly written in the 1830s and 1840s, when the artist was in his seventies and eighties. Hokusai was in the habit of including tiny comic sketches and picture rebuses, several of which take the form of 'self-portraits'. One also includes a single quick sketch of the face of his daughter Eijo (artist name Ōi, about 1800–after 1857; Paris 2014, no. 537). It is no coincidence that these all have to do with negotiations with publishers and others about commissions and fees. Particularly lively and engaging is the self-portrait sketch that Hokusai made when he was eighty-three years old (cat. 184).

Quite different in feeling is a large and respectful preparatory drawing in red and black ink, with working corrections, which shows the aged Hokusai full-length, leaning on a walking stick (cat. 189). This drawing was first recorded around 1900. It contrasts with Hokusai's own modest, self-deprecating portraits in his letters, and so may be by a close pupil. Certainly, a related head and shoulders portrait was used as the frontispiece of Iijima Kyoshin's biography, published in 1893, and has become the face by which the artist has subsequently been known to the world. Also in preparation for the 1893 biography, Hokusai's pupil Tsuyuki Kōshō (Iitsu III, died after 1893) made a sketch from memory of his visit to the humble lodgings of Hokusai and Eijo in the early 1840s (cat. 193). Maddeningly – and surely out of respect for his aged master – Tsuyuki partially hides Hokusai's face behind a pillar. TC

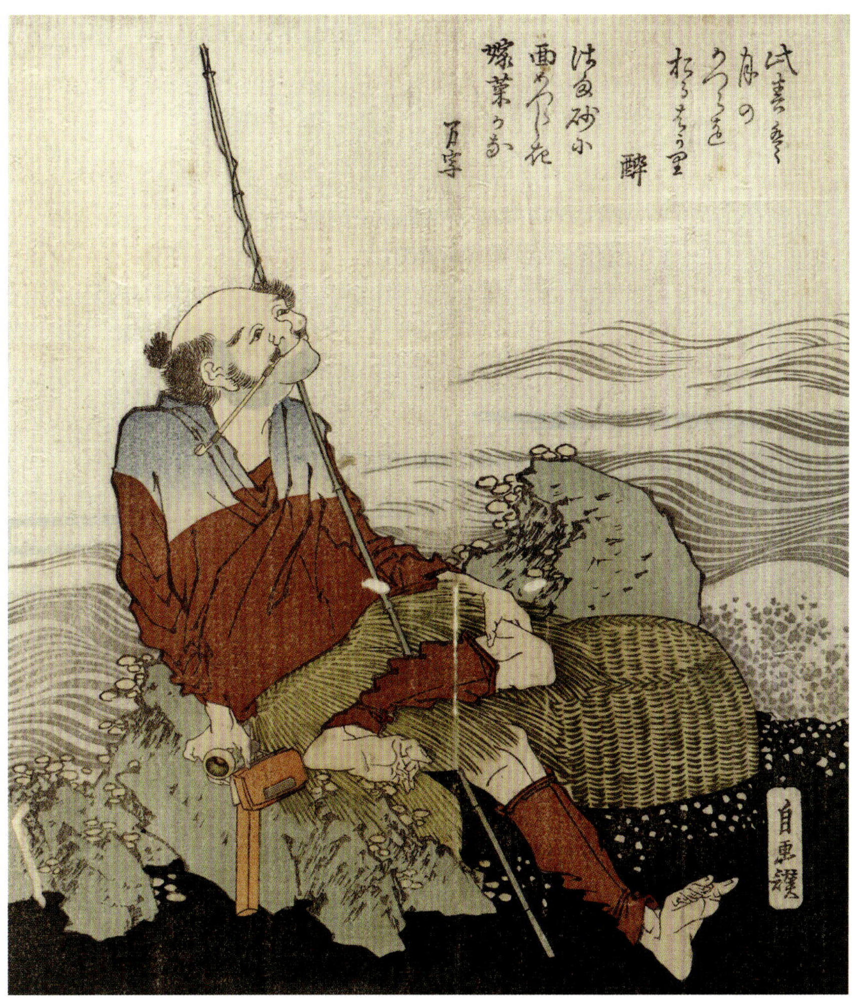

Fisherman seated on a rock

Mid-1820s (?)
Signature: Jigasan ('Drawn and inscribed by myself')
Inscribed poems signed Ei, Manji
Surimono, colour woodblock with metallic pigment and
embossing, 21.8 × 18.4 cm
Provenance: Arthur Morrison
Literature: Forrer 1988, no. 409; Kubota 2015, no. 17;
Keyes & Morse 2015, no. 1595
British Museum, 1906,1220,0.479

Kono haru wa / tsuki no katsura o / oru bakari, Ei
This spring / we broke a branch from / the cassia tree
on the moon, Ei
Hama suna ni / tsura mezurashiki / yomena kana, Manji
How rare for bride asters / to make an appearance /
on the sandy shore, Manji

In this collaboration between father and daughter, Eijo
signed her verse, punningly, Ei ('Tipsy'), while Hokusai
signs his 'Manji', after making reference to 'bride asters',
an autumn flower. Hokusai adopted Manji as his
principal art name with the publication of *One Hundred
Views of Mt Fuji* (from 1834, cat. 176), but used it
frequently from the late 1810s as a poetry name when
composing light comic verse (*senryū*). From 1830, he
regularly and effectively incorporated Prussian blue in
his prints, but here he has employed subtle indigo blue,
as in other square *surimono* of the 1820s, suggesting a
possible date for the work. Eijo's mention of breaking
a branch from a cassia tree is a reference to great
achievement. Perhaps this *surimono* celebrates their joint
successes of the previous few years, which included the
'Dutch paintings' (cats 20–25) commissioned by von
Siebold. That Hokusai produced both the illustration
and one of the poems has led some to interpret the
fisherman as an idealized self-portrait, reflecting
Hokusai's longing for a simple life close to nature. MR

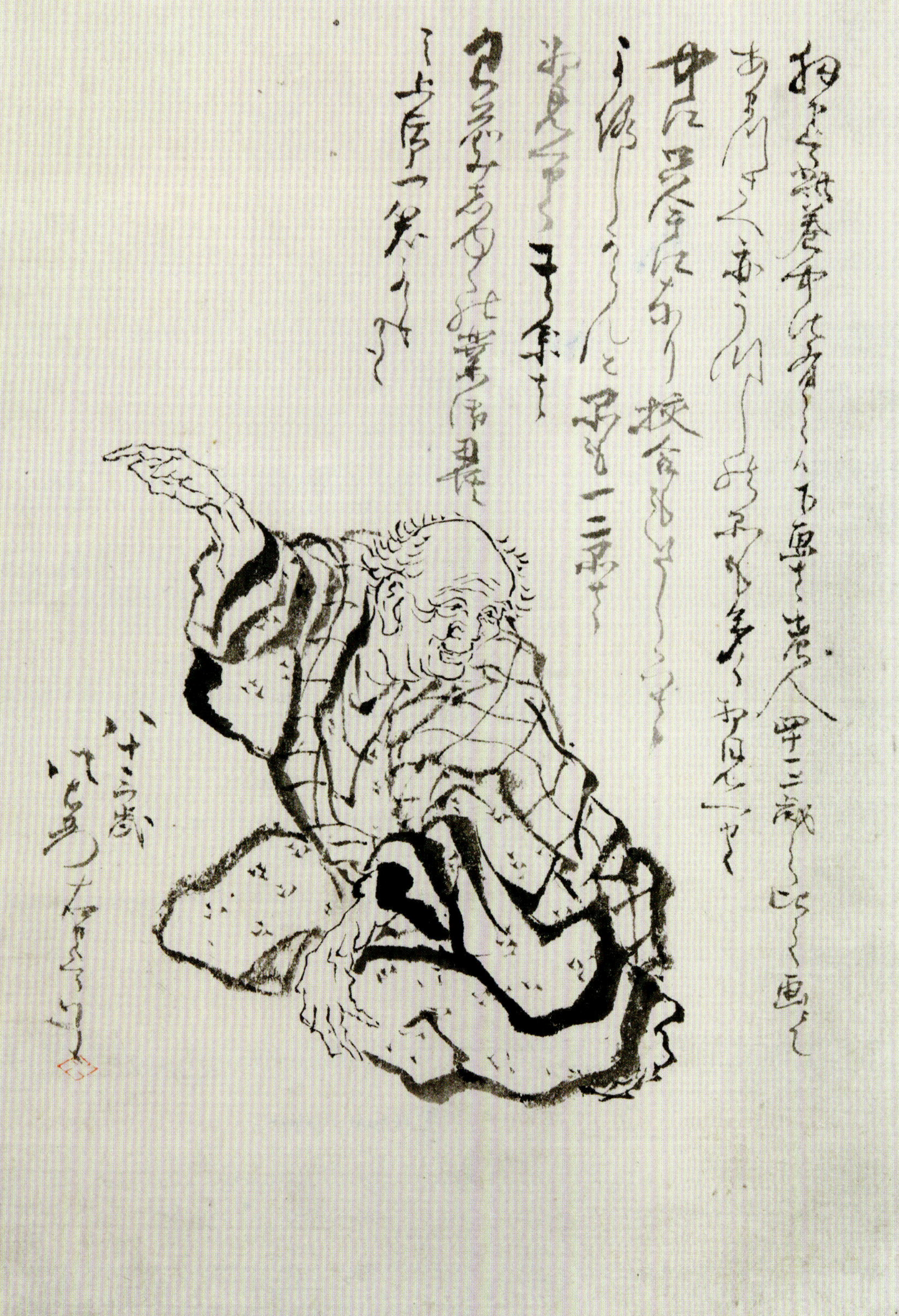

184
Self-portrait, aged eighty-three

1842
Signature: Hachijūsan sai / Hachiemon migi
mōshiage sōrō ijō ('The aforementioned recounted
by Hachiemon, [at] eighty-three years')
Seal: Manji
Drawing in a letter, ink on paper, 26.9 × 16.9 cm
Provenance: Kaneko Fusui; Felix Tikotin; F. Lieftinck
Literature: Ozaki 1934, p. 87; Forrer 1988, no. 483;
RA 1991, no. 111; Kobayashi 1996–1997, vol. 16,
pp. 184–195; Edo Tokyo 2007, no. 238
National Museum of Ethnology, Leiden,
RMV3513-1496

Hokusai includes a lively self-portrait in this letter sent
at the age of eighty-three to a publisher. The heavily
wrinkled visage is similar to that in cat. 189, and the
elderly artist seems to point at something energetically.
The text of the letter tells us that it is accompanied by
drawings that Hokusai had produced much earlier,
around the age of forty-one or forty-two, and which
he is now giving to the publisher unchanged. Hokusai
notes that the drawings were from a time when he had
not yet fully matured as an artist, and that they include
copies of other pictures, but he suggests that some might
still be of use if suitably 'edited' (*kyōgō*). The colophons
to volumes 1–10 (1814–1819) of *Hokusai's Sketches*
(*Hokusai manga*, cats 164, 165) also use the term 'edited
[or compiled] by' to identify several of Hokusai's pupils
who, by implication, seem to have been responsible
for gathering together the master's casual sketches for
publication as a teaching manual. This letter thus sheds
interesting additional light on Hokusai's approach
to book production. MR

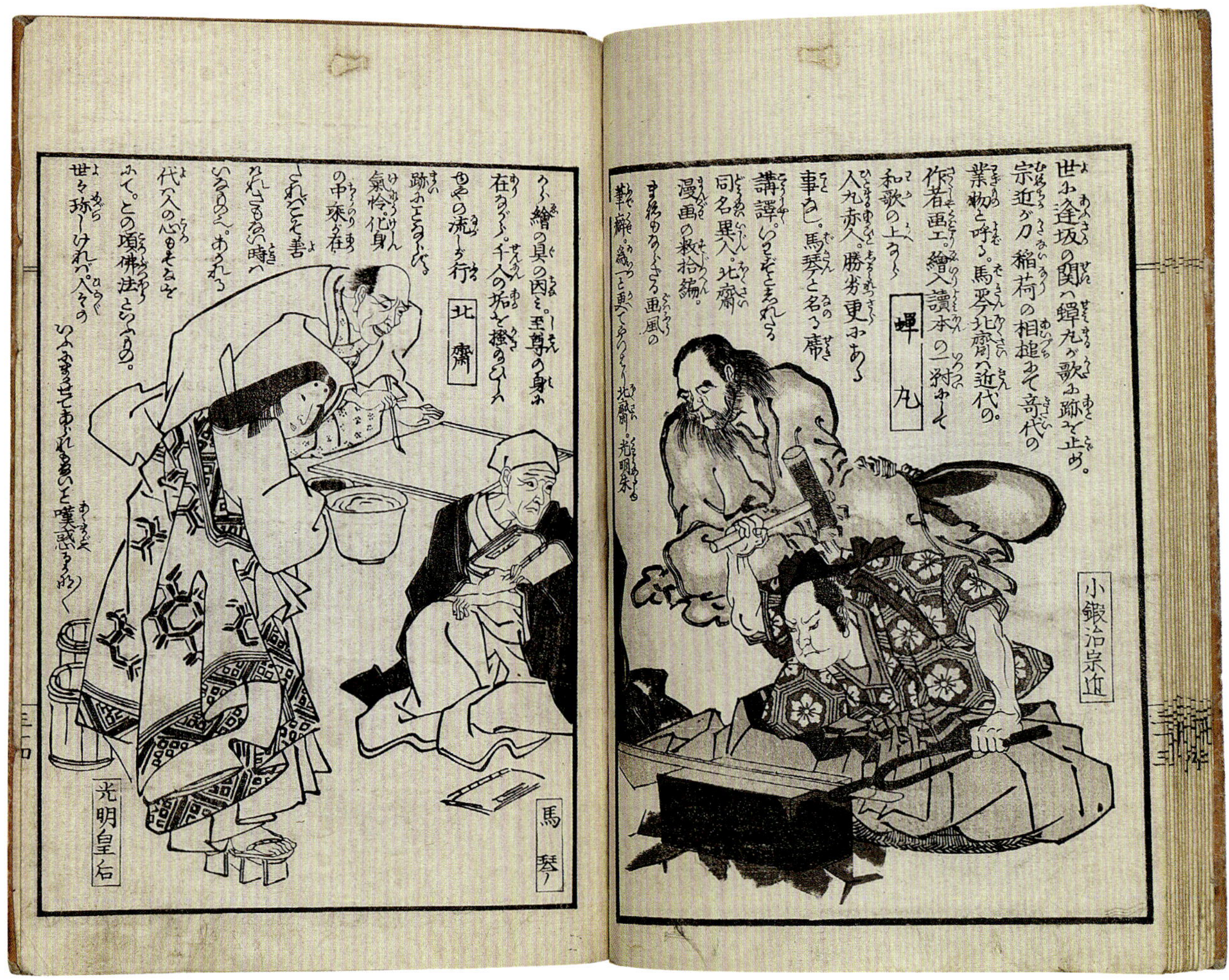

**Hanagasa Bunkyō (text, 1785–1860) &
Utagawa Kuniyoshi (illustrations, 1797–1861)
Portraits of Hokusai, Bakin and others
from *Biographies of Eccentric People
of Japan* (*Nihon kijin den*), vol. 2**

After 1848
Illustrated book, woodblock, published by Kawachiya
Mohei (Gungyokudō) and others, 22.6 × 14.2 cm
(covers)
Literature: Ozaki 1934, p. 88; Suzukī Jūzō, 'Kuniyoshi
ga *Nihon kijinden* no sujō: Ransetsu henjite Bakin to
kasu', *Shoshigaku geppō* 31, 1987, pp. 1–16; Paris 2014,
no. 225
Museum of Fine Arts, Boston, 1997.957, source
unidentifed
Osaka only

This two-volume book presents portraits and short
biographies of famous actors, authors and ukiyo-e
artists, past and present. Hanagasa Bunkyō (1785–1860)
was an author of popular fiction and kabuki dramas
(p. 22), while Utagawa Kuniyoshi (1797–1861) trained
under Utagawa Toyokuni I (1769–1825), but is said to
have regarded Hokusai as his master. Hokusai and the
author of popular fiction Takizawa Bakin (1767–1848)
are depicted together in the top and centre of the
image as 'the duo that produces illustrated adventure
stories [*yomihon*]'. The text praises Hokusai for having
'a style that no one else can imitate'. As in Tsuyuki
Kōshō's sketch (cat. 193), Hokusai appears,
characteristically, kneeling before a sheet of paper
and busy with his brush. His large ears accord with
various reports of the artist's appearance. MR

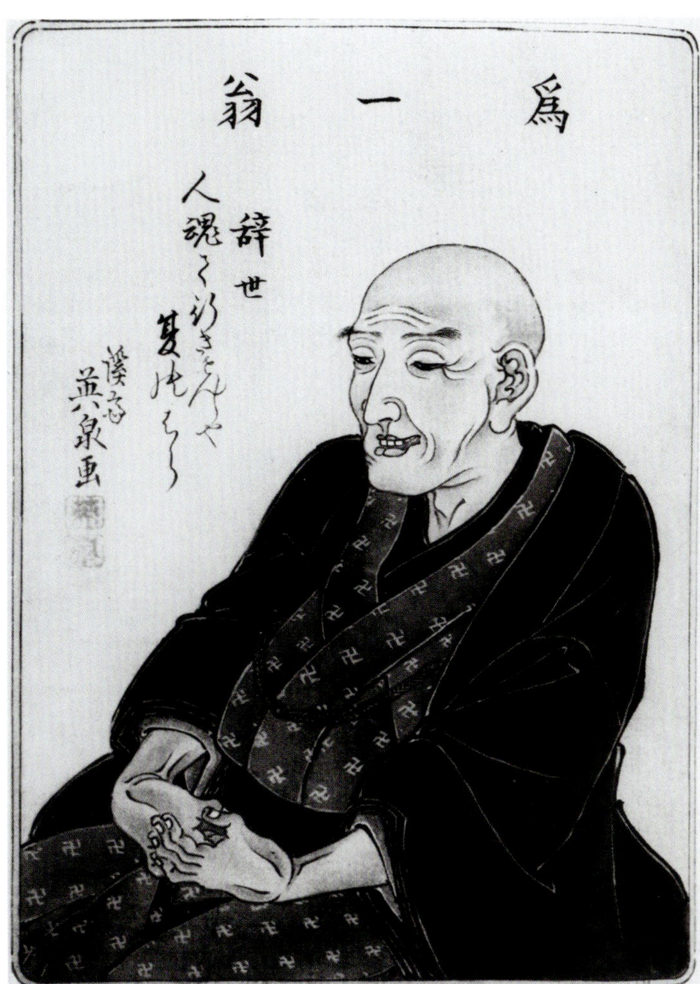

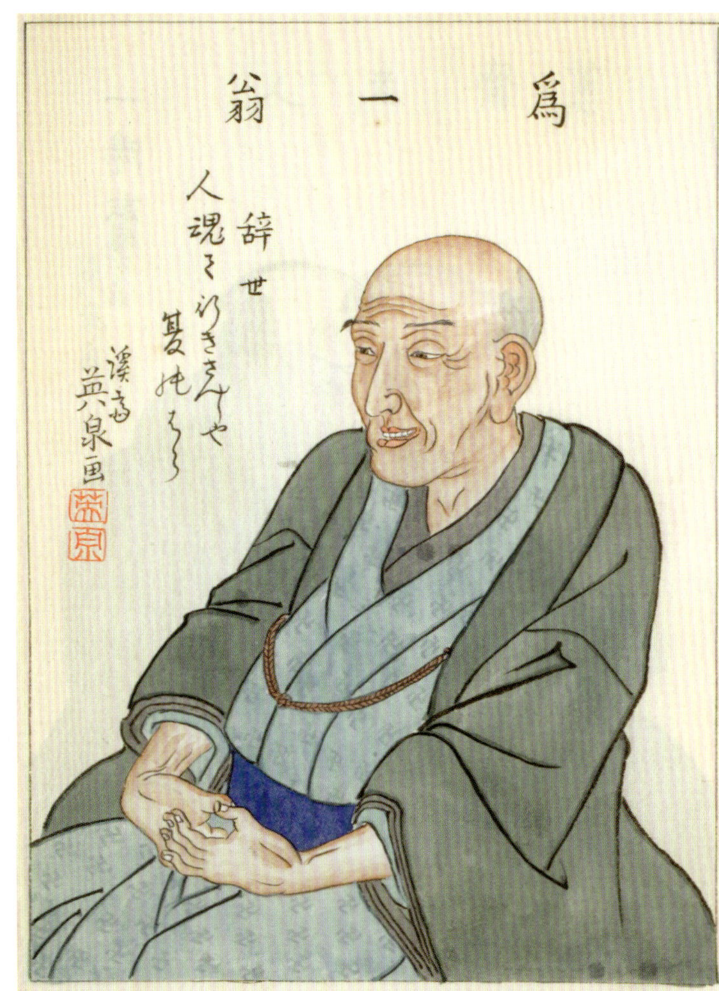

186, 187

After Keisai Eisen (1790–1848)
Portrait of Hokusai

Original early 1840s
Signature: Keisei / Eisen ga
Seals: Ei, Sen
Illustrated book, ink and colour on paper, 2 vols,
26.3 × 18.6 cm (covers) (right)
Literature: Suzuki Jūzō, 'Hokusai shōzō zu no iroiro',
Ukiyo-e geijutsu 10, 1965, p. 14; Paris 2014, p. 10
Photo courtesy of the National Diet Library Digital
Collections (left); Keiō University Library, Tokyo (right)
Catalogue only

Hitodama de / yuku kisanji ya / natsu nohara
Maybe I'll unwind / by roaming the summer fields /
as a will-o'-the-wisp. (Hokusai's death poem.)

Kimura Mokurō (1774–1856), a close friend of author
Takizawa Bakin (1767–1848), included this portrait
of Hokusai in his manuscript *Supplement to Thoughts on
Popular Authors* (*Gesakusha-kō hoi*), compiled in the tenth
month, 1845. The original painting, by the artist Keisai
Eisen (1790–1848), is now lost, possibly as a result
of fire during the Second World War. Fortunately,
however, a monochrome facsimile had been published
in 1935 (left). It is likely, therefore, that it depicts the
artist in his early eighties. Eisen died a year before
Hokusai, so the death poem here must have been
added later. Given that Hokusai was alive at the time,
it is almost certain that Eisen drew him from life, and
this may well be the most accurate and reliable among
the extant portraits of the artist. The painted copy
on the right, from Keiō University Library, suggests
what the original colours might have been. MR

Old man Hokusai urinating, from
Biography of Katsushika Hokusai

1893
Seal: Shun/Toshi
Illustrated book, published by Kobayashi Bunshichi,
23.2 × 15.8 cm (covers)
Provenance: Jack Hillier
Literature: Iijima 1893, vol. 2, p. 14; Iijima 1999,
pp. 209–211
British Museum, 1999,1130,0.1
Osaka only

Biography of Katsushika Hokusai was written by Iijima
Kyoshin (1841–1901) and published in 1893 by
Kobayashi Bunshichi (1861–1923) (Iijima 1893, 1978,
1999). Iijima was employed by the Meiji government
to compile instructional materials, but in private life
he participated in cultural circles and wrote important
biographies of ukiyo-e artists. Notable among these,
and with Kobayashi's encouragement, was his major
study of Hokusai. Illustrated here is Hokusai's reply
to a request from the publisher Kobayashi Shinbei
for illustrations for a *One Hundred Poets* anthology.
The figure in profile is Hokusai himself, presented like
a portrait of a classical poet, but with a blanket thrown
over his head and a piss bottle at his side. The publisher
seems to have been in a great hurry, urging the thin
old man (as Hokusai portrayed himself) not to fuss over
small matters and to make a decision about the project
quickly. In contrast, Hokusai replies with a witty text
saying that he is not to be rushed. MR

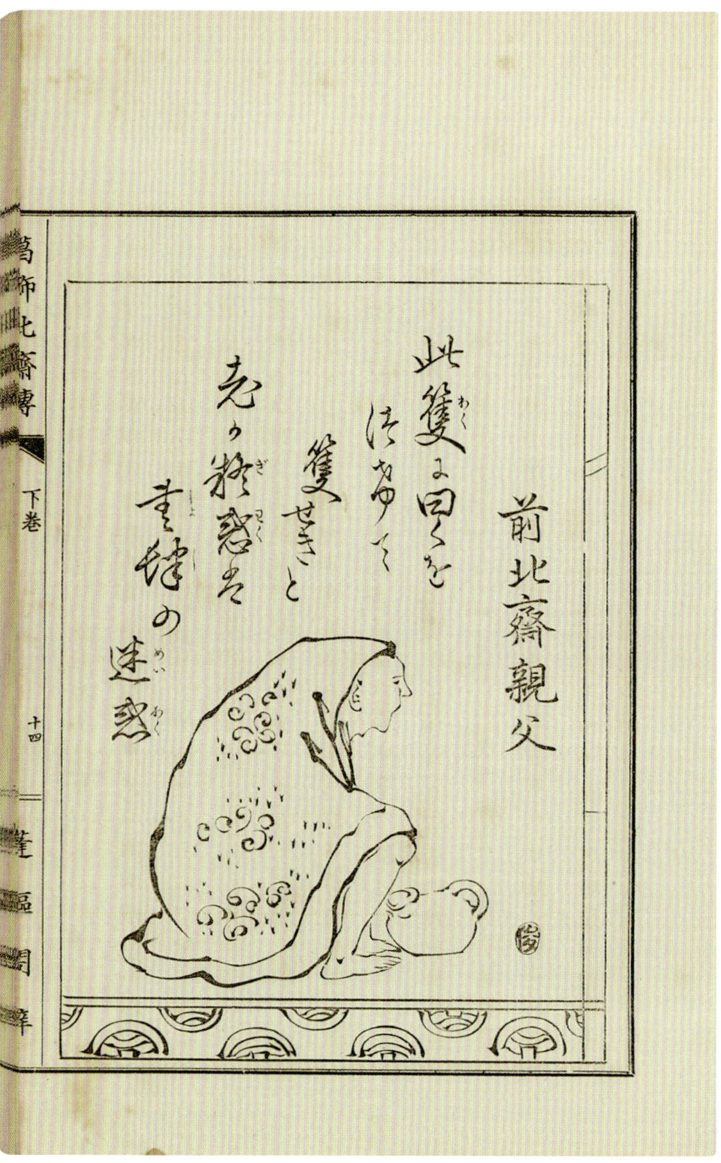

189

Hokusai in old age

1840s–1890s
Unsigned (attributed to Hokusai or a pupil of Hokusai)
Ink and red pigment on paper, with pentimenti,
37.2 × 23.7 cm
Provenance: Siegfried Bing; Henri Vever
Literature: Fenollosa 1901, no. 191; HUT 1987–1990,
vol. 6, no. 8; Kobayashi 1996–1997, vol. 16, pp. 184–
195; HK 20, April 1996, pp. 130–135; Guimet 2008,
nos 102 a, 102b
Musée national des arts asiatiques Guimet, Paris,
EO.1456, given by Henri Vever, 1912
London only

This is the face by which Hokusai has been known to
the world since 1893, when a similar head and shoulders
portrait was used as the woodblock frontispiece to
Iijima Kyoshin's biography of the artist (cat. 188).
Historian Sekine Shisei (1825–1893) described Hokusai's
appearance to Iijima as follows: 'Hokusai indeed had
a lean face: his nose and eyes were not particularly
different from those of other people, but his ears were
very large' (Iijima 1999, p. 199; Yasuhara 2015, part 2,
p. 14). This drawing reflects Sekine's description, and
has sometimes been regarded as a self-portrait of the
artist. It first surfaced in 1900 in the possession of
the Paris art dealer Siegfried Bing (1838–1905), and its
authenticity as a work by Hokusai was attested by the
Paris ukiyo-e dealer Hayashi Tadamasa (1853–1906).

Although the drawing displays lines characteristic
of Hokusai's style, it is not certain that it is in fact
by the artist himself. The technique resembles that in
preparatory drawings for *One Hundred Views of Mt Fuji*
(cats 177–182): the red underdrawing switching to black
suggests that here, too, the artist was producing an
image intended for realization as a woodblock print.
The portrait is carefully drawn and well balanced, but
its brushwork and character contrast with the vigorous
and humorous self-portrait that Hokusai included in
one of his letters (cat. 184). It may be, therefore, that
the drawing is a respectful portrait drawn by a pupil,
who sought to capture the master's appearance for
reproduction as a print that was then never produced.
The date of execution also remains unclear. MR

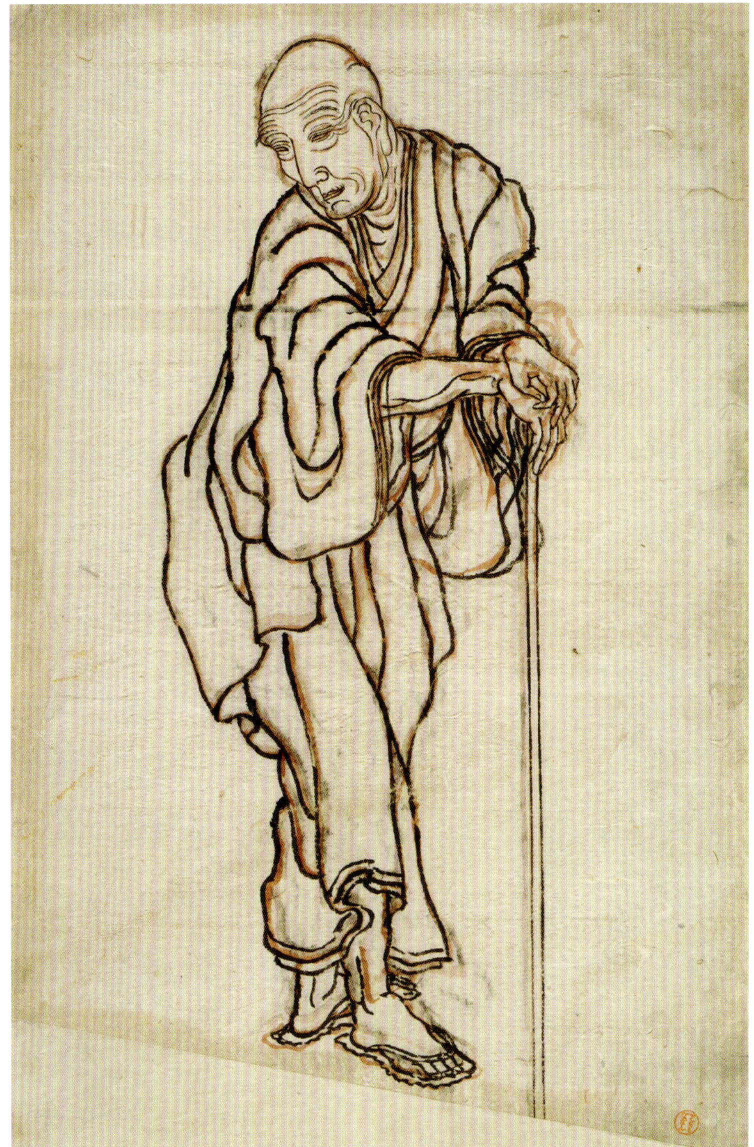

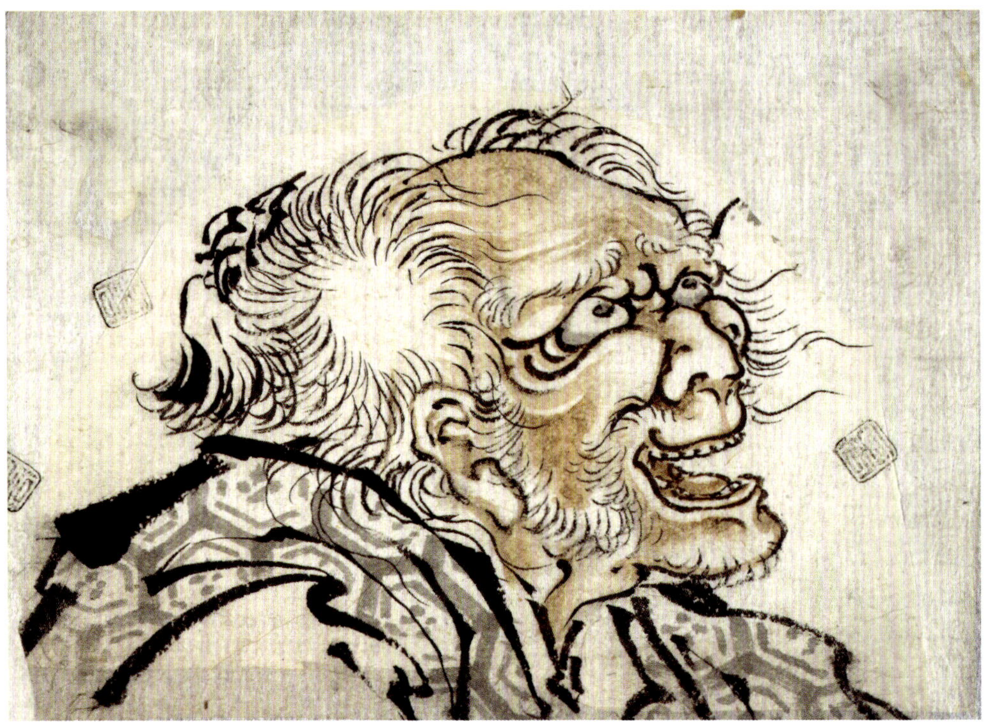

190

Head of an old man

Early 1840s
Unsigned (attributed to Hokusai)
Seal: 'Sū' (?)
Ink and slight colour on paper, irregular fragment
pasted on a sheet, 11.0 × 14.0 cm
Provenance: Kobayashi Shinbei (?)
Literature: Forrer 1988, no. 455; RA 1991, no. 110
National Museum of Ethnology, Leiden, 2736-11/2

This vigorous brush sketch depicts the head of a
white-haired old man viewed in three-quarter profile.
The drawing is on a small fragment of paper cut from
a larger sheet, with slight colour added for the modelling
of the features and the pattern on the robe. The dynamic
lines and ecstatic, open-mouthed expression compel
the viewer's attention. Wearing a simple jacket (*haori*)
and blessed with prominent earlobes, the figure
resembles a self-portrait from the same period (cat. 184),
while the face also recalls *Thunder God* (Freer-Sackler
Gallery, Washington, DC, 00.47), a painting that Hokusai
produced at the age of eighty-eight. The unusual seal
may be that of publisher Kobayashi Shinbei, who used
the business name Sūzanbō. Kobayashi and Hokusai
had a close relationship, as recorded in their
correspondence (Iijima 1999, pp. 143–151). MR

Daily Exorcisms

Dated '23rd day, tenth month' [1842–1843]
Unsigned (attributed to Hokusai)
Ink on paper, 32.0 × 23.0 cm
Provenance: Honma Hokuyō, Honma Tsunesuke
Literature: HK 11, Dec. 1975, pp. 4–17; Hashimoto
2012; Hokusaikan 2015, pp. 146–151
Hokusai Museum, Obuse

In his last years, Hokusai made it a practice to draw
pictures of Chinese lions and lion-dancers every day.
He called these brush drawings 'Daily Exorcisms'
(*Nisshin joma*). Several explanations have been proposed
for this custom: to ward off the influence of his
trouble-making grandson; to prevent fire (an idea first
put forward in 1839); and to pray for long life as he
approached the age of ninety. The lion-dancer, wearing
a mask, brandishes sacred paper streamers (*gohei*) to
avert misfortune. It is said that Hokusai tossed his daily
exorcisms out of the window, but his daughter Eijo,
his students and his neighbours collected them, and
he readily accommodated their requests to add an
inscription. This drawing was formerly in the collection
of Hokusai's student Honma Hokuyō (1822–1868;
see also cat. 208), who seems to have received it from
the artist personally. MR

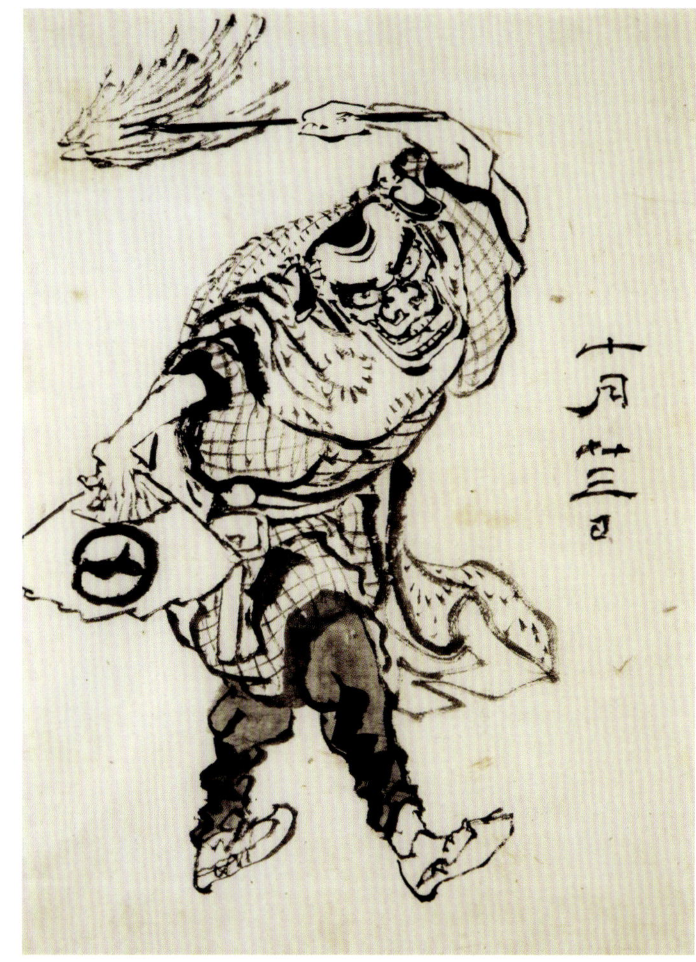

Chinese lion

Dated '21st day, intercalary ninth month' [1843]
Unsigned (attributed to Hokusai)
Ink on paper, 34.7 × 25.4 cm
Provenance: Hayashi Tadamasa
Literature: Taki 1906, pp. 483–493; Hashimoto 2012;
Hokusaikan 2015, pp. 144–145
Hokusai Museum, Obuse

No lion [lying] around – / implion [implying] that this
lion / feels quite sullion [sullen], / except when he
starts to draw: / then he feels he's flion [flying] high.
(*Isogashishi* / *sewashishi shishi mo* / *muzukashishi* / *kaki
hajimetaru* / *kokoro okashishi*)

Hokusai's inscription is a comic poem (*kyōka*) consisting
of words and phrases that incorporate the syllables
'*shishi*', which is also the Japanese term for Chinese
lion. Hokusai seems to be describing himself, as the
poem literally means: 'Being busy and overworked
makes this lion crotchety, but when he begins to draw,
his heart is light and cheerful.' The poem conjures up
an image of Hokusai cheerfully drawing Chinese lions,
even on the busiest of mornings, producing what he
called 'Daily Exorcisms' (cat. 191). In the painting
manual *Picture Book: Essence of Colouring* (1848, cat. 211),
Hokusai provides detailed instructions on how to draw
a Chinese lion. This remarkable painting is fully equal
to the drawing there in regard to the balance of the
standing lion and the vigorous, flowing rendering of
the fur. The viewer comes close to Hokusai the man,
his marvellous, free handling of the brush, and the
spiritual aspect to his daily practice. MR

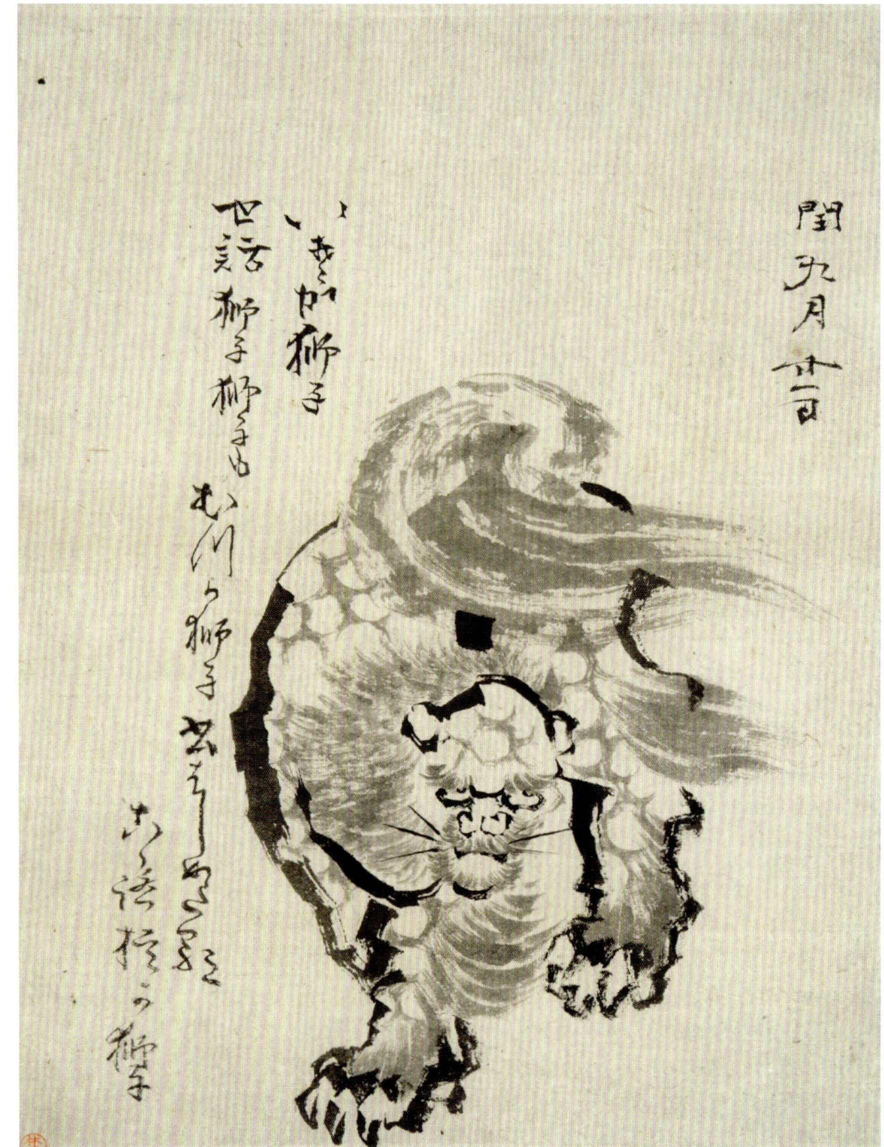

Tsuyuki Kōshō (Iitsu III, died after 1893)
Hokusai and Eijo in their lodgings

Before 1893
Ink on paper, 25.0 × 17.5 cm
Literature: Iijima 1999, pp. 201–203, Kubota 2015,
no. 16
National Diet Library, Tokyo, WA 31-12
Catalogue only

Hokusai's pupil Tsuyuki Kōshō (Iitsu III, died after
1893) has drawn from memory a visit at the beginning
of the 1840s to his master, then in his early eighties,
and Eijo at their temporary lodgings at Kamezawa-chō
in the Fukagawa district of Edo. The drawing was
apparently made for Iijima Kyoshin when he was
working on his biography of Hokusai (Iijima 1999,
pp. 201–203; cat. 188) and provides a vivid picture of
the life the father and daughter led together. Hokusai
crouches forwards in the *kotatsu* (a table brazier with
a quilt) to work on a painting, watched intently by
his daughter, who leans on her long pipe. The text tells
us that Hokusai remained huddled under his *kotatsu*
from autumn to spring, whether sleeping, drawing
or greeting visitors. The brazier and quilt provided
a warm environment for lice to breed, and the room
is littered with crumpled food wrappings. Hanging
from the wall on the left is an old box for *mikan*
tangerines, which houses an image of monk Nichiren
(1222–1282), founder of an important sect of Japanese
Buddhism (cat. 4). Notwithstanding their frugal living
conditions, father and daughter maintained their
religious faith. MR

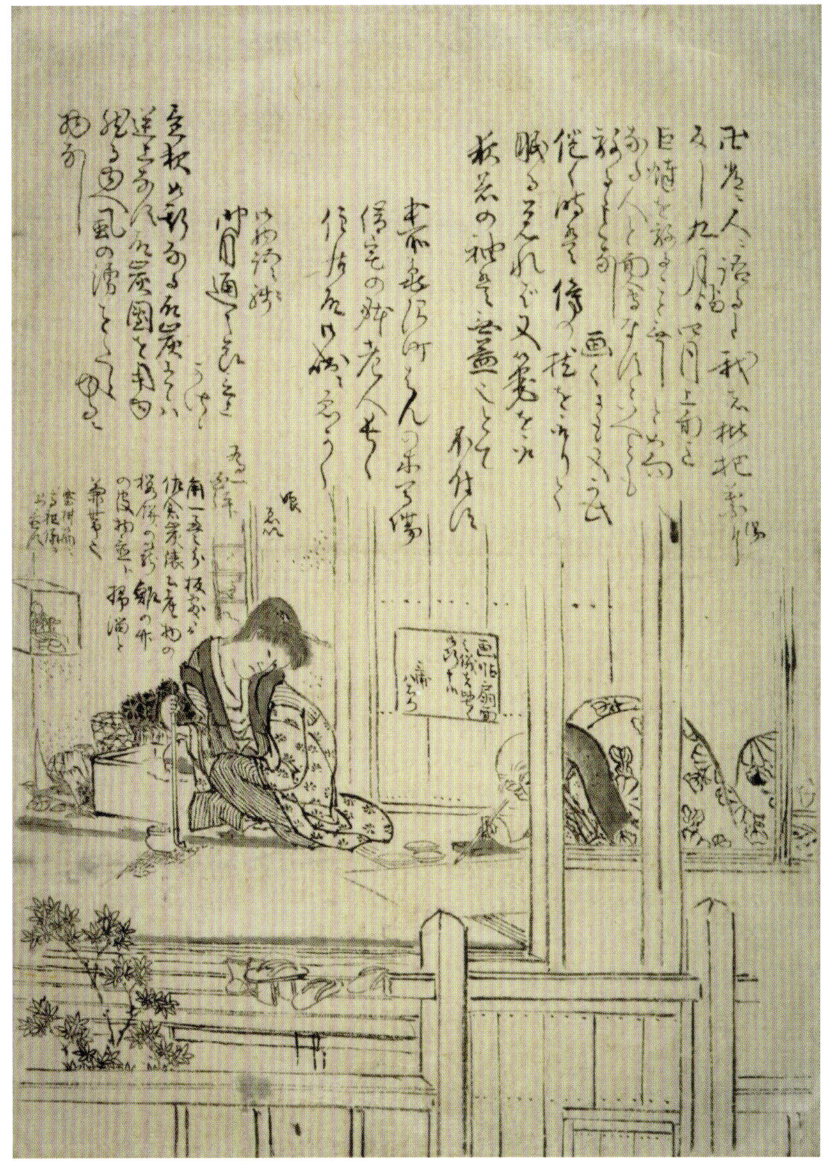

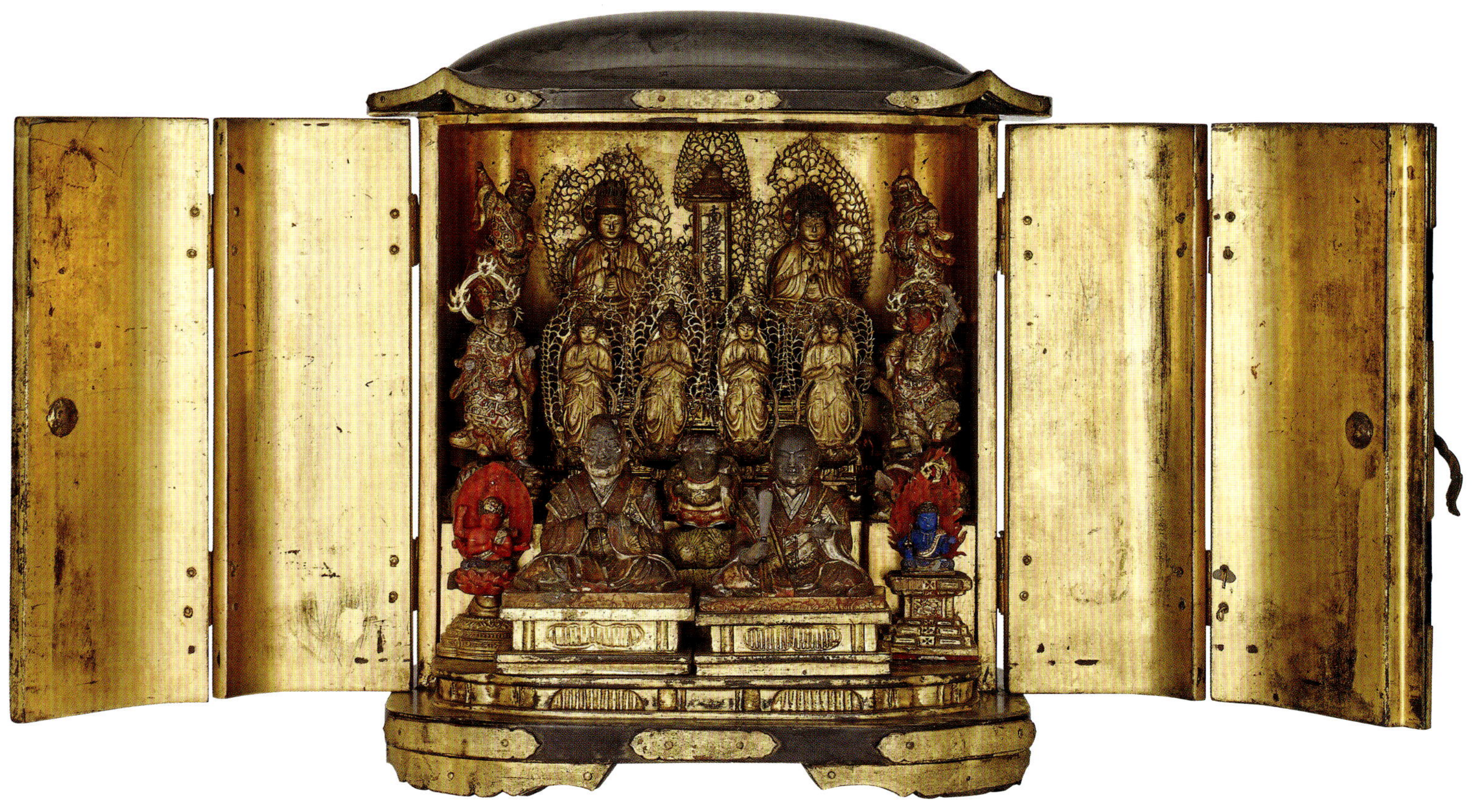

Shrine with Nichiren and Nichizō

1700s–1800s
Portable shrine, ink, colour, gold, gold leaf and lacquer
on wood, with metal fittings, 32.0 × 27.5 × 25.0 cm
British Museum, 1885,1227.37, given by Augustus
Wollaston Franks

This double-doored, portable lacquer shrine houses
sacred images of monk Nichiren (1222–1282) and,
possibly, his follower monk Nichizō (1269–1342),
along with fourteen Buddhist deities and Japanese
kami deities associated with the *Lotus Sutra*, the central
text of Nichiren belief. Such shrines have their origins
in alcoves where sutras, along with Buddhist sculptures
and paintings, were placed. They have been used since
ancient times as portable religious paraphernalia,
making faith more personally accessible. A sketch
by the artist's student Tsuyuki Kōshō (cat. 193),
recalling the living quarters of Hokusai and his
daughter in the early 1840s, shows on one wall a simple
altar made from a tangerine box containing an image
of Nichiren. Hokusai and his daughter evidently had
nowhere in their humble dwelling to place a proper
altar, making their determination to venerate Nichiren
in a temporary box all the more moving. Hokusai's
artistic practice was closely linked with his faith in
Nichiren Buddhism throughout his life. MR

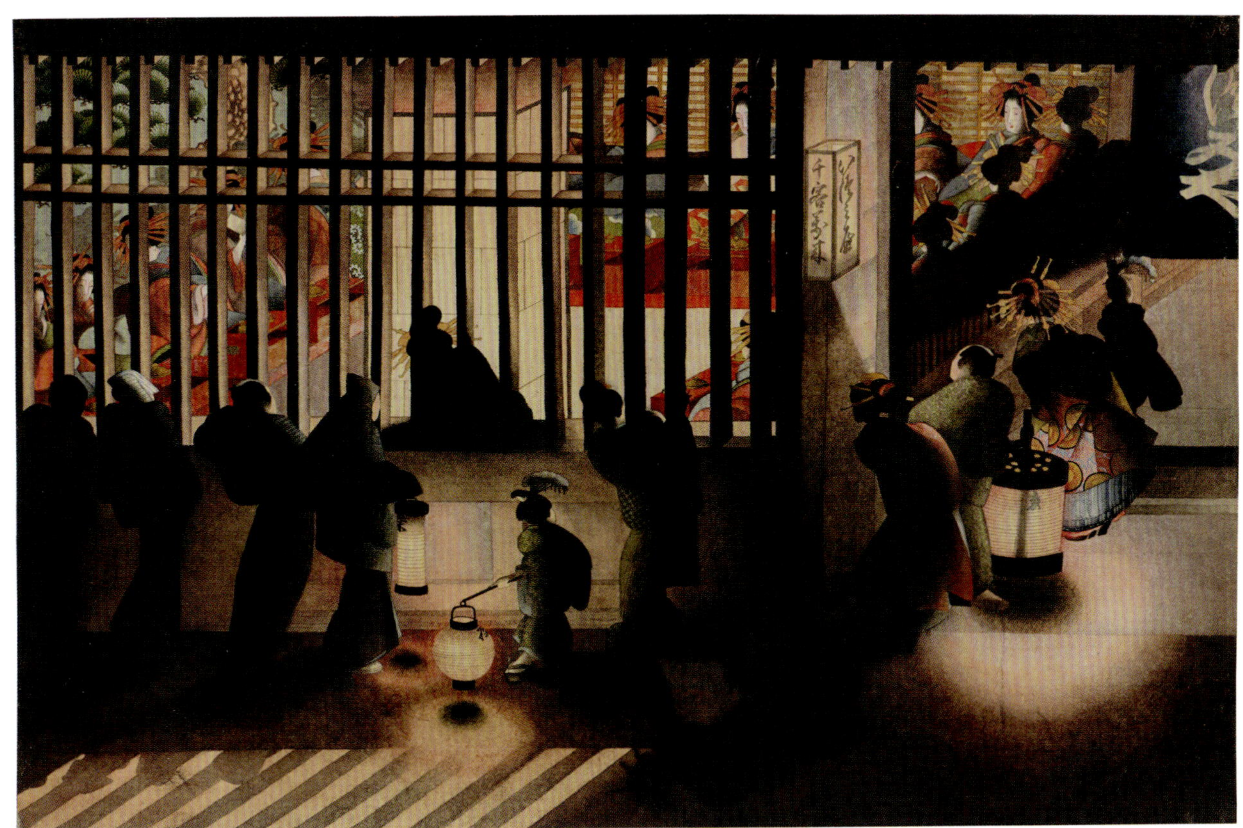

195
Katsushika Ōi (about 1800–after 1857)
Display room in Yoshiwara at night

1844–1854
Unsigned (the characters 'Ō', 'I' and 'Ei' appear on
three lanterns)
Literature: UTS 1932, no. 24; NU 1982, no. 50; Kubota
2015, no. 3; Ōta 2015
Hanging scroll, ink and colour on paper,
26.3 × 39.8 cm
Ōta Memorial Museum of Art, Tokyo
Osaka only

The scene is the display room and entrance to a
brothel in the Yoshiwara pleasure quarter, seen from
the street. Courtesans (female sex workers) are seated
in the display room facing the street, hoping to attract
customers. Most are lined up formally on three sides
of the room, with just one woman at the lattice window,
shown in silhouette and lit from behind by the lamps,
talking to a client outside. The name of the brothel,
'Izumiya', appears on the entrance curtain and an
illuminated sign. There were several establishments
in the Yoshiwara quarter with this name, so it is not
possible to say which is depicted here. The formal
procession of a courtesan is seen returning to
the brothel, past the half-lattice (*sō-hanmagaki*) of the
entrance passage. The memorable style of the painting
emphasizes effects of light, shadow and subtle gradations
between the two, evoking a dream-like atmosphere.
Although unsigned, three characters from the names
'Ōi Eijo' appear on the lanterns, and the work can
be attributed to Hokusai's artist daughter with
confidence. AS

Katsushika Ōi (about 1800–after 1857)
Hua Tuo operating on the arm of Guan Yu

1840s
Signature: Ōi Eijo hitsu ('Brush of Ōi, the woman Ei')
Seal: Katsushika (3)
Hanging scroll, ink and colour on silk, 140.2 × 68.2 cm
Provenance: Kaneko Fusui; Yamagata Shotarō;
Azabu Museum of Arts and Crafts
Literature: NUT 1994–1996, vol. 6, no. 61; Kubota
2015, no. 2
The Cleveland Museum of Art, Kelvin Smith Fund
1998.178

Renowned physician Hua Tuo (died AD 208) slices
into the arm of general Guan Yu (died 220) to remove
a section of bone infected by a poisoned arrow. For
anaesthesia Guan Yu has accepted nothing beyond
a few cups of rice wine and a game of *go*. Even as blood
pours from his arm and servants cringe in revulsion,
the general and his son Guan Ping (upper right) remain
as cool as the surgeon. The scene corresponds to an
episode in part five of the Chinese historical novel
Romance of the Three Kingdoms (*San guo yanyi*; Japanese:
Sangokushi, 1300s), a popular favourite throughout
the late Edo period.

   Artist Ōi was Hokusai's third daughter, and perhaps
his most devoted student. A superb talent in her own
right, she here develops the Katsushika style with a
powerful composition enhanced by an almost eerie
use of European-style shading. Her application of this
technique and the rich detailing of the background
still life reveal the formidable skill that collectors and
other artists of her day also recognized. Ōi remained
close to her father throughout his late years (cat. 193)
and Hokusai's own 'Katsushika' seal has here been
impressed after his daughter's signature, perhaps to
validate her remarkable achievement. This painting
is one of the rare confirmed examples of Ōi's work. AH

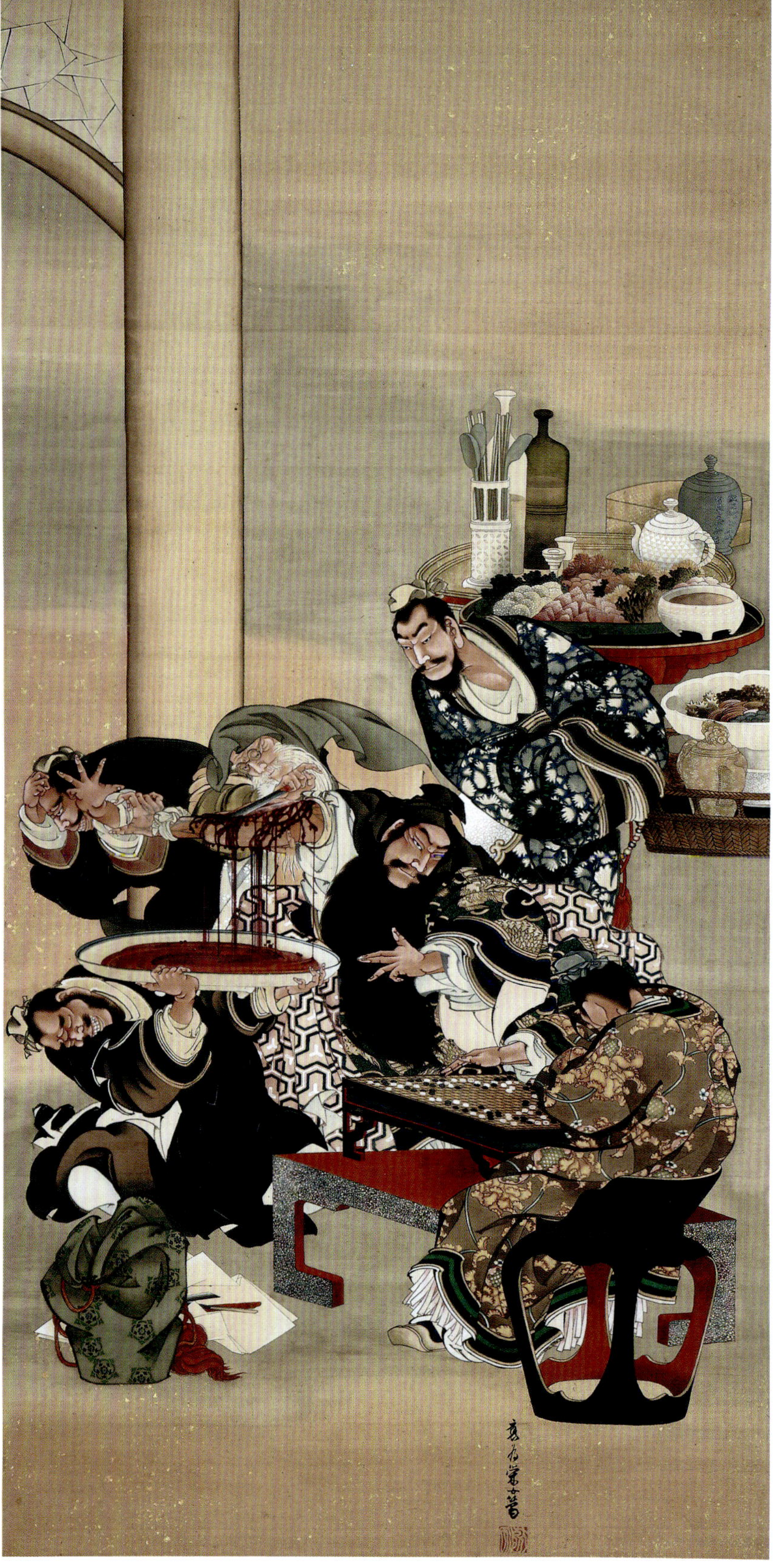

197
Katsushika Ōi (about 1800–after 1857)
Woman fulling cloth by moonlight

1840s
Signature: Ōju Eijo hitsu ('Brush of the woman Ei,
at special request')
Seal: 'Ō'
Ink and colour on paper, 113.4 × 31.3 cm
Provenance: Sugawara Tetsunosuke
Literature: NUT 1994–1996, vol. 2, no. 48; Carpenter
2005, p. 100; Kubota 2015, no. 4
Tokyo National Museum, A-11653

Under a full moon, a woman pounds fabric on a fulling
block. Japanese poetry and painting have often taken
as their subject the emotions evoked by the steady,
echoing 'knock, knock, knock' of fulling in remote rural
areas on an autumn night. This painting is a fine example
of Ōi's detailed brushwork, particularly in the beautiful
rendering of the autumn grasses on the woman's robes,
the fine gradations of blue and the pattern of the wood
grain. One bare foot extending from beneath her
robes adds to her allure, with the abbreviated toenails
characteristic of both Hokusai and Ōi (Hayashi 1967,
pp. 64–67). The signature appears to have been partly
scraped away, perhaps by a dealer who, noting the
similarity to Hokusai's style, sought to pass Ōi's painting
off as a work by her father. MR

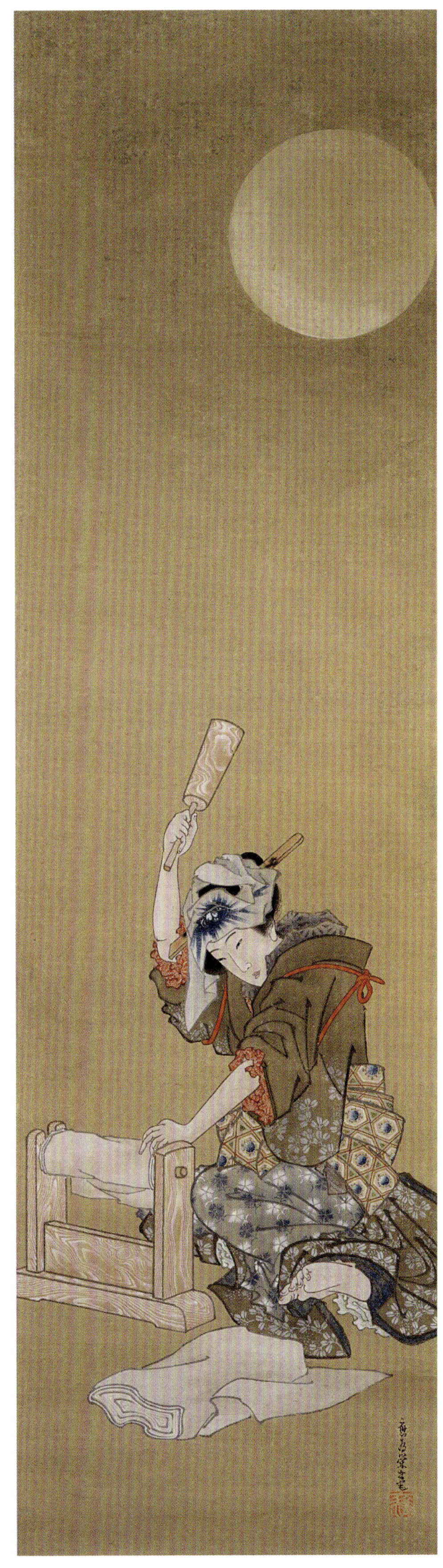

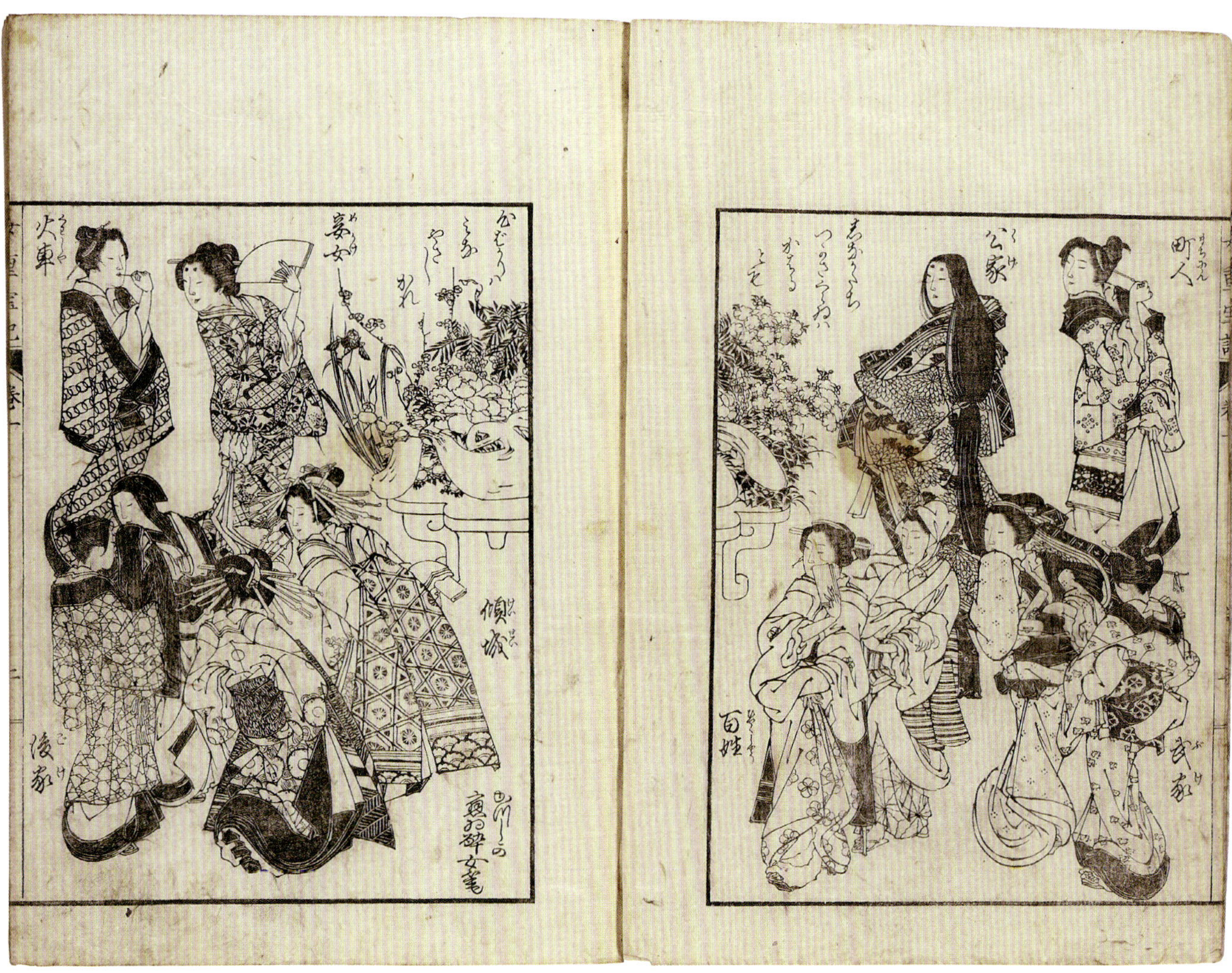

**Katsushika Ōi (about 1800–after 1857),
Types of women, from *Treasury of
Education for Women (Onna chōhōki)***

1847
Signature: Katsushika Ōi Eijo hitsu ('Brush of
the woman Ei, Katsushika Ōi')
Illustrated book, woodblock, published by Suharaya
Mohei, Kawachiya Kihei and others, 25.0 × 18.0 cm
(covers)
Provenance: Jack Hillier
Literature: Carpenter 2005, p. 95; Paris 2014, no. 538;
Kubota 2015, no. 32
British Museum, 1979,0305,0.558
Osaka only

First published in 1629, *Treasury of Education for Women*
brought together practical information that would be
useful for a woman in her daily life. Hokusai's daughter
Ōi designed the illustrations for this new edition
published in 1847. The text was edited by Takai Ranzan
(1762–1838; his preface is dated 1829), who had earlier
worked with Hokusai on a number of illustrated books
(cat. 120). The pages illustrated depict women of
different social classes: a merchant's wife, a court lady,
a courtesan, and so on. Despite the differences in their
outward appearances, all the women nevertheless share
a quality of gentle femininity. In her signature, Ōi has
used the character for 'tipsy', which she also used to
sign her poem on cat. 183. She is known to have been
fond of alcohol and conveyed this through a pun on
her name. MR

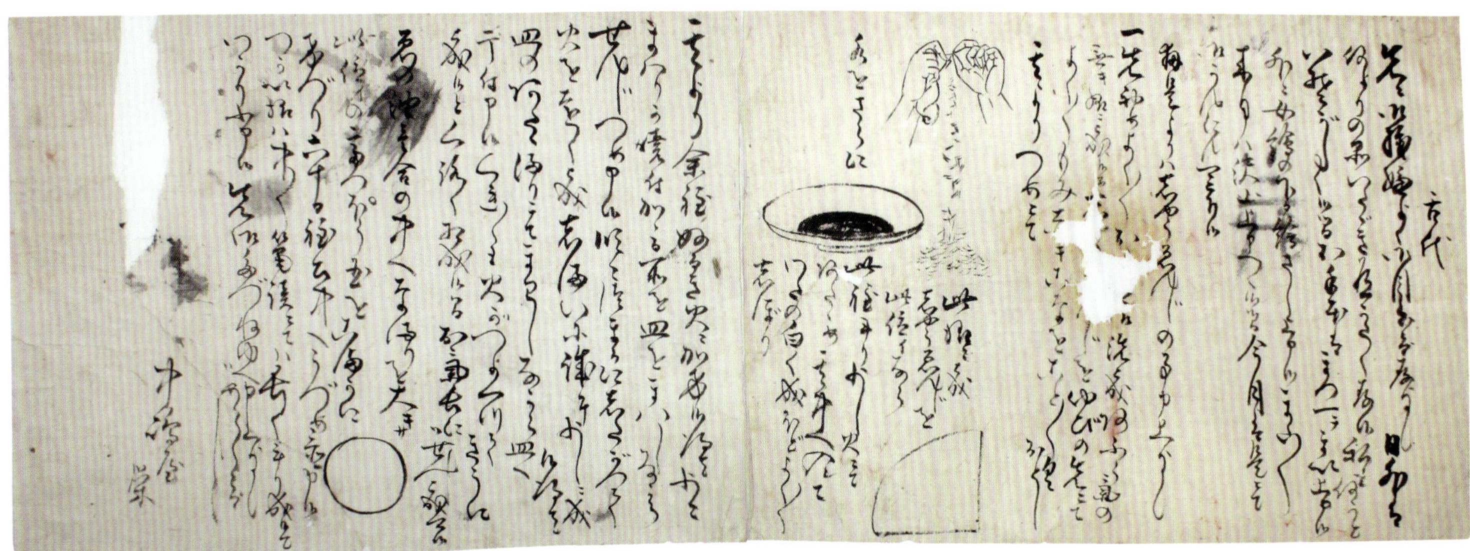

Katsushika Ōi (about 1800–after 1857)
Letter with instructions for mixing pigment

About 1840–1860
Signature: Nakajimaya Ei
Ink on paper, 23.0 × 61.0 cm
Literature: Calza & Carpenter 1994, pp. 243–245;
Hokusaikan 2015, p. 180; Kubota 2015, no. 10
Private collection, Japan

Three letters by Hokusai's daughter Ōi (Eijo) are known.
One is addressed to Hokusai's student Hokushin,
informing him that the master has passed away (cat. 225).
The other two, including this one, have the names of
the addressees cut out, but seem to have been sent to
a resident in Obuse. In this letter, Ōi provides a detailed
discussion of the production of an organic red pigment
(*shōenji*), accompanied by an illustration, and mentions
that at a later date she will send a preparatory drawing
for a painting of a beautiful woman. The addressee
thus seems to have been a pupil. Her instruction,
'Grind a bullet (*teppōdama*) about this size [she draws
a circle] to a fine powder and bury it in the ground
for around sixty days', is similar to one of Hokusai's
instructions for producing pigments in his painting
manual *Picture Book: Essence of Colouring* (cat. 211). **MR**

Hokusai and/or Katsushika Ōi
(about 1800–after 1857) (?)
Chrysanthemums

Late 1840s (?)
Signatures: Hachijūhachi rōjin Manji hitsu ('Brush
of Manji, old man of eighty-eight'; right); Yowai
hachijūhachi sai Manji hitsu ('Brush of Manji,
aged eighty-eight years'; left) [both false?]
Seal: Katsushika [false?]
Pair of hanging scrolls; ink and colour on silk, each
about 95.5 × 31.4 cm
Literature: Calza & Carpenter 1994, pp. 252–255;
Calza 1999, pp. 70–71; Kubota 2015, no. 28
Hokusai Museum, Obuse

This pair of hanging scrolls, with their remarkable
forms and colours, conveys the full power of the
Katsushika style. They depict 'tomoe brocade' (tomoe-
nishiki) chrysanthemums and other varieties of
the flower in hyper-naturalistic detail. In some parts,
the compositions recall Hokusai's *Large flowers* series
of prints (cats 82–88), while in style they resemble
late paintings by him such as *Scattered fans* (cat. 219).
However, it was highly unusual for Hokusai to use
different signatures on paired paintings, and both
the signatures and the seals here are unlike those on
paintings accepted as genuine, raising questions about
the authorship of this pair. It has been suggested that
they may have been produced by Hokusai's daughter
Ōi. Bold colours and delicate details are characteristic
features of her attested works, while the varying
tonalities of the blue pigment resemble *Woman fulling
cloth by moonlight* (cat. 197). MR

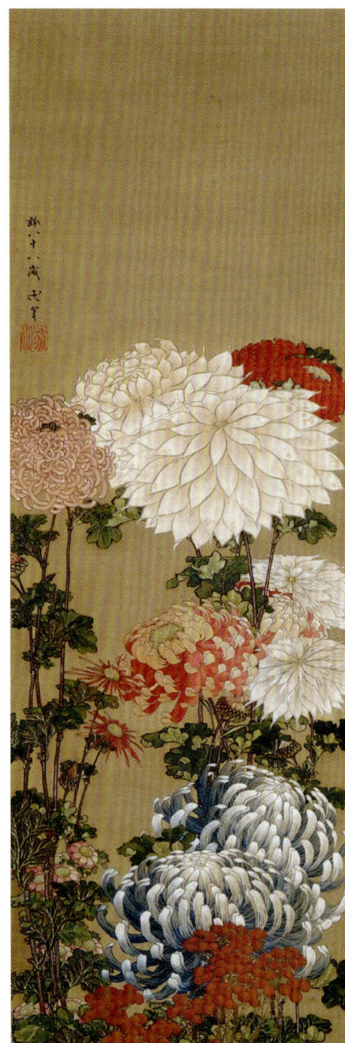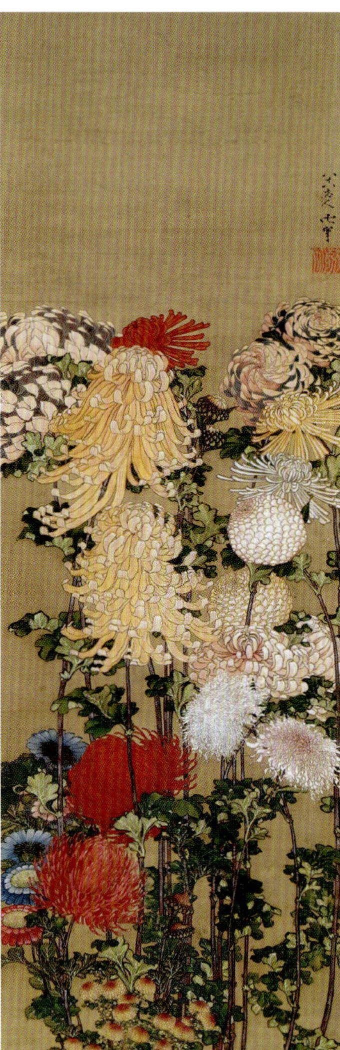

201, 202

Takai Kōzan (1806–1883)
Chrysanthemums

About 1840s (?)
Signatures: Kōzan (left); Kōzan (right)
Seals: Kōzan, [unread] (left); Takai Ken in,
Shijun (right)
Two hanging scrolls; ink and colour on silk,
101.0 × 34.0 (left); 121.0 × 41.0 (right)
Literature: Shibui 1983, suppl. no. 5 (right);
Kubota 1989, II, pp. 8–9; Kubota 2015, no. 28
Takai Kōzan Memorial Museum, Obuse (left);
Ichimura Tsugio collection, Japan (right)
Osaka only

After spending his youth travelling and learning how
to paint in Kyoto and Edo, Takai Kōzan (1806–1883)
returned to his home town of Obuse in 1836 to
manage the family business of manufacturing saké.
Some years later, he invited Hokusai to Obuse and
took care of the artist during his visit. He was involved
in Hokusai's commission to design a ceiling painting
for the Ganshōin temple there (cats 203, 204), as well
as four panel paintings for festival carts, which are also
preserved in Obuse today (cats 206, 207; Haft essay
fig. 28). Like the previous works (cat. 200), these two
scrolls depict the 'tomoe brocade' (*tomoe-nishiki*) variety
of chrysanthemum cultivated in Obuse. References
indicate that Kōzan did produce chrysanthemum
paintings, but someone has tampered with the signatures
here, raising questions about the paintings' authorship.
The manner of painting the chrysanthemums here differs
from the standard Katsushika style, suggesting rather
someone working at a certain remove from the Hokusai-
Ōi partnership. In that respect, it seems reasonable to
consider these two scrolls as Kōzan's work. MR

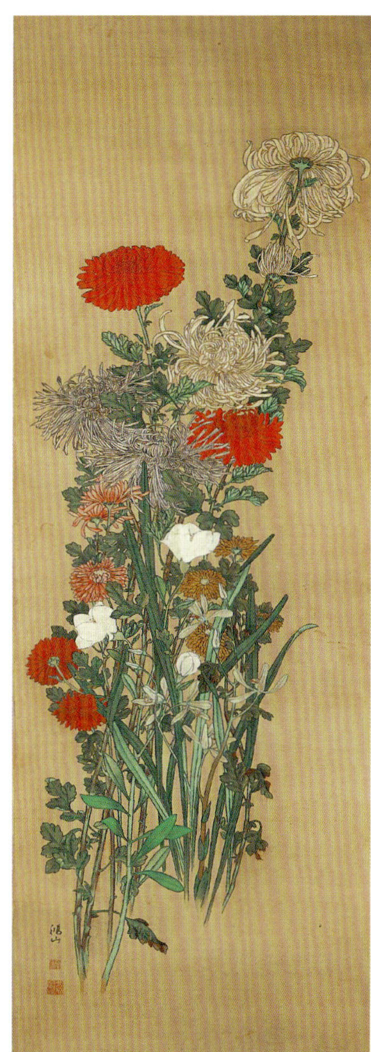
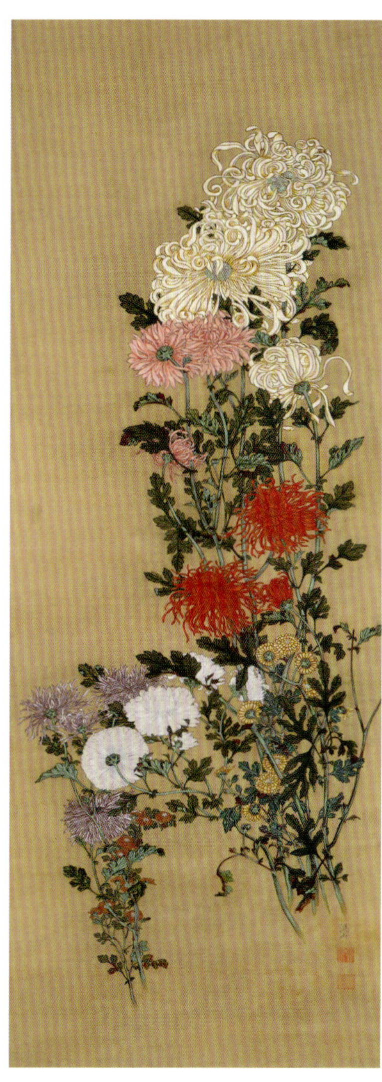

Phoenix for Ganshōin temple ceiling

1845

Unsigned (attributed to Hokusai)

Preparatory drawing, ink and slight colour on paper,
38.9 × 44.4 cm

Literature: Sankei Shinbun 1977 [pages not numbered];
Calza & Carpenter 1994, fig. 15.9

Private collection, Japan

Phoenix for Ganshōin temple ceiling

About 1845

Unsigned (attributed to Hokusai)

Preparatory drawing mounted as hanging scroll, ink
and colour on paper, 38.5 × 52.0 cm

Literature: Sankei Shinbun 1977 [pages not numbered];
Calza & Carpenter 1994, fig. 15.8; Nagata 2000,
no. 287; Suwa 2001, p. 106 ff.

Ganshōin temple, Obuse

These two preparatory drawings provide a rare insight
into how Hokusai designed on a grand scale. The *hōō*,
or 'phoenix', depicted here was eventually painted
on the ceiling of the main worship hall at Ganshōin
temple, covering a space of almost 35 square metres
(or 21 tatami mats; 377 square feet). Its production
was coordinated by Hokusai's local patron and pupil,
Takai Kōzan (1806–1883); Ganshōin was his family's
mortuary temple. The initial design apparently took
some time to emerge – Hokusai apologizes for the
delay in a letter that may originally have accompanied
the drawing (Hokusaikan 2015, p. 183). What is
presumably the first stage drawing divides the
composition into a grid of sixteen squares, indicating
how it should be transferred to the ceiling (above).
In an inscription, Hokusai requests that Kōzan (?)
prepare a total of 4,400 pieces of gold leaf and 11 gold
ryō in cash. A note on the right side of the later hanging
scroll (below) – from Kōzan back to Hokusai (?) –
requests that colour be added. When the actual ceiling
was finished, several years later, some of the subtlety
and power of Hokusai's design was inevitably lost,
but still it overawes the worshipper in the hall beneath.

A multi-coloured harbinger of peace and prosperity,
the *hōō* in East Asia is a more illustrious, complex bird
than the phoenix in the West. Over the centuries it
acquired a diverse range of auspicious meanings and
artistic interpretations. By 1845, Hokusai had been
depicting *hōō* for some four decades, drawing on this
long tradition, and also extending it. Most distinctive
are the roundels he adds to the tail feathers, which serve
to amplify the bird's watchful gaze. Before coming to
Obuse, though, Hokusai had tended to depict the bird
in flight or with wings spread, as in a magnificent
eight-panel screen now in the Museum of Fine Arts,
Boston (Calza & Carpenter 1994, no. 13.10). In Obuse
the previous year, he had painted some ceiling panels
for a festival cart (Hokusaikan 2015, pp. 14–19), one
of which, also of a *hōō*, anticipates, but does not fully
match, the compact, coiled composition here. The
powerful design compresses the bird's magnificent
plumage into a whirlpool of pattern and colour,
surrounding the unmoving central eye. Green, fan-like
feathers on the creature's back give way to cascades of
red and blue, in turn plunging towards two magnificent
gold tail feathers. The swirling movement echoes the
roiling waves he painted the same year, 1845, for a
second festival cart for the town (cats 206, 207). AL

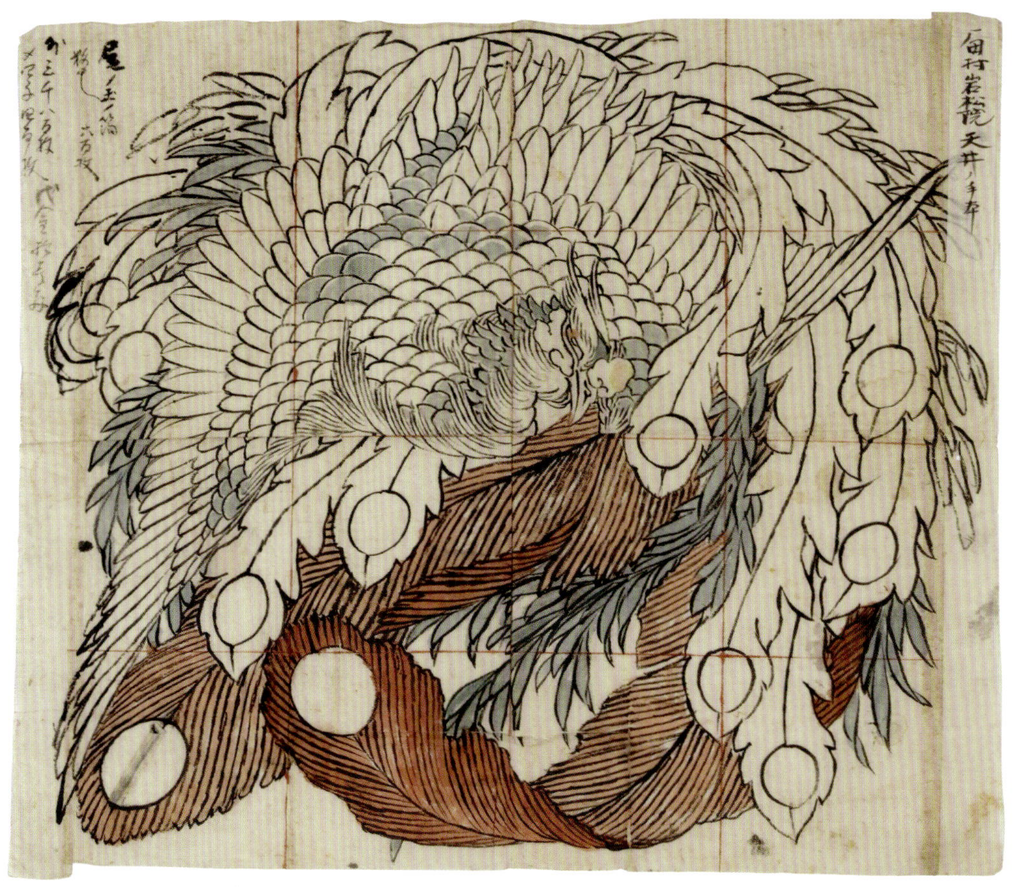

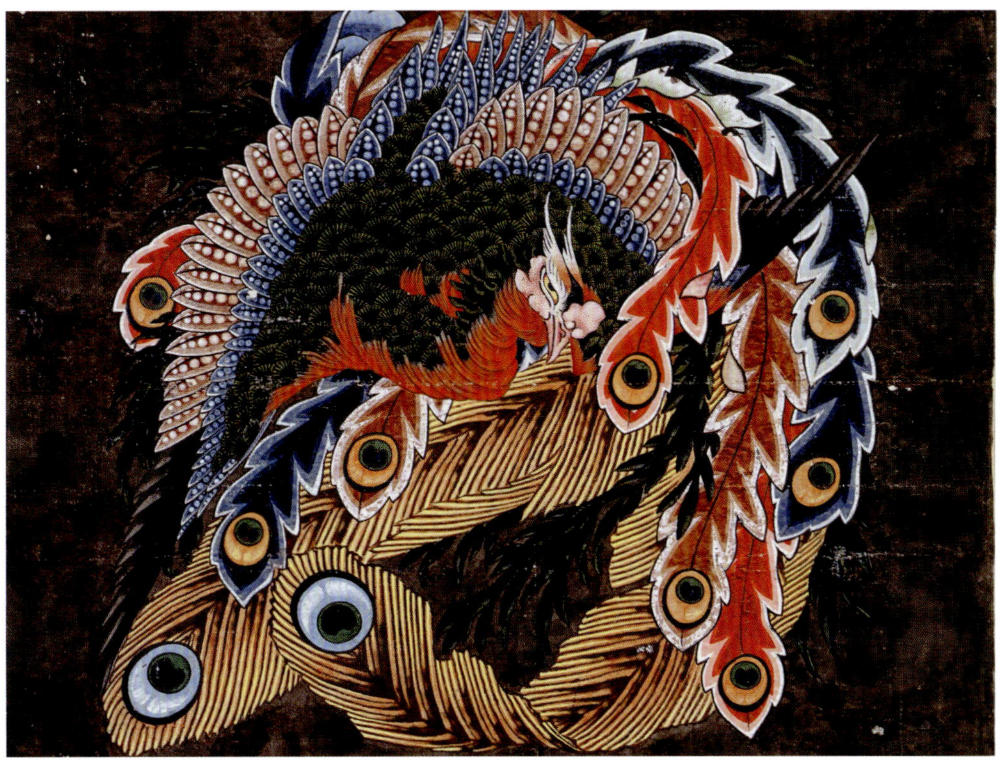

Preparatory drawings for the border decorations of 'Wave'

1845
Unsigned (attributed to Hokusai)
Four preparatory drawings, ink and slight colour on paper. 112.6–116.5 × 11.3–11.8 cm
Literature: Sankei Shinbun 1977 [pages not numbered]
Private collection, Japan
Osaka only

These preparatory drawings are for designs to decorate the frame of one of the two paintings of waves for the festival cart of the Kanmachi neighbourhood (cat. 207, Haft essay, fig. 28, p. 52). The process of actually executing the decorations is described in an inscription on the back of the wave panel they frame, by Takai Tatsuji, the son of Takai Kōzan: 'Colouring of the birds and flowers on the frames was done based on drawings by Old Man [Hokusai] by his pupil Takai Ken [Kōzan].' In general, Kōzan has faithfully followed Hokusai's drawings, although there are some small modifications – for example, the bird of paradise in the preparatory drawing has been changed to a decorative rock (*taiko seki*) and flower in the finished painting. Also of note is the figure of the winged cherub, which was probably copied from a European source. AS

206, 207 (overleaf)
Waves

1845
Unsigned (attributed to Hokusai, with frame paintings completed by Takai Kōzan)
Two ceiling panels for a festival cart, ink and colour on paulownia wood, each about 118.0 × 118.5 cm
Literature: Ozaki 1967, nos 33, 34; Calza & Carpenter 1994, nos 15.4 and 15.5; Suwa 2001, p. 99 ff.; Hokusaikan 2015, pp. 20–25
Kanmachi Neighbourhood Council, Obuse, Nagano
Prefectural Treasure

Hokusai's association with Obuse went back to the 1830s, when he first met Takai Kōzan (1806–1883), a wealthy and cultivated young saké merchant from the town. In the 1840s, Hokusai visited Obuse and stayed with Kōzan, who helped obtain the commissions for four ceiling panel paintings for two festival carts, each owned by a neighbourhood within the town. Kōzan's son Takai Tatsuji wrote inscriptions on the back of the panels in 1900, lending confidence to their attribution and dating (Kobayashi 1996–1997). In 1844, Hokusai produced a dragon (Haft essay, fig. 27, p. 51), surrounded by waves, and a *hōō* (phoenix), outlined with flecks of gold, for the cart of Higashimachi. The following year, he completed two slightly smaller panels for the somewhat larger cart of Kanmachi (Haft essay, fig. 28, p. 52). Hokusai also seems to have provided the designs for the decorative borders surrounding each panel – large, mythical birds and beasts for the so-called 'male wave' (p. 308), and plants and smaller animals, as well as a small winged cherub, for the 'female wave' (p. 309) – which were executed by Kōzan in the spring of the following year, 1846 (cat. 205).

Hokusai was fascinated by water, and particularly waves, throughout his life. Already in the 1810s, his waves had begun to develop the foamy tentacles seen here. With 'The Great Wave' (cat. 51) and 'Fuji from the sea' (cat. 35), in the 1830s, the viewer is plunged into the water. Now, though, we are completely surrounded by the sea, suggesting a portal into an entirely different dimension. The spiralling of the waves throws off white specks that dot the surface of both panels. Foam, at first pale grey-green, then cornflower blue, yields to a deep blue tunnel. The effect is vertiginous, combining waves that curl back on themselves with a whirlpool whose depths remain obscured. Some scholars have interpreted the waves as a Daoist diagram of the 'supreme ultimate' (Japanese: *taikyoku*), a state of undifferentiated potential from which everything originates (Suwa 2001). For Hokusai, it is clear, these panels represented far more than just the sea. AL

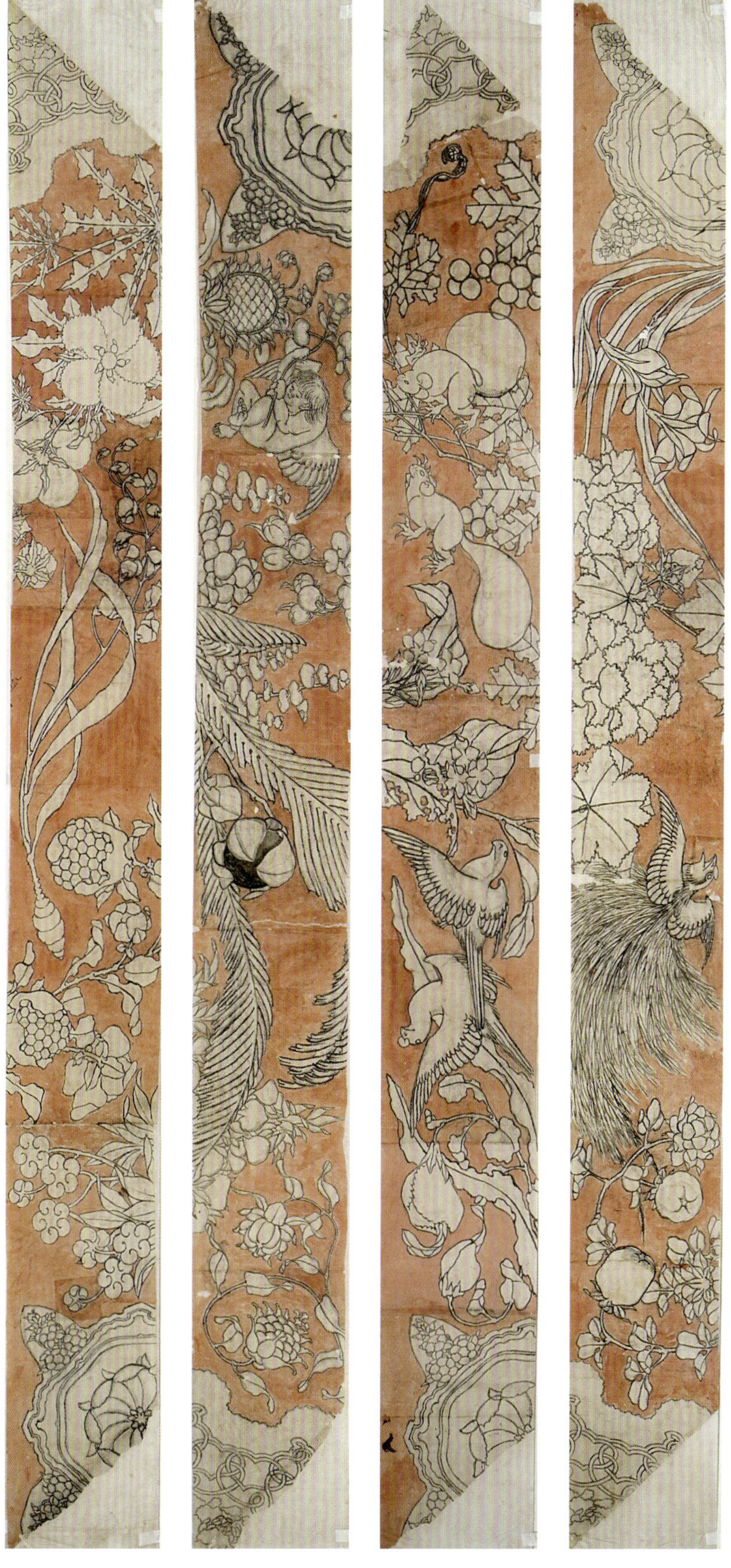

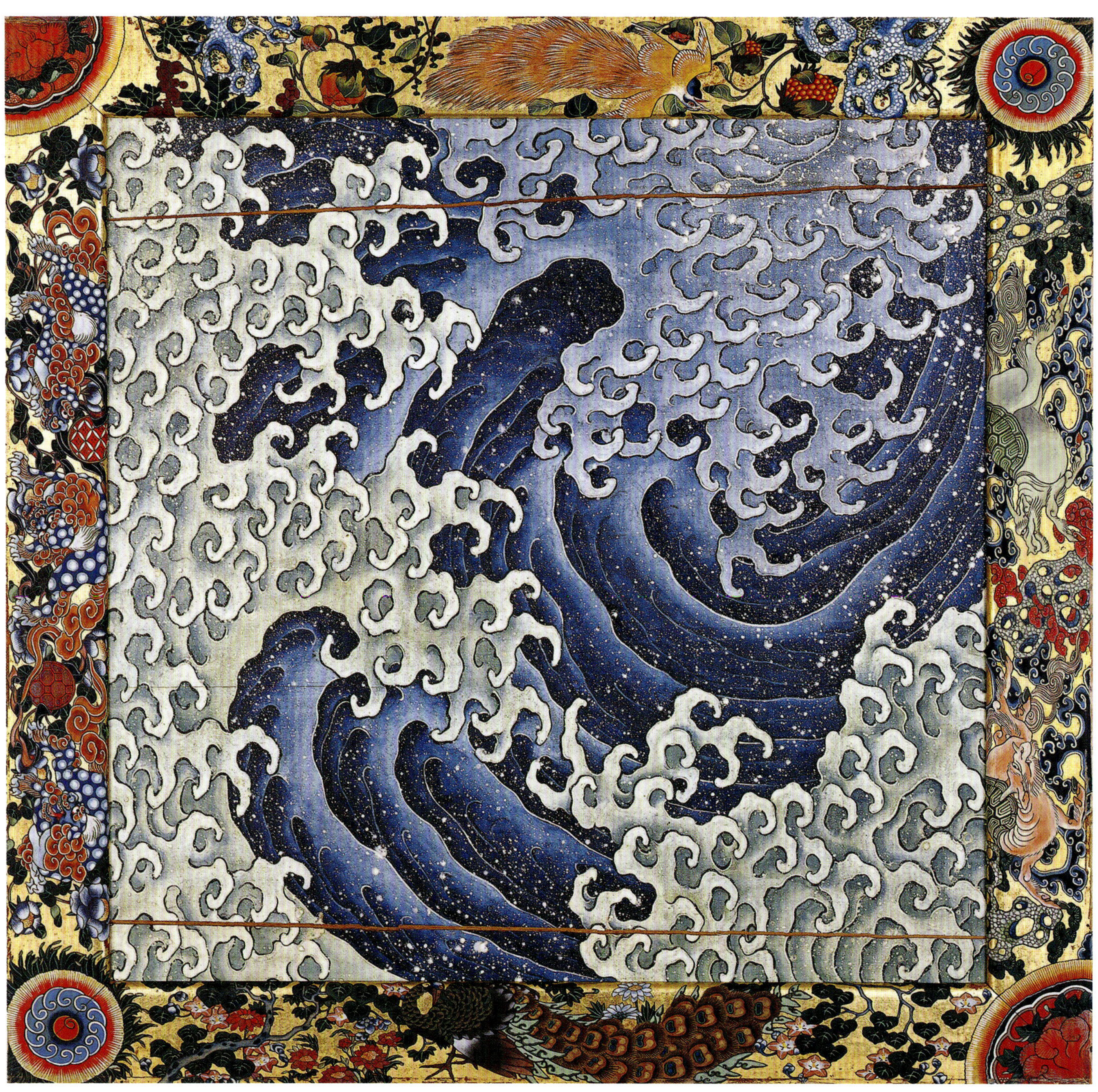

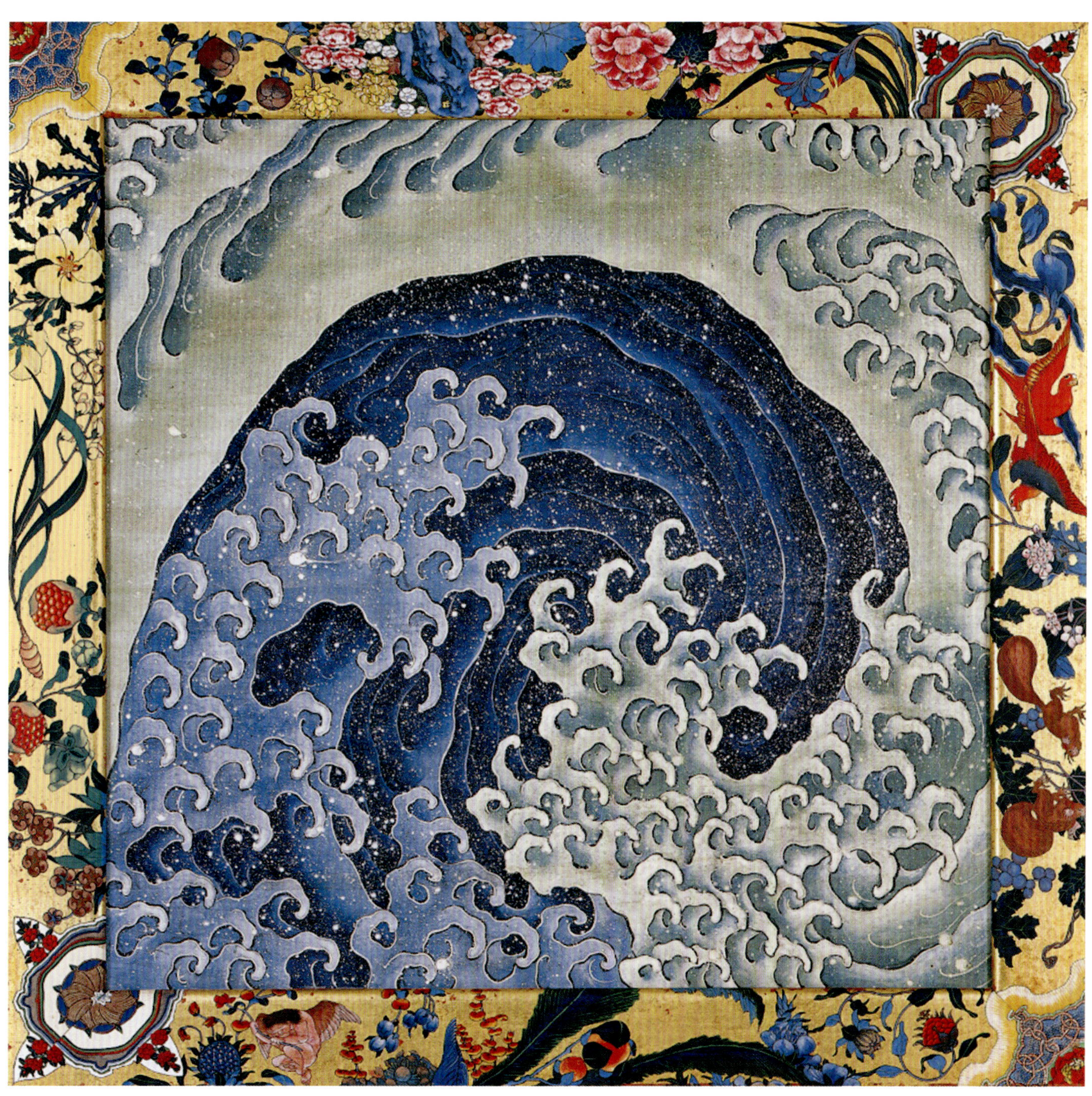

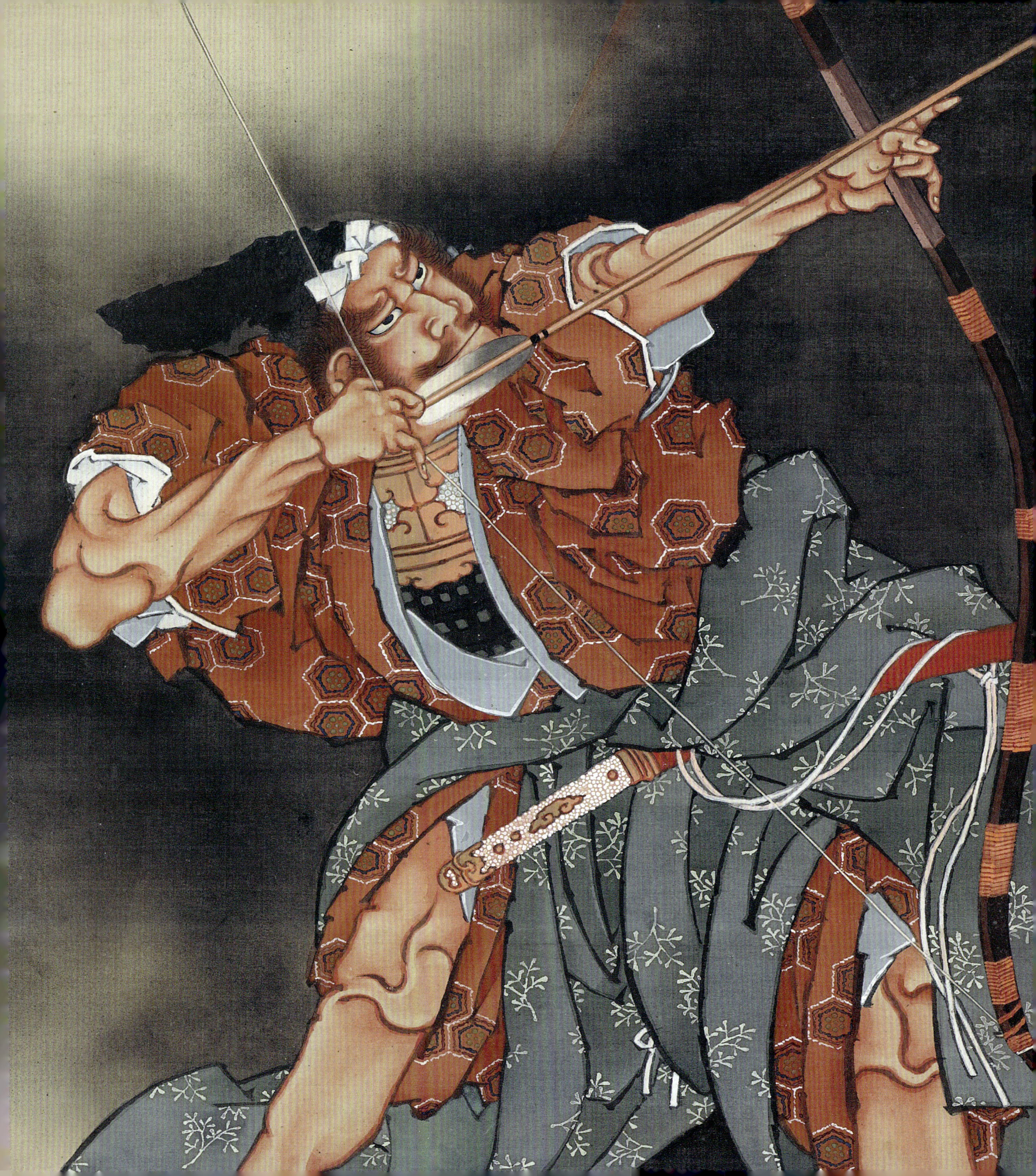

Immortality

Numbers were vital for Hokusai. In 1820, at the age of sixty-one, the beginning of his second sexagenary cycle, he assumed a new art name that announced his turning 'one again'. He usually combined it with a seal, Katsushika, which referred to the county in which he had been born. Fourteen years later, with the publication of *One Hundred Views of Mt Fuji* (cat. 176), he changed again. His new seal, incorporating Mt Fuji, proclaimed an identification with the mountain, while the new name, Manji, declared his affiliation to 'ten thousand things', or, 'everything'. In a postscript to that book, Hokusai also announced his determination to live long enough, at one hundred, to achieve a 'divine state' in his art, so that at one hundred and ten 'every dot and every stroke will be as though alive'. In 1847, aged eighty-eight, the desire became even more urgent and Hokusai began exclusively using 'hyaku', the character for one hundred, in a large new seal. He died just two years later. But the last paintings, stamped with this seal, are witness to both ambition and accomplishment. They are an extraordinary final outpouring and summation of a life lived in devotion to the power of art to connect to the world.

Hokusai's art was founded on meticulous, patient observation, such as that depicted in his painting of the classical Chinese poet Li Bo (AD 701–762) (cat. 220). His encyclopaedic command of style and technique, honed over six decades, gave Hokusai the freedom to reveal new truths: how light brings to life a casual heap of fans (cat. 219); how ducks, leaves and weeds move in flowing water (cat. 210), or a cuckoo rides the wind (cat. 218); and how Fuji, glimpsed through pines, compels rapt attention (cat. 209).

Hokusai did not remain an impartial observer, however. Art gave him a way to imagine himself into the world, to identify with his subjects – and so, like the philosopher Zhuang Zhou (fourth century BC) (cat. 214), to question the very boundary between 'dream' and 'reality'. Sometimes his late paintings encourage quiet contemplation (cat. 212). Sometimes they crackle with energy (cat. 208). And sometimes they inspire awe and ecstasy, connecting the human world to the divine (cat. 215).

Hokusai did not stay Hokusai, therefore. Not for the first time (cat. 101), he could project himself into the underwhelming figure of a cormorant, ignoring his unprepossessing surroundings to contemplate the wider world (cat. 213). He could feel like a tiger, snarling into pouring rain (cat. 222). Or, most protean of all, repeatedly, he could become a dragon, coiling up out of a storm (cat. 223) and ascending above Mt Fuji (cat. 221). AL

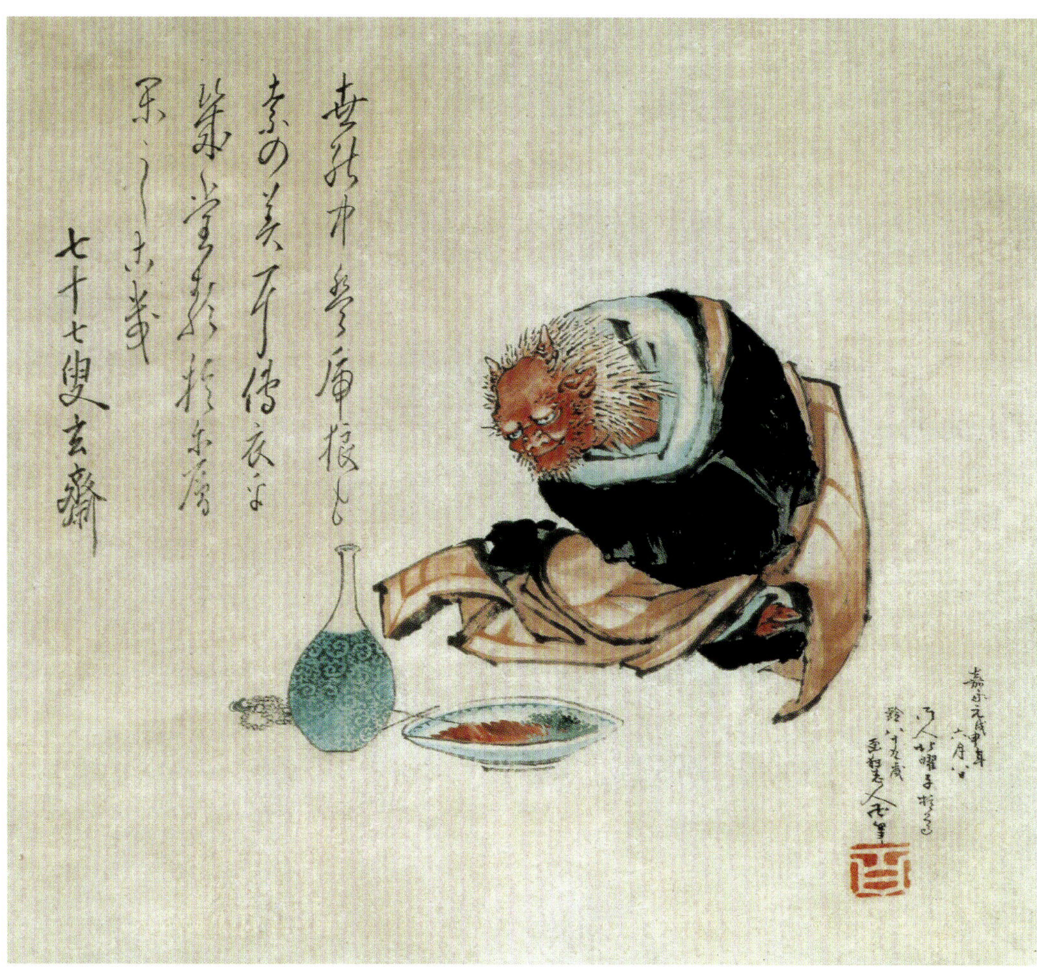

Demon feasting

Early sixth month, 1848
Signature: Ka'ei gan tsuchinoe saru nen / rokugatsu
yōka / monjin Hokuyō-shi okuru / yowai hachijūkyū
sai / Gakyō rōjin Manji hitsu ('Brush of Manji, aged
eighty-nine years, old man crazy to paint, given to my
pupil Hokuyō, 8th day, sixth month, Ka'ei 1 [1848]')
Seal: Hyaku ('Hundred')
Inscription signed Nanajūnana sō Gensai ('Gensai,
old man of seventy-seven')
Hanging scroll, ink and colour on paper, 52.8 × 56.2 cm
Provenance: Honma Hokuyō (1822–1868); exhibited at
Honma Museum of Art, Sakata (June, 1947)
Literature: Nagata 1983; Nagata 2000, no. 137;
TNM 2005, no. 493; Paris 2014, no. 513
Sano Art Museum, Mishima

A red devil in priestly robes leans longingly towards
a dish of appetizing raw fish and a bottle of saké.
His rosary is beside the bottle. Buddhist priests were
not supposed to enjoy such delicacies, so perhaps it
is temptation that has transformed him into a devil?
Quickly and informally done, the painting's every detail
crackles with sprightly energy. Hokusai's inscription says
he gave the work to his pupil Hokuyō on the 8th day of
the sixth month, 1848. Hokuyō's diary confirms that,
after worshipping at the Asakusa temple, he spent the
rest of the 5th day talking with Hokusai at his home,
and then returned on the 8th. Honma Mitsuyoshi
(1822–1868) was from a wealthy family of shipping
transport agents (*kaisen-doiya*) in Sakata, Dewa province
(modern Yamagata). He became a pupil of Hokusai
in about 1843 and was awarded the name Hokuyō.
The inscription is by Ikeda Gensai (1775–1852) of the
neighbouring Shōnai fief, and was added in 1851. TC

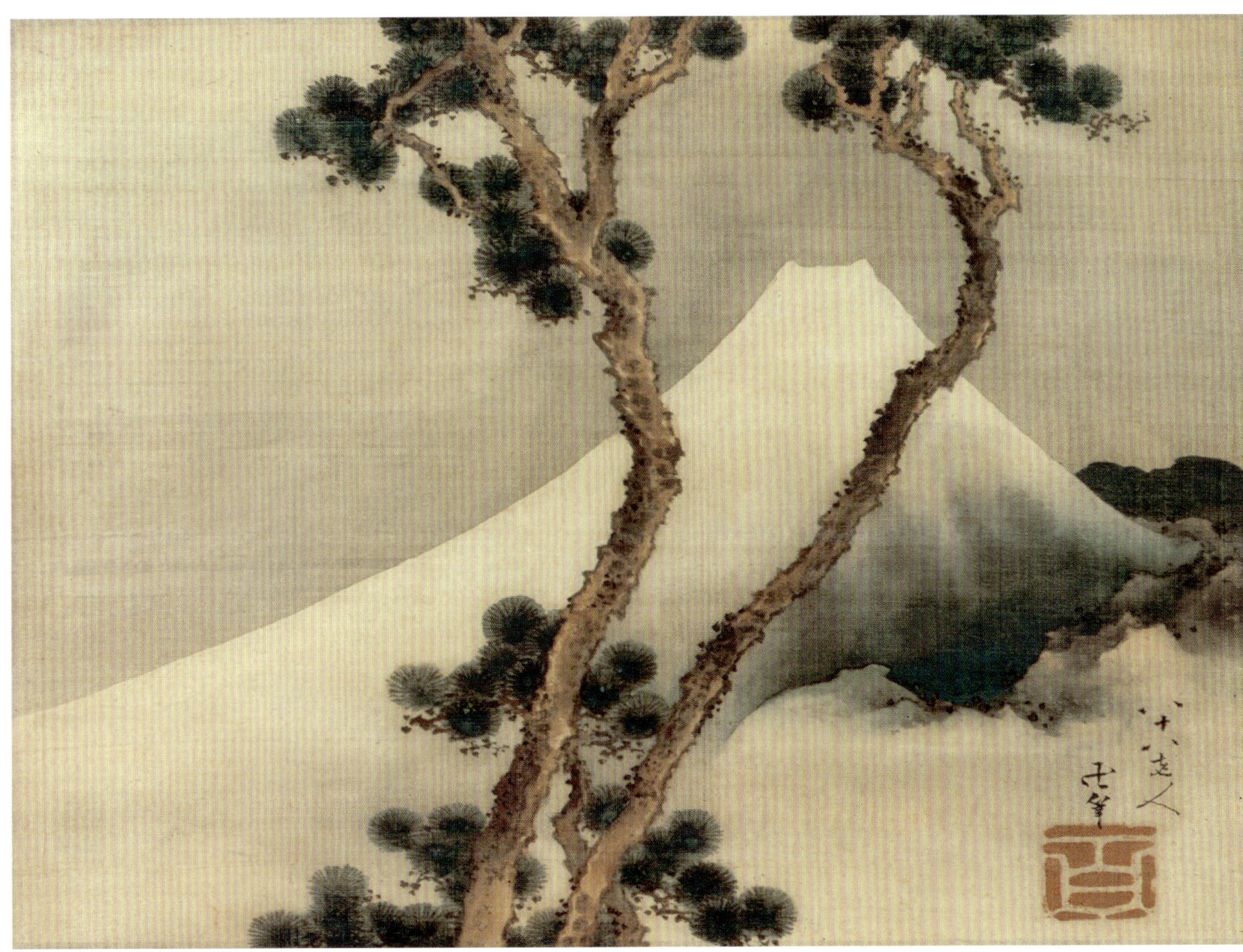

209

Mt Fuji through pines

1847
Signature: Hachijūhachi rōjin / Manji hitsu ('Brush of
Manji, old man of eighty-eight')
Seal: Hyaku ('Hundred')
Hanging scroll, ink and colour on silk, 28.7 × 37.6 cm
Provenance: Sumishō, Tokyo (2000)
Literature: Kobayashi Tadashi, 'Katsushika Hokusai
hitsu *Fugaku zu*', *Kokka* 1268, June 2001, p. 2; Edo Tokyo
2007, no. 207
Private collection, Japan

The relatively small size of this painting belies its
monumental composition. The snow-covered peak of
Mt Fuji, left unpainted in the natural colour of the silk,
is glimpsed between the attenuated trunks of two pine
trees. This conceit recalls 'Hodogaya' from the print
series *Thirty-Six Views of Mt Fuji*, as well as several
compositions from the book *One Hundred Views of
Mt Fuji* (cat. 176) – particularly 'Fuji through pines'
(*Matsugoshi no Fuji*) in volume 2. Foothills on the right
side are painted with unexpectedly colourful scumbling,
including a deep blue, which is also used for the
looming mountain range that continues round to the
back of Mt Fuji. Tree trunks, branches and rock are
all enlivened with energetic ink dots. TC

Ducks in flowing water

1847
Signature: Yowai hachijūhachi Manji ('Manji, aged eighty-eight')
Seal: Hyaku ('Hundred')
Hanging scroll, ink and colour on silk, 111.0 × 40.0 cm
Provenance: Arthur Morrison
Literature: Clark 1992, no. 103; Nagata 2000, no. 131; TNM 2005, no. 488; Paris 2014, no. 509
British Museum, 1913,0501,0.320, given by Sir W. Gwynne-Evans, Bt

One male mallard looks quizzically out at us; the other dives for pond weed. Ripples eddy towards us, creating complex visual effects – clearly of particular interest to Hokusai – suggesting light and reflection. Fallen maple leaves sink into the water and start to disappear, and the richly coloured weed fades to indistinct silhouettes in the depths. Far beyond mere naturalism, there is an almost symbolic reverence for the moment, a sense of personal identification with the natural world, a mood shared with some of the other final paintings (cat. 218). In *Picture Book: Essence of Colouring* (cat. 211), published the following year, Hokusai gives instructions on how to paint just such a duck, as well as many other birds, creatures and plants, providing black-and-white illustrations while also giving recipes for preparing the necessary pigments. TC

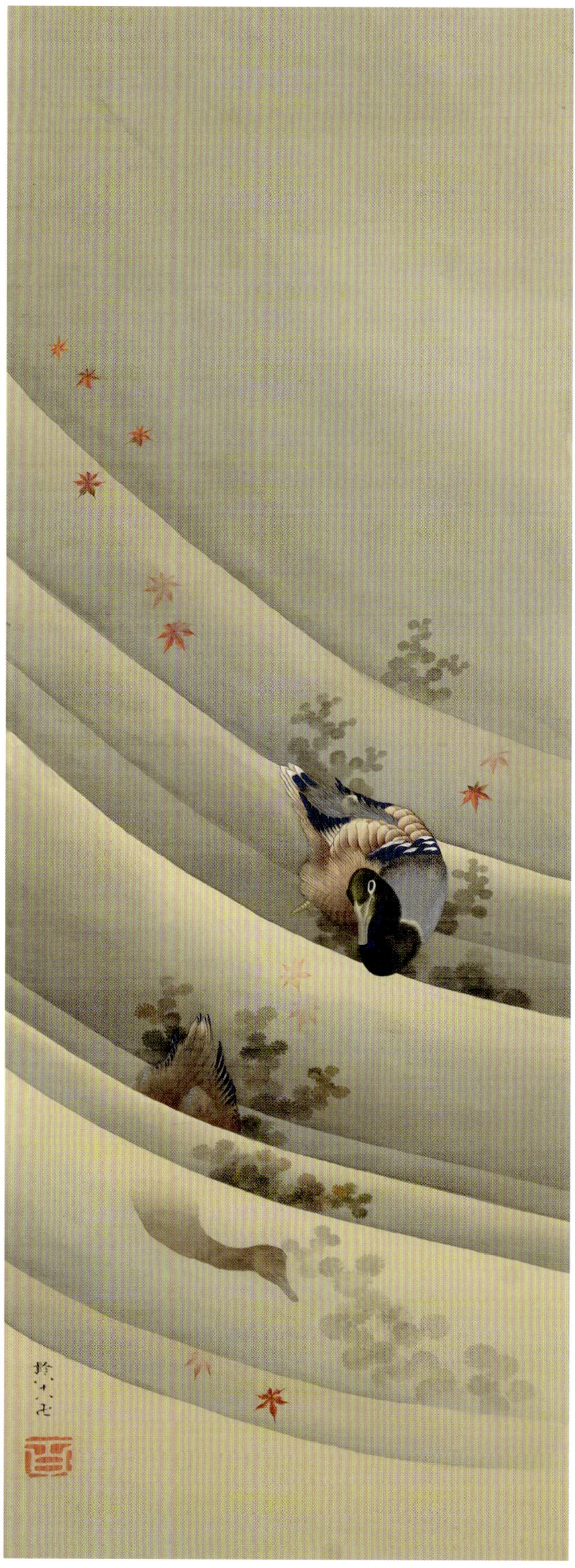

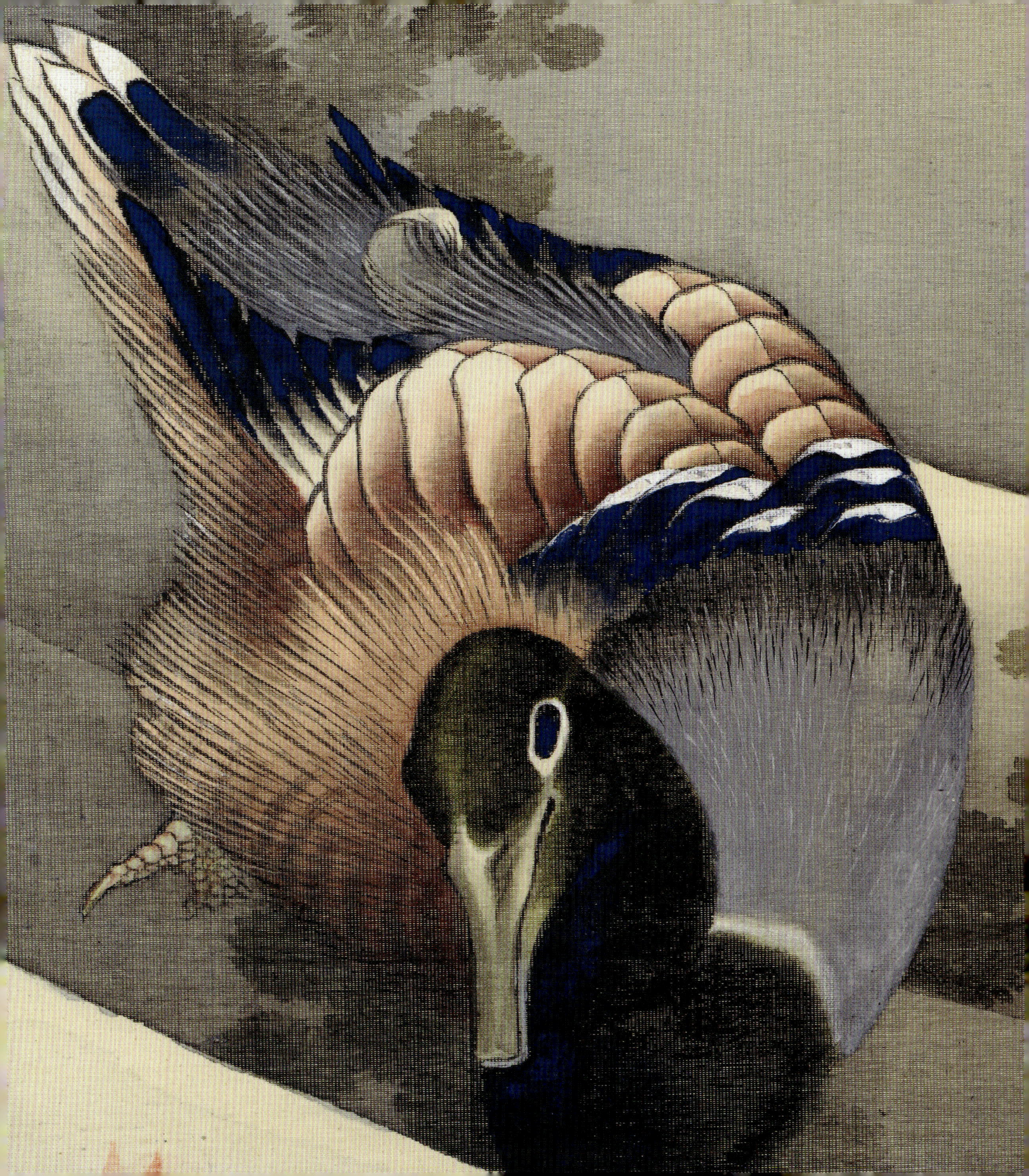

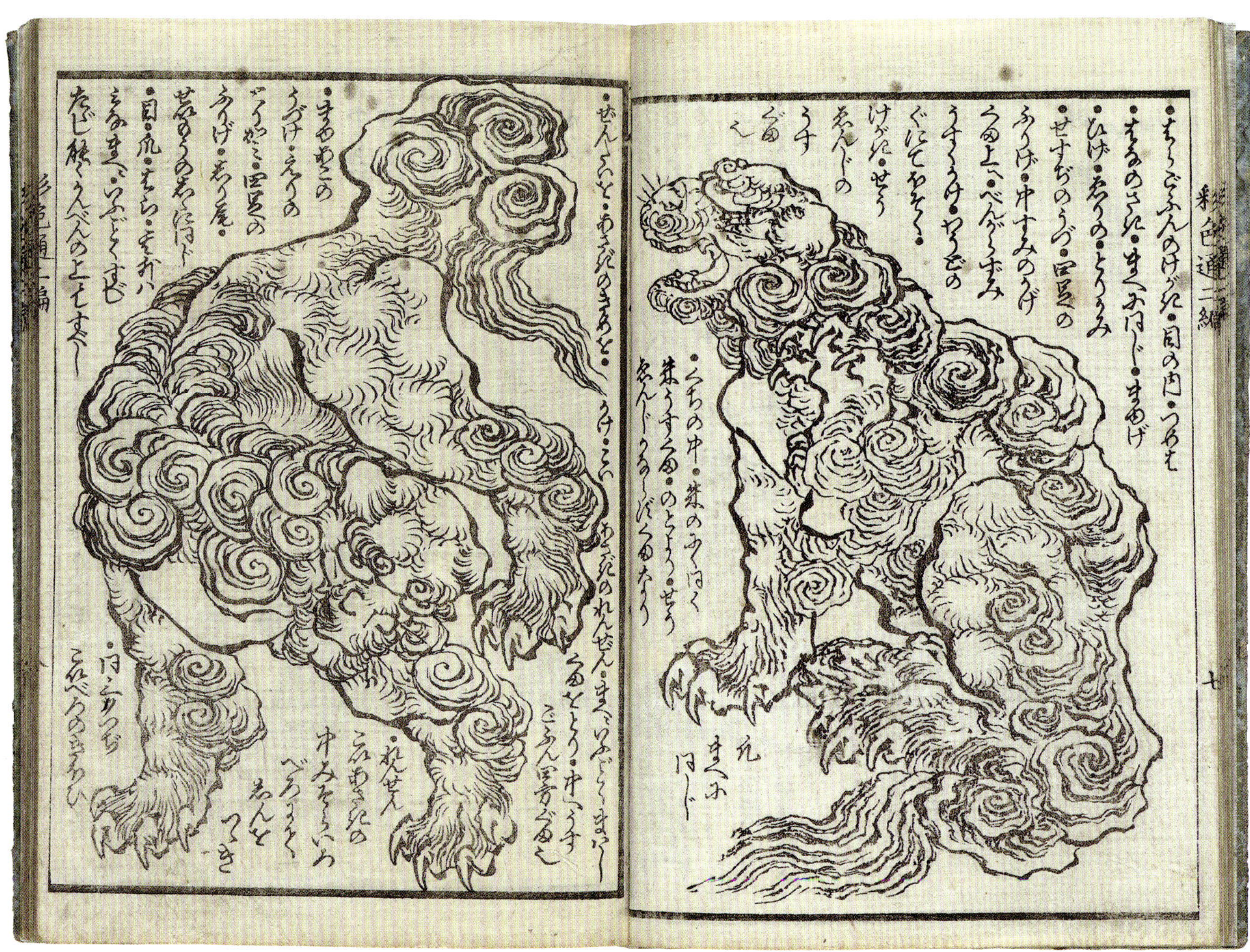

211

Chinese lions, from *Picture Book: Essence of Colouring (Ehon saishiki tsū)*

1848
Signature: Muhitsu Hachiemon ('Brushless
Hachiemon', vol. 1); Saki no Hokusai Manji rōjin cho
('Written by old man Manji, the former Hokusai', vol. 2)
Illustrated book, woodblock, 2 vols, published by
Yamaguchiya Tōbei and others, 18.0 × 13.0 cm (covers)
Provenance: Jack Hillier
Literature: Nagata *Edehon* 3, 1985–1986, vol. 3;
Retta 1994
British Museum, 1979,0305,0.465

Chinese lions, like ones in Hokusai's 'Daily Exorcism'
brush drawings (cat. 192) are shown in controposto
poses, with mouths open and closed. Their manes,
tails and fur are formed into eccentric swirls, and both
mythic beasts exude a strong personality. In the text,
mostly written in easy-to-read phonetic script, Hokusai
gives advice on colours and how to apply them. Far
more painted works have survived from Hokusai's
eighty-eighth year than from any other year of his life.
This book, compiled in 1847 when he was eighty-eight,
supports the impression that the artist's prime concern
during this time was his legacy in painting. Hokusai
writes as much in the postscript to volume 1, and
anticipates getting better and better after ninety and
one hundred. He expresses satisfaction at the modest
price of each small volume of a projected set of four;
in the event only two were published. TC

Mountain landscape

1847
Signature: Hachijūhachi rō Manji hitsu ('Brush of
Manji, old man of eighty-eight')
Seal: Hyaku ('Hundred')
Hanging scroll, ink and colour on paper,
127.0 × 53.5 cm
Literature: Ozaki 1967, no. 38; Hokusaikan 1985, p. 34;
Nagata 2000, no. 133; Hokusaikan 2015, pp. 86–87
Hokusai Museum, Obuse

In the rugged foreground formation of rocks and cliffs
a village nestles among trees; softer hills occupy the
middle ground; and in the distance rises a lofty peak
– each done in a different style and connected by banks
of mist in pale ink. The location does not seem to be
specific, although the angular brushwork and rich
tonalities of the foreground rocks evoke China.
The azure blue of the distant peak even suggests a
mythological realm, as also seen in the *Woodcutter*
painting of Hokusai's ninetieth year (Freer-Sackler
2006, vol. 1, no. 162). Within this expansive, monumental
late landscape, Hokusai perhaps invites us to identify
with the four boatmen straining to pole their loads
of rushes upstream. Falling cherry blossoms scatter
lyrically on the water around them. TC

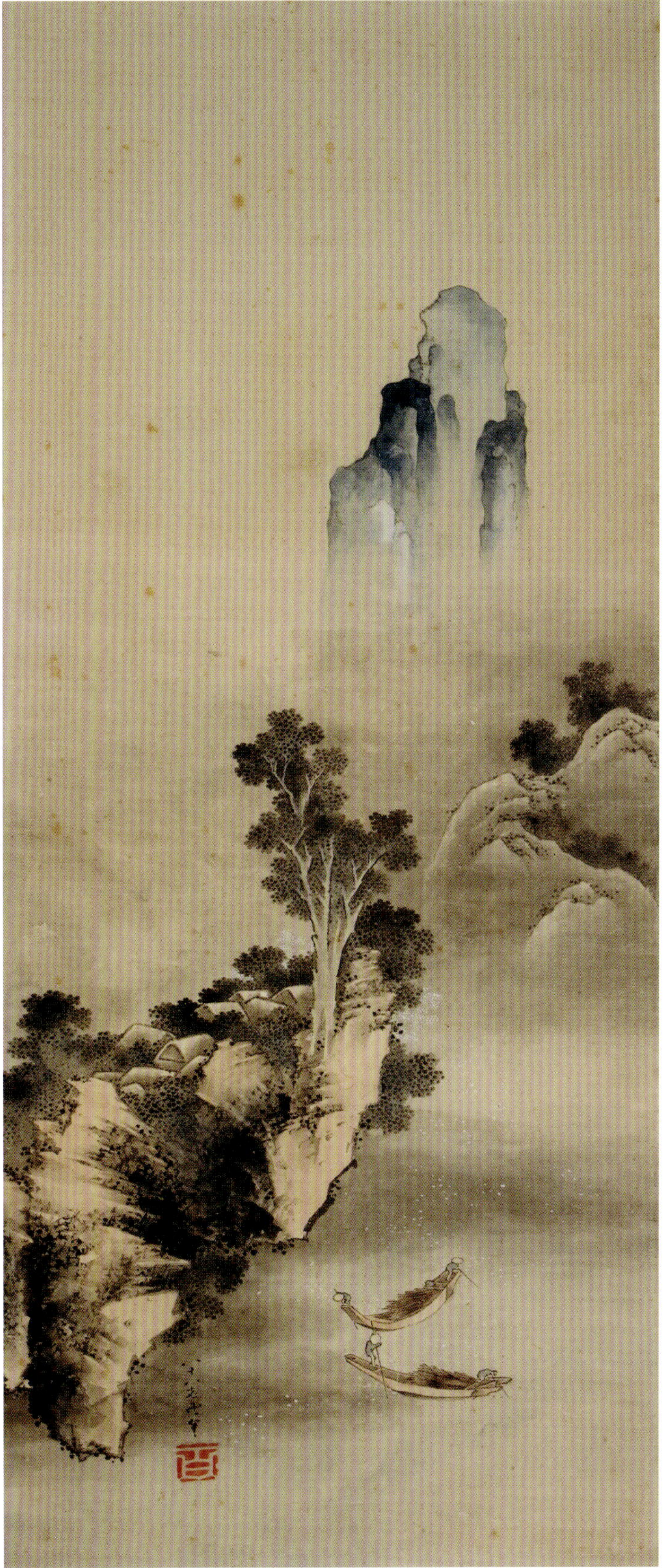

Cormorant on a post

1847
Signature: Hachijūhachi rō Manji hitsu ('Brush of
Manji, old man of eighty-eight')
Seal: Hyaku ('Hundred')
Hanging scroll, ink and colour on paper,
126.1 × 47.8 cm
Provenance: James Martin White
Literature: Fenollosa 1901, no. 211; BM 1948, no. 171;
Clark 1992, no. 104
British Museum, 1950,1111,0.16, given by the Trustees
of James Martin White

This is a deliberately eccentric painting: subject –
an ungainly cormorant inspecting us warily out of
one eye; viewpoint – looking up from mudflats that
surround encrusted breakwater posts; technique –
a different treatment used for each part of the
composition. Perhaps the willed insistence here from
eighty-eight-year-old Hokusai that we should focus on
an un-picturesque scene is in fact the point? When we
look longer, secondary qualities are revealed: yellow
candock (*kōhone*) plants emerging from the water at
different stages of flowering; iridescent deep blue
flashes within the plumage of the bird; rich colouring
beneath the scumbled textures on the post; the stalks
and leaves of the flowering water plant stretched taut.
Hokusai gives instructions for painting candock plants
in volume 1 of *Picture Book: Essence of Colouring* (cat. 211),
probably written in the same year that this hanging
scroll was painted. TC

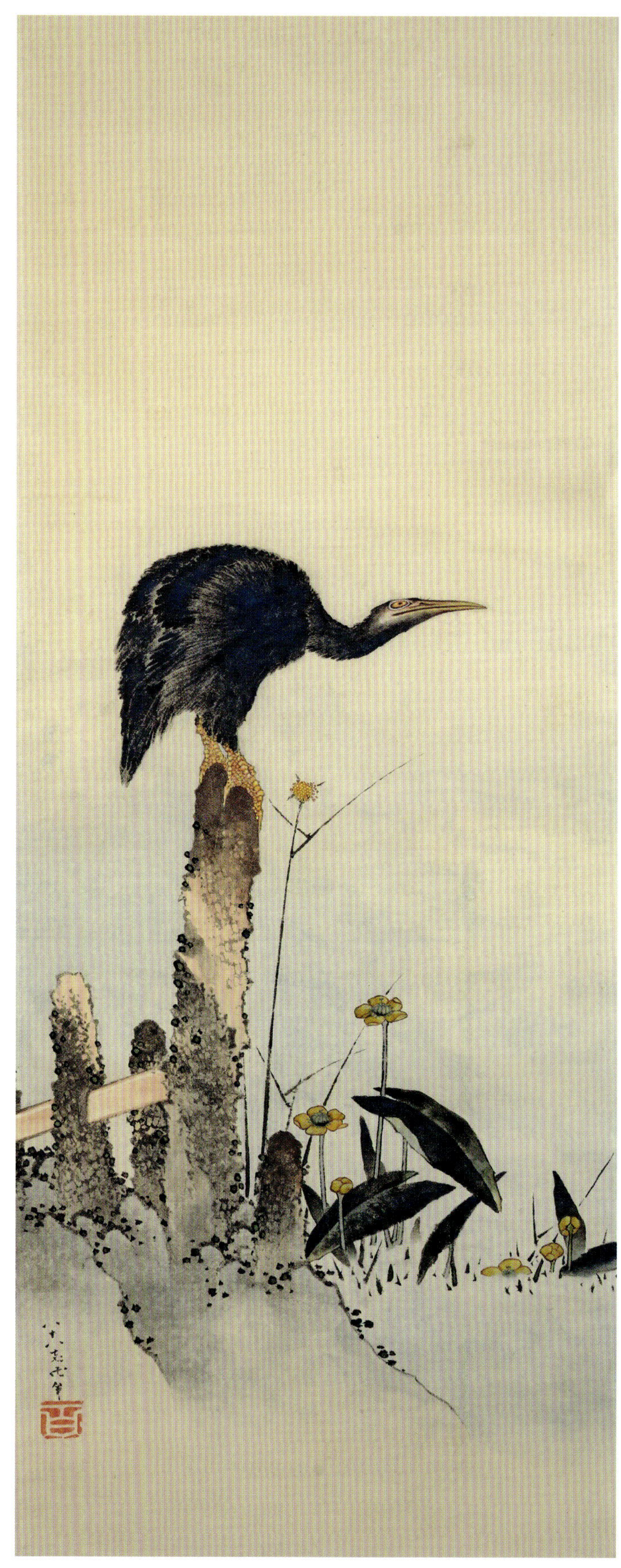

Zhuang Zhou dreaming of butterflies

1847
Signature: Hachijūhachi rō Manji hitsu ('Brush of
Manji, old man of eighty-eight')
Seal: Hyaku ('Hundred')
Hanging scroll, ink and colour on paper, 93.1 × 28.3 cm
British Museum, 1996,1105,0.1, purchase funded by
Brooke-Sewell bequest

The painting illustrates a conundrum posed by the
ancient Chinese philosopher Zhuang Zhou (also
Zhuangzi, fourth century BC): *If you make too clear a
distinction between dreaming and being awake, then how do you
know which state you are actually in?* 'Once, Zhuang Zhou
dreamed he was a butterfly.… He didn't know that
he was Zhuang Zhou. Suddenly he woke up … [b]ut he
didn't know if he was Zhuang Zhou who had dreamed
he was a butterfly, or a butterfly dreaming that he was
Zhuang Zhou. Between Zhuang Zhou and the butterfly
there must be *some* distinction! This is called the
Transformation of Things.' (Burton Watson, *Zhuangzi:
Basic Writings*, New York, Columbia University Press,
1964, repr. 2003, p. 44.) Hokusai had transformed his
art over many decades in order to identify ever closer
with his subjects; so what better illustration of his
credo? As with so many of the late paintings, he focuses
attention on the face of the protagonist – the calm,
rapt expression of the philosopher who is literally
lost in reverie. Quickly and deftly brushed, each
idiosyncratic line and subtle wash locks together to
form an inspired whole. TC

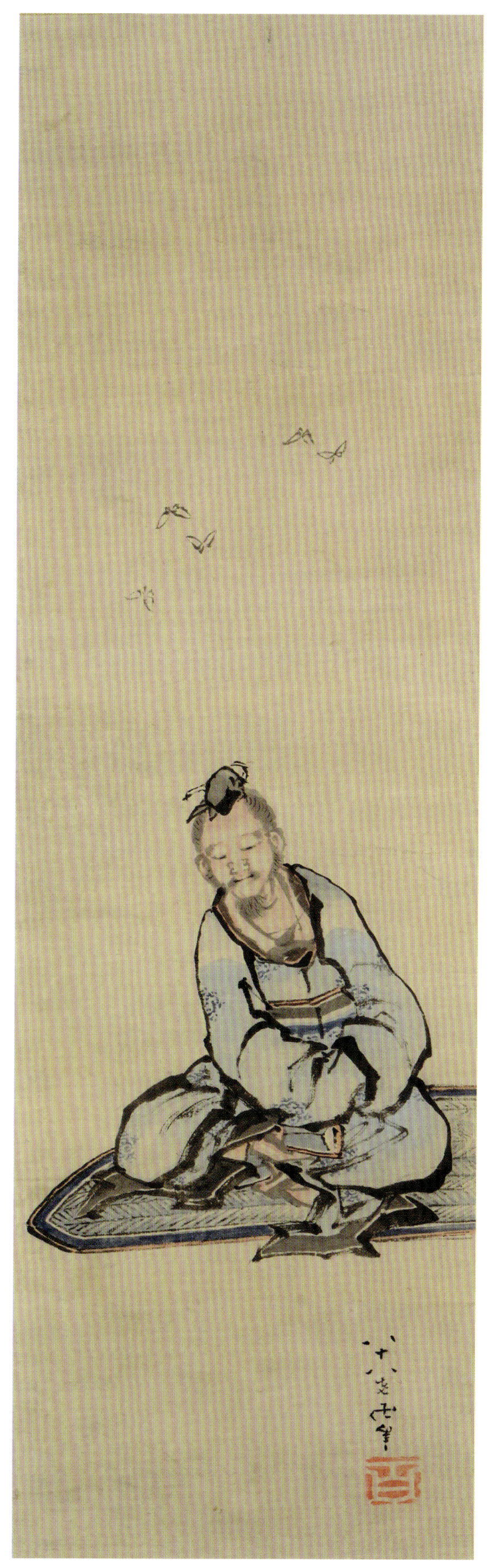

215

Monk Nichiren and the seven-headed dragon deity

1847
Signature: Hachijūhachi rōjin Manji keihitsu
('Respectfully brushed by Manji, old man of
eighty-eight')
Seal: Hyaku ('Hundred')
Hanging scroll, ink and colour on paper,
132.3 × 59.3 cm
Literature: NU 1982, no. 39; Narazaki 1984, pp. 47–48,
plate; TNM 2005, no. 491
Myōkōji temple, Koga

In the eleventh month of 1277 monk Nichiren
(1222–1282) preached at a great rock on the summit
of Mt Minobu in Kai province (modern Yamanashi
prefecture). The congregation were suspicious of
a mysterious, beautiful woman who listened intently.
When challenged by Nichiren she revealed herself
to be the seven-headed dragon deity Shichimen
Daimyōjin, or Shichimen Tennyo, of nearby Mt
Shichimen. In this work, Hokusai, a lifelong and devout
believer in Nichiren Buddhism, makes perhaps his
ultimate artistic statement of that faith. The seven-
headed dragon stares hypnotically straight out from
deep black storm clouds, while two groups of the
congregation cower and huddle together in ecstasy
and awe. The fulcrum of the composition, Nichiren is
calm and resolute as he reads from a holy sutra scroll,
his priestly robes and decorated rug tugged at by a
violent wind. Black ink flicked from the brush to add
final excitement has been skilfully aimed so as to avoid
the faces of the dragon and Nichiren. TC

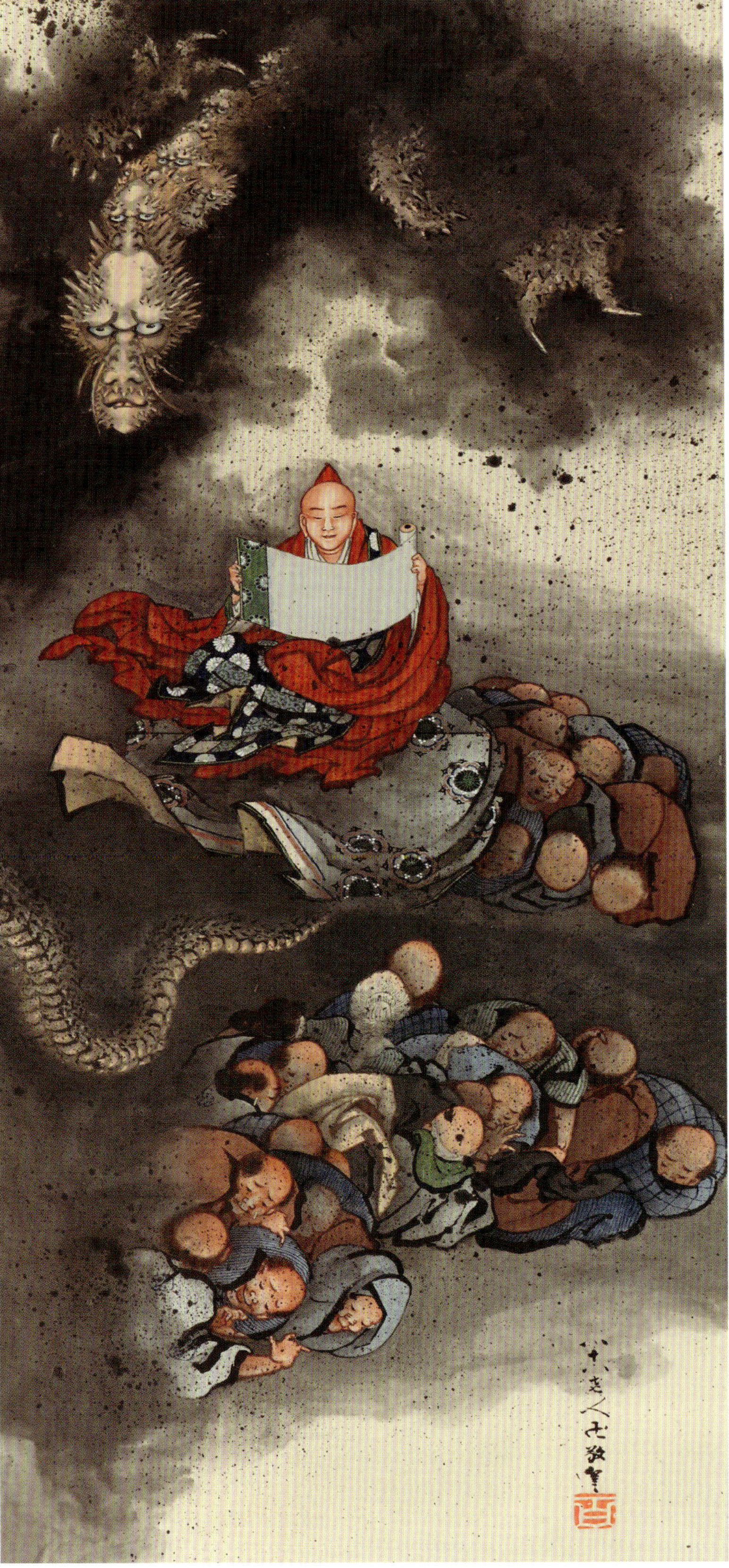

Yorimasa killing the Nue monster

1847
Signature: Hachijūhachi rōjin / Manji hitsu ('Brush of
Manji, old man of eighty-eight')
Seal: Hyaku ('Hundred')
Hanging scroll, ink and colour on silk,
99.0 × 42.2 cm
Provenance: Akiyama Chikanori/Jokō (1919)
Literature: UT 1931, no. 89; Nagata 2000, no. 130;
TNM 2005, no. 489
Private collection, USA

A muscular warrior aims an arrow up into pitch
blackness with grim intensity. The strong diagonal of
his arms and the arrow, intersected by the bow-string
and a sliver of lightning, focuses attention on his hirsute,
resolute features. This is Minamoto no Yorimasa
(1104–1180). The warrior chronicles *Heike monogatari* and
Genpei seisuiki recount how in the fourth month of 1153
he was ordered to subdue a monster that had been
appearing above the Shishinden palace each night
and disturbing Emperor Konoe (reigned 1141–1155).
Yorimasa's inspired shot into the dark found its target:
a fantastic creature with the head of a monkey, body
of a raccoon-dog, tail of a serpent and legs of a tiger
– the mythical Nue monster – fell from the sky, to be
finished off with a dagger by the warrior's henchman
I no Hayata. Hokusai, as in many of his late paintings,
dispenses with extraneous elements and condenses
the scene to its essence. Brilliant technique is used for
complex patterning of the robes, modelling of the
features and subtle gradation of the ragged edge of
the black cloud. TC

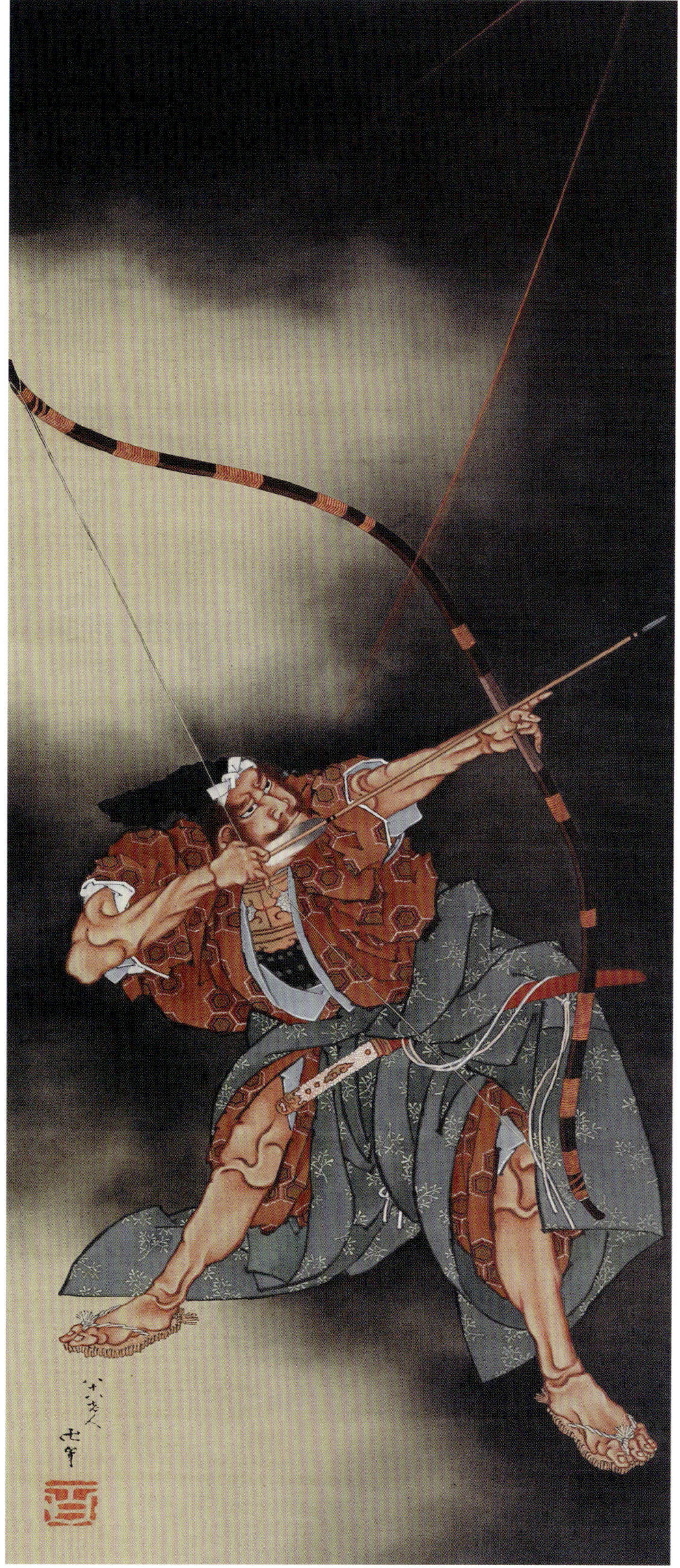

Fox priest (right) and raccoon-dog priest (left)

1848
Signature (both): Manji rōjin hitsu / yowai hachijūkyū
sai ('Brush of old man Manji, aged eighty-nine years')
Seal (both): Hyaku ('Hundred')
Pair of hanging scrolls, ink and colour on paper,
each about 123.6 × 57.9 cm
Provenance: Hatta Hikojirō, Nagano prefecture (1914,
1926); Manno Art Museum, Osaka
Literature: *Kokka* 284, 1913–1914, p. 167, *Kokka* 423,
Feb. 1926, p. 55; NUT 1994–1996, vol. 7, nos 52, 53;
Nagata 2000, nos 135, 136; TNM 2005, no. 492;
Paris 2014, no. 512
Private collection, Japan, Important Art Object
Osaka only

Both paintings, evidently a pair, feature shape-shifting
animals who have morphed into Buddhist priests.
The bushy-tailed fox impersonates a priest called
Hakuzōsu, protagonist of the comic *kyōgen* drama *Konkai*
(or *Tsurigitsune*). After admonishing a hunter for setting
traps, he is nonetheless unable to resist the dead mouse
that hangs as bait in a noose. Meanwhile, the legend
of the 'plentiful tea kettle' (*bunbuku chagama*) is set at
the Zen temple Morinji, in Kōzuke province (modern
Gunma prefecture) in the early 1400s. People were
mystified that no matter how much water was ladled
from the tea kettle, it never ran dry. The mystery was
solved when the priest Shukaku was revealed to be a
trickster raccoon-dog (*tanuki*) in disguise. The paintings
are quickly and confidently done in rich tonalities,
using a variety of dry and moist brushwork. A pleasing
contrast is established between the fox in a wind-blown,
darkening landscape and the raccoon-dog snugly
ensconced next to the kettle on the hearth, from which
a meandering trail of smoke slowly drifts up the scroll. TC

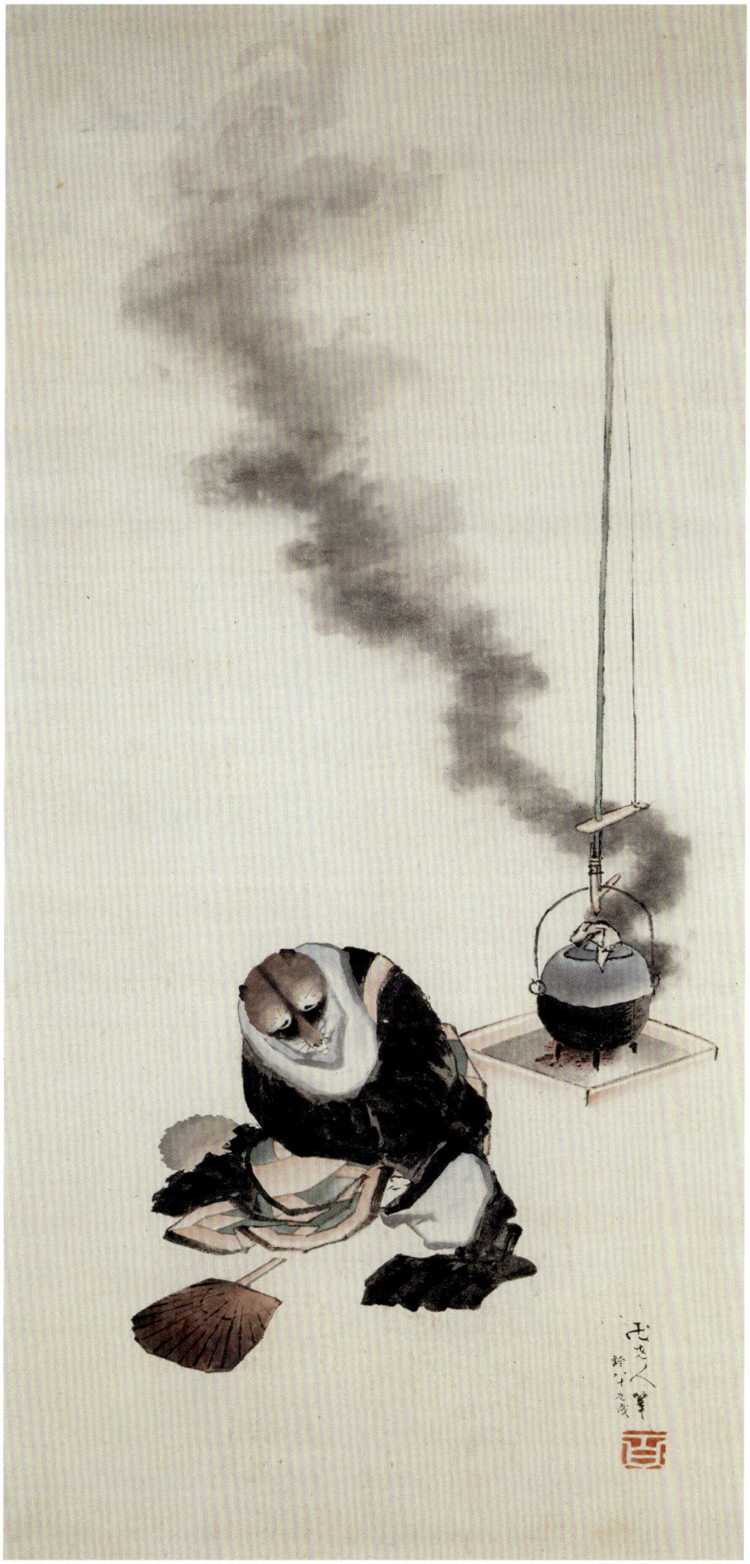

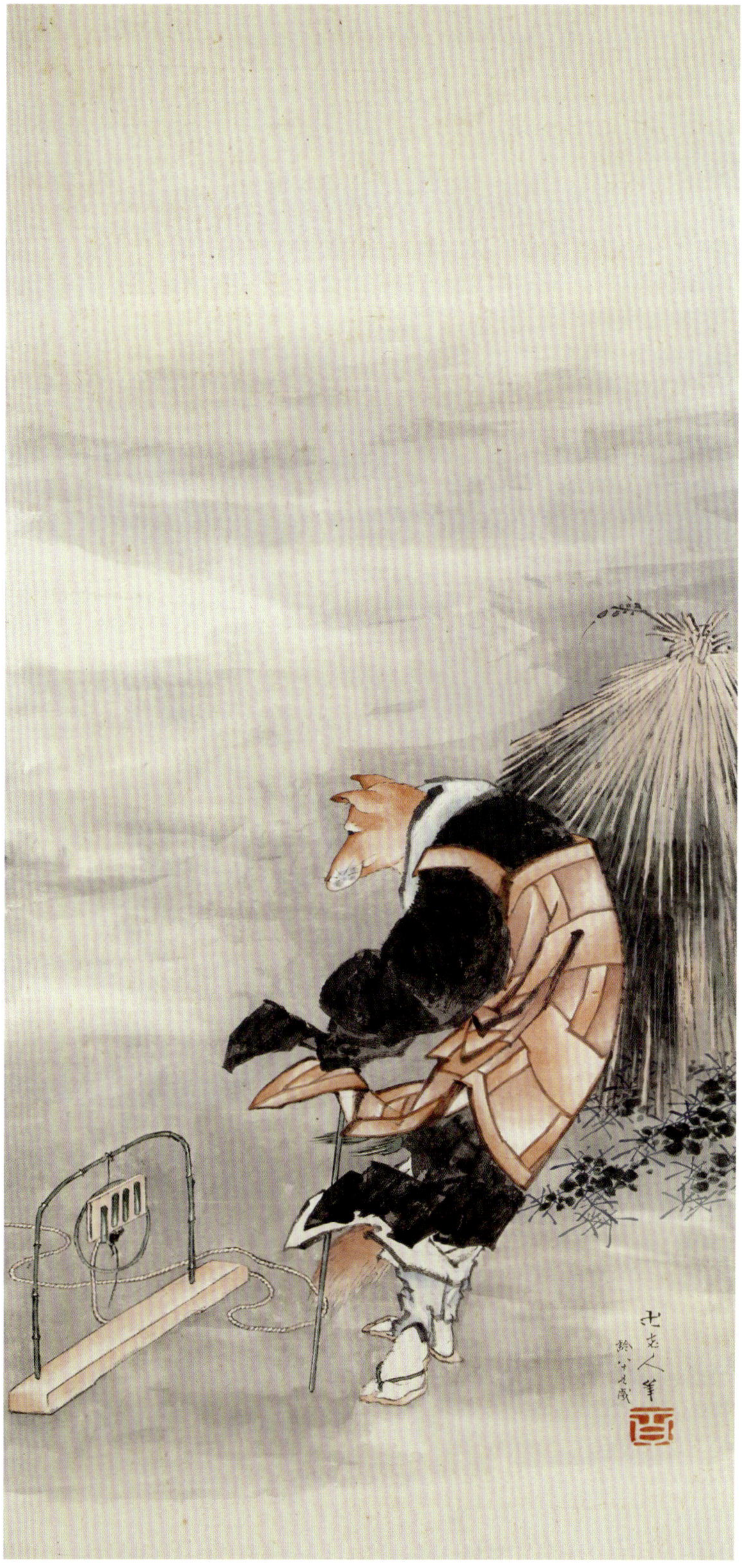

Cuckoo and rainbow

1848
Signature: Manji rōjin hitsu / yowai hachijūkyū sai
('Brush of old man Manji, aged eighty-nine years')
Seal: Hyaku ('Hundred')
Hanging scroll, ink and colour on paper,
116.0 × 49.0 cm
Provenance: Ōtani Yonetarō
Literature: UT 1931, no. 71; Ozaki 1967, no. 89;
Nagata 2000, no. 134
Private collection, Japan
Osaka only

A cuckoo (*hototogisu*) calls out as it falls through the sky.
The grove of trees is buffeted by the winds of the
passing shower, signalled by the rainbow above. This
vignette of early summer is presented like a pictorial
haiku poem (*hokku*), reduced to emblematic elements.
Hokusai's signature and age, too, are written with
appropriate informality. The artist had drawn similar
cuckoos several times in his career (cat. 94) and detailed
instructions are given for painting the bird in an
identical pose in *Picture Book: Essence of Colouring*
(cat. 211), recently published at the New Year of 1848.
The combination of cuckoo and rainbow features in
one plate of *Album of model paintings* (cat. 175). New here
is the sense of the rustling movement of the trees,
created by a combination of rough, spontaneous
strokes in ink with blue and green washes, and finished
off with tiny yellow flowers. TC

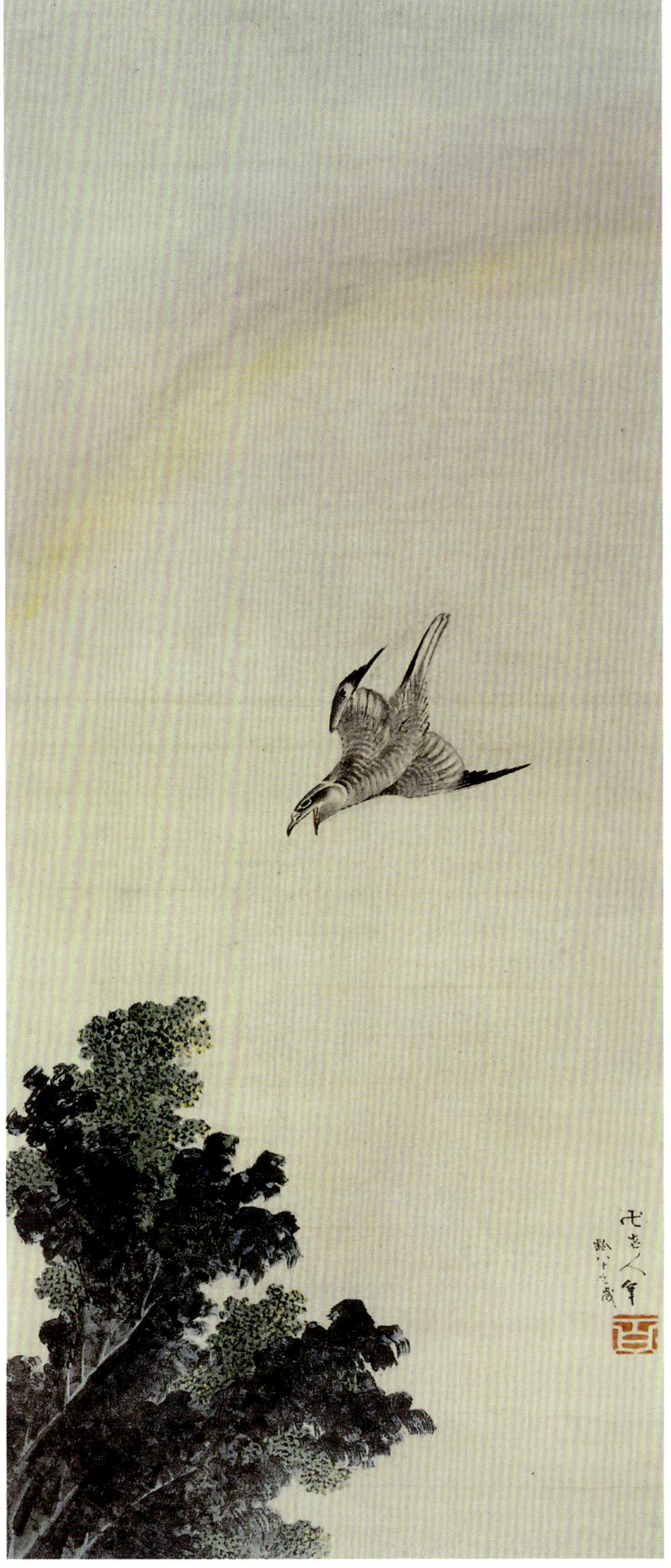

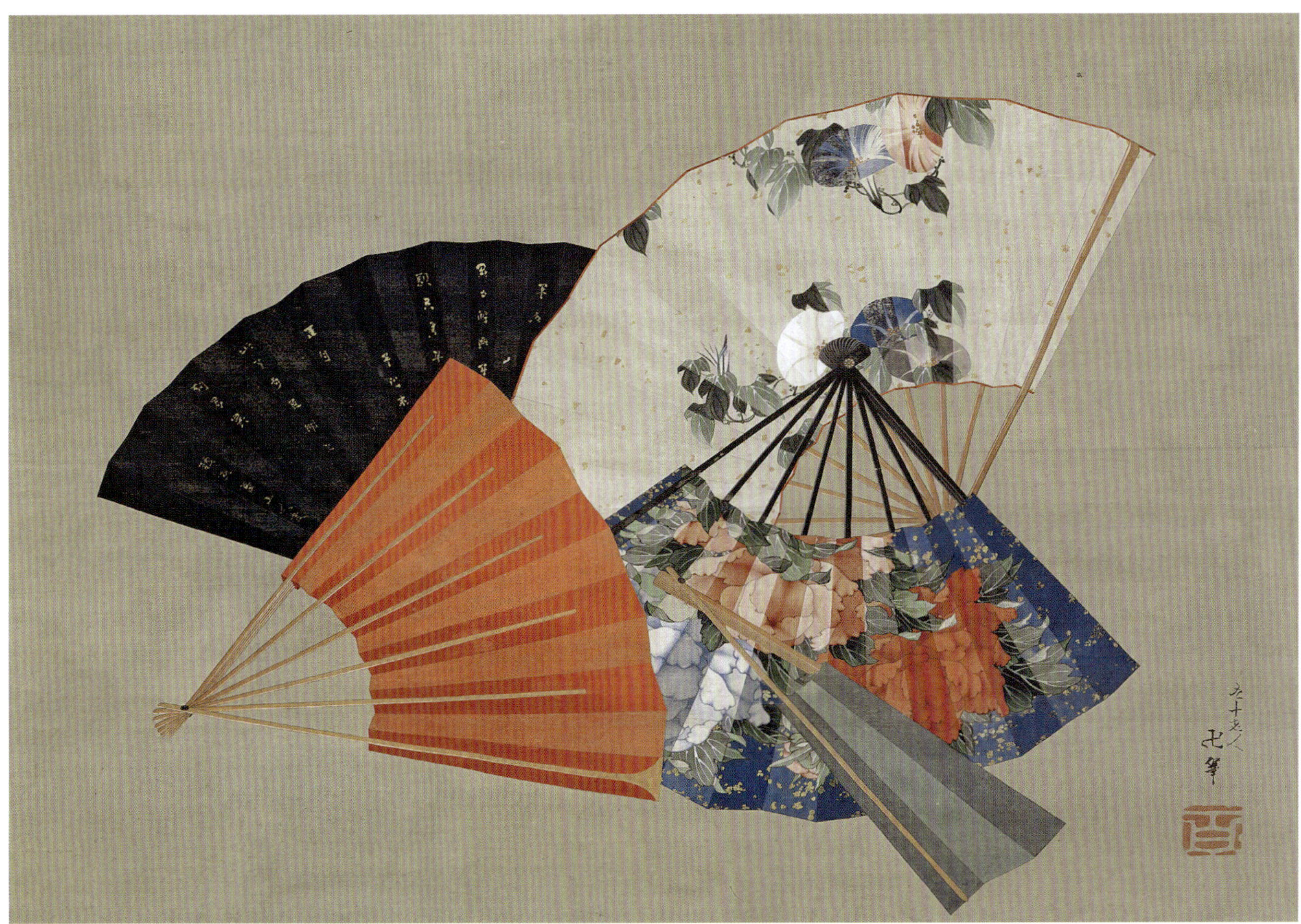

219

Scattered fans

1849
Signature: Kyūjū rōjin / Manji hitsu ('Brush of Manji, old man of ninety')
Seal: Hyaku ('Hundred')
Hanging scroll, ink, colour and gold on silk,
51.5 × 71.4 cm
Provenance: Yamatane Museum of Art
Literature: Nagata 2000, no. 138; TNM 2005, no. 494; Paris 2014, no. 517
Tokyo National Museum, A-12347
London only

Five decorative folding fans, each opened to a different extent, are scattered casually and satisfyingly in a heap. Two are plain colours – red and blue – perhaps shown from the reverse side. Two more have elaborate paintings of flowers – peonies and morning glories – with scattered gold leaf embellishing their bright blue and white backgrounds respectively. The fifth fan has what looks to be a Chinese-style poem written in gold characters on a dark blue background. Extraordinary care has been taken to record how the light catches differently on each of the folds, and the detailing of the ribs and pivot pins is also hyper-realistic. The unpainted background, however, serves to divorce the fans from reality and encourages us to savour their almost animate materiality. Hokusai died on the 18th day of the fourth month of his ninetieth year, 1849, after a short final illness. These paintings, signed 'aged ninety', must have been done – or completed – within a relatively short space of time. TC

Li Bo admiring a waterfall

1849
Signature: Yowai kyūjussai / Gakyō rōjin Manji hitsu
('Brush of Manji, old man crazy to paint, aged ninety
years')
Seal: Hyaku ('Hundred')
Hanging scroll, ink and colour on silk, 93.4 × 30.0 cm
Literature: Nagata 2000, no. 139; Boston 2015, no. 50
Museum of Fine Arts, Boston, 11.7452, William Sturgis
Bigelow collection
Osaka only

Li Bo (AD 701–762), one of the great poets of China's
Tang dynasty, retired to Mt Lu to avoid the rebellion
of AD 755 by the general An Lushan (about AD 703–757).
While there he composed a poem in admiration of a
waterfall. Hokusai had already designed a large colour
print on the subject (cat. 123, with translation of the
poem by Alfred Haft), but in this, one of his final
paintings, the giant waterfall has become the dominant
focus. Light catches the plummeting falls, painted with
slightly wavering freehand lines in myriad shades of
grey, blue and white. Spray flies up from the invisible
pool deep below. We join Li Bo as he faces towards
the spectacular sight, supported by a child attendant.
Together with artist and poet, we contemplate the
eternal forces of nature. TC

221

Dragon rising above Mt Fuji

11th (or 23rd) day, first month, 1849
Signature: Ka'ei ni tsuchinoto tori nen / shōgatsu tatsu
no hi / Hōreki jū kanoe tatsu nen no umare / kyūjū
rōjin Manji hitsu ('Brush of Manji, old man of ninety,
born in the dragon year of Hōreki 10 [1760], [painted
on] dragon day of the first month, Ka'ei 2 [1849]')
Seal: Hyaku ('Hundred')
Hanging scroll, ink and slight colour on silk,
95.5 × 36.2 cm
Literature: *Tanroku* 25 [year 3, no. 8], August 1941,
pp. 12–13, frontispiece; Ōta 1985, no. 584; Nagata
2000, no. 141; TNM 2005, no. 495; Paris 2014, no. 518;
Obuse 2015, pp. 92–93
Hokusai Museum, Obuse

Trailing a long storm cloud in its wake, a dragon has
risen from behind the foreground rocks, flown around
Mt Fuji, and now ascends above the peak into the
heavens. The subtly modulated cloud echoes the writhing
shape of the dragon. Mt Fuji is thickly covered in snow,
etched in unpainted reserve against an ink wash sky,
and the landscape is desolate and devoid of colour,
suggesting deep winter. Dragons generate rain, and an
ascending dragon is conventionally a symbol of worldly
success. For Hokusai the symbolism runs much deeper
here. His inscription recalls that he was born in a dragon
year (1760) and records that this work is painted on
a dragon day in the first month of his ninetieth year.
Successfully passing a major personal milestone –
turning ninety – he, like the ascending dragon, further
aspires to a state of 'divine wonder' (*shinmyō*) in his art. TC

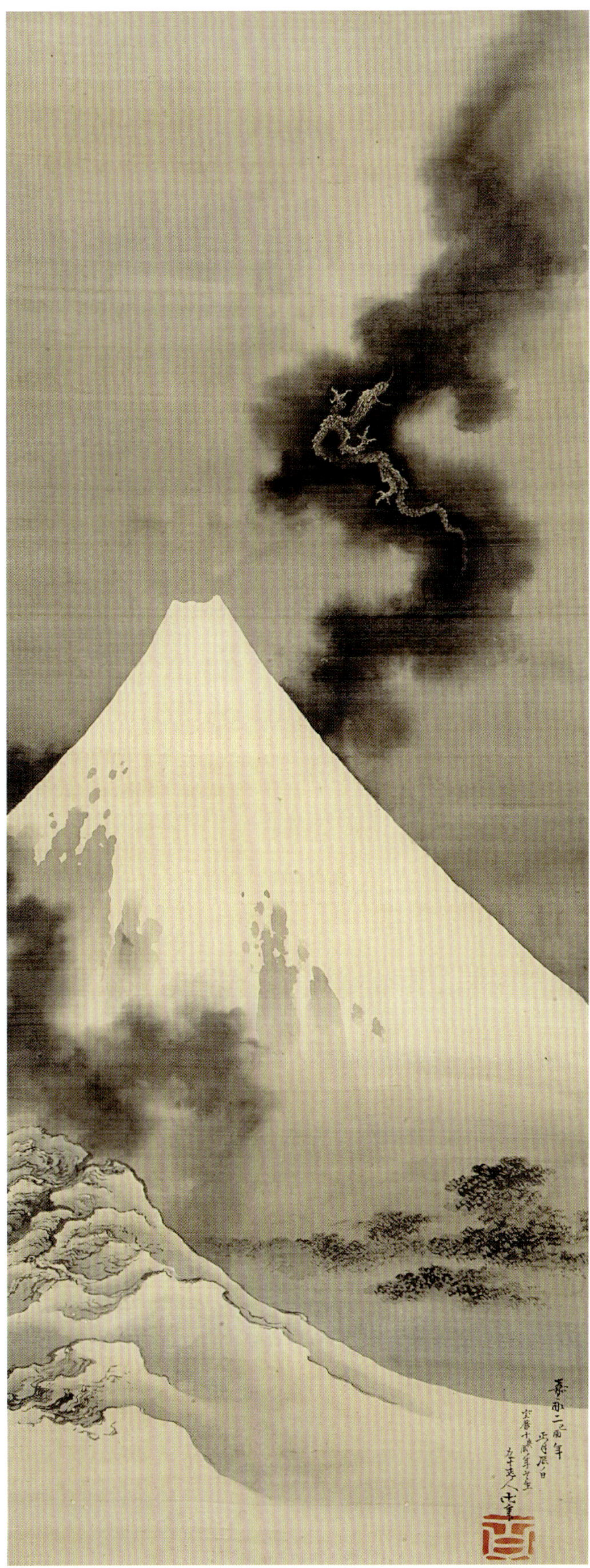

Tiger in rain (left)

1849

Signature: Kyūjū rōjin Manji hitsu ('Brush of Manji,
old man of ninety')

Seal: Hyaku ('Hundred')

Hanging scroll, ink and colour on paper,

120.5 × 41.5 cm

Provenance: Kanō Jigorō (1860–1938) (?);
Ōta Shinkichi (Seizō, 1931)

Literature: UT 1931, no. 1; Ōta 1985, no. 583; Nagata
2000, no. 140; Ōta 2007, no. 1; Guimet 2008, no. 103b

Ōta Memorial Museum of Art, Tokyo

Dragon in rain clouds (right)

1849

Signature: Kyūjū rōjin Manji hitsu ('Brush of Manji,
old man of ninety')

Seal: Hyaku ('Hundred')

Hanging scroll, ink and colour on paper,

120.5 × 42.5 cm

Provenance: Norbert Lagane (1921–2004)

Literature: *Kokka* 1345, Nov. 2007, pp. 36–41; Ōta 2007,
no. 1; Guimet 2008, no. 103a; Paris 2014, no. 516

Musée national des arts asiatiques Guimet, Paris,
MA.12176, given by Nobert Lagane 2001

On the right, a dragon, generating a pitch dark,
blue-black rain cloud, writhes up into the heavens from
out of the tornado visible inside the coil of its tail.
All claws, scales and spines, it glares diagonally down to
the left. On the left, a snarling tiger, jaws gaping, turns
back from where it stands in pouring rain, paws firmly
planted on the ground, to stare diagonally up to the
right. The beast is partially hidden behind a bank
where leaves of a creeper are turning autumnal red.
Although now preserved in separate collections, the
two paintings were created as a complementary pair,
completed in the last few months of Hokusai's life,
after he turned ninety at the New Year of 1849. Both
scrolls, in their different ways, represent the ultimate
development of Hokusai's powers of conception and
technique. The most staggering feature of the dragon
painting is that it was painted in reverse: the highlights
on its head, claws, scales and spines are unpainted paper,
and myriad tones of ink have been applied from light
to dark, with jet-black ink flicked from the brush to
add final excitement. The dragon's intense expression
and gaze exude a living, almost human consciousness.
Equally impressive are the washes of orange, brown
and black, painstakingly built up, that form the stripes
of the tiger. Like the vertiginous falls in the painting
Li Bo admiring a waterfall (cat. 220), also created by
Hokusai when aged ninety, the rain here is suggested
by sensitively brushed parallel lines in a range of ink
tonalities. As Hokusai scholar Nagata Seiji has pointed
out, the dragon is a mythical beast of the eastern
direction, which generates rain in the heavens. The
tiger resides in the west and is associated with the earth.
Although the two creatures had been paired in East
Asian art since ancient times, here they are locked
by Hokusai into a powerful symbiosis whereby the
dragon causes rain to fall on the tiger: heaven irrigates
life on earth. TC

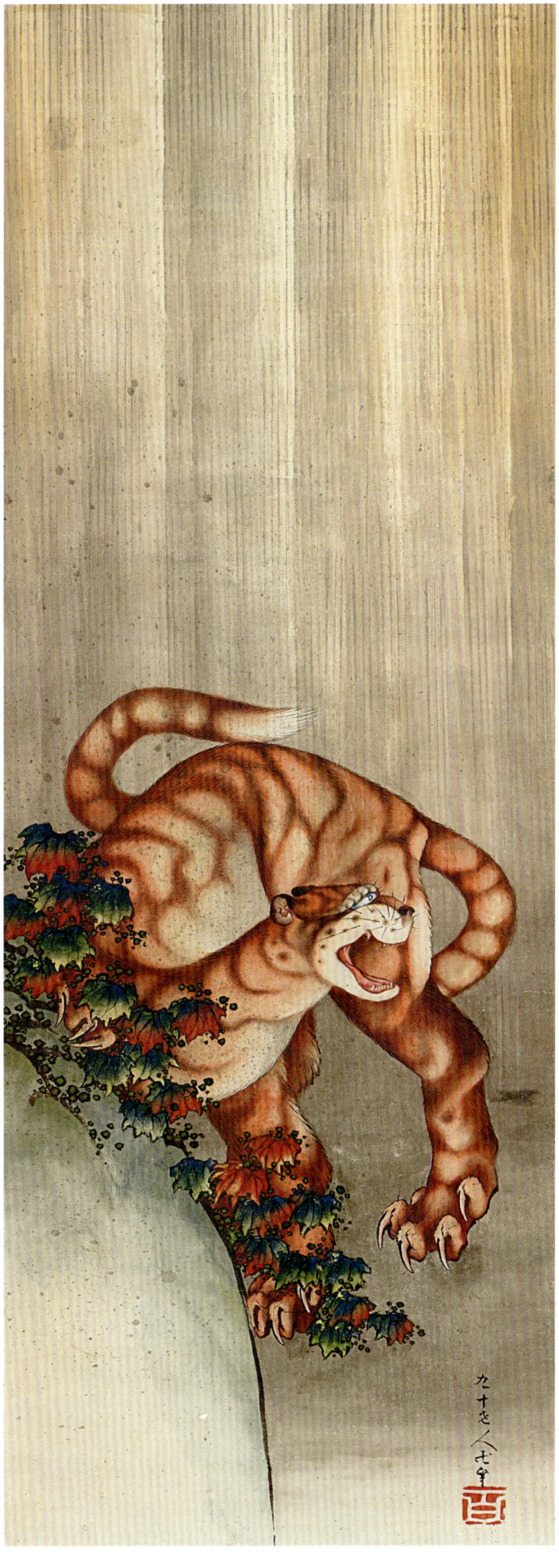

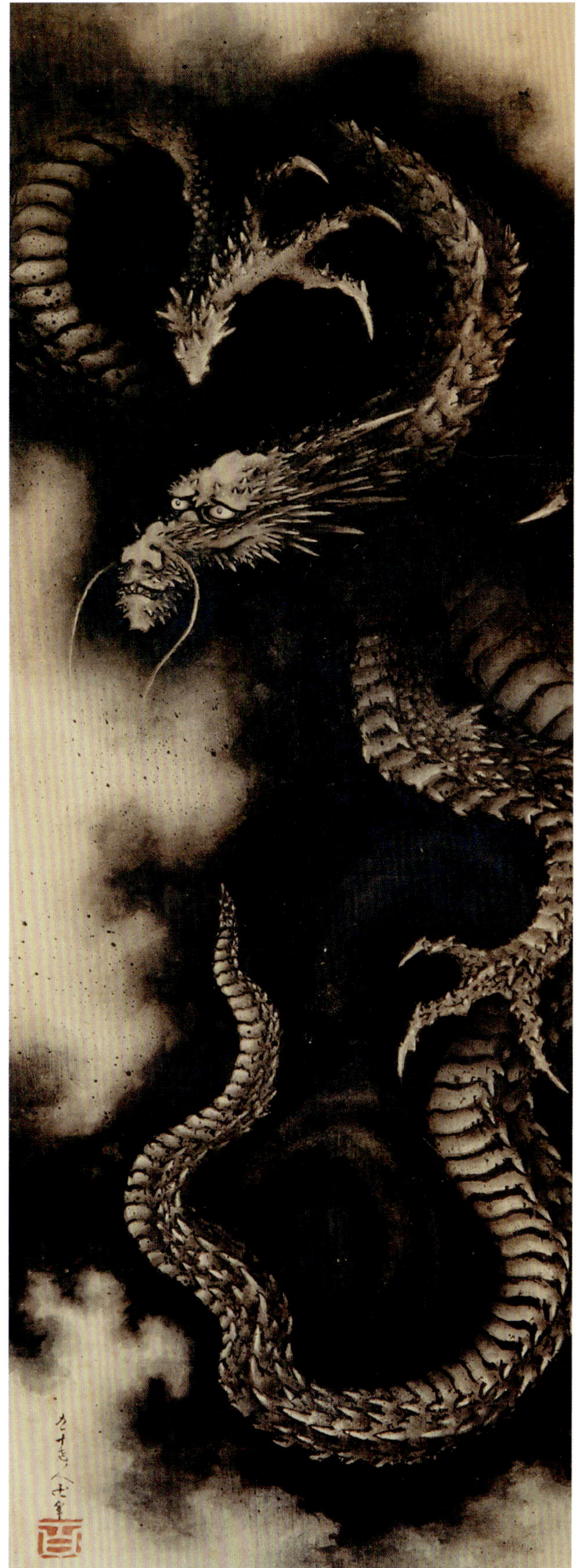

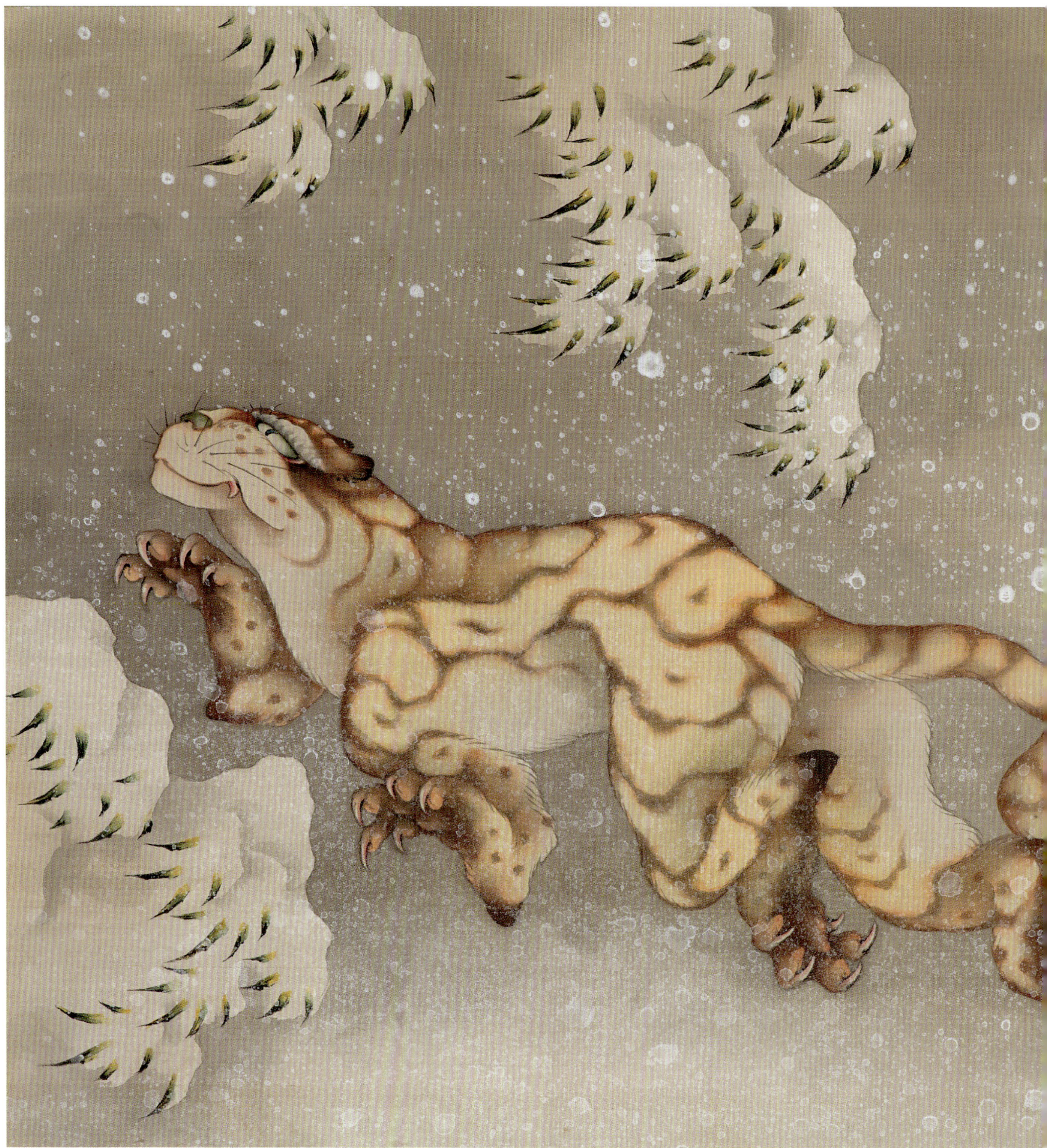

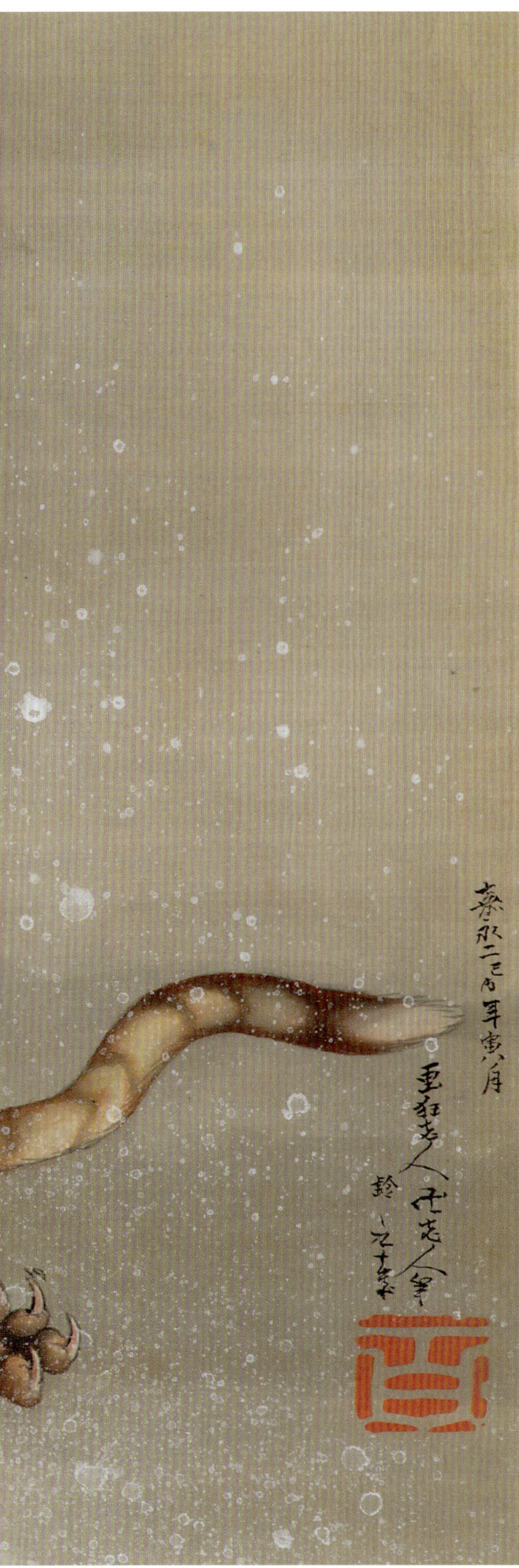

224

Tiger in snow

First month, 1849
Signature: Ka'ei ni tsuchinoto tori nen tora no tsuki /
Gakyō rōjin Manji rōjin hitsu / yowai kyūjussai ('Brush
of old man Manji, old man crazy to paint, aged ninety
years, Ka'ei 2 [1849]')
Seal: Hyaku ('Hundred')
Hanging scroll, ink and colour on silk, 39.4 × 50.5 cm
Provenance: Fenollosa 1901, no. 219, 'loaned by
Mr Nakajima' (?); Raymond Bushell; Azabu Museum
of Arts and Crafts
Literature: NUT 1994–1996, vol. 6, no. 60;
Freer-Sackler 2006, no. 163; Asano 2010, pp. 162–163
Private collection, USA

Gazing heavenwards and seeming to smile, a tiger leaps
through thickly falling snow, surrounded by swaying
bamboo. The snow-laden clumps of bamboo leaves
echo the tiger's paws and claws. In this unprecedented
image, Hokusai is surely expressing a joyous identification
with the cosmos. As with *Tiger in rain* (cat. 222), the
creature's markings have been built up from painstaking
applications of coloured washes. The highlights on
the claws and shadows on the soles of the paws have
extraordinary three-dimensionality. Flicked spontaneously
on to the silk with a brush, white paint representing
dancing flakes of snow has then been softened so as
not to obscure too much of the animal's body. *Dragon
rising above Mt Fuji* (cat. 221) is dated to the day, and this
work is dated to the first (tiger) month of 1849. In the
final time remaining to him, Hokusai is counting out
the days and months, willing additional longevity. TC

Eijo's letter to Hokushin about Hokusai's death

18th day, fourth month, 1849
Signature: Ei hai ('Respectfully [written by] Ei')
Ink on paper, 14.9 × 21.9 cm
Literature: Ōta 1985, no. 747; Paris 2014, no. 536;
Kubota 2015, no. 11
Private collection, Japan
Catalogue only

This note was rapidly brushed by Hokusai's daughter
Eijo (Ōi) on the 18th day, fourth month, 1849, to
inform his pupil Hokushin, of Shimo-no-hashi,
Fukagawa, that her father had just passed away: 'Manji
[Hokusai] was ill and treatment was to no avail. He died
from his illness early this morning at the seventh hour
[about 4 a.m.]. I wanted quickly to inform you of this
situation.' She then adds in smaller characters next
to the name of the addressee: 'Funeral tomorrow,
19th day, fourth hour [about 10 a.m.].' Author and
playwright Yomo no Umehiko (1822–1896) later
recalled how Hokusai's pupils and old friends
contributed funds for a funeral with a modest coffin.
About one hundred mourners joined in the procession
to the mortuary temple Seikyōji, including samurai
with retainers carrying spears and lacquered travelling
boxes. This was unheard of for the funeral of someone
living in the backstreets of the commoner districts
of Edo, and people in the neighbourhood were envious
(Iijima 1999, p. 170). Fukawa (Kōsai) Hokushin (1824–
1876) is said to have become a pupil of Hokusai in 1835,
when he was just twelve (Itabashi 2008, p. 112). Eijo
surely sent out many similar death notices, but this is
the only one known to have survived. TC

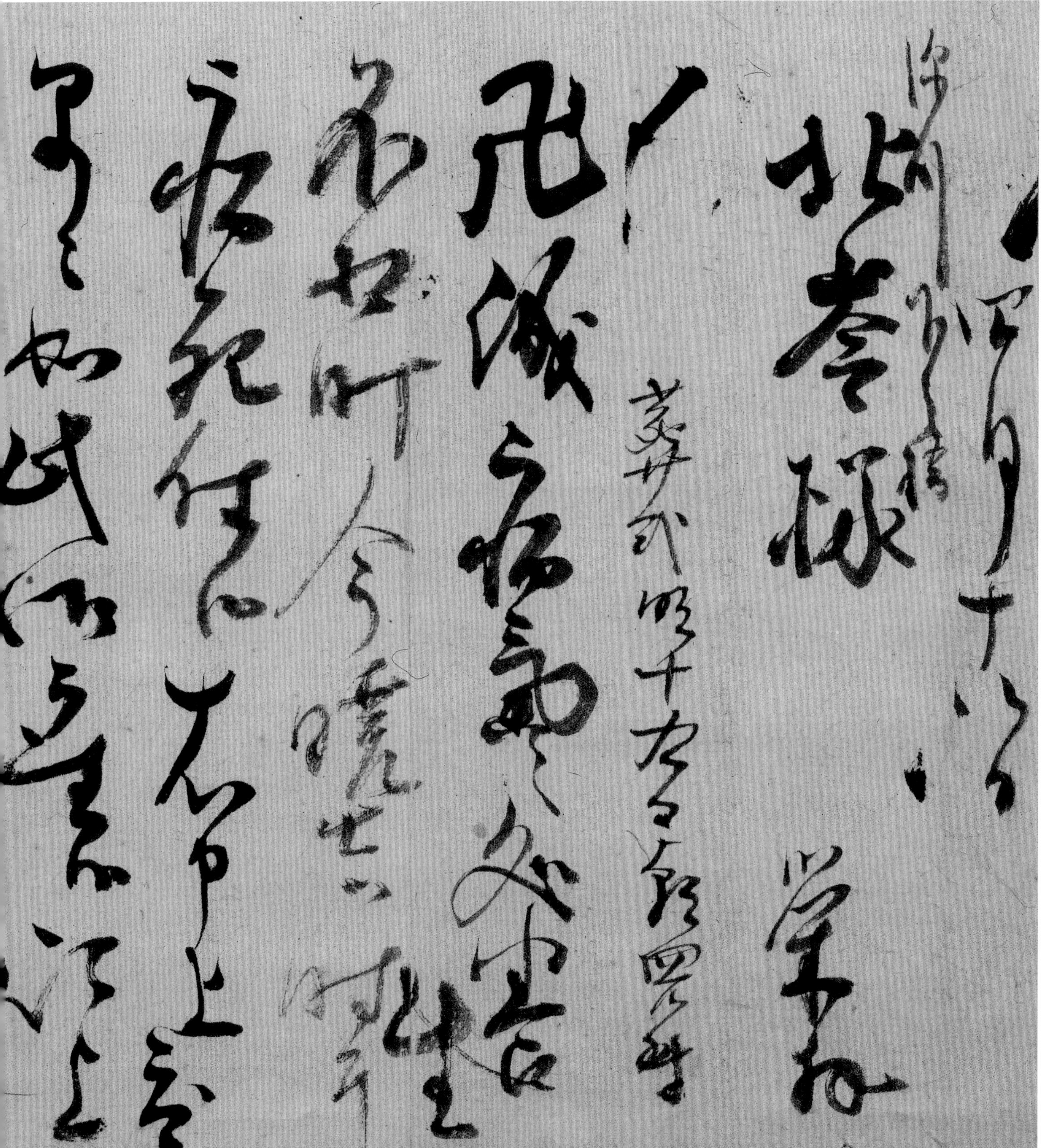

Select bibliography

The journal *Hokusai kenkyū* (HK), nos 1–55, 1972–2017
Tokyo Hokusai Kai (eds), *Hokusai kenkyū* (Hokusai Research) vols 1–55, 1972–2017; all issues available at the National Diet Library, Tokyo; nos 4–55 available in the Department of Asia, British Museum

The journal *Hokusai Kenkyūjo kenkyū kiyō*, nos 1–8, 2008–2015
Hokusaikan, Obuse (eds), *Hokusai Kenkyūjo kenkyū kiyō* (Bulletin of Hokusaikan) nos 1–8, 2008–2015

Fine Art Society 1890
Marcus B. Huish (ed.), *Catalogue of a Collection of Drawings and Engravings by Hokusai Exhibited at the Fine Art Society*, London, The Fine Art Society, 1890

Fenollosa 1893
Ernest F. Fenollosa, *Hokusai and His School: Catalogue of Special Exhibition No. 1* (Museum of Fine Arts, Boston), Boston, Alfred Mudge & Son, 1893

Iijima 1893
Iijima Kyoshin, *Katsushika Hokusai den*, 2 vols, Tokyo, Hōsūkaku, 1893; see also Iijima 1978, Iijima 1999

Goncourt 1896
Edmond de Goncourt, *Hokousaï*, Paris, Bibliothèque Charpentier, 1896

Fenollosa 1901
Ernest F. Fenollosa, *Catalogue of the Exhibition of Paintings of Hokusai Held at the Japan Fine Art Association, Uyeno Park, Tokio, from 13th to 30th January, 1900*, Tokyo, Kobayashi Bunshichi, 1901; repr. Geneva, Minkof Reprint, 1973

Murayama 1906
Murayama Jungo (ed.), *Katsushika Hokusai 'Nisshin jomachō'* (Hokusai's 'Daily Exorcisms'), Tokyo, Kokkasha, 1906; with English translation of preface

Taki 1906
Taki Sei'ichi, '"Daily Exorcisms": The Latest Discovery of Hokusai's Original Drawings', *The Kokka* (International Edition) 17:198, Nov. 1906

Takeoka 1919
Takeoka Toyota, *Yamato-e*, Kōbe, 1919

Ishii 1929
Ishii Kendō, *Nishiki-e no hori to suri*, Tokyo, Unsōdō, 1929

UT 1931
Ukiyo-e taisei, vol. 9: *Ranjuku jidai 4*, Tokyo, Tōhō Shoin, 1931

UTS 1932
Ukiyo-e Kenkyūkai (eds), *Ukiyo-e taika shūsei*, vol. 15: *Katsushika Hokusai*, Tokyo, Taihōkaku Shobō, 1932

Ozaki 1934
Ozaki Kyūya, 'Hokusai shōzō no kenkyū', in *Ukiyo-e hanga taikan*, Tokyo, Taihōkaku, 1934, pp. 82–91

Inoue 1941
Inoue Kazuo, 'Hokusai bannen no tegami', *Tanroku*, vol. 3, no. 8, August 1941, pp. 9–11

Narazaki 1944
Narazaki Muneshige, *Hokusai ron*, Tokyo, Atorie-sha, 1944

BM 1948
Basil Gray (ed.), *The Work of Hokusai: Woodblocks, Illustrated Books, Drawings and Paintings: A Catalogue of an Exhibition Held on the Occasion of the Centenary of his Death*, London, British Museum, 1948

Hillier 1955
Jack Hillier, *Hokusai: Paintings, Drawings and Woodcuts*, London, Phaidon, 1955; 2nd ed. 1957; 3rd ed. 1978

Michener 1958
James A. Michener, *Hokusai Sketchbooks: Selections from the Manga*, Rutland, Vermont & Tokyo, Charles E. Tuttle Company, 1958

Suzuki 1963
Suzuki Jūzō, *Ningen Hokusai*, Tokyo, Ryokuen Shobō, 1963

Bowie 1964
Theodore Bowie, *The Drawings of Hokusai*, Bloomington, Indiana, Indiana University Press, 1964

Kaneko 1964
Kaneko Fusui, *Ukiyo-e nikuhitsu gashū*, vol. 3: *Hokusai-ō shinra banshō gashū*, Tokyo, Ryokuen Shobō, 1964

Freer 1965
Harold P. Stern, *Hokusai: Paintings and Drawings*, Washington, DC, Freer Gallery of Art, Smithsonian Institution, 1960; rev. ed. 1965

Hillier 1966
Jack Hillier, *Hokusai Drawings*, London, Phaidon, 1966

Hayashi 1967
Hayashi Yoshikazu, *Oei to Eisen*, Tokyo, Arimitsu Shobō, 1967

Nihon Keizai Shinbun 1967
Nihon Keizai Shinbun (eds), *Hokusai ten*, Tokyo, 1967

Ozaki 1967
Ozaki Shūdō, *Hokusai*, Tokyo, Nihon Keizai Shinbun, 1967

Yura 1967
Yura Tetsuji, 'Hokusai ni okeru hatō no keifu', *Ukiyo-e geijutsu* 16, 1967, pp. 8–27

Gotō 1969
Gotō Bijutsukan (eds), *Nikuhitsu Katsushika Hokusai ten*, Tokyo, 1969 (text by Kaneko Fusui)

Nihon Keizai Shinbun 1971
Nihon Keizai Shinbun (eds), *Katsushika Hokusai ten*, Kobe, 1971

Nishina 1971
Nishina Yūsuke, 'Hokusai no ema', *Kikan ukiyo-e* 44, Feb. 1971, p. 55

Yasuda 1971
Yasuda Gōzō, *Gakyō Hokusai*, Tokyo, Arimitsu Shobō, 1971

Yura 1971
Yura Tetsuji, 'Nishiki-e no shōgu "baren"', *Ukiyo-e*, no. 44 (February 1971), pp. 57–58

Keyes & Morse 1972
Roger Keyes & Peter Morse, 'Hokusai's Waterfalls and a set of copies', *Oriental Art*, vol. 18, no. 2, summer 1972, pp. 141–147

ZH 1972
Narazaki Muneshige, Suzuki Jūzō, Yasuda Gōzō (eds), *Zaigai hihō*, vol. 4: *Katsushika Hokusai*, Tokyo, Gakushū Kenkyūsha, 1972

Kaneko 1975
Kaneko Fusui et al. (eds), *Nikuhitsu: Katsushika Hokusai*, Tokyo, Mainichi Shinbunsha, 1975

UT 1975
Kobayashi Tadashi (ed.), *Ukiyo-e taikei*, vol. 13: *Fugaku sanjūrokkei*, Tokyo, Shūeisha, 1975

Kano 1976
Kano Hiroyuki, 'Hokusai "garon" no kentō', *Bijutsushi* 93–96, March 1976

Miyazawa 1977
Miyazawa Shirō, 'Shinshū Obuse de hakken sareta nazo no Hokusai in', *Geijutsu shinchō* 333, Sept. 1977

Sankei Shinbun 1977
Sankei Shinbun (eds), *Nikuhitsu Katsushika Hokusai ten*, Tokyo, Sankei Shinbun, Hokusaikan, Nihon Ukiyo-e Kyōkai, 1977

Hillier 1978
Jack Hillier, *Hokusai: Paintings, Drawings and Woodcuts*, London & New York, Phaidon, 1978; 1st ed. 1955; 2nd ed. 1957; 3rd. ed. 1978

Iijima 1978
Iijima Kyoshin, *Katsushika Hokusai den*, 2 vols, Tokyo, Hōsūkaku, 1893; repr. ed., Tokyo, Zōkeisha, 1978, ed. Segi Shin'ichi; see also Iijima 1893, Iijima 1999

Suzuki 1979
Suzuki Jūzō, *Ehon to ukiyo-e: Edo shuppan bunka no kōsatsu*, Tokyo, Bijutsu Shuppansha, 1979

Hillier 1980a
Jack Hillier, *The Art of Hokusai in Book Illustration*, London, Sotheby Parke Bernet & Berkeley, CA, University of California Press, 1980

Hillier 1980b
Jack Hillier, *Japanese Drawings of the 18th and 19th Centuries*, Washington, DC, International Exhibitions Foundation, 1980

Marais 1980
Jacqueline Guillard, Maurice Guillard et al., *Le fou de peinture: Hokusai et son temps*, Paris, Centre Culturel du Marais, 1980

Yasuda 1980
Yasuda Gōzō, 'Hokusai no musume Ōi-Eijo: zenden', *Kikan ukiyo-e* 86, 1980, pp. 32–44

GUDHJ 1980–1982
Nihon Ukiyo-e Kyōkai (eds), *Genshoku ukiyo-e daihyakka jiten*, 11 vols, Tokyo, Taishūkan Shoten, 1980–1982; see especially vol. 8 for Hokusai and his school

Haarlem 1982
Matthi Forrer, W. R. van Gulik and H. M. Kaempfer (eds), *Hokusai and His School: Paintings, Drawings and Illustrated Books*, Haarlem, Frans Halsmuseum, 1982

NU 1982
Narazaki Muneshige et al., *Nikuhitsu ukiyo-e*, vol. 7: *Hokusai*, Tokyo, Shūeisha, 1982

Sasaki 1982
Sasaki Seichi, 'Obuse Higashimachi yatai tenjō-ga "Ryū zu" no gihō shiteki kenkyū', *Tama Bijutsu Daigaku kenkyū kiyō* 1, 1982, pp. 12–26

Tsuji 1982
Tsuji Nobuo, *Hokusai (Book of Books Series, Nihon no bijutsu)*, Tokyo, Shōgakukan, 1982

Higuchi 1983
Higuchi Niyō, *Ukiyo-e to hanga no kenkyū: Ukiyo-e hanga no gakō horikō surikō*, Tokyo, Seishōdō Shoten, 1983

Nagata 1983
Nagata Seiji, 'Saihakken "Oni zu" o meguru Hokusai saibannen no sho mondai', *Kobijutsu* 68, Oct. 1983, pp. 141–145

Shibui 1983
Shibui Kiyoshi (ed.), *Nikuhitsu ukiyo-e bijinga shūsei*, vol. 2: *Hokusai oyobi Hokusai ichimon shū*, Tokyo, Mainichi Shinbunsha, 1983

Edogaku jiten 1984
Nishiyama Matsunosuke et al. (eds), *Edogaku jiten*, Tokyo, Kōbundō, 1984

Nagata 1984a
Nagata Seiji, *Ukiyo-e hakka*, vol. 5, *Hokusai*, Tokyo, Heibonsha, 1984

Nagata 1984b
Nagata Seiji, 'Saihakken Nishiarai Daishi "Kōbō Daishi shūhō zu" ni tsuite', *Kobijutsu* 69, Jan. 1984, pp. 117–122

Narazaki 1984
Narazaki Muneshige, 'Hokusai saibannen no nikuhitsu', *Kokka* 1072, March 1984, pp. 43–49

Nagata 1984–1993
Nagata Seiji, 'Katsushika Hokusai nikuhitsu kanshō, nos 1–48', *Kobijutsu* 71–105, July 1984–Feb. 1993; the articles are individually listed in the bibliography to Calza & Carpenter 1994

Forrer 1985
Matthi Forrer, *Eirakuya Tōshirō, Publisher at Nagoya*, Amsterdam, J. C. Gieben, 1985

Ganshōin 1985
Ganshōin temple (eds), *Katsushika Hokusai ga: Ganshōin hondō tenjō hō-ō zu*, Obuse, 1985

Hokusaikan 1985
Hokusaikan (eds), *Nikuhitsu Katsushika Hokusai*, Obuse, 1985

Nagata 1985
Nagata Seiji, *Katsushika Hokusai nenpu*, Tokyo, Sansai Shinsha, 1985; see also rev. ed. Nagata 1997

Nagata Edehon 1985–1986
Nagata Seiji, *Hokusai no e-dehon 1–5*, 5 vols, Tokyo, Iwasaki Bijutsusha, 1985–1986

Ōta 1985
Ōta Kinen Bijutsukan (eds), *Hokusai ten*, Tokyo, 1985

Nagata Manga 1986–1987
Nagata Seiji, *Hokusai manga 1–3*, 3 vols, Tokyo, Iwasaki Bijutsusha, 1986–1987

Suzuki 1986
Suzuki Jūzō, *Hokusai Fugaku hyakkei*, Tokyo, Iwasaki Bijutsusha, 1986

HUT 1987–1990
Narazaki Muneshige (ed.), *Hizō ukiyo-e taikan*, 13 vols, Tokyo, Kōdansha, 1987–1990; 'English Supplements' provided for purchasers in Western countries

Nagata Ehon sashi-e 1987
Nagata Seiji, *Hokusai no ehon sashi-e 1–3*, 3 vols, Tokyo, Iwasaki Bijutsusha, 1987

Sadamura 1987
Sadamura Tadashi, 'Obuse no Hokusai ni tsuite: atarashii jijitsu to kaishaku', *Ukiyo-e geijutsu* 91, 1987, pp. 24–34

Yamato Bunkakan 1987
Yamato Bunkakan (eds), *Hokusai*, Nara, 1987

Forrer 1988
Matthi Forrer, with texts by Edmond de Goncourt, *Hokusai*, New York, Rizzoli & Paris, Flammarion, 1988

Smith 1988
Henry D. Smith II, *Hokusai: One Hundred Views of Mount Fuji*, London, Thames & Hudson & New York, George Braziller, 1988

Kubota 1989
Kubota Kazuhiro, 'Shiryō kenkyū – Hokusai saibannen: Obuse Hokusai no shūhen, I–III', *Ukiyo-e geijutsu* 95: 1–37, 96: 3–31, 97: 3–15, 1989

Lane 1989
Richard Lane, *Hokusai: Life and Work*, London, Barrie & Jenkins & New York, Dutton, 1989

Morse 1989
Peter Morse, *Hokusai: One Hundred Poets*, New York, George Braziller, 1989; see also Morse 1992

Nagata 1990
Nagata Seiji, *Hokusai bijutsukan*, 5 vols, Tokyo, Shūeisha, 1990

Nagoya 1991
Nagoya-shi Hakubutsukan (eds), *Fukutsu no gajin-damashi – Hokusai*, Nagoya, 1991

MSU 1991
Narazaki Muneshige & Nagata Seiji (eds), *Meihin soroimono ukiyo-e 8: Hokusai I*, Tokyo, Gyōsei, 1991

Nakata 1991
Nakata Katsunosuke (ed.), *Ukiyo-e ruikō* (*Iwanami bunko*, 30-240-1), Tokyo, Iwanami Shoten, 1941; 5th ed., 1991

RA 1991
Matthi Forrer, *Hokusai: Prints and Drawings*, Munich, Prestel-Verlag & London, Royal Academy of Arts, 1991

Sakai 1991
Sakai Gankō, 'Hokusai hennen shiryō', in *Nihon Ukiyo-e Hakubutsukan shozō: Hokusai*, Akita Senshū Museum of Art, 1991

Clark 1992
Timothy Clark, *Ukiyo-e Paintings in the British Museum*, London, British Museum Press, 1992

Morse 1992
Peter Morse, 'Additional Drawings in Hokusai's "Hundred Poets" Series', *Andon*, vol. 11/2, no. 42, Oct. 1992, pp. 50–52; see also Morse 1989

MSU 1992
Nagata Seiji (ed.), *Meihin soroimono ukiyo-e 9: Hokusai II*, Tokyo, Gyōsei, 1991

Tōbu 1993
Tōbu Museum of Art (eds), *Edo ga unda sekai no eshi: Dai Hokusai ten*, Tokyo, Asahi Shimbunsha, 1993

Calza & Carpenter 1994
Gian Carlo Calza & John T. Carpenter (eds), *Hokusai Paintings – Selected Essays*, Venice, International Hokusai Research Centre, 1994

Kano 1994
Kano Hiroyuki, *E wa kataru 14 – Katsushika Hokusai hitsu 'Gaifū kaisei'*, Tokyo, Heibonsha, 1994

NUT 1994–1996
Kobayashi Tadashi (ed.), *Nikuhitsu ukiyo-e taikan*, 10 vols, Tokyo, Kōdansha, 1994–1996

Retta 1994
Carolina Retta, 'Hokusai's Treatise on Coloring: *Ehon saishiki-tsū*', in Calza & Carpenter 1994, pp. 237–246

Edo Tokyo 1995
Edo Tokyo Museum (eds), *Katsushika Hokusai ten*, Tokyo, 1995

Kamiya 1995
Kamiya Hiroshi, 'Hokusai to Nagoya: kenkyū joshō – Maki Bokusen shūshū hangajō no shōkai o chūshin ni', *Nagoya-shi Hakubutsukan kenkyū kiyō* 18, 1995, pp. 1–34

Lane 1995
Richard Lane, *Denki gashū – Hokusai*, Tokyo, Kawade Shobō Shinsha, 1995

Imahashi 1996
Imahashi Riko, 'Densetsu no kigō – Katsushika Hokusai hitsu "Suika zu" to tanabata', *Tōkai daigaku kiyō* (*bungakubu*) 65, 1996, pp. 1–18

Kobayashi 1996–1997
Kobayashi Tadashi, 'Gakyōjin Hokusai no tegami 1–3', *Edo bungaku* vol. 15, pp. 188–199, vol. 16, pp. 184–195, vol. 17, pp. 172–184, 1996–1997

Kōno 1996
Konō Motoaki, *Hokusai to Hokusai-ha* (*Nihon no bijutsu 367*), Tokyo, Shibundō, 1996

Mostow 1996
Joshua S. Mostow, *Pictures of the Heart: The Hyakunin Isshu in Word and Image*, Honolulu, University of Hawai'i Press, 1996

Asano 1997
Asano Shūgō, 'Hokusai no nikuhitsuga no inshō ni tsuite', *Sairen* (Chiba City Museum of Art) 1, March 1997, pp. 13–35

Christie's 1997
Christie's New York (eds), *Important Japanese Drawings – The Nisshin Joma (Daily Exorcisms) of Katsushika Hokusai*, 3 November 1997

Nagata 1997
Nagata Seiji, 'Katsushika Hokusai nenpu', *Hokusai kenkyū* 22, April 1997, pp. 4–175

Nikkei 1998
Nihon Keizai Shinbunsha (eds), *Hokusai – Tōzai no kakehashi*, Tokyo, 1998

San Francisco 1998
Asian Art Museum of San Francisco (eds), *Hokusai and Hiroshige*, Honolulu Academy of Arts and University of Washington Press, 1998

Calza 1999
Gian Carlo Calza et al., *Hokusai, Il vecchio pazzo per la pittura*, Milan, Electa, 1999

Iijima 1999
Iijima Kyoshin, *Katsushika Hokusai den*, Tokyo, Iwanami Shoten, 1999 (edited by Suzuki Jūzō); see also Iijima 1893, Iijima 1978

Boston 2000
Tsuji Nobuo (ed.), *Bosuton bijutsukan nikuhitsu ukiyo-e III*, Tokyo, Kōdansha, 2000

Itō 2000
Itō Megumi, 'Nikuhitsu gajō ni tsuite – seisaku no haikei to kenkyū-jō no sho mondai', in Nagata 2000, pp. 248–256

Nagata 2000
Nagata Seiji, *Hokusai nikuhitsuga taisei*, Tokyo, Shōgakukan, 2000

Clark 2001
Timothy Clark, *100 Views of Mt Fuji*, London, British Museum Press, 2001

Suwa 2001
Suwa Haruo, *Hokusai no nazo o toku – seikatsu, geijutsu, shinkō*, Tokyo, Yoshikawa Kōbunkan, 2001

Calza 2003
Gian Carlo Calza et al., *Hokusai*, London, Phaidon, 2003

Chester Beatty 2003
Clare Pollard, *The Art of Hokusai: Masterpieces of Japanese Printing in the Chester Beatty Library*, Dublin, TownHouse, 2003

Carpenter 2005
John T. Carpenter (ed.), *Hokusai and His Age*, Amsterdam, Hotei Publishing, 2005

Hashimoto 2005
Hashimoto Osamu et al., *Katsushika Hokusai shozuri Hokusai manga, zen*, Tokyo, Shōgakukan, 2005

Matsui 2005
Shimoyama Susumu, Shimoyama Yasuko, Matsui Hideo, 'Nishikie seishoku chakushokuryō no hihakai dōteihō ni motozuku berurin burū dōnyū katei to *Fugaku sanjūrokkei* o kōshi to suru ukiyo-e fūkei hanga no kakuritsu kei'i no kenkyū' (The introduction of Berlin Blue in Ukiyo-e prints and the development of landscape prints, beginning with the *Thirty-six Views of Mt Fuji*, based on non-destructive method of determining blue colorants in Nishiki-e), *Hokusai kenkyū* 37, Sept 2005, pp. i–liv

Smith 2005
Henry D. Smith II, 'Hokusai and the blue revolution in Edo prints', in Carpenter 2005, pp. 234–269

TNM 2005
Tokyo National Museum (eds), *Hokusai ten*, Tokyo, 2005; see also Nihon Keizai Shinbun (eds), *Hokusai: English Text Supplement*, 2005

Freer-Sackler 2006
Freer Gallery of Art and Arthur M. Sackler Gallery, Smithsonian Institution (eds), *Hokusai*, 2 vols, Washington, DC, 2006 (text by Ann Yonemura et al.)

Hokusaikan 2006
Hokusaikan (eds), *Hokusai tokubetsuten zuroku*, Obuse, 2006

Edo Tokyo 2007
Edo Tokyo Museum (eds), *Hokusai ten* (*Siebold and Hokusai and His Tradition*), Tokyo, 2007 (text by Matthi Forrer et al.); see also English Text Supplement 'Siebold and Hokusai and His Tradition'

Ōta 2007
Ōta Kinen Bijutsukan (eds), *Gime Tōyō Bijutsukan shozō ukiyo-e meihin ten*, Tokyo, 2007

Guimet 2008
Musée Guimet (eds), *Hokusai (1760–1849), 'l'affolé de son art'*, Paris, 2008 (catalogue by Hélène Bayou)

Keyes 2008
Roger S. Keyes, 'Pink Fuji: The Print Hokusai Saw', *Impressions* 29, 2007–2008, pp. 68–75

Kobayashi 2008
Kobayashi Tadashi, 'Katsushika Hokusai hitsu tango no sekku kazari zu', *Kokka* 1354, August 2008, pl. 3, pp. 31–32

Itabashi 2008
Yasumura Toshinobu, *Hokusai ichimon nikuhitsuga kessaku sen*, Tokyo, Itabashi Kuritsu Bijutsukan, 2008

McMillan 2008
Peter McMillan, *One Hundred Poets, One Poem Each*, New York, Columbia University Press, 2008

Nagata 2008
Nagata Seiji, '*Fugaku hyakkei* kō (mitei kō)', in HK 42, October 2008, pp. 5–61

Iwakiri 2009
Iwakiri Yuriko, 'Hanmoto "Iseichi" no hangi gun', in *Nishiki-e wa ika ni tsukurareta ka*, National Museum of Japanese History, 2009, pp. 76–84

Machotka 2009
Ewa Machotka, *Visual Genesis of Japanese National Identity – Hokusai's 'Hyakunin Isshu'*, Brussels, Peter Lang, 2009

Sumida 2009
Sumida-ku Bunka Shinkō Zaidan (eds), *Sumida-ku shozō Piitaa Moosu korekushon Hokusai zuroku*, Tokyo, 2009

Asano 2010
Asano Shūgō et al., *Hokusai ketteiban (Bessatsu taiyō, Nihon no kokoro 174)*, Tokyo, Heibonsha, 2010

Takemura 2010
Takemura Makoto, 'Hokusai no ko, mago, himago – Kase Sakijūrō, Yajirō, Chōjirō ni tsuite', HK 45, March 2010, pp. 4–23

Berlin 2011
Martin Gropiusbau, *Hokusai*, Berlin, Nicolai, 2011 (edited by Nagata Seiji)

Clark 2011
Timothy Clark, *Hokusai's Great Wave*, London, British Museum Press, 2011

Hashimoto 2012
Hashimoto Kenichirō, 'Gakyōjin Hokusai "Nisshin jomazu" ni tsuite – *Katsushika Hokusai nisshin jomachō* o chūshin toshite', *Zaidan Hōjin Hokusai Kenkyūjo kenkyū kiyō*, Hokusaikan, Obuse, vol. 4, 2012, pp. 97–114

Iwakiri 2012
Iwakiri Yūriko, 'Hokusai "Shiika shashin kyō" gadai shōkō', in HK 49, March 2012, pp. 8–16

Machida 2012
Machida Shiritsu Kokusai Hanga Bijutsukan (eds), *Hokusai to Hiroshige – kisoi-au Edo no fūkei*, Tokyo, 2012

Osaka 2012
Osaka Shiritsu Bijutsukan (eds), *Hokusai – fūkei, bijin, kisō*, Osaka, 2012

Boston 2013
Nihon Keizai Shunbunsha (eds), *Bosuton Bijutsukan ukiyo-e meihin ten – Hokusai*, Tokyo, 2013

Hinohara 2013
Hinohara Kenji, 'Katsushika Hokusai *Shokoku taki meguri* o megutte – shasei to kisō', *Ōta Kinen Bijutsukan kiyō* 4, 2013, pp. 35–60

Cluzel 2014
Jean-Sébastien Cluzel (ed.), *Hokusai: le vieux fou d'architecture*, Paris, Bibliothèque nationale de France, 2014

Paris 2014
Paris, Grand Palais, *Hokusai*, Paris, Éditions de la Réunion des musées nationaux, 2014

Guth 2015
Christine M. E. Guth, *Hokusai's Great Wave: Biography of a Global Icon*, Honolulu, University of Hawai'i Press, 2015

Hokusaikan 2015
Hokusaikan (eds), *Hokusaikan nikuhitsuga dai zukan*, Obuse, 2015

Keyes & Morse 2015
Roger S. Keyes & Peter Morse, *Catalogue Raisonné of the Surviving Single Sheet Woodblock Prints of Katsushika Hokusai*, 90 vols, unpublished manuscript, 1972–2007 (deposited at the Department of Asia, British Museum in 2015)

Kubota 2015
Kubota Kazuhiro, *Hokusai musume, Ōi Eijo shū*, Tokyo, Geika Shoin, 2015

Ōta 2015
Ōta Kinen Bijutsukan (eds), *Katsushika Ōi kanshō gaidobukku*, Tokyo, 2015 (text by Hinohara Kenji)

Thompson 2015
Sarah E. Thompson, *Hokusai*, Boston, Museum of Fine Arts, 2015

Tinios 2015
Ellis Tinios, 'Hokusai and his Blockcutters', *Print Quarterly*, vol. XXXII, 2015, 2, pp. 186–191; see also Tinios 2016

Yasuhara 2015
Akio Yasuhara, 'English translation of Iijima Kyoshin, *Katsushika Hokusai den*', unpublished manuscript, 2015

Sumida 2016
Sumida Hokusai Bijutsukan (eds), *Hokusai no kikan*, Tokyo, 2016

Thompson 2016
Sarah E. Thompson, *Hokusai's Lost Manga*, Boston, Museum of Fine Arts, 2016

Tinios 2016
Ellis Tinios, 'Hokusai to sono horishi', *Aato risaachi* (Art Research Center, Ritsumeikan University), vol. 16, pp. 39–44; see also Tinios 2015

TNM 2016
Tokyo National Museum (eds), *Hokusai (Tokyo National Museum Selections)*, Tokyo, 2016 (text by Tazawa Hiroyoshi)

Illustration credits

The publisher would like to thank the copyright holders for granting permission to reproduce the images illustrated. Every attempt has been made to trace accurate ownership of copyrighted images in this book. Any errors or omissions will be corrected in subsequent editions provided notification is sent to the publisher.

Further information about the Museum and its collection can be found at britishmuseum.org

All works © The Trustees of the British Museum unless stated otherwise below.

Fig. 1 © Private collection , UK
Fig. 2 © Freer Gallery of Art and Arthur M. Sackler Gallery, Smithsonian Institution, Washington, D.C. / Gift of Charles Lang Freer, F 1907.579
Figs 3, 6, 10, 14, 19, 20, 21, 22, 24, 25. Cats 30, 40, 131, 157, 163, 168, 170, 171, 185, 220 © 2017 Museum of Fine Arts, Boston
Fig. 4. Cat. 202 © Ichimura Tsugio collection, Japan
Fig. 8. Cats 26, 27, 34,121, 148, 156, 199, 203, 205, 209, 217, 218 © Private collections, Japan
Fig. 9 © Musée d'Orsay / Photo: RMN-Grand Palais
Fig. 12 © Board of Trustees of the Royal Botanic Gardens, Kew
Fig. 23 © International Research Center for Japanese Studies, Kyoto, KG/159/Ak
Fig. 27 © Higashimachi Neighbourhood Council, Obuse, Nagano Prefectural Treasure
Fig. 28. Cats 206, 207 © Kanmachi Neighbourhood Council, Obuse, Nagano Prefectural Treasure
Fig. 29 © Ritsumeikan University Art Research Center, hayBK03-0544-06
1, 9, 85, 86, 104, 108, 197, 219 © Collection: Tokyo National Museum / Image: TNM Image Archives
2, 31, 106, 143 © Victoria and Albert Museum, London
3, 225 © Shimane Art Museum (Nagata Seiji Collection)
4 © Hikaru Museum, Takayama
5, 224 © Sebastian Izzard
8, 149, 175, 191, 192, 200, 212, 221 © Hokusai Museum, Obuse
10, 100 © MOA Museum of Art, Atami
11, 150 © Okada Museum of Art, Hakone
12 © Osaka City Museum of Fine Arts
15 © Kobe City Museum
16 © The Museum Yamato Bunkakan, Nara
18 © Nagoya City Museum
19 © Kawasaki Isago-no-Sato Museum
20–25, 184, 190 © Collection Nationaal Museum van Wereldculturen, Coll. No. RMV1-4482-L, RMV1-4482-A, RMV1-4482-C, RMV1-4482-M, RMV1-4482-H, RMV1-4482-K, RMV3513-1496, 2762-11/2
28, 120, 158, 164, 165, 176 © Uragami Mitsuru collection, Japan
32 © Chiba City Museum of Art
36 © Hie Jinja shrine, Kisarazu

37 © Leiden University Library, Special Collections, Ser. 373

42–45, 107, 160, 169, 172 © 2017 The Metropolitan Museum of Art /
  Art Resource / Scala, Florence

48, 49, 74, 174, 195, 222 © Ōta Memorial Museum of Art, Tokyo

52, 109–112, 154, 177–182, 223 © Musée national des arts asiatiques Guimet, Paris
  / Photo: RNM-Grand Palais

68, 71 © Tōyō Bunko (The Oriental Library), Tokyo

72, 125 © Courtesy of the Art Research Centre, Ristumeikan University, Ebi
  Collection, Ebi0562, Ebi0127

73 © Fukui Prefectural Museum of Fine Arts

87, 88, 124, 144, 166 © Fitzwilliam Museum, Cambridge

101 © Hayashibara Museum of Art, Okayama

103, 113, 122 © Ujiie Ukiyo-e Collection, Kamakura

117 © The Museum of the Imperial Collections, Sannomaru Shōzōkan, Tokyo

118 © Fukada Art Museum, Kyoto

119 © The British Library Board, Maps 188.v.3

159 © Kumamoto Prefectural Museum of Art

161 © The Sumida Hokusai Museum, Tokyo

162 © Japan Ukiyo-e Museum, Matsumoto

186 © The National Diet Library Digital Collections

187 © Keiō University Library, Tokyo

193 © National Diet Library, Tokyo

196 © The Cleveland Museum of Art

201 © Takai Kōzan Memorial Museum, Obuse

204 © Ganshōin temple, Obuse

208 © Sano Art Museum, Mishima

215 © Collection: Myōkōji temple, Koga / Image: TNM Image Archives

216 © Collection of Robert and Betsy Feinberg, USA / Photo: Imaging Department
  © President and Fellows of Harvard College

List of lenders

The British Museum would like to thank all the lenders to the
exhibition 'Hokusai: beyond the Great Wave' for their generosity:

The British Library, London
Chiba City Museum of Art
The Cleveland Museum of Art
Ebi collection, UK
Robert and Betsy Feinberg collection, USA
Fitzwilliam Museum, Cambridge
Fukada Art Museum, Kyoto
Fukui Prefectural Museum of Fine Arts*
Ganshōin Temple, Obuse
Hayashibara Museum of Art, Okayama*
Hie Jinja Shrine, Kisarazu*
Hikaru Museum, Takayama
Hokusai Museum, Obuse
Ichimura Tsugio collection, Japan*
Sebastian Izzard collection, USA
Japan Ukiyo-e Museum, Matsumoto
Kanmachi Neighbourhood Council, Obuse
Kawasaki Isago-no-Sato Museum
Kobe City Museum*
Kumamoto Prefectural Museum of Art*
Leiden University Library, Special Collections
Metropolitan Museum of Art, New York
MOA Museum of Art, Atami
Musée national des arts asiatiques Guimet, Paris
Museum of Fine Arts, Boston*
The Museum of the Imperial Collections, Sannomaru
    Shōzōkan, Tokyo

The Museum Yamato Bunkakan, Nara
Myōkōji Temple, Koga
Nagoya City Museum
National Museum of Ethnology, Leiden
Okada Museum of Art, Hakone
Osaka City Museum of Fine Arts*
Ōta Memorial Museum of Art, Tokyo
Private collections, Japan
Sano Art Museum, Mishima
The Sumida Hokusai Museum, Tokyo*
Sumishō Art Gallery, Inc., Tokyo
Takai Kōzan Memorial Museum, Obuse*
Tokyo National Museum
Tōyō Bunko (The Oriental Library), Tokyo
Ujiie Ukiyo-e Collection, Kamakura
Uragami Mitsuru collection, Japan
Yanagi Shigeyuki collection, Japan*
Victoria and Albert Museum, London

* Lenders exhibiting works in Osaka only

List of contributors

Timothy Clark FBA is Honorary Research Fellow in the Department of Asia at the British Museum. Until 2019 he was Head of the Japanese section at the Museum.

Asano Shūgō is Director of The Museum Yamato Bunkakan, Nara, Director of the Abeno Harukas Art Museum, Osaka and President of the International Ukiyo-e Society.

Roger S. Keyes (1942–2020) was a leading scholar of early modern print culture in Japan, particularly Hokusai. Together with Peter Morse (1935–1992) he created the *Catalogue Raisonné of the Surviving Single Sheet Woodblock Prints of Katsushika Hokusai.*

Alfred Haft is JTI Project Curator for Japanese Collections at the British Museum. He is the author of *Hiroshige: artist of the open road* (2025).

Angus Lockyer taught history at SOAS University of London from 2004 to 2019. He currently teaches at the Rhode Island School of Design. *Japan: A History in Objects*, based on the collection of the British Museum, will be published in 2026.

Matsuba Ryōko is Professor of Digital Humanities for Arts and Cultures at Ritsumeikan University and will become a new faculty member at the College of Arts and Design and Graduate School of Science in Arts and Design, which expects to welcome its first students in April 2026.

Initials at the end of each catalogue entry denote the author:

TC   Timothy Clark
AS   Asano Shūgō
RK   Roger Keyes
AH   Alfred Haft
AL   Angus Lockyer
MR   Matsuba Ryōko

Author acknowledgments

The authors would first like to express their gratitude to Mitsubishi Corporation for their sponsorship, which has made this exhibition possible.

We would also like to thank the owners of Hokusai's works – the many museums and private collections in Japan, the USA and Europe in the list on p. 342 – who have loaned to the exhibition. In Japan, NHK and The Asahi Shimbun have assisted with the organization of loans.

Research for the project has been supported by the Arts and Humanities Research Council of the UK. The research project *Late Hokusai: Thought, Technique, Society* will continue until March 2019, in collaboration with a number of international partners: primarily, Abeno Harukas Art Museum, Osaka, where a version of the exhibition will be staged in October 2017; Art Research Center, Ritsumeikan University, Kyoto, leaders in the digital humanities in Japan; and the Freer-Sackler Gallery, Smithsonian Institution, Washington, DC, with their unrivalled collection of Hokusai works. We look forward to further joint discoveries and to sharing these online via the British Museum's ResearchSpace platform, assisted by our colleagues Dominic Oldman and Stephanie Santschi.

We respectfully acknowledge Hokusai research by scholars past and present, particularly Hélène Bayou, Gian Carlo Calza, John Carpenter, Matthi Forrer, Jack Hillier, Kano Hiroyuki, Kobayashi Tadashi, Peter Morse, Nagata Seiji, Narazaki Muneshige, Henry D. Smith II, Suwa Haruo, Suzuki Jūzō, Sarah Thompson, Yasuhara Akio and Ann Yonemura. We are also grateful to those helping with the production and editing of the catalogue – Susanna Ingram and Sarah Vernon-Hunt at Thames & Hudson, and Claudia Bloch and Kara Green at the British Museum – for keeping our work in order and on track.

Colleagues in Japan and the UK have worked tirelessly to help secure loan permissions and images for the catalogue: at Abeno Harukas Art Museum, Fujimura Tadanori and Kitagawa Hiroko; at NHK, Osaka, Hirata Naoki and Obuchi Yūko; at NHK PlanNet, Inc., Kinki Branch Office, Tsunoo Akiko; at The Asahi Shimbun, Osaka, Kuwano Mina and Morimoto Shunji; at the British Museum, Sadamura Koto, Christopher Stewart and Yano Akiko. We express our warm thanks to them all. In Japan, the following institutions and individuals have further assisted with exhibition research, loans and catalogue images: Akama Ryō, Art Research Center, Ritsumeikan University, Arute Kikaku, Robert Campbell, Hokusai Museum, Obuse, International Research Center for Japanese Studies, Itō Keiko, Keiō University Library, Kyoto National Museum, National Diet Library, Tokyo, The Sumida Hokusai Museum, Tokyo, Tokyo National Museum, Yamamoto Yoshitaka.

Hokusai's extraordinary artistic achievement in a wide range of painted and printed media means that his surviving work can be enjoyed by many around the globe. We have been welcomed by a number of institutions with major Hokusai collections. In Japan: Hokusai Museum, Obuse; The Sumida Hokusai Museum, Tokyo; Tokyo National Museum; in the USA: Museum of Fine Arts, Boston; Metropolitan Museum of Art, New York. In Europe: The British Library, London; Fitzwilliam Museum, Cambridge; Musée Guimet, Paris; National Museum of Ethnology, Leiden; Victoria and Albert Museum, London. Our warm thanks are extended to the staff of these museums for their kind cooperation. Robert Feinberg, Israel Goldman, Ichimura Tsugio, Sebastian Izzard, Kochūkyo Co., Ltd, Sumishō Art Gallery, Inc., Ellis Tinios, Tsunoda Hideo and Uragami Mitsuru have all assisted in securing important loans to the exhibition.

The digital realm offers extraordinary potential for sharing the results of our research with the widest possible audience. This is an ambition which Hokusai, supported by his daughter Eijo (Ōi), would surely have embraced wholeheartedly. Working in the mass media of their day – woodblock-printed books and colour prints, as well as autograph paintings – the single-minded goal of Hokusai and Ōi was to inspire us all by celebrating on paper and silk our shared humanity and the world we live in.

Asano Shūgō, Timothy Clark, Alfred Haft, Roger S. Keyes, Angus Lockyer, Matsuba Ryōko

Index